AF228375

FROM THE REALM OF A DYING SUN

FROM THE REALM OF A DYING SUN

Volume III: *IV. SS-Panzerkorps* from Budapest to Vienna, February–May 1945

DOUGLAS E. NASH SR.

CASEMATE

Philadelphia & Oxford

Published in the United States of America and Great Britain in 2021 by
CASEMATE PUBLISHERS
1950 Lawrence Road, Havertown, PA 19083, USA
and
The Old Music Hall, 106–108 Cowley Road, Oxford OX4 1JE, UK

Copyright 2021 © Douglas E. Nash Sr.

Hardcover Edition: ISBN 978-1-61200-956-8
Digital Edition: ISBN 978-1-61200-957-5

A CIP record for this book is available from the British Library

All rights reserved. No part of this book may be reproduced or transmitted in any form or by any means, electronic or mechanical including photocopying, recording or by any information storage and retrieval system, without permission from the publisher in writing.

Maps by Thomas Houlihan and Phillip Schwartzberg

Printed and bound in the United States of America by Sheridan

Typeset in India for Casemate Publishing Services. www.casematepublishingservices.com

For a complete list of Casemate titles, please contact:

CASEMATE PUBLISHERS (US)
Telephone (610) 853-9131
Fax (610) 853-9146
Email: casemate@casematepublishers.com
www.casematepublishers.com

CASEMATE PUBLISHERS (UK)
Telephone (01865) 241249
Email: casemate-uk@casematepublishers.co.uk
www.casematepublishers.co.uk

Contents

Introduction　　　　ix
List of Maps　　　　xv

1　　A South Wind Brings Hope, 13–24 February 1945　　　1
2　　Operation *Spring Awakening*, 1–15 March 1944　　　19
3　　The Defense of Stuhlweissenburg, 16–19 March 1945　　　57
4　　The Storm Breaks, 20–23 March 1945　　　89
5　　The Retreat from Hungary, 24–29 March 1945　　　133
6　　The Cuff Title Order, 26–28 March 1945　　　177
7　　Withdrawal to the *Reichsschutzstellung*, 30–31 March 1945　　　187
8　　Defending the Reich, 1–17 April 1945　　　201
9　　War's End, 17 April–28 May 1945　　　237

Appendix A: IV. SS-Pz.Korps *Battle and Campaign Participation Credits awarded for the period 23 February to 8 May 1945*　　　267
Appendix B: IV. SS-Pz.Korps *Orders of Battle, 5 February to 8 May 1945*　　　269
Appendix C: 6. Armee Orders of Battle, 1 and 17 April 1945　　　273
Appendix D: German Order of Battle, Operation Frühlingserwachen, *5 March 1945*　　　277
Appendix E: Third Ukrainian Front Order of Battle, Vienna Operation, 16 March 1945　　　279
Appendix F: German Army, Waffen-SS *and U.S. Army Rank Equivalents*　　　283
Appendix G: Glossary　　　285
Endnotes　　　293
Bibliography　　　313
Index　　　323

SS-Obergruppenführer Herbert Gille (left) confers with *SS-Brigadeführer* Helmuth Becker during the early stages of *Unternehmen Konrad I,* January 1945. The awards of both men can be clearly seen, including Gille's Knight's Cross with Oak Leaves, Swords and Diamonds and Becker's Knight's Cross with Oak Leaves and his German Cross in Gold. Also visible are his Iron Cross First Class, Wound Badge in Silver, and Infantry Assault Badge in Silver. On the left sleeve of Becker's jacket, the rare skull-embroidered *Totenkopf* Division cuff title can be clearly seen. Both general officers are also wearing insulated *Luftwaffe* aircraft crewman's boots. (Bayerl)

Introduction

This is the final volume of three volumes, which together trace the history of the *IV. SS-Panzerkorps* (*IV. SS-Pz.Korps*) from its inception in August 1943 until the end of the war. The first volume focused on the activation of the corps, its structure and organization, leadership, and the history of its two core divisions—the *3. SS-Panzerdivision Totenkopf* and the *5. SS-Panzerdivision Wiking*. It then traced the history of the corps after its introduction to battle on 28 July 1944, its participation in the massive tank battle of Praga, its role in the three defensive battles of Warsaw, and ended on 26 November 1944 with the siege of Modlin and the transfer of the corps to *2. Armee*. The first volume described some of the heaviest fighting ever witnessed on the Eastern Front, which forged the *IV. SS-Pz.Korps* into a responsive and lethal instrument of war. This phase of the corps' history, which began with its participation in a highly mobile, fluid battle, ended with its troops engaged in static trench warfare reminiscent of World War I.

The second volume traced the history of the corps from the end of November 1944, where the first left off, with the corps still engaged in defending the so-called "Wet Triangle," that tactically significant chunk of terrain situated between the Narew and Vistula Rivers. Seemingly relegated to a secondary front, the corps was jolted out of its holiday preparations when the *Oberkommando der Wehrmacht* (*OKW*) ordered it to begin moving by rail to another theater of operations on Christmas Eve. Thus would begin the final phase of the war in the East, with the corps once again called upon to carry out one of the most audacious attacks of World War II—the relief of an encircled city. During the see-saw fighting that ensued, the *IV. SS-Pz.Korps*, including several divisions of the *Heer*, sought in vain to relieve the embattled garrison of Budapest and to re-establish the old front line along the lower Danube.

This final volume of this trilogy picks up the thread of the corps' history where it left off in mid-February 1945, and focuses on the last three months of the war, which witnessed not only the Third Reich's last large-scale offensive of the war, Operation *Frühlingserwachen* (*Spring Awakening*), but the Red Army's Vienna Operation, which drove German and Hungarian forces completely out of Hungary and advanced deeply into southeastern Austria until the Third Reich finally capitulated on 8 May 1945. During this period, the corps witnessed the fall of Vienna, though fortunately it was not directly involved in that final, fateful battle. Volume 3 concludes with the last-minute surrender by the *IV. SS-Pz.Korps* to U.S. forces and the postwar fate of some of its leading members.

This period of the war witnessed the near-destruction of *Obergruppenführer* Herbert Gille's beloved *IV. SS-Pz.Korps* in the ill-fated defense of the operationally important Hungarian city of Stuhlweissenburg (Székesfehérvár) that began one day after the cancellation of Operation *Frühlingserwachen* on 15 March 1945. Overwhelmed by the combined power of three attacking Soviet armies and outnumbered by 10 to one, the corps was split in two, with the *Totenkopf* Division being forced to pull away in one direction, never to rejoin the corps again, while the *Wiking* Division and Gille's headquarters went in another. As the *Wiking* Division barely escaped from the city, it, along with the rest of the *IV. SS-Pz.Korps*, would then undergo a harrowing retreat along the northern shore of Lake Balaton, which witnessed the near-collapse of *General der Panzertruppe* Hermann Balck's *6. Armee*.

Partly due to Balck's uncharacteristically poor direction of his army, and partly to the incredible combat power and deft handling of the Third Ukrainian Front under its commander, Marshal Fyodor Tolbukhin, Balck's army, along with the remnants of the *IV. SS-Pz.Korps*, barely made it back to the presumed safety of the *Reichsschutzstellung* defensive wall in southeastern Austria. Here, Gille and his weary troops would engage in heavy defensive warfare until the last week of April 1945. Throughout, Gille and his staff would have to undergo increasingly meddlesome and petty interference by Balck in the corps' operations, leading to yet another demand by Balck for Gille's relief of command. Shortages of ammunition, fuel, and above all the armored fighting vehicles upon which his *panzer* divisions relied, the *IV. SS-Pz.Korps* was forced to wage positional warfare in the Styrian Mountains, where infantry skills once again became paramount in order to keep the Red Army at bay.

The corps' history ends after its hectic withdrawal from the front lines east of Graz and its surrender to U.S. forces between 8 and 9 May 1945. To do this, Gille first had to order his troops to pull out from their positions without attracting the attention of Soviet forces and conduct a road march of over 200 kilometers through the Austrian Alps to reach the Allied demarcation line along the Enns River by midnight on 8 May. Shadowed by the Red Army throughout its withdrawal, Gille's rear guards managed to keep their opponents at a safe distance while simultaneously fighting off attempts by the Austrian resistance to impede their movement. Upon reaching the Enns, the corps had only 24 hours to cross to safety, only to endure months or even years of privation in Allied prisoner of war camps, de-Nazification, and re-education.

Finally, after being released from internment camps throughout Europe in the late 1940s (and even longer if held captive in the U.S.S.R.), Gille and his troops, especially those who had fought in the *Waffen-SS*, returned to a West Germany that no longer welcomed them. Back home, the survivors faced the reality that their organization had been made the scapegoat for all of the Third Reich's war crimes and crimes against humanity. Slowly, the survivors of the *IV. SS-Pz.Korps* reintegrated into civil society, a trend that accelerated when West Germany's *Wirtschaftswunder* (economic miracle) began to gather momentum in the mid-1950s. Some returned to their previous professions, while others found new employment, and not a few joined the new West German Army, the *Bundeswehr*. Throughout this period, former *Waffen-SS* members, led by prominent men like Felix Steiner and Herbert Gille, began to organize and formally establish SS veterans' associations, and seek a political voice to address some of their concerns arising from their perceived second-class citizenship status. Although they were only partially successful in achieving their goals, by the early 1960s, nearly all of the survivors of the *IV. SS-Pz.Korps* had been accepted as full-fledged citizens by their countrymen, except for those few accused of having committed war crimes.

Unlike the first two volumes, where archival materials were relatively plentiful, the author found that sources covering the last three months of the *IV. SS-Pz. Korps'* history were sparse in comparison. To tell the story, heavy use was made of the *Kriegstagebuch* (war diary) of *Heeresgruppe Süd* (*H.Gr. Süd*, or Army Group South), which covers the events described in this volume fairly comprehensively until 31 March 1945. After that, only partial daily summaries provided to the *OKH* (*Oberkommando des Heeres*) survive, and even these end after 22 April 1945. Contemporary diaries, postwar accounts, and even unit histories written afterwards about this period of the war tend to taper off by the end of April 1945, leaving the researcher with precious little material to work with.

Fortunately, there are still solid reference works available, representing a tremendous amount of work by dedicated researchers and writers who did their best to accurately chronicle the events described, and the author refers to these works frequently in the text. The first and foremost reference work, as it was in Volume 2, is Georg Maier's *Drama Between Budapest and Vienna*. Though serving on the staff of *Oberstgruppenführer* Sepp Dietrich's infamous *6. Pz.Armee*, Maier also took the time to accurately record the events taking place elsewhere in neighboring armies' areas of operation, including Hermann Balck's *6. Armee*, under which the *IV. SS-Pz.Korps* mostly served from the end of December 1944 until 8 May 1945. Though clearly writing from the perspective of the *Waffen-SS* senior leadership and highly critical of *Gen.d.Pz.Tr.* Balck, Maier backs up his conclusions with solid evidence, including reproductions of actual documents from official *Wehrmacht* records that bolster his case.

The other is Dr Manfred Rauchensteiner's meticulously and thoroughly researched *Der Krieg in Oesterreich 1945* (*The War in Austria 1945*), which covers the war from the fall of 1944 until the end of the war and beyond, including the Allied bombing campaign against Austrian towns and cities. Although writing as an Austrian citizen

40 years after the events described, Dr Rauchensteiner provides equal coverage of the fighting in Austria from the perspective of the combatants, including the plans and operations of Soviet forces and the units of the Third Reich, including the sinister role of the SS and the Nazi Party. In addition to giving behind-the-scenes accounts of the key events that took place, he also describes the impact that the war had upon ordinary citizens, from the *Gauleiter* (District Leader) down to the average member of the *Volkssturm* (People's Militia) or ordinary homemakers and children. As a bonus, his book has highly detailed orders of battle for both sides and reproduces the entire "missing" portion of the *H. Gr. Süd Kriegstagebuch* daily summaries for 1–22 April 1945.

Taken together with the existing reference materials, the author believes that he has accurately traced the history of the *IV. SS-Korps* during the final stages of war on the Eastern Front as much as possible. This chaotic period encompassed the collapse of the German front in northern Hungary during the last week of March 1945, the hasty retreat to the Austrian border, and the final battles in the mountains and valleys along the *Reichsschutzstellung*. It must be stressed that this work is intended as an operational history, focusing on the campaigns of one German corps among many, and is not intended to be a comprehensive account of the campaign in Hungary or the end of the war in Southern Europe—there are a number of previous works by distinguished authors who have already done that, as previously mentioned.

With this concluding volume, therefore, a portion of the missing history of the *Waffen-SS* in general and of the SS armored corps in particular has been fulfilled. As with any work of this nature, it would not have been possible without the generous assistance of a number of contributors, many of whom I have already singled out for thanks in both Volumes 1 and 2. For this particular volume, I would once again like to thank Mirko Bayerl of Sweden, who generously provided copies of division histories, maps, and photographs; Martin Block of Germany, who provided copies of official records of the *Panzertruppe*; Andrew Found of the Netherlands, who also provided photographs; Tommy Natedal of Norway, who provided copies of individual accounts by veterans of *I. Batallion/SS-Panzergrenadier Regiment Norge*; and Kamen Navenkin of Bulgaria and Charles Trang of France, who provided photographs. And last but certainly not least, I would like to thank the former Aide-de-Camp of Herbert Gille, Günther Lange, and his son Wolfgang of Handeloh, Germany, who graciously lent their time to answer the many queries that arose during the drafting of this book.

I would be remiss if I did not mention the professionalism and patience of the Casemate editorial and graphic design staff, in particular publisher Ruth Sheppard, managing editor Isobel Fulton, editorial administrator Felicity Goldsack, and production designer Declan Ingram for their organizational skills and helpfulness, and copy-editor Tony Walton for his knowledge and attention to detail. Casemate not only granted me permission to expand this volume beyond what was originally intended, but allowed me the time needed to incorporate the additional material that was sent to me by some of the individuals mentioned above. It is not every day when an author finds a publishing house so easy to work with, and I have been blessed to have been invited to become one of their contributing authors. My hat's off to all of you!

Douglas E. Nash Sr.
Washington, D.C., August 2020

List of Maps

1. Situation as of 12 February 1945 — 2
2. Operation *Frühlingserwachen*, 5–15 March 1945 — 22
3. Situation as of morning, 16 March 1945 — 59
4. Opening Stages, Vienna Operation, 16–22 March 1945 — 64
5. Escape from Stuhlweissenburg, 22–26 March 1945 — 106
6. Withdrawal to the *Reichschutzstellung*, 27–31 March 1945 — 136
7. Defense of the Reich, 1–17 April 1945 — 202
8. Withdrawal to the Enns, 8–9 May 1945 — 245

A South Wind Brings Hope
13–24 February 1945

With Budapest and its garrison now removed from the playing board, relative calm settled over the front lines of most of *A. Gr. Balck/6. Armee*, with the exception of its right flank, where the *III. Panzerkorps* was concluding its mission of safeguarding the *Margarethestellung* (Margaret Position southwest of Budapest). By 13 February 1945, Lt.Gen. N. A. Gagen's Soviet 26th Army had finally stabilized its section along the line Soponya–Nagy Lang–Jaslang–Agatok–Bal–Bozsok–Gamasa and halted opposite the German main defense line, which Gagen's troops had been unable to penetrate.[1] Lieutenant General Zakharov's 4th Guards Army had already come to a stop for all intents and purposes several days earlier.

From that point onwards, the focus of all of Marshal Tolbukhin's armies, as well as Balck's *Armeegruppe*, were on rebuilding their worn-out and depleted units, restocking ammunition and other supplies, and incorporating replacements, including the three Soviet corps confronting the *IV. SS-Pz. Korps* between Zámoly and Stuhlweissenburg—the XX and XXI Guards Rifle and I Guards Mechanized Corps (see Map 1). Of course, that did not mean that no combat activity took place at all, rather that it reverted to the usual "static front" activities—constant patrolling, infantry raids, artillery harassment and registration fires, mine-laying, and improving fighting positions. Life in the front lines was never dull, and relaxing one's guard often resulted in fatal consequences.

Depending on the weather, the air forces of both sides carried out a limited amount of ground interdiction operations, especially north of the Danube, but during this period most of their efforts were directed towards low- and high-altitude reconnaissance in a bid to determine their opponent's future intentions. The weather changed little during the next several weeks, alternating between freezing temperatures and partial thawing, with rain showers becoming more prominent than snow. Since nearly all of the units of *A. Gr. Balck/6. Armee* were now either occupying defensive positions in the front lines or, as in the case of the *Heer's panzer* divisions, in reserve behind the front lines, the weather affected them relatively little.

On 12 February, the *Wiking* Division reported that it was chiefly involved in regrouping its units and moving into new positions further to the north, stretching

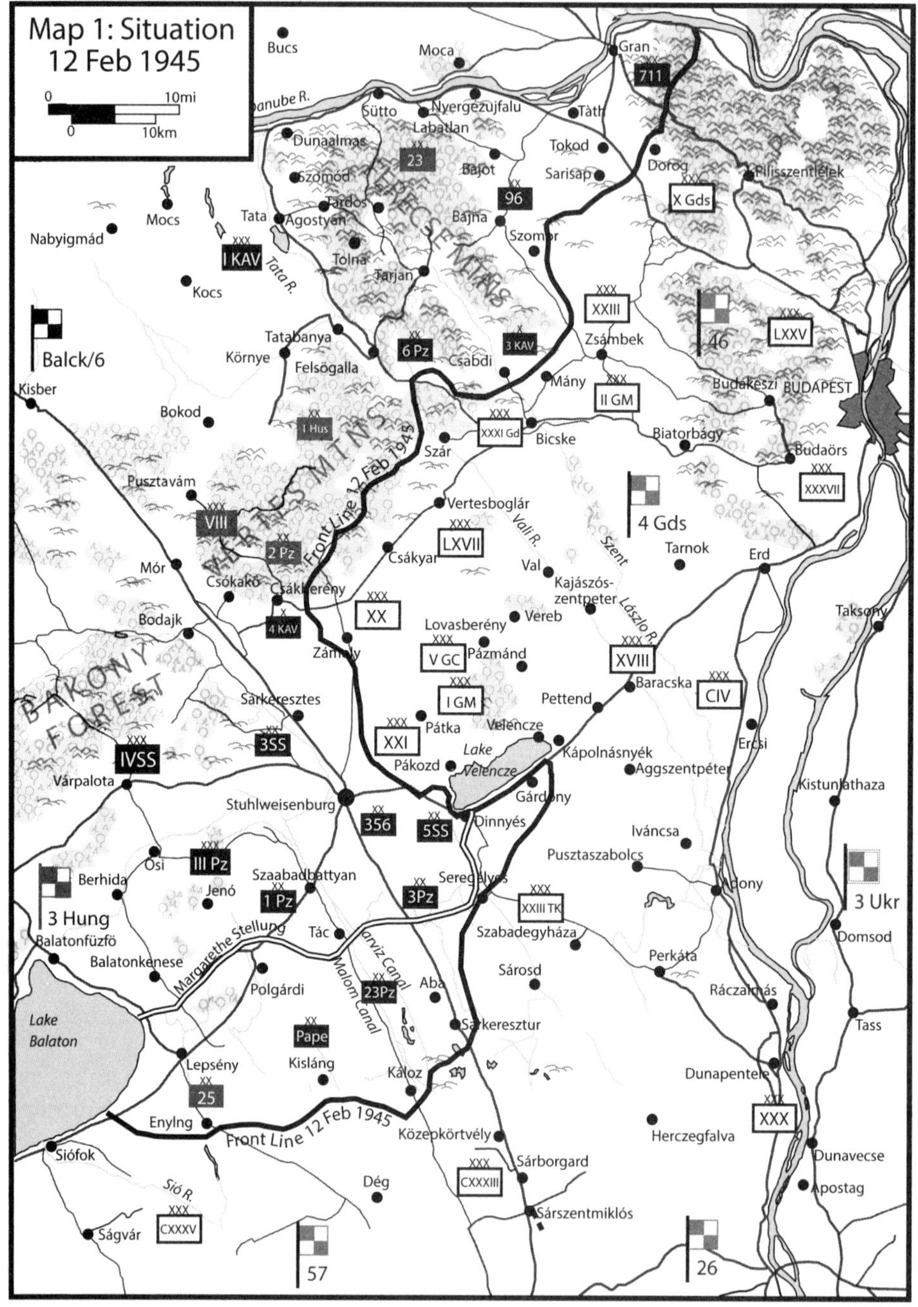

Map 1: Situation 12 Feb 1945
0   10mi
0   10km
Bucs
Moca
Gran
711
Danube R.
Sütto
Nyergezujfalu
Tàth
Labatlan
Tokod
Dunaalmas
Szomód
Bajót
Sarisap
Dorog
Pilisszentlélek
23
Tardos
96
Szomor
X Gds
Mocs
Tata
Bajna
Nabyigmád
Agostyan
Szomor
Tolna
Tarjan
I KAV
Tata R.
Kocs
XXIII
46
LXXV
Tatabanya
X
Balck/6
Környe
6 Pz
3 KAV
Zsámbek
Felsögalla
Csabdi
Kisber
Mány
II GM
Budakeszi
BUDAPEST
Bokod
1 Hus
XXXI Gd
Bicske
Biatorbágy
Budaörs
Pusztavám
Szár
4 Gds
XXXVII
VIII
Front Line 12 Feb 1945
Vertesboglár
Vali R.
Tarnok
Erd
2 Pz
LXVII
Csákyar
Val
Mór
Kajászós-
zentpeter
Taksony
Csókakö
Csákberény
Lovasberény
Vereb
Bodajk
4 KAV
XX
V GC
Pázmánd
Szent László R.
XVIII
Zámoly
Baracska
CIV
I GM
Pettend
Sárkeresztes
3SS
XXI
Pátka
Velencze
Ercsi
IVSS
Pákozd
Lake
Velencze
Kápolnásnyék
Aggszentpéter
Kistunlathaza
Várpalota
Gárdony
Stuhlweisenburg
356
5SS
Dinnyés
Iváncsa
III Pz
Osi
Szaabadbattyan
Seregelyes
Pusztaszabolcs
Adony
3 Ukr
Berhida
Jenó
1 Pz
3Pz
XXIII TK
3 Hung
Tác
Szabadegyháza
Domsod
Balatonfüzfö
Margarethe Stellung
Perkáta
Balatonkenese
Sárosd
Ráczalmás
Polgárdi
Aba
Malom Canal
Sárvíz Canal
23Pz
Sárkeresztur
Tass
Lake
Balaton
Pape
Kisláng
Dunapentele
Lepseny
Káloz
25
Herczegfalva
XXX
Enylng
Front Line 12 Feb 1945
Közepkörtvély
Dunavecse
Siófok
Sárborgard
Apostag
Sió R.
Dég
CXXXIII
CXXXV
Sárszentmiklós
Ságvár
57
26

as far as the southern outskirts of Stuhlweissenburg, where it linked in with the *356. Infanterie-Division*. The division's *O1* remarked that this defensive terrain was mostly swampland and could be observed in its entirety by Soviet units entrenched on the heights east of the city. Furthermore, to adequately position itself to command and control this new defense sector, *Oberführer* Karl Ullrich had ordered his division's *Gefechtstand* (command post) that same day to displace to a castle in Sarpentele, a village located 8 kilometers southwest of Stuhlweissenburg.[2]

Between 13 and 24 February, the *IV. SS-Pz.Korps* reported no significant activity occurring other than the ordinary activities mentioned above. Most of what did occur was administrative or logistical in nature, such as the withdrawal of *s.Pz.Abt. 503 FHH* on 14 February, which was sent north of the Danube to join its new *Feldherrnhalle* headquarters, the *IV. Pz.Korps FHH* commanded by *Gen.d.Pz.Tr.* Ulrich Kleemann. The battalion was in dire need of *Auffrischung* (reconstitution), having been reduced to an operational daily strength of four to five vehicles after three months of non-stop combat. Other units were soon to follow. During this same period, the corps was finally augmented by the arrival of *s.SS-Art.Abt. 504* and *SS-Beob.Abt. 504* after a lengthy training and working-up process at the SS training area in Beneschau. The corps' *ARKO*, *Oberführer* Brasack, would finally have all of the tools that his position required.

That same day, *A.Gr. Balck/6. Armee* issued a proclamation recognizing the achievements of the *1.* and *3. Pz.Div.*, as well as that of the *Panzergruppe* from the *6. Pz.Div.*, during the fighting between the Sárviz Canal and Lake Balaton on 9 February.[3] Balck's headquarters did not issue any similar proclamations to recognize the accomplishments of Gille's corps during the fighting of 3–5 February north of Stuhlweissenburg or the efforts of the *Wiking* Division between 7 and 11 February; yet another example of the double standard Balck and Gaedke employed concerning *Waffen-SS* units. Whether Balck intended to snub Gille and his troops can only be surmised; in any case, this omission would not have improved the morale of the men of the *IV. SS-Pz.Korps*, whether of the *Waffen-SS* or *Heer*.

On 15 February, a shuffling of the corps' order of battle took place, and although the two above-mentioned SS artillery units had arrived, they had not yet gone into operation. On that date, the corps' ground combat units consisted of the *Totenkopf* Division, with the subordinated *I. Btl./Norge* and *I. Btl./Danmark*; the *Wiking* Division, with a battalion subordinated from the Hungarian *23. Inf.Div.*; the understrength *356. Inf.Div.*; and *Div.Gr. Holste*, with the *4. Kav.Brig.*, Hungarian *2. Pz.Div.*, one battalion from the Hungarian *20. Inf.Div.*, a battalion from the *356. Inf.Div.*, and *Btl. Holczer*. In addition to the usual corps troops, the *IV. SS-Pz.Korps* also had subordinated to it the *Volks-Art.Korps 403*, *Volks-Werf.Brig. 17*, *Heeres-Sturm. Art.Brig. 303*, *Pz.Flamm-Kp. 351*, *Taifun-Kp. 870*, and *Pz.Pio.Btl. 23*.[4]

On 16 February, the *IV. SS-Pz.Korps* reported that its far right and far left flanks had been probed by strong Soviet reconnaissance units, but these were driven off.

Except for reporting the arrival of stragglers arriving from Budapest, *Korpsgruppe Harteneck/I. Kav. Korps'* front was also quiet. On that same day, *H. Gr. Süd* submitted an after-action report, signed by *Gen. Oberst* Otto Wöhler, to *OKH* headquarters summing up the Budapest operation from its beginning on 24 December until its end on 10 February. It tallied Soviet losses claimed during ground combat by *A. Gr. Balck/6. Armee*, including those inflicted during the course of the city's encirclement as well as the abortive *Unternehmen Spätlese* (Operation *Late Harvest*). In all, during this 67-day period, Balck's troops claimed to have killed 20,132 Soviet troops, captured a further 5,138 troops, knocked out or rendered inoperable 1,981 armored fighting vehicles, destroyed 946 artillery pieces, 273 mortars, and 1,700 antitank guns, and shot down 63 enemy aircraft using its own *Flak* units. Its own losses had also been rather high. During the same period, *A. Gr. Balck/6. Armee* reported losing 34,108 killed, wounded, and missing, not including the 70,000-man garrison of Budapest, who were completely lost except for the few men who managed to escape between 11 and 16 February and the wounded flown out in the early days of the siege when aircraft could still take off and land.[5]

On 17 February, the *OKW* recognized the accomplishments of all of the troops fighting in Hungary with the following announcement, which gave credit where Balck and Wöhler would not. Rather than focusing on the fighting described above, the *Wehrmachtsbericht* issued on that day noted the accomplishments of all of the units involved in the relief effort:

> In the course of the recently completed offensive and defensive battles between Lake Balaton and the Danube, troops of the army and the *Waffen-SS* have smashed a large number of Bolshevik units. In the period from January 1 to February 15, the enemy lost more than 5,100 prisoners, 2,045 tanks and assault guns, 2,727 guns of all kinds, 3,114 mortars and 2,774 vehicles in the area of one of our armies. The *Luftwaffe* carried out numerous missions during the battles and destroyed another 202 tanks and assault guns, 322 guns of all kinds and 1,600 vehicles. The bloody losses of the enemy are considerable.[6]

On that same day, the *Wiking* Division conducted a brief ceremony, presided over by *Ogruf.* Gille, commemorating the first anniversary of the breakout from the Cherkassy Pocket. It was hard to believe that this had happened only a year before; so much had happened since then. In many ways, the *Wiking* was no longer the same division it had been in February 1944. Heavy losses at Kovel, in battles east of Warsaw, in the Wet Triangle, and during *Konrad I–III* had stripped it of many of its veteran officers and *Unterführer* (NCOs). It had bounced back repeatedly from these losses, but how much longer could it sustain such a high rate of attrition? At some point, the well would run dry. Saturday, 17 February also marked the first day of *Unternehmen Südwind* (Operation *Southwind*, referred to below in subsequent paragraphs).

That same day also marked the end of another week in which to report the combat worthiness of its divisions to *H. Gr. Süd*. This provides a useful barometer to measure how well the SS divisions of the *IV. SS-Pz.Korps* were recovering after nearly 40 days of constant battle from 1 January to 12 February 1945. This also reveals how much little progress the Third Reich was making in trying to replace the enormous losses in men and matériel since the great withdrawal battles of the previous autumn. Allied bombing and loss of occupied and home territory had also made deep inroads into German industrial capacity, which had been heavily reliant upon these areas for not only raw materials such as coal, iron ore, and oil, but on the manufacturing plants in Silesia, Pomerania, northeastern France, and Hungary.

On this date, the *Totenkopf* Division was reported as having four strong and three average infantry battalions, one average combat engineer battalion, and a strong field replacement battalion. It also fielded 14 operational 7.5cm antitank guns, two *Jg.Pz. IV* tank destroyers, 13 operational *StuG III/VI* assault guns, 11 *Pz. IV*s, 12 *Pz. V* Panthers, and six *Pz. VI* Tiger Is, for a total of 44 armored fighting vehicles, a very respectable figure indeed so long as there was sufficient gasoline to power them. Its artillery status had remained unchanged since the previous week, with five light and five heavy batteries. Mobility had decreased somewhat to 80 per cent, though this still allowed *Brig.Fhr.* Helmuth Becker to evaluate his division's *Kampfwert* or combat power as a II (the second-highest rate, the lowest being IV).

The *Wiking* Division, since it had been in heavy combat for a longer period of time, was still working its way back to a higher level of readiness. Still being rated as a *Kampfgruppe*, it reported one strong and one average regimental group (formed by the *Germania* and *Westland* Regiments), one average-strength *Pionier-Bataillon*, and one very strong *Feld-Ers.Btl. 5*, a sign that it had received a large group of replacements. *Oberführer* Ullrich's antitank and armored vehicle status had improved somewhat since the last submission, with the division reporting eight operational antitank guns, two *StuG III/IV*s, four *Pz. IV*s and 12 *Pz. V* Panthers, giving Fritz Darges as many as 18 operational AFVs. Its artillery regiment could still field five light and three heavy batteries, though the division's overall low mobility rating (44 percent), ensured that *K.Gr. Wiking's* commander could only award his division *Kampfgruppe* a conditional "II" evaluation.

Beginning as early as 13 February, the *SS-FHA* had required all of its units in the field to begin submitting a weekly *Stärkemeldung* (strength report) directly to Berlin via separate SS reporting channels, laying yet another requirement upon the hard-pressed staffs of SS separate brigades, divisions, and corps. These reports were prepared by the next-higher SS headquarters (in this case, the *IV. SS-Pz.Korps*) and were sent directly via telex (*Fernschreiber* or teletype) to the office of *Gruf.* Hermann Fegelein, Heinrich Himmler's liaison officer to Hitler's headquarters in the *Führerbunker*. The format of these reports were simplified versions of those required to be submitted through *OKH* channels.

Not every copy of these weekly SS strength reports has survived, but on 19 February, the *IV. SS-Pz.Korps* informed Berlin that the *Totenkopf* Division had an

Iststärke (total daily strength of men actually in the field) of 12,499 men, including a *Kampfstärke* of 5,272. It reported that during the past three days it had suffered the loss of 10 men, including two killed in action. Compared against the previous month's losses, this was very low indeed. It also reported having a total of nine *Pz. VI* Tigers, of which five were *Einsatzbereit* (ready for action), 16 *Pz. V* Panthers (12 ready for action), 17 *Pz. IV*s (11 ready), 17 *StuG III/IV*s (12 ready), and seven *Jg.Pz. IV*s (three ready). This particular report also mentioned that there were 200 tank crewmen available, though without any tanks to operate.

The submission for the same date of the *Wiking* Division is also available. It reported an *Iststärke* of 11,063 men and a *Kampfstärke* of 4,534, a significant improvement since the end of heavy fighting a week before. The report also stated that the division had suffered 41 casualties during the past three days, including 21 men killed in action, most of them during fighting in Dinnyés. In regards to equipment, it was much weaker than the *Totenkopf* Division, reporting 15 *Pz. V* Panthers (12 ready), no *Pz. IV*s at all, five assault guns (two ready), and 10 *Jg.Pz. IV*s (none ready). It also stated that it had 400 armored vehicle crewmen without vehicles. Thus, within the two divisions, there were at least 600 men who could be manning tanks, assault guns, and tank destroyers if only they had them.[7] However, German industry was falling further behind in meeting the demand, and much of the *OKH* armor allocation for the *Waffen-SS* had gone to re-equipping the tank battalions of the four SS divisions comprising the *6. Pz. Armee*.

The remaining operational tanks of Fritz Darges' *SS-Pz.Rgt. 5* were grouped into one company-size "battalion" and positioned behind *Regimentsgruppe Germania*, defending a 7-kilometer-wide defensive sector with few natural obstacles to its front.[8] It was perhaps the most obvious avenue of approach for Soviet armor and had to be backed up by Darges' tankers should this occur. There had also been some changes within the *Totenkopf* Division's *panzer* regiment, which had three times as many tanks as its *Wiking* Division counterpart. On 13 February, the acting commander of *SS-Pz.Rgt. 3*, *Obersturmbannführer* Dr. Adam, was replaced by the newly confirmed commander, *Stubaf.* Anton Berlin. With the shifting of the *Totenkopf* Division's defensive sector to the north, the *panzer* regiment itself had to establish its new headquarters in Mór, while most of the operational *panzers* were located in a reserve position at Magyaralmás, several kilometers west of Zámoly.[9]

In regards to the total casualties suffered by the divisions of the *IV. SS-Pz.Korps* in the period 1 January to 28 February 1945, the number was staggeringly high. During this eight-week period, the *Totenkopf* Division lost 1,032 officers and enlisted men killed in action, another 4,760 wounded, and 409 missing, for a total of 6,201 casualties. This does not include those who were so sick they had to be evacuated to a field hospital, though it was a significant number. From 16 January to 15 February, the division irrecoverably lost 39 tanks, assault guns, and tank destroyers, including two *Pz. VI* Tiger Is.

The *Wiking* Division, during the same period, lost 905 officers and enlisted men killed in action, another 3,541 wounded, and 538 missing, a total of 4,984 men lost to the division. Many of these men were veterans who could not be replaced by anyone with the same degree of skill, which had been developed during years of campaigning. Together, both SS divisions had lost up to 28 February a total of 11,185 men, a staggering amount, nearly half of their combined strength on that date. In terms of irrecoverable losses in armor, Ullrich's division—since it had far fewer tanks, assault guns, and tank destroyers to begin with—lost "only" 19. These tank loss figures are partially misleading, because it includes only those vehicles that were declared total write-offs, which usually meant that they burned out, suffered a catastrophic internal explosion, or been captured.

The numbers presented for losses suffered by the *I. Btl./Norge* and *I. Btl./Danmark* are only partial figures, because they only included those incurred throughout February. As we have already seen, the losses that both battalions suffered during January were very high, especially Vogt's battalion. During February alone, each battalion lost 27 officers and men killed in action, 78 officers and 142 men wounded, and a combined total of 28 missing in action. All told, Vogt's battalion lost 115 men in February, while *Stubaf.* Hermann im Masche's battalion lost 187, but his had more men to begin with than Vogt's. Most of these losses were incurred at Pettend, Kápolnás Nyék, and Dinnyés.

Losses suffered by corps troops are only partially recorded. The *303. Sturm-Art. Brig.* lost 46 men to all causes, and 25 assault guns as total write-offs. *Schwere-Panzer Abteilung 509* had to write-off 10 *Pz. VI* Tiger IIs, while *I. Abt./Pz.Rgt. 24* had to strike a further 19 *Pz. V* Panthers off its balance sheet. Again, this does not include vehicles that were badly damaged but not destroyed, but would still need weeks to be repaired or sent back to Germany for factory-level repairs. The number of dead and wounded in the headquarters, headquarters battalion, and SS corps troops are not known, despite checking with the *Deutsche Dienststelle* in Berlin; however, the German Red Cross shows that 22 men were still declared as missing in action for January and February 1945, including *Stubaf.* Fritz Rentrop and his driver, as well as eight men from the newly arrived *s.SS-Art.Abt. 504*.

Besides tallying casualties (the task of the *IIa* and *IIb* staff officers in the *Adjutantur*) and counting destroyed or damaged armored fighting vehicles (the task of the *Ia* in conjunction with the *Korps Ing./TFK* in the *Führungsabteilung*), there was also the happier task of recognizing deserving soldiers for their performance in battle or in support of those fighting in the front lines. Though the surviving records of the *IV. SS-Pz.Korps* awards approved by Gille are incomplete, enough remain to paint a picture of their comprehensiveness. While divisions and separate units administered their own awards systems, approving medals up to and including the Iron Cross, First Class, any award higher than that, such as the Knight's Cross or German Cross in Gold, had to be processed through the chain of command, reaching up to the *Führerhauptquartier*, where they were approved by Hitler himself.

In recognition for their valor displayed while laying or recovering field telephone cables in the presence of the enemy or maintaining radio communications while under attack, six enlisted men from *SS-Nachr.Abt. 104* were approved for the Iron Cross, Second Class on 30 January 1945. For their performance in battle as tank crewmembers or for their leadership as tank commanders, 41 members of *s.Pz. Abt. 509* were recognized with the Iron Cross on 30 January and 6 February 1945; 34 with the Iron Cross, Second Class and seven with the Iron Cross, First Class, including *Ltn.* Werner Böttger, commander of the battalion's *2. Kompanie.* In addition to receiving the medal itself, they also received a certificate signed by Gille, such as with the War Service Cross, Second Class presented to *Oscha.* Willy Kirchmeier of the corps *Hauptquartier* on 30 January. Although this is just a small sampling of the awards presented during this period, it can be safely said that many more men besides these were recognized by Gille.

Meanwhile, the front remained relatively quiet throughout most of the month, though on 18 February this period of relative calm was temporarily shattered when a Soviet infantry regiment attacked Dinnyés along with five tanks and seized it from the troops of the *Wiking* Division still holding it. Several counterattacks failed to dislodge the village's new occupants, forcing both Gille and Ullrich to accept a 500-meter withdrawal to the railroad line running along the southwestern corner of Lake Velencze, where the defenders had to dig in and fortify their position in expectation of further assaults.

The Soviet attack at Dinnyés was supported by another one at the same time that attempted to link up with it along the western shore of Lake Velencze near Mariamajor. This attempt, however, was unsuccessful when it was driven off by a counterattack launched by the *Totenkopf* Regiment, which suffered the loss of one self-propelled *Flak* gun from its *14. Kompanie* when it was struck by a shell from a Soviet antitank gun. That same day, the *4. Kav.Brig.* was subjected to three company-sized reconnaissance attempts south of Zámoly, but these were forced back without having to give up any ground.[10]

The incident at Dinnyés was considered so significant that it was submitted to the *OKH* as part of *H.Gr. Süd's Tagesmeldung* (daily reports). Reflecting on this event shortly after the war, the chief of staff of the *IV. SS-Pz.Korps* noted that the "*Heeresgruppe* considers this loss to be serious … accordingly, the *IV. SS-Pz.Korps* must be made aware that they have to hang on to this place," which he interpreted as an indirect order that the corps would have to recapture Dinnyés.[11] Fortunately, before an attack to retake it could be carried out, two days later on 20 February, *A.Gr. Balck/6. Armee* weighed in on the matter and informed Wöhler and his staff that it was pointless to risk more men's lives retaking Dinnyés since the enemy there could be kept at bay using artillery alone. Convinced, *H.Gr. Süd* backed off from its demand.

On that same day, the 210 excess tank crewmembers from the *Totenkopf* Division's *SS-Pz.Rgt. 3* were organized into a tank training company under the command of

Ostuf. Martin Ernst and began movement by rail from Veszprém to Sennelager outside of Paderborn. Here, they would await the delivery of new tanks for the regiment's *I. Abteilung.* Once new vehicles were issued, the troops would accompany them during shipment back to Hungary, where they were supposed to rejoin the division. In the meantime, Ernst and his troops would be incorporated into the *SS-Panzer Ersatz- und Ausbildungs Regiment* at the Sennelager SS training center. As fate would have it, they never rejoined their division but were instead incorporated into *SS-Pz.Brig. Westfalen* at the end of March 1945. The brigade fought against American forces throughout April before most of it was compelled to surrender in the Harz Mountains.[12]

The following day, 19 February, *Stubaf.* Max Kühn reassumed command of *SS-Pz. Gren.Rgt. 5 Totenkopf,* replacing *Stubaf.* Fritz Eckert, who in turn took command of the division's field replacement battalion from *Ostuf.* Alfred Atzrott. Kühn, who had been wounded on 3 January 1945 at the beginning of *Konrad I,* had commanded the *Totenkopf* Regiment until the summer of 1944, when he was temporarily placed in command of the *Eicke* Regiment. A proven leader who had been with the *Totenkopf* Division since its inception, Kühn would lead the regiment until he was killed in action on 17 April. On the same day, several hundred survivors of the *8.* and *22. SS-Kav.Div.* were assigned to the *Totenkopf* Division.

These men had either been located outside of Budapest when the encirclement began or had survived the breakout from Budapest. Since neither division was ever re-formed after their destruction, any remaining personnel still in the Hungarian *Kampfraum* (area of operations) were assigned to the *Totenkopf* Division, since all three units traced their origins back to the original *Totenkopfverbände.* Having these experienced veterans assigned was a pleasant surprise, especially when compared to the thousands of untrained *Luftwaffe* and *Kriegsmarine* replacements who were pouring into *SS-Feld-Ers.Btl. 3* at the same time. On 20 February, *I. Btl./Norge* was detached from the *Totenkopf* Division and sent to Veszprém in the corps rear area, where it could continue with its *Auffrischung,* a task nearly impossible to carry out in the front lines.[13]

On 21 February, the *303. Sturm-Art.Brig.* was once again attached to the *Wiking* Division, which it had fought alongside throughout most of *Unternehmen Konrad III* and where both units had developed a strong working relationship. That same day, *Gen.Maj.* Rudolf Holste and his *4. Kav.Brig.* received orders to detach themselves from the *IV. SS-Pz.Korps* and to be subordinated to the neighboring Hungarian *VIII. Armee-Korps,* beginning at noon on 22 February. The sector being vacated was to be filled by the *Totenkopf* Division, which had to extend its left flank to cover the entire Zámoly area by the following day. Also on that same day, a German *Jagdflieger* (fighter pilot) shot down an American four-engine bomber over the *IV. SS-Pz.Korps,* whose crew bailed out and were taken prisoner.

On 22 February, in furtherance of the plan being developed for the offensive by the *6. Pz.Armee,* the *Wiking* Division was directed by *A.Gr. Balck/6. Armee* to switch places with the *356. Inf.Div.* by midnight on 23 February. The latter division had been arrayed within Stuhlweissenburg and as far south as the leftmost boundary of the *Margarethestellung*, while the *Wiking* had been in position within the *Margarethestellung* itself between the southwest corner of Lake Velencze and the western outskirts of Seregélyes. For the first time in nearly three weeks, the *Germania* and *Westland* Regiments would be able to move out of the swamps along either side of the Nádas Canal and into much drier fighting positions. This move was brought about because Balck wanted to strengthen the crucial defense line between Lake Velencze and the southern foothills of the Vértes Mountains as much as possible in case the 4th Guards Army should make another attempt to cut off German and Hungarian forces south of the lakes, as it had attempted earlier in the month.

As a result of the shift to the north by the *Wiking* Division, as well as the departure of Holste's *4. Kav.Brig.*, the *Totenkopf* Division had to move its own boundaries further to the north on 23 January while it gave up terrain in the south. On the left, this had necessitated Becker's troops to array themselves in positions on either side of Zámoly, which had remained in Soviet hands after 5 February, and on the right along a straight line parallel to the highway, ending 9 kilometers south of the town. Here, Becker's division tied in with the left flank unit of the *Wiking* Division, *Rgt.Gr. Germania*. The Hungarian *2. Pz.Div.*, thought to be unreliable if left to its own leadership, was subordinated to Becker's division, as well as the Hungarian *Inf. Btl. Holczer*, and thus *Div.Gr. Totenkopf* was born. The Hungarian *2. Pz.Div.*, still considered one of the best in the *Honvéd* (the Royal Hungarian Army), was the left-most unit in the *IV. SS-Pz.Korps*, sharing a boundary with the Hungarian *1. Hus. Div.*, part of their *VIII. Armee-Korps*, which was in turn responsible for defending a line running through the eastern slopes of the Vértes Mountains ending at Felsőgalla.

On account of this latter shift, the *Wiking* Division had to reposition its division headquarters once again, this time to Iszkaszentgyörgy 7 kilometers west-northwest of Stuhlweissenburg, which had been recently occupied by the *Gefechtstand* of the *Totenkopf* Division. In turn, Becker's command post had to move to the village of Bodajk, several kilometers south of Mór, where he could keep his eye on the Hungarian *2. Pz.Div.* acting commander, *Oberst* vitéz-Zadar.[14]

In looking over the village of Iszkaszentgyörgy, *Ostuf.* Günther Jahnke liked this new position more than the previous one, writing in his diary that night: "The division's sector is far more favorable in terms of terrain and the ability to supply ourselves. The roads are paved between Stuhlweissenburg, Várpalota, and Veszprém, where nearly all of our administrative and logistical services are located."[15] The front had seemingly settled down into a relatively quiet phase, which experienced troops knew only signified the calm before the storm.

While the command and staff of the *IV. SS-Pz.Korps* and the divisions under its command enjoyed a relative period of calm in the campaign, events elsewhere demonstrated that by mid-February 1945, the war was grinding towards its inevitable bloody end. Although the situation in Pomerania had been temporarily stabilized by the *Sonnenwende* counteroffensive spearheaded by *Ogruf.* Felix Steiner's *11. Pz.Armee* under the auspices of Himmler's newly created *H.Gr. Weichsel,* East Prussia had been lost except for a narrow coastal strip occupied by the new *H.Gr. Ostpreussen* (formerly known as *H.Gr. Nord*), *H.Gr. Kurland* was isolated and serving no strategic purpose whatsoever, and the badly battered *H.Gr. Mitte* (renamed *H.Gr. Nord* as of 26 January) had barely managed to reconstruct a very wobbly front line. *Heeresgruppe A,* which had not been as badly affected by the Soviet winter offensive, had been renamed *H.Gr. Mitte.*

In the frozen north, the *20. Gebirgsarmee* had been completely driven out of Finland and was now defending northeastern Norway along the Arctic Circle. While the Italian Front had remained relatively static, the front in Western Europe had not. American, British, Canadian, and French armies were rapidly approaching the Rhine River along its entire length, from the Swiss border to Holland. Defeat was certain within the next three or four months. German industry was approaching collapse, fuel supplies were dwindling rapidly, German cities had been pounded into rubble, and the Red Army had almost reached the Oder River, the last natural obstacle before Berlin. With Germany's situation worsening by the day, the stage was set for the *Wehrmacht's* last successful counteroffensive of the war, the reduction of the Gran Bridgehead, *Unternehmen Südwind.* Occurring less than 90 kilometers north of Gille's headquarters, it would indirectly affect the course of the fighting in Hungary in a way that no one had envisioned.

Generaloberst Wöhler had been advocating the elimination of the Soviet bridgehead at Gran, officially designated as the *Parkány Brückenkopf,* since mid-January, when *Gen.d.Pz.Tr.* Friedrich Kirschner's *LVII. Pz.Korps* had attempted to do so in the wake of the 6th Guards Tank Army's own unsuccessful counterattack that had nearly reached Komorn. When Kirschner's troop were on the brink of success, the two *panzer* divisions spearheading the operation, the *8.* and *20. Pz.Div.,* were recalled to aid *H.Gr. Mitte,* thus causing the counterattack to culminate prematurely. In the time since that effort ended, the 6th Guards Tank Army had been pulled out to be reconstituted east of the Danube opposite Budapest, but the remaining troops of the 7th Guards Army hung on grimly. By early February 1945, based on intelligence intercepts, Wöhler had begun to worry that this bridgehead would soon become the launch pad for the renewal of the Soviet offensive towards Vienna expected in late March or early April 1945.

Until that point, *H.Gr. Süd* lacked sufficient forces that could be spared to carry out any sort of counteroffensive. This time, the prosecution of any counteroffensive against the Soviet bridgehead would be the responsibility of *Gen.d.Geb.Tr.* Hans Kreysing's *8. Armee,* not *A.Gr. Balck/6. Armee,* which in any case was preoccupied at that time, though his *Korpsgruppe Harteneck* would play a brief supporting role. However, the only force that Kreysing had north of the Danube that could participate in such an operation was *Gen.d.Pz.Tr.* Ulrich Kleemann's *IV. Pz.Korps FHH*. Despite its title, this corps lacked any appreciable armor of its own, except for *Pz.Abt. 208*, and consisted chiefly of two weak *Volks-Grenadier* divisions (the *211.* and *357.*) and the *44. Reichs-Gren.Div. HuD*. Another infantry division (the *46.*) would be brought down from the Carpathian Front to strengthen the attacking force, but this would not be enough to tip the balance in Kreysing's favor.

When the advance parties of the two SS *panzer* corps of the *6. Pz.Armee* began to arrive in the area south of the Danube beginning in early February, Wöhler saw an opportunity. During the period while these corps were preparing for their role in Hitler's impending counteroffensive, he proposed to "borrow" one of them to join with the *IV. Pz.Korps FHH*, thus securing the combat power that Wöhler believed was necessary to destroy the two Soviet corps defending the bridgehead. Then, the attacking force could quickly carry out the operation under the control of the *8. Armee* and wipe out the Parkány Bridgehead, bring all of the western bank of the Gran River back under German control, and then release the SS corps from the *6. Pz.Armee* in sufficient time for it to still play its intended role in the impending offensive.

While in Berlin being briefed on the upcoming *6. Pz.Armee* offensive on 8 February, as previously mentioned, Wöhler had gained Hitler's tentative approval of his concept, with the proviso that the borrowed SS corps would be returned to its assembly areas south of the Danube in time to recover for it to be ready for the much larger attack that would begin two weeks later. Wöhler's argument was further buttressed by Hitler's own concern that the presence of such a large Soviet bridgehead immediately north of the *6. Pz.Armee* might pose a threat to the security of his own counteroffensive scheduled for early March. Upon returning from Berlin to his own headquarters in the Esterháza Palace the following day, Wöhler and his chief of staff immediately got the army group's *Führungsabteilung* at work fleshing out the operations plan for what would become *Unternehmen Südwind*. Its intended start date was only eight days away—Saturday, 17 February.

In general, *Südwind* would be conducted in three phases. During the first phase, the northern flank of the Soviet salient would be attacked by the four infantry divisions of Kleemann's *IV. Pz.Korps FHH*. Their mission was to penetrate the enemy's front lines and seize advantageous jump-off positions for the SS armor. The next phase, beginning the same day, would involve attacks by two SS *panzer* divisions to make deep inroads towards Parkány, opposite the city of Gran on the northern bank of the Danube.

Simultaneously, a *Kampfgruppe* from the the *96. Inf.Div.* of *Korpsgruppe Harteneck/I. Kav.Korps*, taking advantage of the defenders' preoccupation with the attack against their northern flank, would conduct an amphibious operation over the Danube in support of the SS *panzer* corps, to be followed by a similar attack from Gran by the *711. Inf.Div.* once German spearheads drew near Parkány. Finally, once Parkány was in German hands, the two combined German corps would establish several bridgeheads over the Gran River in order to be able to conduct future operations and the SS corps would be released. The operation was intended to be completed by 24 February.[16]

The SS unit selected to carry out its part of the operation was *Gruf.* Hermann Priess's *I. SS-Pz.Korps*, consisting of the *1. SS-Pz.Div. Leibstandarte SS Adolf Hitler* (*LSSAH*) and the *12. SS-Pz.Div. Hitlerjugend* (*HJ*). Since it was the first corps scheduled to take part in the March 1945 offensive to arrive in Hungary in its entirety, it was tasked by *OKH* with Hitler's consent to carry out this attack. Both divisions had arrived in Hungary under conditions of great secrecy and had been assigned codenames to deceive and mislead Soviet military intelligence, part of the elaborate German attempt at *Maskirovka* (the Soviet term for military deception). For example, the *I. SS-Pz.Korps* headquarters was designated as *SS-Abschnittstab Süd* (SS-Sector Staff South), the *1. SS-Pz.Div. LSSAH* as *SS-Ersatzstaffel* (Replacement Echelon) *Totenkopf,* and the *12. SS-Pz.Div. HJ* as *SS-Ersatzstaffel Wiking.*[17] The *6. Pz.Armee* was designated as *Höherer Pionier-Führer Ungarn* ("Higher Engineer Command, Hungary").[18]

This was an obvious attempt to mask their true identity and to portray their sudden appearance between Raab and Komorn as part of Himmler's effort to rebuild Gille's two battered divisions, whose presence the Third Ukrainian Front was already aware of. An additional part of this operational security plan was the accompanying directive that all SS personnel taking part in *Südwind* had to remove their cuff titles, cover up division insignia on their vehicles as well as license plates, and use the abovementioned fake titles in all radio and telephonic communications. The possibility that the "cover" of the *I. SS-Pz.Korps* could be exposed during *Unternehmen Südwind* was probably considered, but ruled an acceptable risk.[19]

The area was defended by the XXIV and XXV Guards Rifle Corps of Col.Gen. M. S. Shumilov's 7th Guards Army, with a total of six rifle divisions and one airborne division, supported by 31 tanks and SP (self-propelled) guns. They had been dug in for over a month and had erected a series of formidable defensive barriers, so breaking through their positions would not be easy. The IV Guards Mechanized Corps was positioned on the opposite bank of the Gran River near Ipolysag, but its 27th Tank Brigade had been attached to the XXV Guards Rifle Corps to lend support if needed. Neither corps was at full strength and their divisions had been defending this area for over two months, having endured the after-effects of the failed counterattack of the 6th Guards Tank Army the previous month.

Unternehmen Südwind began on schedule at 4 a.m. on 17 February. The evidence indicates that the Germans achieved complete surprise. Following a two-hour preparatory artillery barrage, the four infantry divisions of the *IV. Pz.Korps FHH* penetrated Soviet defenses in several locations, thus allowing the commitment of the *I. SS-Pz.Korps*. During the next seven days, the attack advanced steadily, despite an extremely determined and skilled Soviet defensive effort. Losses were heavy on both sides. The Soviet defensive effort was undone when *Kampfgruppe Hüppe* of the *96. Inf.Div.*, supported by 20 assault guns from *Sturm-Art.Brig. 239*, successfully crossed the Danube during the night of 17/18 February and attacked the Soviet 93rd Guards Rifle Division in the rear. On 19 February, a battlegroup from the *711. Inf.Div.* crossed the Danube at the city of Gran and with the aid of tanks from *Ostubaf.* Joachim Peiper's *SS-Pz.Rgt. 1* seized Parkány.

During the next five days, the bulk of the German forces closed up along the Gran and pushed the remnants of the two Soviets corps back to the river, while follow-on forces mopped up bypassed enemy centers of resistance. Unsure of whether the 7th Guards Army would contest the German offensive with its remaining forces, the two German corps paused during 23 February while they waited for the rest of their units to catch up. The attack concluded the following day when the XXIV and XXV Guards Rifle Corps blew up their own bridges over the Gran to deny them to their pursuers, leaving their remaining troops on the opposite bank no choice but to abandon their equipment and either swim across the river or surrender. By 24 February, it was over. At 5:20 p.m., the *8. Armee* commander notified *H.Gr. Süd* of the operation's success, which was then relayed to *OKH* 25 minutes later. That same day, the *I. SS-Pz.Korps* began moving back across the Danube to its previous assembly areas to recover from this battle before their next one was scheduled to begin.

Overall, *Generaloberst* Wöhler and Hitler were satisfied with the results of the brief counteroffensive, regarded as the last large-scale German victory of World War II. Although no bridges over the Gran were taken, the threat to the left flank of the *6. Pz.Armee* had been eliminated, two Soviet rifle corps had been crushed, and the Soviet spring offensive towards Vienna had been delayed, at least in the short term. However, losses had been very heavy for all of the units involved. According to Soviet sources, the casualties in both the XXIV and XXV Guards Rifle Corps amounted to 8,194 men killed, wounded, and missing, plus as many as 54 tanks and self-propelled guns knocked out or destroyed, and 459 artillery pieces and antitank guns captured or destroyed.[20]

Had they considered it, both Wöhler and Hitler might have wondered why the rest of the 7th Guards Army had not been committed to the defense of the Gran Bridgehead, and why the VI Guards Tank Corps or Cavalry-Mechanized Corps Pliyev (officially designated by the Red Army as the 1st Guards Cavalry Mechanized Group) had not been committed there either. If both German leaders had done so, they might have realized that the Second Ukrainian Front was focused on something else entirely and was prepared to accept the loss of the bridgehead as an acceptable price to be paid in exchange for a future advantage.

German losses, though not as high as those suffered by the 7th Guards Army, were all but irreplaceable. The *8. Armee* reported that all told, both attacking corps suffered the loss of 6,471 men, including 969 killed in action, 4,601 wounded, and 901 missing in action. Undoubtedly, some of the losses in the latter category were men taken prisoner, including SS men from the *I. SS-Pz.Korps*. In addition, up to 130 tanks, assault guns, and tank destroyers were knocked out or rendered inoperable, though most of these were later repaired. Many of the armor losses were incurred within the tank battalions of the *I. SS-Pz.Korps*, which began the operation with 102 *panzers* of all types and ended up seven days later with only 43 deemed operational. Now, Priess's mechanics had only two weeks to restore as many of these vehicles to operational condition as soon as possible before they were needed again.

Although individual manpower losses for each division during this operation are not known, within Priess's *I. SS-Pz.Korps* they were heavier than they seemed at first glance. All told, the corps had suffered the loss of 2,989 men, including 413 killed, 1,923 wounded, and 653 missing in action. Most of these casualties were suffered in the corps' 12 *Panzergrenadier* battalions. Among the killed and wounded were 83 nearly irreplaceable officers.[21] *Brigadeführer* Otto Kumm, commander of the *1. SS-Pz.Div. LSSAH*, had the following to say after *Unternehmen Südwind*:

> The division was in miserable shape, only a shadow of itself. After the heavy casualties in Normandy and in the Ardennes, it had received an emergency fill of poorly trained personnel replacements from the *Heer, Luftwaffe, Kriegsmarine, Reichsarbeitsdienst* [the Reich Labor Service], and *Ordnungspolizei*. There had been no time for proper training as a result of the continuous moves … most were without any combat value. Many had managed to avoid any front-line service for five years. Certainly, many were honorable men, but they had not yet had the opportunity of firing a single shot in anger—they certainly did not wish to be killed in the last days of a lost war.[22]

Interestingly, the same assessment could probably be made of the replacements that the *Totenkopf* and *Wiking* Divisions were receiving at the same time. *Obersturmbannführer* Hubert Meyer, the *Ia* of the *12. SS-Pz.Div. HJ*, which took part in the offensive along with Kumm's division, wrote about his division's experience west of Gran:

> Although the division received replacements after being employed against the Gran Bridgehead—23 officers, 60 non-commissioned officers, and 1,040 enlisted men—most of them were [former] naval personnel … The offensive had cost us considerable losses. Among others, the commander of one of the two *Panzergrenadier* regiments had been killed. The soldiers had fought splendidly under difficult conditions.[23]

A better barometer of the conditions of these two units is provided by the *H.Gr. Süd* weekly *Kampfstärke* report submitted on 24 February. Both of these divisions had arrived in Hungary less than two weeks before at nearly full strength, after undergoing complete unit reconstitution following their experience in the Ardennes.

The *1. SS-Pz.Div. LSSAH* (aka *SS-Ersatzstaffel Totenkopf*) reported having three strong battalions, three average battalions, and two weak ones. One week later, its actual strength, including non-combat elements, totaled 18,871 men, an indication that it had absorbed a large number of replacements. An undetermined number of these were still in Germany awaiting transportation to Hungary. Its tank strength was very low, consisting of 11 *Pz. IVs*, two *Pz. V* Panthers, three *StuG III/IV* assault guns, 17 *Jg.Pz. IVs*, and only two operational *Pz. VI* Tiger IIs from the attached *s.SS-Pz.Abt. 501*. The division's maintenance services had less than a week to get as many armored fighting vehicles as possible back into operation by 5 March.[24]

The *12. SS-Pz.Div. HJ* (aka *SS-Ersatzstaffel Wiking*) was not much better off, also reporting only three strong infantry battalions, three average battalions, and two weak ones. On 1 March, it reported a total strength of 17,423 men, which included men still awaiting movement to Hungary as well as convalescing wounded. However, its armor strength was decidedly better, including 19 *Pz. IVs*, seven *Pz. V* Panthers, and 21 *Jg.Pz. IV* tank destroyers. In addition, the division had been augmented by 14 operational *Jagdpanther* (Hunting Panther) tank destroyers from the attached *Pz.Jäg. Abt. 560*, each mounting a powerful 8.8cm gun. The *Kampfwert* of both divisions was rated as "II." All told, both divisions were slightly over half-strength in armor, were filled with poorly trained replacements, and would need much longer than two weeks to recover from their ordeal, but there was no time for that.[25]

While the elimination of the Gran Bridgehead was an impressive tactical victory, especially during this late stage of the war, it had not been an easy one. In addition to the heavy losses sustained by the *I. SS-Pz.Korps*, which by themselves were a cause of concern, something of even greater consequence had been lost—the cloak of secrecy that had been drawn around the *6. Pz.Armee*. It did not take long for the Red Army to detect the presence of the *1. SS-Pz.Armee* once *Unternehmen Südwind* began. SS troops had been captured and interrogated, and the southward movement of Priess's *panzer* corps across the Danube bridge at Komorn after the operation had been concluded had been not gone unnoticed either.[26]

The *STAVKA* (the Soviet high command) quickly assembled the facts and guessed their import. They were aware that Dietrich's SS army had last been reported in the West during January, undergoing reconstitution after its failure in the Ardennes during *Wacht am Rhein*; the fact that the premier corps of the *Waffen-SS* had reappeared in Hungary less than a month later could only mean one thing—that Hitler, for whatever reason, had moved his strongest *panzer* army to that theater of war. If not properly countered, this unwelcome development might jeopardize the Soviet Union's plans for the spring that were intended to bring the war to an end.

Although Josef Stalin, the members of the *STAVKA*, and the commanders of the two fronts who would lead it certainly had cause to reconsider the start date of the Vienna Operation, they chose not to do so. They knew that any German offensive at this late stage of the war would be conducted on a logistical shoestring and could not last long. They most likely weighed the possible course of the German counteroffensive, considered the risks, and concluded that the Second and Third Ukrainian Fronts could both absorb the German blow when it came and still launch the Vienna Operation on schedule anyway, a sign of the supreme confidence they felt by this stage of the war.[27]

Meanwhile, Saturday, 24 February was another quiet day at the front around Stuhlweissenburg. The *Wiking* Division's *O1* summed up the situation when he wrote later that evening: "The situation at the front is peaceful, except for the usual amount of light reconnaissance activity by both sides. Hardly any artillery fire, no air activity. Everyone is enjoying this well-earned rest."[28] Although the *IV. SS-Pz.Korps* commander and his staff officers, including Günther Jahnke, were well aware of what was occurring to their north, the corps played no part whatsoever in *Unternehmen Südwind*. Focused primarily on defending their portion of the front line on either side of Stuhlweissenburg, Gille, his staff, and the leaders of the divisions under his command were doing their utmost to hasten the recovery of their units in order to prepare them as much as possible for the start of the Second and Third Ukrainian Front's next offensive. Except for Gille and a few select others, they had no idea that a large German counteroffensive was about to begin, and resolved to make the most of the "quiet" period while it lasted.

CHAPTER 2

Operation *Spring Awakening* 1–15 March 1944

After the successful conclusion of *Unternehmen Südwind*, the focus of *H.Gr. Süd* immediately returned to concluding the preparations for what was to be the last German offensive of World War II. Never before had the Third Reich devoted so many resources towards what would soon become one of the most pointless and wasteful operations it had ever undertaken. Fortunately for the *IV. SS-Pz.Korps*, it would not play a direct role in this misbegotten offensive, though it would suffer the immediate consequences of its failure. How this grand offensive had come about has been subjected to great debate over the years, but one thing is certain: the last remaining armored reserves that the *Wehrmacht* and *Waffen-SS* still possessed in early 1945 were thrown away in an attack in a secondary theater of war that, even had it succeeded, would have had no material impact on the outcome of the war whatsoever.

The offensive was the brainchild of Adolf Hitler's, and his alone. Code-named *Frühlingserwachen* (Spring Awakening), it would involve the commitment of the entire *6. Pz.Armee*, portions of *A.Gr. Balck/6. Armee*, *2. Pz.Armee*, and *H.Gr. E*. Its ostensible purpose was twofold: to secure the Nagykanizsa oilfields located southwest of Lake Balaton and to destroy the group of Soviet forces located west of the Danube–north of the Drava River–south of Lakes Balaton and Velencze (in other words, most of the Third Ukrainian Front). The Nagykanizsa oilfields, located safely behind the lines of the *2. Pz.Armee*, had become the source of 80 percent of the Third Reich's remaining oil reserves by early 1945. Hitler had been obsessing about the safety of this source of raw material to fuel his modern war machine since early November 1944, when it was first threatened by the Soviet offensive into Hungary. Though it had been safeguarded since then by the *2. Pz.Armee*, he knew that if this strategic asset was lost, so was the war. Therefore, his concern was understandable.

The other purpose of the offensive was less practical, but was intended as a spoiling attack to weaken the Third Ukrainian Front, or even destroy it if possible in order to render it unable to take part in any offensive aimed at Vienna or the oilfields. While there were still sufficient forces within *H.Gr. Süd* to protect the oilfields, there were not enough to carry out the latter objective. To do this, Hitler needed *Obst.Gruf* (equivalent in rank to the *Wehrmacht's Generaloberst*) Sepp Dietrich's *6. Pz.Armee.*

Generaloberest Wöhler was in favor of Hitler's plan, because as an army group commander he needed to eliminate the biggest threat to his command's survival as well as to carry out his standing orders to prevent the Red Army from gaining access to Vienna along either side of the Danube. Should this happen, there would be few natural obstacles blocking the approach of any large enemy force seeking to penetrate southeastern Austria and break through all the way to Bavaria. Wöhler was determined to ensure that this would not occur on his watch. With the *6. Pz.Armee* joining his army group, he would finally have the tools to carry out his mission, or so he thought.

One of the few naysayers to any offensive carried out in Hungary was *Gen.O.* Heinz Guderian, who as the chief of staff of the *OKH* was responsible for operations on the Eastern Front. He saw it as a potentially costly waste of precious manpower and matériel, which could and should have been used to defend the approaches to Berlin and not be squandered away in pursuit of an illusory objective. All of his efforts to convince Hitler otherwise were in vain; although Guderian understood and sympathized with Hitler's desire to safeguard the oilfields, sending the *6. Pz.Armee* to Hungary to gain a temporary advantage over the Red Army in a secondary theater of operations amounted to little more than strategic insanity. It would be interesting to speculate how the war might have ended differently had Sepp Dietrich's *panzer* army been used east of the Oder River instead of on the sodden Hungarian *Puszta* (plain); but that is a topic for another day.

Three different operational concepts or *Lösungen* (solutions, or courses of action) were developed, one by Wöhler and the staff of *H.Gr. Süd*, supported by Dietrich and his staff from *6. Pz.Armee* (labeled *Lösung "B"*), and two by Balck and Gaedke (*Lösungen "C1"* and *"C2"*). Course of action "B" involved eliminating Soviet forces west of Budapest as a prerequisite before the attack south of the lakes could begin; the other two (actually, "C2" was a variation of "C1," only with more flank protection) envisioned attacking towards the south and southeast first to link up with the approaching force from *H.Gr. E*, and then dealing with the forces west of Budapest later, if the need arose. Hitler, Guderian at *OKH*, and Balck favored "C2," which in theory would achieve the desired results more quickly, while only Wöhler, Helmuth von Grolman (Wöhler's chief of staff), and Dietrich preferred *Lösung "B,"* which they believed was more realistic given the forces available, as well as less risky.[1]

On 25 February, despite Wöhler and Dietrich's misgivings, Hitler made his decision—it would be *Lösung "C2."* He would live long enough to see the unfortunate consequences of this fateful decision. In its essence, *Frühlingserwachen* would consist of one main effort and two supporting efforts. Much like the previous month's ultimately aborted *Unternehmen Eisbrecher* (Operation *Icebreaker*), this counteroffensive would involve supporting attacks by the *2. Pz.Armee* towards Kaposvár from the west and by *H.Gr. E* across the Drava River from the south. These were designed to tie down Soviet, Bulgarian, and Yugoslav forces and, in the case of the attack by *H.Gr. E*, to meet the approaching spearheads of the main effort south of Lake Balaton and trap the bulk of the Third Ukrainian Front in a pincer movement, where it would be destroyed (see Map 2).

The main effort would be carried out by Dietrich's *6. Pz.Armee* between Lakes Balaton and Velencze with three corps (two SS *panzer* and one cavalry corps), supported on its left by a *panzer* corps from *A.Gr. Balck/6. Armee*. Its stated mission was to encircle and destroy Soviet units south of Lakes Balaton and Velencze, west of the Danube, and north of the Drava. By doing so, Hitler and Wöhler hoped that this would achieve their goals of protecting the oilfields and preventing the Red Army from carrying out any offensive aimed towards Vienna. For this ambitious plan, the *IV. SS-Pz.Korps* was not assigned an offensive role, but was instead tasked with defending the *Enge* (the narrows or "gap") between Lake Velencze and the southern foothills of the Vértes Mountains. The importance of this task was emphasized by the admonition that Gille's corps had to hold the Stuhlweissenburg area "with an iron grip."[2]

Whether Hitler or Dietrich realized it, *Frühlingserwachen* would be the third major German counteroffensive attempted between the two lakes with nearly the same goals. The first, *Unternehmen Spätlese* conducted by *III. Pz.Korps* from 21–22 December 1944, was designed to forestall the Soviet encirclement of Budapest and re-establish the *Margarethestellung*. It failed when *Gen.d.Pz.Tr.* Hermann Breith's tanks got stuck in the mud, which subjected them to furious Soviet counterattacks that quickly forced the *panzers* back to their starting line.

The second offensive, *Unternehmen Konrad III*, was conducted between 18 and 28 January 1945 and was far more ambitious. Launched by the *IV. SS-Pz.Korps*, its purpose was to relieve Budapest, destroy all Soviet forces north of Lake Velencze, and throw all remaining Soviet forces back across the lower Danube. The course of the fighting has been described in previous volumes, but it failed to achieve any of these goals and resulted in the loss of Budapest and its entire garrison. It also prompted a Soviet counteroffensive that had managed to regain all of the ground that they had lost by 12 February.

The only ways in which the *6. Pz.Armee* plan differed significantly from *Konrad III* was in the size of the attacking force (three *panzer* corps and one cavalry corps abreast instead of one *panzer* corps) and there being no requirement to relieve the garrison of *Festung Budapest*, who of course by 5 March were either dead or prisoners of war. Because an entire *panzer* army was being committed to the attack, the amount of supporting artillery and rocket artillery, engineer assets, antiaircraft batteries, and so forth was subsequently increased compared to the relatively small force employed by the *IV. SS-Pz.Korps*. However, the increase in the scale and scope of this latest operation came at a cost—in order to fit nearly 200,000 men and several

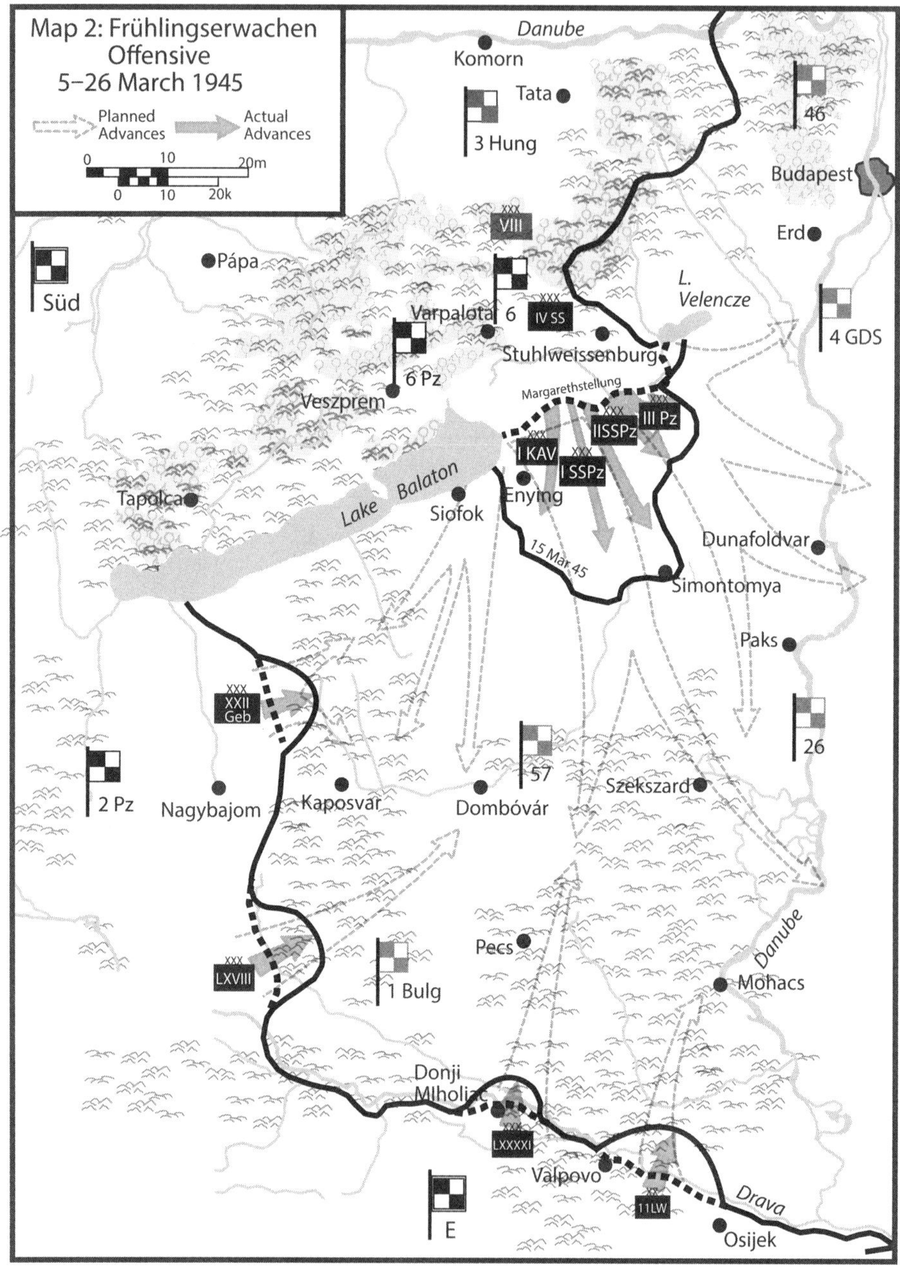
Map 2: Frühlingserwachen Offensive
5–26 March 1945
Planned Advances
Actual Advances
0 10 20m
0 10 20k
Danube
Komorn
Tata
3 Hung
46
Budapest
Süd
Pápa
Erd
L. Velencze
Varpalota 6
VIII
IV SS
Stuhlweissenburg
4 GDS
6 Pz
Veszprem
Margarethstellung
III Pz
IISSPz
I KAV
I SSPz
Tapolca
Lake Balaton
Siofok
Enying
15 Mar 45
Dunafoldvar
Simontomya
Paks
XXII Geb
57
26
2 Pz
Nagybajom
Kaposvar
Dombóvár
Szekszard
LXVIII
Pecs
1 Bulg
Danube
Mohacs
Donji Mholic
LXXXXI
Valpovo
Drava
E
11LW
Osijek

thousand vehicles, including over 500 tanks and other armored fighting vehicles, into the confined spaces between Veszprém and Várpalota, an enormous strain would be placed on the road network, which was being already being impacted by the continuing thaw as late winter turned into early spring.

As previously mentioned, the initial movement of the *6. Pz.Armee* was carried out in conditions of the greatest secrecy and enjoyed considerable initial success. During the *Südwind* operation, for instance, the Second Ukrainian Front and its 7th Guards Army had been surprised by the sudden appearance of the *I. SS-Pz.Korps* on the northern bank of the Danube. This element of surprise contributed substantially to the Germans' success. By the time *Gruf.* Hermann Priess's SS corps had crossed the Danube to return to its assembly area, *Ogruf.* Wilhelm Bittrich's *II. SS-Pz.Korps* (designated for deception purposes as *SS-Ausbildungsstab Süd*, or SS Training Staff South) and its two divisions had begun to arrive. Based on observations of these movements, the *STAVKA* and the two fronts were able to develop a fair assessment of the size of the force assembling between the Bakony Forest and the Danube, as well as its units' actual identities, despite the elaborate deception plan. It would be interesting to speculate how the course of the battle would have changed had the reduction of the Gran Bridgehead not been attempted at all, and whether the *6. Pz.Armee* could have maintained such a tight degree of operational security for two more weeks and still achieve a measure of surprise when its offensive finally began.[3]

Based on its location and composition, Soviet intelligence determined that the *6. Pz.Armee* would most likely attempt to carry out two courses of action—one between Lakes Balaton and Velencze aimed towards the south and southeast aimed at cutting off the bulk of the 26th Army, as *Konrad III* had, and the other between Lake Velencze and the southern foothills of the Vértes Mountains against the 4th Guards Army. Unbeknownst to *H.Gr. Süd*, behind the 4th Guards Army one of the two armies constituting the main effort for the Vienna Operation, the 9th Guards Army, was concentrating its corps and divisions; any German attack in its direction might force a premature commitment and upset the *STAVKA*'s timetable. Based on this analysis, a German attack out of the *IV. SS-Pz.Korps* sector to the east was deemed the most dangerous course of action. However, by early March, when Soviet ground and air reconnaissance had confirmed that *H.Gr. Süd* was concentrating the *6. Pz.Armee* behind the *Margarethestellung*, it was obvious that the Germans would attempt an attack towards the south between the lakes.

The Soviet defenses south of the *Margarethestellung* consisted initially of the 26th Army, later joined by the 27th Army of the Third Ukrainian Front. Although three mechanized corps were being withheld in Marshal Tolbukhin's front reserve (the XVIII and XXIII Tank Corps and the I Guards Mechanized Corps), the bulk of the forces that lay directly in the path of the *6. Pz.Armee* attack consisted of rifle divisions or fortified regions reinforced by more than the usual amount of artillery and antitank guns. Though the infantry units had been replenished somewhat, they were still at half strength of between 5,000 and 6,000 men per division, but they had nearly a month to prepare their defenses.

Just as they had done prior to the initiation of *Konrad III*, the six rifle corps and their divisions had heavily mined avenues of approach, dug numerous antitank ditches, laid hundreds of kilometers of barbed wire, and established dozens of tank kill zones peppered with numerous *Pakfronts* (antitank gun defences). The concept behind this defensive array was to wear out the German armored units, separate them from their protecting infantry, and leave them vulnerable to counterattacks. The same defensive strategy had succeeded at Kursk nearly two years before and had also worked well against *Konrad III*. By the time that the *Frühlingserwachen* offensive began, the Third Ukrainian Front was ready and waiting for the *6. Pz.Armee*'s attack.

Besides the formidable enemy forces arrayed against them, the weather had also seemingly conspired against the Germans and Hungarians. The thaw that had begun in mid-February persisted into the first week of March. Nearly every road, except the few paved highways running through the region, quickly became rivers of mud as over half a meter of snow melted within a few days. Canals, creeks, and streams soon overflowed their banks, posing mobility problems for the tanks that needed to get across them in order to maintain the offensive's momentum. Off-road movement in such conditions would become extremely difficult, as the 45-ton Panthers and massive 60-ton Tigers tended to sink into the mud unless drivers exercised great caution, but well-trained tank drivers were in short supply.

To add to the misery, during the first half of March, the weather alternated between rain and snow, and temperatures seldom fell below freezing point. The movement of so many armored units from their assembly areas north of the Bakony Forest into their crowded *Verfügungsräume* (forward attack area or jump-off positions) along the limited road network was a nightmarish experience, exacerbated by bad roads, traffic jams, and Red Air Force interdiction. Fuel shortages added to the problem, and units were once again ordered to park any vehicles that were not absolutely necessary in order to conserve fuel. The conditions of the roads also hindered the delivery of ammunition, since truck convoys carrying the shells and rockets needed to support the advance had to compete with other movements deemed equally high-priority. Overall, nothing augured well for the success of the operation, but it had been ordered by the *Führer* and consequently it must be carried out regardless of the cost. These repeated delays forced the postponement of *Frühlingserwachen* from 5 to 6 March, but even that 24-hour delay was insufficient.

As the final preparations for Operation *Frühlingserwachen* went forward, the situation in the *IV. SS-Pz.Korps*' area remained relatively peaceful. Since it had no significant role to play in the attack except to safeguard the left flank of Breith's neighboring *III. Pz.Korps*, which would see its share of heavy fighting, the *IV. SS-Pz. Korps* and its divisions spent most of the time between 25 February and 15 March improving defensive positions, incorporating new replacements into their depleted and worn-out battalions, and getting as many armored fighting vehicles as they could back into operation as quickly as possible. *Obergruppenführer* Gille and his corps *Führungsabteilung* would frequently travel to Sepp Dietrich's headquarters, where they received updated briefings on the *Frühlingserwachen* concept of operations. They would also brief Dietrich and his staff on what the *IV. SS-Pz.Korps* had learned about the terrain conditions south of Lakes Balaton and Velencze and between the lakes and the Danube.

It was also a time to meet old friends and get reacquainted, since many of the officers in Gille's corps had previously served in one of Dietrich's four SS divisions at one time or another, or they had attended the *Junkerschule* together. Marking this moment in time, *Ostuf.* Günther Jahnke wrote:

> During these days, Dietrich's army showed up. Numerous old comrades came by to visit us. We tried to solve the puzzle of why so many panzer divisions were being amassed nearby. In our experience, we had learned that an attack by panzer divisions at this time of the year in this swampy terrain crisscrossed with canals was not possible.[4]

The leaders of the *Totenkopf* and *Wiking* Divisions also worked out tentative plans to be put into effect should the corps be called upon to play a role in the coming battle. In turn, the commanders of each division's regiments, battalions, and even companies worked out their own local defense plans, organized local reserves, and conducted training if time and resources permitted.

Several changes in the corps staff occurred during this time. The vital *Ia* position, the duties of which were performed temporarily by Hans Velde following the loss of Fritz Rentrop on 2 February, was finally filled on 1 March by *Stubaf.* Friedrich Rauch, a recent graduate of the 15th wartime *Generalstabslehrgang* (general staff course) at the *Kriegsakademie* who had matriculated on 26 January 1945. The 33-year old Rauch, a Berliner who had joined the *SS-Verfügungstruppe* on 9 November 1938 with the rank of *SS-Junker*, had initially served for several years in the *Heer* and attained the rank of *Leutnant* before transferring to the SS.

An artilleryman by trade, after being promoted in the SS to *Untersturmführer* he was posted to the artillery regiment of the *Totenkopf* Division on 1 November 1939. Here he served until 1940, when he was transferred to the *SS-Junkerschule* in Bad Tölz as an instructor. From November 1943 until March 1944, he was a battery commander in *SS-Art.Rgt. 3*, then as a general staff aspirant on the staff of the *II. SS-Pz.Korps* in Normandy from June–August 1944. Awarded both classes of the Iron Cross, the Infantry Assault Badge, and the Black Wound Badge, Rauch soon proved himself to be a competent staff officer and a worthy successor to Rentrop. Hans Velde reverted to his previous role as the corps' *O1*, where he was able to use the experience gained during the past month as acting *Ia* to assist Rauch in transitioning to his new duties.

During this same period, *Ustuf.* Günther Lange, who had gone to serve on the staff of *SS-Pz.Rgt. 5* as its acting *Ordonnanz Offizier* for the past two months, returned to the corps *Hauptquartier* to resume his previous duties as Gille's *Begleitoffizier* (aide-de-camp, or *O5*). During Lange's absence, he had been temporarily replaced by *Ustuf.* Joachim Barthel, who had to serve simultaneously as both Gille's and his chief of staff Manfred Schönfelder's aide-de-camp. Barthel, who until December 1944 had served as the *O1* of *I. Btl./Germania*, had received a head wound that rendered him no longer fit for front-line duty, though he could still fulfill the role of a general's aide. For his part, Gille was glad to have his old *O5* back, and as a friendly gesture allowed Lange to continue with his amateur photography, which was normally a forbidden practice. Thankfully, most of Lange's photographs survived the war.

In addition to these two officers, at some point after 24 February, *Stubaf.* Hubert Hüppe was assigned to the vacant position of the commander of *SS-Nachr.Abt. 104*, which had been filled by a *Stellvertreter* (acting commander) after its previous commander, *Stubaf.* Karl Krüger, died on 2 February 1945 in an Austrian hospital from wounds received in battle during January. Until that point, Hüppe had been competently serving as commander of *SS-Nachr.Abt. 5* of the *Wiking* Division and had been a signal officer in SS communications units since 1939. He was replaced as the commander of the *Wiking's Nachrichten* (signals) battalion by the equally able *Stubaf.* Herbert Schmeisser. The tall and physically imposing Hüppe would be seen frequently at Gille's side, and as the corps signal officer, Gille would rely heavily on Hüppe's *SS-Nachr.Abt. 104* to ensure that radio, telex, and landline telephone communications with higher, adjacent, and lower units were continuously maintained.

Besides the numerous personnel changes described above, another administrative task was levied on the corps on 1 March when it received an order from the *SS-FHA* in Berlin that its two *panzer* divisions were to begin transitioning to the new *SS-Panzer-Division 1945* organizational structure. As an economizing measure, this would have brought the organization of the seven SS *panzer* divisions into roughly the same as that used by the *Wehrmacht's Panzer-Division 1944* structure. In order to bring this about, each of a division's two SS *Panzergrenadier* regiments would be reduced from three to two battalions, the artillery regiment would lose one light howitzer *Abteilung*, and the division's *Flak* battalion would be reduced from four to three batteries. One of the remaining *Panzergrenadier* battalions would be equipped with bicycles instead of motor vehicles. The *panzer* regiment would continue to consist of two battalions, one equipped with *Pz. IVs* and the other with *Pz. V* Panthers. This would have reduced the *Gesamtstärke* (total end strength) of a division to 13,966 men (excluding *Hiwis*, auxilliary recruits from Eastern Europe), 3,459 men less than the previously authorized number of 17,425. There is no evidence that any of the SS units operating in Hungary, including the *IV. SS-Pz.Korps*, ever converted to this new structure, due partly to the pressure of events as well as the end of the war, at that point only slightly over two months away.[5]

With but a few exceptions, the sector defended by the *IV. SS-Pz. Korps* was relatively uneventful during the period 25 February–15 March 1945. The most important exception was the regiment-sized attack carried out south and west of Zámoly by elements of the XX Guards Rifle Corps against the front line held by the *Totenkopf* Division on 25 February. Supported by a few tanks (no more than a company) and a preparatory artillery barrage, the Soviet attack struck an extended bulge in the lines defended by the *II. Bataillon* of the *Totenkopf* Regiment and the neighboring infantry battalion from the Hungarian *2. Pz. Div.*[6]

The attack managed to penetrate the defenders' forward outpost line, but before the attackers could achieve a penetration in the *HKL* (main combat line, or front), their assault was brought to a bloody halt by concentrated artillery fire from *SS-Pz. Art. Rgt. 3* as well as by the fire of the *Totenkopf* Regiment's own heavy weapons. "At least," said *Sturmmann* Gerstel of *II. Btl./Totenkopf*, "now they know where we are."[7] Some of the battalion's members speculated that the attack had been carried out to seize more favorable jump-off positions for a future attack; it could just as likely have been an attempt to find where the division boundary lay between the *Totenkopf* Division and the Hungarian *2. Pz. Div.* If nothing else, the Soviet regiment found this boundary in the course of its unsuccessful attack, though it paid a high price for it.

The only other event of note that took place that day was that the *Kampfgruppe* designation was removed from the title of the *Wiking* Division. Ullrich's organization had received sufficient replacements to bring it back up to its authorized strength, thereby earning the right to call itself a "division" again. It would be evaluated as a full division from this point onwards and assigned tasks appropriate to its size and strength. Should it be cut down in strength again, it would revert to its previous title. This would prove to be the last time in the war that the *Wiking* Division would reach anywhere near its full wartime strength.[8]

On 26 February, a day when the thermometer reached 50 degrees Fahrenheit (10 degrees Centigrade), the skies partially cleared and the Red Air Force appeared in significant numbers, bombing and harassing the front lines of both the *IV. SS-Pz. Korps* and the *8. Armee* north of the Danube. The only event worthy of note that day was that this was the first time that the officers of the *IV. SS-Pz. Korps Führungsabteilung*, including Schönfelder, Rauch, Jankuhn, and Velde, were briefed by the staff of the *6. Pz. Armee* on the overall *Frühlingserwachen* plan.[9]

On 27 February, the new commander of *HARKO 306, Gen. Lt.* Eduard Aldrian, briefed the *IV. SS-Pz. Korps* staff and *SS-ARKO 504* and told them that reconnaissance had determined that the number of artillery batteries being employed by the 4th Guards Army opposite the corps' main defense line had been reinforced by a further 23 batteries, bringing the total number of identified batteries up to 122, compared to the 66 batteries within the *IV. SS-Pz. Korps*, almost a two-to-one advantage.[10] At the time, this was not seen as anything to worry about, since experience had shown that the Red Army preferred at least a four-to-one advantage in artillery before it launched a general offensive. However, this was still more than three times as many batteries as those arrayed against the sector defended by the *III. Pz.Korps* to the south of Gille's headquarters, which could have been seen as an indicator of future Soviet intentions, though apparently no one drew that conclusion. On that same day, both the *3.* and *4. Kav.Brig.* were formally upgraded to division status, a precursor to both being withdrawn and employed as part of the *I. Kav.Korps* in its order of battle for *Frühlingserwachen*.[11]

Wednesday, 28 February was the last day that *Korpsgruppe Harteneck/I. Kav. Korps* was to serve as part of *A.Gr. Balck/6. Armee*'s order of battle. That evening, *Gen.d.Kav.* Gustav Harteneck's command prepared to hand over responsibility for the left wing of *A.Gr. Balck/6. Armee* to the Hungarian *3. Armee*, which had to move from its positions along the northern shore of Lake Balaton to take over the sector to the left of Gille's corps stretching all the way across the Vértes, Gerecse, and Pilis Mountains to Gran in the northeast. Apparently, *H.Gr. Süd* believed this area to be the least critical sector and that *Gen.Lt.* József Heszlényi's army was capable of defending it. The commander and chief of staff of the *6. Pz.Armee* were unsettled by this aspect of the plan, and informed *H.Gr. Süd* of their misgivings, echoing the concerns expressed by the previous commander of *H.Gr. Süd, Gen.d.Inf.* Johannes Friessner, who stated in October 1944: "It is now quite apparent that the Hungarians will not stand fast anywhere."[12] Settling into the same headquarters installation in Tata that had been used by Harteneck's headquarters, the Hungarian *3. Armee* would take control of its new defensive sector the following day, 1 March.

Otherwise, there was no fighting or any other enemy activity worth mentioning that day in the *A.Gr. Balck/6. Armee* area of operations. The weather continued its warming trend and scattered rain showers became more prevalent. Unpaved roads were still a terrible mess, and rivers, streams, and canals continued overflowing their banks. According to one eyewitness, the *Ia* of the *6. Pz.Armee*:

> The timetables and the movement tables had been waste paper for a long time. Only improvisation and the tireless efforts of the commanders down to company and battery level enabled the suffering troops to make slow progress. Mud, everywhere one looked. Mud, wherever one stepped. Mud, wherever one moved or rode![13]

The *IV. SS-Pz.Korps* was not immune from the effects of the mud. In its defensive sector, the *I. Btl./Norge* had begun moving to the rear to continue its reconstitution in the vicinity of Veszprém. While doing so, Vogt and the remaining survivors of his battalion had to struggle on foot to make their way through the never-ending traffic jams. Likewise, *SS-Rgt. Ney* was moved out of its positions on the eastern outskirts of Stuhlweissenburg to the town of Sur to begin its own period of reconstitution in the Hungarian *3. Armee* rear area.

On 1 March, the movement of the start date for *Frühlingserwachen* to 6 March was finally approved by the *OKH*, after the commanders of *H.Gr. Süd* and the

6. Pz.Armee had lobbied for a 24-hour extension due to the difficulties being encountered in moving up units into their attack positions on account of the terrible traffic situation. Two important events also took place that day in the *IV. SS-Pz. Korps* sector. The first was the detachment of the *356. Inf.Div.* and its subsequent assignment to the neighboring *III. Pz.Korps* south of Lake Velencze. Although the *IV. SS-Pz.Korps* did not regret the departure of *Oberst* Kühl's division, which it had characterized as having "debatable defensive strength," this necessitated a shift of several kilometers to the south by the *Wiking* Division, which had to take over the positions being vacated by the *356. Inf.Div.*[14]

Shortly after this had taken place, the battalion from the *Wiking* occupying the ground just given up by the *356. Inf.Div.* was attacked by a battalion-sized enemy force. Although it successfully fought off this attempt, it was a clear indication that Soviet troops were keeping a sharp eye on German troop dispositions. The shift of the *Wiking* Division's right flank to the south also required the *Totenkopf* Division to do the same; by shuffling its battalions, Becker and Ullrich determined that the new boundary between the two divisions should be the northern edge of Stuhlweissenburg, which would be taken up by *Hstuf.* Peter Stienen's *I. Bataillon* of the *Totenkopf* Regiment. Adjudging that they both needed to move their division command posts once again to place them in the most advantageous position to facilitate command and control, by that evening Becker's command post was relocated from Bodajk to Fehervarcsurgo, while Ullrich's was shifted to Iszkaszentgyörgy.

The *IV. SS-Pz.Korps* commander, his *ARKO*, and his three division commanders were disappointed when they learned in the evening that *Volks-Art.Korps 403* and *Volks-Werf.Brig. 17* were being removed from the corps' order of battle the following day in order to reinforce the artillery of the *III. Pz.Korps* as it was being assembled to support the *6. Pz.Armee*'s attack. Thus, in one fell stroke, Gille's corps lost a third of its dedicated artillery support. Opposite the positions held by the *Wiking, Totenkopf,* and Hungarian *2. Pz.Div.*, forward outposts had detected a significant amount of activity taking place at night behind Soviet lines. This included the laying of new minefields, constructing or reinforcing fighting positions, and the movement of troops in and out of the lines in such as manner as to render it difficult to determine the enemy's plans and intentions.

The first day of March also marked the date when both of Gille's SS divisions were required to submit their monthly *Zustandsbericht* (status report) to the *OKH* Inspectorate of *Panzer* Troops covering the previous month. With this report, as with previous ones, a staff officer in Berlin could gain a solid appreciation of not only a division's *Kampfstärke* and *Kampfwert*, but also how it was faring in specific categories, how it was organized in terms of its *K.St.N* (*Kriegsstärkenachweisung*, or War Strength Inventory Directive), as well as the commander's personal narrative summarizing how he viewed the readiness of his division. These were first reviewed by their immediate higher headquarters, in this case the *IV. SS-Pz.Korps*, before being passed up the reporting chain to Berlin.

Viewing the *Zustandsbericht* of the *Totenkopf* Division for this date, the division reported that in terms of manpower, it had 14,896 men present for duty. During the last 28 days, it had lost 109 men killed, 683 wounded, and 111 missing—a total loss of 903 men—with an additional 127 men sick or absent from duty for other reasons. This was less than half of the losses suffered during the previous month. In turn, it had received 1,058 replacements and 154 returning convalescent wounded personnel. Included in the present for duty number was a large number of new replacements assigned to the division, but being held back in the *H.Gr. Süd* rear area in a large pool of *Waffen-SS* replacements, so while they were technically "assigned," they were not present at the front line.

In regards to armored vehicles, the division reported 11 operational *StuG III/ IV*s with four in short-term repair (ready in less than three weeks), 16 operational *Pz. IV*s with two in short-term repair, 11 *Pz. V* Panthers with five in short-term repair, and six *Pz. VI* Tiger Is combat ready with another one in short-term repair. Finally, it had four operational *Jg.Pz. IV*s and one in short-term repair. Overall, the division at that particular moment could field 48 operational armored fighting vehicles with 13 more in short-term repair. Though this was less than a quarter of the total number of armored fighting vehicles authorized, it was average for a *panzer* division in *A.Gr. Balck* at that time.

In terms of *SPW* (*Schützenpanzerwagen*, or armored personnel carriers), the division had only 72 operational (out of 272 authorized) and eight more in repair. In regards to soft-skinned vehicles, the situation was mixed. It had 1,658 of all types deemed operational, out of 2,075 authorized, enabling the division to carry only 80 percent of its mandatory tonnage carrying capability. An additional 180 trucks were under short-term repair. Of the 176 half-tracked prime movers authorized, the division still had 122 operational on hand, including eight unauthorized *Raupenschlepper Ost* (*RSO*) fully tracked cargo vehicles. Another 22 were under repair. Moving to heavy weapons, the *Totenkopf* had 13 operational 7.5cm Pak antitank guns out of 28 authorized, 42 combat-ready artillery pieces out of 59 authorized (with another 10 in short-term repair), and 20 antiaircraft guns out of 50 authorized by the *K.St.N.*

The last section of the condition report was reserved for the commander. Not known as a man to mince words, Becker rated the training level of his division as "Sufficient," the morale of his troops as "Good, despite unbroken combat since 1 January 1945," and some particular difficulties such as "Severe shortages of tanks, assault guns, *Geschützen* [artillery, antitank and *Flak* pieces], and *SPW*s." On this date, he rated his division's mobility as 85 percent, and assessed its *Kampfwert* as a surprisingly low "II/III," which was below what it had been assessed for the weekly status report for *H.Gr. Süd* the week before. In other words, he subjectively viewed it as being somewhere between conditionally ready for offensive operations and fully ready for defensive missions. Why he rated it this way is not explained, but it could have been due to the overall effect of the equipment shortages, so many new recruits, shortages of experienced officers and NCOs, and other intangibles. Nevertheless, it was still the strongest division in Gille's corps.[15]

For the same reporting period, the *Wiking* Division's numbers also reflect the huge number of replacements it had received during the past month, with its present for duty strength listed as 15,445 men. During the previous period, it had suffered the loss of 1,041 men—including 190 killed in action, 735 wounded, and 116 missing in action—with an additional 1,255 men reported as sick or absent for other reasons. This does not include the 4,014 men assigned to the division but laying in hospital or recovering from previous injuries in the *Vaterland* (Fatherland). To balance these losses, it had received 1,771 replacements and 74 returning convalescents. As with the *Totenkopf* Division, many of the new replacements were assigned to the division, but held back in a large *Waffen-SS* replacement pool in the *H.Gr. Süd* rear area. Although it reported an excess of 532 *Unterführer* during the period, nearly all of these were transfers from the *Luftwaffe* or *Kriegsmarine* with no front-line experience or infantry leadership skills.

The condition of its armored fighting vehicle fleet was simply discouraging. Although not authorized any assault guns by this stage of the war, it reported two as being operational and another three in short-term repair. Only three *Pz. IV*s were reported as being combat-ready, with one more in repair. The condition in regards to *Pz. V* Panthers was only slightly better, with nine reported as operational and six under short-term repair. Thus, out of 183 authorized armored fighting vehicles, it only had 14 operational and 10 more in repair, approximately 13 percent on hand in all, barely a single tank company. It no longer had any *Jg.Pz. IV* tank destroyers at all. The condition of its *SPW*, so necessary for armored warfare, was not particularly good, fielding only 103 operational armored half-tracks, with another 30 in repair.

As bad as the situation was concerning armored vehicles, that of its soft-skinned vehicles was even worse. Authorized 2,075 trucks of all types, it could only report 1,235 operational and 155 in repair. This enabled the division to only carry 3,753 short tons (3,405 metric tons) of supplies, only 60 percent of the 6,240 short tons (5,660 metric tons) it was required to carry in one lift. Concerning tracked prime movers, it reported 91 operational (out of 176 required) and 13 more in short-term repair. It had 11 operational 7.5cm Pak guns (out of 28 authorized) with four in repair, 46 out of 59 required artillery pieces with five in repair, and six SP infantry guns. Its *Flak* battalion was in comparatively good shape, reporting that it had 11 3.7cm guns and eight 8.8cm *Flak*. The division was still suffering chronic shortages of light machine guns, reporting only 449 out of the 1,108 authorized. Considering that German infantry squad tactics were based around the firepower provided by the *MG-34* or *MG-42*, this was a serious shortage indeed. Additionally, this report on machine-gun readiness had a note affixed to the bottom of the page stating "only conditionally combat ready due to constant loading stoppages." Whether this was due to mechanical problems or overuse of lacquered cartridge cases was not stated.

The *Wiking* Division's commander was slightly more of a wordsmith than his counterpart in the *Totenkopf* Division, saving his literary skills for his commander's assessment. In Section 4, *Kurzes Werturteil des Kommandeurs* (Commander's Evaluation), Ullrich wrote: "On account of the heavy losses in personnel suffered in January and during the first half of February, as well as the insufficient training time in the second half of the month while employed close to the front line including manning defensive positions, the training condition of the division is deficient." Despite these conditions, he assessed the morale of this troops as "Very good." During the following paragraph, echoing Becker, Ullrich wrote that "the shortage of tanks and tank destroyers is very acute and the few still on hand, on account of the heavy over usage they have endured, can only be considered as partially mission-capable." As Gille would have known, most of these *panzers* were over a year old and had survived long beyond their expected lifespans. The fact that they were operational at all should stand as a monument to the skills of the recovery and maintenance crews.

Oberführer Ullrich reminded his chain of command, who were probably already well aware of the situation, that there were sufficient trained tank crews available within the *panzer* regiment to operate a great deal more, should the division ever be issued with replacement vehicles while fighting in Hungary or Austria (it never was). This statement was aimed at officials in the *OKH Heeresrüstungsamt*, who decided the basis of allocation of replacement vehicles for both the *Wehrmacht* and *Waffen-SS*. Besides these shortages, he wrote, the division still needed an additional issue of rifles, machine guns, field telephone sets and telephone cable, as well as trucks and *SPW*.

Due to the shortage of the latter two items, he assessed his division's mobility as only 45 percent. He accordingly assessed his division's *Kampfwert* as "IV," suitable only for limited defensive missions, the lowest category available. What the division really needed, and what it would not get, was at least a month in a training area to rest, incorporate new equipment, and train at the individual, collective, and unit level, but of course by this stage of the war this was impossible—it simply could not be spared, as much as Gille would probably have liked it to be.[16]

Unfortunately, the *Zustandbericht* for the corps *Hauptquartier*, its *Flak* battery, and *Begleit Kompanie*—as well as the other corps troops and attached *Sondertruppen des Reichsführung-SS*, such as *s.SS-Art.Abt. 504* and *SS-Werf.Abt. 504*—are not available, so it is impossible to know what their exact matériel and personnel conditions were. But taking the two divisions together, although battered and worn, and stocked with half-trained replacements, they still represented a considerable amount of combat power, especially when compared to comparable Soviet units, and were still led by competent and experienced leaders at the battalion, regiment, and division level.

The greatest weakness of these two battle-scarred divisions, besides the afore-mentioned lack of tanks, was the shortages of experienced and talented small unit leaders at the squad, platoon, and company level—it was here where the losses had been the highest and where the best men were needed. If there was to be any of the legendary "SS spirit" to be found at all, it would be found here, in the trenches, in the form of the few remaining senior privates, corporals, sergeants, lieutenants, and captains who had somehow survived the past five years of war. There were never enough of them, especially now.

Perhaps the greatest concern felt by SS commanders at all levels was the reliability of the Hungarian *2. Pz.Div.*, aligned to the left of the *Totenkopf* Division. Still considered one of the few remaining elite units of the *Honvéd*, it had been brigaded under the *Totenkopf* so that *Brig.Fhr.* Becker could keep a close eye on it. Although this division, led by the reliably pro-German commander *Gen.Maj.* vitéz-Zsedényi, who had returned to assume the leadership of his formation on 1 March 1945, the division had not suffered much from a high desertion rate, unlike many other Hungarian units. It had reached such a point in some areas, that *H.Gr. Süd* was compelled to institute draconian measures, including summary execution if soldiers were seen crossing into Soviet lines. Any soldiers apprehended in the process of desertion were to be tried by summary courts and hanged. This could not have anything other than a deleterious effect on Hungarian morale; suffice to say, once the Soviet spring offensive got underway, the troops of the *Totenkopf* Division would be looking anxiously over their left shoulder in the hopes that the *2. Pz.Div.* would stand its ground and fight.[17] Only time would tell.

On 2 March, temperatures continued to hover well above freezing, though the wind had increased. Isolated thundershowers and partly cloudy skies completed the scene. While all of the German and Hungarian units earmarked for *Frühlingserwachen* struggled to get into their positions despite the atrocious state of the roads, the troops from the *IV. SS-Pz.Korps* holding the line in what was now being called the "Stuhlweissenburg Gap" continued carrying out their usual duties.[18] Aside from this, the only other activities of note reported that day consisted of reconnaissance and combat patrols being conducted by both sides, as well as the "normal" amount of artillery harassing fire. Little aerial activity took place, except for the seemingly ever-present Soviet and German reconnaissance aircraft.[19] According to one observer from the *Wiking* Division, "The front line situation has become completely becalmed … only light reconnaissance activity, hardly any artillery fire, no enemy air activity."[20]

The situation continued in the same manner the following day, 3 March. Although temperatures during the evening frequently dipped below the freezing mark, during the day it would warm up again, bringing rain showers alternating with snow. The wind continued its blustery behavior, although while it chilled it also hastened the drying-out process. Conditions had become so bad along the roads and traffic jams so frequent, that the *H.Gr. Süd* chief of staff was compelled to place groups of officers at key intersections to act as traffic police to resolve disputes on the spot, using deadly force if necessary. Units that had torn up the roads were required to make any necessary repairs before they were allowed to continue. *Strassenbau* (road construction) battalions were brought in to lend a hand. With draconian measures such as these, including the impressment of local Hungarian civilians into labor gangs, the units earmarked for *Frühlingserwachen* slowly filed into their forward assembly areas.[21]

On 4 March, the weather remained the same as it had been the day before. Enemy activity was unchanged too. The situation along the *IV. SS-Pz.Korps'* front at the time was summed up in a report written by an unnamed *SS-Kriegsberichter* that was published in the division newsletter of the *Totenkopf* Division, *Der Totenkopfmelder*:

> The warming yellow spring sun has been shining for many days now over the ground we have recently occupied as well as in our new defensive positions. Its rays penetrate into the hard-caked earth covered with the last remains of snow and transforms paths and trails into deep, brown mud. In places, the wide asphalt roads that crisscross the landscape become lost in small lakes full of meltwater from the thick snow walls shoveled up to the left and right. This marks the beginning of the age-old muddy period, a time of suffering for the drivers, which they must become accustomed to once again … the grenadiers in the trenches do their best by making homemade wooden grates to stand on and reinforce their embankments with wooden planks [to prevent trench walls from collapsing]. They often stand guard in their foxholes with mud up to their knees as anti-tank teams stand watch behind their "stovepipes" [i.e.., *Panzerschreck* antitank rocket launchers], with carbines, machine guns and hand grenades always ready at hand. Flanks are secured by one antitank gun after another. When the Soviets become restless over on the other side, our *Nebelwerfer* fire, the mortars spit their bombs, and heavy shells from our own artillery are sent howling towards the threatened area. Enemy deployments are soon recognized, efforts that are soon nipped in the bud. In the air, German fighter aircraft secure the area.[22]

Behind the front lines, rear echelon troops from both the *Totenkopf* and *Wiking* Divisions were able to watch as troops from the *3.* and *4. Kav.Div.* and their horses moved south along the highway between Mór and Stuhlweissenburg, followed shortly thereafter by the battalions and regiments of the *44. Reichs-Gren.Div. Hoch und Deutschmeister (H.u.D.)*, which until a week before had been fighting against the Gran Bridgehead north of the Danube. Their morale seemed to be good, with at least one *Landser* being overheard saying: "One more big push in the East will change things in our favor!"[23]

Sunday, 4 March began with road conditions relatively unchanged. Worried by the slow movement of the assault troops into their assembly areas, German senior commanders began debating the wisdom of rescheduling the beginning of the offensive to a later date, perhaps by two or three days, but when the question was submitted to *OKH* headquarters, Hitler was adamant that it would proceed on 6 March as scheduled. This would result in some of the attacking formations beginning their operations behind schedule so that instead of a simultaneous attack along the entire front line, it would commence in a rippling fashion, but nothing could be done about it in the face of Hitler's obstinacy.

Within the *IV. SS-Pz.Korps'* sector, there was hardly any enemy activity at all, other than the usual. As an example, between 2 and 4 March, the *Totenkopf* Division suffered only 21 casualties, all wounded in action, while during the same period, the *Wiking* Division reported just 24 men being wounded.[24] In contrast, the division's newspaper, *Der Totenkopfmelder*, presented its monthly *Erfolgseite* (success page) listing the amount of Soviet tanks, other weapons, and equipment it had destroyed between 1 January and 28 February during *Konrad I–III* and the battles that followed—it was an impressive number indeed. During this period, the division claimed to have captured or destroyed 110 Soviet tanks, one assault gun, 100 antitank guns, four artillery pieces, seven mortars, 71 machine guns, 18 trucks, and three aircraft, as well as considerable amounts of land mines, artillery rounds, and hand grenades. Although it claimed to have captured a number of Soviet troops, the total was not specified.

The following day, 5 March, proved to be just as quiet for the roughly 40,000 men of the *IV. SS-Pz.Korps*. For the first time in nearly a week, a cold front had moved in, bringing renewed light snowfall and the return of freezing temperatures. This boded well for the attack by the *6. Pz.Armee*; hopefully it would continue long enough for the ground to sufficiently freeze before the attack began, rendering cross-country movement by armored vehicles easier. This promising situation did not continue throughout the day, as temperatures once again rose above freezing point, dashing the hopes of the men who would lead the attack.

On Gille's left flank adjacent to the Hungarian *3. Armee*, the *6. Pz.Div.* was heavily engaged in fighting around Csabdi, which changed hands no less than six times during the day, ending with the Red Army in possession of the devastated town that had been in the front line for nearly two months. The following day, the *6. Pz.Div.* was scheduled to be withdrawn and become the *A.Gr. Balck/6. Armee* reserve, being replaced around Csabdi by the still-untried *SS-K.Gr. Ameiser*. This was the designation of the regiment-sized battlegroup formed around the combat-ready troops of the *37. Freiwilligen SS-Kav.Div. Lutzöw* commanded by *Stubaf.* Anton Ameiser, which was placed under the operational control of the *96. Inf.Div.*[25]

At 4 a.m. the following day, the *Frühlingserwachen* offensive began. Because the *IV. SS-Pz.Korps* did not directly take part in the fighting itself until 16 March, by which point it had already run its course, the offensive will be only briefly summarized here, since it is already covered in great detail in other works. In essence, the attacking forces were arrayed as follows, from right to left: on the far right or western zone of attack, *General der Kavallerie* Harteneck's *I. Kav.Korps* with his two mounted divisions (the newly upgraded *3.* and *4. Kav.Div.*) would protect the right flank of the *6. Pz.Armee* by advancing towards the Sió River. Next to it was positioned *Gruppenführer* Priess's *I. SS-Pz.Korps*, with two SS divisions (the *1. SS-Pz.Div. LSSAH* and *12. SS-Pz.Div. HJ*) and the Hungarian *25. Inf.Div.* These divisions would attack southwards towards the intermediate objective of Simontornya, with their left flank anchored along the Sárviz Canal. Positioned adjacent to Priess was *Ogruf.* Wilhelm Bittrich's *II. SS-Pz.Korps* with the *2. SS-Pz.Div. Das Reich* and the *9. SS-Pz.Div. Hohenstaufen*, along with the *23. Pz.Div.* and the *44. Reichs-Gren.Div. H.u.D.*, which would advance with its right flank along the Sárviz and Malom Canals, with an intermediate objective of Czecze. Finally, covering Dietrich's left flank was *General der Panzertruppe* Breith's *III. Pz.Korps*, operating under the command of *H.Gr. Balck/6. Armee* with the *1. Pz.Div.*, *3. Pz.Div.*, and *356. Inf.Div.* (see Map 2).

From the west, *Gen.d.Geb.Tr.* Rudolf Konrad's *LXVIII. Armee-Korps* of the *2. Pz.Armee* with two divisions (the *13. SS-Waffen-Geb.Div. Handschar* and *71. Inf.Div.*) and the *XXII Geb.Korps*, also with two divisions (the *118. Jäg.Div.* and *1. Volks-Geb. Div.*), would attack from Nagybajom and Marcali towards Kaposvár to tie down the Soviet 57th Army and continue advancing along the southern shore of Lake Balaton. From the south, *Gen.d.Inf.* Werner von Erdmannsdorff's *XCI Armee-Korps* of *H.Gr. E* with its two divisions (the *104. Jäg.Div.* and *11. Lw.Feld-Div.*) would cross the Drava River, advance north towards Pecs and Mohacs, and attack the 1st Bulgarian Army and XII Yugoslav Army Corps. If the situation developed favorably, Erdmannsdorff's troops would link up with the spearheads of the *6. Pz.Armee* by slicing through the rear of the Third Ukrainian Front. Even at the time, given the limited combat power of these two infantry divisions, this aspect of the *Frühlingserwachen* plan appeared to be wildly optimistic.

In terms of correlation of forces, both sides were roughly evenly matched. Marshal Tolbukhin's Third Ukrainian Front reported having 407,000 men and 407 tanks and guns available at the beginning of March, while the combined forces of the *6. Pz.Armee*, *A.Gr. Balck/6. Armee*, *2. Pz.Armee*, and *H.Gr. E* would commit up to 430,000 men and 900 (of which approximately 700 were operational) armored fighting vehicles to the offensive. In terms of artillery and antitank guns, Tolbukhin enjoyed a quantitative advantage of a least two to one. These numbers do not include anything from the Second Ukrainian Front or the *STAVKA* strategic reserve, which were ultimately not committed to the fight.[26]

With the element of surprise lost by 6 March, Lieutenant General Gagen's 26th Army, which lay in the immediate path of the attack, was ready for the German assault when it finally began that morning. Preceded by a 30-minute artillery barrage, the attack, especially along the right flank by the *I. Kav.Korps* and *I. SS-Pz.Korps*, made good progress initially, covering the same ground that had been repeatedly fought over during the *Konrad III* offensive and the subsequent counteroffensive by the 26th Army. Soviet troops resisted ferociously, making the Germans pay for every inch of ground they gained. Antitank guns and mines slowed the SS troops' advance, forcing them to take out each defensive position individually. Soviet artillery pounded German troops nearly every step of the way, causing most of the casualties they suffered during the offensive. However, unlike the conditions in January, by early March the thaw period was well underway, and off-road movement by armored vehicles had become problematic; unwary drivers could easily mire their *panzers*, so in many instances the SS *Panzergrenadiers* had to dismount and fight on foot in mud up to their mid-calves. German superiority in the number of armored vehicles employed was thus nullified.

Left of Priess's corps, Bittrich's SS corps, which was late getting into position, made even less progress. Attacking behind schedule, his troops found the defenses of the 26th Army nearly impregnable. Although his troops were able to take the town of Aba, his advance was stymied at Sárkeresztur. Because the *I. SS-Pz.Korps* was enjoying greater success, the *23. Pz.Div.* was taken away from Bittrich and used to support Priess's attack along the western side of the Sárviz Canal, the division's old battleground from early February. The mud and overflowing canals and streams in his area of operations impacted the *II. SS-Pz.Korps* just as decisively as they had its sister formation to the west.

On Bittrich's left, Breith's *III. Pz.Korps*, with three divisions (the *1.* and *3. Pz.Div.* and *356. Inf.Div.*), was able to push the front line as far east as Gárdony along the southern shore of Lake Velencze. Seregélyes, where the *Wiking* Division had fought so desperately during early February, finally fell to the *1. Pz.Div.* As the 26th Army began to show signs of stress, the bulk of Lt.Gen. Sergei Trofimenko's 27th Army was brought out of reserve east of the Danube by 7 March and sent to buttress the defense on the right flank of Gagen's army. The XVIII Tank Corps was also thrown into the battle. The high water mark of the offensive was reached on 15 March, when the *1. SS-Pz.Div.* was able to seize a bridgehead across the Sió River at Simontornya, but by then it was a spent force and no German formation was approaching from the south to meet it.

To the west, the two corps from the *2. Pz.Armee* initially achieved only limited local successes and failed to break through Soviet defenses, despite the commitment of the army's reserve, the *16. SS-Pz.Gren.Div. Reichsführer-SS.* The Soviet VI Guards Corps and LXIV Rifle Corps of the 57th Army fought well, expertly employing their six rifle divisions and limited mechanized assets to good effect. There was never any chance of the Germans reaching Kaposvár, especially since neither corps possessed any significant amount of armored fighting vehicles and had no *panzer* divisions. In the *H.Gr. E* attack zone along the Drava River, though both divisions employed by the *LXXXXI Armee-Korps* were able to seize bridgeheads at Donji Miholjac and Valpovo, their attack floundered on the opposite bank when the Soviet CXXXIII Rifle Corps with five infantry divisions and the Yugoslav 3rd Army's XII Army Corps with two divisions counterattacked and kept the Germans penned in their bridgeheads.

Upon reflection, neither of these supporting attacks ever stood any real chance of success, both being insufficiently strong for the overly ambitious objectives assigned to them. Had the two supporting attacks been mounted in conjunction with *Konrad III* on 18 January (*Unternehmen Eisbrecher*), as *H.Gr. Süd* had requested at the time, these two operations would have stood a much greater chance of success; but by 6

March, they had become mere annoyances to the Third Ukrainian Front when they were finally carried out as part of the *Frühlingserwachen* offensive.

When the last great German offensive of World War II reached its culminating point on 15 March, the *6. Pz.Armee's* spearheads were located along a broad arc stretching from the eastern shore of Lake Balaton, southeast along the Sió Canal, to the north along the Sárviz Canal, and to the east towards the eastern tip of Lake Velencze. Four German corps—nearly 200,000 men, representing the Third Reich's last appreciable armored reserve and the cream of the *Waffen-SS*—were thus exposed in a salient over 50 kilometers deep that drew its entire sustenance between the 30-kilometer-wide gap between Lakes Balaton and Velencze. With the Soviet defenses having absorbed the blow by the *6. Pz.Armee* for the past 10 days without having to commit any appreciable reserves of their own (the 6th Guards Tank Army and 9th Guards Army had been untouched, as well as Cavalry-Mechanized Group Pliyev), the stage was thus set for their own counteroffensive.

German losses had been enormous, and ultimately nothing appreciable had been gained by this supreme gamble. During the first week alone, the *6. Pz.Armee* lost 12,358 men killed, wounded, and missing, illustrating the fact that this was initially more of an infantry battle than an armor one. Only 31 tanks and other AFV were declared total write-offs; though this number seems low in comparison to the number available (722), this apparent undercount was considered to be due more to the fact that, on account of adverse terrain conditions, few tanks could actually be deployed off-road, or that, while damaged, some were deemed repairable and thus not a total loss.[27] The *6. Pz.Armee* had failed to reach the Danube, failed to trap and destroy the Third Ukrainian Front, and failed to link up with the *H.Gr. E* attack from the south. The two supporting attacks in the west and south never stood a chance of success, especially since they lacked the means required to achieve their objectives. Even worse, losses within *Gen.d.Art.* Maximilian de Angelis's *2. Pz.Armee* had been so heavy that its continuing ability to secure the Nagykanizsa oilfields was cast into doubt, which was one of Hitler's stated objectives for the counteroffensive.

While *Frühlingserwachen* raged a few kilometers south of his command post in Inota, *Ogruf.* Gille and his corps maintained a watchful eye on the Soviet forces arrayed against them along its *HKL* stretched from the southwest corner of Lake Velencze to the southern foothills of the Vértes Mountains at Csákberény. On 6 March, the corps reported that east of Stuhlweissenburg, troops from the *Wiking* Division had carried out a small-scale attack to seize a tactically advantageous local terrain feature and incorporate it into its main defense line. An assault unit from the *I. Bataillon* of the *Totenkopf* Regiment carried out a similar attack at the same time to seize terrain northeast of the city. The *I.* and *II. Abteilung* of *SS-Pz.Art.Rgt. 3* provided limited direct fire support. Unfortunately, these two attacks drew an immediate Soviet response, and both forces were counterattacked by superior forces that soon drove them back to their starting line.

Wednesday, 7 March proved to be another cold, cloudy day. Scattered snowfall was reported by the *H.Gr. Süd* weather service during the morning hours, which gradually cleared up throughout the afternoon. The road conditions due to the ongoing thaw had hardly improved. That day, the only action that the *IV. SS-Pz.Korps* reported was an enemy combat patrol 4 kilometers southeast of Stuhlweissenburg that was driven off by the *Wiking* Division, although both the *Totenkopf* and *Wiking* Divisions continued their efforts to seize more terrain to improve their front-line positions.[28]

That same day, *Sturm-Art.Brig. 303* was taken away from the *Wiking* Division and reassigned to the *356. Inf.Div.* north of Seregélyes, where it was needed more. This unit, with its 20 operational *StuG III/IV* assault guns, would soon be sorely missed. Additionally, the heretofore-reliable Hungarian *Btl. Holczer*, which had been fighting alongside the two SS divisions of Gille's corps for over a month, was renamed the *I. Btl./Inf.Rgt. 14* and told to be prepared to join the Hungarian *20. Inf.Div.* Its attachment to the *Totenkopf* Division remained in effect for the time being. Throughout this period, one of Gille and Becker's biggest worries remained the Hungarian *1. Hus.Div.* defending the adjacent sector east of Pusztavám controlled by their *VIII. Armee-Korps*. According to Becker, this division—assessed to have only six weak infantry battalions, six light artillery batteries, and just eight antitank guns—was not thought to be strong enough to hold if attacked. He was later proven correct.

Most of the men in its infantry battalions, Becker told Gille, were recently assigned from rear-area services and had no combat experience whatsoever. Was it surprising, he asked, that many of these men were no longer willing to fight? After all, a large proportion of them came from areas of Hungary that had since been occupied by the Red Army. Therefore, it came as no shock that this division, the offspring of the once-proud *1. Kav.Div.* that had fought magnificently alongside the *Totenkopf* at the gates of Warsaw the previous summer, was now regarded as a weak link, vulnerable to the propaganda efforts of the Soviets.[29] Arrayed along its front line along a series of isolated strongpoints in the forests and southern slopes of the Vértes Mountains, its less-than-dedicated men were presented with ample opportunities to desert without being seen by their German neighbors, a situation that many of them apparently took advantage of. However, Becker had his hands full with supervising the Hungarian *2. Pz.Div.*, so the most that he and Gille could do at this point was express their concerns to the *6. Armee/A.Gr. Balck* commander.

Throughout this period, the initiation of the *Frühlingserwachen* offensive had one positive result, at least as far as the troops of the *IV. SS-Pz.Korps* were concerned. The daily attacks by the Red Air Force, including strafing and bombing attacks by fighter-bombers and ground-attack aircraft, had noticeably slackened in the airspace over the Stuhlweissenburg Gap, having been redirected to bomb and harass the troops of the *6. Pz.Armee* instead. This development allowed Gille's troops to carry out some necessary daytime activity, such as bringing up supplies without having to stand next to an air raid trench. Reconnaissance flights persisted, a sign that the Third Ukrainian Front had not completely forgotten about the *IV. SS-Pz.Korps*.

Freezing temperatures returned once more during the night of 7/8 March. Snow was reported in some areas. The condition of the roads remained the same—terrible. Once again, there was little combat activity of any kind occurring along the front line held by Gille's corps.

That day, the *Totenkopf* Division was instructed to take any tank crews without tanks that had not yet been sent back to Germany as part of the *Abholkommando* (*panzer* ferrying detachment) the previous month, and form them into an infantry *Kampfgruppe*, being equipped accordingly. This idea was understandably received without much enthusiasm by the *Totenkopf's* tankmen.[30] At the end of March, the *Wiking* Division was ordered to do the same with its own surplus crews, forming a small provisional infantry battalion led by *Ostuf.* Otto Schneider.

On this same day, the fourth of the counteroffensive, the attacking forces of the *6. Pz.Armee* continued to encounter difficulty in the face of stiff Soviet resistance; the offensive was clearly falling behind schedule. Wöhler asked his commanders for various ideas about how to increase the attack's momentum by drawing the enemy's attention elsewhere. One of these proposals had been previously voiced by *Gen.d.Pz.Tr.* Balck, who had earlier suggested that perhaps the *IV. SS-Pz.Korps*, reinforced by the *6. Pz.Div.*, could carry out a surprise attack north of Lake Velencze to "create uncertainty among the enemy." This idea was not discussed in the evening conversation between Wöhler and Guderian, perhaps because at the time this was thought to be the last place they should weaken the *H.Gr. Süd* main defense line, given the unknown status of reserve armies in the *STAVKA* strategic reserve and lack of knowledge of their future plans.[31]

The evening of 8/9 March was shattered by a spate of shelling by Soviet artillery and mortars all along the front of *A.Gr. Balck/6. Armee*, but when the sun rose, the usual ground attack that followed such bombardments did not occur. Otherwise, the front line along the *IV. SS-Pz.Korps* sector in the Stuhlweissenburg Gap had grown very quiet, except for the usual reconnaissance activity being carried out by both sides, if such a deadly cat-and-mouse game could be labeled as "usual." A soldier could have been forgiven for thinking it was peacetime. The corps was surprised that day when *A.Gr. Balck/6. Armee* issued orders removing the Hungarian *Btl. Holczer* (now *I. Btl./Inf.Rgt. 14*) from the *Totenkopf* Division and sending it south to be attached to the *6. Pz.Armee* somewhere east of Lake Balaton.[32]

During a visit by the *H.Gr. Süd* commander on 9 March, Balck once again brought up his proposal to use the *IV. SS-Pz.Korps* along with the *6. Pz.Div.* in an attack north of Lake Velencze, eastwards as far as the line Lovasberény–Velencze. Subsequently sent by teletype to the headquarters of *H.Gr. Süd*, he urged Wöhler to use the corps to "deny the enemy the free use of his forces west and southwest of Budapest." When Wöhler discussed this idea shortly thereafter with the *Führungsabteilung* of the *6.*

Pz.Armee, they were surprisingly unenthusiastic, telling him that this would require that Gille's corps leave their prepared defensive positions, fight through an unknown number of Soviet units, and establish a new defense line in unfamiliar terrain further to the east. Dietrich and his *6. Pz.Armee* staff had also been counting on using the *6. Pz.Div.* in their own attack, and this proposal would essentially take it off the table. Wöhler agreed with them.[33] That evening, Wöhler brought up Balck's proposal in his nightly conversation with Guderian, who, much to his surprise, enthusiastically approved it, causing Wöhler to order his staff to begin studying the concept.

Interestingly, that evening in the *H.Gr. Süd* war diary, Wöhler recorded his thoughts concerning his visit to *A.Gr. Balck* that day. He had also visited the headquarters of the *IV. SS-Pz.Korps* and the *6. Pz.Armee* that same day to discuss operational matters. In addition to these topics, Wöhler attempted to smooth things over between Gille and Balck. Apparently, their continuing animosity towards one another had not gone unnoticed, for Wöhler noted: "In addition, I have endeavored [today], through discussion with *Gen.d.Pz.Tr. Balck* on the one hand and *SS-Ogruf.* Gille on the other hand, to eliminate the tension that always exists between the two officers." Apparently he was unsuccessful, and may even have hardened Balck's determination to rid himself of the proud and self-confident SS general.[34]

The only other event of note that happened that day was the receipt of a *Führerbefehl* (*Führer* directive) addressed to every member of the *Wehrmacht* and *Waffen-SS*. Meant to address the growing number of incidents of desertion throughout the German Armed Forces, this was the so-called *Sippenhaft Befehl* (Family Arrest Order), signed by *G.F.M.* Wilhelm Keitel, chief of staff of the *OKW*, which read as follows:

> The Führer has ordered: Whoever falls into enemy hands who is not wounded or has not fought with his utmost until being overpowered, has betrayed his honor. The community of decent and brave soldiers rejects him. Thus, his relatives are liable for him. Any payment of wages or support to his relatives shall be forfeited. This must be announced immediately. The details are regulated by the chief of the *OKW* on behalf of the *Führer*.

This order was countersigned by Wöhler, who added: "This *Führerbefehl* is to be made known to the troops immediately."[35] This order probably had two immediate effects. Firstly, it accomplished its primary purpose, in that it forced men to seriously consider the consequences should they decide to desert, because their family would pay for the offense. The other effect was that it may have hardened soldiers even further against the Nazi regime, which had become so ruthless in its bid to keep men in the ranks at any price, that it would arrest or remove financial support from families whose bread-winners, through no fault of their own, had decided to flee. It was another warning sign of the rot to come.

While 10 March was yet another uneventful day in the Stuhlweissenburg Gap, the fighting in the *6. Pz.Armee* area was intensifying. Losses had been very heavy and most of the army's reserves had already been committed to maintain what little amount of momentum the offensive still had. There were, however, signs that after five days of relentless pounding by the *6. Pz.Armee*, Tolbukhin's defenses might be beginning to crack after all. On that date, *H.Gr. Süd* ordered *A.Gr. Balck/6. Armee* to send the *6. Pz.Div.* the next day from its reserve position near Mór to the *III. Pz.Korps* south of Lake Velencze, instead of to the *6. Pz.Armee*.

It was also the day that Balck's scheme to have the *IV. SS-Pz.Korps* attack to the east (labeled as a *Teilangriff*, or partial attack) was approved by *OKH*, despite the fact that the *6. Pz.Div.* was in the process of being transferred to the *III. Pz.Korps*. According to German intelligence sources, Soviet formations were being transferred south from the area north of Lake Velencze to aid the defenses against the *Frühlingserwachen* offensive (these reports later turned out to be incorrect).[36] Accordingly, *H.Gr. Süd* thought that the objective should be less ambitious than what Balck proposed, limiting the advance to a line drawn between Pákozd and Pátka, which would only require the *IV. SS-Pz.Korps* to advance to the east for approximately 5–8 kilometers. It was thought that even such a limited attack would be sufficient to tie up any Soviet reserves in that area, and would not overly tax the capabilities of Gille's corps. Balck was apparently not too concerned, assuming that even without the *6. Pz.Div.*, the *IV. SS-Pz.Korps* still had enough "internal" reserves to carry out the mission. This was to prove a faulty assumption.[37]

Although evidence indicates that Guderian himself was beginning to have second thoughts about the necessity for this operation, the orders went out from *H.Gr. Süd* to the *IV. SS-Pz.Korps* that night anyway. The only redeeming feature about this order was that it made it clear that this operation was not to be conducted without the *6. Pz.Div.* If the attack succeeded, the *IV. SS-Pz.Korps* could possibly join in with a follow-on attack by the *III. Pz.Korps* to its south in order to re-establish a defense line along the Váli River between the Danube and Lake Velencze. Should it succeed, the Hungarian *VIII. Armee-Korps* was also to extend its right flank all the way to Lovasberény to free up the *Totenkopf* Division for future employment.

Final authority for launching the attack was reserved to *H.Gr. Süd*, because only its commander, and not that of *A.Gr. Balck*, could judge whether or not the *6. Pz.Div.* could be spared for this attack or sent to aid the *III. Pz.Korps*, or whether the *Teilangriff* should be attempted at all. When the *IV. SS-Pz.Korps* received the order, Gille and Schönfelder got the *Führungsabteilung* to work developing the corps' own version of the operations plan to issue to the divisions. The exact date for the attack had not been set, but was envisioned to be within four or at most five days from receipt of the order.[38]

The rest of the day in the *IV. SS-Pz.Korps* defensive sector passed without further incident. On that same day, the *III. Pz.Korps* halted its attack east of Seregélyes and went over to the defense while it waited for the *6. Pz.Div.*, though the *3. Pz.Div.* continued with its attack to the south alongside the *II. SS-Pz.Korps*. How this would impact the planning for the *Teilangriff* by the *IV. SS-Pz.Korps* was unknown; at least it appeared that there would be no linking up with Breith's corps east of Lake Velencze after all. Gille's corps had already fought in that area during *Konrad III* and his commanders most likely had no remaining appetite to go there again and repeat the process, especially since Budapest had already fallen.

The morning report for *A.Gr. Balck/6. Armee* for 11 March, which proved to be a stormy day in terms of the weather as well as along the battlefront, began with the words "Sixteen men from the Hungarian *1. Hus.Div.* deserted to the enemy." *Brigadeführer* Becker's worst fears were being realized. How long would this Hungarian unit survive when it was attacked, if it was already disintegrating when it was under no enemy pressure at all? In the *IV. SS-Pz.Korps'* sector in the Stuhlweissenburg Gap, no combat activity was reported, thus allowing the corps and division staffs to continue focusing on preparations for their impending attack. That same day, due to developments in the *III. Pz.Korps'* attack zone, the *6. Pz.Div.* was finally released from *Armeegruppe* reserve and attached to Breith's corps, thereby ending its role in any possible *Teilangriff* alongside the *IV. SS-Pz.Korps*. The introduction of the *6. Pz.Div.* to battle did spur the momentum of Breith's corps and helped it retake the *Wiking* Division's old battlefield at Puszta Szabolcs. However, its departure also meant that *A.Gr. Balck/6. Armee* no longer had any significant reserve to fall back upon should the need arise.

In the calm reigning in the corps' rear area, 11 March also marked the 40th birthday of *Hstuf.* Alfred-Ingemar Bernd, the newly appointed commander of *II. Abt./SS-Pz.Rgt. 5*, at its battalion headquarters in Sárkeresztes. Prior to arriving at the front in Hungary, he had worked on and off in the Third Reich's propaganda ministry, serving occasionally in the front lines as a *Panzerjäger* in the *Heer*. A long-time commissioned member of the *Allegmeine-SS*, where he served in the rank of *Obersturmbannführer*, he was promoted to *Leutnant* in the *Heer* and was shipped to North Africa, where he served as *G.F.M.* Erwin Rommel's publicist and record keeper in the field marshal's *Afrikakorps* headquarters from 1941–43. After a falling out with Josef Goebbels during the late summer of 1944, he was fired from the propaganda ministry and subsequently volunteered for front-line combat duty. Himmler arranged to have him promoted to *Hauptsturmführer* and transferred to the *Wiking* Division in early March 1945.[39]

The weekly unit combat strength reports were submitted on 11 March for the period ending the previous day. These provide a last glimpse into the condition of both SS divisions before the collapse of the front a week later. The numbers provided reveal the last point in time when the *Totenkopf* and *Wiking* Divisions were anything close to being full strength; after 15 March, both divisions began a precipitous decline. As before, the *Totenkopf* Division was the most capable of the two, reporting one strong and six mostly strong *Panzergrenadier* battalions, one mostly strong *Pionier* battalion, and one strong *Feld-Ersatz* (field replacement) battalion. In addition, it fielded 17 antitank guns, 12 operational assault guns, five *Jg.Pz. IVs*, 16 *Pz. IVs*, eight *Pz. V* Panthers, and seven *Pz. VI* Tiger Is, for a grand total of 48 operational AFVs. It also reported the usual amount of operational field pieces (five light and five heavy batteries). Becker evaluated its mobility as 80 percent and once again rated his division as having a *Kampfwert* of "II," higher than the previous month.

The *Wiking* Division had made great strides since the last weekly report in improving its matériel and personnel readiness, reporting two strong, three mostly strong, and two average *Panzergrenadier* strength battalions, one average-strength *Pionier* battalion, and one strong *Feld-Ersatz* battalion. In addition, it reported that it had two battalions undergoing reconstitution under its administrative control—*I. Btl./Norge* (strong) and *I. Btl./Danmark* (average). Neither had completed the process yet and were not considered ready for combat. The division reported 10 operational 7.5cm antitank guns, one assault gun, eight *Jg.Pz. IV*s, four *Pz. IV*s, and 13 *Pz. V* Panthers, the largest number of operational AFVs in over a month, with a total of 26 vehicles. Ullrich reported his division's mobility as only 46 percent, and had increased his subjective evaluation of its *Kampfwert* from a "III" to a "II." These numbers indicated that this was as ready as either division would ever be again.

Since it was part of Gille's corps and did contribute some measure of combat power, the report by the Hungarian *2. Pz.Div.* for the same period is also relevant. Its commander, *Gen.Maj.* vitéz- Zsedényi, reported one strong, one mostly strong, and two weak infantry battalions, along with one fought-out *Pionier* battalion. It also reported having only two serviceable antitank guns but 16 operational *Pz. IV*s, a sizeable number. Its artillery situation was not as good, having only four light batteries assigned. Its degree of motorization was relatively unchanged at 43 percent. Overall, based on these factors, vitéz-Zsedényi rated his division as being only a "IV."

Interestingly, on 11 March, the commander of the Hungarian *3. Armee, Gen.Lt.* vitéz-Heszlényi, along with *Generaloberst* Wöhler, visited the quarters of *SS-Rgt. Ney*, which was undergoing reconstitution in the town of Sur a few kilometers behind the front. By this point, the regiment had grown to a strength of a brigade, with nearly 4,000 men, most of whom were untrained volunteers from the segment of the Hungarian population that was fanatically prepared to defend their homeland. *Sturmbannführer* Ney, who had been a mere *Leutnant* in the *Honvéd*, was a controversial character who had repeatedly refused to kowtow to the Arrow Cross-led government of Szalási. Apparently, some heated words were exchanged between Ney and Heszlényi, prompting Wöhler to write in his journal that evening: "I consider it necessary for *SS-Sturmbannführer* Ney to be incorporated into a division of the *Waffen-SS* as soon as possible, so that he does not start to harbor ugly thoughts of an internal political nature."[40] Shortly after recording these thoughts, Ney's regiment was once again subordinated to Gille's corps.

As the fighting south of the lakes was beginning to reach it culminating point, the situation in *IV. SS-Pz.Korps'* defensive sector on 12 March remained the same, as described by the oft-repeated refrain "Along the rest of the *Armeegruppe's* front, other than localized unsuccessful enemy attacks, there was no combat activity worth mentioning." Only the "normal" amount of artillery harassment fire was reported. Once again, temperatures hovered around freezing point in the morning, with partly cloudy skies, scattered rain showers, and unchanged road conditions as temperatures increased. In consideration of the impending attack of the *IV. SS-Pz. Korps*, the *I. Bataillon* of the *Totenkopf* Regiment had been pulled out of the line during the night of 11/12 March and quartered in the village of Söréd to serve as the corps reserve. However, in view of how the situation was developing in the *6. Pz.Armee* area of operations and increasing indications of Soviet troop movements into the area north of Lake Velencze, the limited attack by the *IV. SS-Pz.Korps* was quietly shelved. though *I. Btl./Totenkopf* remained where it was.

Besides the temperature, other things began heating up for the *IV. SS-Pz.Korps* from 13 March. Although the night before had been quiet, daylight revealed a considerable amount of Soviet traffic moving along the highway linking Lovasberény and Stuhlweissenburg, heading towards the southwest. In the area south and north of Zámoly, defended by the *Totenkopf* Division, daylight movement of bodies of up to 700 troops could clearly be seen marching towards the front lines. One report from *Totenkopf* Division detailed the sighting of four Soviet *Katyusha* multiple rocket launchers moving from Csakvár to the west, to the area north of Zámoly, a sure sign of future offensive intent.[41] In the area of the neighboring Hungarian *3. Armee*, a similar amount of Soviet vehicular and troop movement was spotted between the area of Bicske and Csakvár, moving in a westwards direction. Nearly everywhere, Soviet air activity had also increased, especially reconnaissance flights between Lakes Balaton and Velencze.

Other than these significant sightings, nothing out of the ordinary occurred that day, except the usual activity that has been frequently repeated elsewhere in the narrative.[42] When the news about suspected Soviet troops' movements began to arrive at the field headquarters of the *6. Pz.Armee* in Balatonfüzfő, an anxious staff officer contacted Gille's headquarters in Inota and was reassured by the *IV. SS-Pz. Korps* commander that, "His corps was in well-constructed positions and capable of defending against even a major enemy attack of long duration."[43] The corps had ensured that units in the front line in the Stuhlweissenburg Gap had been warned and were ordered to assume a higher level of readiness than usual.[44]

Some apprehension was noted in the ranks of the Hungarian *2. Pz.Div.*, an understandable emotion considering that many of its new recruits had never fought in a major battle before. When reports of this attitude filtered up to Becker at his headquarters, he sent forward *Stubaf.* Friedrich Messerle, the commander of *IV. Btl./ SS-Pz.Art. 3*, to investigate. Messerle later wrote:

> After an adventurous ride in my motorcycle sidecar through dense forests and mountains, I was able to determine that the areas [held by the Hungarian division] were sufficiently fortified, but the *HKL* appeared to be too thinly manned. Many of the Hungarian infantry were occupying

their bivouacs behind the lines. Most of them seemed indifferent about reports of approaching columns of enemy troops.

Upon his return, Becker asked him what he had seen. After Messerle finished, Becker thanked him and said that the *Totenkopf* Division should expect to see a lot of the enemy coming from that direction.[45]

Probably more than one staff officer in *H.Gr. Süd* or the *6. Pz.Armee*, although mainly occupied with the *Frühlingserwachen* offensive, breathed a sigh of relief when the overly optimistic *Teilangriff* plan of Hermann Balck directing the *IV. SS-Pz.Korps* to attack eastwards along the northern shore of Lake Balaton was cancelled. Had it been carried out, Gille's corps may very well have been slaughtered, its defenses built with such care left unmanned, and the *6. Pz.Armee* would most likely have been trapped south of Lakes Balaton and Velencze, though as will be demonstrated in the following chapter, this almost happened anyway.

On the morning of 14 March, all three divisions in Gille's corps were ratcheting up their level of readiness and preparing for action. The corps commander ordered each division to implement its defensive plans and increase the number of reconnaissance patrols to look for any signs within the enemy's forward positions that would indicate offensive preparations. The *Westland* Regiment, occupying a defensive sector southeast of Stuhlweissenburg, sent out one combat patrol to inspect a cluster of empty houses near the hamlet of Nádas Csárda at the southwest corner of Lake Velencze, where they encountered and drove out a similarly sized Soviet force. Obviously, the Germans were not the only ones concerned with determining their enemy's intentions. A company-sized Soviet combat patrol attempted to penetrate the forward outpost line of the *Wiking* Division held by the *Germania* Regiment northeast of Stuhlweissenburg in the vineyard area, but was spotted and driven off by artillery fire.

The most alarming report that day originated from the Hungarian *3. Armee*, which still had two experienced German divisions in its order of battle—the *96.* and *711. Inf.Div.* On 14 March, although it had experienced no combat activity worth mentioning, forward outposts reported that they had observed heavy motor vehicle traffic in undeterminable numbers moving from Csakvár towards the northwest, along with 60 vehicles moving from Szár to the southwest, and 200 more moving toward the northwest along the road leading out of Bicske. Finally, that afternoon the army reported that one of its forward units (most likely the *96. Inf.Div.*) had observed 1,000 motor vehicles moving along the road in a southwesterly direction from Bicske toward Bodmér.

This last sighting got everyone's attention at the *A.Gr. Balck/6. Armee* headquarters. To verify the reports, *Luftwaffe* reconnaissance flights were immediately conducted over the area east of the *IV. SS-Pz.Korps* and the Hungarian *3. Armee*. The results confirmed the sightings, and much more: aerial photographs confirmed that more than 3,000 Soviet vehicles were assembling between Bicske and Lovasberény, with concentrations spotted in the eastern Vértes Mountains and in the areas due east of Zámoly and Stuhlweissenburg. These numbers were in addition to the Soviet units that were already there, representing a significant concentration of combat power.

German intelligence analysis quickly concluded that these sightings indicated that the Soviet 9th Guards Army had begun moving into position, as well as portions of a mechanized corps, or perhaps the long-missing 6th Guards Tank Army that had reappeared after a long sojourn on the east bank of the Danube or even the famed Cavalry-Mechanized Pliyev Group. Based on these troop concentrations and direction of movement, it appeared that the Soviet reserves had moved to the area north of Lake Velencze and were primarily oriented towards the mountain passes in the western Vértes near Tatabanya and Mór, as well as the Stuhlweissenburg Gap. As one observer later wrote, "There was no longer any doubt possible that the beginning of a major Soviet operation was to be expected shortly."[46]

The chief of staff of the *IV. SS-Pz.Korps* summed up the situation that evening:

> The attack by the *6. (SS) Pz.Armee* had come to a halt after running into stiffening enemy resistance and had become increasingly stuck in the mud. Aerial reconnaissance had revealed the movement of long columns of enemy vehicles approaching from the operational depths around Budapest, with the bulk of them headed towards Zámoly and some headed towards the Vértes Mountains. The enemy thus revealed his intentions for an operational-level counteroffensive.[47]

All too late, the reality of the situation began to sink in at the headquarters of *A. Gr. Balck/6. Armee*. The time for operational flights of fancy was over. That evening, in his report to *H.Gr. Süd*, Balck stated that based on observations made that day, the enemy's objective was clear:

> … the enemy would carry out his attack mainly against the left wing of the *IV. SS-Pz.Korps* at Zámoly, where conditions were suitable for the employment of motorized formations. It was also possible that the enemy was willing to put up with the terrain difficulties in the Vértes Mountains, which do not permit the employment of large-scale formations of motorized forces, in order to take advantage of the weak Hungarian defenses there.[48]

This was ironic, to say the least, as the *IV. SS-Pz.Korps*—at the time surely considered a large-scale motorized formation—had conducted just such an attack in early January during *Unternehmen Konrad I* and been able to navigate its way through the mountainous terrain of the Vértes and Gerecse Mountains, despite stiff Soviet resistance along the way.

Based on this report as well as others, the *H.Gr. Süd* leadership determined that the objective of this attack, should it materialize in the next several days, was most likely the plains south of the Danube between the Bakony Forest and the Raab–Komorn area. This would have the effect of not only cutting off the bulk of *H.Gr. Süd*, but would set the conditions necessary for the initiation of the Vienna Operation by the Second and Third Ukrainian Fronts. At this point, Balck was probably regretting that he had sent away the *6. Pz.Div.*, his army's only remaining armored reserve, to the *III. Pz.Korps*, where it arrived in time to accomplish very little. Now he had no reserves at all. In addition, his gamble to assign the defense of the left flank of his army to the Hungarian *3. Armee* was now being seen as a bad bet.

In his orders for the following day that he issued that evening, Balck directed the *IV. SS-Pz.Korps* and the Hungarian *3. Armee* to reinforce their defensive measures, occupy previously reconnoitered antitank blocking positions, and form tank destruction teams to be positioned behind the front lines in the areas of Zirc and Kisber. In Gille's two SS divisions, most of these tasks had already been put into operation, but the defensive sectors held by Hungarian units remained a source of constant worry. Fearing that Mór, a town in the Hungarian *3. Armee* rear area between the Bakony Forest and the Vértes Mountains, might fall to a Soviet tank attack, Balck decided to reinforce its defenses with the only reserves he could find—six non-mobile companies from *Festungs-Pak-Verband IX*, equipped with 7.5cm antitank guns—with possibly a heavy *Flak* battalion from the *Luftwaffe* to be brought in later.[49]

Balck also informed *H.Gr. Süd* that the *IV. SS-Pz.Korps* had "considerable reserves," but no one on Gille's staff would have known what he was talking about. Each division had its own *panzer* regiment (actually, only less than a battalion in each regiment) and two additional *Panzergrenadier* battalions in reserve, but these forces were being rotated in and out of the front lines for rest purposes and would all be needed to hold the front line when the enemy attack came. Then there was the additional matter concerning the new *Luftwaffe* and *Kriegsmarine* replacements that had been organized into four training battalions kept behind the front. None of these battalions were in any condition to be thrown into battle until they had undergone rudimentary infantry training.

Describing the actual situation concerning these reserves, Schönfelder wrote: "The *IV. SS-Pz.Korps*, which was serving as the strongest point in the main defense line, had behind its front lines four battalions that were designated as 'fully ready' and four as 'filled with new recruits,' as well as the *SS-Kampfgruppe Ney* which was not actually under the corps' jurisdiction at that particular moment."[50] There was also *I. Btl./ Norge* and *I. Btl./Danmark*, but both of these were still undergoing *Auffrischung* and could not be considered ready or strong enough to repel a large-scale breakthrough. The only other forces available within *H.Gr. Süd* that could be sent immediately to augment the *IV. SS-Pz.Korps* were *Heeres-Art.Brig. 959* and *Werf.Brig. 17*. Although these would be a welcome addition to the *IV. SS-Pz.Korps'* artillery command, they were not particularly well-suited to fight tanks on an open battlefield, and that was what Balck seemed to fear the most.[51]

In addition to these forces, *H.Gr. Süd*, which was well aware of the threat by now, was able to take *Sturm-Art.Brig. 325* away from the *8. Armee* and send it to Mór to reinforce the Hungarian *3. Armee*. The army group also ordered that *Gren. Brig. (mot.) 92* be detached from the *2. Pz.Armee*, where it was positioned as that army's last reserve force, and attached to the *3. Armee* as well. While this measure would provide a belated "German backbone," it would take two or three days for either of these units to arrive. These were measures that Balck should have already carried out, but were now almost too late. He would soon regret his failure to follow through on his earlier directive that German units had to be interspersed between Hungarian forces to serve as "corset stays" in the Vértes Mountains.[52]

As for the *IV. SS-Pz.Korps*, it had done everything that it could to prepare for the impending attack. Describing the situation, the corps' chief of staff wrote shortly after the war that Gille and his staff had previously looked at these possibilities and as a result, "A large number of security measures against the enemy's imminent large-scale attack against the pass at Mór and the gap between Lake Velencze and the Vértes Mountains had been considered" from a planning standpoint.[53] But with such a limited number of available reserves, the corps could only do so much with its own resources. Help had to come from outside once its own reserves were exhausted.

The only other event out of the ordinary to occur on 14 March was the spectacular attack against the oil refineries at Szöny and Almás Füzitö, as well as the marshaling yards at Komorn and Neuhäusel, carried out by a group of at least 50 American four-engine bombers of the Fifteenth Air Force flying out of Italy. This was part of a 634-aircraft armada consisting of both B-17s and B-24s, with fighter escorts, that also struck targets in Austria and Czechoslovakia the same day. Smoke from the burning refineries could be seen as far away as Zámoly and Stuhlweissenburg. The damage inflicted was considerable, later estimated as having reduced their output capacity by 70 percent. According to the *OKW* war diary, this loss equated to the entire production capability of all the synthetic oil refineries still operating in Germany.[54] Since most of the fuel for the *6. Pz.Armee*'s armored fighting vehicles also relied upon these refineries for their direct supply, this would soon have severe consequences.

Late that evening, the *Ic* of *H.Gr. Süd*, *Oberstlt.* Karl-Heinrich Graf von Rittberg, released his revised intelligence estimate for the following day. An associate of *Gen. Maj.* Reinhard Gehlen's *Fremde Heere Ost* (Foreign Armies East) intelligence organization, von Rittberg had taken into account all of the ground and air observations from that day and previous days, and arrived at the following conclusion:

> The enemy revealed his intentions for an operational level counterattack on the ninth day of the friendly attack [*Frühlingserwachen*]. Initial movements yesterday toward the Stuhlweissenburg–Zámoly front from the east to the west were observed. They could have indicated local reinforcements for holding actions or relief forces, but movements today leave no further doubt concerning enemy intentions … This means that the enemy will launch his main assault against the front southwest and west of Zámoly with the objective of attacking toward Lake Balaton to cut the rearward lines of communications of the German assault forces [i.e., *6. Pz.Armee*] attacking from the Stuhlweissenburg Gap. Secondary attacks can be directed against the front in the Vértes Mountains with the objective of opening the pass at Mór to the road through Söréd and through the mountains northwest of Csákberény and taking other passes through

the mountains. The attack may be expected to begin either tomorrow [15 March] or the day after, since the enemy has revealed his approach in such an open way. He may even attack from the line of march.[55]

This assessment was remarkably prescient, though late. Written as it was only two days before the enemy initiated its counteroffensive, it gave the major subordinate commands of *H.Gr. Süd* involved in the *Frühlingserwachen* offensive precious little time to react and craft a credible response. In broad terms, the impending Soviet attack had already successfully achieved the operational surprise that its commanders were seeking.

The last relatively peaceful day that the men of the *IV. SS-Pz.Korps* would enjoy for a long time, 15 March, also marked the last day of the *Frühlingserwachen* offensive. In its morning report to *H.Gr. Süd, A.Gr. Balck/6. Armee* mentioned that there had been no fighting overnight in the *IV. SS-Pz.Korps'* sector and that all of the enemy movement into the area opposite the Hungarian *3. Armee* appeared to have stopped. It had rained during the night, and temperatures had hovered three to seven degrees above freezing point, creating conditions that gave rise to dense fog during the morning hours.[56] As the day lengthened, it rose to as high as 48 degrees Fahrenheit (9 degrees Centigrade). This miserable weather continued throughout the day, severely limiting air operations by both sides.

Although the evening report from *A.Gr. Balck/6. Armee* stated that no combat activity had taken place against the *IV. SS-Pz.Korps*, two small engagements did occur that morning, one in the *Wiking* Division's sector on the right and the other in the *Totenkopf* Division's sector in the center. The *Wiking* Division reported that its troops had stopped and forced the withdrawal of a tank-supported armed reconnaissance force that approached its positions along the road leading from Stuhlweissenburg to Pákozd after a short engagement on the northeastern outskirts of the city. No Soviet tanks were reported to have been knocked out. At roughly the same time, another Soviet reconnaissance force, though without armor support, attempted to carry out a similar mission against the center of the *Totenkopf* Division's position, but was driven off. On the division's right, the *Eicke* Regiment sent out a foot patrol across the highway linking Zámoly and Stuhlweissenburg, which managed to work its way into the vineyards on the eastern side of the highway to look for any signs of the enemy. Encountering strongly defended Soviet positions established throughout the vineyard, the patrol quickly retreated and reported what it had seen.

Based on these reports, as well as others provided by *SS-Pz.Aufkl.Abt. 3* which had scouted out the corps' left flank in the sector defended by the Hungarian *2. Pz.Div.*, Gille ordered that the corps' alert status be increased to its highest level, including the aforementioned defensive measures involving the positioning of reserves. This heightened level of alert was clearly warranted, as evidenced by a telephone message sent out to all units of the corps that evening, stating that "German reconnaissance has sighted a 30 kilometer-long motorized Russian [sic] column approaching."[57]

That evening, *Gen.d.Pz.Tr.* Balck, overriding Gille, ordered the *III. Bataillon* of the *Totenkopf* Regiment out of its reserve position in Bodajk, where it had been serving as Gille's own corps reserve, and directed it to be moved out of the corps' sector to a position 2 kilometers north of Csákberény. Here, in the Hungarian *3. Armee* area of operations, it would be positioned behind the Hungarian *1. Hus.Div.* to ensure that connectivity between Gille's corps and the neighboring Hungarian *VIII. Armee-Corps* was maintained once the attack began. However, in such an isolated position, it would be nearly impossible for the commander of the *Totenkopf* Division to control the battalion's actions, placing its fate in the hands of the commander of the *1. Hus.Div.*, *Oberst* Zoltán Schell.

A curious incident occurred at about this same time, shortly before the Soviet counteroffensive began, involving *Ustuf.* Erich Kernmayr, the *Zugführer* (platoon leader) of *SS-Kampfpropaganda-Zug Ungarn*, a psychological warfare unit that had previously served with *SS-Rgt. Ney*. Since February, his platoon had been attached to the staff of the *IV. SS-Pz.Korps*, where it worked under the auspices of its *Ic*, *Stubaf.* Herbert Jankuhn. In addition to his translator duties (Kernmayr spoke fluent Hungarian and Russian), he also worked as the *Ic* counterespionage officer in the corps' rear area as well as an interrogator of prisoners of war.

While carrying out his duties, Kernmayr was summoned to the corps' forward *Gefechtstand* by Jankuhn, who told him that two Soviet deserters had been brought in by one of the *Panzergrenadier* battalions. When he arrived, he quickly discerned that one of them was a Ukrainian who was eager to talk. The deserter asked Kernmayr for a map, and he quickly showed the German officer where he had come from and pointed to a spot where he said he had seen large numbers of Soviet vehicles assembling along the front between Mór and Stuhlweissenburg and north of Lake Velencze, including thousands of trucks. While interrogating him further, the telephone rang, bearing a summons for Kernmayr and the two deserters to report to *Ogruf.* Gille along with Jankuhn at the corps' primary *Hauptquartier* in Inota. Finally, here was proof that the Soviet counteroffensive was not a mirage, but a reality.

After briefing Gille that evening, Kernmayr was ordered to drive immediately to the *H.Gr. Süd* headquarters at the Esterháza Palace over 150 kilometers away, along with his driver and the two prisoners, and present them to the *Ic* of *H.Gr. Süd*, *Oberstlt.* Graf von Rittberg. After driving all night in blackout conditions, a half-frozen Kernmayr arrived at the army group's intelligence office at 8 a.m. No one was on duty, save for a sleepy *Feldwebel* who was annoyed that Kernmayr had woken him up. Finally, after waiting for several hours for an audience with von Rittberg, Kernmayr was waved into his office, along with the two prisoners and his driver, *Rottenführer* Gottlob. After speaking with them for a few moments, with Kernmayr interpreting, von Rittberg showed them the latest aerial photographs of the area in question, and both POWs pointed out where the Soviet troop concentrations were. The *Oberstleutnant* informed the SS lieutenant that he would brief *Generaloberst* Wöhler about this valuable intelligence later that afternoon. Until then, Kernmayr was asked to remain as his guest.

After the 4:30 p.m. army group meeting concluded, von Rittberg returned several hours later and told Kernmayr that he had briefed the general, and that he found the entire story very interesting. "Please send *Obergruppenführer* Gille our warmest regards," he said. "*Jawohl*," replied Kernmayr, somewhat hesitantly. "Is there anything else?" von Rittberg asked him. To which the *Untersturmführer* responded with a stutter: "W-what about the danger to our flanks?" Seemingly amused by Kernmayr's concern, von Rittberg replied airily: "The Hungarian Hussars are positioned there. They only have to last an hour. Then Gille will send in his *Feuerwehr* [fire brigade] again. He's used to that." Kernmayr merely stood there in amazement, well aware that the Hungarian *1. Hus.Div.* would not even last that long when pressed hard. Observing the look of concern on his face, von Rittberg clapped him on the shoulder reassuringly and said: "Don't worry, the army group will initiate the appropriate actions in time." With that, he turned around and left. Disappointed, Kernmayr left the prisoners with the *Heeresgruppe* provost guard and he and Gottlob returned to Inota. His trip had been for nothing; to him, it had seemed that the army group headquarters was far too complacent, despite the clear evidence to the contrary.[58]

As the commanders and troops within the *IV. SS-Pz.Korps* scrambled throughout the day to get into position to be able to resist the coming attack, a great deal of back-and-forth was taking place within the ranks of the leadership of *OKH*, *H.Gr. Süd*, *6. Pz.Armee*, and *A.Gr. Balck/6. Armee* concerning the future course of the *Frühlingserwachen* offensive. By 15 March, it had become evident to nearly everyone that the attack had stalled and had no prospects of achieving any of its original objectives. Despite the supreme efforts and heroic sacrifices of the German and Hungarian troops involved, the Soviet 26th and 27th Armies committed by the Third Ukrainian Front had absorbed the hammer blows of the *I.* and *II. SS-Pz. Korps* and had steadily whittled away at their strength.

The attack by the *III. Pz.Korps* had stalled early during the operation, though there had been many moments when the Red Army's situation was seemingly precarious. Tolbukhin had already sent additional reinforcements from his other two armies (the 4th Guards and 57th Armies), including elements of the V Guards Cavalry Corps to assist them. The situation had grown so serious in his estimation that he begged for more help from the *STAVKA* reserve on 9 March and requested permission to move his command post to the eastern bank of the Danube. He was subsequently called personally by Josef Stalin, who told him:

> Comrade Tolbukhin, if you are thinking of prolonging the war for another five or six months, then by all means order your troops to move back. It will undoubtedly be quieter there. But I

don't think that is what you want. The defense must therefore be conducted on the left [i.e., the western] bank of the Danube, and you too should remain there with your staff.[59]

Stalin had no intention of rescheduling the Vienna Operation, which meant that the armies being set aside to conduct it were not to be touched. The Third Ukrainian Front would therefore have to make do with its own resources. Thus admonished, Tolbukhin set about his duties with a greater sense of determination. The situation finally began to turn in his favor by 12 March, when the crisis passed. Still, considering how close that Tolbukhin thought he was to being defeated, one wonders what *Frühlingserwachen* might have achieved had it not been for the mud, rain, and flooded *Puszta*.

The specter of a large-scale counteroffensive about to unfold along the left flank of *A.Gr. Balck/6. Armee* restored clarity of thinking among the senior German commanders. Realizing the looming danger, Sepp Dietrich (one of the most clear-headed of all the senior commanders in *H.Gr. Süd*, despite the negative stereotypes) requested permission to pull out the *I. SS-Pz.Korps* and "reposition" it alongside the *III. Pz.Korps*, where both corps would then attack towards the Danube in an effort to cut off the Soviet force assembling north of Lake Velencze before it was too late. The *II. SS-Pz.Korps* would remain where it was and continue attacking, along with the *I. Kav.Korps*. However, this could not be done without Hitler's permission, which he withheld until the last possible moment. Perhaps a wiser course of action would have been to cancel the offensive altogether at that very moment and withdraw all of the *6. Pz.Armee* back to its starting line, where it would be able to position itself in time to counter the Soviet attack.

However, by this point in time it was all too late, because the Soviet offensive began the following morning. All of *6. Pz.Armee*'s sacrifices during the "offensive to nowhere" had been in vain. That evening, *Frühlingserwachen* was unofficially *abgestellt* (shut down) at 11 p.m. when *H.Gr. Süd* ordered the *I. SS-Pz.Korps* to regroup to the left wing of the *6. Pz.Armee*. Guderian himself informed Wöhler that he expected that this movement would take up to three days, but that the *6. Pz.Armee* needed to carry it out as quickly as possible, within 48 hours or less.[60] Three days might as well have been three years, because it would have been too late in either case. Even three days was optimistic; moving the corps through the mud from the southern courses of the Sió River to a new position south of Lake Velencze would take longer than that.

The draft of the first report stating the overall number of German and Hungarian losses between 6 and 13 March was compiled by *H.Gr. Süd* on 17 March, but was incomplete since the fighting was still ongoing. Final numbers were not compiled until nearly a week later, and when it was completed, it painted a more complete picture of the scale of the defeat. From 1–17 March, German forces deployed for the *Frühlingserwachen* offensive suffered the loss of 15,117 men killed, wounded, and missing in action. In terms of losses per forces engaged, the *6. Pz.Armee* lost 5,919 men, the *2. Pz.Armee* 3,563, *A.Gr. Balck/6. Armee* 3,175, and *H.Gr. E* 2,460.

Although the number of armored fighting vehicles deemed irrecoverably lost was reported as low as only 46, this tells only half the story. Of the 153 operational tanks, assault guns, and tank destroyers reported by the *III. Pz.Korps* on 1 March, before the offensive began, only 63 were still battle-ready by 13 March. In the much larger *6. Pz.Armee,* of its 595 tanks, assault guns, and tank destroyers reported ready for battle on 1 March, only 185 were still operational 13 days later.[61] This represents a total of only 248 vehicles, out of the approximately 900 that had been on hand on 1 March (when 722 of these were reported as being operational), slightly over 27 percent of what *H.Gr. Süd* began the offensive with.

Though many of the inoperable tanks were repairable, those left on the battlefield needed to be recovered and hauled back through the mud to the rear, where they could be worked on and placed back into operation. Many of these could not be recovered in time, forcing crews to blow them up to prevent them from falling intact into the hands of the Red Army. After nearly three months of non-stop armored combat, the plains west of the Danube, south of Lakes Balaton and Velencze, and north of Simontornya had been transformed into an enormous tank graveyard, with hundreds—perhaps thousands—of wrecked and destroyed German and Soviet armored vehicles strewn along its length and breadth.

Postwar Soviet claims of German losses were enormously inflated, as was usually the case during the Cold War; Marshal Tolbukhin's biographer claimed that losses inflicted on the Germans during the battle were as high as 45,000 men killed, wounded, and missing, and that 1,000 armored fighting vehicles were destroyed.[62] Soviet losses were not insignificant; *H.Gr. Süd* claimed to have killed or captured up to 6,407 Soviet troops by 17 March, and destroyed as many as 237 enemy tanks and assault guns. In addition to these, German statisticians in *H.Gr. Süd* claimed that its troops had destroyed or captured 532 artillery pieces and antitank guns and shot down 30 Soviet aircraft.[63] While impressive, these statistics could not compensate for the tremendous losses suffered by German forces. Modern Russian historians state that the Third Ukrainian Front's losses were actually higher than first estimated, amounting to 32,899 men, including 8,492 killed or missing and 24,407 wounded.[64]

For all practical intent, 15 March marked the high-water mark as well as the last day of the *Frühlingserwachen* offensive. The following day would see the forces of *H.Gr. Süd* begin hastily transitioning to a defensive posture to repel the Soviet offensive that began that morning. Buoyed along initially by Hitler's high hopes for its success, *Frühlingserwachen* had been launched under great secrecy with a large proportion of Germany's last remaining reserves, but delivered no gains worth the high price its troops had paid. Even had it succeeded, it most likely would not have made any material contribution to advancing the Third Reich's strategic goal of regime survival.

The last strategic reserve of the *Wehrmacht* had been frittered away in a series of meaningless attacks, and the most that the offensive had accomplished was the temporary occupation of some worthless ground that its troops could not hope to successfully defend for more than a few days. It had all been a colossal waste of troops, tanks, and time, confirming what some of the senior leaders—such as Wöhler, Dietrich, von Grolman, and Guderian—had feared all along. Now, the check had finally come due for these men to begin paying for their unquestioning obedience, indeed, their blind loyalty to the *Führer*. Ironically, the first unit to be presented with the bill was the *IV. SS-Pz.Korps*, and the bill collector arrived in the form of the 9th Guards Army.

CHAPTER 3

The Defense of Stuhlweissenburg 16–19 March 1945

Once *Frühlingserwachen* began to show signs of slowing down as early as 8 March, it became apparent to the Soviet high command that the immediate crisis had passed and that the 26th and 27th Armies would be able to withstand any further assaults by the *6. Pz.Armee*, notwithstanding Marshal Tolbukhin's initial jitteriness. By this point, nearly all of Dietrich's powerful army, as well as the *III. Pz.Korps*, had placed themselves in an extremely vulnerable position, having continued their attacks south and east of the Sárviz Canal where most of their armor was stuck in the mud or blocked by determined Soviet resistance. What few German units were still able to advance were moving farther and farther south, increasing the distance from their starting point east of Lake Balaton.

By this stage of the battle, all that protected the *6. Pz.Armee* left flank were the *IV. SS-Pz.Korps* with its three divisions (two German SS and one Hungarian) in the Stuhlweissenburg Gap and the Hungarian *3. Armee's* unproven *VIII. Armee-Korps* with four divisions (two German and two Hungarian, plus a Hungarian *SS Kampfgruppe*), holding a thinly spread line stretching across the Vértes, Gerecse, and Pilis Mountains. Virtually all of *A.Gr. Balck/6. Armee's* reserves had been committed by this point, except for a variety of small and inconsequential units. In all of military history, few armies had ever been presented an opportunity to stage a repeat of the Battle of Cannae. Here was such an opportunity and the *STAVKA* supreme command was determined not to let it slip through their hands.

Originally, the *STAVKA* had intended for Marshal Rodion Malinovsky's Second Ukrainian Front and Tolbukhin's Third Ukrainian Front to simultaneously initiate the Vienna Operation along both sides of the Danube once the German counteroffensive had run its course; however, presented with the chance to bag both the entire *6. Pz.Armee* and *6.Armee* in one fell stroke, Stalin ordered a change of plan on 9 March. Rather than have the Third Ukrainian Front concentrate all of its attacking forces from the area west of Budapest in a northwesterly direction against the Hungarian *3. Armee* in the Vértes and Gerecse Mountains, as originally intended, Tolbukhin was directed instead to attack in two directions at the same time beginning on

16 March. One of these attacks would be aimed at the Hungarian *3. Armee* as per the original plan, while the other would be aimed at the *IV. SS-Pz.Korps* in the Stuhlweissenburg Gap (see Map 3).[1]

The direction of attack in the north was aimed at Tatabanya, a town located in the gap between the Vértes and Gerecse Mountains northwest of Felsőgalla. Once this objective was taken, the attacking spearheads would advance northwest across the open plains towards Komorn. The attack in the south, once it broke through the 31-kilometer-wide gap between Stuhlweissenburg and the southern foothills of the Vértes Mountains, would advance westwards towards Várpalota and Veszprém, where it would cut off and trap the *6. Pz.Armee* as well as most of *A.Gr. Balck/6. Armee*. The southern attack would be carried out by Col.Gen. Nikanor Zakhvatayev's 4th Guards Army, which was already in place, and Col.Gen. Vasily Glagolev's 9th Guards Army.[2]

The Soviet attack through the mountains towards the northwest would be carried out initially by Col.Gen. Aleksandr Petrushevskiy's 46th Army, which would attack along two primary axis—one towards the boundary between the Hungarian *1. Hus. Div.* and *2. Pz.Div.*, and the other between the *1. Hus.Div.* and the German *96. Inf.Div.* Petrushevskiy's initial objectives would be the towns of Mór and Tatabanya, which, once taken, would put the 46th Army in the position of either cutting off the *IV. SS-Pz.Korps* from the rear or the entire Hungarian *3. Armee*.[3] To prosecute his attack, Petrushevskiy's army had 66 of its own tanks, with the II Guards Mechanized Corps in reserve with 99 more.[4] To the south, the attack between the Stuhlweissenburg Gap would be reinforced by Col.Gen. Andrei Kravchenko's 6th Guards Tank Army once it had completed its movement across the Danube by 19 March. Kravchenko's army had initially been intended for use by the Second Ukrainian Front, but as a result of the *STAVKA*'s decision, Malinovsky's attack north of the Danube would be weakened at a critical moment and delayed until 25 March, to the short-term benefit of *Gen.d.Geb.Tr.* Hans Kreysing's *8. Armee*.

While Dietrich's *6. Pz.Armee* and Breith's *III. Pz.Korps* had been fruitlessly pounding away at the southern flank of the Third Ukrainian Front for the past 10 days, with little to show for their efforts, the other elements of Tolbukhin's front and all of the Second Ukrainian Front, including the 6th Guards Tank Army, had been quietly increasing in strength. According to one source, nearly all of the Red Army's units designated to take part in the Vienna Operation had been brought up as near as possible to their authorized table of organization in both manpower and equipment. Instead of rifle units operating at only 30–40 percent strength, most of them had been brought up to 80 men in normal rifle units, and 140 men in the Guards Rifle companies.[5]

When the Vienna Operation began, the correlation of forces would be overwhelmingly in the Red Army's favor. Hitler had inadvertently helped the Soviet plan when he insisted on continuing the *Frühlingserwachen* offensive as long as his did, giving the Red Army plenty of time to prepare. Against the German and Hungarian forces

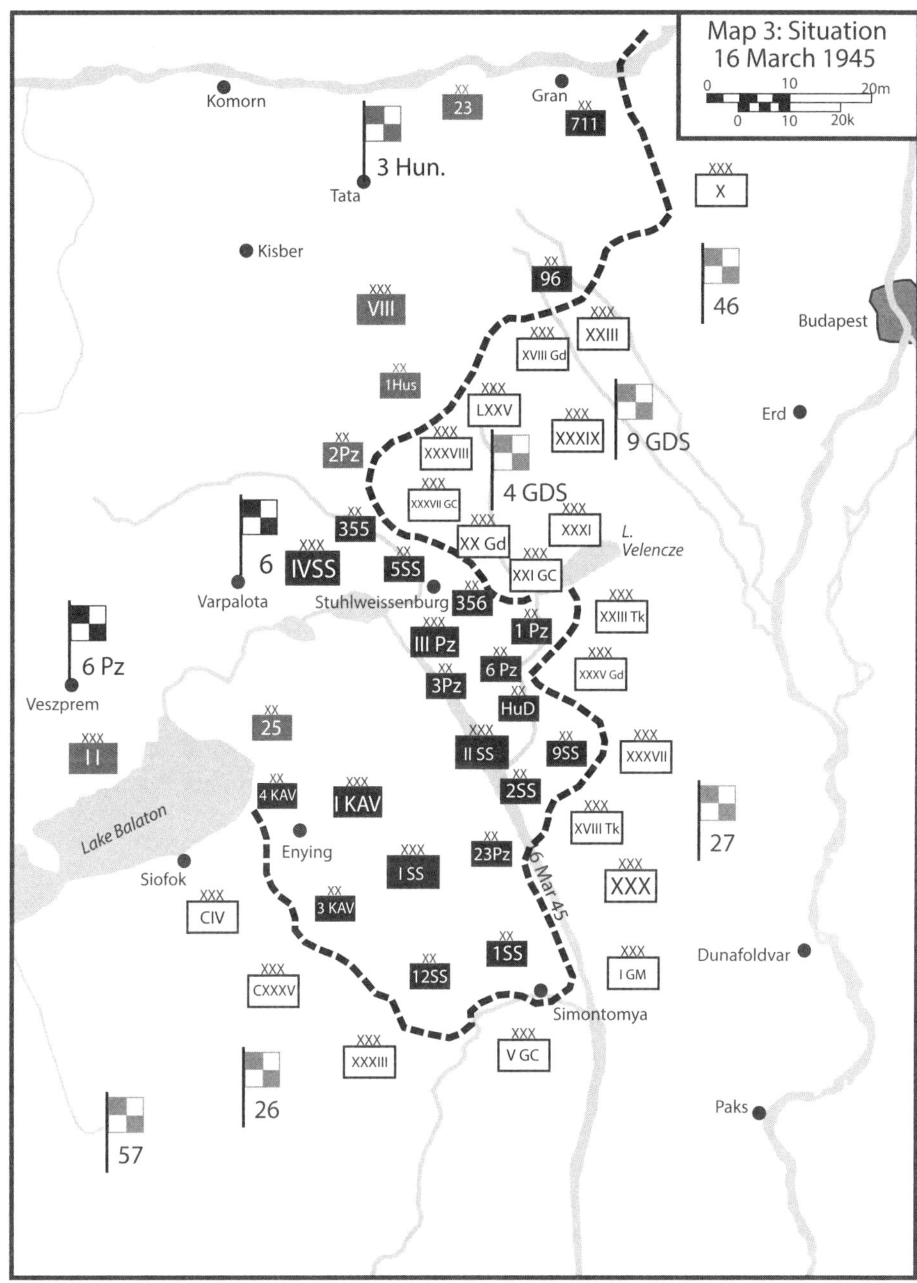
Map 3: Situation 16 March 1945
0 10 20m
0 10 20k
Komorn
23
Gran
711
X
3 Hun.
Tata
Kisber
96
46
Budapest
VIII
XXIII
XVIII Gd
1Hus
LXXV
XXXIX
Erd
9 GDS
2Pz
XXXVIII
XXXVII GC
4 GDS
XXXI
L. Velencze
6
IVSS
355
XX Gd
5SS
XXI GC
Varpalota
Stuhlweissenburg
356
1 Pz
XXIII Tk
III Pz
6 Pz
6 Pz
3Pz
XXXV Gd
Veszprem
HuD
II
25
II SS
9SS
XXXVII
Lake Balaton
4 KAV
I KAV
2SS
27
Enying
23Pz
XVIII Tk
Siofok
I SS
16 Mar 45
XXX
CIV
3 KAV
1SS
Dunafoldvar
CXXXV
12SS
I GM
Simontomya
XXXIII
V GC
26
Paks
57

defending the 31-kilometer-wide Stuhlweissenburg Gap, the 4th and 9th Guards Armies would be able to commit 5,425 artillery tubes, mortars, and rocket launchers, averaging 175 tubes per kilometer. In contrast, *SS-ARKO 504*—with approximately 434 tubes of all calibers, including mortars and antitank guns—would only be able to muster 14 field pieces, mortars, and rocket launchers per kilometer, giving the Soviet attacking force a 12.5 to one advantage in firepower.[6]

According to post-USSR data, the Third Ukrainian Front had increased in strength to a force numbering more than 745,000 men (counting forces arrayed in the south against the *6. Pz.Armee*), while the Second Ukrainian Front north of the Danube reported 272,200 men. In contrast, *H.Gr.* Süd reported a total troop strength of 270,000 men between Lake Balaton and the Danube, excluding the *2. Pz.Armee* and *8. Armee*. Even more impressive was the number of armored fighting vehicles the Red Army had marshalled to prosecute the offensive—approximately 1,600 of all types, with more in reserve. While *H.Gr. Süd* reported 1,796 armored fighting vehicles of all types assigned, including both the *2. Pz.Armee* and *8. Armee*, approximately 1,024 of them were in either short- or long-term repair, leaving commanders only 772 operational tanks, assault guns, and tank destroyers on 15 March. That number would shrink even further once fuel shortages became widespread after the destruction of the Komorn and Füzitö fuel refineries on 14 March.[7]

After reviewing these numbers describing the correlation of forces, one has to wonder why *H.Gr. Süd* carried out the *Frühlingserwachen* offensive at all and why Hitler demanded to continue waging it as long as he did, long after signs of its failure were evident. It was not as if *OKH* and *H.Gr. Süd* were in complete ignorance of Soviet strengths and intentions; German intelligence services had been sounding the alarm about signs of enemy troop movements west of Budapest for nearly a week. When one officer from *H.Gr. Süd* later asked the *OKH* chief of staff why continuing to carry out the offensive had been so important despite the warnings, Guderian replied that when Hitler saw the words "oil fields," for him they were always "spelled out in capital letters."[8]

Squarely in the path of this looming juggernaut lay the *IV. SS-Pz.Korps*. By this point, its three divisions, corps troops, and attachments—approximately 40,000 men in all—had been occupying the same defensive positions for over a month. Its troops had dug deep into the earth and constructed a well-laid-out series of defense lines, alternate positions, antitank-gun nests, and command posts. Thousands of land mines had been laid and barbed wire had been strung along the most likely avenues of approach. Communications wire had been dug in to reduce its vulnerability to indirect fire. Mortar and machine-gun positions and even artillery pieces had been emplaced in dug-in firing positions, many reinforced with layers of logs and earth-filled sandbags. These field defenses should have held up well, despite the fact that there had been no concrete available to reinforce any of it. It was in these positions, as well as the troops manning them, that Gille and his three division commanders had placed their trust, as Gille had already expressed in his phone call to the staff of the *6. Pz.Armee*.

While each of his two SS divisions were filled with several thousand new replacements, both Becker and Ullrich still had confidence in their small-unit leaders and were sure that once they got over their initial shock of combat, they would do well. Becker was not so certain about the Hungarian *2. Pz.Div.*, but most of his worries concerned their *1. Hus.Div.* in the adjacent corps' sector. Although all three of the corps' armored divisions fielded less than 100 combat-ready tanks, assault guns, and tank destroyers combined, their crew members were all veterans who were confident in the lethality of their weapons and their ability to employ them to deadly effect. By all previous measures, there was every reason to be confident that the *IV. SS-Pz. Korps* would hold when the storm struck the Stuhlweissenburg Gap, except for the wild card in the form of the Hungarian division.

The Red Army's Vienna Operation was scheduled to begin in the early hours of Friday, 16 March, but dense ground fog and heavily overcast skies postponed the initial assault until noon, by which point the weather had finally cleared. Earlier that morning, *Brigadeführer* Becker had personally visited each unit of his division designated as his *Eingreifreserve* (emergency reserve) to ensure that they were alerted and had time to move into their designated reserve positions behind the front lines. He also took additional measures to ensure that once the battle began, he had on-the-ground contact on the left with the Hungarian *2. Pz.Div.* One soldier from *II. Bataillon* of the *Totenkopf* Regiment who was there, *Ustuf.* Peter Renold, later wrote:

> *SS-Brigadeführer* Becker appeared at our battalion command post around 4 a.m. [on 16 March] to order all of us reserve units to begin moving into our positions [note: *II. Btl./Totenkopf* at Csákberény]. With a portion of our new men, mostly replacements from the *Luftwaffe*, and parts of the *5. Kompanie*, we moved into our *Auffangstellung* [interception line] around Söréd. At the double time we reached the area and occupied our positions. Shortly afterwards, a motorcycle sidecar driven by a messenger named Hermann arrived and picked me up to take me to battalion headquarters.[9]

When he arrived at the battalion command post, *Ustuf.* Renold was told by its commander, *Hstuf.* Christian Bachmann, to take two Hungarian *Volksdeutsche* SS men standing next to him and personally establish contact on the left with the right-most unit of the Hungarian *2. Pz.Div.*

He was also told to take two machinegun teams from *2. Kp./SS-Pz.Aufkl.Abt. 3* and place them where they could fire in support of the adjacent Hungarian unit should it require assistance. If the Hungarians should run away, it would have left the division's left flank wide open to envelopment, therefore Renold and his troops were to be placed there as a safeguard measure.[10] Bachmann directed him to keep the two Hungarian SS men and use them as runners. Renold said that this was not an ideal way to go about it, but since he had no radio or telephone contact with the neighboring unit, it was the best that he could do under the circumstances. At least he had a field telephone connecting him to his battalion headquarters. This arrangement would very soon be put to the test.

Becker also instructed the *III. Bataillon* of the *Totenkopf* Regiment, commanded by *Hstuf.* Herbert Brunst, to move beyond the left flank of the corps to its new position behind the Hungarian *1. Hus.Div.* in the woods east of Mór, as previously directed by *Gen.d.Pz.Tr.* Balck. Here, the battalion's position abutted the far right flank of the Hungarian division, serving as the only solid connection between the *IV. SS-Pz.Korps* and its neighbor, the Hungarian *VIII Armee-Korps*. Although Becker had complied with his instructions from corps headquarters to ensure that the integrity of the boundary between the *IV. SS-Pz.Korps* and the Hungarian *VIII. Armee-Korps* was secured, it also meant that Brunst and his battalion would be isolated from the rest of the *Totenkopf* Division once the shooting began.[11]

Although the troops of the *IV. SS-Pz.Korps* had been placed on high alert that evening, the night of 15/16 March went by relatively uneventfully. The morning report for *A.Gr. Balck/6. Armee* simply stated: "The night passed quietly along the entire *Armeegruppe*'s front."[12] No sounds of motor vehicles on the opposite side of the lines were reported, and the usual nightly artillery and mortar fire dwindled to almost nothing. Whether they knew it or not, this would be the *IV. SS-Pz.Korps*' last peaceful night for a long time, and for many of the soldiers of the *Totenkopf* and *Wiking* Divisions, as well as the Hungarian *2. Pz.Div.*, their last night on earth.

Much of the focus of the *H.Gr. Süd* and *6. Pz.Armee* leadership that morning was on the preparations being made to reposition the *I. SS-Pz.Korps* to the northeast in order for it to carry out the attack to the Danube south of Lake Velencze alongside *III. Pz.Korps*, which Hitler had only approved late the previous evening. Even this attack, had it been carried out, stood no chance whatsoever of achieving any meaningful success, but because Hitler had insisted on it, the *6. Pz.Armee* had no option but to carry it out. As events were to prove, even this plan could not be executed in time on account of the Third Ukrainian Front's offensive that began the same day. The delay in the transmission of the request and the final receipt of Hitler's approval had cost *H.Gr. Süd* 48 valuable hours, time it would never be able to make good.

Not mentioned in most of the post-war accounts were the secret discussions that Dietrich and his chief of staff had with Wöhler's chief of staff, *Gen.Lt.* Helmuth von Grolman, on 14 March concerning an alternate plan that would have diverted Priess's *I. SS-Pz.Korps* to the area south of Stuhlweissenburg instead of towards the Danube. In this location, it would be in a better position to assist the *IV. SS-Pz.Korps* should the Soviet spring offensive be carried out earlier than anticipated. Based on von Grolman's tentative approval, Dietrich ordered his staff to begin secretly working on the plan, but even this one could not be carried out in time before the blow struck.[13] However, its concept of operations would come in handy six days later.

At precisely 12:30 p.m., German and Hungarian positions were bombarded by a one-hour artillery and rocket barrage of an intensity that had never before been experienced, even greater than what the corps had gone through during the second battle of Warsaw.[14] It ranged back and forth from the front line as far back as artillery positions, with the intent of obliterating everything in the path of the infantry assault, which followed behind as soon as the curtain of fire lifted. In the words of Schönfelder, Gille's chief of staff: "After a drumfire artillery barrage, masses of [Soviet] infantry attacked, consisting of large bodies of troops from 500 to 1,500 men at a time that appeared out of the folds in the terrain or from ravines, supported by packs of tanks. These were shortly followed by a second wave that attacked partially from the column of march."[15] These were part of the initial force of 122 tanks that had be apportioned for use by the attacking 4th and 9th Guards Armies, but even more were being held in reserve (see Map 4).[16]

The men of the *IV. SS-Pz.Korps*, who had been alerted hours before, were already standing to in their fighting positions, kneeling beside their antitank guns, artillery pieces, and mortars, or sitting in their warmed-up *panzers* waiting for the orders to attack. All they could do until the storm passed was to crouch behind cover and hope or pray that their position would not receive a direct hit. Once the barrage lifted, they would spring to their posts, load their weapons, and sight in on their pre-planned fields of fire while they awaited the inevitable infantry assault. New replacements, facing ground combat for the first time, would have displayed the usual jitteriness, but the presence of the few remaining *Alte Hasen*—old front-line veterans—was reassuring. In one or two days, if they survived, they too might become "old hares."

The daily report by *H.Gr. Süd* outlined the course of the fighting that day in sharp, terse terms:

> After a heavy drumfire artillery barrage supported by multiple rocket launchers and mortars, around noon the enemy initiated his anticipated major offensive with attacks along a broad front in battalion- to regiment-strength against the defensive sectors of both corps [i.e., the *IV. SS-Pz.Korps* and Hungarian *VIII. Armee-Korps*] as well as the right flank of the *96. Inf. Div.* The assault was supported by several groups of tanks, about 30 in all … in the sector between Lake Velencze and Sárkeresztes, the enemy force, supported by 10 tanks, was able to achieve several local penetrations, that were mostly cleared out by counterattacks. In the sector of the Hungarian *2. Pz.Div.* between Sárkeresztes and Gánt, the enemy attacked and broke through along a wide frontage with at least four regimental-size assault groupings, forcing the Hungarians to fall back a distance of 4 kilometers, while being pursued by the enemy. The breakthrough area … 4 kilometers north of Stuhlweissenburg and up to 4 kilometers north of the line Sárkeresztes–Magyaralmás–Csákberény has been sealed off and [our] counterattack is ongoing. In all, 10 enemy tanks have been destroyed so far.[17]

Throughout that day, though struck hard and under enormous pressure, Gille's two SS divisions held on, and by evening had prevented any major breach in their *HKL*.

Obergruppenführer Gille, in a telephone conversation with a staff officer from the *6. Pz.Armee*, provided a brief update, telling him that both of his SS divisions had

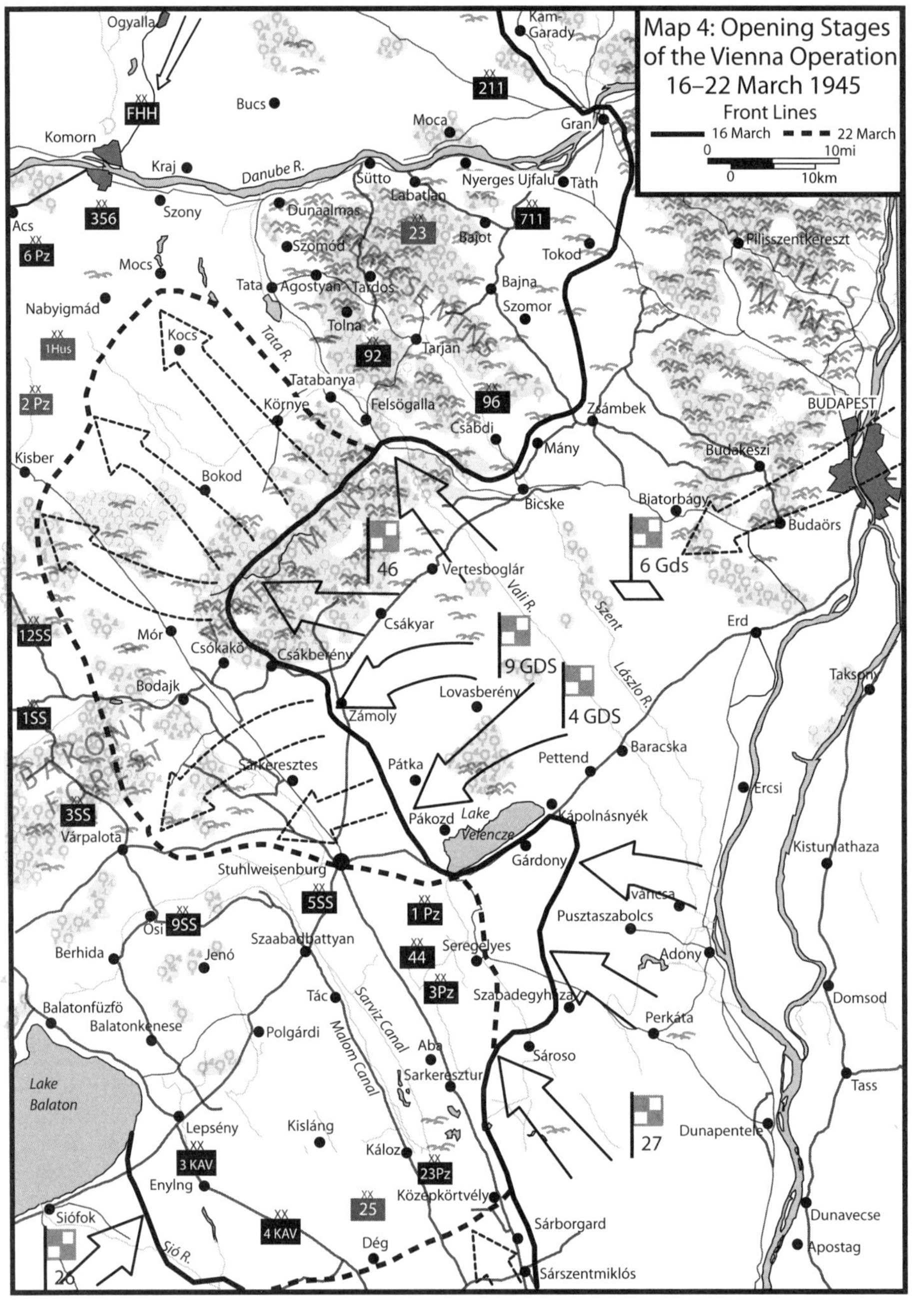
Map 4: Opening Stages
of the Vienna Operation
16–22 March 1945
Front Lines
16 March
22 March
0
10mi
0
10km
Ogyalla
Kam-Garady
FHH
Bucs
Moca
Gran
211
Komorn
Kraj
Danube R.
Sütto
Nyerges Ujfalu
Tàth
Acs
Szony
Dunaalmas
Labatlan
711
356
Szomód
Bajot
Tokod
6 Pz
Mocs
Tata
Agostyan
Tardos
Bajna
23
Nabyigmád
Tolna
Szomor
Kocs
Tarjan
1Hus
Tatabanya
92
Zsámbek
2 Pz
Környe
Felsögalla
96
Csábdi
BUDAPEST
Kisber
Bokod
Mány
Budakeszi
Bicske
Biatorbágy
Budaörs
Vertesboglár
6 Gds
46
12SS
Csákyar
Erd
Mór
Csókakö
Csákberény
9 GDS
Taksony
Bodajk
Lovasberény
4 GDS
1SS
Zámoly
Baracska
Sarkeresztes
Pátka
Pettend
Ercsi
3SS
Pákozd
Lake
Velencze
Kápolnásnyék
Várpalota
Gárdony
Kistunlathaza
Stuhlweisenburg
Ivancsa
5SS
1 Pz
Pusztaszabolcs
Osi
9SS
Szabadbattyan
Seregelyes
Adony
Berhida
Jenó
44
Tác
3Pz
Szabadegyhaza
Perkáta
Domsod
Balatonfüzfö
Balatonkenese
Polgárdi
Aba
Sároso
Lake
Balaton
Sarkeresztur
Tass
Lepsény
Kisláng
27
Dunapentele
3 KAV
Káloz
Enylng
23Pz
Dunavecse
Siófok
Középkörtvély
Sárborgard
Apostag
26
Sió R.
4 KAV
25
Dég
Sárszentmiklós

been able to withstand the Soviet attack so far, but that his division commanders had told him that the infantry assaults were "unusually strong" and had "very heavy fire support." Although he felt that the *Totenkopf* and *Wiking* Divisions were doing well, he was very worried about vitéz-Zsedényi's division west of Zámoly, where the attacking Soviet troops had made deep penetrations, forcing Gille to commit his reserves to seal them off.[18] Indeed, the Hungarian *2. Pz.Div.* was having a difficult time, but other than the forces that Gille had already sent, *A.Gr. Balck/6. Armee* had no other reserves available. The only other formation that Balck could possibly have used, the *6. Pz.Div.*, had already been sent elsewhere to reinforce the *III. Pz.Korps'* futile attack east of Seregélyes several days before.

In the sector of the adjacent Hungarian *VIII. Armee-Korps*, which ran through the eastern slopes of the Vértes Mountains, the situation was even more serious. Soviet troops quickly made numerous penetrations in the main defense line held by the Hungarian *1. Hus.Div.*, including the right flank where *Sturmbannführer* Messerle had carried out his inspection tour on a motorcycle three days before. What *Brig.Fhr.* Becker had predicted would happen then had now come to pass: the spearheads of the 46th Army, taking advantage of the Hungarians' lax security, had easily located the positions of their opponent's widely spaced defensive positions and had simply gone around them.

In the lowlands east of the Vértes Mountains northwest of Bicske, Soviet troops made up to seven penetrations in the Hungarian line, as well as in the adjacent defenses on the right flank of *Gen.Maj.* Hermann Harrendorf's *96. Inf.Div.* Ominously, breakthrough attacks directed towards Tatabanya had been attempted southwest of Felsőgalla and near Csabdi, but these were temporarily fended off. On the far left flank of the Hungarian *VIII. Armee-Korps*, *Gen.Maj.* Josef Reichert's *711. Inf.Div.* had been attacked by a battalion-sized force against its thin security line southwest of Kirva (Máriahalom), and although Reichert had launched a counterattack, its outcome was still unknown by the evening reporting deadline.

In many places, Hungarian and German counterattacks failed to make any impression at all on the overwhelming numbers of enemy troops being sent against them, forcing them to fall back and establish hasty defensive positions. This became especially evident when the *A.Gr. Balck/6. Armee* evening report was submitted at 5:55 p.m. It stated:

> The Hungarian *2. Pz.Div.* on the left wing of the *IV. SS-Pz.Korps* has run away. The enemy is continuing to advance from Borbála Puszta to the southwest. He is even approaching Csákberény and is pushing into the woods to the northeast of it. The reserves of the *IV. SS-Pz.Korps* have already been employed for the most part against these penetrations … based on impressions gained from the course of today's fighting, one is dealing with the expected enemy offensive. So far, however, surprisingly few enemy tanks have appeared. Up to 30 have been identified up to this point, of which eight have been knocked out … The situation in the Vértes Mountains could become difficult if the Hungarian *1. Hus.Div.* pulls back any further. The *Armeegruppe* requests that *Gren.Brig. (mot.) 92* moving in from the *2. Pz.Armee* be attached in order for it to assemble at Környe [note: it was attached to *A.Gr. Balck* at midnight].[19]

Although in this report *Gen.d.Pz. Tr.* Balck had claimed that the Hungarians simply ran away, this is not true. Their *2. Pz.Div.* and *1. Hus.Div.*, along with the two German divisions in the Hungarian *VIII. Armee-Korps*, did carry out a series of counterattacks, but the sheer size of the enemy force bearing down on their units was simply too great for them to bear, and many of the companies and battalions were simply obliterated.

The German reserves positioned behind the Hungarian *2. Pz.Div.* earlier that morning were all that remained to prevent a rout and they did what they could, but now there was nothing left to send. *Hauptsturmführer* Brunst's battalion from the *Totenkopf* Regiment, positioned along the seam between both corps earlier that day, initially held back the Soviet attack, even after the weaponless soldiers from the adjacent battalion of the *1. Hus.Div.* fled past him shouting: "The Russians are coming! They're right behind us!" His battalion was soon surrounded and fighting for its life. Only later that evening was Brunst able to order a breakout, rejoining the division west of Mór after suffering heavy losses.[20]

Balck's insistence on 15 March downplaying the possibility of any major Soviet offensive taking place in the Stuhlweissenburg Gap, as well as his assertion that Gille's corps was sufficiently strong to withstand any attack if one did occur, were now seen by the senior leaders of *H.Gr. Süd* as having been unrealistically optimistic. This was a trend of his that was becoming all too evident, even to those who had initially been well disposed towards him. Balck's report prompted *Generalleutnant* von Grolman to pen a note for entry into the official record to that effect.[21] Additionally, Balck's earlier failure to place any German units within the *1. Hus.Div.* sector to act as "corset stays" after *H.Gr. Süd* recommended that he do so was proving to be a fatal omission, and the belated commitment of a single German two-battalion infantry brigade (*Gren.Brig. 92*) in Tatabanya was not going to be sufficient to address the situation, even if it did arrive in time (which it did not).

During the fighting that day, the *Wiking* Division's commander ordered Fritz Darges to carry out a counterattack with his "regiment," which was only a company in size by this point. After the initial barrage had lifted, the *5. Kompanie* (with *Pz. V* Panthers) was sent forward. The acting commander of the company, *Ostuf.* Heinrich Kerckhoff, later wrote:

> Towards noon, the Russians put down a barrage with all available calibers like they had at Warsaw and Kovel. We fired up the engines, slammed the hatches shut, and remained alert. After a good hour, the Reds attacked. The grenadiers stood their ground; we provided high-explosive rounds to good effect. Together, the attack was turned back and abated towards the evening.[22]

On the main defense line around Stuhlweissenburg, the *Westland* Regiment fought off several attacks. The regimental commander, Franz Hack, later wrote that he and his troops first smashed a frontal attack from the northwest, then "packs of tanks and infantry rolled over our outpost line, and we were only able to get them to turn around when we fired our *Sperrfeuer* [artillery blocking barrage].” During the afternoon, Hack's regiment lost contact on its left with the *Germania* Regiment, which was holding on to its sector with difficulty.[23]

The Soviet attack was able to penetrate the left flank of the *Germania* Regiment in the afternoon, which led to the temporary encirclement of *Hstuf.* Hans Müller's neighboring *III. Btl./Eicke*. Despite a minor wound caused by a shell fragment in his shoulder, Müller continued leading his battalion in an all-round defense until contact could be restored. The momentum of the Soviet attack was relentless. One survivor of that day, *Sturmmann* Börger of *6. Kp./Eicke*, later wrote:

> Due to the concentrated enemy artillery fire on our position that had us completely covered, many of our comrades were killed and many more were wounded. As soon as the firing stopped, the Russians and their tanks were already in front of us and jumped into our trenches with a loud “Urrah!” They killed nearly everyone who wasn't able to escape at the last moment.[24]

The fighting southeast of Sárkeresztes was exceedingly bitter, and only by committing its reserves was the *Eicke* Regiment able to restore its positions. In the middle of the fighting, the regimental commander, Knight's Cross holder *Ostubaf.* Franz Kleffner, was killed in action when his command vehicle was hit by a high-explosive shell. He was replaced shortly thereafter by *Ostubaf.* Wilhelm Breimeier.

A counterattack initiated by Kleffner before his death that included *Haupsturmführer.* Frommhagen's *I. Btl./Eicke*, supported by the tanks of *SS-Pz.Rgt. 3*, was able to restore the situation after destroying several of the enemy's tanks. A Hungarian battalion attached to the *Eicke* Regiment from their *20. Inf.Div.* was overrun during the assault, and the Soviet attack rushed forwards through the gap in their vacated positions until it reached the guns of *I. Abt./SS-Pz.Art.Rgt. 3* positioned several kilometers behind the front lines. Only by firing over open sights with high explosives was the enemy attack stopped just before its riflemen penetrated the gun positions. The battalion had trained for such a possibility and was ready when it came.[25]

Dozens of similar scenes to these played out up and down the lines that day, as the *IV. SS-Pz.Korps* struggled to keep the attackers at bay. Losses on both sides were high. On the left flank behind the Hungarian *2. Pz.Div.*, the reserve that had been positioned between Csákberény and Csillaki Puszta to man a blocking position, Bachmann's *II. Btl./Totenkopf*, was overrun and Bachmann was killed in action. *Untersturmführer* Renold and his 20-man platoon were barely able to return to their battalion after the neighboring Hungarian battalion vanished, where Soviet loudspeaker trucks were reportedly blaring recordings entreating the Hungarians to surrender.[26]

During his attempt to rejoin his battalion, Renold was captured 24 hours later and was marched through the village with several other prisoners to the spot where his battalion's command post had been. The village was strewn with the bodies of dead German and Soviet soldiers and Hungarian civilians. Four knocked-out T-34s and a JS-II Stalin heavy tank smoldered next to Bachmann's destroyed command car in the courtyard where he had once occupied his command post. Bachmann lay dead on the ground nearby, wearing his distinctive fur-lined leather jacket and cradling a *Panzerfaust*.

His Soviet captors were none too happy about the number of men they had lost while storming the village, and up until the last moment Renold thought he would be shot in retribution.[27] But the sacrifice of *II. Btl./Totenkopf* had not been in vain, for it had bought the time needed for three of the division's assault guns along with its *Stosszug* (special assault platoon) led by *Oscha*. August Zingel to be sent to the threatened area that afternoon, where the small *Kampfgruppe* immediately launched a counterattack that destroyed several enemy tanks and scattered the accompanying infantry. Overall, 13 Soviet tanks were destroyed in the corps' defensive sector that day.

On account of the seriousness of the fighting, Gille had nothing to spare to help relieve the neighboring Hungarian *VIII. Armee-Korps*, except the two independent battalions undergoing *Auffrischung*, the *I. Btl./Norge* and *I. Btl./Danmark*. Although neither were considered to be "combat ready," he sent them anyway to assist the *Totenkopf* Division, which had been hit the hardest. Before it had arrived, Vogt's *I. Btl./Norge* was recalled and ordered to march to Inota instead, while im Masche's *I. Btl./Danmark* proceeded to Söréd. The *SS-Rgt. Ney*, located in Sur, was also alerted by *A.Gr. Balck/6. Armee*, but it was not under Gille's direct control at that moment. The reserves that Balck had requested the previous day, the six fortress antitank companies to defend Mór and the artillery *Heerestruppen*, had not yet arrived, nor had *Oberst* Herbert Grosser's *Gren.Brig. (mot.) 92*.[28]

Overhead, waves of Soviet ground-attack aircraft from the 17th Air Army scoured the countryside seeking targets, attacking anything that moved. Dogfights between German and Soviet aircraft swirled in the sky above, while Allied four-engine bombers were seen flying over the battlefield at high altitude, heading for targets in Austria or Czechoslovakia. Amazingly, *Luftflotte 4* was able to generate 300 sorties that day and its fighter squadrons claimed the downing of 28 Soviet aircraft throughout the entire *H.Gr. Süd* area of operations.[29] During the same day, 30 Soviet bombers targeted Veszprém and the area west of the city, barely missing Gille's headquarters in the town of Inota.

That evening, *Ogruf.* Gille would have been busily trying to keep track of what was happening on the battlefield and as was his habit, he would have attempted to reach the headquarters of his three divisions to speak with their commanders and look them in the eye to gauge the seriousness of the situation. Becker and Ullrich were known quantities who never buckled in a crisis; so far, vitéz-Zsedényi had done well, though his division clearly would not be able to hold out for very long if the attack continued at this pace. Gille had sent the divisions everything he had, and his corps troops, especially *s.SS-Art.Abt. 504* and *SS-Werf.Abt. 504*, had been firing practically non-stop in support. The most that he and his staff could do was to ensure the continuous supply of fuel, ammunition, and food to the forward units and that the wounded were evacuated and sent to field hospitals as soon as they could be moved. The corps staff would do whatever they could in regards to requesting *Luftwaffe* close air support as well.

That same evening, it appeared that *Gen.d.Pz.Tr.* Balck still did not understand the seriousness of the situation, for his intentions for the following day were simply stated as "Sealing off the breakthrough and re-establishing the old *HKL*." This conveys a certain air of unreality; either it was a deliberately false statement or he had no idea of the true situation. Gille's command post was only a few kilometers away from his, and Balck could have easily gone to that location to see for himself. If he had, he would have known that it was impossible to carry out this mission with the meager forces that Gille had available. As far as changes to troop dispositions, Balck's only official act was to direct the *96. Inf.Div.* to detach its *Füs.Btl. 96* and assign it to the Hungarian *1. Hus.Div.* that night. *Grenadier-Brigade (mot.) 92*, the bulk of which was still in transit, was placed under the control of *A.Gr. Balck/6. Armee* as soon as it arrived, but only its lead motorized elements had begun to trickle into its assembly area in Nagyigmánd that evening due to the terrible road conditions. The rest, travelling by rail, would unload in Raab and then trek to their assembly area near Tatabanya.

Both Wöhler and Dietrich were focused on extracting the *I. SS-Pz.Korps* from its vulnerable position in the south near Aba and Sarkeresztur, and repositioning it south of Stuhlweissenburg, later followed by the withdrawal of the *III. Pz.Korps*. Although Hitler had not yet given up the idea of continuing with *Frühlingserwachen*, nearly everyone else had, especially Wöhler and Dietrich. Both commanders had quickly realized the mortal threat posed by the Third Ukrainian Front's attack against the *IV. SS-Pz.Korps*. If the Vienna Operation had followed the plan as originally conceived that directed the Soviet 4th and 9th Guards Armies toward Komorn–Tatabanya–Felsőgalla, it would have been bad enough, but at least *H.Gr. Süd* would still have had room to maneuver and its northern flank would have been shielded by the Bakony Forest. But with this new assault clearly aimed in a westerly direction towards Várpalota and Veszprém, both Wöhler and Dietrich, as well as their chiefs of staff, quickly recognized the mortal danger.

From the late evening onwards, their efforts would be directed towards extracting the *6. Pz.Armee* from its vulnerable position south of Lakes Balaton and Velencze and turning it around. Everything now depended upon how quickly these movements could be carried out. What is curious is that nothing more was done to strengthen the *IV. SS-Pz.Korps*, other than the unimpressive amount of reinforcements that Balck had already asked for. This, in turn, points to something else: that Balck deliberately downplayed the severity of the situation in order to conceal his error, especially since he had displayed such an over-optimistic assessment the day before. Had he truly concealed how bad the situation was, especially in the Hungarian *3. Armee* sector?

Or were he and his chief of staff simply ignorant of what was happening? After all, the sounds of heavy fighting near Stuhlweissenburg would have been clearly audible at the army's headquarters in Várpalota, less than 20 kilometers away.

If Wöhler himself had been properly apprised of the true severity of the crisis that day, he most likely would have done more to ensure that Gille got the reinforcement he needed, such as pulling out the *6. Pz.Div.* (the closest force available) and sending it immediately to aid the *IV. SS-Pz.Korps* or, even better, help out the Hungarian *3. Armee*. None of these topics were discussed that evening, and it appears that everyone who was not in *A.Gr. Balck/6. Armee*, with the exception of the commanders and chiefs of staff of the *IV. SS-Pz.Korps* and the Hungarian *3. Armee*, believed that Balck had everything under control. As we have seen, this was certainly not the case.

As far as Marshal Tolbukhin was concerned, the attack so far was developing as he had intended. While the *IV. SS-Pz.Korps* was proving to be a difficult nut to crack—which was probably to be expected, given the reputation the corps had earned during *Konrad I–III*—the right flank of the Hungarian *VIII. Armee-Korps* was collapsing as anticipated. Although the two German divisions on the Hungarians' left flank were holding steady, they were not in the direct path of the steamroller and would soon find themselves on their own with nowhere to retreat to should the Third Ukrainian Front reach the bridges at Komorn before they did. Within the Vértes Mountains, the attacks by the Soviet 46th Army had progressed very well indeed, and its troops were finding little difficulty in moving along the narrow mountain roads. Unlike the *IV. SS-Pz.Korps* in early January, the 46th Army did not have to worry about having to fight their way through resolutely manned roadblocks erected in its path by the *Honvéd*. Instead, the defenders, at least those who chose to stand and fight, were brushed aside with hardly any difficulty. The rest were either trying to escape towards the west as fast as possible or surrendering in droves.

Saturday, 17 March was marked by increasingly warm temperatures, with a high of 50 degrees Fahrenheit being recorded, punctuated by widely scattered rain showers that fell upon the already soaked landscape. The *H.Gr. Süd* morning report stated: "In the [*6. Pz.Armee*] sector, the successful attacks against the enemy bridgehead over the Sió [River] continued, as well as the defense against several enemy assaults." This was an indication that the bulk of the army had not yet moved, but was still defending a pointless salient. The morning report by *A.Gr. Balck/6. Armee* was not only misleading, but alarming as well, if anyone knew what was really happening. It simply stated: "The enemy continued his attacks in the Stuhlweissenburg area and in the Vértes Mountains, but was unable to achieve any significant ground."[30]

By the time the evening report was submitted, a truer assessment of the day's events were revealed. It was no longer possible to conceal the extent of the unfolding disaster. The bulk of *6. Pz.Armee* was still engaged along the Sió River and bogged down in heavy fighting near Simontornya, and that day's attempt by the *II. SS-Pz. Korps* to seize the heavily fortified town of Sárkeresztur failed despite the best efforts of the troops involved. The *I. SS-Pz.Korps* had not yet completed its move to the left flank between the *II. SS-Pz.Korps* and Breith's corps. *H.G. Süd* issued orders for *A.Gr. Balck/6. Armee* to begin extracting the *Panzergrenadiers* from the *III. Pz.Korps* and send them to the Vértes Mountains as a stopgap, but that had not yet happened by the close of the day.

The reason why *H.Gr. Süd* would want to take away the infantry from the *1., 3.,* and *6. Pz.Div.* and send them to the left flank of *A.Gr. Balck/6. Armee* is evident in the consolidated *H.Gr. Süd* report that evening:

> In the *A.Gr Balck* area, the enemy continued his anticipated breakthrough attack, mostly in the sector between Stuhlweissenburg and the southern edge of the Vértes Mountains, with the partial assistance of newly brought-up masses of infantry supported by tank formations [of up to 20 tanks]. Despite our tough resistance even after the Hungarian forces had fallen out, our remaining forces could not prevent the enemy from reaching the Stuhlweissenburg–Söréd highway along a broad front. South of Lake Velencze, the enemy carried out several attacks intended to tie up our forces and managed to make a small penetration between Lake Velencze and Stuhlweissenburg that threatens the northern flank of the *III. Pz.Korps*. The enemy was also able to seize additional ground in the Vértes Mountains; although he employed only a minimal amount of his forces, he was still able to seize the mountain's western exits near Oroszlány.[31]

Several things are clear after re-reading this report. The first is that *Gren.Brig. (mot.) 92* would never make it all the way to Tatabanya unless as prisoners. The enemy's presence at Oroszlány meant that they had nearly outflanked the town already and that better use could be made of the brigade instead of sacrificing it before it could even be assembled.

The consolidated daily report also provides a glimpse of just how serious the situation was. Since Soviet troops had reportedly reached the Söréd–Stuhlweissenburg road "along a broad front," it meant that the *IV. SS-Pz.Korps'* front line between the northern edge of Stuhlweissenburg and the southern outskirts of Zámoly had been pushed back between 5 and 10 kilometers, which constituted a major setback; in fact, the corps' old front line no longer existed.

A Soviet division-sized attack attempted to force its way into Stuhlweissenburg, but the assault by its regiments were thwarted north and northeast of the city by the *Westland* Regiment, which inflicted *blutige* (bloody) losses on its enemy. In contrast, the attack that forced the *Totenkopf* Division and the *Germania* Regiment back from the Stuhlweissenburg–Zámoly highway was devastating. Numerous attacking groups in regimental strength (approximately 1,500 men each), supported by up to 10 tanks, began bypassing German centers of resistance in Söréd, Sárkeresztes, and Magyaralmás, leaving follow-on units to eliminate them with concentric attacks. A gap separating the *Totenkopf* and *Wiking* Divisions began to appear, but there were insufficient reserves to do anything about it. A large attacking force approached to within 3.5 kilometers of Mór before they were stopped by a joint counterattack by the *Totenkopf* Division and the Hungarian *2. Pz.Div.* North of Mór, a 5-kilometer gap yawned between it and Pusztavám, defended by the nearest element of the Hungarian *1. Hus.Div.*

On the *IV. SS-Pz.Korps'* left, the right flank of the neighboring Hungarian *1. Hus. Div.* had begun to swing back to the north, so that by sundown its front faced south, with its center of mass in Pusztavám, where it attempted to form a new defense line. Mór remained as an isolated outpost defended by Bachmann's *III. Bataillon* of the *Totenkopf* Regiment and portions of the Hungarian *2. Pz.Div.* The Hungarian *VIII. Armee-Korps'* center was being shredded as Soviet columns, led by as many as a dozen tanks each, appeared out of the mountains and bore down on Kozmá, Környe, and Oroszlány. The villages of Puszta Majk and Vértessomlo were seized against hardly any resistance. The leading battalion of *Gren.Brig. (mot.) 92* was ordered to carry out a counterattack as soon as it arrived northwest of Vértessomlo and managed to throw back a Soviet assault group that had attempted to attack Tatabanya from the south, but it was the only unit with any fighting potential in the entire *1. Hus.Div.* sector and was outnumbered by 10 to one. *Sturm-Art.Brig. 325* was on its way to reinforce the brigade, as was *Pz.Aufkl.Abt. 1* from the *1. Pz.Div.*, but whether these would arrive in time to be of much assistance before Tatabanya fell to the advancing Soviets was an open question.

On the center and left wing of the Hungarian *VIII. Armee-Korps*, a series of battalion-sized Soviet attacks west of Csabdi, north of Mány, and northwest of Zsámbék were thrown back by *SS-K.Gr. Ameiser*, supported by the *96. Inf.Div.* Another attempt by the *96. Inf.Div.* to restore the old *HKL* by a counterattack northwest of Kirva failed. The Hungarian *3. Armee* was clearly falling apart, and unless drastic action was soon taken it would be split into two pieces—the *1. Hus. Div.* and *23. Inf.Div.* on the right and the two German divisions on the left, with *SS-K.Gr. Ameiser* somewhere in between.

The last thing that the evening report makes clear is that the attacks against the front of the *III. Pz.Korps* were intentionally designed to tie up and prevent any of its divisions from being pulled out and sent to aid the *IV. SS-Pz.Korps*. Thus, all that Balck could spare from Breith's *III. Pz.Korps* and send to Gille's aid was the abovementioned non-armored elements of their *Panzergrenadier* Regiments, which after 12 days of heavy fighting during *Frühlingserwachen* were practically worn down. Tolbukhin knew exactly what he was doing.

The "minor" penetration the report mentioned between the right flank of the *IV. SS-Pz.Korps* south of Stuhlweissenburg and the left flank of the *III. Pz.Korps*, carried out by an infantry force supported by 20 tanks, would soon have far more serious consequences. Although this attack was stopped for the time being by a counterattack launched by the *III. Pz.Korps* that destroyed six of the enemy's tanks, some ground had been lost that would allow Soviet forces to jam more troops into the narrow gap between Lake Velencze and the southeast corner of the city. However, on 17 March, the *III. Pz.Korps* was subordinated to the *6. Pz.Armee*, leaving *A.Gr. Balck/6.*

Armee with only the *IV. SS-Pz.Korps* and the Hungarian *3. Armee* to command.[32] This move, which had been in its planning stages for the past several days and was unrelated to the present situation, would soon unnecessarily complicate the German command and control situation south of Stuhlweissenburg at a critical moment.

In the air, the *IV. SS-Pz.Korps* and *III. Pz.Korps* were pummeled mercilessly throughout the day by hordes of IL-2 *Sturmoviks*, A-20 Bostons, and other ground-attack aircraft. Any town or locality near or behind the front lines was bombed and staffed, as well as anything moving along the roads. The *Luftwaffe* was only able to fly 180 sorties that day in response. German ground-attack aircraft reported destroying two Soviet tanks and *Luftwaffe* fighter aircraft shot down three Red Air Force airplanes, but in terms of the number of aircraft the Soviet 17th Air Army was able to launch, this amounted to nothing.[33]

In regards to his intentions for the following day, Balck had modified those he had stated the night before. Instead of "restoring the previous main defense line," his plans had changed to "hold and fortify the current position," an admission that bore witness to his realization that things indeed had gotten away from him. However, even these more modest objectives were still beyond the capability of the *IV. SS-Pz.Korps* and Hungarian *3. Armee*. They would need more help than a mere infantry brigade, an assault gun battalion, and an armored reconnaissance battalion to fix things.

In a message sent to *H.Gr. Süd* at 00:45 a.m. on 18 March, Balck finally confessed the extent of the true situation: "There was a danger that the enemy could break through unimpeded to the northwest." In addition to *Gren.Brig. (mot.) 92*, which had already been sent, and *Pz.Aufkl.Abt. 1* (which had to be pulled out of the line near Nádasdladány), Balck also requested that he be given permission to withdraw the entire *356. Inf.Div.* from the *III. Pz.Korps* and use it to "secure" the Vértes Mountains, stating that, "If one did not reposition the *356. Inf.Div.*, a situation would arise in the next few days *that would upset all previous plans and require even more forces than those requested now* [emphasis added]."[34] This was an understatement, but this miniscule force (the *356. Inf.Div.* at the time only had four weak infantry battalions) would be a mere drop in the ocean compared to what was needed to stop the 46th Army's advance, and the 6th Guards Tank Army had not yet been committed to battle.

Balck's belated cries of alarm in regards to the situation between Stuhlweissenburg and the Vértes Mountains had even drawn the notice of *Gen.O.* Heinz Guderian, who had been following events closely. After reading a subsequent message from Balck that stated he could "no longer hope to be able to re-establish a front tonight with the available German reserves," Guderian contacted the *H.Gr. Süd* chief of staff, who was still fixated on the fighting along the Sárviz Canal, and informed him that he had:

> given considerable thought to the situation in the Vértes Mountains and had come to the realization that it was very serious. If the enemy succeeded in breaking through, then all other plans were invalid. Any loss of terrain there went straight for the marrow. The *Armeegruppe* [i.e., *A.Gr. Balck*] had to do everything to prevent it.[35]

Consequently, *H.Gr. Süd* received a planning directive from *OKH* informing it of the following intentions, pending Hitler's approval:

> *H.Gr. Süd* shall prepare to perform the following tasks:
> 1) Immediate preparations for bringing in the following reinforcements:
>   a) *16. SS-Pz.Gren.Div. RFSS* from the *2. Pz.Armee*.
>   b) Withdrawal of the *356. Inf.Div*.
>   c) Allocation of transport capabilities to move both divisions.
>   d) Operational planning to commit the *I. SS-Pz.Korps* in a northerly direction.
> 2) Immediate measures to be put into effect:
>   a) Deployment of *Gren.Brig. (mot.) 92* and all available reconnaissance battalions in a blocking position behind the Vértes Mountains.
>   b) Allocation of *Volks-Art.Korps 403* and *Werf.Brig. 17* to the *IV. SS-Pz.Korps* to support the defensive operations.[36]

When this plan was presented to Hitler later that evening for his approval, he refused to allow the *16. SS-Pz.Gren.Div. RFSS* to be moved (it had to remain behind to secure the Nagykanizsa oilfields) and insisted that the *I. SS-Pz.Korps* remain where it was pending a thorough estimate of the situation by *H.Gr. Süd*. He did permit the *Volk-Artillery Korps'* movement and that of the *Panzeraufklärungs-Abteilungen*, as well as *Werf.Brig. 17* and the *356. Inf.Div*.[37] He had already approved the movement of *Gren.Brig. (mot.) 92* the day before. While on paper this represented a respectable force, it was still insufficient for the task at hand.

For his part, Wöhler was considering a plan to move the entire *I. SS-Pz.Korps* to the Várpalota area instead of the region south of Stuhlweissenburg, an indication that he was beginning to understand Tolbukhin's true intentions. At Várpalota, the corps would be much more able to react to a push by the 4th or 9th Guards Armies to cut off the elements of the *6. Pz.Armee* still fighting south of Lake Balaton. Additionally, Várpalota was much closer and the *I. SS-Pz.Korps* would be able to get there more quickly than to Stuhlweissenburg. But again, this move would have to be approved in advance by Hitler, a process that required between 24 and 48 hours before he could make a decision, a policy that effectively tied the hands of his generals at this critical moment.

This impediment to rapid decision-making instituted by the dictator in Berlin conferred an enormous advantage to the Red Army, whose generals were no longer encumbered by such restrictions as they had been in 1941. Frequently, the leaders of *H.Gr. Süd*, *6. Pz.Armee*, and *A.Gr. Balck/6. Armee* did not receive an answer to their requests for Hitler's approval until a crisis had already fully developed, by which point many of their plans had already been overtaken by events. It was a terrible decision-making process, especially in fluid situations where the need to act quickly was essential, but this trend only grew worse as the war shuddered to its grisly end.

That evening, *H.Gr. Süd* issued the as-yet unapproved guidance for the next day, which can be characterized as a "concept plan" intended to counter the Vienna Operation, then in its second day. According to this concept, which had been worked out and agreed upon by Wöhler, Guderian, and their respective chiefs of staff, the *6. Pz.Armee* was directed to hold the front line it had established on the Sio River and Sárviz Canal with the *I. Kav.Korps*; the *2. Pz.Armee* was instructed to continue with its attack towards the east in accordance with the original *Frühlingserwachen* plan (although by this point it was nothing more than a sheer waste of troops since "Spring Awakening" had for all intents been cancelled); the *III. Pz.Korps* was to seal off the penetration southeast of Stuhlweissenburg; the *I. SS-Pz.Korps* would attack towards Zámoly from the area southwest of Mór along with the *356. Inf.Div.*; the *II. SS-Pz. Korps* would follow behind the *I. SS-Pz.Korps*; and finally, *Gren.Brig. (mot.) 92* would counterattack from the area around Kecskéd–Környe to the southeast to recover the southeast edge of the Vértes Mountains.[38] As we shall see, portions of this plan began to be implemented the following day, though Hitler, as the supreme "decider," would balk on the movement of the two SS corps. While the generals nervously waited for Hitler's response, the Vienna Operation rolled forwards inexorably.

The fighting continued without letup the following day. On 18 March, after a cold night when the thermometer read a low of 23 degrees (-5 degrees Celsius), the temperatures during the day reached a high of 59 degrees (15 degrees Celsius), with partly cloudy skies and local rain showers. Despite this sporadic precipitation, the roads throughout the area were finally beginning to dry out. Spring had finally begun arriving on the Hungarian *Puszta*. However, these improving weather conditions had come far too late and would benefit the forces of the Third Ukrainian Front more than those of *H.Gr. Süd*.

During the night of 17/18 March, *A.Gr. Balck/6. Armee* reported that most of the enemy's actions directed against the *IV. SS-Pz.Korps* were focused against the *Wiking* Division's defenses north of Stuhlweissenburg, where its *Westland* Regiment beat back a Soviet nighttime attempt to seize the suburb of Kiskecskemét. Northwest of the city, a local breakthrough that had reached the railroad line leading out of the city was eliminated in heavy fighting by a *Germania* Regiment counterattack. In the Hungarian *3. Armee* sector, or rather what was left of it, it reported that numerous company-sized attacks were launched during the night against the *96. Inf.Div.* defenses in Felsőgalla, but all were beaten back and no appreciable ground was lost.

North of Bicske, German troops reported that during the evening they had spotted long columns of motorized vehicles approaching from the east that appeared to be moving in a southwesterly direction. This could only signify more enemy forces being moved forward. On the *Armeegruppe*'s right flank, the *III. Pz.Korps*, whose attachment to the *6. Pz.Armee* had still not been approved by Hitler, reported that during the night Soviet units had managed to achieve a penetration 5 kilometers northeast of Seregélyes, but its units had managed to seal off the breach after destroying eight enemy tanks.[39]

Before the sun had risen on 18 March, the Soviet 4th and 9th Guards Armies and 46th Army continued their attacks between Stuhlweissenburg and Tatabanya, with masses of infantry supported by small groups of tanks. Announced by punishing artillery barrages that swept the defenders' newly dug fighting positions several kilometers behind the old ones they had been driven from after only two days, the attackers surged forward towards the German and Hungarian lines. Although in Stuhlweissenburg the *Wiking* Division continued its successful defense, the 4th and 9th Guards Armies were able to continue advancing between the city and the town of Mór, as well as along the western edges of the Vértes Mountains.

In the *Totenkopf* Division's sector, overwhelmingly superior Soviet forces had managed to bypass Mór to the south and achieve a penetration several kilometers deep on the northeastern edge of the Bakony Forest northeast of Várpalota, less than 20 kilometers away. North of Mór in the sector defended by the remnants of the Hungarian *1. Hus.Div.*, equally strong Soviet forces managed to reach the outskirts of the town of Csäszar (according to von Grolman, this division "had panicked and left their positions, abandoning weapons, equipment and horses").[40] South of the industrial district including Felsőgalla and Alsőgalla, nearly all of the commanding heights were now in enemy hands. The Hungarians' headquarters reported that further Soviet attacks were expected towards the line demarked by Kisber and Nagyigmánd.

According to aerial reconnaissance, a large mechanized formation including many tanks was spotted moving through the Vértes Mountains towards the northwest. This was just the consolidated report for that day. The individual field army reports were even more specific. In the *III. Pz.Korps'* sector, it reported that a large enemy force of up to 1,000 men had attacked its front line 4 kilometers southeast of Stuhlweissenburg, in the same place where they had tried to break through the day before. The fighting to eliminate this attempt to break through was still ongoing at the evening reporting deadline.

In the *IV. SS-Pz.Korps'* area that day, the fighting was brutal, intense, and costly. Despite the corps' heavy defensive artillery fire, which inflicted "very bloody losses" upon the massed Soviet troops, the German defenders, especially the *Totenkopf* Division, also suffered heavy casualties in return. A large Soviet force attacking from Sárkeresztes sliced across the highway between Mór and Stuhlweissenburg, brushed its way past the defenders, and continued advancing to the southwest. When Soviet forces reached the small town of Iszkaszentgyörgy, which was serving as the forward headquarters of the *Wiking* Division, Ullrich's staff were forced to evacuate. Despite bitter house-to-house fighting, the town fell that afternoon to the enemy's assault. The division's *O1*, who was there at the moment the attack began, described the scene:

> Suddenly, around midday, the Russians approached our division command post with a strong tank force that broke through into Iszkaszentgyörgy. The *kleine Führungsstaffel* [forward command post] was barely able to escape at the last moment and moved out to Csór [located along] the Stuhlweissenburg–Várpalota highway. Enemy fighter-bombers were flying all over the place attacking towns and highways with bombs … When we reached Csór, we had to leave immediately and move to an open vineyard 4 kilometers west of the town. We only had radio communications to control the division. We had no contact on the left with any unit

at all. For this reason, we realized that we needed to have the division's left defensive sector swing back to the south. The village of Csór was still in our hands, but the situation to the north was completely unclear. The *Germania* Regiment was only able to maintain contact with Stuhlweissenburg by setting up a series of strongpoints between the city, Csór, and Várpalota, oriented towards the north.[41]

Csór was only 6 kilometers east of Gille's command post in Inota, so close to the fighting now that sounds of battle could be plainly heard.

Another large group of Soviet troops attacked out of Magyaralmás towards the west and seized the village of Fehervarcsurgo, despite the determined efforts of the *Totenkopf* Division to hold on to it. Söréd, defended by troops from the *Totenkopf* Division as well as the *I. Btl./Danmark*, fell to a massive attack supported by 20 tanks. The commander of the Danish battalion, *Stubaf.* Hermann im Masche, was killed in action during this engagement after he was wounded in the abdomen by a burst of machine-gun fire. As he attempted to climb onto a German armored vehicle that was withdrawing, he slipped off and was run over and crushed by another *panzer* following closely behind. What was left of his battalion, which lost between 250 and 300 men during the fighting, was taken over by *Hstuf.* Ewald Linsmeier, the commander of the battalion's *4. Kompanie.*[42]

The remnants of the Hungarian *2. Pz.Div.* were thrown out of Csólkakő and bustled off towards the west. Despite this series of reverses, by nightfall, the *IV. SS-Pz.Korps* had managed to establish an intermediate defense line consisting of a series of strongpoints along the Gaja Canal running from Iszkaszentgyörgy–Guttámási–Bodajk that was loosely tied in on the far right with the *Wiking* Division in Stuhlweissenburg. *Brigadeführer* Becker reported that the small defending force from his division holding Mór, consisting of some *Panzergrenadiers* and the big guns of its *Flak* battalion, was under attack from all sides, except for a narrow corridor facing southwest, but so far was standing firm.

SS-Regiment Ney, which had been undergoing reconstitution in Súr, was released from *H.Gr. Süd* reserve and attached by 7 p.m. that day to the *Totenkopf* Division, where it was immediately involved in several counterattacks that night and throughout the next day to retake the defensive positions southwest of Bodajk, along with remnants of the Hungarian *2. Pz.Div.* During the course of the heavy fighting that took place over the next three days, *SS-Rgt. Ney* became separated from the *Totenkopf* Division and was pushed by Soviet attacks towards Aka Súr, a village northwest of the eastern edge of the Bakony Forest. Here, Ney's regiment was combined with the survivors of the Hungarian *1. Hus.Div.* to form *Kampfgruppe Schell* under the Hungarian division's commander, *Oberst* Zoltan Schell, who in turn was still operating under the Hungarian *VIII. Armee-Korps.*[43] It would take nearly a week for Ney's regiment to find its way back to the *Totenkopf* Division.

In the Hungarian *3. Armee*'s sector, the town of Pusztavám, defended by remnants of the *1. Hus.Div.*, fell to an enemy assault composed of at least two infantry regiments that managed to advance as far as Csakvár. Bokod, held by a small Hungarian *Kampfgruppe* from their *23. Inf.Div.*, fell to a Soviet assault, while the neighboring town of Dad was also overrun. *Generalleutnant* vitéz-Heszlényi was attempting to establish a new main defense line northwest of Dad with the remnants of his *1. Hus.Div.* and *23. Inf.Div.*, but it was almost too late—the 46th Army had reached the western edge of the Vértes Mountains along nearly its entire length and the *3. Armee* did not have many troops left to carry out its mission unless the reserves that Balck was sending arrived in time.

Oroszlány, defended by the Hungarian *23. Inf.Div.*, fell that day to a large-scale attack, followed shortly thereafter by Kecskéd, though when the same enemy force advanced on the village of Kömlöd, it was stopped when troops from *Oberst* Grosser's *Gren.Brig. (mot.) 92* quickly knocked out nine Soviet tanks. The main body of the brigade, fighting in Környe, successfully beat back numerous enemy assaults, but by this stage of the battle it was nearly surrounded. The defenders from *Gren.Rgt. 283* of the *96. Inf.Div.* holding Felsőgalla and Alsőgalla also managed to prevent these two industrial towns from falling into enemy hands, but they were nearly surrounded as well. Along the remaining front lines of the Hungarian *3. Armee*, the rest of the *96.* and *711. Inf.Div.* were tied up in repulsing a series of battalion-sized attacks that were apparently being conducted to prevent them from pulling any of their units out of the line to be sent to assist friendly forces elsewhere.[44]

In the air, a series a savage battles raged as the *Luftwaffe* sought to do its utmost to relieve the pressure being placed on the forces fighting between Stuhlweissenburg and the Vértes Mountains. *Luftflotte 4* performed very well that day, a remarkable feat for this late stage in the war, especially with the difficulties the *Luftwaffe* was having in procuring fuel. It managed to carry out 300 sorties on 18 March, including missions directed against Soviet tanks by *Ju-87 Stukas* and other ground-attack aircraft, others against enemy artillery emplacements, and deep attacks directed against the rail network and locomotives aimed at stopping or at least delaying the movement of more Soviet reserves into the battle area. The Red Air Force's 5th and 17th Air Armies were equally active that day, conducting the same kind of ground-support missions, while its LaGGs and Yaks dueled with *Focke-Wulf 190*s and *Messerschmitt 109*s for control of the air.

At the unit level in both of Gille's SS divisions, the fighting went on without pause throughout the day. Small groups of soldiers, supported by a handful of tanks or assault guns, carried out numerous counterattacks to throw back the advancing enemy or prevent them from seizing key terrain features or towns. Both divisions, especially the *Totenkopf*, were steadily being ground down, including their two *Panzergrenadier* regiments that bore the brunt of the battle. The *Wiking* Division, entrenched on the edges of Stuhlweissenburg, was able to maintain its unit cohesion to a greater degree, simply because built-up areas provide better shelter against heavy artillery and air bombardments. But it was feeling the pressure too.

All along the line, the combat troops fought as best they could. The new replacements either learned quickly or became casualty statistics. The smart ones listened to their squad or platoon leaders and did as they were told; those who panicked died. It was as simple as that. Even veterans were shaken at the intensity of the fighting. One veteran tank commander, *Ostuf.* Heinz Kerkhoff, who was an eyewitness to the fighting on 18 March, later wrote:

> The Russians started the dance really early with artillery and mortar fire. That was followed by support from fighter-bombers. Ivan was setting off fireworks like the good old days. Infantry and tanks then attacked. There were nine of us Panthers and we were positioned under good cover right on the Stuhlweissenburg–Mór road. The 5. and 6. *Kompanie* initially concentrated on the enemy tanks, some 50 to 60 of them. In short order, we knocked out six of them. That motivated the grenadiers and gave the Russians weak knees … towards noon, the sounds of battle swelled back to a hurricane. It appeared to me that the Russians were trying to force a decision. Just like the *Wiking*, the *Totenkopf* … was greatly weakened. The enemy knew that as well; consequently, [his] forces were massed to force a breakthrough. A crisis started to arise in the sector around Stuhlweissenburg. Wave after wave of fighter-bombers came in. We had the impression that the barrage of fire of the [enemy] artillery was getting even stronger.[45]

As it turned out, this was merely a prelude. So far, large numbers of Soviet tanks had not yet been introduced to the battle, those that had been being employed primarily in support of the infantry. But this attack was different. Kerkhoff continued:

> The Russians had formed up their tanks and started to attack. We opened fire at 1,400 meters. After working it out with [*Ostuf.* Alfred] Grossrock, the 6. *Kompanie* took the Russians from the right to the left and the 5. *Kompanie* from left to right. In short order, seven enemy tanks were immobilized on the battlefield; another six had been destroyed by direct hits. By 4 p.m., we had suffered only one loss … around 5 p.m., it started to turn dark and, with the darkness, enemy tanks suddenly surfaced along [our] left flank on the Mór–Stuhlweissenburg road. We gave battle immediately, and the first three enemy tanks were knocked out surprisingly quickly. Grossrock then concentrated on the enemy attacking to the front and the 5. *Kompanie* on the flank attack of the Russian tanks.

That was the last entry in Kerkhoff's diary; that same evening, while repositioning his tank, it was knocked out and he was seriously wounded and evacuated to a field hospital, where he underwent emergency surgery. He survived but never fought again.

It was the same story in the *Totenkopf* Division. One survivor of the battle, a young *Untersturmführer* named Peter Renold who was at Söréd with a *Kampfgruppe* from the 5. *Kompanie* of the *Totenkopf* Regiment, along with a few troops from the division's *Feld-Ersatz* battalion, remembered the day very clearly, writing:

> At the crack of dawn, Russian tanks rolled towards us in front of the swamp. We were able to identify three Shermans [*n.b.*: more than 4,000 M4 Shermans were provided by the USA to the Soviets during the war through the Lend-Lease scheme]. A young recruit and I waded forward carefully armed with four *Panzerfausts* through the swampy area. Towards the direction of the bridgehead at Söréd we could hear the constant sound of revving engines. Also in front of our own position we could hear the same noises.

He and his young recruit were able to knock out the three M4 Shermans with their single-shot rocket launchers, but this seemed to draw more tanks. He continued:

> Two tanks were burning, the third had been immobilized. About 9:45 p.m., we were completely cut off and were attacked by a bunch of tanks with Soviet cadets hanging on them and were literally overrun. In a shell hole *Oscha.* Pfefferkorn was crouching along with *Rottenführer* Lothar Tremmel, August Sigmund and me. We were completely out of ammunition. My imagination fails to adequately describe how I felt … it was all over for us. The Russians ruthlessly stripped us of our valuables then they led us off. A little while later, a Russian approached us and without any provocation whatsoever pulled *Oscha.* Pfefferkorn out [of our ranks] and shot him to death with his machine pistol right in front of us … I knew I was the next one to get a bullet in the head. But before that could happen, a Russian officer ordered us to climb up onto this tank, where some [wounded] Ivans were already lying or crouching, and we drove off to Csillaki Puszta[46]

Despite the enormous pressure being exerted upon it, the *Totenkopf* Division bent but did not break. Although it had suffered a tremendous number of casualties, its men kept on fighting, as long as they had the means to do so.

The *9. Kp./SS-Pz.Rgt. 3* of the *Totenkopf* Division was busily engaged that day, with its four remaining battle-ready *Pz. VI* Tiger Is in great demand (three had been destroyed the previous day during the fighting for Magyaralmás). Several of the division's Tigers were defending the railroad station in Bodajk, but had to pull back once they received news that the Soviets had captured Söréd and Mór. In order to avoid being surrounded, they withdrew to Balinka, but six *Pz. IVs* from *II. Abt./ SS-Pz.Rgt. 3* moving with the *9. Kompanie* were shot up and destroyed between Bodajk and Balinka. The commander of the company's tank recovery platoon, *Oberscharführer* Bauer, was killed in Sárkeresztes, while several other of the company's members were killed along the Kisber–Mór road while attempting to recover some mired or brokensdown *SPWs*.[47]

Too many of the old hands knew what would happen if they surrendered; the example of *Oberscharführer* Pfefferkorn was hardly an isolated example. Fighting all the way, most of the division managed to extract itself across the Gaja Canal and establish hasty defensive positions along the arc running from the town of Balinka west of Bodajk, east to the village of Guttámási, and thence south to the northern outskirts of Iszkaszentgyörgy, while another battalion from the division was holding out in Mór. A portion of the *Totenkopf* Division's *Hauptquartier* was overrun at Guttámási, an attack that resulted in 39 members of the division headquarters staff and headquarters company being taken prisoner and 93 motor vehicles captured, though Becker and most of his *Führungsabteilung* were not present at the time.[48]

While the divisions and corps of *A.Gr. Balck/6. Armee* fought for survival, a different sort of battle was being waged at the headquarters of *H.Gr. Süd*. To nearly everyone's surprise, Hitler had approved most of Wöhler's suggestions, except regarding the attack by the *2. Pz.Armee*, which *der Führer* wanted to continue. Even more surprising, Hitler granted Guderian the leeway to continue fighting the battle around Lake Balaton and Stuhlweissenburg as he saw fit; in turn, Guderian allowed

The Corps Command and Staff During the War

During the lead up to the *Frühlingserwachen* offensive, Sepp Dietrich visits Gille's headquarters in Inota in early March 1945 to discuss the upcoming operation. From left to right, Manfred Schönfelder, Gille, Dietrich, and Friedrich Rauch, Gille's *Ia*. (Photo courtesy Günther Lange from his personal archive)

Gille (back to camera) confers with (from L to R) *SS-Ustuf.* Joachim Barthel, Schönfelder (in foreground), *SS-Ostubaf.* Fritz Braune, and *SS-Stubaf.* Friedrich Rausch (Corps *Ia*, leaning over map) in late March 1945 during the retreat from Stuhlweissenburg. (Lange)

Gille with (from L to R) *SS-Hstuf.* Hans Velde (Corps *O1*), *SS-Oscha.* Schlemmer (the *Ia Schreiber*), and Barthel. (Lange)

Gille (center) with *Oberst* Hans-Ulrich Krantz (left), *Ia* of the *1. Pz.Div.*, Gille, and Thünert, commander of *1. Pz.Div.* during the retreat from Veszprém, in late March 1945. The SS officer standing behind Thünert is *SS-Ostubaf.* Hubert Hüppe, commander of *SS-Nachr.Abt. 104*. (Lange)

Gille with (from L to R) Schönfelder (on crutches), Schlemmer, and Rausch west of Veszprém during the retreat from Veszprém in late March 1945. (Lange)

Gille (second from right) with (from L to R) *SS-Hstuf.* Hans Velde (with hands folded behind his back), *SS-Stubaf.* Herbert Oeck (commander of *SS-Pz.Jäg.Abt. 5*), Schönfelder (with crutch), and Rausch (holding maps) observing troops from *SS-Feld-Ers.Btl. 5 Wiking* as they withdraw from Veszprém during late 22 March 1945. (Lange)

Gille with (from L to R): Rausch (Corps *Ia*) and *SS-Hstuf.* Wilhelm Riemek, acting commander of *SS-Feld-Ers.Btl. 5*, who was killed in action on 8 March 1945. (Lange)

Gille with *SS-Ostuf.* Otto Schneider, the commander of the infantry battalion formed from tank crews without tanks, near Ödenburg, Austria, in April 1945. (Lange)

Joachim Barthel with Manfred Schönfelder, who wears a special glove to protect his injured left hand, in April 1945. (Lange)

Gille with Schönfelder and *SS-Brig.Fhr.* Kurt Brasack, commander of *SS-ARKO 504*, in early April 1945. (Lange)

Gille receiving a commemorative photo album presented to him on behalf of the corps staff at the *Hauptquartier* in Inota, Hungary. During the informal ceremony, conducted at some point in February 1945, key staff personnel joined together to present Gille with the gift, including (from L to R) *SS-Stubaf.* Karl-Willi Schulze (Corps *IIa* or *Adjutant*), *SS-Stubaf.* Herbert Jankuhn (Corps Intelligence Officer, or *Ic*), *SS-Hstuf.* Dr Herbert Metowsich (Deputy Intelligence Officer), and *SS-Hstuf.* Johann Velde (Corps *O1*). (Lange)

While looking at the photograph album, *SS-Ostubaf.* Fritz Braune, the corps *Pionierführer*, stands on the right. Manfred Schönfelder stands behind Gille. Parked in the background is a Büssing-NAG Type 4500 S 4½-ton cargo truck modified with a closed box body to enable it to serve as a mobile command post. (Lange)

At the same ceremony, Gille speaks with (from R to L) *SS-Hstuf.* Dr Franz Wehofsich (Corps *VI* or *NSFO*), *SS-Ostubaf.* Dr Hans Heinz (*Korpsrichter* or Staff Judge Advocate), and Joachim Barthel. (Lange)

Also present at this ceremony was (from L to R) *SS-Staf.* Kurt Schlamelcher, commander of the *SS-Art. Schule II* in Beneschau (Benešov, now in the Czech Republic) and a former artillery battalion commander in the *Wiking* Division, with Rausch and Barthel. Schlamelcher was visiting the battlefront during an official tour pertaining to his duties, focusing on the needs and performance of the corps' SS artillery units. (Lange)

Smiling Soviet troops march through the ruins of Budapest in the aftermath of the siege on their way to the Balaton front in late February 1945. By 16 March, Marshal Tolbukhin had amassed sufficient reinforcements to finally commence the Vienna Operation. (NARA)

A Soviet tank unit equipped with T-34/85s awaits the order to advance in mid-March 1945, as two Hungarian prisoners carry one of their wounded comrades to the rear on a stretcher. By this stage of the war, many Hungarian troops chose to either surrender or desert and join with Soviet-sponsored Hungarian forces to fight their former ally. (Author)

Wöhler to do the same, within limits. Most of the efforts of the senior commanders and staff were spent that day crafting a response to the Soviet offensive. Many of these plans had already been worked out, as previously noted, as well as one that Hermann Balck had coordinated with the *H.Gr. Süd* chief of staff that was to prove controversial.

In essence, the *I. SS-Pz.Korps* would be shifted to the north and prepare a counterattack between Mór and Moha. The *II. SS-Pz.Korps*, following behind, would attach itself to the left flank of the *I. SS-Pz.Korps* and conduct counterattacks between Mór and Kisber as soon as it arrived. The *IV. SS-Pz.Korps* would remain in its current positions, but would be subordinated to Dietrich's command. The *356. Inf.Div.* had already been put in motion and was in the process of moving around a wide arc to the area west of Tata, where it would fall under the control of the *6. Pz.Armee* once it arrived. Because the *I. SS-Pz.Korps* had been attached to *A.Gr. Balck/6. Armee* on 17 March to carry out the attack south of Lake Velencze alongside the *III. Pz.Korps*, it was already on the move and was now diverted to a new assembly area northeast of Várpalota/Inota with its *1. SS-Pz.Div. LSSAH* and *12. SS-Pz.Div. HJ*, instead of the previous assembly area south of Stuhlweissenburg.

To control this operation, Wöhler selected Dietrich's *6. Pz.Armee*. The reason why was not stated, though perhaps it was due to Wöhler's increasing lack of confidence in Balck's judgement, or because he thought it was best to have an SS headquarters controlling so many SS corps and divisions. Perhaps it was done simply because Balck wanted Wöhler to rid him of a troublesome subordinate; he had been complaining to Wöhler and von Grolman incessantly about Gille's performance, and had previously made several attempts to have both him and his chief of staff relieved of their duties, but was thwarted each time. Thus, for whatever underlying reason—whether warranted by the situation or due to petty personal grievances—Wöhler made the controversial decision to "castle," or switch, the controlling field army headquarters while they were in the middle of a decisive phase of the battle.[49]

This plan directed the *6. Pz.Armee* to exchange its area of operations with that of *A.Gr. Balck/6. Armee* during the night of 18/19 March. Effective from 2 p.m. on 19 March, Dietrich would assume responsibility for the entire defensive sector from the southwest corner of Lake Velencze all the way north to the Danube, including the area held by the Hungarian *3. Armee*, although he had not yet been able to reposition his headquarters to its new location in Martinsburg. The *IV. SS-Pz.Korps* would remain where it was and would be subordinated to Dietrich's command. This would be the first and only time, however briefly, the corps would be assigned to an SS higher headquarters, probably to the relief of Gille and his staff.

To assist the *6. Pz.Armee* with controlling the variety of units assembling behind the Hungarian *3. Armee*—including the inbound *356. Inf.Div.* and *6. Pz.Div.*—the headquarters of the *XLIII. Armee-Korps* would be released by *8. Armee* and would be made responsible for defending the area between Kisber and Tata, a decision that would require this corps to hand over its command and control responsibilities to another corps headquarters and move south across the Danube. Another outcome of the decision on 18 March was the dropping of the elaborate cover names for all of the SS units involved in *Frühlingserwachen*, which had only sown confusion and had already lost their usefulness after the elimination of the Gran Bridgehead, by which point the Red Army had already figured out what the code names meant.

Balck's *Armeegruppe*, which would revert to its old title of simply *6. Armee* the following day, would assume responsibility for the area south of Lakes Velencze and Balaton, including the *I. Kav.Korps*, the Hungarian *II. Korps*, and the *III. Pz.Korps*. The *II. SS-Pz.Korps* would be subordinated to Balck until it could be pulled out of its sector, a process that was expected to require several days. Balck's army would orient its defenses towards the south, southeast, and east, where the enemy forces were believed to pose a lesser threat.

In his treatise on the campaign, the former *Ia* of the *6. Pz.Armee, Ostubaf.* Georg Maier, believes that this switch of headquarters at the last moment (in German, the *Rochade*) had been planned surreptitiously by Hermann Balck to escape the blame for the looming catastrophe in the Vértes Mountains (what he labeled an *aufgebürdete Niederlage*, or "a defeat saddled on someone else"), though the facts supporting this assertion are ultimately inconclusive.[50] Whatever the case, the change of controlling headquarters at such a critical point in the battle and the resulting confusion soon proved to have been a very unwise decision that ultimately worked to the benefit of the Third Ukrainian Front.

Another disgruntled participant in this affair was Gille's chief of staff, who by this point had become thoroughly disenchanted with Balck as well as Gaedke. *Obersturmbannführer* Manfred Schönfelder suspected that something out of the ordinary was in the works and that Balck and Gaedke, whether accidentally or by design, were setting up both him and Gille—and by extension, the entire *6. Pz.Armee*—for failure. Shortly after the war, he wrote:

> At midnight, the *Heeresgruppe* expressed to the commander of the *6. Pz.Armee* [Dietrich] that the *IV. SS-Pz.Korps* had lost control of its sector. [Wöhler] was concerned that the corps had allowed the enemy to cross the canal [the Gaja Canal, beyond the Mór–Stuhlweissenburg highway], although according to Balck, the commander in chief of the *6. Armee*, the [Gaja] canal sector could only be crossed at a few "locks." Balck had said that it was necessary to stop this advance "by full deployment of the *IV. SS-Pz.Korps* as well as with the approaching *I. SS-Pz.Korps*" [next to this statement, Schönfelder added a sarcastic note in his journal: "had not the corps been fully deployed thus far?"].[51]

Unfortunately, calculated insults like this from their *Armeegruppe* commander had become all too common. At least for the next several days, the *IV. SS-Pz.Korps* commander and his staff, while serving under Sepp Dietrich's *6. Pz.Armee*, would enjoy a reprieve from Balck's constant harping, micro-managing, and overbearing prejudice against the *Waffen-SS*.

One thing that is clear from events leading up to this "castling" of headquarters, is that once the front collapsed shortly after the *6. Pz.Armee* arrived to take control (in fact the *A.Gr. Balck/6. Armee*'s front was already in the process of doing so before Dietrich's headquarters even arrived), the *6. Pz.Armee* would receive most of the blame for the failure during and after the war, though Balck had already made most of the bad decisions before Dietrich and his army got there. As Balck had told Guderian in a telephone conversation that evening, "I had no desire to let myself get drawn into a new, completely unnecessary catastrophe"; a "catastrophe" largely of his own making, it must be noted.[52] Thus, the scene was set for the ultimate defeat of *H.Gr. Süd*.

Of course, the commander of the Third Ukrainian Front was not going to wait while the German command structure within *H.Gr. Süd* sorted itself out. Tolbukhin aggressively continued his relentless attacks overnight and well into the next morning. With the withdrawal of the *I. SS-Pz.Korps*, followed shortly thereafter by half of the *II. SS-Pz.Korps*, the opportunity that Tolbukhin had been waiting for finally came about. The departure of Dietrich's two SS corps had reduced the armor available to the Germans south of Lake Balaton by half, finally creating the necessary conditions for the two Soviet formations in the south, the 26th and 27th Armies, to go over to the attack. Instead of having to advance against seven *panzer* divisions, now they only had to face three, and very weakened ones at that. Very soon, Balck's army would be placed under enormous pressure because it would not only have to continue fighting against Soviet forces approaching east of Stuhlweissenburg and Seregélyes, but additional forces attacking from the south as well, where previously both of Tolbukhin's armies had been on the defense.

Armeegruppe Balck/6. Armee, in its last morning report before it handed over its sector on 19 March, stated that the *Wiking* Division successfully held off numerous tank-supported assaults against the southeastern corner and northern boundary of Stuhlweissenburg. It had also managed to insert a blocking force 1.5 kilometers east of the highway connecting the city with the village of Csór, and had blocked another Soviet advance along the heights 2 kilometers north of the village. However, this did nothing to close the 8-kilometer-wide gap west of Stuhlweissenburg through which the 9th Guards Army was inexorably advancing. The *Totenkopf* Division reported that it had successfully cut off another penetration in its new outpost line on the outskirts of Guttámási. The *I. SS-Pz.Korps* was moving to its new assembly area during the night, so its two *panzer* divisions did not take part in any fighting until they had arrived. Incredibly, Balck's headquarters reported that nothing out of the ordinary had happened overnight in the Hungarian *3. Armee*'s sector, other than the usual artillery harassment fire.[53] What did this portend?

Monday, 19 March proving to be another warm day, with clear skies and little precipitation. When the evening report was submitted by 6 p.m., Dietrich's *6. Pz.Armee* had been in control of its new defensive sector for only four hours, but a great deal of fighting had already occurred that day before the change of operational control took place. In the *IV. SS-Pz.Korps'* sector, the heaviest fighting that day took place within Stuhlweissenburg itself, when a powerful tank-supported Soviet assault penetrated all the way into the city center during the course of a pincer attack, clearly aimed at cutting off the city and the bulk of its *Wiking* Division garrison. Extremely bitter house-to-house fighting immediately ensued. That evening, taking into the account the events of that day, the division's *O1* wrote:

> The enemy keeps attacking. The division is still holding on to the east and northern edge of Stuhlweissenburg. Our opponent attacked north of [our defense line] and plunged in a westerly direction along the Stuhlweissenburg highway and railroad towards Várpalota … The division's [forward] command post once again was forced to move around midday towards the south into the gap between the village of Réti Puszta and the railroad station in order to prevent [it] from being cut off from the rest of the division. Corps headquarters was also forced to relocate and position itself in a new location behind the withdrawing *Totenkopf* Division. In the evening, our opponent reached the area around [Meritö Puszta], forcing the division command post to be moved once again to join the *Ib* staff at Nádasdladány [less than 6 kilometers southeast of Réti Puszta].[54]

The other arm of the Soviet pincer passed north of the city and continued pushing towards the west until it was stopped in heavy fighting by the *Germania* Regiment before it reached Csór. Northwest of the city, the *Totenkopf* Division continued its efforts to hold the line between Isztimér and Bodajk, reporting that it had managed to repulse all of the enemy's attacks, including the destruction of six tanks near Balinka.[55]

Although he had given up control of his army's previous sector, *Gen.d.Pz.Tr.* Balck continued meddling with the *IV. SS-Pz.Korps* and sent a message at 9:26 p.m. that evening to *H.Gr. Süd* stating that he had the impression that the fighting capability of the garrison of Stuhlweissenburg (i.e., the *Wiking* Division) to defend the city was effectively at an end. Not only was this matter beyond Balck's span of control, since he had taken over the adjacent sector earlier that afternoon, it was manifestly untrue.

In a similar vein, that same evening, Wöhler informed Guderian that the entire front line held by the Hungarians had simply disappeared and that he had seldom witnessed such a catastrophe in his entire career.[56] This disregards the fact that many Hungarian units had, in fact, fought very well until they were destroyed by the overwhelming power of their attackers. Perhaps the commander of *H.Gr. Süd* should have considered the shortcomings of the Hungarian *3. Armee* and its *VIII. Armee-Korps* before assigning it such a critical sector to defend in the first place, especially without adequate German reserves positioned within and behind it.

Meanwhile, throughout the day the two divisions of the *I. SS-Pz.Korps* began filing into their new assembly area behind the *IV. SS-Pz.Korps*. The *1. SS-Pz.Div. LSSAH* (referred to hereafter as simply the *LSSAH*) was ordered to establish a security line running from the south to the north to ensure that it and the *12. SS-Pz.Div.*

HJ (hereafter the *Hitlerjugend*) were able to occupy their designated areas before the advancing Soviet troops did. During the day, this security line was probed at numerous points by enemy forces that had slipped past the screen line established by the *Totenkopf* Division, with one Soviet attempt even reaching as far as the edge of the wood line 2 kilometers east of Inota.

Elements of the *LSSAH* Division, commanded by *Brig.Fhr.* Otto Kumm, along with *K.Gr. Streith* from the *1. Pz.Div.*, were able to lend a hand to the *Wiking* Division in its efforts to block advancing enemy forces in front of Csór, and were able to retake Bakonykúti, a village that lay 5 kilometers to the north of Gille's headquarters.[57] Not wishing to undergo the same experience at Inota as it had the previous month, when it was nearly cut off and captured in Seregélyes, Gille wisely ordered his *Gefechtstand* to move to the village of Öskü, 11 kilometers to the southwest and out of range of all but the heaviest Soviet artillery.

The state of affairs in the neighboring Hungarian *VIII. Armee-Korps* of Heszlényi's *3. Armee* can best be described as "in flux." The advance elements of the 46th Army began pushing their way out of the Pusztavám–Dad area in the morning and took the region encompassing the villages of Császár, Szák, and Szend, despite the efforts of *K.Gr. Wolf*, composed of the reconnaissance battalion of the *1. Pz.Div.* and *Sturm-Art.Brig 325*, to keep them from breaking through. The Soviet advance was finally stopped before it reached the larger towns of Kisber and Kocs by elements of the *356. Inf.Div.* and *K.Gr. Wolf*, which had arrived the previous day. Both units took over the defense of the area from the Hungarian *1. Hus.Div.*, which had virtually ceased to exist, consisting of mainly scattered groups of survivors by this point. Both German units were immediately attached to the just-arriving *XLIII. Armee-Korps*. For its part, this corps, led by *Gen.d.Geb.Tr.* Kurt Versock, was tasked with establishing a screening line between Nagyigmánd–Mocsa–Naszály and Füzitö Puszta.

In the sector still defended by the Hungarian *3. Armee*, it was unable to prevent the 46th Army from seizing the town of Kocs and Tata Tóváros, and could not keep the Soviets from pushing further to the northwest. *Grenadier-Brigade (mot.) 92* and *SS-K.Gr. Ameiser*, the only combat-effective units remaining on its right flank, were thrown back to the west as far as the southern tip of the lake east of Tata Tóváros and Bánhida. The leading elements of the 46th Army had finally seized a significant portion of the *Puszta* west of the Vértes and Gerecse Mountains, and it had become clear that a major effort was needed to prevent them from taking the important transportation centers of Komorn, Raab, and Acs. Along the rest of the army's front, the *96.* and *711. Inf.Div.* reported that they were bound up in heavy fighting but had been able to hold their positions.

In the air, the majority of the Red Air Force's attention was directed against the *6. Pz.Armee* and Balck's *6. Armee*, particularly any movement along roads and highways. Soviet fighter, fighter-bomber, and ground-attack aircraft aggressively sought to block or impede German reserve forces from changing position as well as assembly areas. Once again, the *Luftwaffe* rose to the occasion, managing to carry out 270 sorties that day, during which its pilots claimed the destruction of 11 Soviet tanks and 21 enemy aircraft. During the night of 18/19 March, *Luftflotte 4* also reported its squadrons had flown 80 night missions targeting Soviet troops' concentrations and road movement near Csólkakő and Bicske.

During the evening, a number of organizational changes were hurriedly made, as *Generaloberst* Wöhler did his best to strengthen the center of his army group, particularly in the area between the Danube and the northern edge of the Bakony Forest, which as of 2 p.m. on 19 March became the responsibility of the *6. Pz.Armee*. A great deal of its combat power in the form of the divisions of the *I. SS-Pz.Korps* and corps troops were still moving to their new assembly areas, but the bulk of their combat elements were expected to arrive by the evening of 19/20 March. The assembly areas of the *LSSAH* and *Hitlerjugend* Divisions were respectively designated as the area southwest of Várpalota and Bakonycsernye, a village 20 kilometers to the north.

Heeresgruppe Süd and *6. Pz.Armee* had moved remarkably fast to counter the 46th Army's move, as well as to shore up the crumbling defenses of the *IV. SS-Pz.Korps*. In addition to Priess's SS corps, Wilhelm Bittrich's *II. SS-Pz.Korps* was also ordered to begin moving into the area south of Komorn, with its *2. SS-Pz.Div. Das Reich* (referred to hereafter as the *Das Reich*) and the *6. Pz.Div*, which would be attached to the corps. Bittrich's other division, the *9. SS-Pz.Div. Hohenstaufen* (hereafter the *Hohenstaufen*), was held back by *6. Armee*, which insisted that it remain under its control in order to secure the area south of Stuhlweissenburg, where it would be placed under the control of Breith's *III. Pz.Korps*. This was soon to prove a wise decision on Balck's part.

Once all its forces were gathered, the *6. Pz.Armee* would have three SS panzer corps (the *I.*, *II.*, and *IV.*), the *XLIII. Armee-Korps*, and the Hungarian *VIII. Armee-Korps* under its command, with a total of five SS *panzer* divisions (the *1.*, *2.*, *3.*, *5.*, and *12.*) and possibly one more (the *9.*), the *6. Pz.Div.*, and the *356. Inf.Div.*, as well as the Hungarian *2. Pz.Div.*, *1. Hus.Div.*, and *23. Inf.Div.*, though by this point these were mere remnants. The exact role of the Hungarian *3. Armee* by this time was not quite clear; technically, it would be under the command of the *6. Pz.Armee*, which meant that Dietrich's army should have been renamed *A.Gr. Dietrich*, but for unknown reasons this designation was never made.

That evening, the intentions for the following day were issued to the *6. Pz.Armee* by Wöhler's headquarters:

> a) Subordination of portions of the *Hohenstaufen* Division under the *IV. SS-Pz.Korps* for clearing up the situation at Stuhlweissenburg;
>
> b) The *I. SS-Pz.Korps* will attack from the area west of Bakonykúti–Isztimér towards the east with the objective to seize the heights east of Csór–Fehervarcsurgo–Bodajk and from there, depending on the development of the situation, attack towards the southeast in order to destroy enemy forces located northwest of Stuhlweissenburg;

c) Assembling the *6. Pz.Div.*, the *Das Reich* Division, and the *356. Inf.Div.* in the area between Kisber and the Danube [initially under the control of the *XLIII. Armee-Korps*] in order to prevent an enemy breakthrough in the direction of Komorn by carrying out a counterattack in the adjacent sector in the direction of Dad–Kocs.[58]

At least the *6. Pz.Armee* would not have to worry about defending Komorn; that city was placed under the jurisdiction of the neighboring *8. Armee*. Its defenses were to be reinforced by the addition of several heavy *Flak* batteries from the *19. Flak-Div.* *Generalmajor* Günther Pape, commander of the then-rebuilding *Pz.Div. FHH*, was named as its *Kampfkommandant*. The *6. Pz.Armee* by this point was not expecting the *II. SS-Pz.Korps* to arrive by the next morning, hence it was not mentioned; the *Das Reich* was on the move, as was the *356. Inf.Div.*, but their expected time of arrival was uncertain.

For its part, Balck's *6. Armee* was ordered to hold the line between the southeast corner of Lake Balaton and the southwestern corner of Lake Velencze. The *I. Kav.Korps* was directed to begin withdrawing, along with the *23. Pz.Div.* and the Hungarian *25. Inf.Div.*, to a much shorter and more defensible line running east of the shore of Lake Balaton that would encompass sections of the *Margarethestellung*. The *III. Pz.Korps*, which had reverted to Balck's control as part of the castling order, was directed to pull back its forces to the western outskirts of Seregélyes, with its left flank anchored on the southwest tip of Lake Velencze. Balck ordered Breith to pull out the *1. Pz.Div.* in order to prepare it to serve as the army's reserve, where it was expected to serve as an emergency force to block any armored thrust southeast of Stuhlweissenburg or an attack from the south directed against Várpalota. Meanwhile, the *3. Pz.Div.* and the *44. Reichs-Gren.Div. HuD* would remain in the line and continue blocking any enemy attempt to break through from the area south of Lake Velencze.

Despite instructions from *H.Gr. Süd* to release it, Balck continued holding on to most of the *Hohenstaufen* Division, which he insisted that the *6. Armee* needed to keep in the line to allow him to pull out the *1. Pz.Div.* to become his army's reserve. As events were to show, after repeated complaints by the *6. Pz.Armee* to Wöhler, Balck still continued holding on to at least two of the *Hohenstaufen*'s battalions, but without the attachment of all of the division, Gille could not hope to "clear up the situation around Stuhlweissenburg," because by this point his other two divisions were too weak.

Although Marshal Tolbukhin's 4th and 9th Guards Armies and 46th Army had been attacking without letup for the past four days and had made several breakthroughs, these were insufficiently deep to deploy all of his forces. Two of the three Hungarian divisions confronting him had been completely destroyed, but most of his attacking spearheads had been blocked, slowed down, or sealed off by desperate last-minute counterattacks by relatively small numbers of German units, and these would be shortly augmented by the weight of the *6. Pz.Armee* and its *II.*

SS-Pz.Korps. Tolbukhin's armies had also suffered heavy losses, particularly in front of the stubbornly defending *IV. SS-Pz.Korps,* and his troops were approaching a state of exhaustion like those of his opponent. After four days, a critical moment in the battle had arrived, but the initiative still lay with the Third Ukrainian Front. The next move was up to Tolbukhin.

In order to maintain the offensive's momentum and achieve the objective of trapping the German armies between Stuhlweissenburg and Lake Balaton, Tolbukhin decided to commit Kravchenko's full-strength 6th Guards Tank Army into the gap northwest of Stuhlweissenburg the following day, oriented along the southwest axis of Bakonycsernye–Várpalota. It had taken several days for the army to cross the Danube and occupy its forward assembly areas southwest of Budapest, but it was now finally ready to play its role in the Vienna Operation. The commitment to battle of this overwhelmingly powerful tank army would quickly overtake most of the reactionary troop movements belatedly ordered by *H.Gr. Süd* and drag both Dietrich's *6. Pz.Armee* and Balck's *6. Armee* to the brink of catastrophe.[59]

CHAPTER 4

The Storm Breaks
20–23 March 1945

On the morning of 20 March, the *IV. SS-Pz.Korps* controlled two greatly weakened divisions (the *Totenkopf* and *Wiking*), its corps troops, and attached *Heerestruppen*. The bulk of the *Hohenstaufen* Division had been subordinated to Gille's corps the previous evening, but its forces had not yet been released by the *6. Armee*. On the left, a 20-kilometer-wide gap yawned between Bodajk and Kisbér, where there were only a few scattered German and Hungarian units. The corps' infantry strength, especially that of the *Totenkopf* Division, had been cut nearly in half and its regiments and battalions jumbled up. The Hungarian *2. Pz.Div.* had been nearly obliterated, its survivors scattered or incorporated into various *Kampfgruppen* in the *6. Pz.Armee's* new area of operations.

There was no longer a solid front line connecting the *Totenkopf* and *Wiking* Divisions. On the morning of 20 March, they were separated by an 8-kilometer-wide salient that Soviet troops had carved between Mohr and Stuhlweissenburg, with only a thin line of German outposts from both of Gille's depleted divisions. The *Westland* Regiment with supporting elements was tied up defending Stuhlweissenburg, while the *Germania* Regiment, positioned south of the railroad line running westwards from the city to Várpalota, maintained a tenuous connection with the *Totenkopf* Division near the village of Bakonykúti. Gille had no more reserves with which to plug any new enemy breakthroughs, and was dependent upon the *I. SS-Pz.Korps* or his new field army headquarters to help him restore the situation, despite the aforementioned addition of the *Hohenstaufen* Division.

The night of 19/20 March had been cold and clear, with temperatures hovering around 39 degrees Fahrenheit (4 degrees Celsius) and no measureable precipitation. Fighting within Stuhlweissenburg had not stopped with the approach of darkness, but had continued without pause. In its morning report, the *IV. SS-Pz.Korps* stated that a Soviet battalion had broken through the *Wiking* Division's defense line to a depth of approximately 500 meters between the city and Lake Sóstó on the city's southern outskirts. This attack was perhaps linked to the same unit that the *1. Pz.Div.* had encountered at roughly the same time (see below).

In the neighboring *6. Armee's* sector, the *1. Pz.Div.* of the *III. Pz.Korps* reported that it had tried to carry out a counterattack during the evening against a Soviet breakthrough, possibly by the 62nd Guards Rifle Division, which had managed to advance as far as the agricultural estate 3 kilometers southeast of Stuhlweissenburg. However, *Gen.Maj.* Eberhard Thünert's division was unable to re-establish physical contact with the *Wiking* Division by sunrise. To the west of the city, another Soviet force of indeterminable size that had brushed past Csór the previous evening continued advancing westwards during the night, reaching the former location of the *Wiking* Division's command post at Réti Puszta before sunrise. The town of Balinka, held by the *Totenkopf* Division, fell after a Soviet assault supported by heavy artillery fire overwhelmed the thin line of defenders. This setback, in turn, forced *Brigadeführer* Becker to pull back the few troops still under his control several kilometers, where they finally established a new screen line west and northwest of Balinka.[1] The other portion of his division, concentrated southwest of Mór, was fighting virtually a separate battle and would eventually fall under the command of the *II. SS-Pz.Korps* before being eventually reunited with Becker's command weeks later.

Behind the *IV. SS-Pz.Korps*, the *I. SS-Pz.Korps* continued moving into its new assembly areas northeast of Inota throughout most of the daylight hours of 20 March. *Gruppenführer* Priess established his corps headquarters in the village of Tés, 12 kilometers northwest of Gille's at Öskü. During the night, as it was getting settled into its assembly area, Kumm's *LSSAH* Division had to fight off a strong enemy attack 4 kilometers east of Inota. At 4 a.m., Kumm initiated his division's attack to seize its first objective, the heights 3 kilometers northeast of Inota. By 5 a.m., Priess's headquarters had still not received any reports from the *Hitlerjugend* Division, which was supposed to be carrying out its own attack southeast from Bakonycsernye towards Isztimér at about the same time. Priess's corps reported that it had already destroyed up to 12 enemy tanks the previous day as its divisions were moving into their respective assembly areas.

On the far left flank of the *6. Pz.Armee*, Dietrich's newly established headquarters in Martinsberg reported that on 20 March the *XLIII. Armee-Korps* had already begun establishing its designated security line with a series of blocking positions along the line Csép–Nagyigmánd–Mocsa–Naszály–Füzitö Puszta. No morning report was submitted by the Hungarian *3. Armee*, but a rather alarming one sent by the *711. Inf.Div.* reported that during the night a Soviet force of undetermined size had landed behind it on the opposite bank of the Danube, 7 kilometers east of Nyerges Ujfalu, using as many as 70 small boats, a move that threatened to cut off a significant portion of Heszlényi's army.

By this point, the advancing Soviet 46th Army, supported on its left by elements of the 4th Guards Army, had managed to fight its way completely through the Vértes Mountains between Kisber and Tata Tóváros and had cut off German forces located to the east in the Gerecse and Pilis Mountains, including the *96.* and *711. Inf.Div.*,

SS-K.Gr. Ameiser, and *Gren.Brig.(mot) 92*, as well as remnants of the Hungarian *23. Inf.Div.* The landings reported that evening at Nyerges Ujfalu completed their isolation and had effectively split Dietrich's *Armeegruppe* in half.[2]

Dawn on 20 March brought more bad news. Along the boundary between the *III. Pz.Korps* and *IV. SS-Pz.Korps*, a powerful Soviet attack during the day against the village of Börgönd threw out the defenders from *II. Btl./Westland* of the *Wiking* Division, clearing the way for a much larger force to begin making a penetration. Shortly afterwards, an enemy force consisting of at least 1,200 men supported by 23 tanks began pouring through the gap thus created between Stuhlweissenburg and Lake Velencze, and headed southwest.

The *IV. SS-Pz.Korps* had no forces nearby that could counter this attack, nor did the *6. Pz.Armee*, so *Gen.d.Pz.Tr.* Balck was compelled to order the commander of the *III. Pz.Korps* to direct the *1. Pz.Div.* to carry out an immediate counterattack, which was able to push back this Soviet assault and re-establish contact with the *Wiking* Division inside the city. To the west, the enemy force that had advanced past the southern outskirts of Csór after attacking through the Mohr–Stuhlweissenburg gap the previous day was finally stopped southeast of Réti Puszta by a counterattack launched by *SS-Pz.Aufkl.Abt. 9* and *II. Btl./Pz.Gren.Rgt. 19* of the *Hohenstaufen* Division. Both units had been positioned in this area by the *III. Pz.Korps* the night before to cover the corps' deep (rear) flank in the vicinity of Nádasdladány, before they were officially attached to the *IV. SS-Pz.Korps* later in the day.[3]

Which corps headquarters the *Hohenstaufen* Division was subordinated to during this period is somewhat unclear. While *H.Gr. Süd* had directed the *II. SS-Pz.Korps* to release the division to the *IV. SS-Pz.Korps* on 19 March, Bittrich's corps headquarters had at the time already departed for its new mission south of Komorn. To ensure continuous command and control until it could be subordinated to Gille the next day, the *Hohenstaufen* was initially subordinated to the *III. Pz.Korps* and temporarily remained in its current front-line position near Seregélyes until it could be pulled out and sent to the Falubattyán area, where it would join the *IV. SS-Pz.Korps*. However, Balck refused to release all of it to Gille's corps as he was directed, claiming that it was currently too badly needed in the *III. Pz.Korps'* front line.

As a consequence, a portion of the division remained under Balck's control, while another went to Dietrich's army, under which the *IV. SS-Pz.Korps* was subordinated at the time. This was a topic of considerable importance; on 20 March, *Oberf.* Sylvester Stadler's division still possessed 29 operational tanks and 29 assault guns and tank destroyers, and a reported *Kampfstärke* of 4,614 men.[4] As a result, a tug-of-war ensued during the course of the next several days regarding the control of the division; the resulting confusion and conflicting orders seriously complicated German efforts to halt the Soviet offensive in the *6. Armee's* area of operations.[5]

Throughout 20 March in the *IV. SS-Pz.Korps'* sector, heavy fighting continued in and around Stuhlweissenburg as the *Wiking* Division fought to keep the city from falling into Soviet hands. Continued possession of the city meant that its value as a major transportation hub could not be exploited by the enemy to facilitate the further movement of supplies and reinforcements. The northern suburb of Kiskecskemet, lost during an earlier attack, was retaken by a counterattack by Hack's *Westland* Regiment. House-to-house fighting was still underway in the city, where Hack's troops were attempting to evict the remaining Soviet troops from the 80th Guards Rifle Division who had broken into the city the previous day. The two previously mentioned battalions from the *Hohenstaufen* Division that were attached to Gille's corps that day were ordered to remain in the area west of Stuhlweissenburg in the vicinity of Csór to continue blocking Soviet forces advancing through the gap north of the city.

The *I. SS-Pz.Korps* commenced its main attack on the morning of 20 March to support the *IV. SS-Pz.Korps* and reconstruct the front line between Mór and Stuhlweissenburg by regaining the commanding terrain northeast of Inota. Shortly after commencing its attack, Kumm's *LSSAH* immediately ran into an equally strong enemy armored force carrying out a concentric attack oriented towards Várpalota. A bitter defensive battle immediately ensued, in which 30 Soviet tanks were reportedly knocked out by time of the evening report. The division's own losses were heavy. To the north of Kumm's division, the *Hitlerjugend* Division, under the command of *Brig.Fhr.* Hugo Kraas, initiated its own attack to the southeast but ran into another large enemy force composed of infantry supported by numerous armored fighting vehicles near the town of Balinka.

During exceptionally heavy fighting, Kraas's division, supported by remnants of the *Totenkopf* Division, managed to destroy at least eight enemy tanks, though because of the heavy fighting, the division could not proceed with its own attack. To the south, Soviet forces persisted in their attacks to break through towards the west along the Stuhlweissenburg–Várpalota highway between Csór and Réti Puszta. The two battalions from the *Hohenstaufen* Division, along with elements of the *Germania* Regiment, were involved in very heavy fighting throughout the day to prevent a further breakthrough from occurring.

In his report that evening to *OKH*, a frustrated Wöhler wrote: "While the enemy used few tanks during the early days of his attack, groups of up to 50 tanks are now making an appearance. It must be assumed that the enemy has brought in new tank forces to use against our assembly areas. It is not yet known what forces are involved."[6] Although the commanders and troops of the *I.* and *IV. SS-Pz.Korps* did not yet know it, they had been attacked that day by the vanguard of the 6th Guards Tank Army, which was advancing towards them with as many as 425 tanks, assault guns, and SP guns.[7] Once again, German military intelligence agencies had failed to detect the approach and commitment of a *STAVKA* strategic reserve, a testimony to the effectiveness of the Red Army's camouflage techniques, *Maskirovka* operations, and speed.

On the left flank of the *6. Pz.Armee*, the headquarters of the *II. SS-Pz.Korps* had arrived, establishing itself in Per, 7 kilometers north of Martinsberg. The lead elements of the *Das Reich* Division and *6. Pz.Div.* also arrived at roughly the same time. While these units began to spread out and prepared their counterattacks to regain ground lost the day before, the *XLIII. Armee-Korps* was already involved in heavy fighting as its units—primarily *K.Gr. Wolf,* composed of troops from *Pz.Aufkl. Abt. 1*, the Hungarian *VIII. Armee-Korps*, and the leading elements of the *356. Inf.Div.*—sought to prevent the attackers from penetrating the mostly unmanned security line that the corps had established the previous day.

On Dietrich's far left flank along the Danube, the now-isolated Hungarian *3. Armee*, with its predominately German force, slowly withdrew the units on its right flank, while retaining a tight grip on to the Felsőgalla–Alsógalla industrial area, where a regiment of the *96. Inf.Div., Gren.Brig. (mot.) 92*, and *SS-Kgr. Ameiser* were soon exposed to encirclement. The army's area south of the Danube was now called a "bridgehead," a sure sign that it had been cut off from any land connections with neighboring units. Unless the land link with the *6. Pz.Armee* could be re-established, vitéz-Heszlényi's army would have to withdraw across the Danube or accept defeat. No decision to do so had yet been made, but time would soon force Wöhler's hand.

Air activity over the battlefield between Stuhlweissenburg and the Danube was intense. Soviet ground-attack aircraft concentrated their efforts on German movement routes, shooting and bombing vulnerable convoys of trucks, armored vehicles, and horse-drawn wagons as the divisions of *H.Gr. Süd* scrambled to get into position to carry out their assignments. Once again, the fatally flawed decision to switch field army headquarters and constituent elements in the middle of a decisive battle paid significant dividends to the Red Army. The roadsides throughout the area north and east of Lake Balaton and south of Komorn were soon littered with the carcasses of burnt-out trucks and the bodies of dead horses. Soviet pilots did not differentiate between civilian refugees fleeing to the west or troops in uniform moving about; they bombed and strafed them all.

Even the *Rückwärtiges Gebiet* (rear operations area) of *H.Gr. Süd* was not immune from their depredations, as Soviet fighter-bombers flew deep strike missions designed to disrupt or damage rear communications and supply dumps.[8] On 20 March, the city of Komorn was attacked by as many as 30 A-20 Boston light bombers from the 5th Air Army, which bombed and strafed the area south of the city, focusing their efforts on the *Flak* batteries that had recently been brought in to reinforce the city's defenses.

In response to the activities of the Red Air Force, the *I. Fliegerkorps* of *Luftflotte 4* conducted 300 sorties that day, focusing on the enemy's ground assault in the *6. Pz.Armee* area and in the skies over Stuhlweissenburg. Its fighter aircraft claimed the downing of 23 Soviet aircraft, as well as the destruction of one tank and a locomotive. During the night of 19/20 March, the *Luftwaffe* flew 40 sorties against

Soviet traffic along the highway leading from Stuhlweissenburg to Bicske in an effort to interdict and destroy as many of the enemy's vehicles and supplies as possible. In contrast, the Soviet 5th and 17th Air Armies flew over 800 sorties. That *Luftflotte 4* was able to successfully launch so many aircraft at this stage of the war was simply incredible, especially compared with its operations in the west, which were mostly carried out at night because of Allied air superiority.[9]

That evening, Wöhler participated in a number of individual telephone discussions with Dietrich, Balck, and Guderian; likewise, the chief of staff of the *6. Pz.Armee*, *Brig.Fhr.* Fritz Kraemer, conducted his own with *Generalleutnant* von Grolman, Wöhler's chief of staff, while that of the *6. Armee, Generalmajor* Gaedke, did the same.[10] Both of the army commanders had a unique set of challenges and requirements, and both aggressively competed for Wöhler's ear. The evidence suggests, however, that Balck usually succeeded in bringing his army group commander around to his own viewpoint, to the detriment of a unified effort. Meanwhile, in Berlin, Guderian, no matter how sympathetic he was to Dietrich's situation, was walking a tightrope balanced between the practical needs of the other field armies on the Eastern Front and an increasingly mercurial Hitler, who acted more irrationally with each passing day.

By the evening of 20 March, it can be said with certainty that Dietrich and his *6. Pz.Armee* faced the most insurmountable challenges of the two armies. His army had just been assigned responsibility for defending a sector over 120 kilometers wide with four German corps and a Hungarian corps that were being attacked by four Soviet armies in at least three and perhaps four different locations, if one counts the amphibious operation over the Danube at Nyerges Ujfalu conducted the previous evening. Balck had only two corps to worry about and a rather limited (and rapidly shrinking) defensive perimeter between Lakes Balaton and Velencze. His greatest concern was his left flank that tied in to that of the *IV. SS-Pz.Korps* of the *6. Pz.Armee* south of Stuhlweissenburg.

Balck demanded that Gille, and by extension Dietrich, do something to strengthen the defenses there, but the *6. Pz.Armee* had nothing to send. Dietrich's army was already throwing everything it could into stopping the attack by the 4th and 9th Guards Armies north of Stuhlweissenburg, joined later that same day by the even more dangerous attack by the 6th Guards Tank Army. On his left, the *6. Pz.Armee*'s commander had to address the equally dangerous situation unfolding south of the Danube, where the 46th Army had destroyed Hungarian defenses in the Vértes Mountains and isolated the bulk of the Hungarian *3. Armee* with its two German divisions.

South of the Danube, Dietrich had to build up a new defensive front almost from scratch using the two corps headquarters and three divisions that had been hurriedly brought in to prevent his opponent from seizing Komorn, Raab, and Acs, as well as remnants from two Hungarian divisions. The question arose at that time concerning why Balck could not do more to help the *IV. SS-Pz.Korps*, and by extension the *6. Pz.Armee*, on 20 March. Balck certainly had more forces available at that particular moment (two corps and nine divisions) than Dietrich did.

Oddly, the *6. Armee* commander seems to have been unaware that his army was in grave danger of being trapped and wiped out in the "sack" slowly beginning to form between the lakes as the bulk of two Soviet armies (the 26th and 27th) began to close in around his two corps. Despite his reputation as a tactical genius and man of action, Balck acted uncharacteristically, seemingly satisfied with defending a static front line when the unfolding situation seemed to dictate the need for bolder and more imaginative actions. Unfortunately, that is a question that may never be answered. As shall be seen, several days later, Balck would be compelled to act, if for no other reason than his self-preservation.

That evening, the *H.Gr. Süd* headquarters sent out Wöhler's intentions for the following day's operations by *Fernschreiber* or messenger to the headquarters concerned. These intentions fell under the guidelines of the orders previously approved by *OKH* and therefore did not require the *Führer*'s approval. The *6. Pz.Armee*, as anticipated, drew the greatest amount of taskings. According to the orders sent out that evening, Dietrich's army was directed to carry out the following:

a) *IV. SS-Pz.Korps*: Eliminate the enemy forces that have advanced towards Réti Puszta and retake Csór [note: unbeknownst to Wöhler, Csór was still in German hands, though surrounded];

b) *I. SS-Pz.Korps*: Intercept the enemy's assault spearheads through offensive operations and hold the line Inota–Ácsteszér [note: this sector was over 30 kilometers wide];

c) *II. SS-Pz.Korps*: Conduct a counterattack along the line Kisber–Nagyigmánd to destroy the enemy grouping located south of Mocsa;

d) *XLIII. Armee-Korps*: Support the passage of lines of the attack by the *II. SS-Pz.Korps* on the right flank while holding the left; and finally,

e) Hungarian *3. Armee*: Defend current positions.

This was a very long list of tasks to be accomplished, especially by the two German corps operating between Komorn and Kisber, because the main bodies of most of the units designated to carry out the counterattack from the *Das Reich, 6. Pz.Div.*, and *356. Inf.Div.* had still not arrived.

Fortunately, as mentioned previously, the defense of Komorn itself was assigned to the *8. Armee*, which was using the headquarters of *Generalmajor* Pape's still-rebuilding *Pz.Div. FHH* to control its defense. A number of *Luftwaffe* heavy *Flak* batteries also ringed the city in fortified positions. As an additional precaution, the road and railroad bridges over the Danube at Komorn were wired for demolition. However, neither *8. Armee* nor the *6. Pz.Armee* appears to have planned any sort of counterattack to restore connections with the Hungarian *3. Armee*, now isolated south of the Danube in the area around Gran. For the moment at least, *Gen.Lt.* vitéz-Heszlényi—with his two German divisions, a motorized brigade, and an SS battlegroup, as well as splinter Hungarian elements from the *23. Inf.Div.*—would have to fend for themselves.

Even the *I. SS-Pz.Korps* had a difficult mission, because most of its attacks would require its two divisions to advance through the hilly and densely wooded Bakony Forest, where *panzer* divisions were least suited. However, there were no other forces available to carry out this vital mission. *Gruppenführer* Priess's corps was also the only force that could withstand an assault by the 6th Guards Tank Army. For its part, the Soviet tank army did not encounter as many problems moving through such inhospitable terrain as Priess's forces, because Kravchenko's tanks had been augmented by a number of rifle divisions from the 9th Guards Army.

In regards to the *IV. SS-Pz.Korps*, its mission of throwing back the enemy's tank assault and re-establishing contact with Csór was a tall order, given that all it had to carry out this task was a battalion from the battered *Germania* Regiment and the two battalions from the *Hohenstaufen* Division, with hardly any armor. Half of the *Wiking* Division was tied down defending Stuhlweissenburg and could contribute nothing to the fight, while the *Totenkopf* Division had been split up and pushed into the sector being occupied by the *I. SS-Pz.Korps* or was attempting to defend Mór. Regardless, Wöhler insisted during the evening that "it must be absolutely clear to the *IV. SS-Pz.Korps* that it is of decisive importance that it bring the situation at Réti Puszta and Csór back under control."[11] Both Dietrich and Gille insisted that they needed the entire *Hohenstaufen* for this mission, and Wöhler had ordered Balck to release it, not once but at least six times on this date, but for unknown reasons, Balck simply refused to carry out his instructions. Unaccountably, *H.Gr. Süd's* commander did not reprimand him for this blatant disobedience.[12]

The tasks assigned to Balck's *6. Armee* for 21 March were relatively simple in comparison to the gargantuan assignment that Dietrich had been given. Although not mentioned in the day's orders, Balck's army also had the *1. Pz.Div.* occupying a position northwest of Seregélyes, where it was technically serving as his army's reserve, its position having been taken over by the *Hohenstaufen* Division. According to the nightly guidance, Balck's army was to carry out the following the next day:

a) Withdraw the *23.* and *3. Pz.Div.* to the line specified in Paragraph 2 above [this was an intermediate defense line stretching from the west to the east, encompassing the eastern shore of Lake Balaton–Bozsok–Hill 163–Kisláng–Bel major–Sarkeresztur–Seregélyes, then ending south of Börgönd];

b) Withdraw the last remaining elements of the *9. SS-Pz.Div. Hohenstaufen* [at the time positioned near Falubattyán] and relieve them by the *3. Pz.Div*;

c) In the rest of the army's area, continue holding and reinforcing its current positions [by this point, the *I. Kav.Korps'* two cavalry divisions had been pulled back along a shortened line stretching eastwards from Balatonkenese].[13]

Although neither of its commanders knew it yet, both the *1. Pz.Div.* and *Hohenstaufen* Division were about to play a crucial role in the survival of the *IV. SS-Pz.Korps.*

A very real crisis was looming over all of these deliberations which was not directly connected to the advancing Third Ukrainian Front, and that was the worsening fuel shortage that threatened to bring all operations by *H.Gr. Süd* to a halt. The *Oberquartiermeister* of the army group had been sounding the alarm ever since the bombing of the Komorn and Füzitö refineries several days earlier. The fuel situation had grown so bad that on 20 March, Wöhler's chief of staff was compelled to issue an army group-wide order directing even stricter economizing of the lifeblood of *panzer* divisions—gasoline. The order, issued that afternoon, read in part:

> The systematic air raids against the Hungarian refineries have now brought the last production of fuel in Hungary to a standstill—at least temporarily. In spite of all efforts, the restoration and reactivation of these facilities cannot be foreseen in terms of time and quantity, as further attacks are to be expected. The *Heeresgruppe* will therefore have to live on its small stocks indefinitely. *The supply of fuel has thus become the most serious question for the Army Group* [emphasis added]. It can only be mastered by the most severe restrictions and measures.[14]

The order then listed the restrictions and measures to be carried out by every unit in the army group's four armies, including fuel allocations for ground combat units, such as the divisions of the *IV. SS-Pz.Korps* and its accompanying *Heerestruppen*. It also required commanders to prioritize their vehicles into categories earmarked for destruction based on their combat value and urgency of need. The destruction of superfluous vehicles, except in crisis situations, was still dependent on the approval of *H.Gr. Süd's Oberquartiermeister*, acting in concert with the army group's chief of staff. Finally, the order stated that all motor vehicles not required for combat or urgent supply purposes were to be evacuated by rail to *Heeresgruppe* motor vehicle parks or to areas behind the *Reichsschutzstellung* in Austria. Coming at such a critical time in the battle, the fuel shortage and resulting stringent economizing measures would soon influence every event that was to follow.

The night of 20/21 March was cloudless, with very light fog and temperatures that were hovering in the low 40s Fahrenheit. The drying trend continued throughout the day, improving the condition of unpaved roads, which up until this point had still been muddy. Off-road movement had also greatly improved. During the day, it warmed up to 54 degrees Fahrenheit (12 degrees Centigrade), the warmest day of the campaign so far, and became partly sunny, perfect conditions for a spring outing, for flying, or indeed for a major spring counteroffensive.

The morning report for 21 March reflected no slackening of the fighting on the right wing of the *6. Pz.Armee* overnight. In the *IV. SS-Pz.Korps'* sector, Stuhlweissenburg's defenders were engaged in deadly house-to-house fighting, but by dawn, Hack's *Westland* Regiment had managed to iron out the deep penetration that had reached the city center two days before, as well as another one that had taken place on the city's southwest corner. Laboriously, and at great cost in human lives, the *Wiking* Division was able to re-establish its defense line curving around the city to the southwest and south, but its commander still faced the specter of envelopment. By this point, the *Westland* Regiment and its attachments, including a battalion formed from the remnants of the Hungarian *1. SS-Sturmjäger Regiment*, were connected to the rest of the corps by a narrow corridor running along the Stuhlweissenburg–Várpalota highway. This route was only kept open by an improvised *Kampfgruppe* from the *Wiking* Division that was surrounded in Csór during the day, but could move freely at night.

This scratch force was composed of *I. Abt./SS-Pz.Art.Rgt. 5* with two howitzer batteries, *K.Gr. Stichnoth* from elements of *SS-Pz.Aufkl.Abt. 5* commanded by *Ostuf.* Erich Stichnoth, and stragglers from both the *Wiking* and *Totenkopf* Divisions, as well as the *14. Kompanie* of the *Eicke* Regiment, equipped with 2cm self-propelled *Flak*. During the night of 20/21 March, it was reinforced by a platoon from the division's *Begleitkompanie* and *SS-Pz.Rgt. 5*'s five remaining assault guns.[15] South of Csór, the portions of the *Hohenstaufen* Division under Gille's control had established a defense line running west of Réti Puszta and east of Ösi after eliminating in a violent night battle a Soviet unit that had managed to advance as far as the area southeast of Várpalota. To put it mildly, the situation was extremely fluid.

The previous night's fighting was just a warm-up exercise for what would happen during the day. On 21 March, the Soviet XX and XXI Guards Rifle Corps redoubled their attacks against Stuhlweissenburg, spearheaded again by the 80th Guards Rifle Division, and by the end of the day, the 4th Guards Army had taken most of Stuhlweissenburg except for the southern portion. The *IV. SS-Pz.Korps* reported the resumption of westward movement by a powerful infantry grouping, which had resumed its attacks towards Nádasdladány and Ösi, which fell later in the day. To counter this development, the two battalions from the *Hohenstaufen* Division, supported by a few *panzers*, carried out counterattacks towards the north from Ösi and from Öskü in the direction of Várpalota.

Throughout the day, heavy fighting raged in and around Várpalota, as a series of tank-supported Soviet infantry units attacked the town from the southeast, east, and north. Losses on both sides were characterized as extremely heavy, and by the end of the day, Várpalota fell to the Red Army. As a sign of the intensity of the fighting, within the *IV. SS-Pz.Korps'* sector alone that day, Gille's headquarters reported that its troops had destroyed 46 Soviet tanks.[16] Taking into consideration how the events of the day had affected the *IV. SS-Pz.Korps*, the commander of *H.Gr. Süd* made several key decisions that would alter its order of battle in several important ways, in some ways negatively.

First, the *Wiking* Division was once again attached to the *III. Pz.Korps* to ensure better coordination between Ullrich's division and the adjacent *1. Pz.Div.*, especially concerning the fighting for Stuhlweissenburg. Having served under Breith's corps before, this did not pose a problem for Karl Ullrich, though being under Balck's command again was no cause for celebration. Describing the situation that evening, the division's *O1* wrote:

> We're again with the *III. Pz.Korps* and subordinated to General Breith. If our neighbor on the right [i.e., the *1. Pz.Div.*] pulls back the situation in Stuhlweissenburg will become untenable

... [We heard] that the Russians reached Várpalota today and crossed over the swampy area at Nádasdladány. With this, holding on to Stuhlweissenburg no longer makes any sense. The situation is completely unclear ... only one road to the southwest is open.[17]

The second decision was to attach the *Totenkopf* Division to the neighboring *I. SS-Pz. Korps* on Gille's left flank, which was a logical move, given that what was left of Becker's division—now designated as *K. Gr. Totenkopf*—was practically serving under Priess's corps already. *Volks-Art.Korps. 403* was also removed from Gille's control and attached to the *I. SS-Pz.Korps*. This momentarily left Gille corps' in control of the largest portion of the *Hohenstaufen* Division, including its division headquarters and the *Germania* Regiment, but little else except corps troops.

The *Hohenstaufen* Division, commanded by *Oberführer* Stadler, had finally been released by *6. Armee* (which had kept two of its battalions in the line near Seregélyes) and was employed in the Ösi–Nádasdladány area throughout the day, where it had established a main defense line facing to the north. To its right, Thünert's *1. Pz.Div.* was positioned in the area east of Falubattyán–Szabad, where it was keeping the lines of communication open with the elements of the *Wiking* Division in Stuhlweissenburg. To the south of Thünert's division, the *3. Pz.Div.* and *44. Reichs-Gren.Div. HuD* were still holding on to their defensive positions around Seregélyes. As a result of the Soviet advance force being near Várpalota, Gille had to order his command post to displace once again to Vilonya, a village 5 kilometers west of Berhida.[18]

On the southern wing of the *6. Pz.Armee*, Dietrich's intelligence staff had definitely identified the presence of the 6th Guards Tank Army, which had been introduced into the battle the day before when it initiated its attacks against the *I. SS-Pz.Korps* that had stopped Priess's two advancing divisions in their tracks and prevented them from carrying out their assigned missions. Despite the loss of the towns of Ösi and Várpalota that day, as well as a local breakthrough directed towards Zirc, by and large the *I. SS-Pz.Korps* was able to prevent the operational breakthrough that Tolbukhin had sought by employing active defense tactics. As a result, little ground was lost and the enemy suffered heavy losses in men and matériel, including the destruction of 15 tanks.

On the northern wing of Dietrich's army, his staff reported that the 46th Army had strengthened and renewed its efforts between Kisber and the Danube. The joint counterattack carried out at 2 p.m. that afternoon by the *II. SS-Pz.Korps* and *XLIII. Armee-Korps* from the Nagyigmánd area towards the east and southeast was able to regain some of the ground lost the day before, destroying 12 Soviet tanks in the process. In the new "bridgehead" south of the Danube defended by the Hungarian *3. Armee*, Heszlényi's staff reported that the enemy was carrying out attacks against both flanks.

After a bitter and sustained battle, the industrial areas of Felsőgalla–Alsógalla were finally abandoned by *Gren.Brig. (mot.) 92*, in contravention of a *Führerbefehl* to hold it at all costs because of the iron and coal mines that Hitler deemed "essential" for German arms production. Gran, held by the *711. Inf.Div.* since early January, was also abandoned when its garrison was threatened with encirclement. The *6. Pz.Armee*, based on reports from all of its corps, had identified no fewer than 42 rifle divisions and seven or eight mechanized or tank corps participating in the Vienna Operation so far, and this did not include those divisions and corps "warming up" on the northern bank of the Danube to take part in the Second Ukrainian Front's impending attack.[19]

In the *6. Armee*'s area of operations, Balck's headquarters that evening reported that between Lakes Balaton and Velencze, elements of the Soviet 26th and 27th Armies had increased the pressure of their attacks against its divisions, employing large numbers of tanks from the I Guards Mechanized Corps that concentrated on German defenses west of the Sárviz Canal, where they drove a 12-kilometer-deep wedge in the area defended by the *23. Pz.Div.* The attacking enemy force was able at first to advance as far as the *Margarethestellung* on the right flank of the *I. Kav. Korps*, adjacent to the eastern shore of Lake Balaton, before it was intercepted and destroyed by the *3. Kav.Div.* Balck personally acknowledged the contributions of the "bravely fighting" troops of the *Wiking* Division in Stuhlweissenburg, which had been attached to his *6. Armee* earlier that day, the first time he had singled out that division for praise.[20]

Within the southwestern portion of Stuhlweissenburg still held by the *Wiking* Division, the situation had begun to deteriorate even faster, as Soviet pressure increased against the desperately fighting *Westland* Regiment. Late that evening, *Obersturmführer* Jahnke wrote:

> Communications with the *III. Pz.Korps* have been interrupted … The corridor linking us to the west has shrunken to a length of only 15 kilometers and a width of 3 to 8 kilometers. We are holding at the front, but everything behind us appears to have dissolved, where will the front line be tomorrow? Around noon, we receive for the first time a *Führerbefehl*. We are to hold Stuhlweissenburg. We think this order is crazy, for we have only a few remaining troops available. And the possibility of a retreat is becoming more and more unlikely, and [we've heard] that the Russians are already in Papa [this was actually an incorrect report].

A glance at a situation map revealed that complete encirclement of the city and its *Wiking* Division garrison was only a few hours away, half a day at the most. *Oberführer* Ullrich made several calls that day to request permission to evacuate the city; his immediate superior, *General der Panzertruppe*. Breith of *III. Pz.Korps*, refused to commit, and passed the request up the chain of command to Balck's chief of staff, who insisted that the division stay where it was, although there was no longer any military advantage to be gained by holding Stuhlweissenburg.

In addition to the *Führerbefehl* to hold the city, there had been a great deal of back-and-forth messages between *H.Gr. Süd, 6. Pz.Armee, 6. Armee*, and the *OKH* concerning another order from Hitler that directed *H.Gr. Süd* to employ the *6.*

Pz.Armee to carry out an extremely ambitious two-pronged attack through the Stuhlweissenburg Gap using the *I. SS-Pz.Korps*, and another through the Vértes Mountains with its *II. SS-Pz.Korps*. The first attack was to drive to the Váli River, execute a left turn, and destroy the three Soviet armies attacking in the south; the second was to recapture the lost industrial area at Felsőgalla–Alsógalla, destroy the 46th Army, and re-establish contact with the Hungarian *3. Armee* and its divisions trapped in the "bridgehead" south of the river. Somewhere in the course of this counteroffensive, both of Dietrich's SS corps would link up in the mountains. This order was fantastic in its scope and completely impossible to carry out, especially when the *6. Pz.Armee* and its five corps were fighting for their lives and outnumbered by a factor of four to one.

Nevertheless, Dietrich's headquarters put together a concept plan to carry this out, even though he and his chief of staff knew that it would never come to pass. The amount of time dedicated towards drafting it was a complete waste of effort, requiring Kraemer and the staff to drop what they were doing to concentrate on developing the concept of operation, fire support plan, and everything else besides. This concept plan was approved that evening by *H.Gr. Süd*, but fortunately for all the units involved, it was never attempted because it was literally overcome by events on the ground during the next 24 hours.

Towards the end of the day (after the evening report was submitted), Balck's front line was pierced in numerous places between Lake Balaton and Dinnyés. Although at this moment he had two corps with eight divisions lined up closely next to one another, they were insufficiently numerous to stop the tidal wave surging towards them. Slowly, his army was forced to give ground as it backed to the north. Soon, Stuhlweissenburg would be completely isolated once the *1. Pz.Div.* withdrew past Sárszent Mihaly, a move that would have cut off the *Wiking* Division's escape route.

The reasons for holding Stuhlweissenburg were never completely clear; it was evident to nearly everyone on the ground, even Balck, that leaving the better part of a division behind to die made no military sense at all. However, Balck's chief of staff disagreed, writing at the time: "If one gives up contact with Lake Velencze and Stuhlweissenburg, then the enemy would have the opportunity to attack west along a narrow front with his 22 freed-up divisions as his main effort. That would be a massing of forces that one could only tough out with difficulty."[21] Back in Berlin, Hitler saw things in the same light, believing that the city's garrison was tying up a significant amount of Soviet troops (the old discredited *Wellenbrecher*, or Breakwater Doctrine) that could be turned around to reinforce other ongoing attacks once the city was given up.

In retrospect, neither Gaedke's nor Hitler's claims make any sense whatsoever because the 6th Guards Tank Army and the two other armies operating between Stuhlweissenburg and the Vértes Mountains had more than enough combat power to continue pushing back *H.Gr. Süd*, as they were clearly demonstrating, and still leave behind two or three divisions to carry on investing the city. Gaedke's estimate also did not take into consideration the other two Soviet armies—the 26th and 27th—that were about to attack the *I. Kav.Korps* and *III. Pz.Korps* from the south and southeast.

Surprisingly, Guderian was also in favor of holding the city, but for a different reason—he felt that should the city be abandoned and if "one were to give up here," then the entire front between the Danube and Lake Balaton would waver and "lose its footing all the way to Komorn," and Wöhler would be unable to establish a firm front anywhere.[22] Thus for him, holding Stuhlweissenburg had become more significant for morale purposes than for tactical reasons. Had Guderian been there on the spot that day at Balck's headquarters in Farkasgyepű, he would have seen with his own eyes that *6. Armee* and *6. Pz.Armee* were both "slipping" anyway, and that unless Balck's entire army was withdrawn past the eastern shores of Lake Balaton as quickly as possible, it would be trapped in the same way that the *Wiking* Division was about to be.

Oberführer Ullrich was aware that Franz Hack had been named *Kampfkommandant* for Stuhlweissenburg, which was the usual language accompanying any *Führerbefehl* involving the establishment of a *Festung*, so technically Hack's name was bound to the order. Because Ullrich and his *Führungstaffel* were no longer located within the city (at the moment it was being reestablished in the vicinity of Veszprém), he was unable to personally take charge of the situation. At that time, the *Westland* Regiment controlled about 3,000–4,000 members of the division in Stuhlweissenburg, including some artillery, the few remaining tanks of *SS-Pz.Rgt. 5*, a Hungarian SS battalion, and a large number of wounded. Hack had watched in alarm as he witnessed the jaws of the pincer slowly closing around the city and knew that it was only a matter of time before his troops were completely trapped. Well aware that his division had barely survived the encirclement and breakout from Cherkassy the year before, and that he and his men had been forced to stand by as the garrison of Budapest had been slaughtered during their breakout attempt, Hack was determined not to allow that to happen to his *Westland* Regiment.[23]

Having had no luck in convincing *III. Pz.Korps* or *6. Armee* headquarters of the urgent need to break out, Hack, in an act of desperation, radioed his former division commander, Herbert Gille, at his headquarters in Vilonya to ask for his advice. Later that afternoon, he received his response. Gille's radio message was short and succinct: "Collect all of your vehicles and disengage to the west, get your wounded out with you too."[24] Despite every attempt to contact the division headquarters and request permission or to get further guidance from *Oberf.* Ullrich, Hack was on his own (the division's headquarters was still displacing to Veszprém and was out of radio contact). Having at least received guidance from his former corps commander, though Gille was not technically in his chain of command at the time, Hack made his decision at 8 p.m. to disobey the *Führerbefehl* and ordered his battalion commanders to be prepared to evacuate the city, commencing shortly after midnight. At least this way, as much of the garrison and their equipment as possible might be saved, rather than waiting until daylight, when the chances for success would be much less.[25]

The route that the division would have to take would not be a direct or easy one. The most direct road out of the city running to the west through Csór had been cut at numerous places; the gap between it and Stuhlweissenburg was now filled with thousands of troops and tanks from the 6th Guards Tank Army. This information had been gained the hard way when the commander of *SS-Pz.Rgt. 5*, Fritz Darges, and his regimental surgeon, *Ostubaf.* Dr Hans Thon, had tried to use that same route into the city the previous evening. Darges, discharged from the field hospital that day after recovering from a case of bronchial pneumonia, was travelling in his staff car behind a Volkswagen driven by *Ostuf.* Kurt Schumacher, the division's new *O1*-in-training, and *Hstuf.* Georg Glanert, the division *Ic*. At first, as they headed east, they had passed columns of German troops from units of the *III. Pz.Korps* (primarily from the *1.* and *3. Pz.Div.*) that were withdrawing to the west.

After a few moments, Darges noted that the traffic had dwindled to only a handful of passing vehicles, then saw just a few disabled or burning vehicles, then nothing. As they drove around a bend in the road, they noticed that Schumacher and Glanert had stopped to repair a flat tire, so he and Dr Thon drove past them as they shouted words of encouragement. Continuing eastwards in the gathering darkness, they soon encountered a line of tanks illuminated by their headlights. Both Darges and Dr Thon thought they were German vehicles, but when they stopped to ask the commander of the leading tank a question, the man looked at them in an odd way. Darges immediately grasped he was speaking to a Soviet soldier at the same moment the tank commander realized that his questioner was a German. The tank was a T-34/85.

In the ensuing confusion, both Darges and Dr Thon jumped out of their staff car and ran across the open field next to the road, with machine guns firing at them from behind. Only the darkness had saved them. Neither had a chance to warn the two officers following behind in the Volkswagen, which was fired upon when it unsuspectingly drove up to the lead tank. Both men also bailed out and tried to run away. Glanert was seriously wounded and was found the following day when a German military policeman accidentally stepped on him. He was evacuated to hospital, where he recovered. Knight's Cross holder Schumacher's body was never found. Somehow, both Darges and Dr Thon survived and made it to the southwest corner of Stuhlweissenburg on foot, their clothing rent by bullet holes. Clearly, this was not the route to take whether entering or leaving the city.[26]

The only road not being used by the enemy that still lay open by this point was the one leading southwest out of the city past the western shore of Lake Sóstó and southwest of the east–west railroad line along the route passing through Urhida and Sárkeszi before finally ending at Nádasdladány. Shortly after midnight, the city's defenders had withdrawn to the railroad marshalling yards between the southern edge of the city and Lake Sóstó. There are no official estimates regarding the size of the force preparing to break out, only that it consisted of the bulk of the *Westland* Regiment, a few men from the *Germania* Regiment, the battalion from the Hungarian *1. SS-Skijäger Regiment,* half a dozen tanks from the *panzer* regiment, most of the engineer battalion, some artillery, and various *Flak* and support troops; perhaps 3,000–4,000 men in all. The garrison was able to disengage from the enemy unnoticed and quietly assembled behind the front line. The column then moved out in the darkness towards Urhida, where Hack intended to reorganize the group before progressing further.

There was no physical contact to the east or west with the *1. Pz.Div.*; Hack and his staff only knew that its westernmost boundary lay somewhere between Falubattyán and the southern edge of Stuhlweissenburg. No coordination arrangements could be made, since Hack's orders were in direct violation of a *Führerbefehl.* To the north and northwest lay the enemy in vast numbers. Somewhere to the west in the vicinity of Nádasdladány lay the right flank of the *Hohenstaufen* Division, which had been subordinated to the *I. Kav.Korps* earlier that afternoon (incidentally, Stadler's division had been subordinated to four different corps headquarters within the past 72 hours).[27] The *Westland* Regiment had no radio or physical contact at all with the *Wiking* Division by this point, although apparently the *IV. SS-Pz.Korps* headquarters had notified the commander of the *Hohenstaufen* Division to be on the lookout for it sometime that night and to assist if possible, though technically at that moment Gille's corps was still assigned to the *6. Pz.Armee* while Stadler was under the *6. Armee.*

Once the group arrived in Urhida at first light, Hack shuffled its composition to ensure that the combat-ready elements of his *Westland* Regiment would screen to the north to protect the column, where the major enemy threat was believed to be located. The main group, led by Darges's armored element, would head west and southwest down the road towards Nádasdladány or to the shore of Lake Balaton if necessary. For at least the first 15 kilometers, the column would be travelling in close proximity to the enemy; after that, it would have to travel at least a dozen kilometers more before it safely reached its destination. Coincidentally, the morning of 22 March also marked the beginning of the large-scale attack by the Soviet 26th and 27th Armies and the subsequent collapse of the southern front of Balck's *6. Armee,* which Hack's escaping column did not learn about until it had marched directly into the path of the Soviet attack (see Map 5).

The column had initially begun moving along the route with little interference, while the infantry elements of the *Westland* Regiment screened to its north. Shortly afterwards, the leading tanks in the column, which by that point had been apparently joined by some retreating elements of the *III. Pz.Korps,* collided with a large column of Soviet vehicles approaching from the south. Though the term "all hell broke loose" is an overused cliché, in this case it was an appropriate description for what happened next. Attacked along its entire left flank, the German column had to fight its way through several attempts to block its escape route. Nearly all of the division's surviving armored vehicles—including its last three tanks, assault guns, *SPWs*, and the SP artillery from *II. Abt./SS-Pz.Art.Rgt. 5*—were sacrificed in fighting that kept the enemy at bay long enough for most of the column to escape.[28]

Slowly, the column fought it way westwards. Around noon, its vanguard had reached a point several kilometers east of the northeastern edge of Lake Balaton, where it was augmented by more fleeing German and Hungarian troops from the *I. Kav.Korps*. Somehow, the *Wiking* column maintained unit integrity and did not panic as it grimly fought its way through the gauntlet, although some elements were separated and had to fight through "using storm troop tactics," according to one eyewitness.[29] During mid-afternoon, the column finally encountered combat troops from the *Hohenstaufen* Division, whose commander had extended his front line towards the south to help the survivors by establishing an escape corridor.

Most of the men from the *Wiking* Division who had participated in the breakout attempt made it out safely, but an unknown number of men were killed or listed as missing in action. Most of the wounded were brought out, though at least one *SPW* loaded with wounded was destroyed by a tank shell right in front of the battalion surgeon of *II. Abt./SS-Pz.Rgt. 5*, *Ostuf.* Dr Edwin Kalbskopf.[30] Dozens of trucks and other soft-skinned vehicles were destroyed or abandoned when they broke down or were damaged. Many of the accompanying troops from the *Heer* and *Honvéd* travelling with the *Wiking* had thrown away their weapons during their flight to safety, and had become little more than a mob. As for the leaders of the *Wiking*, who had endured Cherkassy and Kovel, they understood the importance of maintaining discipline during a breakout from encirclement and knew what to do to keep their troops in hand. Units that were able to maintain their integrity and remained together stood a far better chance of success than those that disintegrated at a critical moment of the breakout.

At 4 p.m. that day, Hack and his staff arrived at the division headquarters of the *Hohenstaufen* Division in Papkeszi to personally thank *Oberführer* Stadler for doing so much to save their division. An hour after that, they reached the new headquarters of the *III. Pz.Korps* at Balatonfüzfő, where Breith congratulated him for successfully leading his regiment out of Stuhlweissenburg. Nothing was said about disobeying the *Führerbefehl*. Two hours later, all of the *Westland* Regiment and divisional units that had escaped encirclement assembled behind the front line of the *Hohenstaufen* Division.[31]

That same evening, the *Wiking* Division, now reunited with the *Westland* Regiment, reverted once again to the control of the *IV. SS-Pz.Korps*, much to the relief of Jahnke and his fellow staff officers. By 9 p.m., the division had moved

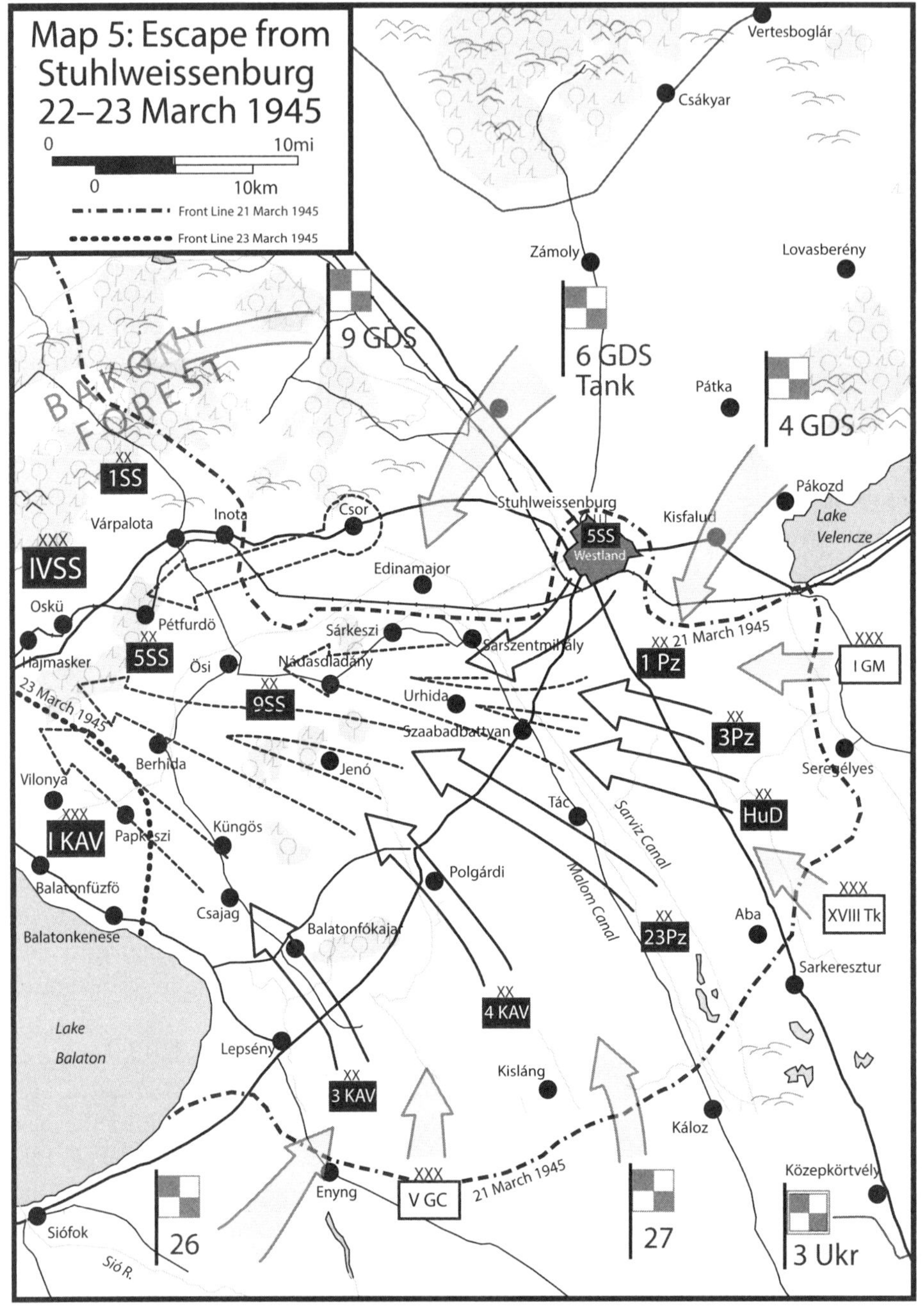
Map 5: Escape from Stuhlweissenburg 22–23 March 1945
0 10mi
0 10km
Front Line 21 March 1945
Front Line 23 March 1945
Vertesboglár
Csákyar
Zámoly
Lovasberény
9 GDS
6 GDS Tank
Pátka
4 GDS
Pákozd
Lake Velencze
1SS
Várpalota
Inota
Csor
Stuhlweissenburg
Kisfalud
IVSS
5SS
Westland
Oskü
Pétfurdö
Sárkeszi
Sarszentmihály
21 March 1945
1 Pz
I GM
Hajmasker
5SS
Ösi
Nádasdladány
Urhida
3Pz
23 March 1945
9SS
Szaabadbattyan
Seregélyes
Berhida
Jenó
Tác
HuD
Vilonya
Sarviz Canal
I KAV
Papkeszi
Küngös
Polgárdi
Malom Canal
XVIII Tk
Balatonfüzfö
Aba
Csajag
23Pz
Sarkeresztur
Balatonkenese
Balatonfókajar
4 KAV
Lake Balaton
Lepsény
Kisláng
Káloz
Közepkörtvély
3 KAV
Enyng
V GC
21 March 1945
26
27
3 Ukr
Siófok
Sió R.

into its new assembly area 6 kilometers south of Veszprém around the village of Veszprémfajsz to reorganize its units, which had become intermingled during the breakout. The division's logistics units were already located here, which allowed the combat units to be resupplied to some extent. Jahnke later wrote: "We believed that because we had made it out, we had earned a few days of rest and time to put everything back in order." But he was mistaken.[32]

Interestingly, the little *Kampfgruppe* from the *Wiking* defending Csór also broke out at about the same time, bringing with them their four *Sturmgeschütze*, two artillery batteries, four *SPWs*, and a company of infantry, regaining the German front lines at Inota shortly thereafter. They also had to fight their way through, but because their attack took place in the darkness, it was achieved with only minimal losses.[33] Describing the day's events in his own notebook, Gille simply wrote: "Although *Div. W[iking]* not subordinated to [the corps, I] ordered it to pull out by radio, otherwise it would be encircled and lost."[34]

While Hack was leading his regiment to safety, a series of back-and-forth telephone calls were made during the night of 21/22 March between the *6. Armee*, *6. Pz.Armee*, *H.Gr. Süd*, and *OKH*, wherein Wöhler repeatedly requested Guderian to ask Hitler to reconsider his decision to allow the *Wiking* Division to withdraw and abandon Stuhlweissenburg. In each case, Hitler refused. Therefore, *H.Gr. Süd* had no option but to pass on the order to *6. Armee* that the division was to continue holding the city. Balck's headquarters passed on the order to the *III. Pz.Korps*, which had direct control over the *Wiking* Division, although he must have known that by doing so, Ullrich's division would be lost.[35]

Nearly 24 hours passed before *H.Gr. Süd* was to learn that the city was completely occupied by the enemy and that the *Wiking* Division had escaped. Because of the collapse of the *6. Armee* that occurred on 22 and 23 March, the unauthorized breakout of the *Wiking* Division in violation of a *Führerbefehl* had become of minor importance; remaining records from *H.Gr. Süd* reveal that the subject was not even brought up afterwards. In his memoirs, Balck claimed credit for withdrawing the Stuhlweissenburg garrison and thereby saving them, but the facts prove quite the opposite.[36]

Rather than honestly acknowledge his own failure of leadership when he chose to blindly follow the *Führer*'s orders to hold on to the city, by default Balck left that decision to the local commander, just as he had done in the case of Budapest and Pfeffer-Wildenbruch, which conveniently left Balck free of blame for the failure of the breakout attempt. Instead of giving credit where it was due, Balck blamed the *6. Pz.Armee* in general and the *Hohenstaufen* Division in particular for its failure to "hold the line" when, in fact, it had saved his army, not once, but twice, as will be seen.

While the final act of the drama of Stuhlweissenburg was beginning to play out during the evening of 21/22 March, *H.Gr. Süd* issued guidance to its four field armies for the following day's operations. Given the actual military situation, with the Red

Army's Vienna Operation beginning to unfold in full strength, these instructions have something of an air of unreality about them. While the orders issued to the *2. Pz.Armee* and *8. Armee* were mundane ("continue current mission"), those provided to the *6. Armee* and *6. Pz.Armee* for 22 March, in light of what the enemy was about to do, are nothing short of fantastic:

> The *6. Armee* will:
> a) Pull the front line back to the line Balatonfökajar–Füle–Falubattyán; from this point, with the exception of the Stuhlweissenburg garrison, pull back the *3. Pz.Div.* and the *4. Kav.Div.*;
> b) Assemble the *3. Pz.Div.* and the *4. Kav.Div.* in the area encompassing Küngös–Papkeszi–Balatonkenese.
>
> The *6. Pz.Armee* will:
> a) Counterattack to clear out the enemy penetration in the area of Ösi–Várpalota [using the *I.* and *IV. SS-Pz.Korps*];
> b) Continue its attack towards Kocs [with the *II. Pz.Korps* and *XLIII. Pz.Korps*];
> c) Continue holding the bridgehead south of the Danube by withdrawing reserves to prop up the western front [the Hungarian *3. Armee*].[37]

These orders were already impossible to carry out. Apparently, Hitler still labored under the belief that the formations depicted on his situation map in Berlin corresponded with the condition of the actual units on the ground nearly 800 kilometers away. Where he saw fresh, full-strength units, in reality the troops in Balck's and Dietrich's armies were exhausted, nearly out of fuel and ammunition, and were feeling the effects of the heavy losses in men and matériel they had suffered during and after the abortive *Frühlingserwachen* offensive.

For his part, Marshal Tolbukhin and his Third Ukrainian Front continued adhering to their plan. The 26th and 27th Armies, which had begun smashing through the *6. Armee* from the south and southeast on 21 March, would increase the tempo of their attacks, perhaps sensing that they had their opponent on the run. At a point northeast of Lake Balaton, in the area encompassing the Polgárdi–Balatonfökajar sector, Tolbukhin intended them to link up with the approaching spearheads of the 6th Guards Tank Army and 4th Guards Army, thereby trapping all of the *6. Armee*. In the center, the 9th Guards Army would continue pushing west and northwest into the Bakony Forest, while in the north, the 46th Army would continue advancing towards Komorn.

The Soviet 5th and 17th Air Armies would continue carrying out aerial interdiction attacks against German rear area installations, chokepoints, and bridges, while bombing and harassing the movement of front-line troops. Although the attack by the 6th Guards Tank Army had not yet achieved the decisive breakthrough as hoped, having been stymied by the counterattacks of the *I. SS-Pz.Korps*, Tolbukhin would ensure that his army commanders redoubled their efforts on 22 March. What would unfold the following day would be a race towards safety by the *6. Armee* that would make the harrowing escape from Stuhlweissenburg by the *Wiking* Division pale in comparison.

The fateful day of 22 March began with temperatures in the low 40s Fahrenheit, low ground fog, mist, and cloudy skies. During the day, temperatures rose once again into the low 50s, as the skies cleared. Road conditions in general were excellent for both wheeled and tracked vehicles. The *H.Gr. Süd* morning report at 9:20 a.m. stated that within the *IV. SS-Pz.Korps*'s defensive sector, the *Wiking* Division (which at that point in the day was still technically attached to the *III. Pz.Korps*) had lost Stuhlweissenburg during the evening of 21/22 March despite fighting bitterly to hold it. "Heavy defensive fighting" was reported taking place south of the city.[38] At the time the report was submitted, neither the *6. Armee* nor *H.Gr. Süd* knew that Hack had pulled his troops out of the city without permission, and had initially assumed they were lost.

For reasons that will become evident, at 3 p.m. that day, the *IV. SS-Pz.Korps* was once again placed under the tactical control of Balck's *6. Armee*. When this order went into effect, the corps was to control the *Wiking* Division, *3. Pz.Div.*, and the splintered portions of the *Totenkopf* Division that were not already attached to the *I. SS-Pz.Korps*. The subordination of the *Hohenstaufen* Division to Gille's corps also ended that day at the same time, when it was attached to the *I. Kav.Korps* as previously mentioned. Despite their hopes to the contrary, neither the *Wiking* Division nor the *3. Pz.Div.* received any of the well-earned rest period that they richly deserved. Instead, both were immediately thrown back into battle. By this point, the corps' headquarters had been relocated to the area 3.5 kilometers southwest of the town of Nemesvámos, approximately 3 kilometers southwest of Veszprém and 3 kilometers west of the *Wiking* Division's new headquarters at Veszprémfajsz.

The evening report for 22 March submitted by the *IV. SS-Pz.Korps* provides a summarized version of that day's activities:

> From the Várpalota area, the enemy attacked with massed infantry and armor forces towards the southwest and reached the line Gyárt Puszta–Sóly–Kádárta–Gyulafirátót … enemy tank spearheads that had reached to within 3 kilometers east of Veszprém were driven off after three of his tanks were knocked out. The *9. SS-Pz.Div. Hohenstaufen* and elements of the *4. Kav.Div.* were able to establish a screen line running from south of Berhida–north of Papkeszi–north of Vilonya–north of Sita and were able to ward off several tank-supported enemy attacks.[39]

By the time this information had been included in the evening report, the *Hohenstaufen* Division had been attached to the *I. Kav.Korps* since 3 p.m., when it became involved in the effort to assist the units breaking out from what became known as the Jenö Pocket. While the report does not mention the ordeal of the *Wiking* Division or the return of Ullrich's division to the *IV. SS-Pz.Korps'* order of battle, those submitted by the other adjacent and higher units do provide accounts of what occurred throughout the day in the remaining areas between Lake Balaton and the Danube.

The consolidated *H.Gr. Süd* evening report for 22 March summarized what had happened that day, stating that in the area southwest of Stuhlweissenburg, the enemy continued its massed attacks begun during the evening of 21/22 March, with its center of mass aimed at the *6. Armee* area northeast of Lake Balaton. Despite the massive losses in troops and tanks that the 26th and 27th Armies had suffered (the *3. Kav.Div.* claimed to have knocked out 34 tanks on 22 March alone), the two combined armies had still been able to push back the defensive line held by the *I. Kav.Korps* "several" kilometers towards the northwest (an understatement—in actuality, it was nearly 20 kilometers). Further to the north, the 6th Guards Tank Army had been able to advance southwest of Stuhlweissenburg into the midst of the withdrawing *Kampfgruppen* from the *III. Pz.Korps* (presumably including the *Wiking* Division) which were trying to fight their way through to safety in the west.

The evening report submitted by the *III. Pz.Korps* paints a starker picture of what actually happened, which Balck's consolidated report glosses over. In stark terms, Breith or his chief of staff wrote:

> During the morning, a strong enemy force supported by numerous tanks attacked towards the Polgárdi area and seized Falubattyán from the northeast. From there, he turned his forces towards the north and continued his advance. As a result, he tore apart the new defense line being established by the *III. Pz.Korps*. Elements of the *1. Pz.Div.* and the *44. Reichs-Gren. Div. HuD* were involved in heavy defensive fighting this afternoon along the heights west of Falubattyán against numerous enemy tanks attacking from the south, east, and northeast directions. During the night [of 21/22 March] an enemy force attacking from the north seized the towns of Ösi, Nádasdladány, and Berhida, and during the late morning, the town of Jenö as well. The *3. Pz.Div.* and the *5. SS-Pz.Div. Wiking* defending Stuhlweissenburg were able to fight their way through the enemy in a generally westwards direction, initially reaching Balatonfüzfő.[40]

The exact number of German and Hungarian casualties resulting from the breakout from the Jenö Pocket are unknown; nor are the number of tanks destroyed or abandoned, or troops taken prisoner, but the losses must have been considerable. Those of the *Wiking* Division would not be tabulated until the end of the month.

In his memoirs, Balck claimed that the *44. Reichs-Gren.Div. HuD* was wiped out, that it had "ceased to exist," and that it was "the only major unit under my command that was destroyed during World War II."[41] This claim is sheer fantasy; while the division's commander, *Gen.Maj.* Hans-Günther von Rost, was killed along with his division *Ia* in an *SPW* loaned to him by *1. Pz.Div.* while leading the breakout, most of his troops made it out safely to the northeastern corner of Lake Balaton, although "the losses, especially in the Grenadier Regiments, were very high." A large proportion of its horse-drawn vehicles were lost, as well as all but 12 of its remaining artillery pieces, and there were a large number of stragglers reported afterwards. Shortly thereafter, following a few days spent reorganizing under *Oberst* Hoffmann as its acting commander, the *44. Reichs-Gren.Div.* would be back in action as a *Division-Kampfgruppe*.[42]

The *1. Pz.Div.*, which had formed the rear guard for the *III. Pz.Korps'* escape, had held open the corridor to the west for as long as possible, and was still able to fight its way through as a cohesive unit, bringing along with it numerous stragglers from the *3. Pz.Div.*, the *44. Reichs-Gren.Div. HuD*, and the *Wiking* Division. Most of its remaining tanks were lost in hard fighting against numerous Soviet barricades erected at Jenö, Küngös, and Berhida or against their attempts to cut up and destroy the column in segments, but thanks to the leadership of *Generalmajor* Thünert and *Oberst* Bradel, the division was also able to reach the safety of the German lines at Balatonfüzfő late on the evening of 22 March. For the moment, the *III. Pz.Korps* was too disorganized and broken up to operate as a unified whole, forcing Wöhler to order Balck to move it and its divisions behind the front lines to spend the next two days reorganizing.[43]

The evening report submitted by *Gen.d.Kav.* Gustav Harteneck's *I. Kav.Korps* was just as chilling as Breith's, providing mute evidence of the complete collapse of the front line commanded by Balck:

> The *3.* and *4. Kav.Div.* and *23. Pz.Div.* of the cavalry corps were attacked during the evening of 21 March … along a wide front by massed enemy infantry and tank forces. In the forest region southwest of Polgárdi the enemy broke through with tanks and infantry. In the night of 21/22 March the enemy advanced with numerous tanks from the area of Lepseny towards the northwest in a night attack and seized Balatonfökajar. At the same time, the enemy attacked with tanks and infantry southwest from the direction of Polgárdi. During the day [22 March], the enemy's assault continued to gain momentum through the increased commitment of armored forces along the shore of Lake Balaton towards the northwest and was finally brought to a stop by the defenses set up along the line south Balatonkenese–south of Küngös. From 21 and 22 March, the *3. Kav.Div.* alone knocked out 34 enemy tanks.[44]

By this point, the Hungarian *25. Inf.Div.* was no longer being mentioned in the corps' reports, since it had been virtually destroyed as an organized fighting force several days prior to this attack. Although the *Hohenstaufen* Division is not mentioned in this report either, even though it had been subordinated to Harteneck's corps at 3 p.m. that day, the unauthorized extension of its lines to the south and southeast was most likely responsible for the ability of the *I. Kav.Korps* to withdraw in a semblance of order. Although there is no record of Harteneck issuing any orders to Stadler to carry out this action, there is no mention in the official records of him expressly forbidding it, either.

The situation to the north of the *6. Armee* in the large sector held by the *6. Pz.Armee* was just as discouraging, though not as catastrophic. In his evening report to *H.Gr. Süd*, Dietrich's chief of staff wrote that a large Soviet armored concentration with up to 50 tanks had thrust through Priess's front line southwest and west of Várpalota, clearly oriented towards Veszprém, where the signs of an envelopment from the north were beginning to unfold. The attempts by the *I. SS-Pz.Korps* to close the widening gap on its right flank failed. A staff officer from *H.Gr. Süd* reviewing the report added after the statement: "A counterattack by the forces currently being regrouped in the area northeast of Veszprém [i.e., *III. Pz.Korps*] are to be used in an attack intended to throw the enemy located at and south of Hajmáskér back towards the northeast." But as events were to show, the *III. Pz.Korps* would not be used in this attempt.[45]

In the northern sector of the *6. Pz.Armee* between the Danube and northern edge of the Bakony Forest, the *II. SS-Pz.Korps* and *XLIII. Armee-Korps* were both tied up in heavy defensive fighting against Soviet forces attacking from the east and southeast. The counterattacks planned by both corps had to be postponed, since they had to fight off persistent Soviet attacks throughout the day. One enemy attack attempted to gain access to the road connecting Veszprém with Kisber by going around the right flank of the *II. SS-Pz.Korps* before it was stopped by a counterattack from the *6. Pz.Div.* Had this succeeded, it would have allowed the 46th Army or the 9th Guards Army to send some of their troops behind the right flank of the *6. Pz.Armee*, raising the specter of yet another pocket forming.

Between Kisber and the Danube east of Komorn, the *8. Armee* reinforced the defenses of Komorn by sending in more elements of *Generalmajor* Pape's *Pz.Div. FHH*. One enemy spearhead that had advanced too far ahead of the rest of the advancing forces was encircled and wiped out near Csép by a concentric attack by a *Kampfgruppe* from *Pz.Div. FHH* and the *Das Reich* Division. Additional division-sized Soviet forces, including 25 tanks, continued pushing northeast towards the line Nagyigmánd–Mocsa before they were blocked by a counterattack by the *Das Reich* after advancing only a few kilometers. The *XLIII. Armee-Korps*, operating in conjunction with *Pz.Div. FHH*, claimed the destruction of six tanks and two assault guns that day.

In the "Danube Bridgehead" west of Gran, Soviet troops supported by tanks continued pushing to the west and southwest along the river highway in an effort to split up the grouping of German and Hungarian troops, but these attacks were finally brought to a halt after the Hungarian *3. Armee* had committed all of its remaining reserves. The Soviet bridgehead at Nyerges Ujfalu, which had been growing in size after several nighttime attempts by their Danube Flotilla to reinforce it with more troops, was hemmed in by a counterattack launched by the *96. Inf. Div.* Despite these local successes, the defenders were slowly being forced into a smaller and tighter bridgehead with each passing day. German efforts to convince the Hungarians to commit their own Danube Flotilla to counter the Soviet river fleet were unsuccessful, thus ruling out the one force that might have been able to cut off the Red Army's bridgehead at Nyerges Ujfalu.

The situation in the air was characterized by the constant activity by large numbers of Red Air Force bombers, ground-attack, and fighter aircraft, with most of their efforts focused against the northern side of Lake Balaton, where the German and Hungarian forces from the *6. Armee* were attempting to escape the trap being rapidly drawn around them. German air operations were not nearly as robust as they had been the previous day, because many of the *Luftwaffe*'s airfields had been forced to relocate further to the west or northwest on account of the withdrawal of the *6. Armee* to its new positions. As a result, the divisions of the *6. Pz.Armee* and *6. Armee* were rendered even more vulnerable to enemy air attack, placing most of the air defense burden on their own *Flak* units.

During discussions conducted individually by Wöhler with his subordinate commanders, the evidence indicates that he, von Grolman, Balck, Gaedke, Dietrich, and Kraemer were beginning to realize the enormity of the predicament that the two center armies of *H.Gr. Süd* faced. The size, scope, and momentum of the Vienna Operation on the south side of the Danube had caught all of them by surprise. Soviet units seemed to be breaking through everywhere, and small clusters of their tank and infantry forces had appeared at some of the least likely locations behind the front lines, where rear-echelon troops were unprepared to counter them. Despite all of the orders that *H.Gr. Süd* had issued during the past several weeks for these administrative and logistics units to have antitank teams standing at the ready and equipped for such a possibility, these *Tross* units proved to be completely incapable of stopping Soviet tanks spearheads supported by motorized infantry when they actually had to face them. Perhaps the idea of expecting non-combat troops to fulfill this role was unrealistic to begin with, something that should have been self-evident.

In addition, a phenomenon the Germans called *Kessel-Psychose,* or "cauldron fever," was beginning to sweep the ranks. This definitely negative trait was characterized at the time as the fear of being trapped by the enemy and abandoned by one's own command.[46] First diagnosed at Stalingrad in 1942–43, it was initially manifested as a form of extreme nervousness displayed by front-line troops that tended to make them appear unduly nervous or jittery. One officer who had observed this phenomenon first-hand at another battlefield during the same phase of the war, *Gen.d.Geb.Tr.* Valentin Feuerstein, wrote in his 1963 book *Mistaken Duty*:

> In general, these troops no longer possessed the hard-nosed will to fight. Many small units defending isolated strong points remained squatting in their shelters long after air attacks had passed and allowed themselves to be taken prisoner without a fight. A few of their officers even committed suicide. Leaflets, telephone calls, and encouraging words, even visits to the front line no longer sufficed [to boost their will to fight]. The bowstring had been stretched too far.[47]

It is likely that this same mood was beginning to affect the senior leaders as well, though it was something that they would have attempted to conceal. Even Balck himself remarked to Wöhler during the latter's visit to his headquarters on 22 March that he had never personally experienced what it was like to "stand on the edge of a catastrophe," and that this day marked "the worst situation that I have ever experienced."[48] Indeed, he certainly had cause to believe this, because his army had nearly collapsed that day and had only escaped due to the heroic actions of a few units and individual leaders, not to any decisive actions he had taken.

Until this point, Balck had regarded this and many previous situations outside of Budapest with an unbridled optimism that was not warranted by the facts. He was certain that both the *III. Pz.Korps*, with its four divisions along with a portion of the *Hohenstaufen* Division, and the *I. Kav.Korps*, with three divisions, were more than enough to hold the 50-kilometer-long line between Seregélyes and the eastern shore of Lake Balaton, but he was wrong. The power of the attack by the two Soviet armies, supported by at least two Guards mechanized corps from the 6th Guards Tank Army, against his own forces had exceeded anything that he had expected, leaving him mentally unprepared when it happened.

Increasingly concerned about what was happening in the *6. Armee* area of operations, based on numerous unfavorable reports pouring into his headquarters, Wöhler visited Balck later that day to see for himself what was actually going on, as mentioned above. Perhaps he was looking for reassurance that Balck had things under control, but found the truth was quite the opposite. Later that evening, summing up what he had seen and heard there that day, the *H. Gr. Süd* commander wrote:

> [I found a] serious deterioration of the situation northeast of Lake Balaton. Wild confusion reigns. As there are no telephone connections, it is difficult to get a clear picture. [I ordered that] it was necessary to apprehend deserters and shirkers and treat them very severely. *Gen.d.Pz.Tr.* Balck pointed out the serious weaknesses of the *Waffen-SS* (partly insufficient leadership, bad reporting systems, undisciplined behavior behind the front).[49]

Once again, Balck appeared to be placing the blame for his army's reverses on the *Waffen-SS*, but based on Wöhler's observations, it was evident that the *6. Armee* commander did not have a firm grip on the situation. Rather than focusing on how best to handle stragglers, shirkers, and deserters, Balck should instead have directed his energy towards regaining control on the battlefield. At any rate, it is evident that the *H. Gr. Süd* commander came away from his visit with anything except the reassurances he sought.

What Balck had anticipated to be an orderly and phased withdrawal by the *I. Kav. Korps* to shorten its lines and free up forces for *6. Armee* to use as reserves devolved into a near rout that nearly destroyed three of his divisions and badly damaged the other four. While Breith's, Harteneck's, and Gille's corps could claim a large number of Soviet tanks knocked out, again this mattered little in the calculations when determining the correlation of forces; while the Red Army could replace lost tanks quickly, the *Wehrmacht* could not. The trend was definitely not working in Hermann Balck's favor.

It was becoming just as evident that Dietrich's *6. Pz.Armee* was not going to be able to carry out its objectives either. Wöhler's directive for the SS general to plant his headquarters in Martinsberg was a mistake. With the responsibility for such a wide defensive sector, where the two wings of his army were fighting separate battles and a third part was trapped on the southern bank of the Danube dozens of kilometers to the east, what the situation really called for was another field army headquarters to be established. Such an army could handle the battle between the Danube and Bakony Forest, allowing *6. Pz.Armee* to concentrate on the battle north of Lake Balaton.

Wöhler could also have reassigned Balck and his *6. Armee* to his old headquarters location in Martinsberg and handed over the entire battle north of Lake Balaton to Dietrich, as a sort of reverse castling movement. However, by this point, neither arrangement would have worked because it would taken too much time, time that had already been wasted when Wöhler ordered the first unwise "castling movement" during the evening of 18/19 March. It was now far too late. If Wöhler, Dietrich, Balck *et al.* could create a unified front line by this point in the battle, it would be a near miracle.

Regardless of the true situation, or perhaps unaware of it, *H.Gr. Süd* issued guidance that evening for the following day's operations. That given to the *6. Pz.Armee* the previous evening remained unchanged; it was directed to continue ongoing operations to stop the Soviet offensive, throw it back, and relieve the Hungarian *3. Armee*. In contrast, a number of changes were given to previous instructions issued to Balck's *6. Armee*. One of Wöhler's biggest concerns at that moment was the possibility that his two center field armies might become separated from one another. To prevent this from happening, Balck's *6. Armee* was instructed to carry out the following tasks, beginning 23 March:

> The *I. Kav.Korps* [*3.* and *4.Kav.Div.*, *23. Pz.Div.*, and *Hohenstaufen* Division] will hold the current line Balatonkenese–2 kilometers south of Berhida–Vilonya;
>
> The *IV. SS-Pz.Korps* will assemble the *3. Pz.Div.* in the Veszprém area and the *5. SS-Pz. Div. Wiking* in the area southwest of Litér to carry out an attack to the northeast towards Vilonya–Hajmáskér; and
>
> Pull back the Hungarian *25. Inf.Div.* behind Lake Balaton and return it [to Hungarian control] to be used on the lake's northern shore.[50]

The only reserve Balck had was the *1. Pz.Div.*, but after serving as the rear guard during the breakout, it was not in very great shape either, but at least still functioned as a unified whole under the firm control of its commander.

Upon receipt of his instructions, Gille and his staff would have had very little time to carry out a mission or terrain analysis and develop courses of action to achieve these stated objectives. The two divisions expected to carry out this attack had only just returned to his control late in the afternoon after breaking out, and both were in a shambolic situation; it would normally require several days for them to sort themselves out, count heads, and reorganize for battle. They would not get that time, and were instead being thrown into battle the very next day.

What they really needed was a month at a rest camp, as well as a substantial amount of replacements, new weapons, and equipment to replace what they had just lost, but there was no time for that or any other forces available to perform the mission. It was yet another recipe for disaster. If Gille's attack succeeded, his two divisions would be able to safeguard Veszprém, the most important railroad and highway center on the northern shore of Lake Balaton; if they failed and the city passed into enemy hands, Balck's army might become separated from Dietrich's and *H.Gr. Süd* would split into two wings. The consequences should that occur were unthinkable.

That evening, in a bid to boost the morale of the troops and instill a greater sense of urgency to their mission, Wöhler issued an accompanying order to all four of his field armies, though most of it was undoubtedly directed towards the *6. Armee* and *6. Pz.Armee*. The order, Number 1068/45, went out via telex at 11:15 p.m. and stated:

> The enemy has launched a major attack between Lake Balaton and the Danube to force the decisive breakthrough on Vienna. The extension of this operation to the Gran Front in the foreseeable future, as well as against the front between the Drava and Lake Balaton, must find us fully prepared to defend ourselves. Every German and Hungarian soldier must be aware that the designs of the enemy must be destroyed! If not, the whole of Hungary would fall into the enemy's hands, and the Vienna area and thus the entire southeastern part of the Reich would be threatened. In addition, essential economic goods, which are vital for the continuation of successful warfare, would be lost.
>
> I therefore command:
>
> No step of ground shall be given up without a fight. I forbid any voluntary withdrawal from the front. We must attack and destroy the enemy's spearheads everywhere and at all times. Where the enemy is attacking with superior forces, the position must be held until the last. More determined than ever, we shall fight and win![51]

By this point, such exhortations to stand fast and fight to the last round had lost their efficacy; mere words would not stop the Red Army's Vienna Operation, only an infusion of fresh forces under new leadership or a major withdrawal that would shorten the front lines. The time for empty words had passed. The small circle of those who still believed in the power of such proclamations was probably limited to the *Führer* himself and to the commanders of *H.Gr. Süd* and *6. Armee*; that is, if they still believed their own words. By 22 March, the handwriting on the wall of looming defeat could clearly be seen, and no amount of bold wordplay could prevent it.

The following day, 23 March, can be regarded as that when any effective German defense of Hungary became impossible. The troops from the two armies of *H.Gr. Süd* defending between the Danube and Lake Balaton may have woken up after a cool, dry evening expecting a warm, sunny day, but what they got instead was heavy fighting against an irresistible opponent. Understandably, they probably felt that they had earned the right to a rest after what they had lived through during the past several days, especially the troops of the *6. Armee* who had managed to successfully extract themselves from the "sack" that had threated to close around them south of Lake Balaton. They probably even believed that this was the day when German arms would at long last prevail. If anyone in the *6. Armee*, including its commander, had thought this way, he was shortly to be proven mistaken, for there was still another trap that the army would have to avoid. What occurred during the evening of 23 March would set the stage for later events that would forever tarnish the reputation of the *Waffen-SS* and create a rift in the German high command that would endure until the end of the war.

The paragraph summarizing the day's events that was entered into the official record of *H.Gr. Süd*'s *Tagesmeldung* was illuminating and remarkable for its straightforwardness in describing the disaster that rapidly unfolded throughout the day:

> The defensive battle between Lake Balaton and the Danube continued with undiminished ferocity. Directly north of Lake Balaton, vastly superior enemy infantry and tank forces broke through towards Veszprém and seized the city. Strong tank units of the attacking enemy forces continued following the westward course of the great highway leading [west] out of Veszprém and were not stopped until Márkó when they were intercepted by *Flak* artillery; according to the most recent reports they lost 20 tanks. The emplacement of a new defense line and the concentration of our forces that have been scattered during the past few days of fighting is currently underway using every means available.[52]

The town of Márkó was approximately 10 kilometers northwest of Veszprém; a quick glance at a situation map reveals what this meant—that the 6th Guards Tank Army had finally achieved the operational breakthrough that Marshal Tolbukhin had been seeking. What is noteworthy is that this advance had been brought to a temporary halt not by front-line troops, but by a *Luftwaffe Flak* unit positioned 10–15 kilometers behind the front along the unfinished *Klarastellung* (the "Klara" Defense Line). Blame and recriminations quickly shot back and forth along the chain of command; but what had actually happened to bring this about?

To understand what went on that day and the role that the *IV. SS-Pz.Korps* played in this disaster, it is instructive to read the more detailed report submitted by Balck's *6. Armee* headquarters late that afternoon for inclusion in the *H.Gr. Süd* evening report to the *OKH*. In cold, military language, the report stated that the enemy had continued its attacks throughout the previous evening and into the early morning, with increasingly powerful assaults against the already-weakened army front line. The units on the ground reported that they had identified three main directions of attack by the Red Army using forces that consisted chiefly of armored units: one along the northern shore of Lake Balaton with 70 tanks; another from the area of Sóly–Vilonya in a general southwesterly direction with approximately 60 tanks; and a third from the Hajmáskér area towards the west with about 50 tanks, meaning some 180 tanks in all. The attack was supported with powerful artillery fire and close air support carried out by waves of ground-attack aircraft.

Severe traffic jams caused by withdrawing columns of German *Tross* vehicles, stragglers, Hungarian refugees, and Jewish slave laborers, worsened by air attacks that destroyed trucks and other soft-skinned vehicle by the score, had markedly slowed the eastward movement of ammunition and fuel to the forward fighting units. In turn, the lack of these vital items began to exert a negative effect on the fighting potential of the *I. Kav.Korps*, *III. Pz.Korps*, and *IV. SS-Pz.Korps*, whose divisions now had to face the possibility of not having enough of either item of supply they urgently needed to continue fighting effectively as mechanized units.

Ironically, the *6. Armee*, along with its five *panzer* divisions and two cavalry divisions, had a total of 121,936 men (excluding Hungarians) serving in the ranks and a large number of armored fighting vehicles (excluding *SPWs*) assigned.[53] On 17 March, it reported having at least 134 operational AFVs, not including those of the *Wiking* or *Totenkopf* Divisions, which was nearly as many as the attacking V Guards Tank and I Guards Mechanized Corps combined, but without fuel and ammunition, Balck's tanks were little more than static pillboxes.[54] As an excuse for his army's failure that day, the *6. Armee* commander explained that his divisions had been bled white and could not gain control of the situation in the face of such an overwhelmingly powerful enemy.[55] While this was undoubtedly a contributing factor, something else was responsible for his army's inability to operate effectively that day. Balck had certainly operated successfully in the past with divisions that were just as weakened and debilitated.

The *IV. SS-Pz.Korps*, which was preparing early that morning to carry out the orders it had been issued the previous night, reported that it was attacked during the early morning by about 60 tanks supported by infantry from the direction of Sóly, which quickly took Litér, the designated jump-off position for the *Wiking* Division's attack scheduled for later that morning. Along the corps boundary on its right, where it connected with the *I. Kav.Korps*, Gille's headquarters reported that a large enemy force had attacked the *Hohenstaufen* Division and penetrated 2 kilometers into the corps' defensive sector near the town of Szentkirályszabadja, a mere 8 kilometers southeast of the city center of Veszprém.[56]

Another tank attack launched by the V Guards Tank Corps from the direction of Hajmáskér quickly overran the corps' hasty defenses erected outside the towns of Kádárta and Gyulafirátót on the corps' northern boundary that it shared with the *I. SS-Pz.Korps*. Not satisfied with these accomplishments, the spearhead of the V Guards Tank Corps then pushed into Veszprém, which quickly fell after the small *Kampfgruppe* from *Gen.Maj.* Wilhelm Söth's *3. Pz.Div.* that had been tasked by Gille with the city's defense withdrew without a fight. Evidently, it was supposed to be relieved in Veszprém by *Div.K.Gr. LSSAH* of the *I. SS-Pz.Korps*. Why it pulled out without notifying anyone or waiting until it was relieved can no longer be determined.

On the northern edge of the city, a *Panzergruppe* from the *LSSAH*, consisting of nine operational tanks of *SS-Pz.Rgt. 1* under the command of *Stubaf.* Werner Pötschke, had been preparing to counter the Soviet thrust. This unit was part of *Brig. Fhr.* Otto Kumm's *Div.K.Gr. LSSAH* that was supposed to relieve the *3. Pz.Div.* At the time this occurred, Kumm's battlegroup was operating under the direct control of the *6. Armee* and was due to be returned to Priess's SS corps once this mission was completed. It would have made more sense for Balck to place Kumm's force under the temporary control of the *IV. SS-Pz.Korps*, but Balck chose to direct it himself, perhaps not trusting Kumm or Gille to follow his orders.

Consisting of most of *Ostubaf.* Max Hansen's *SS-Pz.Gren.Rgt. 1* and Pötschke's *Panzergruppe*, plus other elements of the division including its *Flak* and antitank battalions, *Div.K.Gr. LSSAH* had been assigned the mission of preventing enemy forces from seizing Veszprém and ensuring that a solid connection was maintained between the *6. Armee* and *6. Pz.Armee*. Although the battlegroup had been able to make its way into the city, the situation quickly deteriorated when the Soviets initiated a surprise attack before the *Leibstandarte* was ready for it. One eyewitness, *Ustuf.* Roland Reiser, later described what happened:

> It was morning, shortly after [6 a.m.]. We were driving through Veszprém with nine *Panzers*, a radio *SPW* and two *Schwimmwagen* in order to occupy positions on the edge of the city to the northeast. The city was almost dead. Here and there we ran into vehicles racing through. I drove in a *Schwimmwagen* with *Sturmbannführer* Pötschke to reconnoiter the terrain at the edge of the town. The *Panzers* followed. It was a cloudless day and already warm at that early hour. We left the vehicle and walked through a garden in order to get a look at the terrain laying before us. Through binoculars we saw an armored column advancing from out of Kodarta—it could have been thirty to forty vehicles—approaching Veszprém from the south. Our *Panzers* caught up and Pötschke fetched all of the commanders in order to brief them on the town and the position.

While Pötschke was briefing them, an artillery or mortar salvo struck nearby, mortally wounding him and killing several other officers under his command.[57]

Left momentarily leaderless, the SS *Panzergruppe* struggled to reorganize in time to prepare its defense of Veszprém. Before it could move into position, Kumm, acting as both the division commander and commander of *Div.K.Gr. LSSAH*, ordered the tanks to withdraw to the northwest towards the Kádárta–Hajmáskér area so it could rejoin the rest of his *Kampfgruppe*.[58] Explaining his action, Kumm later wrote in his after action report:

> In heavy fighting, the division withdrew to Kárdáta. Veszprém was already lost to a strong enemy attack from the north. During the day the division was thrown out of Veszprém by an armored attack and pushed back to the eastern edge of Márkó by enemy forces pursuing from the direction of Hajmáskér. Besides numerous tanks, a Soviet 15.2cm assault gun was also destroyed. The captured driver said that the battalion, with 60 such guns, was sent immediately into combat after a 200 kilometer march.[59]

Kumm's report is not completely accurate because his defenses had not yet been fully established in the city and he had withdrawn his troops before the Soviet attack had begun to fully develop, so he is partially responsible for what happened next.

Why Kumm pulled his tanks out instead of directing them to stay in Veszprém as he had been ordered is also unknown. Perhaps he made the decision on the spot when he learned that the *3. Pz.Div.* had already pulled out before all of his own troops had arrived, which would have made any successful defense of the city problematic. Or maybe he had received conflicting orders to the contrary. The few *Panzergrenadiere* from *SS-Pz.Gren.Rgt. 1 LSSAH* endeavoring to defend the city were also withdrawn before they could become decisively engaged with a superior Soviet force already penetrating the outskirts. This operationally and tactically important city fell shortly thereafter to advancing Soviet forces with hardly a fight; the commander of the leading tank unit most likely could not have believed his good fortune.

Balck, whose headquarters had been controlling Kumm's task force since the previous day, admitted that evening that he had been unable to contact any of his subordinate units by radio that day, so Kumm, lacking any clear guidance from above, may have acted on his own initiative.[60] The *LSSAH* Division commander's decision to pull out may also have been influenced by the fear that his troops might be trapped within the city if they remained there too long. That alone may have led to his decision that it was not worth sacrificing half of his division in exchange for the temporary control of a city that was already as good as lost. The rest of Kumm's battlegroup, arrayed along the city's northwestern outskirts, also withdrew to the northwest after a brief attempt to delay approaching Soviet forces.

During a late-night telephone conversation with Wöhler at 12:30 a.m. on 24 March, Balck placed the blame for the loss of Veszprém squarely on the shoulders of Otto Kumm, claiming that he had simply marched off with his troops; in doing so, Balck failed to acknowledge that he shared part of the blame for failing to keep his subordinates properly informed of the developing situation.[61] There is no evidence either that Balck ever reprimanded Söth for giving up this key locality without a fight or waiting to be relieved by Kumm's task force before departing. Once again, Balck had successfully placed the blame for his faulty leadership upon the *Waffen-SS*, which was becoming a noticeable trend since his army had been experiencing an increasing number of battlefield reverses since 16 March.

That evening, instead of being released to the *I. SS-Pz.Korps* as the *6. Pz.Armee* had urgently requested, *Div.K.Gr. LSSAH* was held back on the direct orders of Balck himself. Here it would remain for several more days, despite continuing pleas by the *6. Pz.Armee* for its immediate release. Dietrich needed to reassemble the division because Priess's *I. SS-Pz.Korps* at the moment only had the understrength *Hitlerjugend* Division, *Div.K.Gr. Totenkopf*, and *SS-Pz.Gren.Rgt. 2 LSSAH* to hold its now 50-kilometer-wide defense line in the Bakony Forest. This force was insufficient to either retain control of the key road nexus of Papa or delay the Soviet advance long enough to re-establish a coherent front line in the face of concerted attacks by the 4th Guards and 6th Guards Tank Armies.

Balck stubbornly continued refusing to carry out a series of direct orders from *H.Gr. Süd* to return Kumm's *Kampfgruppe*, despite repeated attempts by both Wöhler and von Grolman to force his compliance. Inexplicably, Wöhler made no attempt to reprimand his out-of-control subordinate, whose stubbornness and willingness to disobey his chain of command was threatening the survival of the entire army group. At one point that day, Balck even threatened to resign his command if he was forced to relinquish control of *Div.K.Gr. LSSAH*. Shamefully, Wöhler yielded to Balck's demands and failed to enforce his own directives.[62]

Unopposed, the V Guards Mechanized Corps' armored juggernaut then continued moving towards the northwest along the highway, as previously related, and was not brought to a stop until 6:30 p.m. when its lead tanks were shot up by *Flak-Abt. I./25* 3 kilometers east of Márkó, where it lost the aforementioned 20 tanks. The Soviet attack along the *IV. SS-Pz.Korps'* left flank continued advancing towards the northwest, where it encountered the defenses of *Div.K.Gr. LSSAH*, which finally brought it to a halt northeast of Márkó that evening. The *Div.K.Gr. LSSAH* eventually returned to its division several days later when the *H.Gr. Süd* chief of staff simply ordered Kumm to disregard any further orders from *6. Armee* and return to the *I. SS-Pz.Korps* on his own authority.[63] Fortunately for the *6. Armee*, the arrival of the *1. Volks-Gebirgs Division* eased the departure of Kumm's *Kampfgruppe* and helped to fill the gap during the next several days (see following chapter).

Compelled to fall back to the southwest, during the afternoon of 23 March the *IV. SS-Pz.Korps* assembled its divisions (at this point, the scattered units of the *Wiking*, *3. Panzer*, and *Hohenstaufen* Divisions) behind the unfinished *Klarastellung*. Gille was informed that this would become the new *6. Armee* main defense line, although events would quickly prove this to have been a rather ambitious goal. Construction had begun on this position as an alternate main defense line in November 1944, but work had been discontinued when *H.Gr. Süd* decided that the *Margarethestellung* would become the primary focus of its defensive efforts instead. Work on the *Klarastellung* had barely begun, and in many places consisted only of an imaginary line drawn on a map. As events were soon to prove, the *6. Armee* would not occupy it for long.

In the neighboring sector on Gille's right, the *I. Kav.Korps* that day initially reported good news when an attack by the *23. Pz.Div.* against a Soviet tank force during the night of 22/23 March succeeded in clearing the way for the escape of 1,700 men from the Jenö Pocket, consisting of the rear guards of the *1. Pz.Div.* and *3. Pz.Div.*, as well as the *44. Reichs-Gren.Div. HuD*, who had been fighting all day to reach friendly lines. The *23. Pz.Div.* reported that it had destroyed 15 enemy tanks during this engagement and was able to establish a new defense line west of Küngös. This was the only good news that the *6. Armee* was able to report that day.[64]

When the sun finally rose, it was the signal for the better part of two Soviet mechanized corps to begin their attacks with 180 tanks. The flimsy front line established overnight by the *3.* and *4. Kav.Div.* and *23. Pz.Div.* "collapsed like a house of cards," in the words of one German historian, and was penetrated at multiple points, joined shortly after by another attack from the Papkeszi area in the northeast.[65] Within a remarkably short time, organized resistance disappeared and the bulk of *I. Kav.Korps* began hastily withdrawing to the west, until it reached the *Klara* defense line between Szentkirályszabadja and Balatonalmádi late that afternoon.

It could have been much worse, were it not for the stout defense offered by a *Kampfgruppe* from the *Hohenstaufen* Division west of Papkeszi that fought a delaying action for most of the day, buying the time needed for Harteneck's corps to escape. According to the division's postwar history:

> [Our] tanks and *Flak* held their fire and allowed the approaching enemy to draw near, waiting for the first tank to strike an [antitank] mine. That was the signal to open fire. Our own tank crews fired shot after shot from the barrels of their 7.5cm cannon and the 8.8cm *Flak* fired like the devil was after them. This was the moment that the men of the *Hohenstaufen* had been waiting for, now they had the enemy in the jaws of a trap. Our own tanks occupied a well-camouflaged ambush position in the vineyards, every crewmember knew their assignments down to the smallest detail. Over there was a column of [Soviet] tanks that was terrible to behold, but many of them were already on fire, others were trying to withdraw but got stuck in the swamp on either side of the road and began to sink into the mud … the [enemy's] accompanying infantry sought cover in the flat terrain but we could see them clearly from our positions; there was no cover for them at all … The enemy attack stalled in the face of our merciless fire … Around midday, the fireworks display was all over. It grew quiet, suspiciously quiet. Shot-up tanks still burned, while others sank halfway into the mud. Black smoke obscured the meadows all the way to the railroad embankment.[66]

By 5 p.m., the force blocking the western exits from Papkeszi began pulling out and an hour later had established another blocking position at the Balatonkenese–Veszprém road junction that held out until the last of Harteneck's corps had escaped.

As an indicator of the severity of the fighting, on 22 and 23 March, Stadler's division alone claimed to have knocked out 108 Soviet armored fighting vehicles, including 15 JS-II Stalin heavy tanks destroyed by the eight *Jagdpanthers* from the division's attached *s.Pz.Jag.Abt. 560*.[67] During the fighting to hold open the southern shoulder of the 3-kilometer-wide escape corridor from the Jenö Pocket at Berhida several kilometers southeast of the northern shoulder at Papkeszi, *Obersturmbannführer* Hofmann's *SS-Pz.Gren.Rgt. 19* was reduced to 200 men, while the *1. Batterie* of *SS-Flak-Abt. 9*, fighting a rear guard action at Pétfürdő, was reduced to a single 8.8cm antiaircraft gun.[68] In his memoirs, Balck makes no mention of the efforts and sacrifice of the *Hohenstaufen* Division, which for the second time in as many days had fought against superior enemy forces to keep open another escape corridor between Lake Balaton and Veszprém long enough for the troops of the *6. Armee* to make their way out of yet another trap.

Despite its sacrifice, Balck blamed the *Hohenstaufen* Division for the mauling experienced by the rest of the *I. Kav.Korps*.[69] Stadler's division had suffered heavy losses while covering the escape of the *6. Armee* from the "sack" south of Lake Balaton while assigned to the *I. Kav.Korps* (by 1 April, it reported only one operational *panzer*). Despite the division's sacrifice, Balck held the SS commander personally responsible for the destruction of the *44. Reichs-Gren.Div.*, stating that Stadler had the blood of its troops on his hands. Balck later wrote in his memoirs:

> [W]e were able to pull the *Panzer* divisions out more or less intact. In the same manner, we withdrew the *I. Kav.Korps*, which was calmly and confidently commanded by General Gustav Harteneck. Only the *44. Inf.Div.* was mauled during the process. That was entirely the fault of the *9. SS-Pz.Div. Hohenstaufen*. Against specific orders, it failed to remain in place and left its positions without orders and without waiting for and orienting its relief force. *It just marched off to rejoin the 6. SS-Panzer-Armee* [emphasis added]. It took two days for us to figure out what had happened there. The commander, *SS-Oberf.* Sylvester Stadler, had not deemed it necessary to orient his relieving division.[70]

This statement is patently untrue and is disproved by the official records; it also appears that Balck conflated the separate events of 22 and 23 March into one enormous act of malfeasance. In addition, the withdrawal of the *I. Kav.Korps* had been anything but orderly; at times, it seems to have been a pell-mell rush to the rear.

There is also no evidence in the *H.Gr. Süd* war diary, including the *6. Armee* daily reports for the two days in question, showing that another division was tasked with the relief of the *Hohenstaufen*. Despite Balck's claim to the contrary, it had *not* marched off to rejoin Dietrich's *panzer* army at all, but instead for two entire days had steadfastly held its position until everyone had made it out of two rapidly closing pockets, at great cost to itself. Had the *Hohenstaufen* not assisted these breakouts, the number of escapees would have been far less and the destruction of the *I. Kav. Korps* and *III. Pz.Korps* would have been complete.

Not surprisingly, Stadler and Balck had not been on friendly terms with one another, and this incident only made things worse. As an example of the bad feelings growing between the two, during the only visit to the division command post the *6. Armee* commander made during the fighting on 23 March, Stadler began by giving Balck a situation report. Before he could complete his briefing, Balck cut him off in mid-sentence and "spat out" that one of his combat engineer companies had been intercepted fleeing to the rear. Stadler's explanation that he had ordered it to pull back to an alternate defensive position as part of Balck's own phased withdrawal plan fell on deaf ears (an investigation carried out immediately afterwards revealed that the battalion in question had, in fact, belonged to the *Wiking* Division).[71]

Balck then told the commander in no uncertain terms that the present defense line had to be held "under all circumstances," as spelled out in a recent *Führerbefehl*, and that he would hold the commander of the *Hohenstaufen* personally responsible if he failed to carry out his orders, threatening him with a court martial. Although Stadler responded by stating that of course he would hold the line, but would not senselessly sacrifice his men, Balck swore at him and said "the *Führer* has ordered it so and that is that!" before storming off.[72]

Obersturmbannführer Maier of the *6. Pz.Armee* staff later wrote that he suspected Balck was intentionally misinforming Wöhler in an effort to discredit the *Waffen-SS* in general and the *Hohenstaufen* Division in particular, and was deliberately trying to burn the division out, which he perceived as yet another sign of his loathing for the *Waffen-SS*.[73] As an indication that Stadler believed Balck was attempting to do just that, at 11:35 a.m. on 23 March, he sent a telex message to the *6. Armee* boldly requesting his division's relief from Balck's army and reassignment to the *6. Pz.Armee*: "Division [is] completely shattered and is being used up to the last man. Request immediate release." Stadler also sent a courtesy copy of the request to Dietrich's headquarters.

Outraged with what he saw as Stadler's impertinence and disregard for his chain of command, Balck told Wöhler about the message. In response, the *H.Gr. Süd* commander sent a strongly worded reply by telex to the *Hohenstaufen*'s commander at 9:40 p.m. that evening: "I expect you to carry out the orders of General Balck unconditionally and more precisely. It is my imperative to hold out unconditionally until the arrival of reinforcements. As always, I require the greatest devotion to duty from both officers and men."[74] Stadler claimed after the war that he never saw this order and never knew it had been issued. Although Dietrich and Bittrich, his nominal army and corps commanders, were sympathetic, there was nothing they could do to help Stadler, since operational matters in the *Kampfraum* were strictly the purview of the army group commander, even regarding the *Waffen-SS*.[75]

It is not known whether *Obergruppenführer* Gille, for his part, intervened in the matter, possibly because the command relationships had become so murky and confused by this point. He may have simply told Stadler to obey the orders he had been given. Although the *Hohenstaufen* Division was not officially subordinated to his corps at this moment, the force of events had left no one on the scene except Gille who could give Stadler directions, since it appeared as if no one else would or could. Whether he influenced Stadler to submit his controversial request through the chain of command to rejoin the *6. Pz.Armee* is unknown, but in Gille's remarks in his notebook that evening he wrote: "The withdrawal was quite difficult, but they were able to make their way out towards the west, assisted by the *Hohenstaufen* Division, which provided the greatest assistance by holding on to its positions despite orders to the contrary."[76]

In the *6. Armee*'s *Tagesmeldung* that was submitted that evening, in an attempt to explain how the disastrous collapse of the *I. Kav.Korps* and the loss of Veszprém could have taken place, Balck—or his representative acting in his name—wrote: "Due to the heavy fighting of the last several days, our cavalrymen and *Panzergrenadiers*, who have been subjected to immense physical and mental stress, gave their last ounce of energy to stop an overwhelmingly strong, onrushing enemy, but could not withstand his attacks."[77] This partially explains why such a huge number of stragglers were reported that day, a first in terms of Balck's experience. The army's report ended on an ominous note:

> In the area of both corps the intervention of general and general staff officers with *special judicial powers* [emphasis added] along with other available officers from headquarters units and the military police were able to intercept scattered and partially leaderless bands of soldiers, as well

as parts of units separated from their headquarters, and employ them in fighting positions behind the partially constructed front line.[78]

Indeed, Balck expressed his surprise at the numbers of stragglers, especially *Waffen-SS* troops, many of whom he suspected of desertion or being detested *Drückeberger* (*Wehrmacht* slang for shirkers or quitters). At 9:35 a.m. that day, he telephoned the *H.Gr. Süd* headquarters to inform Wöhler that:

> The units are no longer fighting as they should. Some are saying that the war is lost anyway and they do not want to get killed before the imminent end of the war. Everyone is afraid of being encircled. The trust that the leadership is capable of mastering the situation has been lost. [I] wanted to talk to *Gen.O.* Guderian immediately about the situation.[79]

It does not seem to have occurred to Balck that this critical assessment by his troops might have applied to his own leadership as well. While it is true that the SS divisions in the *IV. SS-Pz.Korps* were not immune from straggling, because they were already located north and west of Veszprém they were for the most part not in the highway corridor along the northern shore of Lake Balaton through which the bulk of the troops of the *I. Kav.Korps* were retreating. Regardless, Balck continued to direct a significant part of his ire towards the *Waffen-SS*, a service arm of which he had been critical for some time.

Perhaps Balck would have fared better if he had modelled his conduct after that of the Allied commander, General Dwight D. Eisenhower, who once said: "Leadership consists of nothing but taking responsibility for everything that goes wrong and giving your subordinates credit for everything that goes well."[80] Apparently, Balck believed in just the opposite. In a subsequent telephone call to Wöhler's headquarters that same day, Balck complained about the alleged inability of *Waffen-SS* officers under his command to carry out orders, following up on a similar complaint he had made the previous day. He also called Guderian directly shortly afterwards and repeated the complaint, bypassing his army group commander once again. In response, Guderian wired Wöhler, informing him that Balck's assessment had been sent to the *Führer* as well as to Himmler "in all urgency."

According to Guderian, this had been the first time that "such a failure on the part of the SS has been reported." In the *H.Gr. Süd* war diary that evening, Wöhler wrote in his commander's comments portion that, upon receiving Guderian's thoughts, "[the failure of the *Waffen-SS*] is a serious indicator, almost like a sign of an impending storm."[81] No longer satisfied with merely expressing his discontent with the *Waffen-SS* to his army group commander, Balck had now elevated his complaint to the highest authority in the Third Reich—Adolf Hitler himself. Yet while he was complaining about the performance of *Waffen-SS* units under his command, he continued demanding that his field army be given more of them.

However, perhaps influenced by Balck, Wöhler followed up later that evening with a two-page missive sent by telex titled simply "*Waffen-SS*." In all of the annals of Himmler's vaunted "asphalt soldiers," this stands out as one of the most detailed official complaints ever sent during the war. Most likely penned with the help of the *6. Armee* commander, who had aired similarly worded sentiments to his army group commander over the past several days, this message most likely laid the groundwork for the notorious "cuff title order" that followed several days later. Relayed to *OKH* Headquarters in Zossen at 11:50 p.m., it was addressed to Guderian but meant to be read by Hitler. It stated:

1) It again appears that reporting procedures area in urgent need of improvement. For example, the situation of the *9. SS-Pz.Div. Hohenstaufen* could not be clarified for two days during its operations at Ösi. There is too little use made of tactical radio. On the other hand, this division radioed to the *6. Armee* and the *II. SS-Pz.Korps* at 1135 hours [11:35 a.m.] on 23 March 1945 "Division completely destroyed and is being used up to its limit. Request immediate relief from *Verband Balck* and return to the Headquarters of the *6. SS-Pz.Armee* …" I have left no doubt that the division is to unconditionally carry out the orders of its superiors at the *6. Armee*. Basically, I have emphasized frequent and clear reporting procedures at every opportunity. Before the *6. Pz.Armee* went into action, I discussed this thoroughly with *SS-Oberstgruppenführer* Dietrich.

2) I have the impression that the leadership of the *9. SS-Pz.Div. Hohenstaufen* is too slow. *SS-Oberstgruppenführer* Dietrich and *SS-Obergruppenführer* Bittrich protested against this opinion quite energetically today and described *SS-Oberführer* Stadler as a superb officer.

3) *SS-Oberstgruppenführer* Dietrich described the situation of his vehicles as very poor. The vehicles had been in use for 2–3 years. For this reason, there were large numbers continuously out of service. Indeed, one sees very many towed vehicles on the roads. [The] *9. SS-Pz.Div. Hohenstaufen* is said to have only 30 per cent of its vehicles that it is authorized. For that reason, some elements march on foot. Bittrich underscored this.

4) [The] Armored vehicle replacement situation was "catastrophic" a week ago. Now there is some improvement.

5) Dietrich and Bittrich stated that the replacements for the *II. SS-Pz.Korps* had become very poor. The *II. SS-Pz.Korps* had received:
   a. 3,500 *Luftwaffe* soldiers and Ukrainians to make up losses of 8,500 men prior to the battle of the Ardennes.
   b. Now, 1,300 briefly trained naval personnel.

6) On 21 March, the *6. Armee* caught 140 stragglers, that is, *Drückeberger* [shirkers]. 70 percent of them belonged to the *Waffen-SS*.

7) The local population has made many complaints concerning plundering by the *Waffen-SS*. Livestock, in particular, are being taken.

8) It has met with the disapproval of Army units that the *Waffen-SS* has female *Hiwi* with the staffs and in the units.

Signed, Wöhler
General der Infanterie
Oberbefehlshaber, H.Gr. Süd[82]

The most remarkable aspect of this message is that Wöhler's headquarters dedicated the time and energy to compose and send it, especially given that the army group was in the middle of a very critical and dynamic battle and his staff must have been very busy. Upon reading it 75 years later, what stands out most to the reader is the pettiness of the complaints contained in the message, few of which rise to the level where the supreme commander of the German Armed Forces (Hitler) needed to become involved in or even to be aware of. Wöhler should have never sent it. Whether he regretted sending it will never be known; all that is known is that it began to poison the previously good working relationships between the staffs of *H.Gr. Süd* and the *6. Pz.Armee*.

In his book, Maier dedicates a great deal of ink refuting this message point by point, but the author will refrain from going into them here, except to say that Maier's points are well-reasoned and convincing.[83] One point that Maier does dwell on though, is that this document bore the unmistakable signs of Balck's authorship, in that it repeated many of the same accusations against the *Waffen-SS* that he had been making ever since *Unternehmen Konrad I*, when he first came face-to-face with Herbert Gille.

While the message does not specifically accuse the *IV. SS-Pz.Korps* of any of the enumerated offenses, the message's author undoubtedly included it in his general criticism. Coming as it did at the same time that *H.Gr. Süd* was struggling to mount a credible response to the Vienna Operation, all it managed to accomplish was to instill a sense of increasing distrust in Hitler of his elite bodyguard units, at a time when he could least afford it, especially considering that Wöhler was depending upon the fighting prowess of Dietrich's *panzer* army to mount a successful defense. If sowing distrust was Balck and Wöhler's intent, it succeeded beyond their wildest dreams, for it laid the groundwork for what was soon to come.

As the palace intrigues continued at *6. Armee* headquarters, the attack by Gille's corps did not take place on 23 March because instead of advancing, the *Wiking* and *Hohenstaufen* Divisions and the *3. Pz.Div.* were immediately forced to defend their jump-off positions and in some cases were even forced to withdraw a short distance to the west. Gille and his commanders were certainly too occupied to worry about such high-level intrigues, even if they were aware of them. It was difficult enough to simply maintain a level of situation awareness of what was happening in the moment, so rapidly were events overtaking one another.

As an example of how the disruption of command and control at the field army level was beginning to influence the fighting divisions, the *Wiking* Division's *O1* described the confusion that occurred on 23 March when he wrote later in the evening:

> The division had begun assembling it the area of Veszprémfajsz. Strong enemy air activity. The division believed that it would get three to four days' time to collect everyone together. Around noon, General Gille arrived at our division command post and spoke to us about the real situation. The Russians were already north of Veszprém carrying out a wide, circular advance towards the west. At that time, Veszprém was already in Russian hands and his troops there were [already] moving towards the southwest. We were ordered to go immediately with all of our available forces to the area north of Veszprémfajsz into a defensive position. When we got there, we looked for a connection to a unit on our right. Who our left neighbor was, we weren't sure. At 3 p.m., the division command post was moved to a forest ranger's house 8 kilometers southwest of Veszprémfajsz. [84]

The *Wiking* Division could not remain there long because it was in danger of being cut off, so the next morning it was forced to move yet again to a new position further to the west. Gille's only remarks in his notebook for that day read: "*Wiking* Division once more subordinated to the *IV. SS-Pz.Korps*. [We are] constantly withdrawing."[85] That evening, even his own headquarters was forced to displace further to the rear, on this occasion to a new location in the village of Tótvázsony, 8 kilometers southwest of Nemesvámos.

The *6. Armee* was not the only German field army facing a difficult challenge that day. North of Balck's army, the *I. SS-Pz.Korps* of Dietrich's *6. Pz.Armee* was having a hard time holding its ground in the densely wooded and hilly country of the Bakony Forest. Here, the *Hitlerjugend* and *Totenkopf* Divisions, as well as the other half of the *LSSAH* Division, were having to conduct a number of holding actions in the face of strong enemy pressure. The various *Kampfgruppen* sought to carry out their mission of re-establishing a front line, but failed when they were attacked or bypassed by superior enemy forces at numerous locations and compelled to pull back step by step to the west. By the end of the day, the *I. SS-Pz.Korps'* units had finally managed to successfully withdraw into the northern portion of the *Klara* defense line.

On the right flank of the *I. SS-Pz.Korps*, the remaining portion of the *LSSAH* Division, minus Kumm's *Kampfgruppe* (which was still under the control of the *6. Armee*) had the dual mission of preventing the Soviet attack from bypassing Veszprém from the north and preventing the enemy from breaking through the *LSSAH* Division's front lines in the forest region south of the *Hitlerjugend* Division. The key towns of Zirc and Lókút fell after being attacked by several tank-supported infantry regiments. More importantly, the town of Gyulafirátót, 8 kilometers north of Veszprém, fell to Soviet leading units; combined with the loss of Kádárta in the neighboring sector, the northern approaches to Veszprém now lay open and, more ominously, a 10-kilometer-wide gap had been created between the *6. Pz.Armee* and *6. Armee*, a gap that both armies would strive to close in vain during the next 48 hours.

To the north of Priess's corps, in the area between Kisber and the bridgehead at Komorn defended by elements of the *8. Armee*, the leading elements of the Soviet 46th Army continued their attacks against the *6. Pz.Armee* front line that had been recently strengthened by the arrival of all of the *II. SS-Pz.Korps* (except the *Hohenstaufen* Division) and *XLIII. Armee-Korps*. Although Soviet troops attacked at multiple points using powerful, tank-supported infantry forces, they were thrown back, with the exception of a few locally isolated instances, by the counterattacks of the *6. Pz.Div.*, the *Das Reich* Division, and the *356. Inf.Div.* During the course of the fighting, five enemy tanks were destroyed, though more were arriving to make another attempt the following day.

On that same day in the Hungarian *3. Armee* bridgehead at Gran, both the *96.* and *711. Inf.Div.* and two brigades (*Gren.Brig. 92* and *SS-K.Gr. Ameiser*) were involved in heavy defensive fighting against enemy troops attacking from the south and east. Heszlényi's army was now beginning to experience significant shortages of supplies, especially ammunition, which contributed to its inability to prevent Soviet forces from splitting the bridgehead in two. The *711. Inf.Div.*, located on the eastern side of the bridgehead, received the order that day to begin attacking towards the northwest to reconnect the two sections of the bridgehead before it was too late.

That afternoon, the Hungarian *3. Armee* was finally attached to the *8. Armee*, the most commonsense decision that *H.Gr. Süd* had made in several days. That made one less crisis for Sepp Dietrich to worry about.[86] That day, Hitler had finally granted permission for the troops south of the Danube to be evacuated. Ferrying operations were ordered by the *8. Armee* to begin evacuating troops trapped on the southern bank of the river that evening, the only escape route for the *96.* and *711. Inf.Div.*, *Gren.Brig. (mot.) 92*, and *SS-K.Gr. Ameiser*, as well as a few thousand survivors of the Hungarian *23. Inf.Div.* Due to the hasty evacuation order, which should have been issued two days earlier, much of the army's heavy equipment would have to be left behind.

The prevalence of Soviet air power was frequently remarked upon in German reports that day, which made any movement in daylight hours, especially by road, very hazardous, particularly along the northern shoreline of Lake Balaton. The *Luftwaffe's* ability to generate enough sorties to keep up with the Red Air Force was beginning to show signs of faltering, though it was still able to launch a few interceptor missions on that day against Soviet ground-attack aircraft active over Lake Balaton and in the Kisber–Nagyigmánd area. In order to resupply the *I. Kav. Korps* with some of the ammunition it badly needed during the night of 22/23 March, 10 Ju-52s flew aerial resupply missions that managed to deliver 9 tons of munitions, though no fuel, which was needed just as badly.[87]

Despite the worsening fuel shortage, German bureaucratic obstinacy could still prevail. During the evacuation of Veszprém on 23 March, supplies that could not be removed in time were ordered to be destroyed to prevent them from falling into enemy hands, although many units were already experiencing severe shortages. One regimental commander of the *Hohenstaufen* Division, *Ostubaf.* Eberhardt Telkamp, was notified that a large amount of gasoline was about to be destroyed, so he hurried to the city before it was too late. Finding the fuel dump already prepared for demolition, he demanded that the quartermaster officer in charge allow him to take it for the division, but was told that the order had already been given to blow it up. Drawing his pistol, Telkamp forced the officer at gunpoint to issue it anyway. The fuel thus obtained was sufficient for the *Hohenstaufen* Division to continue operating for several more days, with enough left over to help supply the neighboring division. Consequently, the *Hohenstaufen* was able to save most of its vehicles, while the other divisions in the *I. Kav.Korps* were not.[88]

The *H.Gr. Süd* commander's intentions for the next day, 24 March, were spelled out in short and succinct terms, and few of them were realistically achievable, given the condition of most of the units. Balck's *6. Armee* was ordered to build a new continuous front line that tied in with the right flank of the *6. Pz.Armee*, while simultaneously reorganizing its shattered and splintered units and holding on to the northern shore of Lake Balaton. Dietrich's army was tasked with holding its current *HKL*, closing the gap in the Bakony Forest between the *I.* and *II. SS-Pz.Korps*, and reinforcing the right wing of the army, where it was also ordered to re-establish its connection to the left wing of the *6. Armee*.

That night, the *IV. SS-Pz.Korps* now had more or less two tank divisions (*3. Pz.Div.* and the *Wiking* Division) subordinated to it. However, each one was little more than a brigade in strength, and in the case of the *Wiking* Division, had lost most of its armored fighting vehicles during its escape from Stuhlweissenburg. The *Div.K.Gr. LSSAH* was operating independently to the left (or north) of Gille's corps, and was still under the direct control of Balck's *6. Armee* headquarters. The *Hohenstaufen* Division was subordinated that same day to Harteneck's *I. Kav.Korps*, which had lost almost all of its armor during its narrow escape. The *Wiking* Division's commander reported that he had only one tank still operational. The few armored vehicles in the repair shops in Veszprém from *SS-Pz.Rgt. 5* were evacuated in time before the city fell, but Darges's regiment still needed time for its mechanics to get them running again. All three divisions were in dire need of a rest halt and were finding basic necessities such as fuel and ammunition in short supply.

This day, 23 March, marked the end of a chapter in the history of the *IV. SS-Pz. Korps*. The beginning of the month had found the corps occupying static defensive positions arrayed between Stuhlweissenburg and the Vértes foothills. It had then initially withstood a powerful Soviet attack on 16 March, heralding the beginning of the Red Army's long-awaited Vienna Operation. After valiantly holding its positions for two days, its divisions were finally forced to give way in the face of an irresistible attack by two powerful Soviet field armies with over 150,000 men. After the corps was split in two by the enemy assault, the *Totenkopf* Division was splintered and forced westwards and northwestwards into the Bakony Forest, while half of the *Wiking* Division was ordered into Stuhlweissenburg, a virtual death trap. The Hungarian *2. Pz.Div.*, which faced the brunt of the Soviet attack, had virtually ceased to exist as an organized unit.

Although Gille had attempted to reconstruct a coherent front line that was to include both of his SS divisions (the Hungarian *2. Pz.Div.* had been pushed completely out of the corps' sector), the enlargement of the Soviet attack on 19/20 March, signified by the commitment of Kravchenko's 6th Guards Tank Army, separated the two divisions forever, as the main body of the *Totenkopf* Division was subordinated to the *6. Pz.Armee* from 21 March until the end of the war. Except for a few fragments of the division, primarily stragglers from the *Eicke* Regiment and a few guns from *SS-Pz.Art.Rgt. 3* that had "drifted" into the *IV. SS-Pz.Korps'* defensive sector between 21 and 23 March, the powerful one-two punch combination of the *Totenkopf* and *Wiking* Divisions was no more.[89]

Brigadeführer Becker's division had been an integral part of Gille's corps since the end of July 1944 and was instrumental in helping the *IV. SS-Pz.Korps* achieve battlefield successes in Poland during the defense of Warsaw and during *Unternehmen Konrad I–III*. Its aggressive spirit, exemplified by the performance of its tough soldiers and equally tough commanders, would be sorely missed. Its official departure from the *IV. SS-Pz.Korps'* order of battle during the evening of 21/22 March and its subsequent subordination to the *I. SS-Pz.Korps* was not accompanied by a proclamation or a farewell message from Gille to the men of Becker's division; there had been simply no time for that.

Most of the *Wiking* Division that was trapped in Stuhlweissenburg only survived because Hack, the city's *Kampfkommandant*, disobeyed a direct order from the *Führer* at the urging of Gille and ordered his troops to break out. Caught up in the collapse of the *6. Armee* front line on 22/23 March, the *IV. SS-Pz.Korps*—along with the *Wiking*, *Hohenstaufen* and *3. Panzer* Divisions—managed to carry out a fighting retreat to a new defensive line, the so-called *Klarastellung*. How long this line would hold was an open question; but after 23 March, it had become increasingly evident that the *6. Armee* and *6. Pz.Armee* might not be able to reconnect their forces in time to carry out a coordinated defense of what was left of Hungary. The complete dissolution of the *IV. SS-Pz.Korps* would gradually unfold during the next 45 days, though at one point it seemed that this process would be reversed. Still, 8 May 1945 seemed like a lifetime away from the perspective of 23 March.

CHAPTER 5

The Retreat from Hungary 24–29 March 1945

By midnight on 23 March, it had become abundantly clear that the German Armed Forces were no longer in control of the situation between Lake Balaton and the Danube. The same thing could also be said about any of the Third Reich's other remaining battlefronts, with perhaps the exception of northern Italy and Norway; but nowhere else was the confusion among the higher ranks and disorganization of the units on the ground as bad as they were within *H.Gr. Süd* on that day. And all of this was taking place before the Red Army had even launched the second phase of its Vienna Operation.

In the west, the Rhine River bridge at Remagen had fallen into American hands on 12 March and the Mosel had been crossed on 15 March at Coblenz. Meanwhile, in the east, the Heiligenbeil Pocket had been split in two on the same day. Kolberg fell to Soviet forces on 18 March. Soviet armies already stood on the eastern bank of the Oder and had seized a bridgehead at Küstrin. On 23 March, the western Allies launched their largest offensive of the war, when over 300,000 American, British, and Canadian troops crossed the Rhine at Xanten while carrying out the largest airborne operation of World War II. On that same day, Soviet troops began fighting their way into Danzig.

Meanwhile, between 6 and 15 March, the largest and most powerful grouping of German armies still remaining in the Third Reich's order of battle had been allowed to fritter away its last remaining reserves in a series of pointless attacks under the worst terrain and weather conditions against an enemy force that had anticipated the attack and prepared a thoroughly integrated defence to counter it. After giving its opponent 10 days to wear himself out, the Red Army then initiated an even more powerful operation of its own designed to do nothing less than conclude the war in southeastern Europe by destroying all German armies remaining between Budapest and Vienna.

How these two great German armies—Hermann Balck's *6. Armee* and Sepp Dietrich's *6. Pz.Armee*—were improperly used and the command decisions that squandered their military potential has been described in the previous chapters;

what remained after 23 March was a week-long period in which their remnants vainly sought to halt or delay the Soviet onslaught and keep their enemy as far away as possible from the Reich's borders. After the collapse of the *6. Armee* between 22 and 23 March, this was no longer possible because the integrity of the front line between the Danube and Lake Balaton had been irrecoverably disrupted.

The consequences of the poorly conceived and untimely decisions made by the *OKH, H.Gr. Süd,* and its two central armies between 16 and 23 March could no longer be made good. The period that followed, beginning on 24 March, would begin the last, saddest phase of the war in southeastern Europe from a German perspective. During this period, the *IV. SS-Pz.Korps* would be swept up in an irresistible tide that would transport it from the northern shores of Lake Balaton and deposit it in the area southwest of Vienna within the relatively brief period of seven days, during which the limits of its human endurance and fighting spirit would be sorely tested.

Every organized effort by *H.Gr. Süd* to block the initial phase of the Red Army's Vienna Operation between 16 and 23 March had failed; every attempt to create a working command and control relationship between the army group, and its *6. Armee* and *6. Pz.Armee* had been unsuccessful. Not only were the ways and means that *H.Gr. Süd* required to accomplish its overly ambitious objectives inadequate, but at nearly every step of the way, *OKH* and *H.Gr. Süd* headquarters' red tape, meddling by the commander of the *6. Armee,* and Hitler's own penchant for delaying necessary decisions had resulted in slow and sluggish responses to a rapidly evolving situation when speed and decisiveness were required. As a result, the Third Ukrainian Front was able to repeatedly operate within *H.Gr. Süd*'s decision-making cycle, even though Marshal Tolbukhin was not a particularly gifted operational commander, and inflict a series of devastating defeats on some of the *Wehrmacht* and *Waffen-SS*'s proudest formations.

The *IV. SS-Pz.Korps* was one of these formations. Throughout the three attempts to relieve Budapest, it had performed well, very nearly reaching Budapest on three separate occasions before it was recalled at the brink of success each time. During the defensive phase lasting from 28 January to 17 March, it had also fought extremely well, inflicting casualties on the enemy much greater than its own forces had suffered. The collapse of its front on 18 March, though no fault of its own, had been followed by a series of reverses, until by 23 March, the several divisions subordinated to it had been reduced to a shadow of their former strength.

As a corps commander operating within the framework of an army group, *Obergruppenführer* Gille had very little latitude in regards to his decision-making authority. Under the mistrustful and authoritarian command of *General der Panzertruppe* Balck, the remaining records indicate that Gille had rarely been asked for his thoughts or advice on how best to accomplish the field army's objectives. By this point in the campaign, there seems to have been hardly anyone on the staff of the *6. Armee* willing to lend a sympathetic ear to Gille or to appraise the *Waffen-SS*'s performance objectively.

On several occasions, Balck had unsuccessfully attempted through *OKH* channels to have both Gille and Schönfelder relieved for incompetence, but each time *Generaloberst* Guderian had demurred, referring the matter to Heinrich Himmler, the only one besides Hitler who had disciplinary authority over the SS. Now that Gille's corps had been once again subordinated to the *6. Armee* on 22 March, after a four-day reprieve under Sepp Dietrich's *6. Pz.Armee*, Gille and his staff could expect nothing but the same unfair treatment until the war's end. In his memoirs, Balck boasted of having been given "disciplinary authority" over *Waffen-SS* commanders or staff officers who were subordinated to his *6. Armee*, including Gille, but if he took any disciplinary action against any of them, there is nothing in the official *H.Gr. Süd* or *Waffen-SS* personnel records to indicate that he had done so.[1] His account is also refuted on this score by the *Ia* of the *6. Pz.Armee*, Maier, who stated that while Balck may have wished to institute some form of punishment against Gille, Stadler, Kumm, *et al.*, he never actually carried through on any of his threats.[2]

Balck's chief of staff, *Generalmajor* Gaedke, loathed the *Waffen-SS* and everything it stood for, and harboured intense personal prejudices against Gille and his chief of staff, *Obersturmbannführer* Schönfelder, dating back to the time they had worked together during the battle of the Cherkassy Pocket. In regards to the growing problem with desertion and straggling within the *6. Armee*, Gaedke found a ready-made scapegoat, remarking that "the discipline and the will to fight had declined even more so in the SS units than in the army divisions," which may have been the ultimate accusation that anyone in such a position as his could have made.[3]

Saturday, 24 March marked the day when the front line north of Lake Balaton was torn asunder. The advance towards Márkó by the V Guards Tank Corps on 23 March had effectively sundered the physical connection between the *6. Armee* and *6. Pz.Armee*. At that point, the only logical move that Wöhler could order to save his armies was to direct them to fall back beyond Lake Balaton to a more defensible line within their capabilities, but Hitler once again interfered by issuing a *Führerbefehl* that ordered that the northern shore of the lake was to be held at all costs.[4] The reason given was that Hitler believed giving it up would uncover the left flank of the *2. Pz.Armee* located southwest of the lake and, by extension, leave the critically important Nagykanizsa oil fields vulnerable to attack. Because of Hitler's obstinacy and single-minded focus on defending everywhere, both armies north of Lake Balaton were being forced into an impossible position, resulting in what nearly everyone at the time predicted would happen—the gap between the armies would continue to grow to the point where it would become nearly impossible for them to carry out any kind of unified defence at the operational level (see Map 6).

The remaining few weeks of the *IV. SS-Pz.Korps*' history can be outlined in four separate phases. The first, lasting from 24–29 March, concerns its participation in the

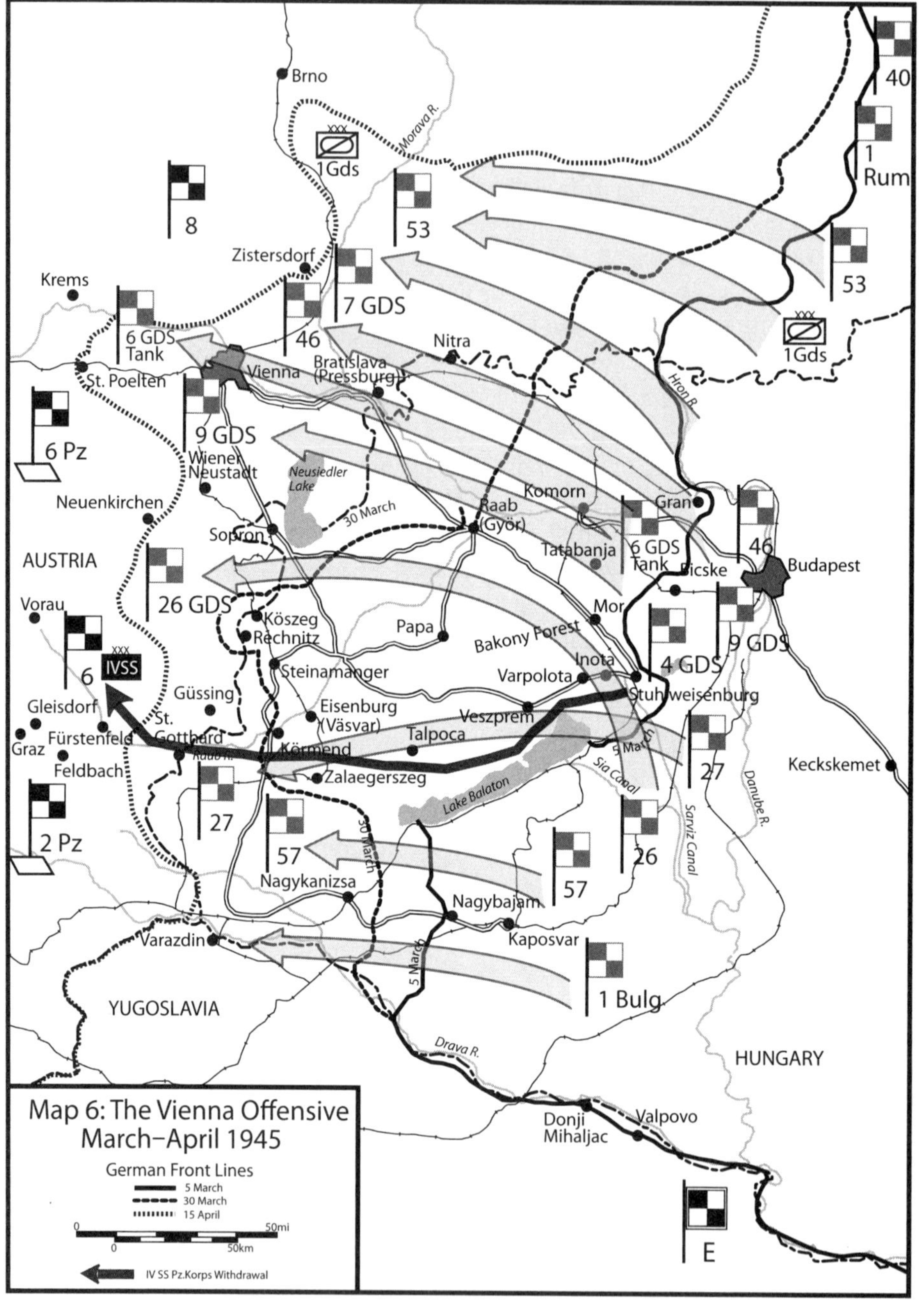
Brno
Morava R.
1Gds
8
53
Zistersdorf
7 GDS
Krems
6 GDS
Tank
46
Nitra
St. Poelten
Vienna
Bratislava
(Pressburg)
Hron R.
1Gds
40
1 Rum
53
6 Pz
9 GDS
Wiener
Neustadt
Neusiedler
Lake
30 March
Komorn
Raab
(Györ)
Gran
Neuenkirchen
Sopron
Tatabanja
6 GDS
Tank
Bicske
46
Budapest
AUSTRIA
26 GDS
Köszeg
Rechnitz
Papa
Bakony Forest
Inota
Varpolota
4 GDS
9 GDS
Vorau
6 IVSS
Steinamanger
Stuhlweisenburg
Mor
Gleisdorf
Güssing
Eisenburg
(Väsvar)
Veszprem
Talpoca
St.
Gotthard
Raab R.
Körmend
5 March
Sia Canal
27
Sarviz Canal
Keckskemet
Graz
Fürstenfeld
Feldbach
Zalaegerszeg
Lake Balaton
Danube R.
2 Pz
27
26
30 March
57
57
Nagykanizsa
Nagybajam
Kaposvar
Varazdin
5 March
1 Bulg.
YUGOSLAVIA
Drava R.
HUNGARY
Donji
Mihaljac
Valpovo
Map 6: The Vienna Offensive
March–April 1945
German Front Lines
5 March
30 March
15 April
0   50mi
0   50km
E
IV SS Pz.Korps Withdrawal

attempt by *H.Gr. Süd* to re-establish a defensible front line within Hungary. During this phase, Gille's corps, along with the neighbouring corps of Balck's *6. Armee*, attempted to carry out "normal" operations within the parameters of a traditional defense using divisions that still retained a semblance of tactical integrity and combat power. The second phase, from 30 March to 17 April, can be characterized by the corps' participation in a series of holding actions as it withdrew towards the *Reichsschutzstellung* and the area south of Fürstenfeld southwest of Vienna, ending with the re-establishment of a cohesive front line in southern Austria. The third phase covers the period from 18 April until the capitulation of the *Wehrmacht* on 9 May, when the *IV. SS-Pz.Korps* and hundreds of other German units sought the safety of the demarcation line along the Enns River established by the western Allies. The fourth and final phase consists of the corps' surrender, its movement to POW camps, and attempts by its members to return home and restore a semblance of normality to their lives in postwar Germany.

On the morning of 24 March, this all seemed so far away. While many officers, regardless of whether they were members of the *Waffen-SS* or the *Wehrmacht*, had begun to realize that Germany, in fact, had lost the war, a sizeable number of the enlisted rank and file still believed that the war was winnable, even if it meant that Hitler might have to make peace with the western Allies in order to continue prosecuting the war against the Soviet Union. Although *H.Gr. Süd* had been unable to regain control of the situation east, north, and south of Lake Balaton, the *Wehrmacht* had heretofore always been able to set things right by deploying reserves from the homeland or by clever strategies employed by front-line generals such as Sepp Dietrich and Hermann Balck, about whom legends were spun. But there were no more reserves and both generals had run out of ideas as well as time.

There would be no reprieve that day. Paradoxically, Saturday, 24 March would be the warmest day of the season so far, with temperatures reaching a comfortable high of 68 degrees Fahrenheit (20 degrees Centigrade) and sunny, clear skies. It would have been a beautiful day for nature seekers or strolling along the banks of the Danube. However, the hundreds of thousands of troops of the Second and Third Ukrainian Fronts were not interested in viewing the delights of spring, but were focused instead on the annihilation of the hated Fascists. The more they killed that day, and the faster they went about it, meant another kilometer closer to Vienna and another day closer to returning home. Tolbukhin's men were not in a sentimental mood.

Nor were the men of Balck's *6. Armee* or Dietrich's *6. Pz.Armee*, who were focused upon personal survival or fighting to the last bullet, with every emotion between the two extremes exerting itself upon their actions in one way or another. The *H.Gr. Süd* daily report for 24 March began with:

> The defensive battle between Lake Balaton and the Danube continued today with unabated intensity. Despite the bitter defence of our divisions, which have been involved in unceasing offensive and defensive battles since 6 March, the enemy once again managed to penetrate

and divide our main defense line along a 40 kilometer wide gap paralleling both sides of the Veszprém–Devecser highway … Our splintered strongpoints and *Kampfgruppen*, though separated, continued to fight under the leadership of their division and corps staffs and managed to delay and stop the enemy's advance through the Bakony Forest and towards the west. Tank-led enemy spearheads reached the westward exists of the forested mountains [i.e., the Bakony Forest] southeast of Papa.[5]

This report was not strictly true, for while *H.Gr. Süd*'s troops had delayed the Soviet advance through the Bakony Forest, they had been unable to stop it, lacking as they did the troops, weapons, and time needed to set up any kind of credible defense.

Within the *6. Armee*, the *I. Kav.Korps* and *IV. SS-Pz.Korps* were involved in heavy defensive fighting that day, while the *III. Pz.Korps* headquarters had been withdrawn behind the front to restore some semblance of order to the army's *Rückwärtiges Gebiet* (rear area), round up stragglers, and supervise the construction of new defense lines. At that time, Breith only had the *1. Pz.Div.* under his corps headquarters' control, which was being reassembled as the *6. Armee*'s emergency reserve, minus a *Kampfgruppe* fighting with the *I. Kav.Korps*.

In the *I. Kav.Korps*' sector on 24 March, Soviet mechanized formations from the 27th Army attacked Harteneck's weakened forces that morning along their newly occupied defense line in the *Klarastellung*, 2 kilometers north-northeast of Vörösbereny–southwest of Szentkirályszabadja, where the *3.* and *4. Kav.Div.*, the *23. Pz.Div.*, as well as *K.Gr. Bradel* from the *1. Pz.Div.* were pushed back 1 kilometer north of the line between Felsőörs and the northern edge of Veszprém.[6]

In the sector defended by Gille's *IV. SS-Pz.Korps*, consisting on that day of the *Wiking*, *Hohenstaufen* and *3. Panzer* Divisions, as well as a battalion-sized element composed of stragglers from the *Totenkopf* Division (*Div.K.Gr. LSSAH* remained under the direct control of *6. Armee*), a number of mechanized elements of the 26th Army likewise continued their attacks west of Veszprém against the corps' newly established defense line and were able to throw back Gille's forces several kilometers to the line running from the eastern edge of Hidegkút to a point 4 kilometers west of Nemesvámos.[7]

Within the *Wiking* Division, the *Panzergrenadier* battalions of the *Germania* and *Westland* Regiments were once again combined within each regiment to form a single *Kampfbataillon*, each now travelling on foot since they had been forced to abandon most of their troops carriers due to lack of fuel. The only truly mechanized formation left within the division was *SS-Pz.Aufkl.Abt. 5*, now commanded by *Stubaf.* Fritz Vogt, who had taken over after its previous commander, *Stubaf.* Heinz Wagner, had been wounded in action. Most of the division's remaining *SPW*s and armored cars had been grouped under his command, and with the addition of a number of new replacements, combined with Vogt's legendary zeal, it had become the division's only full-strength and combat-effective tactical unit.[8] What few tanks and assault guns that had been saved were undergoing repairs in a hurried effort to get as many running as quickly as possible.

North of this line, on the corps' far left flank, Soviet tank forces pushed past *Div.K.Gr. LSSAH*, which was defending in the vicinity of the towns of Márkó and Szentgál, and advanced as far as Úrkút, completely bypassing the *IV. SS-Pz.Korps'* left flank to the north in the process.[9] The last report received that evening stated that this same Soviet force had continued attacking towards the west and was last reported nearing the town of Padragkút far to the rear of Gille's sector. Whether the 27th Army was operating in concert with the adjacent 6th Guards Tank Army and 26th Army could not be determined, but as a result of the fighting that day, the gap between the two German armies had increased to a width of 40 kilometers, as previously mentioned.

Incidentally, Wöhler and von Grolman, as well as Dietrich, had foreseen the danger of this occurring several days before it happened, and had repeatedly requested *OKH* permission to transfer the still-powerful *16. SS-Pz.Gren.Div. Reichsführer-SS* (*RFSS*) from *2. Pz.Armee* to either *6. Pz.Armee* or *6. Armee*. Because Hitler believed it was needed as a reserve to safeguard the oil fields at Nagykanizsa, he denied their request. The best that Guderian could get Hitler to agree upon was to allow the transfer of the *1. Volks-Geb.Div.* from *2. Pz.Armee* and the *232. Pz.Div.* (a tank training division) from *8. Armee*, where it had been fighting in Slovakia.

The first elements of the nearly full-strength mountain division would begin entraining the following day, with the bulk of its combat elements scheduled to arrive by the night of 24/25 March. However, assigning the mission of closing a 40-kilometer-wide gap created by a guards tank army to a "light" mountain division and an understrength, recently mobilized tank training division consisting of only 2,452 men and five armored fighting vehicles (including one *Pz. IV*) was nothing less than a "Hail Mary" gambit, but that was the best that *H.Gr. Süd* could do from within its own limited resources.[10]

Although it was being slowly separated from its neighbor to the south, and was consequently less important to the fate of the *IV. SS-Pz.Korps*, the contributions of the *6. Pz.Armee* towards the defense of Hungary and the withdrawal to Austria deserves brief mention. By 24 March, it had become increasingly evident that Dietrich's army was fighting two separate battles, both of which were of decisive importance. The first and most important for the reader's standpoint was the army's battle in the Bakony Forest on its right wing, where the *I. SS-Pz.Korps* and its three understrength divisions (*1.*, *3.*, and *12. SS-Panzer* Divisions) were still fighting to prevent a deep penetration by the 6th Guards Tank Army.

Priess's corps was having little luck accomplishing this mission, but his troops had at least managed to slow down the Soviet advance after destroying a number of Kravchenko's tanks. On the corps' far right, the other battlegroup from the *1. SS-Pz.Div. LSSAH*, formed around its *SS-Pz.Gren.Rgt. 2*, was trying to maintain contact with its sister regiment operating under the control of the neighboring *6. Armee*, but as has been shown, this was becoming more and more of a fool's errand as long as Balck continued his refusal to release *Div.K.Gr. LSSAH*. The best that Otto Kumm, the division commander, could do in this case was to shuttle from one command post to the other, across the boundary between the *6. Armee* and *6. Pz.Armee*, in an effort to coordinate the actions of his division. It was certainly a less-than-ideal way to fight a war.[11]

On its left wing, on the wide-open Hungarian *Puszta* between Komorn and the northern edge of the Bakony Forest, the *6. Pz.Armee's II. SS-Pz.Korps* and *XLIII. Armee-Korps* were fighting to prevent a breakthrough by the 46th Army, which was supported by at least one tank or mechanized corps, oriented towards Raab and Komorn. Working in conjunction with *Generalmajor* Pape's *Kampfgruppe* from *Pz.Div. FHH* in Komorn, which had been subordinated to the newly arrived *IV.Pz. Korps FHH* headquarters responsible for defending the key city, Dietrich's forces had been enjoying moderate success in slowing or in some cases stopping the Soviet advance, using his three divisions and several smaller German and Hungarian splinter units to good advantage.

Between these two corps operating in the center and left of Dietrich's army, his headquarters claimed the destruction of 32 enemy tanks between 20 and 24 March. The only infantry division in the area, the *356. Inf.Div.*, had suffered heavy losses and was at less than 25 percent strength, so Bittrich's SS corps would need additional reinforcements soon. The best that Dietrich could offer to make up for the shortage of infantry was to attach up to 1,300 new SS recruits, courtesy of the *Kriegsmarine*, to the *Das Reich* Division, but this would hardly help improve its combat power.[12] Although many of the *6. Pz.Armee's* battalions had been reduced to a *Kampfstärke* of less than 100 men, additional training was needed before these inexperienced replacements could be committed to an ongoing battle.

On 24 March, the *6. Pz.Armee* situation report painted a very negative picture. North of Veszprém in the Bakony Forest, its *I. SS-Pz.Korps* was involved that day in establishing a line of blocking positions using every available combat unit, including *Alarm* units from the rear area, in order to buy time until the arrival of *Gen.Lt.* August Wittmann's *1. Volks-Geb.Div.* the following day. The severity of the fighting between 22 and 24 March can be gauged by the fact that *Gruf.* Hermann Preiss's *I. SS-Pz.Korps* claimed the destruction of 78 enemy tanks.[13] Between Bakonyszentlászló and the Danube to the north of Priess's corps, elements of the 46th Army with powerful infantry forces reinforced by tanks attacked the defense sector of Bittrich's *II. SS-Pz.Korps* southwest of Kisber, north of Kisber, and in the *XLIII. Armee-Korps* area between Nagyigmánd and the Komorn. That day, renewed Soviet efforts to break through this hastily erected German defense line were unsuccessful, testimony to the ferocity of the fighting and the determination of the German and Hungarian troops to prevent their opponent from doing so.

Activity by the Red Air Force above the *6. Pz.Armee* and *6. Armee* was described as heavy, with most of it concentrated against the *6. Pz.Armee*, especially in the

Veszprém area along the boundary between both armies and Zirc. *Luftflotte 4* reported that shortages of aviation fuel had severely limited its ability to generate the requested number of sorties, and it was able to launch only 140 aircraft during the day, although its ground-attack squadrons claimed to have destroyed four Soviet tanks. Both sides had resumed flying a number of low-, mid-, and high-altitude reconnaissance missions to reveal each other's troop dispositions and intentions.

By 23 March, German intelligence agencies had been able to positively identify the 26th, 27th, and 46th Armies, the 4th and 9th Guards Armies, and the 6th Guards Tank Army, along with two additional mechanized or tank corps in the south and two in the north. While these forces were more than sufficient to push *H.Gr. Süd* completely out of Hungary, an equally ominous enemy concentration was revealing itself on the northern side of the Danube. East of the Gran River, German intelligence had detected preparations that indicated that the Second Ukrainian Front and its 7th Guards Army and 53rd Army, with at least 10–15 rifle divisions, two tank or mechanized corps, a Romanian Army and the I Guards Cavalry-Mechanized Group (formerly known as Cavalry Corps Pliyev), were being positioned for a major offensive. Indications seemed to show that its probable direction of attack would be westwards over the Gran River, with its main assault originating from the Léva area (modern-day Levice). Unfortunately, *Generalmajor* Gehlen's *Fremde Heere Ost* could not predict the exact date the offensive would begin, but thought it was possible any time after 24 March.[14] They were not far off the mark in their estimate, as events would demonstrate.

Intentions for the next day, 25 March, were formalistic; Balck's *6. Armee* was directed to order the *I. Kav.Korps* with its four greatly understrength divisions (*3. and 4. Kav.Div.*, *23. Pz.Div.*, and *Hohenstaufen* Division) to establish another line of resistance to replace the one it had been forced to abandon earlier in the day. The new one would be located 2 kilometers northeast of a line running (south to north) from Balatonfüred–Hidegkút–4 kilometers west of Nemesvámos. Apparently, the line held by the *IV. SS-Pz.Korps* on the army's left wing along the *Klarastellung* did not require any further significant adjustment on that day.

As a corps commander charged with the heavy responsibility of holding the *6. Armee's* left flank, Gille did not have much to work with. On that day, he still had under his control the shattered *Wiking* Division and *3. Pz.Div.*, both of which had narrowly escaped destruction during the breakout from Stuhlweissenburg and the harrowing passage through the corridor held open at one end by the *1. Pz.Div.* and by the *Hohenstaufen* Division at the other. Both Ullrich's and Söth's divisions had lost most of their armor, as well as a large amount of their heavy weapons and communications equipment, either by enemy action or lack of fuel.

The disruption of the corps' communication networks due to the near-daily need to withdraw to the west meant both division commanders were having difficulty in keeping Gille abreast of what was happening either by radio or landline communication. While Gille could keep in contact with their division command posts and relay orders using couriers, he still attempted his daily practice of visiting the command posts of his divisions, despite the considerable danger to his person this entailed. His corps staff were doing their utmost to carry out their normal duties, but the constant interruptions took a toll on their efficiency. At the division level, the situation was probably much worse.

By the evening of 24 March, *Brigadeführer* Kumm's *Div.K.Gr. LSSAH* had begun to drift out of the *6. Armee* area of operations, not willingly, but in adherence to its orders as it was pushed to the northwest by the attacking Soviet spearheads. The next morning found it in Kislőd, where it blocked the major east–west highway running through the Bakony Forest.[15] Otherwise, it was isolated from the rest of the *LSSAH* nearly 20 kilometers away on its left, and was an equal distance from the *3. Pz.Div.* of the *IV. SS-Pz.Korps* on the right. It was the only thing that tied together the inner flanks of both neighboring armies, but in reality, it amounted to little more than an operational "fig leaf."

Balck continued complaining about the *Waffen-SS* units under his command, although when Wöhler once again directed him to release the *Hohenstaufen* Division and *Div.K.Gr. LSSAH* to the *6. Pz.Armee*, Balck refused, perhaps in recognition of their true value as combat troops despite the amount of negative criticism he had levied against both division commanders.[16] Ironically, the *1. Pz.Div.* had been withdrawn behind the front on 23 March to reorganize and serve as the *6. Armee* reserve, so technically Balck could have released Kumm's battlegroup and replaced it with Thünert's division had he chosen to do so.[17] But to be fair, both armies lacked enough troops to hold the line; without a continuous front, Soviet spearheads would continue finding gaps to exploit to their numerical advantage, which they seemed to do with unerring accuracy.

The army group commander and the commanders of the *6. Armee* and *6. Pz.Armee* all continued to complain about the shortage of infantry needed to defend the ever-widening front line, as well as the increasing number of stragglers they were encountering on the roads during their daily visits to their corps. Many of these men from the 14 German divisions of the *6. Armee* and *6. Pz.Armee* (of which six were *Waffen-SS*) had been separated from their units during the confused fighting of the past four days and were simply trying to make their way back to their *alte Haufen* (old gang) along the crowded roads as best they could. A small number of men were most likely shirking their duty, as soldiers have done in nearly every army in any war throughout history, but almost everyone separated from his unit was increasingly being considered as a *Drückeberger* by the army group commander, who had ordered that they were to be "dealt with ruthlessly."[18]

Wöhler had already ordered all four of his field armies to establish stringent anti-straggler control measures on 23 March, which began to show results, though how willing a soldier was to continue fighting after being press-ganged into an *ad hoc* emergency formation was a question best not asked. How much the phenomenon of straggling continued to weigh on Wöhler's mind is exemplified by an order issued by his headquarters in the early morning of 28 March, five days after his first order concerning the subject:

> I have once again noticed that there are an intolerable number of stragglers in the rear area. These "stragglers" are cowards and *Drückeberger*, and thus war criminals, who do not deserve any protection because they let their comrades bear the hardships of the fight alone. Those who are separated from their units during the fighting must report immediately to the first fighting unit he encounters. Finding them is not difficult. The sound of battle is the safest signpost. I therefore command:
>
> Those who fail to report immediately to the nearest unit and are apprehended will be tried and shot after a summary court. In the same way, all those who are separated from their unit during the fighting without being able to prove their exact whereabouts are to be dealt with harshly. Whoever does not fight due to cowardice will die in disgrace!
>
> Those leaders who, out of convenience or carelessness, fail to discourage straggling are to be dealt with accordingly. This already includes those who provide inadequate support to the responsible disciplinary authorities.
>
> The above order will be announced to the troops immediately.
>
> Details for the organizations of the Wehrmacht responsible for order in the rear areas will be issued later by their commanders.[19]

How many men were subsequently apprehended and given roadside drumhead courts martial are unknown; the number found guilty of desertion and executed on the spot are also unknown, though one report states that as many as 500 men had been executed in the *H.Gr. Süd* area of operations by 3 April.[20] On account of these harsh measures, or in spite of them, it appears that the straggler problem for *H.Gr. Süd* temporarily abated.

Wöhler even meddled in the personnel administrative affairs of the *6. Pz.Armee*, when he attempted on 24 March to instruct Sepp Dietrich how to make the best use of his replacements to bring his units up to strength. In a message sent that day to the *OKH* operations section, Wöhler informed Guderian and his staff that he was aware that Dietrich's army had received 6,000 untrained *Kriegsmarine* and *Luftwaffe* replacements, sent by the *SS-FHA* as a *Führerzuweisung* (an allocation of replacement troops authorized by Hitler) to the *6. Pz.Armee* when it first arrived in Hungary. These men were intended to replace some of the losses the *I.* and *II. SS-Pz.Korps* had incurred during the costly Ardennes offensive. In addition to these men, Wöhler told Guderian that the *SS-FHA* had informed him that four more *Marsch* battalions (comprised of replacement personnel) were "in transit" from Germany with 2,000–3,000 men each, with an unspecified arrival date. The *IV. SS-Pz.Korps* was supposed to receive its share of replacements from this large manpower pool, though how many of them it eventually received by the end of the war is unknown.

To Wöhler, it must have appeared that this large number of replacements would immediately solve Dietrich's manpower shortage and thus end his (and Balck's) complaining, though it should have been obvious to anyone that most of these troops were barely trained recruits and not a genuine addition to *Waffen-SS* combat power in Hungary without a period of additional instruction. The *H. Gr. Süd* commander was also tracking the movement of 2,190 older members of the *Ordnungspolizei* (rear-area paramilitary police) who were being sent to augment Dietrich's army. In his message, Wöhler told the *OKH* that he had directed Dietrich to use these policemen as individual replacements in his army's administrative and logistics units, allowing him to free up younger SS men for service at the front. As if this were not enough, Wöhler mentioned to Guderian that 700 stragglers had been reportedly apprehended in the *6. Pz.Armee* area of operations on 23 March alone, but due to his harsh anti-straggler control measures that he had instituted that same day, that number had shrunk to a mere 60 men by midday on 24 March. Whether these men were from the *Waffen-SS* was not mentioned, but the tone of his message inferred that they were.[21]

Dietrich's dilemma had not gone unnoticed in Berlin. In addition to Wöhler's attempts to assist the *6. Pz.Armee* commander in increasing the number of men available to replenish the *Waffen-SS* fighting units, Hitler also decided to intervene, though typically not in a helpful manner. When informed on 23 March during the middle of his daily *OKW* situation briefing that Dietrich was running low on combat troops in Hungary, the following exchange occurred between Hitler and *Stubaf.* Johannes Göhler, *Gruppenführer* Fegelein's assistant (Fegelein was absent sick that day):

> HITLER: I demand one thing now; that the last man, wherever he may be hidden, be sent immediately to the *Leibstandarte*, to the entire *6. Pz.Armee*. But immediately! Sepp Dietrich is to be informed of that immediately! Right now! If I catch only one man, then God have mercy on him!
>
> GÖHLER: Yes, sir. He has already received a telegram from the *Reichsführer* yesterday; the *Reichsführer* gave [Dietrich] specific orders that the troops strength should not be allowed to decrease under any circumstances.
>
> HITLER: What does "decrease" mean? It means nothing. The last man that the [*6. Pz.Armee*] has must be sent in.
>
> GÖHLER: Yes, sir.[22]

The result of this decree by Hitler was the aforementioned expedited movement of thousands of raw replacements to all *Waffen-SS* units fighting in Hungary. It was to grow to such a state that while thousands of men were being sent immediately to the front, many thousands more were being held back behind the lines in the army rear area until they were needed; neither Priess's nor Bittrich's divisions could absorb that many men so quickly. At least this provided a few lucky individuals an opportunity to undergo further training while they awaited transfer to the front, unlike those unfortunates who were being sent straight into combat as soon as they arrived. The *IV. SS-Pz.Korps* would later receive many of these men during the first weeks of April, once it had withdrawn into Austria when the war was nearly over.

The manpower situation in the SS divisions was not an isolated one, for it affected the troops of the *Heer* units as well. The shortage of infantrymen throughout the *6. Armee* and *6. Pz.Armee* had become so desperate that by 24 March, Wöhler issued another order directing units to comb through their "trains elements, logistical installation, etc. in order to gain combatants for the front. It is essential to quickly and substantially increase the number of *Panzergrenadiere*, regardless of the current or future structure [of the units], in order to secure the front line."[23] Somehow, it had become an acceptable thought that mechanics, clerks, truck drivers, and *Feldpost* (postal) workers would adequately serve as a *Panzergrenadier* in a pitched battle with little or no infantry training. When such specialists were taken out of their duty assignment in a combat division, it provided a short-term gain, but in the long term, their absence only contributed further to that division's decline. Wöhler knew this, of course, but he was acting under pressure from Berlin to carry out such drastic measures.

Hitler's interference almost always made things worse, especially when he interfered in the duties normally the responsibility of the army group or army commander. One excellent example of his interference was a *Führerbefehl* issued on 24 March that stated: "The *Führer* has again expressly ordered that every soldier who can carry a weapon, whether machine gun, rifle, or *Panzerfaust*, is to be used to halt the enemy breakthrough south of the Danube or in a second position behind the Gran Front north of the Danube to prevent an enemy breakthrough." This *Führerbefehl* was distributed to army groups and field armies, and commanders were instructed to take the appropriate measures to ensure that it was properly carried out.[24]

Essentially, it required each division commander to make sure that every able-bodied soldier in their organization was placed in the front line, regardless of their age, specialty, or degree of training. It was a sign of the increasing sense of desperation being felt throughout Hitler's fading realm, as if untrained masses of men could halt the mechanized Allied juggernaut on both Eastern and Western Fronts with light machine guns and *Panzerfaust*. All of these nonsensical orders would have applied equally to the *IV. SS-Pz.Korps* and could have no other effect than further dampening morale. Evidence indicates, however, that most responsible leaders, while giving it lip service, surreptitiously ignored this order and others like it, knowing that to obey them would quickly lead to the dissolution of their command and an even greater loss of ground.

However, despite his occasional echoing of Hitler's frequently nihilistic orders—that seemed to have been designed to harm the war effort—Wöhler at heart was still a decent human being. Although perhaps not as forceful or dynamic a leader as Balck or Dietrich, he still had a good understanding of what Germany's chances of winning the war were by this point, and had perhaps grown tired of having his sound recommendations and advice ignored ever since taking command of *H.Gr. Süd* four months earlier, or, as in the case of his subordinate Hermann Balck, being constantly circumvented. One recommendation Wöhler sent to *OKH* for Hitler's eyes only on 24 March was probably responsible for him being relieved of command shortly thereafter.

This suggestion, written as a top-secret *Blitz* message meant to be read only by Guderian and Hitler, was unofficially titled "Formation of a Solid Front No Longer Possible," and was worded as follows:

> Enemy pressure between Balaton and the Danube is so strong that a solid front, which must be unconditionally held, cannot be established with friendly forces that are almost entirely exhausted [see *Tagesmeldung* for 23 March 1945]. Even so, that was ordered along with the elimination of local penetrations by offensive operations … At the moment, it is not possible to relieve exhausted divisions, since every soldier is urgently needed as a combatant … The decisive significance of the oil refineries is known to every soldier. Their recapture, as well as any attack by any type of substantial forces, is not possible at this time.[25]

Wöhler must have known that this would be the final straw that would end his career, but at least he had made his thoughts known.

He was informed shortly afterwards that he was to be relieved the following day (25 March), but since his replacement would not be available for assignment for at least another week, Wöhler was asked—and agreed—to stay on until 7 April. While Guderian was probably sympathetic, being a former front-line soldier himself, Hitler was more than willing to sacrifice every able-bodied male of military age, if that was required to keep him in power another day longer. This, despite the fact that Germany was quickly running out of able-bodied men and was already drafting boys of 16 into uniform.

Neither would *Generaloberst* Guderian last much longer in his position. On 27 March, he became involved in a heated argument with Hitler in Berlin about the failure of a counterattack to relieve the fortress at Küstrin conducted by *Gen.d.Inf.* Theodor Busse's *9. Armee* the previous day. Hitler first blamed the lack of artillery ammunition for the attack's failure, then the troops, and finally Busse. At each accusation, an outraged Guderian responded with the facts that proved that none of them were true and that Busse was an honorable man who deserved to be allowed to remain in command.

As the recriminations flew back and forth, Hitler stopped and suddenly dismissed everyone from the room except Guderian and *Generalfeldmarschall* Keitel, the *OKW* chief of staff. Hitler then told Guderian that he needed to take a six-week medical leave, and should depart the very next day. Guderian was replaced by *Gen.d.Inf.* Hans Krebs on 28 March. Krebs had taken over as the head of the *OKH Führungsstab* after his predecessor, Walter Wenck, was sent to serve as Himmler's chief of staff of

H.Gr. Weichsel in February. Although Krebs was an able soldier, he was also a "yes" man and not someone who would question or challenge *der Führer.*[26]

Another development that did not auger well was the scheduled departure the following day of Wöhler's chief of staff, von Grolman, who had been a steady hand and the voice of common sense throughout Wöhler's tenure as commander. He had repeatedly stood up to Balck's bullying behavior and unreasonable demands, having seen through him for the kind of man he really was. What role Balck played in his dismissal is unknown. Von Grolman departed from his old position at the *H.Gr. Süd* headquarters in Esterháza Castle on 25 March to assume command of the *4. Kav.Div.*, viewed by many as a demotion for such a high-ranking officer. He was immediately replaced by *Gen.Lt.* Heinz von Gyldenfeldt, an experienced general staff officer with a good reputation who had recently served as the chief of staff of *H.Gr. F/O.B. Südost.*[27]

Even Hermann Balck was beginning to sense that the end was near. In regards to this period in the wake of his army's close-run escape from the trap south of Lake Balaton and its near destruction between 22 and 25 March, he described the situation in his memoirs as follows:

> After several days of continuous crises the bulk of the *6. Armee* was again out of immediate danger. We had prevented a catastrophe. The *6. Armee* now stood north of Lake Balaton, tied into it with its right flank and with the left flank north of Veszprém. The situation, however, was not a rosy one. Although the *6. Armee* was secure for the time being, it was not in good shape. We had saved most of our equipment, but we were out of fuel. The troops were like headless chickens and their only concern was to avoid encirclement.[28]

This statement, written after the war, is inaccurate on several counts, quite apart from not mentioning his army's left flank was exposed, left hanging in the air. His army had not prevented a catastrophe, but had barely survived one of his own making due to the Red Army's slowness in realizing that the *6. Armee* was in complete disarray. Balck's delay in withdrawing the *I. Kav.Korps* and *III. Pz.Korps* out of the "sack" south of Lake Balaton until it was nearly too late contributed substantially towards the near-collapse that followed. Although he is correct in stating that his army was not in good shape, it was far from secure; its *panzer* divisions had lost most of their equipment, especially their armored fighting vehicles. It was within such a command atmosphere that the *IV. SS-Pz.Korps* had to operate.

The weather at daybreak on Palm Sunday, 25 March, presaged another beautiful day, nearly identical to the previous one, creating the perfect conditions for the initiation of a major offensive operation by the Second Ukrainian Front later in the day. The night of 24/25 March had witnessed the continuing attack by troops and tanks of the Third Ukrainian Front, which had clearly mastered the art of conducting night operations. North of the Danube, Soviet forces were evidently completing preparations for an attack, where the *8. Armee* reported several large-scale armed reconnaissance attempts near crossing sites in front of its defense line along the lower Gran River.

The *6. Pz.Armee* reported that in the sector defended by the *I. SS-Pz.Korps*, the 6th Guards Tank Army had been exerting pressure throughout the day against German strongpoints erected in an arc around the northern, eastern, and southern routes leading into the city of Papa, which lay astride an important road junction in the Bakony Forest. Somehow, the small defending force initially managed to hold out, despite a tank assault against the edge of the city. To strengthen that portion of the army's front line, Dietrich's staff reported that it would continue its attempts to lengthen its right wing by pushing additional forces out to the east to ward off further enemy attempts to take Papa.

This was a critical moment. Should Papa fall into the hands of the Red Army, Tolbukhin's forces would have a high-speed lateral line of communication through the forest that allowed them to be rapidly switched from the north to the south, or vice versa. The forces that the *I. SS-Pz.Korps* had on hand were insufficient compared to the magnitude of the task before them, consisting of little more than a heavy *Flak* regiment of the *Luftwaffe* and an SS *Kampfgruppe*. On the *6. Pz.Armee's* left wing, the Soviet 46th Army persisted in its attempts to break through towards the northwest with powerful infantry formations, but the outnumbered forces of the *II. SS-Pz.Korps* and *XLIII. Armee-Korps* continued their successful active defense and prevented any decisive breakthroughs, although they were continuously being forced to give up ground.

As the day lengthened, the *8. Armee* reported that after short-duration artillery barrages, multiple enemy river crossings had taken place at Kam-Darmoty, Alsovarad, Nagy Kalna, Kis Kalna, Bajka, and Nagy Salló, as well as at other locations. One report by the *357. Inf.Div.* included a message stating that up to 36 Soviet tanks, 17 guns, and numerous trucks had been spotted moving west of the Gran near Garam Szent-Gyorgyi, a sign that at least one large bridgehead had already been established. Phase II of the Red Army's Vienna Operation had clearly begun, as Marshal Malinovsky's Second Ukrainian Front was finally committed to battle.

In the *6. Armee's* area of operations, the divisions of the *I. Kav.Korps*, though pressured by enemy reconnaissance troops, had managed to continue settling into their new defense line between Balatonfüred and Hidegkút. Within the *IV. SS-Pz. Korps*, Gille's headquarters reported that the *Hohenstaufen* Division (once again subordinated to Gille's corps on that day) had destroyed 23 enemy tanks attempting to penetrate between the two corps near Hidegkút during the last 12 hours. Southwest of Nemesvámos, Gille's corps had been attacked by a large infantry force supported by 17 tanks, which was forced to withdraw after seven of them were knocked out by *Pz.Gren.Rgt. 3* of the *3. Pz.Div.* While impressive, these successes could not prevent the Red Army from breaking through as the day progressed, forcing Söth's division to retire to the next switch position several kilometers to the west.[29]

When the army's morning report was submitted, another Soviet attack, this time by a force supported by 15–20 tanks, was still underway.[30] The daily report for 25

March paints a fairly accurate picture of what took place in the *6. Armee* area of operations that day:

> North of Lake Balaton the enemy sought to continue his powerful assault supported by numerous tanks against the front of the *I. Kav.Korps* and the *IV. SS-Pz.Korps* in a southwesterly direction. Despite bitter resistance, during which the town of Tótvázsony changed hands several times, a deep penetration could not be prevented. Along both sides of the highway leading to Jánoscháza the enemy attacked with mechanized forces and penetrated into the town of Devecser.[31]

Devecser was a town 25 kilometers south of Papa, the mention of which signified that the 6th Guards Tank Army had completely bypassed German defenses on the western edge of the Bakony Forest, including *Div.K.Gr. LSSAH*, and that the operational breakthrough Tolbukhin had been seeking since 23 March was now well underway.

In detail, the situation in the *6. Armee* during 25 March unfolded in the following manner. Although the *I. Kav.Korps* was initially able to engage with artillery a large enemy troop concentration forming up opposite its front lines, on account of the ammunition shortage the barrage was unable to achieve the desired effect. This was followed shortly thereafter by a renewed Soviet attack toward the town of Hidegkút on the boundary between Harteneck's and Gille's corps, which finally fell after repeated attacks. The resulting breakthrough at this location forced Harteneck's corps to retreat all along its line. Because it no longer had any fuel to power its armored fighting vehicles, Harteneck had no choice but to order his divisions to blow them up to deny them to the enemy. Dozens of tanks were parked, their remaining fuel and ammunition removed, and destroyed by their crews.[32] In many cases, vehicles were simply abandoned intact, allowing the Red Army to form whole companies of captured vehicles that were immediately turned against their former owners.[33]

Within *s.Pz.Abt. 509*, attached at the time to Harteneck's corps, 25 March was remembered as one of the blackest days in its history. Fighting as part of the *I. Kav. Korps* rear guard, the battalion became embroiled in the enormous traffic jam on the northern shore of Lake Balaton along the highway linking Balatonfüred with Tapolca. Labeled as the "time of the great tank death" in the unit's war diary, the lack of fuel and the impossibility of towing immobilized tanks due to the traffic-clogged roads forced the battalion to blow up 14 of its precious *Pz. VI* Tiger IIs lest they fall into the hands of the pursuing Soviets. This regrettable necessity left the battalion with only 15 operational tanks, a third of what it had on hand when Operation *Konrad III* began two months earlier.[34]

The pressure against the *IV. SS-Pz.Korps* was equally great. After a 2,000-man assault supported by 11 tanks from the northeast, the key town of Tótvázsony was lost in heavy fighting. This town, located within the *Wiking* Division's defense zone, had to be held at all cost, prompting Gille to order Ullrich to retake it. Despite the dwindling strength of his division, which by this point amounted to little more than a reinforced regiment, it did so after heavy fighting, destroying four of the enemy's tanks in the process. Despite this successful counterattack, the corps' front line was forced back by another powerful Soviet assault directed against the *3. Pz.Div.* between Nagyvázsony and Hill 601.[35]

As the day progressed, the increasingly critical fuel situation manifested itself throughout the *IV. SS-Pz.Korps'* sector in a very negative way, just as it had in Harteneck's. At 8:45 p.m., Balck had to inform Wöhler that the *IV. SS-Panzer Korps* reported that it had had to blow up most of its remaining operational tanks late that afternoon due to a lack of fuel needed for the corps' imminent withdrawal movement that evening. The *3. Pz.Div.* was forced to blow up most of its surviving tanks near Sümeg, while the location where the *Wiking* Division had to destroy its tanks is unknown, though it did not have as many to sacrifice as did the *3. Pz.Div.* The loss of the fuel refineries at Pétfürdő and along the Danube due to Allied bombing was now being acutely felt.[36]

Günther Jahnke, the *O1* of the *Wiking* Division, left us his detailed account of the day's activities:

> At 5 a.m., the division's *Gefechtstand* displaced to the forest north of Vörösto. During the day, heavy defensive fighting took place along both sides of the highway [leading to Veszprém] against an ever-increasing attacking enemy force. The commander of the *Germania* Regiment, *Stubaf.* [Helmut] Müller, was seriously wounded. He was replaced by *Stubaf.* [Karl-Heinz] Bühler, commander of the *II. Abt./SS-Pz.Art.Rgt. 5*. When he began his journey at 2 p.m. to take over the regiment, [Bühler] only found the *SPW* of one of his battalion commanders, the *SPW* of the division's radio section, and signal troops of the division headquarters but little else … During the same day, while inside the division command post in the forest, we received many visitors, including the corps commander, the army commander, and *Oberf.* Stadler [of the *Hohenstaufen* Division]. The entire division staff was there, all we needed were troops … during the evening, we changed our position once again, towards Kapolcz [author's note: 11 kilometers from Vörösto].[37]

Most of the German resistance during this phase of the fighting was centered around small battle groups of 100–200 men, all that remained of once-proud regiments, led by a few junior officers or senior sergeants, supported perhaps by one or two tanks or assault guns, determined to do their utmost to stop or at least inflict heavy losses on their opponents. A great deal of the damage inflicted on Soviet tank columns was done by individual soldiers armed with *Panzerfausts* waiting in ambush positions in small towns or alongside defiles through which the forest roads frequently passed. Once a column was brought to a halt when the lead tank went up in flames, Soviet riflemen would be forced to dismount and clear the obstruction, but were often met by a hail of small-arms fire.

If any artillery or heavy mortars were available, the German defenders would attempt a counterattack to retake lost ground, but this sort of organized attack was dependent upon radio or telephone communication with supporting batteries, as well as availability of ammunition. Often, neither of these were available, leaving the defenders no choice but to withdraw to the next town or terrain feature or to die in place where they were. So it went, day after day. After the war, in recognition of the accomplishments of the *Wiking* Division's rank and file during this particularly trying period, its historian Peter Strassner wrote: "In retrospect it can be said that in those days and hours the officers, NCOs, and above all the men accomplished great individual achievements. Everyone fought bitterly against the overwhelming superiority of the enemy."[38]

Along the corps' isolated left flank, another battalion-sized unit supported by 11 tanks broke through its screen line and began moving northwest along the Veszprém–Devecser highway before it was turned back after two of its tanks were knocked out by elements of *Brigadeführer* Kumm's battle group from the *LSSAH*. Soviet tanks seemed to be attacking everywhere along Gille's front. Another attack led by 17 tanks appeared out of the village of Magyarpolány to the northwest of *Div.K.Gr. LSSAH* and advanced to the south in an effort to get around the stubbornly defending SS task force. Fortunately, Kumm had the foresight to place a rear guard at that particular point. After a brief fight, seven Soviet tanks were knocked out, forcing the rest to turn around.

The relief in place of the task force from *Div.K.Gr. LSSAH*, defending the town of Városlöd, by *Geb.Aufkl.Abt. 54* of the *1. Volks-Geb.Div.* was disrupted by a Soviet tank attack that threw the defenders out of the town before they could consolidate their defenses. This enemy attack, conducted with skill and daring, continued advancing westward until it had taken the neighboring town of Kislőd too.[39] For this, Balck blamed *Div.K.Gr. LSSAH*, claiming that it had once again simply marched off without waiting to be relieved.[40] This was demonstrably untrue; as directed by the *H.Gr. Süd* chief of staff, the relief in place of *Div.K.Gr. LSSAH* by the *1. Volks-Geb.Div.* was being conducted platoon by platoon when the attack took place, but no ground was being given up without a fight, as the *6. Armee* commander had unfairly alleged.

In actuality, both *Geb.Aufkl.Abt. 54* and *Div.K.Gr. LSSAH* had been simply overwhelmed by superior Soviet forces. Describing the situation that he and his men faced that day, in an exchange with division historian Ralf Tiemann after the war, Kumm wrote:

> There was heavy fighting against far superior enemy forces in the Hared area. The commanders of the *1.* and *12. SS-Panzer* Divisions met for a long time on the road for discussions. Establishing contact between the two flanks was out of the questions with the few forces available. The fronts of both divisions totaled 40 to 50 kilometers [and] could only be held by strongpoints. The enemy marched unhindered between [them]. New positions were established east of Városlöd and southeast of Ajka Berend [*sic*; actually Ajkarendek]. An attack by 17 tanks out of Magyar-Polyani was repulsed after seven tanks were destroyed … during the fighting on that day, Városlöd was lost. Elements of the *1. Volks-Geb.Div.* arrived [to relieve us].[41]

Nevertheless, Balck and his chief of staff complained mightily to *H.Gr. Süd* about the impending departure of Kumm's division, ever desirous of keeping as many forces to themselves as possible. Despite Balck's disdain for the *LSSAH*, the *H.Gr. Süd* commander, perhaps in sympathy for what it was having to endure under the *6.*

Armee's commander's caustic leadership, singled it out for praise that day, writing in the army group's war diary: "The *1. SS-Pz.Div. Kampfgruppe*, under the leadership of its divisional commander in the *6. Armee* area of operations, stands as a breakwater in a raging storm as enemy forces wash around it."[42]

The enemy force that had broken through at Városlöd was estimated to consist of at least a rifle regiment reinforced by 17 tanks, a much more powerful force than the German defenders could counter. After taking Kislőd, this vanguard continued pressing forward to the southwest and had seized the towns of Ajkarendek and Gyepesi by nightfall. With this, the German defenders were forced back and *Geb. Aufkl.Abt. 54* was forced to establish another defense line while it waited for the rest of the division to arrive. Since the inter-army boundary ran through this area, rather than allowing *Generalleutnant* Wittmann's *1. Volks-Geb.Div.* to become subordinated to the *6. Pz.Armee*—as had been originally intended—*H.Gr. Süd* assigned it to the *6. Armee* due to Balck's insistence that it was needed to replace the departing *Div.K.Gr. LSSAH.*

This decision made no sense whatsoever, because it divided responsibility for the defense of the Bakony Forest between two armies. A single mountain division was now expected to maintain the connection between the two armies, but it had arrived too late—by this point, there was no possibility whatsoever that this division could do so. Rather than agreeing to allow the *Div.K.Gr. LSSAH* to return to the *I. SS-Pz. Korps*, Balck still wanted to keep it, despite orders to release it. In addition to gaining the mountain division, Wöhler also subordinated the Hungarian *II. Armee-Korps* to *6. Armee*, but this brought no appreciable military capability that Balck could hope to use. With only the understrength Hungarian *20. Inf.Div.* and remnants of the *25. Inf.Div.* under its command, this corps was fit only for controlling rear area security operations.

In regards to the next day's operations in the *6. Armee* area, Balck was directed to ensure that the *I. Kav.Korps* pulled its forces back in sufficient time to avoid the envelopment that appeared to be developing on its left flank along its boundary with the *IV. SS-Pz.Korps*. Should this occur, Harteneck's troops would be pinned against the northern shore of Lake Balaton. Balck wanted to prevent this from occurring at all cost and took the necessary steps to get the *I. Kav.Korps* back to a new defense line generally aligned in a north–south direction between Balatonakali and Nagyvázsony. While Harteneck's corps withdrew, the *IV. SS-Pz.Korps* was directed to hold its current positions.

Although its three divisions (on 25 March, the *Wiking, Hohenstaufen,* and *3. Pz.Div.*) were able to hold that line throughout the day, Soviet forces had approached too close to the *IV. SS-Pz.Korps* forward command post, forcing it that night to relocate to Vörösto, 7.5 kilometers southwest of Tótvázsony, while the *Hauptquartier* with the corps *Ib* and *IIa* staff elements was forced to move even farther away, where they could safely re-establish rear area services, including *SS-Lazarett 504*. The headquarters of the *I. Kav.Korps* was also forced to displace to the rear to Dörgicse. For both corps headquarters, daily changes of position had become routine, as the front line continued moving to the west and southwest. Such constant disruptions were making it extremely difficult for Harteneck and Gille to effectively command and control their corps' subordinate elements. For his part, Balck decided to order his own army's command post to move to Vásárosmiske, a small town in the Bakony Forest 40 kilometers southwest of Papa.

The *H.Gr. Süd* daily report for 25 March closed with a paragraph acknowledging the impressive battle accomplishments of the *6. Armee* and *6. Pz.Armee* in terms of Soviet tanks knocked out, including the periods between 6 and 15 March (202 destroyed) and from 16–24 March (405 more knocked out), for a total of 607 enemy tanks in only 19 days. While this is indeed an impressive number, without context it is meaningless. Since this number was presented without comparing it to the armored fighting vehicles lost by the two German armies during the same period, it is nearly impossible to judge what it represents. Besides, once again the Red Army could quickly replace or repair those it had lost, while the *Wehrmacht* could not. Whereas German armored strength declined in absolute terms, that of the Red Army remained the same or increased, demonstrating the growing gap between German and Soviet combat power.

That same day, the shattered *44. Reichs-Gren.Div. HuD*, under acting commander *Oberst* Hoffmann, was ordered to begin moving on foot and rail the following day to a rest area behind the *2. Pz.Armee*, where it would undergo a brief *Auffrischung*, leaving behind a battalion-sized *Kampfgruppe* to operate temporarily under the *I. Kav.Korps*.[43] This is ironic, given that at the time when *H.Gr. Süd* needed more foot soldiers to hold back the Soviet flood, it was instead pulling out its only infantry division. Uncharacteristically, Balck raised no objections to this division's removal from his army's order of battle. When the *44. Reichs-Gren.Div.* did return to battle a week later. under the control of the *2. Pz.Armee* near Radkersburg, it would be no match for Soviet tanks and mechanized infantry, despite an influx of replacements for the men who had been lost in the Jenö Pocket.[44]

Another illustration of the decline in strength of the *6. Armee* was the report submitted that day by the *1. Pz.Div.*, which in theory was functioning as the *Armeereserve* but had a *Kampfgruppe* (*K.Gr. Bradel*) serving in the front line as a rear guard for the *I. Kav.Korps*. It reported having only five *Pz. V* Panthers operational, two *Panzergrenadier* battalions—each with a *Kampfstärke* of approximately 100 men—16 guns in its artillery regiment, and one combat engineer company. Other heavy weapons included four heavy antitank guns, five 2cm *Flak* cannons, eight mortars, and two light infantry howitzers. Although its losses had been extremely heavy, Thünert's battered *1. Pz.Div.* was still the strongest division in the *6. Armee*.[45]

On that same date, German troops serving under the Hungarian *3. Armee* still in the bridgehead south of the Danube near Gran continued their evacuation to the river's northern bank, just in time to avoid being trapped by the offensive taking place a few kilometers to the northeast. Therefore, the hard-fighting *96.* and *711. Inf.Div.*, *Gren.Brig. (mot.) 92*, and *SS-K.Gr. Ameiser* lived to fight another day.[46] Once the evacuation from the bridgehead at Labatlan was completed on the night of 26/27 March, instead of being allowed to return to either the *6. Armee* or *6. Pz.Armee*, all of these German units were subordinated to the *IV. Pz.Korps FHH* of the *8. Armee.*

There was one area in which the German forces were nearly powerless to stop the advancing enemy, and that was in the air. Over the entire *H.Gr. Süd* area, in particular the skies over the *6. Armee*, the Red Air Force's 5th and 17th Air Armies were particularly active that day, not only due to the beautiful flying weather, but the fact that the *Luftwaffe* could only launch 120 sorties to counter it. In contrast, the Red Air Force carried out in excess of 800 sorties. Most of the German aircraft that did make it airborne were ground-attack aircraft that managed to knock out five Soviet tanks. German missions were increasingly being flown at night, a sign that it was compelled to yield the skies to the enemy during the day. On the night of 24/25 March, *Luftflotte 4* flew 150 sorties, mostly against assembly areas and troop movements in the Leva area, where the attack by the Second Ukrainian Front attack was just beginning, as well as against Soviet troop concentrations opposite the *6. Pz.Armee* in the Bakony Forest.[47]

In addition to everything else that had occurred that day, another significant event took place when *Alarmstufe I* (Alert Level I – the highest) was issued to all of the *Volkssturm* home guard units in *Wehrkreis* (Defence District) *XVIII*, which was responsible for the defense of the lower Danube region of the *Reichsschutzstellung*. The 14 battalions activated on 25 March were made responsible for occupying and defending the portion of the "Eastern Wall" fortifications from Rechnitz to Radkersburg, a distance of roughly 160 kilometers. In all, they totaled approximately 5,000 men, or half the strength of a Soviet rifle division. Poorly equipped and trained, and consisting primarily of Hitler Youth and older men, this force would be no match for the approaching Red Army. The most that could be expected of them was that they might delay the invaders long enough for regular troops to withdraw in time to establish a proper defensive system.[48]

The pace of the campaign began to pick up on 26 March. The weather was as warm as the previous day, while the skies remained clear until the afternoon, when they became partly cloudy, ideal weather for the continuation of the Vienna Operation by the Second and Third Ukrainian Fronts. The lead paragraph of the *Heeresgruppe* daily report described the situation it faced at sunset as follows:

> The defensive battle on both sides of the Danube continues. Strong enemy pressure against the *I. Kav.Korps* and the *IV. SS-Pz.Korps* led to several breakthroughs. An envelopment of the field army's [*6. Armee's*] left flank began to become evident. The enemy attacked along both sides of Papa with overwhelming mechanized forces and was able to reach the Marczal Canal and

the Raab River along a wide front to a point 15 kilometers southwest of the city. A crossing of the Marczal Canal at and north of Czelldömölk [note: the town of Kleinmariazell, defended by *SS-Rgt. Ney*] could not be prevented. In the Kisbér–Komorn sector, the enemy launched powerful attacks with predominately infantry forces, which our forces were able to ward off in heavy fighting … north of the Danube, the enemy was able to considerably widen and reinforce his bridgeheads west of Leva along a 25-kilometer-wide stretch with a depth of 15 kilometers. The enemy was able to throw back our counterattacks at several locations. The building of a unified defensive front on account of insufficient forces is at the moment not possible … In this 250-kilometer-wide running defensive battle, leaders and troops are giving their every effort. Their tough resistance for the most part is being carried forth from a series of poorly prepared strongpoints by *Kampfgruppe* composed of fragments of units that have still been able to inflict heavy losses on the enemy's manpower and material.[49]

The *I. Kav.Korps* had indeed experienced a hard time that day. The displacement of its three divisions overnight to its new defense line had been hard-pressed by the enemy, though the *3.* and *4. Kav.Div.* and the *23. Pz.Div.* all managed to make it back to their designated line intact.

Throughout the day, Soviet troops hurled themselves at Harteneck's new front line as if to test it, but the line held except for along his left flank, which he shared with the *IV. SS-Pz.Korps*. Here, the enemy was able to achieve a deep penetration that would necessitate another withdrawal. In the *IV. SS-Pz.Korps'* sector, its divisions had also experienced a difficult evening. A nighttime attack with up to 40 tanks towards Nagyvázsony in the center of the corps defense line succeeded in taking the small town. During the day, the new *HKL* established the previous day along the wood line west of Leányfalu was pushed back as well. On the corps' far left, a battalion-sized infantry attack against Halimba that originated from the town of Padrag was forced back by a counterattack by a small element of *Div.K.Gr. LSSAH* that had not yet departed to join the rest of the division.

The *Wiking* Division participated in much of the fighting on 26 March, though its combat power had declined markedly. Its two *Panzergrenadier* regiments had been so decimated by this point that the division's only combat unit with any remaining capability—Fritz Vogt's new command, *SS-Pz.Aufkl.Abt. 5*—was constantly engaged. That day, the division's *O1* wrote:

> The *Aufklärungabteilung* was practically the only unit employed by the division on this day. Despite constant enemy attacks throughout the entire day against our newly occupied intermediate defensive position that continued late into the evening, the division was able to make in back in good order.[50]

Whether his men loved or hated him, the hard-charging and fanatical Vogt always achieved results.

His battalion was the exception. The corps' chief of staff, Manfred Schönfelder, describing the condition of the units at that point, wrote: "The troops are exhausted. On account of the shortage of fuel, they have little mobility, on account of ammunition shortages, they have little firepower and no armored fighting vehicles."[51] How the troops kept fighting despite these conditions was simply unfathomable, a testimony to their officers' leadership skill and their dedication to one another. However, Balck saw things differently, writing after the war:

> The situation in my sector was getting difficult. As I noted in my journal: the cavalry corps under Harteneck is fighting bravely and well with no signs of dissolving. It is a different picture with the *5. SS-Pz.Div. Wiking*. A stream of troops left their positions and marched back along the side of the road without the corps intervening. The troops were collected up later and sent back forward, but then they immediately slipped back toward the rear. It is a horrible, recurring cycle behind the courageously but barely held forward lines. On 23 March, 75 percent of the troops at a collection point were SS. Thank God the *1. Gebirgs-Division* has arrived and we can still hold the front line intact.[52]

After the war, both Schönfelder and Maier took Balck to task for this statement, which they believed was based on the flimsiest of evidence. If Balck had complained to the *IV. SS-Pz.Korps* commander or staff about this situation, it never got to Schönfelder's ears during the war.[53]

In making their case, the two former SS staff officers later wrote that the road along which Balck was travelling when he made his observation had been the main supply route of Gille's corps. The *IV. SS-Pz.Korps* at the time was composed predominately of SS units (the *Wiking* and *Hohenstaufen* Divisions, along with the *3. Pz.Div.*) and not Harteneck's, which was composed of 100 percent troops from the *Heer* at this point (*3.* and *4. Kav.Div.* and the *23. Pz.Div.*). Therefore, if 75 percent of the troops that Balck observed at a straggler collection point were in the SS corps' defensive sector, then this probably corresponded to the proportion of SS personnel in the corps. Nor does Balck state how many troops he observed were "streaming to the rear," whether it was 75 percent of four, 40, or 400 men; without context, his statement is meaningless and unfair to the troops involved.

Nor does it seem that Balck stopped to question these "stragglers" as he drove by; because all SS units had previously been ordered to remove their cuff titles in February, there was no way for him to determine whether they were from the *Wiking* Division or not. They could just as easily have been from the *Hohenstaufen* Division, *Div.K.Gr. LSSAH*, or from the several thousand SS *Korpstruppen* fighting alongside them. These troops could also have been ordered to the rear area to reorganize or for any number of other possible reasons, but the *6. Armee* commander merely considered these as excuses to explain away their "cowardice." Incidentally, Balck continued in a similar vein for the remainder of his official reports as well as in his memoirs, but this should be sufficient for the reader to understand the former *panzer* commander's mindset, especially in regards to his well-known negative views regarding the *Waffen-SS*. In Gaedke's own autobiography, he constantly describes the conduct of *Waffen-SS* troops in a negative manner.[54]

The first evening report of the newly arrived *1. Volks-Geb.Div.* was submitted on this day, though only two of its six mountain infantry battalions and its reconnaissance battalion had arrived by this point. It had been a most eventful day for the division, which began arriving when the attack by the 6th Guards Tank Army was in full flood. Although the division's troops had been able to knock out seven Soviet tanks on 26 March, enemy forces were able to bypass them near Devecser and continue pushing west until they reached the southern limit of the Marczal Canal east of Jánoscháza. Another Soviet force that had reached the canal at the same time began establishing a bridgehead south of the town.[55] This development forced the division to begin constructing a new *HKL* along a 25-kilometer-wide portion of the canal between the towns of Ukk and Czelldömölk, a sector far too wide for a single division to do anything but establish a screening line. Although it was far removed from Gille's headquarters, this division was still subordinated to his control, even though the *I. SS-Pz.Korps'* command post was much closer.

Soviet air activity remained at the same level of intensity, while that of the *Luftwaffe* grew less and less. The bulk of the aerial combat appeared to be taking place that day over the *6. Pz.Armee* sector south of Komorn and along the northern bank of the Danube, where the Second Ukrainian Front's bridgehead was increasing in size, as Marshal Malinovsky continued shoving troops into it to enable the breakout and pursuit towards Vienna along the Danube Basin. Any movement along the roads north of Lake Balaton was guaranteed to attract the attention of Soviet aviators, ever on the lookout for a staff car or fuel truck to bomb and strafe. One eyewitness account by a soldier from the *3. Pz.Div.* conveys what it was like to endure such an attack as his supply column attempted to move towards the west:

> To the left of us is Lake Balaton … to the right of us [the Bakony] mountains rise into the distance. No other way out is possible. We ask our ammunition driver how much he has on the truck. At that point, the column is attacked from the air. With a few last jumps we throw ourselves into a hole for cover. [The] ammo truck is now on fire. Large quantities of infantry ammunition start burning up. [We] have to wait a long time until the truck finally explodes completely. Russian fighter planes keep coming and attacking us. Let's get out of here! One by one we crawl past the burning truck. We finally reach our field kitchen. But we can't go any further, because the road is blocked. Finally we roll on.[56]

At this point, with a 40-kilometer-wide gap between the two armies growing larger, as well as the initial stages of the offensive by the Second Ukrainian Front clearly unfolding before their eyes, the necessary measures that the German high command in Hungary needed to take were not being made in sufficient time, quickly resulting in a situation which by default completely yielded the initiative to the Red Army.

By this late stage in the war, operations in the Hungarian theater of operations, which rightly should have been the purview of the *H.Gr. Süd* commander, were being dictated exclusively by the *OKH* headquarters in Berlin, with ultimate decision-making authority reserved to Hitler and Hitler alone, who was intervening more frequently in decisions that heretofore had been done by regimental or battalion commanders. This micromanaging left the army group, army, corps, and division commanders little other role than to ensure that Hitler's orders were carried out. This tendency tended to destroy what little initiative that remained and violated the practice of issuing mission-type orders which had traditionally allowed commanders to decide how to carry out their assigned tasks.

According to two general staff officers of the *Heer* who experienced this new way of thinking, many things were no longer the way they were at the beginning of the war, to the detriment of the *Wehrmacht*. Both men had served as principle staff officers in a *Waffen-SS* corps headquarters on the Western Front from August 1944 to May 1945, but their experiences were typical of a corps staff at this point in the war. In a postwar account written for the U.S. Army's Historical Division, *Oberst i.G.* Ullrich Ulms and *Maj. i.G.* Karl Reuther (the chief of staff and *Ia* of the *XII. SS-Armee Korps* respectively) wrote:

> The command mission of corps headquarters had changed quite considerably during the past year of the war, and particularly during recent months. The broadly outlined mission and resulting tactical decisions for its execution was no longer the most important issue. This task of real command, calling for the execution of independently developed ideas and plans, had receded in an ever-increasing measure. The main effort of the command's mission was to be concentrated on organization rather than on tactics, on the supervision of the execution of orders coming from higher levels rather than on initiative. [57]

On these points, both officers most likely would have found a sympathetic ear in *Ostubaf.* Manfred Schönfelder, who was well aware of this tendency regarding the *H.Gr. Süd* command, but in the particular case of Balck and the *6. Armee*, was magnified even further by their army commander's intense dislike of Schönfelder and Gille.

One example of an order issued from Berlin on 26 March arrived at the headquarters of *H.Gr. Süd* early that evening, which concerned reports that Hitler had received about the pace of the *6. Armee's* withdrawal. Passed on by *H.Gr. Süd* to *6. Armee* at 8:50 p.m., the order simply stated: "The *Führer* believes that the recently intended [defense] line is located too far to the rear. He demands that you hold along the line Zanka–Talian Dorgond–Hyirad–Kaptalanfa." At the time he issued his order, the information upon which he had based it was probably at least 24 hours old, since these locations had already been bypassed by Soviet spearheads.[58]

As if this was not bad enough, Hitler had never been on this ground, did not understand the enemy, and did not know the conditions of the troops. Based on all this, as well as other factors, there was no way for him to understand whether his decision would be effective or not, even if he had been able to make one based on information immediately available to him. To make matters worse, he was increasingly inclined to ignore the advice of his own *OKH* chief of staff, Guderian. It was under conditions such as these that Gille and his staff had to labor every day until the end of the war.

The task assigned that evening to the *6. Armee* for the following day, 27 March, was simply: "Re-establish a continuous front line between Lake Balaton and

Czelldömölk [Kleinmariazell]." The distance between these two points, allowing for the terrain, was approximately 77 kilometers, a line running from the southeast to the northwest. To carry out this order, on the evening of 26 March, Balck had eight divisions (the *1. Volks-Geb.Div., 3.* and *4. Kavallerie, 1., 3.,* and *23. Panzer,* and the *Wiking* and *Hohenstaufen* Divisions), the battalion-sized *Div.K.Gr. 44 HuD,* and a small SS *Kampfgruppe* (the last portion of *Div.K.Gr. LSSAH* that had not yet departed).[59] However, on that date only one of these could have been considered ready to be employed as a full division, and that was the newly arrived *1. Volks-Geb. Div.* The remaining divisions were little more than regiment-sized task forces, with hardly any tanks or infantry, little artillery, hardly any fuel, and a minimal amount of ammunition.

To maintain at least the appearance of carrying out his army's orders, which was the most that Balck could actually do given the meagre forces on hand, the *IV. SS-Pz.Korps* would have to extend its line to the northwest 47 kilometers beyond where it ended on 26 March, which was the line running to the northwest from the northern shore of Lake Balaton as far as Sümeg, approximately 30 kilometers. Even this distance was beyond the point where he could safely extend it, since each of Gille's three divisions occupying their present positions to the left of the *I. Kav. Korps* could defend a sector no more than 3 or 4 kilometers wide on account of their weakened condition.

In order to make each of Balck's two corps minimally capable of carrying out their assignments and to carry out his assigned tasks, the composition of both would have to be reshuffled once again to at least spread out their remaining capability, but in truth the result made both corps equally weak. Therefore, on 26 March, Balck subordinated *K.Gr. Bradel* of the *1. Pz.Div.* to Gille, where all of that division's remaining combat power was concentrated. To do this, it would have to come out of army reserve, but Balck had no other choice. He had already subordinated the *1. Volks-Geb.Div.* to the *IV. SS-Pz.Korps,* but in return Balck had made Gille responsible for defending the *6. Armee's* wide-open left flank as far as Kleinmariazell.[60]

In turn, the *I. Kav.Korps* once again received the *Hohenstaufen* Division from Gille's corps, which gave Harteneck four divisions to Gille's four. Assigning the *IV. SS-Pz.Korps* the mission of covering the 47-kilometer-wide sector from Sümeg to Kleinmariazell with a single mountain division and a battalion-sized motorized SS *Kampfgruppe* was also a near-impossible assignment, which Balck must have known. But in truth, the mission that *H.Gr. Süd* had assigned both the *6. Armee* and *6. Pz.Armee* for 27 March was equally impossible to fulfill, although Balck and Dietrich would do their utmost to carry it out anyway. As the old Prussian adage goes, "*Befehl ist Befehl*" (orders are orders).

Tuesday, 27 March was to prove a day of decision. It was a warm day, with temperatures averaging 60 degrees Fahrenheit. There were locally scattered showers and light clouds. With the onset of spring, weather had ceased to play a determining factor in operations, with the exception of air operations. With the *Luftwaffe* nearly out of fuel that it needed to operate, this meant that the Red Air Force was free to operate nearly anywhere and everywhere it wanted. This being the new reality, German ground forces hoped for bad weather because it might limit incessant attacks by waves of the hated IL-2 Sturmoviks, Bostons, and Yaks, which they had grown to dread as much as packs of T-34s.

The first paragraph of the consolidated *Tagesmeldung* for 27 March was alarming, confirming *H.Gr. Süd*'s worst fears:

> Between Lake Balaton and the Danube the defensive battle in the sector north of Lake Balaton, along both sides of Jánoscháza, between Kleinmariazell [Celldömölk] and Marcaltö, and southeast of Raab continued with undiminished ferocity … between Kleinmariazell and Gyirmót, 7 kilometers southwest of Raab, the enemy was able to reach the eastern bank of the Raab River along a wide front, and managed to establish small bridgeheads [over the river].[61]

The distance between Kleinmariazell and Gyirmót, following the curve of the Raab River to the north, was nearly 90 kilometers, representing an irreparable breach between the *6. Armee* and *6. Pz.Armee* that *H.Gr. Süd* would not be able to repair quickly enough. The contents of the report also signified that the spearheads of the 4th and 9th Guards Armies and 6th Guards Tank Army had begun to emerge on the western edge of the Bakony Forest; after this, there was nothing to slow them down until they reached the Austrian border. Unless something was done quickly to stop them, the situation could not be reversed. *Heeresgruppe Süd*'s last hope was the uncompleted defensive line known as the *Susannestellung* by *H.Gr. Süd* plans officers, which ran along the western banks of the Raab River and Marczal Canal.

It was to prove an eventful day for the *6. Armee*, as the attacks by the 26th and 27th Armies north of Lake Balaton continued to build momentum. The *I. Kav.Korps* was hit by an attack in the morning by a strong Soviet force, backed up by 14 tanks, that advanced along the road running parallel to the lake's northern shore. At the same time, a much larger force supported by 40 tanks took the town of Zahaláháp in the center of the defensive line held by the *Hohenstaufen* Division and pushed into the new line the corps had erected the previous evening. Clearly, the 27th Army had not given up its intent to split the corps and envelop its right flank along the northern shore of Lake Balaton. Once again, this move forced Harteneck's corps to withdraw to another position where it would try again to stand firm.

That same day, the *IV. SS-Pz.Korps* did the best it could to hold its widely spaced front line. Against its right flank, a battalion- or regiment-sized attack attempted to slice down the corps' boundary between it and the neighboring *I. Kav.Korps*. In Sümeg, Soviet troops and tanks stormed into the town and briefly encircled a portion of the decimated *Pz.Gren.Rgt. 3* of the *3. Pz.Div.*, which was able to fight its way out during the night.[62] An eyewitness recorded: "The *3. Pz.Div.* is not able to stop the Russian advance … There is a lack of ammunition for weapons, fuel for vehicles, and troops … The Soviet tanks often arrive at a crossroads quicker than our own soldiers who are supposed to occupy them."[63]

Having taken Sümeg, this same large group of Soviet tanks continued pushing to the west. Because of the danger posed by the collapse of the *I. Kav.Korps'* front line and equally serious developments on the corps' far left flank, Gille was directed to move his headquarters to the town of Besenyö, 3 kilometers south of Zalagerszeg and over 30 kilometers away from its present position. Concerning this development, Schönfelder later wrote:

> On account of the overexpansion of the front lines of the *I. Kav.Korps* and the *IV. SS-Pz.Korps*, what we had been fearing the most finally happened. The Russian XVIII Tank Corps drove between both corps and tore a hole between Tapolca and Sümeg. Due to this development, *6. Armee* instructed both corps to pull back. An hour later this order was overridden. The entire *6. Armee* must now fight its way back.[64]

This order to pull back also included each of the corps' divisions, except for the *1. Volks-Geb.Div.*, which was practically fighting on its own in the north. At 4 a.m., the *Wiking* Division's command post was pulled back to Türje; that night, it moved further west to Tutimajor, requiring a "jump" of over 30 kilometers. That night, the division's *O1* wrote:

> Finally the order for the long-awaited leap to the rear. These little dribs and drabs [of withdrawals] served no purpose and cost us unnecessary losses. No one knew what the larger situation was, where our own troops were, where our neighbors were … after a short while, enemy tanks began to appear, sometimes to our front and sometimes in our rear. What a mess.[65]

The defense line (actually a thinly manned outpost line) of *1. Volks-Geb.Div.*, which was holding the largest sector of all, was pierced in multiple locations by elements of the XVIII Tank Corps and V Guards Tank Corps.

Having been forced to spread its units so thinly to cover this wide area, *Generalleutnant* Wittmann's *1. Volks-Geb.Div.* was not strong anywhere, and except for a few locations, such as in the town of Jánoscháza, could not mount an effective defense. Avoiding pitched battle, the enemy spearheads bypassed the town from the north and south, crossed the Marczal Canal, and continued pushing west towards Bögöte, where the division attempted to set up another defense line west of Jánoscháza while it waited for its four remaining battalions to arrive, which in the meantime had been delayed in shipment.[66]

By the evening, the ominous report that *H.Gr. Süd* headquarters had been dreading arrived: a Soviet motorized unit had reached and crossed the Raab River at the town of Kleinzell (Sárvár), far behind the German front line. That evening, *H.Gr. Süd* ordered the *6. Armee* to eliminate the forces that had broken through between Sümeg and Kleinzell, as well as sealing off the other deep penetration along both sides of the highway leading westwards out of Jánoscháza.[67] Even at the time, the commander and chief of staff of *H.Gr. Süd* must have known that this was an unrealistic order. There was no feasible way that Balck could have carried it out with the forces that he had at his disposal. The only formation that could have attempted this mission was a full-strength corps of two or three divisions at the very least; of course, there was no such corps to be had. Demanding that this task be carried out by the 12,000-man *1. Volks-Geb.Div.*, the only force available (by this point, all of Kumm's *Div.K.Gr. LSSAH* had finally departed the area to rejoin the *I. SS-Pz.Korps*), was unrealistic.[68]

To the north, the right wing of the *6. Pz.Armee* was being slowly pushed back towards the Raab River. The town of Kleinzell, the linchpin defended by the *I. SS-Pz.Korps* that connected the *6. Pz.Armee* to the neighboring army to the south, was bypassed in heavy fighting, leaving the army's right flank dangling in thin air. A *Luftwaffe* reconnaissance aircraft flying overhead counted in excess of 200 enemy vehicles moving westwards of the town immediately afterwards. If it were to survive, all of the *6. Pz.Armee* would have to fall back immediately to the Raab River before it was too late. Dietrich's requests to do so had already been caught up in red tape at *H.Gr. Süd* and *OKH* headquarters, which meant that when permission was finally given, the Soviet advance forces might already be waiting there for the *6. Pz.Armee*.

While Dietrich waited for Hitler's answer, the troops of the 46th Army were advancing everywhere between the Danube and Kisber. Papa was lost the day before when the *Luftwaffe* heavy *Flak* regiment from the *20. Flak-Div.* positioned there withdrew without orders, leaving the small SS *Kampfgruppe* from the *I. SS-Pz.Korps* (*K.Gr. Keitel*) that was defending the city no choice but to withdraw before it was surrounded. It simply lacked enough troops to mount any sort of credible defense without the support of the *Luftwaffe's* lethal 8.8cm guns (this lapse led Wöhler to submit an official complaint that night to the commander of *Luftflotte 4*).[69]

Generalmajor Pape's bridgehead at Komorn established by the *8. Armee* would soon find itself isolated as well, especially if the front line along the Gran to its northeast collapsed and Soviet forces advanced as far as Neuhäusel, which appeared imminent. Lacking as it did sufficient command and control mechanisms for the two divisions being brought out of the Gran bridgehead (*96.* and *711. Inf.Div.*), the *8. Armee* commander requested the relief of *Gen.d.Geb.Tr.* Kurt Versock's *XLIII. Armee-Korps* headquarters from the *6. Pz.Armee* and its movement north of the Danube on 26 March. This was approved by Wöhler's headquarters that same day and Versock's headquarters began moving at noon on 27 March.[70] With this transfer, the *356. Inf.Div.* also departed the *6. Pz.Armee's* order of battle, leaving Dietrich with the *I.* and *II. Pz.Korps* with the *1., 2., 3.,* and *12. SS-Pz.Div.* and the *6. Pz.Div.*, as well as a number of splinter units of varying sizes and quality.

North of the Danube, the Second Ukrainian Front, having amassed sufficient combat power to commence the breakout from its various bridgeheads on the west bank of the Gran, penetrated the defensive line of the *8. Armee* at numerous points and began its inexorable advance towards Pressburg (Bratislava). To the south of the

6. Armee, the enemy opposite the *2. Pz.Armee* was quiet, but *Gen.d.Art.* Maximilian de Angelis knew that it would not remain so for much longer. Offensive preparations by the opposing 57th Army had already been detected by German intelligence, and it would only be a matter of time before this army attacked as well.

The *Luftwaffe* hardly took to the skies during the day, citing fuel shortages. There was little its squadrons could do to stop the hordes of Soviet fighter-bombers and ground-attack aircraft from harassing and bombing German positions and troop movements. The few aircraft that were able to take to the skies during the day were caught up in aerial battles with Soviet fighter aircraft, in which its *Jäger* claimed the downing of four Soviet aircraft. While *Luftflotte 4* managed to launch 50 nighttime sorties in the area above Veszprém and Jánoscháza, its attacks against Soviet columns and troop concentrations amounted to mere pinpricks.[71]

By 28 March, the Red Army's Vienna Operation had been well underway for nearly two weeks. The complimentary offensive by the Second Ukrainian Front north of the Danube was beginning to gain momentum, as the 7th Guards Army and 53rd Army, as well as Pliyev's 1st Mechanized Cavalry Group, continued to batter away at the weary *8. Armee*. Unless evacuated, the Komorn bridgehead and its defenders would soon be lost. The Third Ukrainian Front had managed to separate the *6. Pz.Armee* between the Danube and Bakony Forest from the *6. Armee* north of Lake Balaton by deep attacks launched by the 4th and 9th Guards Armies and 6th Guards Tank Army, aimed towards the Raab River and Marczal Canal defense line, where Soviet tank spearheads had seized at least one bridgehead by late afternoon the previous day. The *Susannestellung* was the last remaining significant natural obstacle between the Bakony Forest and the Austrian border; should any sizeable force from the Red Army cross it before the defenders could establish a new front line, nothing could be done to stop them from penetrating the Reich until they reached the Alps.

Another supporting attack on the tank army's left flank south of the Bakony Forest by the 26th and 27th Armies had begun to split the *6. Armee* in two, threatening to push the *IV. SS-Pz.Korps* northwest towards the Raab River and the *I. Kav.Korps* southwest to the western tip of Lake Balaton. By this point, the only logical course of action that *H.Gr. Süd* could have taken was to withdraw to the west as quickly as possible and form a new front line. However, neither the *OKH* chief of staff nor Hitler were prepared to even consider this option; the constant refrain remained: "Stand fast!" In reality, by 28 March, Wöhler no longer had sufficient forces that could stand their ground, let alone prevent the enemy from advancing on Vienna.

The Soviet offensive continued to expand in size and scope that day. Despite this unfavorable development, the daily report of *H.Gr. Süd* began with optimism: "North of Lake Balaton, although the enemy pushed our own *Kampfgruppen* further to the southwest [referring to the *I. Kav.Korps*], they were able to preserve the integrity of the front." This was immediately followed by the gloomy assessment of the situation along the Raab River:

> Along the *Raabfront* [author's note: this is the first time this term appears in the official records] the enemy approached along a wide front and carried out many attacks across the river, establishing wide and deep bridgeheads on both sides of Kleinzell and in the area of Csorna that our forces have not yet managed to seal off. The danger of a breakthrough at Steinemanger [Szombathely] towards the northwest and in the direction of Ödenburg [Sopron] is beginning to emerge. On other points along the *Raabfront* our forces managed to fend off other crossing attempts by the enemy.[72]

The enemy's advance to the Raab forced the *H.Gr. Süd* headquarters to move out of the Esterháza Castle which had been its headquarters for the past eight months and switch to a new location in the city of Eisenstadt, located in southeastern Austria on the western side of the *Neusiedlersee*, where it could operate in safety, at least for the time being.

North of the Danube, the assault elements of the Second Ukrainian Front had reached the outskirts of Neuhäusel and Neutra (Nitra), forcing the *8. Armee* to shorten its front line. In the area of Neusohl (Banská Bystrica), it appeared that Marshal Malinovsky's Second Ukrainian Front was attempting to catch up with Tolbukhin's offensive in the south. Further to the north, Soviet attacks continued against the *8. Armee's* left flank in Slovakia. Events were now occurring so quickly that the *Ia KTB Schreiber* (the NCO who kept and maintained the war diary) at *H.Gr. Süd* probably had a difficult time keeping up with them.

The same thing could also have been said for the *Ia KTB Schreiber* at Balck's headquarters. That evening, the *6. Armee* reported a series of harrowing events across the length and breadth of its area of operations. In the *I. Kav.Korps'* defensive sector, Harteneck reported that his corps had been confronted along its entire front by a series of battalion- to regiment-sized infantry assaults supported by numerous tanks. At the key position of Sümeg, located along its boundary line with the *IV. SS-Pz. Korps*, the understrength *3. Kav.Div.* managed to prevent the enemy from breaking through after inflicting heavy losses on its opponent, although the division's left flank was thrown back westwards as far as the Zala River. This action would soon have profound implications for the *IV. SS-Pz.Korps*.

Attacked on its right by a force similar to that which had attacked Harteneck's corps, the division holding the line at that point, the *3. Pz.Div.*, was also threatened with envelopment. Employing *K.Gr. Bradel* of the *1. Pz.Div.* as his armored reserve, Gille was able to finally stop the Soviet attack along his right flank on the western bank of the Zala after Bradel's few remaining *panzers* and a *Kampfgruppe* from the *3. Pz.Div.* counterattacked and shot up seven Soviet tanks. Should the 27th Army achieve a penetration at this vital point, it would become increasingly difficult for both the *IV. SS-Pz.Korps* and *I. Kav.Korps* to remain tied together. As a result of this maneuver, however, Gille had been forced to refuse his own right flank as well, withdrawing it to the northwest, where the *1. Pz.Div.* moved around to the corps' left flank to take up a defensive position at Zalaszántó.[73]

In the middle of all this chaos, the situation in the *Wiking* Division's sector was deceivingly calm at first. With the bulk of the fighting that day taking place along the front of adjacent units, the Red Army inadvertently gave the division a break. That night, Jahnke wrote in his diary:

> Today began somewhat quieter. The Russians appeared to have not wanted to follow us too closely. One had the impression that the entire front had quit fighting. When we later displaced [that afternoon], the Russians had mostly arrived there before us. We were visited that same day by the army's chief of staff [Gaedke]. He told us that a withdrawal to the German border could no longer be avoided and that hopefully we would arrive there before it was too late … later on, we were alerted that enemy tanks had broken through and that the division commander had been briefly cut off.[74]

On Gille's far left flank, the *1. Volks-Geb.Div.* was forced to conduct a fighting withdrawal to the west from its positions along the Maszcal Canal. It had repelled numerous Soviet tank-supported attacks throughout the day until it was threatened with envelopment. Far away from any help, even if Gille had any to provide, the division was ordered to withdraw to a new defensive line several kilometers to the east of the Raab River, which it managed to accomplish without being overtaken. However, its withdrawal to a new line had opened up another avenue of approach to the north leading towards the Raab for the 6th Guards Tank Army and the other Soviet armies to exploit, but help was on the way.

The withdrawal by the *IV. SS-Pz.Korps* on 28 March was not an orderly one, despite everything that had been done to hold the line as long as possible. Once again, the anonymous eyewitness from the *3. Pz.Div.* has left us a vivid account:

> The *IV. SS-Pz.Korps* arrives with its divisions on the Raab in the course of 28 March. The enemy immediately follows and breaks through the *1. Pz.Div.* The *Kampfgruppen* from the *3. Pz.Div.* are able to hold their security line. Behind them, the remaining units flood over the wide river in the direction of Styria [in Austria]. Some of the *Tross*, repair services and supply depots have already arrived in the territory of the Reich. The Soviets attack from Steinamanger to the southwest and press on Körmend. This creates the danger that the *3. Pz.Div.* will be encircled again. All vehicles that are not absolutely necessary will have to be quickly transferred via Körmend to the road to Graz. Fantastic sights can be seen. [In some places], oxen are pulling some trucks, while in another place, a prime mover has 20 different vehicles in tow.[75]

Hermann Breith's *III. Pz.Korps*, which had been busily engaged in organizing rear area defenses and forming various *Alarm* units to send to the front, was committed once again to battle on Wöhler's urging, much to the relief of the *1. Volks-Geb.Div.* However, its division commander was to quickly learn that Breith was not bringing much along with him, besides his headquarters.

Having established his *Hauptquartier* in Nemeskolta, Breith's mission was to help plug the enormous gap growing between the *6. Armee* and *6. Pz.Armee* on the western side of the Raab River, from the *IV. SS-Pz.Korps* to the nearest element of the *I. SS-Pz.Korps* in the *6. Pz.Armee* sector. For its part, Dietrich's army was hurrying back to the *Susannestellung* along the Raab, with the goal of reaching the western bank before the Red Army did. In most cases, his troops succeeded in fighting their way to safety, though the garrison within Komorn, including *Pz.Div. FHH*, was forced to begin withdrawing to the north bank of the Danube before it was completely encircled.

By this point, the gap between the *6. Armee* and *6. Pz.Armee* had expanded to the operationally significant width of 50 kilometers, beyond the range of German artillery fire to interdict. The newly arrived *232. Pz.Div.*, in reality only a *Kampfgruppe*, attempted to hang on to the bridgehead east of the Raab at Marcaltö that it had occupied on 26 March with its two understrength *Panzergrenadier* regiments, but Soviet advancing elements operating from Egyed crossed the river north of the town and attacked it from the rear, scattering the division before it could carry out an orderly withdrawal. Its division commander, *Gen.Maj.* Hans-Ulrich Back, was seriously wounded during the fighting, adding to the general confusion. This, in turn, forced the now-reunited *1. SS-Pz.Div. LSSAH* to extend its flank to the left to prevent a breakthrough, while on the right it sought contact with the newly arrived *III. Pz.Korps* of the *6. Armee*.

On the first day of its reintroduction to battle, the *III. Pz.Korps* reported that enemy forces took two towns along the Raab River and quickly established bridgeheads, while a larger force attacked westwards and southwestwards out of Kleinzell. Despite the efforts of Breith's mish-mash forces to stop them, Soviet spearheads had reached the town of Vat, 13 kilometers west of Kleinzell, by the evening. Breith's force was a far cry from what he first had under his command a month earlier. On 28 March, all that *III. Pz.Korps* was able to deploy to stop the vanguard of the 6th Guards Tank Army were seven Hungarian fortress battalions, some elements of *Volks-Werf.Brig. 17* and *19* (without launchers), a few assault guns from *Sturm-Art.Brig 303*, the *Feld-Ersatz* battalions of the *1.* and *3. Pz.Div., I. Abt./Heeres-Art.Rgt. 77, s.Pz.Abt. 509*, and portions of *SS-Rgt. Ney.*[76] It would soon be assigned all of the *1. Volks-Geb. Div.*, which would add a considerable amount of combat power.

While on paper this appears to be a significant force, the number of armored fighting vehicles under his control was probably fewer than a dozen. For instance, *s.Pz.Abt. 509* only had five operational *Pz. VI* Tiger IIs, the same number that *Sturm-Art.Brig. 303* had.[77] Most of the other units had been positioned in the rear area of *H.Gr. Süd* and had been thrown together at the last minute. In addition, the seven attached Hungarian fortress battalions were of dubious reliability. This did not auger well for a successful defense or a force that was supposed to attack across the path of advance of two powerful Soviet armies and link up with the neighboring *6. Pz.Armee*.

The *IV. SS-Pz.Korps'* chief of staff has provided a fairly detailed account of what took place on 28 March. From his perspective, unlike Jahnke, he had a better awareness of the "big picture," but had no more idea of the *OKH's* intentions than his younger counterpart:

> On the right flank of the *IV. SS-Pz.Korps*, a strong enemy force broke through to the Zala [River] at Zalaszentgrót before it was brought to a halt by the *3. Pz.Div.* During the evening [of 28/29 March] the enemy was able to bring up enough forces to take this place and cross

the river. North of that spot, the *5. SS-Pz.Div.* and the *1. Pz.Div.* were forced to pull back to the line Zalaveg–Csipkerek. Balck complained that [the] commander of the *2. Pz.Armee* had subordinated the cavalry corps to himself and was already issuing orders to that effect.[78]

While Balck was engaged in this petty infighting with his neighboring field army commander (de Angelis), Schönfelder related: "The gap between the *I. Kav.Korps* and the *IV. SS-Pz.Korps* on the one hand, and the one between it and the *6. SS-Pz. Armee* on the other grew wider."

For the development of this unfavorable situation, Balck appeared to hold the *IV. SS-Pz.Korps* and its commander personally responsible. "Like he had done once before," Schönfelder wrote, "Balck was of the impression that we could somehow take care of the situation … with the present forces under our command."[79] It is apparent that the *6. Armee* commander still believed that Gille, even with the shattered forces under his command, should have been able stitch together a solid front between Lake Balaton and the Raab River. This suggests that Balck really did not understand the actual condition of the corps, the enemy situation, or the seriousness of the dilemma that his army faced. Both Maier and Schönfelder believed that he had simply succumbed once again to his unrealistic sense of optimism.[80]

Wednesday, 28 March also stands out as being the last day that a relatively complete weekly status report was submitted to *H.Gr. Süd* by Balck's *6. Armee*, describing the material condition of its two front-line corps (the *III. Pz.Korps* was still operating in the army's rear area before the report was compiled). It paints a picture of an army that was in a state of dissolution and that bore little resemblance to the force it had been a mere two weeks before.[81]

General der Kavallerie Gustav Harteneck's *I. Kav.Korps* was a shambling ruin. Its strongest unit was the *23. Pz.Div.*, which on that date reported three weak and two exhausted battalions, an average-strength combat engineer battalion, and a strong *Feld-Ersatz* battalion. Its commander, *Gen.Lt* Josef von Radowitz, was able to report that it still fielded 12 heavy antitank guns, though 11 of these were drawn by horses. As to armor, it could boast only having three *Jg.Pz. IV*s and one *StuG III* operational, all of its tanks having been blown up by their crews along the highway north of Lake Balaton for lack of fuel. At least the picture regarding artillery was more encouraging, with four light and four heavy batteries in operation, approximately 28–32 guns in all. The lack of fuel and shortage of vehicles earned it a mobility rating of just 40 percent, resulting in its commander assigning it a *Kampfwert* of only "IV," the lowest.

Both the *3.* and *4. Kav.Div.* were in much worse shape. *Generalmajor* von der Groeben's *3. Kav.Div.* reported three weak and two exhausted battalions and a weak *Feld-Ersatz* battalion. For armor, it reported only two operational assault guns and two heavy antitank guns. It did, however, possess six light howitzer batteries and one heavy mortar battery, as well as six light batteries from the attached Hungarian *Art. Abt. 37*. It had a horse-drawn mobility rating of 62 percent, and a motorized rating of 53 percent. Taken together, the division was also assessed as having a *Kampfwert* of "IV." The weekly report did not provide an overall number of men present for duty.

The *4. Kav.Div.*, temporarily commanded by *Oberst* Axel von Nordenskjöld until *Generalleutnant* von Grolman was released from his duties at *H.Gr. Süd*, was in a similar situation in terms of combat power, reporting only four weak battalions, one exhausted battalion, no *Feld-Ersatz* battalion, three heavy antitank guns, and two operational assault guns. It had three light howitzer batteries and three heavy mortar batteries, but only enough ammunition to supply one battery. Its horse-drawn component was rated as having 70 percent mobility, while its motorized component was only 10 percent. Overall, its combat value was rated by its commander as "IV," like its sister division. The last reporting element of the *I. Kav.Korps* was *Div.K.Gr. Hoch und Deutschmeister*, built around a single weak infantry battalion and two light howitzer batteries of the *44. Reichs-Gren.Div. HuD*; the main body of the division had already departed for its rest area in the *2. Pz.Armee* area of operations. Its acting commander, *Oberst* Hoffmann, awarded the battle group a *Kampfwert* of only "IV." Unfortunately, no weekly report from the *Hohenstaufen* Division for the period is known to exist.

For the same period ending 28 March (but actually submitted on 31 March), the *IV. SS-Pz.Korps* reported that its *1. Pz.Div.* (which had once again been subordinated to it on or about 27/28 March) had two average battalions, two weak ones, one weak combat engineer battalion, and an average-strength *Feld-Ersatz* battalion. In regards to operational armored vehicles, it had four operational *Pz. V* Panthers, no assault guns, and six heavy antitank guns. In regards to artillery, it reported two light and three heavy batteries, and a 60 percent degree of mobility. Because it still possessed a sufficient amount of operational capability, *Generalmajor* Thünert rated its *Kampfwert* as "II," capable of limited offensive operations and fully capable of conducting defensive operations, although this was most likely an overly optimistic assessment.[82]

Generalmajor Söth's *3. Pz.Div.* was nearly as strong, reporting that it still had two average battalions, two weak battalions, a weak combat engineer battalion, but no field replacement battalion. It still had seven heavy antitank guns, four operational *Pz. V* Panthers, and one *Jg.Pz. IV* tank destroyer, even after destroying most of its remaining tanks at Sümeg three days previously due to lack of fuel. Its artillery regiment still had three light batteries and two light ones, with perhaps 15–20 guns. Its mobility was assessed at 61 percent, earning it, at least in its commander's eyes, a *Kampfwert* of "II."

Finally, Ullrich's *Wiking* Division reported that it could still field one average battalion, two weak ones, two exhausted ones, and an average combat engineer battalion. In contrast, it still had an average strength *Feld-Ersatz* battalion and an average "ad-hoc" battalion, along with four weak "ad-hoc" battalions. No description of the composition of these five "ad-hoc" battalions was provided, but it can safely be assumed that they were formed from a combination of rear-echelon troops and stragglers. The chronic shortage of fuel had resulted in *SS-Pz.Art.Rgt. 5* being able to save only one heavy and two light batteries. Finally, Ullrich assessed his division's mobility as being just 40 percent, which earned it, in his eyes at least, a more realistic combat value of "IV" – suited for limited defensive operations only.

While the staff of *H.Gr. Süd* and its four armies were preparing their weekly reports on 28 March, the *Luftwaffe* reported that it had been able to carry out 100 individual daylight sorties that day, and that its aircraft reported destroying one enemy tank and a train carrying fuel. Throughout the rest of the *H.Gr. Süd* area of operations, for the first time in several days, attacks by the Red Air Force appeared to have slackened, perhaps due to the need for their airfields to further displace to the northwest to ensure their aircraft were able to keep providing timely air support to the Second and Third Ukrainian Fronts. In the *LXXII. Armee-Korps'* sector in the *8. Armee*, Hungarian *Flak* gunners shot down one IL-2 Sturmovik and *Flak* troops in the *2. Pz.Armee* also bagged one; while individually impressive, these small victories in no way impeded the operations by the Soviet 5th and 17th Air Fleets.

In addition to the ongoing withdrawal of German and Hungarian forces towards the *Reichsschutzstellung*, another large-scale movement of human beings was taking place that exacerbated the already overburdened road network in the rear area of *H.Gr. Süd*. Besides the thousands upon thousands of Hungarian refugees who were fleeing their homes ahead of the advancing Soviet forces, as many as 20,000 Hungarian Jews were also being force-marched into Austria, per an order issued by Himmler on 28 March that stipulated their "orderly evacuation" from front-line areas. These were the survivors of an initial group of 35,000 Jewish men who had been forcibly conscripted in October 1944 to help construct the *Südostwall* (Southeast Wall) of fortifications along the Hungarian–Austrian border, including the *Susannestellung*.[83]

Guarded by a mixture of SS, SA, *Volkssturm*, *Ordnungspolizei*, and Hitler Youth, their intended destination was the Mauthausen Concentration Camp, several hundred kilometers away in Upper Austria. Most of them marched on foot, and anyone too weak to continue walking was usually shot on the spot and left for dead, to be collected by a detail travelling at the end of the column. Many of the survivors—as many as 7,000, according to some sources—remained in the Austrian border region east of Graz, where they continued to be employed in construction of the incomplete *Reichsschutzstellung* defenses. The prisoners' living conditions and food were terrible; many contracted diseases such as typhus and were either put to death or allowed to die in makeshift infirmaries with little or no medical assistance.

On at least one occasion, three soldiers from the *Wiking* Division—including *Uscha.* Adolf Storms, who had been separated from his battalion in the *Westland* Regiment during the withdrawal from Veszprém—were implicated in the murder of 57 Hungarian Jews out of a group of 500 being evacuated from the Austrian town of Deutsch-Schützen on 28 and 29 March. Acting on orders from the local Hitler

Youth leader, Alfred Weber (a former member of the *Waffen-SS* himself), the three *Wikinger*, along with five members of the *Ordnungspolizei* and a number of Hitler Youth members, shot prisoners who were deemed unable to continue marching.[84] In addition to this crime, one of many being comitted at roughly the same period throughout southeastern Austria, an unspecified number of Hungarian Jews who had escaped from the evacuation columns were shot by German combat units because they had been found in the front-line area, which automatically drew the death sentence.

This was not to be the last time that members of the *Wiking* Division would be implicated in the murder of Jews near the end of the war. All of these events occurred within the *IV. SS-Pz.Korps'* and *III. Pz.Korps'* defense zone during this phase of the campaign, although no mention of such activities exists in any of the surviving official records or contemporary individual accounts. These incidents occurred at such a low level and in accordance with standing operating procedures that Gille and Breith were probably unaware of them occurring, though they could not have failed to notice forced marches of Hungarian Jewish "evacuees" taking place at that time along the same routes their own men were using. Balck makes no mention of them either, even though as the officer in charge of this area of operations, he was legally responsible for everything occurring under his purview.

Despite the worsening situation in the *6. Armee* rear area and the congestion along the highways exacerbated by the last-minute evacuation of forced Jewish laborers, the orders issued that night by *H.Gr. Süd* for the following day, 29 March, simply read: "Hold the front and close the gaps in between, especially at Kleinzell." Other than the remaining elements of the *1. Volks-Geb.Div.* that had finally arrived, and the aforementioned odds and ends subordinated to the *III. Pz.Korps*, no other reinforcements were available to carry out this impossible assignment. Perhaps the *H.Gr. Süd* and *6. Armee* leadership truly believed that the addition of the *III. Pz.Korps* would suffice to put things right. However, the deciding vote as to whether this was true or not would go to General Kravchenko, the commander of the 6th Guards Tank Army, who had no intention of allowing the *6. Armee* to close the gaps that his forces had just carved into the German defensive preparations.

By 28 March, three of *H.Gr. Süd's* four field armies were decisively engaged in battle with two Soviet army groups. On 29 March, the fourth was added to the list, when Lieutenant General Sharokhin's 57th Army attacked the *2. Pz.Armee* along both sides of the town of Nagybajom and forced its troops back several kilometers. Though the forces of the 57th Army were unable to achieve a breakthrough on this day, they would continue until they did. Hitler had repeatedly refused *H.Gr. Süd's* proposal that de Angelis's *2. Pz.Armee* be allowed to withdraw to the old *Margarethestellung* southwest of Lake Balaton. Although this action would have shortened the *2. Pz.Armee's* front line and freed up the *16. SS-Pz.Gren.Div. RFSS* for use as a reserve, Hitler feared that doing so would dangerously weaken the defenses in front of the Nagykanizsa oilfields.

With this next phase of the Vienna Operation unfolding, Hitler's forces would lose the oilfields anyway, as well as a large portion of the troops defending them. The *H.Gr. Süd* morning report for 29 March continued:

> In the defensive sector between Lake Balaton and the Raab River, tank-supported enemy forces broke through [the *6. Armee* positions] near Zalagerszeg and continued moving to the southwest, tearing the connections of [its] front apart. The [*Heeresgruppe's*] intention is to close this gap with forces committed by the *2. Pz.Armee*. West of the Raab, enemy mechanized forces drove through Steinamanger [Szombathely] towards the *Reichsgrenze* [i.e., the border of the Third Reich]. North of this area the enemy seized control of the area around Güns [Köszeg] and stood at several points along the *Grenzstellung* [border defensive position], now weakly held by rear area security forces.[85]

To the north of the *6. Armee*, Dietrich's *panzer* army was struggling to get the last of its units safely over the Raab, while having to shore up its weak flanks and prevent enemy breakthroughs along the river. North of the Danube, the focus of main effort by the Second Ukrainian Front was the battle northwest of Neuhäusel, where Soviet forces were able to cross the Neutra River and seize terrain on the opposite (i.e., western) bank. Forward elements of the 7th Guards Army attacked the German bridgehead in the city of Neutra but were driven off.

Thursday, 29 March was the last day that the *I. Kav.Korps*, including the *Hohenstaufen* Division, would serve under the *6. Armee*. Despite Balck's arguments to the contrary, *General der Artillerie* de Angelis apparently presented a more convincing case, especially since it appears that he had a more logical plan to put Harteneck's corps to better use on his army's left flank than Balck could on his right. When it was subordinated to de Angelis's army at 6 a.m. the next day, Harteneck's headquarters sent their new army commander the message: "We are happy about [our] new Commander-in-Chief, who has our full confidence. We are finally receiving orders to withdraw in a timely fashion, which allow the withdrawal to be conducted in an organized manner." Apparently, Gille and Schönfelder were not the only senior officers in the *6. Armee* who had been dissatisfied with the leadership of their army commander.[86]

But before the change in its higher headquarters could take place, the *I. Kav. Korps* still had to deal with a determined enemy, regardless of whether the corps was assigned to *6. Armee* or *2. Pz.Armee*. It reported that enemy forces attacking from around Zalaszentlaszlo pressed forward aggressively along the northern shore of Lake Balaton. The town of Keszthely on the western corner of Lake Balaton was quickly lost, but retaken by an immediate counterattack. Several other breaches in the corps' front line were sealed off by additional attacks. When the news was received informing Harteneck that his corps was now under the command of the *2. Pz.Armee*, he was directed to hold his present position with a rear guard and move the rest of his command to a new line from Keszthely–Kustany–Udvanok, where the *I. Kav.Korps* would become the left flank corps of de Angelis's command.

In Gille's defensive sector, the *IV. SS-Pz.Korps* reported that Soviet troops continued their attacks towards the southwest using numerous tanks along the highway leading to Zalagerszeg, which soon fell to his advance. The *Wiking* Division was sorely pressed, being compelled to hold its ground as it withstood numerous tank-supported battalion- and regiment-sized attacks throughout the day. After defending its position, by the evening its front line ran from the southern outskirts of Gerse–western edge of Gyorvat–western edge of Oloszka–eastern edge of Felsöoszko. On that same day, the *1. Volks-Geb.Div.* was officially removed from the *IV. SS-Pz. Korps* and subordinated to Breith's newly arrived *III. Pz.Korps*, a logical move that should have been made two days earlier.[87]

On that day, the *IV. SS-Pz.Korps* was ordered to displace to its new front-line position in front of the Raab River in a new bridgehead at Eisenburg (Vasvár). In the center of the corps' bow-shaped defense line, the *3. Pz.Div.* took up a defensive position, while on the corps' left flank stood the fighting elements of the *1. Pz.Div.*, and on the right, the *Wiking* Division took up its position. With its back facing the Raab, the corps was expected to hold its position "to the last" to prevent any further Soviet incursions towards the Reich border.

Uncertain of the enemy's precise location at this point, the division *O1* wrote in his diary that night: "The Russians supposedly have already stormed across [the river] north and south of us."[88] On the same day, *K.Gr. Bradel* from the *1. Pz.Div.* carried out a series of rear guard actions designed to delay the enemy while the corps' non-motorized elements had time to march to safety. Thünert's troops also conducted a spoiling attack against a Soviet assembly area at Felsöoszko, where an armor and artillery combination smashed and scattered the enemy, gaining a short reprieve that lasted nearly a day.[89]

While the *IV. SS-Pz.Korps* was forming a defense line around its bridgehead at Eisenburg with its three divisions, Soviet troops were busily circumventing it from the north and south, as Günther Jahnke had suspected. On this point, Schönfelder had no doubts. At the corps' new headquarters site in Körmend, 20 kilometers west of Eisenburg, where it had moved during the evening of 28/29 March, he wrote:

> The enemy force at Zalagerszeg [author's note: 25 kilometers south along the Zala River] had already turned to the north and south and now practically stood in the rear of the *IV. SS-Pz. Korps*, as well as the *I. Kav.Korps*. Balck had accused Gille of wanting to get back behind the Raab … The "big decision" to take a leap back into the *Grenzschutzstellungen* before the enemy punched through it was long overdue. We were the ones that suffered from the damage that was caused by movement decisions that were always ordered too late.[90]

Regardless of what was actually happening on the ground, Balck once again placed the blame for the growing gap between the *IV. SS-Pz.Korps* and *I. Kav.Korps* squarely on Gille's back. That evening, in a telephone conversation with Wöhler, Balck vented his frustration at what he viewed as the incompetence of the *IV. SS-Pz.Korps'* commander for wanting "to get back behind the Raab." The *H.Gr. Süd* war diary recorded the conversation as follows:

> In a discussion with the commander-in-chief [of *H.Gr. Süd*] at 10:50 p.m., the commander-in-chief of the *6. Armee* said that he saw the main reason for the gap that has arisen north of [his] army was the inadequate leadership of the *IV. SS-Pz.Korps*. The [commander of] *IV. SS-Pz. Korps* [appears to be] anxious to retreat behind the Raab. An artillery regiment of [his] corps had been found near Fürstenfeld. [Gille] had claimed that it had gone back so far because it had run out of ammunition, [so] he had sent the regiment back into the *Grenzschutzstellung*. In spite of [Balck's] order to [establish] his front in front of the Raab, he was not sure whether the *IV. SS-Pz.Korps* had retreated behind the Raab or not. [Balck] had also repeatedly ordered the *IV. SS-Pz.Korps* to link up with the cavalry corps to the right. Nevertheless, the *IV. SS-Pz. Korps* had moved away to the northwest and thus tore a hole wide open. [Balck] had asked the Army Group to once again transmit the order to the Commanding General of the *IV. SS-Pz. Korps* to keep its forward line of defense before the Raab with his front facing to the east.[91]

No mention was made of the Soviet spearhead that had forced its way into the space between the two withdrawing corps, an action that forcefully punched the actual "hole" that Balck described, not any action on the part of Gille's corps.

In such an extremely fluid situation, where orders to withdraw always seemed to come too late, Balck was obviously failing to come to grips with the reality of what was actually taking place on his front lines, where a retreat behind the Raab was the most logical course of action that Gille could have followed. Once again, there is no mention in the official records of the *6. Armee* commander visiting any of his forward units that day. Out of touch with his units, reliant primarily on radio reports, and unsure of the actual situation on the ground, the *6. Armee* commander was left to speculate as to what was happening. That Balck placed the blame for the events of that day upon the *IV. SS-Pz.Korps* is yet another example of how his legendary leadership talents had continued to deteriorate; in this, as in previous incidents, he was demonstrating that even he was unable to re-establish order in such a chaotic situation.

The *IV. SS-Pz.Korps* was not the only element of the 6. Armee experiencing difficulty that day. On its left, the *III. Pz.Korps* also struggled to hold its portion of the line along the Raab on the *6. Armee's* north flank, but Breith's meagre forces were inadequate for the task at hand. The large enemy bridgehead at Kleinzell (Sárvár) could not be contained any longer, as the forces from the XXXVII Guards Rifle Corps of the 9th Guards Army, supported by tanks from the 6th Guards Tank Army, continued surging westwards. The various *Alarm* units and fortress battalions that Breith had to employ were simply scattered and driven away. By evening, the vanguard of this powerful force had taken the important city of Steinamanger (Szombathely). A portion of the *1. Volks-Geb.Div.* was briefly encircled during the fighting, but managed to break out to the southwest, reaching its own lines by dusk. Yet no recriminations were hurled at its division commander.

On the *6. Armee*'s left flank, the *6. Pz.Armee* was having similar problems—too much ground to hold with too few troops (by this point, Dietrich had five divisions under his command, all of them understrength, plus a number of small *Alarm* units), and having to fight an overwhelmingly strong opponent who was carrying out a theater-level operation with impressive skill and speed. On the northern bank of the Danube, the same challenges applied to the *8. Armee*, which had held on to the Gran and Neutra defense lines for too long, as well as the pointless Komorn bridgehead. To the south, the attack against the *2. Pz.Armee* by the 57th Army had also begun to gather momentum.

Although de Angelis's army had fought well, the gap between it and the neighboring *6. Armee* caused by Balck's dithering had continued to widen and begun to expose the left flank of the *2. Pz.Armee* to envelopment. The tug-of-war over the *I. Kav.Korps* between Balck and de Angelis had delayed the decisions necessary to prevent this separation from occurring, and even the last-minute subordination of Harteneck's corps to the *2. Pz.Armee* could not correct this error. Despite this, the *2. Pz.Armee* proudly announced that evening that "its" *I. Kav.Korps* had destroyed 222 Soviet armored fighting vehicles between 20 and 29 March, denying the commander of *6. Armee* the opportunity to brag about this impressive feat himself.[92]

The *6. Armee* mission set by *H.Gr. Süd* for the following day simply stated, "Close the gaps between the *2.* and *6. Panzer Armies*," but in retrospect this seems to have been an aspirational goal, rather than an attainable one, since there was no possibility that Balck's army would be able to accomplish it. The new chief of staff of *H.Gr. Süd*, *Generalleutnant* von Gyldenfeldt, sent a subsequent order addressed to the *IV. SS-Pz.Korps* that read, "Do not withdraw to the west," an allusion to Balck's frequent complaints about Gille's corps.[93] Gille and Schönfelder were both well aware of this instruction and were doing their utmost to adhere to it. They were already doing everything in their power to orient the withdrawal of their corps' divisions to the southwest in order to regain contact with the *I. Kav. Korps* to its south, but it was proving a difficult task. In this case, the Red Army had the deciding vote; it still had the initiative and was sufficiently strong to keep pushing the *IV. SS-Pz.Korps* towards the west, whether Gille wanted to move in that direction or not.

Surprisingly, the *Luftwaffe* was able to show a surge of activity that day, a reflection that most of its squadrons were now flying from bases in southern Austria, where fuel and spare parts were once again available. It was able to carry out 120 daytime sorties, mostly against ground targets. The squadrons of *Luftflotte 4* claimed the destruction of seven enemy tanks, 100 motorized or horse-drawn vehicles, and four antitank guns, an impressive achievement in the face of Red Air Force numerical superiority. *Luftwaffe* pilots also carried out 80 night interdiction sorties, primarily against Soviet troop concentrations in Kleinzell as well as in the Neuhäusel–Neutra area. Red Air Force pilots also flew hundreds of interceptor and ground-attack missions, focusing their efforts against the *6. Armee* and along the front lines of the *8. Armee* fighting west of the Gran River.

If the *6. Armee* and *6. Pz.Armee* managed to withdraw into the *Reichsschutzstellung* in an orderly manner and establish a coherent defensive line, it would be nothing short of a minor miracle, but the odds were against this occurring. Wöhler also had to consider the equally important matter of how to defend Vienna and block the historical approach route into southern Germany. The tactical skill and initiative displayed by Soviet commanders during the Vienna Operation, from army group down to division level, had finally caught up with, and in most cases had surpassed, that of their German counterparts. Unlike the *H.Gr. Süd* commander, Soviet commanders also did not have to rely on a dangerously slow decision-making process presided over by someone in a bunker 800 kilometers away.

Against such an effective combination of competent leadership and overwhelming force, there was little at this point for *H.Gr. Süd* to do except try to get as many of its troops, tanks, and equipment back into the *Reichsschutzstellung* as quickly as possible before it was too late. Last-minute orders, caused by Hitler's flawed and fatally slow decision-making process, were seemingly made as if the dictator deliberately intended to sabotage his own troops. Perhaps this too smelled "like a briefcase" situation, as Gille and his staff might well have thought there was sabotage by a traitor within the ranks. The next several weeks would devolve into a race, not only to hold Vienna, but to reach the borders of the Reich itself ahead of the onrushing foe.

CHAPTER 6

The Cuff Title Order
26–28 March 1945

During the last week of March 1945, another dramatic incident involving the *Waffen-SS* concerning its operations in Hungary took place that has become legendary, an event known as the notorious *Ärmelstreifenerlass* (cuff title order). Based on numerous adverse comments and reports he had been receiving from the *H.Gr. Süd* commander, as well as directly from the commander of the *6. Armee*, between 21 and 26 March, it must have seemed to Hitler that his loyal *Waffen-SS* was failing him everywhere. Not only had the famous *Wiking* Division withdrawn from Stuhlweissenburg despite a *Führerbefehl* commanding it to hold out to the last round, but Dietrich's vaunted *6. Pz.Armee* also seemed to be unable to establish and hold a main defense line anywhere between the Bakony Forest and the Danube.

Despite repeated demands from Hitler and Guderian at *OKH* for Dietrich's SS and *Heer* troops to stand their ground and fight, the *6. Pz.Armee* commander continued withdrawing his corps and divisions gradually towards a more defensible line to the west situated along the Raab River and Marczal Canal known as the *Susannestellung*. Dietrich knew that if his army could reach this position in time, it might prevent it from being completely overwhelmed by numerically superior Soviet forces while buying the time needed to reorganize his exhausted forces.

Either unaware of this necessity or willfully ignorant of it, Hitler, and by extension Guderian, forbade this continuing withdrawal, believing that the *6. Pz.Armee's* failure to stand fast was due to an increasing disloyalty and cowardice of SS troops at all levels. We know that this perception was completely at odds with the reality, for Dietrich's troops had been fighting stubbornly and skillfully, inflicting casualties on their opponent much higher than they themselves suffered. Ironically, the *H.Gr. Süd* commander himself had recommended these withdrawals in his *Blitz* message to Hitler on 24 March, but Wöhler failed to speak up convincingly or emphatically enough in Dietrich's defense when questioned about these incidents by the *OKH*.

Matters came to a head during the daily situation briefing inside the *Führerbunker* in Berlin on 26 March, when Hitler began to ask questions about the situation in Hungary and why the *6. Pz.Armee* had once again been unable to stand its ground;

none of the senior *Wehrmacht* and SS officers present had a ready answer. Because no one was able to give him a satisfactory explanation, he gave vent to his pent-up frustration and began making wild accusations about the loyalty of the *Waffen-SS* that no one dared contradict. In the course of his rage-filled tirade, he told Himmler to order Dietrich's army to remove their cuff titles as a mark of shame due to their failure to stand fast and uphold their oaths of loyalty to *der Führer*.[1] While Himmler was cowed into silence during this outburst, the only person present brave enough to speak up on behalf of the *Waffen-SS* was Hermann Göring, of all people.

Göring told Hitler and the other staff officers and political leaders present at the briefing that the *Waffen-SS*, especially the *Leibstandarte*, had "fought bravely on every front since the beginning of the war and had already taken casualties equal to several times its strength." Göring, whose star was on the wane due to the inability of his vaunted *Luftwaffe* to defend German cities, concluded his remarks by stating that "He considered this [cuff title] action unjustified and insulting to the men, the officers, and especially to Sepp Dietrich." *Obersturmbannführer* Otto Günsche, Hitler's SS *Adjutant* at that time and an eyewitness to the event, later wrote: "Even the *Führer* was silent for a while. Finally, he ordered Fegelein and Himmler to join him immediately in the Reich Chancellery."[2]

In Berlin, far removed from the reality of the battlefield, Hitler refused to consider that his SS troops had fought magnificently against heavy odds and inflicted enormous losses upon the enemy, only that they had been unable to fulfill yet another of his impractical "stand fast" orders. When the rather tense situation briefing was nearing its conclusion, Guderian was compelled to stand his ground when Hitler ordered him to fly to Wöhler's headquarters the next day and demand that all of Dietrich's SS divisions remove their cuff titles as a mark of shame. Guderian demurred, stating that it was an SS matter that was properly in the purview of Heinrich Himmler.

When recalling this incident in his autobiography, Guderian wrote: "Up to now, Himmler had always refused to allow the Army any influence on his SS units; he now tried to change this policy, but it did him no good, since I had far more important matters to attend to." Guderian ended his account by dryly stating: "This mission of his to Hungary did not win him much affection from his *Waffen-SS*."[3] When Hitler spoke to Himmler after Guderian's refusal to follow Hitler's orders, the *Reichsführer-SS*—once the most feared man in occupied Europe—failed yet again to speak up in defense of his soldiers and meekly stood there accepting Hitler's abuse, as verified by Hitler's former *Adjutant's* eyewitness account.[4]

Wöhler first got wind of what was about to happen when Guderian telephoned him late in the evening on 26 March, informing him that "the *Führer* is beside himself about the attitude of the SS *panzer* divisions. He had ordered the *Reichsführer-SS* to go to the *Heeresgruppe* and check which divisions had done their duty and which had not."[5] This proved to be no mere rant on Hitler's part; he had ordered Himmler as the head of the SS to send a top secret telex marked "*KR-Blitz-Führung*" (most urgent priority) to the headquarters of the *6. Pz.Armee* informing its commander about Hitler's decision, which was duly composed and transmitted through *H.Gr. Süd* communications channels after 5 a.m. on 27 March.

Though an actual copy of the notorious "cuff title" message is not known to have survived, the officer at the *Hauptquartier* of the *6. Pz.Korps* who received it, *Ostubaf.* Georg Maier, remembered it vividly:

> The sense of the teletype's contents, however, was that by order of the *Führer* and the supreme commander of the *Wehrmacht*, all the divisions of the *6. SS-Pz.Armee* were no longer authorized to wear the cuff titles that they had once been awarded and that these titles were to be removed because the divisions had failed in their military duty and because they lacked courage. The teletype closed with "/signed/Heinrich Himmler."[6]

When the telex arrived, after reading it over, a shaken Maier brought it to Sepp Dietrich, who, after examining it, ordered Maier not to pass it on to the units. Maier later wrote:

> [Dietrich] turned slowly away and bent over the map table. He propped himself up with both hands so that I could not see his face. He was deeply shaken and moved, and it took him some time before he could pull himself together again. Then, after a long pause, still bent over the map table, he said in an unusually low, almost breaking voice in which the deepest disappointment and bitterness could be heard: "This is the thanks for everything."[7]

Dietrich spoke to each of his SS corps and division commanders either in person or via telephone about the "cuff title" order and told them to ignore it. He also forbade them from informing the rank and file, lest it demoralize them, especially at such a critical moment in the campaign. After regaining his composure, Dietrich pointed to his own gold-embroidered *Leibstandarte SS Adolf Hitler* cuff title on his left sleeve and told Maier "it stays on."[8] Shortly afterward, Dietrich drove off to visit his front-line troops, as was his habit.

The commander and chief of staff of the *IV. SS-Pz.Korps* most likely learned about Hitler's directive shortly thereafter, but whether they were notified by Dietrich or by the *6. Armee* commander is unknown. Gille does not mention the incident at all in his notes, but in a letter to Georg Maier, Schönfelder confirmed that he became aware of the order at about the same time. Apparently, he had learned about it from someone at *6. Armee* headquarters.[9] In his own wartime dairy, Balck commented on this episode shortly after learning about it: "Hitler immediately dispatched Himmler and overshot the objective—as usual—by immediately taking away the SS cuff titles from the troops."

In describing the incident after the war, Balck added in his memoirs: "[T]he troops did not deserve that … they had only been following the orders that they had been given by their leaders, and they were not responsible for Himmler's system of leader selection and his other funny business."[10] His chief of staff was not so circumspect. After the war, Gaedke wrote: "The *6. Armee* gained a certain satisfaction from the *Ärmelstreifenerlass* news. The SS units had not lived up to their reputation" (in saying so, it can be safely assumed that Gaedke was not alone in this sentiment).[11]

Balck fails to mention that he was one of the primary instigators of the incident, either by his constant complaints about the *IV. SS-Pz.Korps* to Wöhler or his frequent unauthorized back-channel telephone calls to Guderian protesting about Dietrich and the performance of the *6. Pz.Armee*. Whether motivated by professional jealously, animosity towards Gille, Stadler, and Dietrich, or hatred of Himmler, Balck's and Gaedke's efforts and the interests of the *6. Armee* would have been far better served if they had devoted their considerable energy towards the task at hand rather than on waging an ungentlemanly and dishonest whispering campaign against the *Waffen-SS*. The only entity to benefit from this conduct was *H.Gr. Süd*'s real opponent—the Third Ukrainian Front.

Hermann Balck apparently had learned about the "cuff title" order from *H.Gr. Süd*, perhaps at the same time that Dietrich did. After all, the telex from Berlin with Himmler's order had gone through *Wehrmacht* message traffic channels and had been read by officers or enlisted men working in the *H.Gr. Süd* communications center before being forwarded to the *6. Pz.Armee* headquarters. No mention of this order was ever made in the *H.Gr. Süd* war diary and no copy is known to exist in the records of the U.S. National Archives and Records Administration or the German Federal Archives. Dietrich's own copy was most likely destroyed in May 1945 when all of the *6. Pz.Armee*'s records were burned per standing orders. As Dietrich forbade his commanders from carrying out the *Ärmelstreifenerlass* or even mentioning it to their men, most of the troops in his SS divisions did not become aware of the order until after the war when they were in POW camps.[12]

Practically speaking, the order could not be carried out; by the end of March 1945, few of the thousands of SS troops fighting in Hungary were still wearing their cuff titles on their sleeves anyway. They had already been taken off their uniforms at the end of the previous month, when an order was issued as a security measure to prevent SS unit identities from being revealed when the *6. Pz.Armee* was marshaling in preparation for its *Frühlingserwachen* offensive. Whether the troops themselves were still wearing their cuff titles or not—bearing such legendary names as *Leibstandarte SS Adolf Hitler*, *Das Reich*, *Totenkopf*, or *Wiking*—any published order to remove them would indeed have had an adverse effect on morale that was already low at this point.

Perhaps the only recorded examples of anyone removing their cuff titles pursuant to this order occurred when the chief of staff of *6. Pz.Armee*, *Brig.Fhr.* Fritz Kraemer, and Georg Maier removed theirs. According to Maier, shortly after Dietrich had departed for the front line on the morning of 27 March, Maier handed Kraemer the copy of the *Ärmelstreifenerlass* and briefed him on Dietrich's reaction. According to Maier, "[Kraemer] became red with anger. We used a letter opener to cut off each other's cuff titles. He was wearing one for the *Leibstandarte*; I was wearing one from my old division, the *2. SS-Pz.Div. Das Reich*. The two of us had had enough." That was as far as it went.[13]

One popular myth that grew out of this incident that has little connection with reality concerns an alleged threat made by certain SS officers serving in Hungary, who upon learning of Hitler's order, threatened to send their cuff titles and decorations to Berlin in a chamber pot, addressed to the *Führerbunker*. There is no factual basis to this story, which made the rounds in the 1950s after being sensationalized in Gerald Reitlinger's book, *The SS: Alibi of a Nation*.[14] Some accounts include the extra detail of a detached arm from a dead SS man clothed in a torn sleeve with the cuff title from the *Götz von Berlichingen* Division still affixed. There are no facts that support any these colorful (and morbid) allegations, but they are nonetheless still believed in some historical circles.[15]

Himmler flew from Berlin to Hungary on the morning of 28 March to speak with Wöhler about this and other complaints that the *H.Gr. Süd* commander had in regards to the *Waffen-SS*, as well as to "personally inspect the condition of the SS armored divisions." Wöhler saw this impending visit by the *Reichsführer-SS* as an opportunity to vent his and Hermann Balck's frustrations about the performance of SS troops in general and the SS leadership in particular. The *H.Gr. Süd* commander asked his staff to prepare a detailed list of talking points that morning to use as a conversational guide for the meeting scheduled to take place upon Himmler's arrival.

This document, titled *Besprechungspunkte für Reichsführer-SS*, was divided into two sections, one addressing a point Wöhler wished to pose to Himmler in his capacity as commander-in-chief of the *Ersatzheer* (Replacement Army) and the other in his capacity as leader of the SS, and included 10 discussion points. His first discussion point was more of a conversation starter, merely notifying Himmler as head of the *Ersatzheer* that lack of replacements for combat duty with the *Heer* from the 1901 year group and younger ought to require him to order a call-up of older age groups, who had thus far been spared. Even if Himmler acceded to this request, it would take weeks if not months for *H.Gr. Süd* to benefit from any influx of extra manpower.

The other portion of this document was mostly a list of complaints against the performance of *Waffen-SS* units fighting in the Hungarian theater of operations, which would have necessarily included the *IV. SS-Pz.Korps*. How many of these complaints were authored by Balck himself is unknown, but many of the accusations had oft been repeated by the *6. Armee* commander and will be familiar to the reader. Some of these had already been aired in Wöhler's 23 March memorandum addressed to Guderian at the *OKH* (see previous chapter). Being a punctilious officer, Wöhler would have had this list of talking points at his fingertips during his initial conversation with Himmler, and may have also used it when Dietrich was invited to join the conversation later that day. These discussion points consisted of the following:

1) Lack of combatants, especially of *Panzergrenadiere*, [and] unhealthy ratio between total and frontline strength.
2) Great shortages of officers as a result of heavy losses. An acting company commander commands a regiment-wide sector in one place.
3) Total exhaustion. In continuous offensive or defensive combat since 6 March 1945. One commander reported that during the defense of Veszprém, men were falling asleep from exhaustion in their foxholes, where they were struck dead by the Russians. Officers fell asleep while talking to them.
4) Terror of the Russians. Fighting on the defense in small groups without units on either side. Fear of being surrounded, as experience had shown no chance of getting relieved.
5) Disadvantages of being accustomed to using motor vehicles when withdrawing. The possibility exists that when squads are not held together by strong-willed noncommissioned officers, who are frequently missing, they get on *Tross* vehicles that are moving back under orders. These vehicles, moving far to the rear, give [these men] an opportunity for a peaceful night's sleep.
6) Fear of artillery fire among the very young year groups based on experiences in the west. If strong-willed officers are not present, the troops pull back right at the beginning of artillery fire.
7) Tendency of middle-level command to pull out companies early for reconstitution that had been battered, but were still entirely fit for combat, in order to maintain a sound cadre.
8) In spite of exhaustion, generally excellent impression of the officers, especially from the *12. SS-Pz.Div. Hitlerjugend.*
9) Poor reporting procedures for the divisions and corps, so that even the field army was sometimes poorly informed. General staff work at the field army [i.e., *6. Pz.Armee*] flawless thanks to a splendid chief of staff and very good *Ia* [i.e., Georg Maier].
10) Perpetual shortage of fuel, artillery ammunition and ammunition for other heavy weapons is influencing the fighting to a very high degree.[16]

A cursory examination of these points reveals that many of these "talking points" could apply just as easily to any of the *Heer* units fighting alongside troops from the *Waffen-SS*. Also noteworthy is that none of these cases matches the description of the deliberate acts of cowardice that Hitler accused the SS troops of having committed during his 26 March rant. Some of these "points" are rather petty or specious, while others, such as the one concerning shortages of fuel and ammunitions, were just as much the responsibility of the army group as they were of the field army.

As far as the SS replacement situation was concerned, much of the fault for this shortcoming lay with Himmler himself, who increased the size of the *Waffen-SS* without a corresponding change in the size of its replacement and training establishments. Without a large and fully mature *Ersatz und Ausbildungs* infrastructure like the one that the *Heer* possessed—which could adequately absorb and retrain hundreds of thousands of former *Luftwaffe* and *Kriegsmarine* personnel—the *Waffen-SS* poured large numbers of similar replacements directly into field units with nothing to prepare them but a two- or three-week administrative and familiarization period. The fact that such poorly trained and conditioned men failed when subjected to Soviet artillery fire for the first time should have surprised no one.

Upon arrival at Wöhler's headquarters on the morning of 28 March, rather than go directly to Dietrich's headquarters or visit any of his SS corps or divisions in the field in person, Himmler—in typically cowardly fashion—summoned Dietrich to meet him at noon at Wöhler's army group HQ in Eisenstadt. According to the *6. Pz.Armee*'s *Ia*: "That suited Sepp Dietrich just fine. He was still furious and grimly determined to tell Himmler what he thought of this and to stand up for his soldiers. At the time he stated that he would demand the retraction of this disgraceful order."[17] While he awaited Dietrich's arrival, Himmler met for several hours in private with Wöhler. Since no note taker was permitted to sit in on the meeting, we only have the army group commander's later notes in the *H.Gr. Süd KTB* as a reference. It is not known whether Himmler made any notes of his own about their conversation.

After a hazardous daylight journey from his headquarters, during which his staff car was vulnerable to attack by the Red Air Force at any moment, Dietrich arrived at Eisenstadt in a convoy escorted by an *SPW* platoon from his headquarters security company along with a 2cm *Vierlingsflak* SP antiaircraft gun. Once all three men had gone into a closed conference room away from prying eyes, both Himmler and Wöhler proceeded to criticize the *6. Pz.Armee*'s performance, as well as to discuss Balck's accusations concerning Gille and Schönfelder's performance and his demand to relieve both men of their duties. Again, no note taker was present to record the conversation.

According to Dietrich, Himmler was conciliatory about the "cuff title" order and said that he had done everything he could to argue the case before Hitler on Dietrich's behalf, but we now know this was a blatant lie, as revealed by Günsche after the war. As previously related, only Göring had spoken up in defense of the *Waffen-SS*, while Himmler had remained silent. Upon his return to his army headquarters in the town of Györsovenihaz several hours later, Dietrich told his chief of staff and *Ia* that he had listened to Himmler's feeble excuses but at least he had been able to argue in defense of his soldiers. The only official mention in the *H.Gr. Süd* war diary that the meeting had taken place stated:

> The *Reichsführer-SS* visited the command post of *Heeresgruppe Süd* in Eisenstadt and had a thorough discussion with the Commander-in-Chief [of *H.Gr. Süd*] and the Commander in Chief of the *6. Panzer-Armee* concerning the condition of the SS armored divisions, means for raising combat power, and for maintaining discipline. [18]

Apparently, Himmler did not ask Dietrich whether the *Ärmelstreifenerlass* had been implemented; the two men did not have a good personal or working relationship with one another, and Himmler most likely wished to avoid a confrontation with the burly and intimidating SS general.

One concession that Wöhler was able to pry from Himmler was the latter's agreement to release a substantial amount of gasoline from an SS fuel stockpile in

Vienna for use by *H.Gr. Süd*. While this hoard had been accumulated for sole use by the Nazi Party, the SS, and *Ordnungspolizei* for their own internal security purposes, Himmler had withheld it from his own combat troops fighting in Hungary, who had been forced to abandon many of their armored vehicles due to lack of fuel. Although *H.Gr. Süd* immediately began taking possession of the fuel depot, this windfall came too late in the campaign to have much effect upon the fighting; by this point, the self-inflicted damage to the *6. Armee* and *6. Pz.Armede* had already been done.[19]

That same day, Wöhler issued an order to his armies concerning the outcome of his conversation with Himmler (based on his own notes) and their mutually agreed-upon points. Issued at 8:20 p.m., the order stated:

> The approach of the Bolshevists must be stopped under any circumstance; the building of a solid defense front, no matter of the difficulties involved, must be carried out.
>
> Every means to raise the level of our combat power is permitted. The *Reichsführer-SS* and I are in agreement that even specialist personnel, whose weapons cannot be employed (for example, tank crews), should all be sent to the front line to be deployed as *Panzergrenadiere*. An attempt should be made to employ these "combed out" soldiers within their own divisions, but it is not an absolute prerequisite.
>
> I know that my army and corps commanders as well as every commander in the front line have never thought of resigning. We are united as one in the belief that we know where our duty lies, now more than ever![20]

How much all of these behind-the-scenes machinations affected the fighting ability of German forces in Hungary can be debated. Whatever the case, Wöhler's order could not significantly enhance *H.Gr. Süd*'s combat potential or make it more effective. It is doubtful whether the Second and Third Ukrainian Fronts even noticed the difference. If anything, removing specialists from their duty positions and employing them as infantrymen would, as previously related, only hasten the collapse of *H.Gr. Süd*'s fighting divisions, not delay it.

Hitler's "cuff title" order and other orders like the one above help us understand today what was going on in the minds of *Waffen-SS* leaders and their men, who were still compelled to keep fighting during the last full month of hostilities despite the affront to their honor ordered by Hitler. Torn between the dictates of their consciences and the oath to Hitler that they had all sworn to obey, the men of the *Waffen-SS* clung together more tightly, firm in the belief that their loyalty to one another was the only thing left they could count on. Despite the knowledge that their divisions were falling apart and their sacrifices might be in vain, most SS officers and enlisted men continued to do their utmost nonetheless, even at the cost of their lives. According to Georg Maier, the most reliable eyewitness to this event, "In spite of everything, the fact that [the *Waffen-SS*] remained obedient—even when difficult—and still did its military duty, fighting bravely to the best of its ability demonstrates that the *6. Pz.Armee* remained loyal to its oath of allegiance to the bitter end."[21]

After all, from the perspective of 28 March, the fighting was still taking place a long distance from Vienna and the end of the war still seemed very far away. Some officers and men probably thought that their sacrifices would still serve a higher purpose, if only they could keep the Red Army away long enough for the Western Allies to join them in their life and death struggle against "Bolshevism." At any rate, on 29 March they had far more important things to concern themselves with, as both the *6. Armee* and *6. Pz.Armee* raced to reach the elusive safety of the *Reichsschutzstellung* before the Red Army did and to prepare its defenses as best they could before Soviet troops set foot on German soil.

CHAPTER 7

Withdrawal to the *Reichsschutzstellung* 30–31 March 1945

The large-scale German withdrawal beyond the western shore of Lake Balaton towards the anticipated protection of the *Reichsschutzstellung* behind the Austrian border continued into 30 March. Another sunny, warm spring day followed a cool and dry evening. Localized light rain showers were reported throughout the day, but on the whole, flying and fighting conditions were good, especially for the attacking Red Army. The *H.Gr. Süd* daily report for 30 March, submitted that evening to *OKH* headquarters in Berlin, read as follows:

> The *2. Pz.Armee* was unable to prevent the enemy from widening his deep breakthrough on the army's southern wing and in the Nagybajom area, which forced the army to withdraw into the *Margarethestellung* in order to preserve the integrity of the front line. A strong tank-led attack west of Nagybajom was intercepted and brought to a halt. West of Lake Balaton the enemy attacked as far west as he could in order to envelop the army's deep left flank and force it to withdraw at several points towards the south … Southeast of Steinamanger [Szombathely], the forces of the *6. Armee* were forced to withdraw to the west bank of the Raab. The extension of its right flank towards the southwest to link up [with *2. Pz.Armee*] is currently taking place. West of Steinamanger on account of his numerical superiority in men and matériel, the enemy was able to penetrate into the *Grenzstellung* [i.e., the *Reichsschutzstellung* on the Austrian border], where he was able to seize an area northwest of Güns [Köszeg] until he was finally intercepted by a blocking unit.

This litany of disasters involved only two of *H.Gr. Süd*'s armies, *2. Pz.Armee* and *6. Armee*. The situation of the other two, the *6. Pz.Armee* and *8. Armee*, were comparatively more encouraging. The report continued:

> Southeast of the Neusiedlersee [in the *6. Pz.Armee* area of operations], strong enemy infantry and tank assaults were for the most part brought to a halt by our magnificently fighting troops in tough defensive fighting. North of the Danube, the enemy continued his grand offensive [against the *8. Armee*] with his focus of main effort being the Neutra defensive sector and the area to the southwest and was able to claw his way a few kilometers towards the northwest. Our counterattacks are currently in progress. On the mountain front [in Slovakia], local enemy attacks were driven back.[1]

This was the neat and tidy "macro" view as reported to *OKH*. Down at the field army, corps, and division level, things looked much messier.

In the *6. Armee* defensive sector, the *IV. SS-Pz.Korps* reported that during the day, elements of Lieutenant General Govorunenko's XVIII Tank Corps of the 27th Army were able to advance into the gap between the *6. Armee* and *2. Pz.Armee*. Some of his tanks reached the Raab River between the towns of Nagycsákány and Nagymizdó, southwest of the corps' location at Körmend, and crossed the river at Rábadorosló unopposed. This force, consisting of two tanks and about 200 men, continued moving to the west against little opposition. Gille's corps had already been outflanked yet again, this time on its right before it could get its divisions properly settled into their new main defense line.

Unless it could establish a solid perimeter connected to the rear by a bridge capable of bearing the weight of its remaining armor, most of the *IV. SS-Pz.Korps* ran the risk of being trapped on the eastern side of the river, where the majority of its fighting troops were positioned, a convincing reason why Gille wanted to withdraw to the river's western bank. Meanwhile, non-combat administrative and logistics units of the *6. Armee* and its constituent elements, including *IV. SS-Pz. Korps*, began moving to the west as quickly as possible to avoid being embroiled in the fighting. Günther Jahnke of the *Wiking* Division was on the scene to record the events from the division's perspective:

> At 5 a.m., the division command post moved to the southern part of the bridgehead near the only remaining bridge over the Raab. About 11 a.m., I was given an assignment to go immediately to the corps headquarters located to the west … here I was supposed to learn that I was to go and collect up all of the elements of the division located in the *Tross* area and assemble them in Fürstenfeld [Austria] and to lead them into the sector designated for our division in the *Reichsschutzstellung*.[2] I learned that the area where the corps command post was [currently] supposed to be … was already occupied by the Russians. At 2:30 p.m. I crossed the *Reichsgrenze*, what a "welcome home" that was. From this point onwards, all of the roads were blocked without exception. On the main highway leading towards Fürstenfeld, there were two to three vehicle convoys sitting side by side on the road.

The young officer was stunned at what he saw. How was he going to get to Fürstenfeld through this traffic jam? Later that evening he wrote:

> Despite the direct intervention of numerous staff officers and *Feldgendarmes*, they could not straighten out this mess. At 11 p.m., I finally found the division *Ib* [*Hstuf.* Heinz Fischer], who was not quite sure of the actual situation of the [division's] *Tross*. Finally, we got to work constructing barriers and started rounding up all the units of the division that we could find and sending them into their new positions in the *Reichsschutzstellung*. Later in the evening, we were briefed by the corps and division commander about our new defensive sector. With this, the *Wiking* Division ended its campaign in enemy [*sic*] territory. The war had [finally] reached the *Reichsgrenze* [national border] too.[3]

Jahnke's fellow observer of these events, Manfred Schönfelder, also recalled what he had seen and experienced that day near the front lines. Writing after the war, he stated that the attack that the *6. Armee* had ordered the *IV. SS-Pz.Korps* to carry out to re-establish contact with the *2. Pz.Armee* that day did not turn out as Balck had intended.

This attack was to have been conducted out of the Körmend bridgehead towards the south through the village of Gersekarát, using the *3. Pz.Div.*, which was intended to link up 25 kilometers beyond that point with the *I. Kav.Korps*. If successful, this operation would re-establish the connection between the two armies as Balck had been ordered to do. However, the attack was forestalled when the Soviets launched their own assault against Eisenburg on the corps' left flank. Schönfelder later wrote:

> [T]hat the part of the bridgehead east of Körmend had been lost and the enemy had pushed into the bridgehead at Eisenburg [Vasvár]. As a result, [Balck] accused the *IV. SS-Pz.Korps*, which was supposed to attack through Gerse[karát] to the south and re-establish contact with the *2. Pz.Armee*, which "had gotten itself into an impossible situation there, as it was dependent on the bridge position at Körmend and Eisenburg for its supplies."[4]

Schönfelder asserts that this accusation was unfounded, since it was Balck himself who had ordered the attack to the south. The corps also lacked the means to carry out an attack of that magnitude—advancing 25 kilometers through enemy-held territory would have been a difficult task for a full-strength *panzer* division, but it was beyond the ability of a corps whose three divisions by this point consisted of little more than weak infantry brigades supported by a platoon of tanks. At the most, Gille could spare one division *Kampfgruppe* for this assignment, lest his left flank and center be weakened to the point where they were exposed to further attack.

Had the corps actually carried through the attack on 30 March as it was originally intended, with just one division *Kampfgruppe*, it probably would have been cut off and destroyed by the 27th Army. When he heard that evening that the attack had not taken place at all, Balck complained again to Wöhler that he was "having a hard time getting the *IV. SS-Pz.Korps* to move out. It doesn't think it'll be ready to attack for two or three days. In addition, it complains that its *panzer* and fuel situation is bleak, and that there is a shortage of artillery ammunition. Its infantry is now just a jumbled-together heap."[5] All of this was true, but the situation in Gille's corps was not much different than what any other corps in *H.Gr. Süd* was experiencing at that time.

As an example, one such "jumbled-together heap" consisted of *Gruppe Lenk* of the former Hungarian *1. SS-Sturmjäger Regiment*, which had attached itself to *IV. Btl./SS-Rgt. Ney*. Ney's regiment at that time was split between the *IV. SS-Pz. Korps* and *6. Pz.Armee*, with the bulk of it fighting just south of the Neusiedlersee under Dietrich's command on 30 March. The *IV. Btl./SS-Rgt. Ney* was operating somewhere to the left or north of the *1. Pz.Div.*, where it maintained a tenuous connection with the neighboring *1. Volks-Geb.Div.* of Breith's *III. Pz.Korps*. In addition to the *Waffen-SS* members in its ranks, *Gruppe Lenk* had also incorporated hundreds of non-SS Hungarian troops who had been swept up in the withdrawal. Lacking heavy weapons, transportation, and communications equipment, *Gruppe Lenk* could do little more than man an outpost line, but it was with such troops as these that *H.Gr. Süd* had to attempt to stem the onrushing tide.

Interestingly, neither Balck at the time nor Schönfelder after the war mention that for part of the day, the *IV. SS-Pz.Korps* command post was out of contact with its three divisions, having been forced to hurriedly escape from Körmend just ahead of the small Soviet task force that had crossed the Raab at Rábadorosló earlier that day. Jahnke alludes to this in his own diary, when he mentions that when he tried to find the corps headquarters inside the town, he discovered that the enemy had arrived there before him. Gille and his staff were nowhere to be found. The division history of the *3. Pz.Div.* also mentions this incident, stating that on 30 March, "The corps stopped leading. It displaced [to the rear] without notifying its divisions … *Generalmajor* Thünert, commander of the *1. Pz.Div.*, the highest ranking officer, took over command of the *3. Pz.Div.* [and] ordered the evacuation of the Eisenburg bridgehead."[6]

In contrast, the highly detailed division history of the *1. Pz.Div.* makes no mention of this situation having occurred at all. Regardless, this was most uncharacteristic of Gille and Schönfelder, who had always striven their utmost to remain in contact with their subordinate units, especially after being reprimanded by Balck for allegedly failing to do so the previous month. Most likely, Gille and the rest of the forward command post staff had to pack up and leave very quickly, with no time to notify their subordinate units. They were probably out of contact for several hours at the most—a relatively short time—since no mention was made of this in any reports submitted by *6. Armee*, whose commander would have made the most of this incident, nor in the *KTB* of *H.Gr. Süd*. The *H.Gr. Süd* evening report did, however, report that the *IV. SS-Pz.Korps* headquarters was now operating in Königsdorf across the Austrian border, 40 kilometers to the west.[7]

One of Gille's increasingly rare comments during this period mentioned this particular movement, when he wrote: "An order, finally a great leap back towards the west into the *Reichsschutzstellung* that will probably be partly occupied by the Russians when we get there. We are to hold this position until the end."[8] The movement of the corps back to the *Reichsschutzstellung* immediately ran into the huge columns of vehicles that Jahnke had already written about, which delayed the *IV. SS-Pz.Korps'* displacement to its new positions longer than anticipated. The process of having to tear down the command post, load equipment into vehicles while under enemy pressure and move along crowded roads to another location, only to set up again, was a tedious and time-consuming process.

Each hour a corps command post was not in operation meant that it would be out of contact with its subordinate units throughout that period and could not exercise effective command and control until it re-established radio communications once again. In such a fluid situation as existed on 30 March, it was pointless to lay wire, which was becoming scarce anyway. What happened to the headquarters of the *IV. SS-Pz.Korps* was not an isolated incident; on the same day, the commander of the *XXII. Geb.Korps* of the *2. Pz.Armee*, *Gen.d.Geb.Tr.* Hubert Lanz, lost contact with his own divisions in a similar situation, leaving the *I. Kav.Korps* to assume temporary control of them until the corps commander could re-establish communications.[9]

On the northern flank of Gille's corps, adjacent to the *III. Pz.Korps'* defensive sector, Soviet troops and tanks from the 6th Guards Tank Army broke through between the towns of Gerse and Döröske and advanced as far as the bridgehead held by the *1. Pz.Div.* over the Raab River at Eisenburg. The Soviet attack forced the elements of the combined *Kampfgruppe*—composed of *Pz.Aufkl.Abt. 1* supported by a small *Panzergruppe* from the *Hohenstaufen* Division (portions of *SS-Pz.Aufkl.Abt. 9*)—to withdraw their right flank back to the river.[10] Another mechanized Soviet formation attacked the bridgehead's left flank and managed to fight its way into the town itself before it was ejected by a German counterattack. Finally, after the Soviet commander on the scene launched a second attack, the defenders withdrew from the town and took up positions in the woods on either side of it, until *Generalmajor* Thünert ordered them to evacuate the bridgehead that evening.

On the *III. Pz.Korps'* left flank near Kis Balogta, elements of the V Guards Cavalry Corps of the 26th Army launched a series of company- and battalion-sized attacks northwest of Güns (Köszeg) that were initially delayed by a blocking detachment formed from hastily assembled German *Alarm* units. Another force took the town of Butsching (Bucsu), and after two attempts finally took Rechnitz (Rohoncz) on the Austrian side of the border after overcoming resistance by a *Volkssturm* battalion and an ad-hoc infantry battalion from a *Volks-Werfer* Regiment. Thereafter, a powerful Soviet attack group including between 40 and 60 tanks advancing from the area of Güns stormed into the Austrian border between the road linking Schachendorf and Rechnitz, turned to the north, and began advancing towards the town of Kirschlag, 60 kilometers away. Finally, the Red Army was well and truly on Austrian soil.[11]

In anticipation of this moment, and dissatisfied with the apparent inability of German forces in Hungary to stand their ground, the *OKH* had issued another *Führerbefehl* via teletype at 6:30 a.m. that morning to *H.Gr. Süd* and all of its subordinate units stating that the army group's mission was:

1) To ensure the protection of German territory in the southeast and the decisive oil region southwest of lake Balaton; and
2) To interdict the enemy breakthrough by harnessing all forces, to close the breakthrough gaps in the frontline and to re-establish a cohesive main line of resistance. For this purpose, the *H.Gr. Süd* center may [pull back] under overwhelming enemy pressure to the line west end of Lake Balaton–*Reichsgrenze* southwest of Steinamanger [Szombathely]–*Reichsschutzstellung* up to Pressburg [Bratislava]–Pribina position up to west of Neutra–Neutra.[12]

The most ironic elements of this entire situation were not only the imminent abandonment of the oil fields, but that at the moment when enemy forces had finally reached the boundary of the Third Reich in southern Austria, *H.Gr. Süd* had no substantial forces whatsoever that could be spared to prevent the Red Army from advancing towards Vienna.

Most of the *6. Pz.Armee*, with its four SS and one *Heer panzer* divisions (all now designated only as *Kampfgruppen* since they had suffered so many losses), was fighting along the northern Raab River defense line and could not spare any forces to defend the city at that moment, nor could the *IV. SS-Pz.Korps* with its single SS division (the *Wiking*). Despite the fact that there were now nine SS divisions operating within *H.Gr. Süd*, the most that the *Waffen-SS* could immediately offer for the Austrian capital's defense on 30 March were administrative and logistics troops in the *H.Gr. Süd* rear area, barely trained replacements from *SS-Gren.Ausb.und Ers. Btl. 11*, and convalescents fresh out of hospital. The forces needed to defend the city would have to be brought in from elsewhere.

Repeated requests by the now lame-duck Wöhler for permission to transfer the *16. SS-Pz.Gren.Div. RFSS* from the *2. Pz.Armee* to *6. Pz.Armee* went unanswered because Hitler still wanted it to protect the Hungarian oil fields, which were as good as lost by this point.[13] The understrength *13. Waffen-Geb.Div. der SS Handschar* had been fighting with *General der Artillerie* de Angelis's army for several months, and the Ukrainians of the *14. Waffen-Gren.Div. der SS* had been brought up from their reserve area southwest of Graz and were in the process of moving to the far left flank of the *I. Kav.Korps*, where it would establish loose contact with the *Wiking* Division on 31 March.[14]

In his memoirs, Balck accused the *IV. SS-Pz.Korps* of causing the tremendous traffic jam on the Austrian border between 28 and 30 March when, during the withdrawal, it allegedly strayed north from its designated route into that specified for the *III. Pz.Korps*:

> [E]verything now was mixed into an insolvable mass of humans and vehicles in the most difficult mountain terrain. All movement had stopped there. At that time, it was impossible to know what reasons had prompted the *IV. SS-Pz.Korps* to attempt such an impossible action … Today I believe that it was rampant fear of encirclement that resulted in their absurd decision. The corps leadership's complete lack of understanding of the big picture and the available operational options did the rest.[15]

Looking at his description of events from today's perspective, it is difficult to understand how or why he made this statement some 35 years later, unless he did not look at a map. The *III. Pz.Korps* was fighting 30 kilometers to the north of the *IV. SS-Pz.Korps*, and its withdrawal route ran westwards from Steinamanger past Rechnitz into the Pinka River valley, not through the Raab or lower Lafnitz River valleys, so if any units were using the improper withdrawal route and causing the traffic jam, they would have been from the *III. Pz.Korps*.

While it is true that there were enormous traffic backlogs in Gille's sector, not all of the vehicles involved could have been from his corps, which at that time consisted of the three aforementioned *panzer* divisions, including the *Wiking* Division. Hundreds of vehicles, if not thousands, operated by *Heerestruppen* from the *6. Armee* and *H.Gr. Süd* were also using the same route that Balck and Jahnke mention, including logistics and administrative units fleeing from Soviet forces advancing from the south as part of Tolbukhin's effort to split apart the *2. Pz.Armee* and Balck's. In addition to military units, the same roads were being used by tens of thousands of Hungarian refugees fleeing from the Red Army, as well as Hungarian Jews being evacuated from the border area where they had been digging fortifications. None of these disparate entities had any other way to reach the Austrian hinterland. Additionally, Jahnke mentions the enormous traffic jam that already existed before he had made his reconnoiter, which the *IV. SS-Pz.Korps* certainly did not cause.

Another factor to consider is that according to German Army doctrine in effect at the time, traffic control in a field army's *Ruckwärtige Gebiet* (rear area) was the responsibility of the field army rear area commander, not a *panzer* corps. Interestingly, on 25 March, Balck had named his *Korück* (rear area zone) commander, *Gen.Lt.* Walther Krause, as the leader of an ad-hoc *Divisions-Kampfgruppe* named after him, fighting to the north of the *IV. SS-Pz.Korps* under the *III. Pz.Korps*. When his energetic talents to sort out the mess were needed the most, Krause was employed elsewhere, though other equally capable senior officers, such as *Gen.d.Geb.Tr.* Julius Ringel, commander of *Wehrkreis XVIII*, were available to lead the battle group.[16] This is yet another example of one of Balck's *ex post facto* attacks against the military competency of the *IV. SS-Pz.Korps* to excuse his army's failure to accomplish its objectives that day.

Between 29 March and 1 April, it seemed as if *H.Gr. Süd* would never be able to put together any kind of coherent defense in its area of operations. The end seemed to be drawing nearer, and every attempt to stop or slow down the Third Ukrainian Front's advance had seemingly failed. Despite the hopelessness of the situation, there was still a war to be fought and it was becoming increasingly apparent that as military professionals, the leaders of the *Wehrmacht* and *Waffen-SS* would have no choice but to continue fighting to the bitter end—after all, the survival of their homeland was at stake. Although handfuls of nonsensical *Führerbefehle* were issued each day from Hitler's bunker in Berlin to the armies defending the ever-shrinking perimeter of his empire, the *Wehrmacht* and *Waffen-SS* would continue to carry them out to the best of their ability.

The defense of what was left of Hungary and the new front in Austria had not been forgotten by the *OKH*. For 31 March, *H.Gr. Süd*, acting on a directive from Berlin, assigned Balck's *6. Armee* the following tasks:

> Defend the northern bank of the Raab between Neumarkt [an der Raab] and Körmend with the *IV. SS-Pz.Korps*; withdraw from the Eisenburg bridgehead; pull the *III. Pz.Korps* back towards the line Körmend–Jak–Torony; clear out the enemy breakthrough at Rechnitz by the use of part of the *1. Volks-Geb.Div.* and by thinning [troops out of] the front line between Rum and Torony [*III. Pz.Korps*].[17]

Most of the forces in the *6. Armee* order of battle lacked the ability to carry out these assignments, since the majority of them had left their tanks, artillery, and other heavy weapons behind on the roadside for want of fuel or had blown them up. On that day, Gille's corps could report having only 23 operational armored combat vehicles within its three divisions, compared to the 200 being operated by the Soviet XVIII Tank Corps alone.[18] Even for these few tanks and guns remaining, there was little ammunition or fuel to be had. Still, the men of the *III. Pz.Korps* and *IV. SS-Pz. Korps* would give their best.

Although 30 March did not mark the official end of the campaign in Hungary or the beginning of a new one in Austria, for the *IV. SS-Pz.Korps* the day represented a milestone in its history, for it was the first day that it had ever fought on home soil. It would never again fight in foreign lands. From 31 March until the end of the war, Gille, Schönfelder, and the rest of his staff, corps troops, and subordinate divisions (including the *Wiking*) would do their utmost to defend Hitler's dying empire in unenviable circumstances, reinforced in their desire to succeed by the need to protect defenseless Austrian women and children, if for no other reason.

The following day also represented another milestone, marking the last day of the last complete month of the war diary for the *H.Gr. Süd Führungsabteilung* that survived the war. Beyond this point, the official record trails away, such that the historian is forced to rely on a reconstructed and incomplete *H.Gr. Süd* operational summary that ends after 22 April, along with personal diaries, veterans' accounts, Allied news reports, postwar histories, and such surviving fragments of official records that can be found in the archives. It also marked the last day that Schönfelder recorded in his postwar manuscript written as a rebuttal to Balck's accusations.

However, for the commanders and staffs of the armies, corps, and divisions of *H.Gr. Süd*, Saturday, 31 March was just another day of the campaign, the 16th day since the initiation of the Red Army's Vienna Operation. Each headquarters had its own peculiar rhythm that tied in with that of its higher headquarters. Periodic reports, morning and evening reports, ammunition and fuel reports, and casualty reports still had to be submitted the same time every day, usually to the same day or night shift staff officer or NCO serving as the on-duty *Schreiber*. Formats generally stayed the same; the only aspect that did change was that it was becoming increasingly difficult to contact the units in the field which were supposed to submit feeder reports with their data. Through no one's fault, units were having difficulty reporting because they were now being forced daily to change locations, their communication systems were out of order, or they had been overrun by the enemy. While the life of a staff officer or NCO was never easy, including chasing down such relevant data from the units, it was still better than living and fighting in the mud, with the ever-present possibility of imminent death weighing heavily on one's mind.

From the perch of *H.Gr. Süd*, everything must have still seemed to be working the way it always had. Its old commander, Wöhler, was still in command, if only in an acting capacity for a few more days. Its new chief of staff, *Generalleutnant* von Gyldenfeldt, was a calm and forceful presence. But from the perspective of nearly everyone else, 31 March would have been remembered as a day of heavy fighting characterized by some planned and some unplanned withdrawals, which must have created the general impression of chaos. In the *2. Pz.Armee*'s area of operations, it was another day of concerted attacks against its front and along its north flank, where the 57th Army was continuing its attempt to unhinge it from the neighboring *6. Armee*, in a series of assaults that gained more ground and continued to widen the distance between the two German armies.[19]

On the *6. Pz.Armee* front, the situation in the area south of Wiener Neustadt and southwest of the *Neusiedlersee* had become increasingly serious. Armor-led spearheads of the 46th Army had been intercepted south of Wiener Neustadt and were stopped before they could penetrate into the city with 17 of its tanks being destroyed. An even deeper breakthrough along the western shore of the lake by a predominately tank-heavy force from the 4th Guards Army posed a serious threat to the blocking line being emplaced there by the *6. Pz.Armee* along both sides of the town of Ödenburg (Sopron), where the small *SS Kampfgruppe* that was supposed to eliminate the breakthrough had not yet finished forming up. Near the town of Fertöboz, 60 Soviet tanks had been spotted moving west. A *Kampfgruppe* from the *Hitlerjugend* Division that had been encircled by the I Guards Mechanized Corps near the Austrian town of Deutsch-Kreutz was able to break out and fight its way back to German lines in the northwest. North of Güns, the *I. SS-Pz.Korps* was unable to stop the advance of the 6th Guards Tank Army, which had seized Oberpullendorf on 30 March and was poised to carry out a deep attack with its IX Guards Mechanized Corps and V Guards Tanks Corps.

North of the Danube on the *8. Armee* front, the 7th Guards Army continued its attacks in a northwesterly direction on 31 March, and west of the Waag River its troops were easily able to penetrate the new defense line being built there by *IV. Pz.Korps FHH*. To counter this move, the *8. Armee* was rapidly assembling the *211. V.G.D.* in the army's rear area, while the *XLIII. Armee-Korps*—operating once again north of the Danube after leaving the *6. Pz.Armee*—was able to pull back its right wing in an orderly manner as it began to prepare its defense of Pressburg. This historically significant city, a crossroads of many invading armies, controlled the narrow pass in the Little Carpathian Mountains through which the Danube flowed. Less than 65 kilometers to the northwest lay Vienna. In addition to having to prepare his forces for this overwhelming task, the *8. Armee* commander, *Gen.d.Geb. Tr.* Hans Kreysing, also had to pay attention to unfolding events on his left flank in the Tatra Mountains, where the *8. Armee* maintained connectivity with *H.Gr. Mitte* in Slovakia.

Balck's *6. Armee* continued being roughly handled throughout the day by two of the three Soviet armies that had been battering it since 21/22 March—the 26th and 27th Armies (the 9th Guards Army had shifted to the north on 27/28 March so that it was now operating between the 6th Guards Tank Army and 4th Guards

Army). During the night of 30/31 March, the *Kampfgruppe* consisting of portions of *SS-Aufkl.Abt. 9* from the *Hohenstaufen* Division and elements of *K.Gr. Bradel* from the *1. Pz.Div.*, operating under the control of the *IV. SS-Pz.Korps*, withdrew to the west bank of the Raab at Eisenburg in the face of heavy enemy pressure from the direction of Steinamanger. That night, Gille's headquarters reported that its divisions were experiencing difficulties as they tried to withdraw to their new defensive positions along the Austrian border due to traffic jams, but that the bulk of the corps except the rear guards had arrived at their new positions on the Austrian border by the evening.

It had been a busy day, especially for the *Volkssturm* units from *Wehrkreis XVIII* who had only begun occupying the *Reichsschutzstellung* after being alerted on 25 March. They had barely moved into their positions when the Red Army began feeling its way into the Raab and lower Lafnitz River valleys. From the east, elements of Govorunenko's XVIII Tank Corps, after advancing over 110 kilometers in six days, were able to push into the weakly held German bridgehead at St Gotthard (Szentgotthárd) along the Raab River and seize the Hungarian border town before any of the *IV. SS-Pz.Korps'* combat units could arrive. The Austrian town of Neumarkt an der Raab was also lost that day when its defenders, *Volkssturm-Btl. Graz-Land*, surrendered without a fight.[20]

The adjacent unit, *Volkssturm-Btl. Jennersdorf*, fled before they were overwhelmed by enemy tanks. The only significant resistance Soviet spearheads faced occurred east of the town of Fehring, 24 kilometers west of St Gotthard, where a mixed *Kampfgruppe* composed of *Volkssturm-Btl. Liezen*, a *Flak-Kampfgruppe* equipped with a battery of 8.8cm guns, border guards, and Labor Service personnel temporarily fought them to a standstill, preventing Govorunenko's tanks from advancing further into the Raab valley that day. Undeterred, a portion of the Soviet force crossed the Raab east of Jennersdorf near the village of Weichselbaum and veered north in an effort to bypass the few defenders.[21]

The *Wiking* Division was ordered to attack from the area southwest of Fürstenfeld and retake Neumarkt an der Raab, but an enemy force including 15 tanks attacked the *Grenzschutzstellungen* east of Heiligenkreuz 6 kilometers northwest of St Gotthard and stopped the *Wiking's* attack before it had progressed very far. The division's O1 remembered that day very well, recording the events in his diary that evening. After experiencing the disorganized chaos the day before, he expected things to improve:

> Parts of the division, mainly the commander, a few officers and those elements of the division that we had been able to intercept occupied the *Reichsschutzstellung*, or rather we merely planted his command flag there. The position is only partially completed in the form of light field works with a few strong points, occupied by *Volkssturm*. The Russians are already there in front of some of the positions with small advance detachments. In the sector to our right, north of Jennersdorf, he is supposed to be already inside our positions. Around midday, we established the division command post at the *Reichsarbeitsdienst* [RAD] camp near Gillersdorf. Since the middle of the afternoon, the first portions of the division began

to arrive by truck and were put into position on our left sector by the division commander without considering to which unit they belonged. This was necessary because [on our left], we could control an important highway leading to Fürstenfeld through the [lower Lafnitz] valley from the heights above.[22]

Slowly, the *Wiking* Division's troops, with the exception of the rear guard, moved into their half-completed fighting positions, but found that they would still require a lot of work before they could be made into anything that might stop an enemy attack or protect them from artillery fire.

Soviet attacks against the *IV. SS-Pz.Korps'* defensive sector throughout that day showed no signs of slowing down. From their bridgehead over the Raab at Nagycsákány, yet another tank-supported force pushed out towards the west along the east–west highway leading towards Heiligenkreuz and took the village of Gaztony. To head off this dangerous development, the *1. Pz.Div.* was ordered to counterattack south towards Inzendorf and cut off the enemy spearhead before it reached the border defensive positions, which were not yet ready to withstand an attack. At roughly the same time, an attack by the *3. Pz.Div.* against the same bridgehead at Nagycsákány from the east nearly succeeded, retaking the village of Rábadorosló before it ground to a halt in front of the Soviet antitank defenses.

Obersturmbannführer Schönfelder recorded his observations of that day shortly after the war, leaving a vivid impression of the chaos that he encountered as well as the visit to the corps' *Gefechtstand* in Königsdorf that day by *General der Panzertruppe* Balck, who had come out from his new headquarters in Stegersbach to examine the corps' defensive preparations:

> Despite an enemy breakthrough due to the desertion of an entire Hungarian unit (an act which General Balck accused the *Szent László* Division of committing, which was false; that division never had any deserters), the *6. Armee* wanted us to occupy and defend the *Grenzschutzstellungen* from the St Gotthard sector to the northwest of Steinamanger. However, we could not do this without first sealing off the south wing of the *IV SS-Pz.Korps* which was threatened by the enemy who had already crossed over [the border] at St Gotthard and was heading in the direction of Feldbach. The *5. SS-Pz.Div.* was supposed to retake the area southeast of Fürstenfeld and Neumarkt. The *1.* and *3. Pz.Div.* were to launch their counterattacks at the same time. Because our troops had been ordered to remain in Eisenburg for too long, the enemy was able to reach the *Grenzschutzstellungen* before our own troops did. Balck saw things differently and said "The *IV. SS-Pz.Korps* has once again failed to put its troops in the proper position as ordered." He now requested once more (how many times did this make?) the relief of the commanding general of the *IV. SS-Pz.Korps*, because "he could no longer be entrusted with the leadership of a corps."[23]

Once again, Balck's efforts to relieve Gille and Schönfelder were unsuccessful. Balck wrote that he later tried to get Gille relieved of command for health reasons:

> [W]hen I found out who the incoming commanding general would have been, I put all wheels in motion to retain Gille. We would have been worse off with his replacement. What proved

decisive in the end was that Gille's troops had a high level of blind trust in him, and that was a capital that had to be valued highly for the coming final operation.[24]

Intriguingly, Balck never revealed who Gille's replacement might have been, but it must have been another *Waffen-SS* general whom he obviously disliked even more than Gille (Stadler, the commander of the *Hohenstaufen*, perhaps?). No mention of this incident can be found in the *H.Gr. Süd* official records, leaving one to wonder who the officer was that he was referring to.

At 7 p.m. that evening, the *IV. SS-Pz.Korps* was informed by *6. Armee* headquarters that it would have to try again the following day to retake the border town of Neumarkt an der Raab, which had fallen to a strong Soviet force earlier that morning. At least 50 tanks from the XVIII Tank Corps had been reported there, and some had even been seen moving along the highway out of the town heading west to Fehring.[25] The town was approximately 17 kilometers southeast of Fürstenfeld; Gille and his staff had to decide which division to assign this task to, well aware that they had all just barely made it back to the border in time. As reported, the *Wiking* Division drew this assignment, but the attack by one of its *Kampfgruppen* did not get very far before it ran into Soviet resistance. It would have to try again the next day.

While the *IV. SS-Pz.Korps* was conducting a fighting withdrawal along the course of the lower Raab into southern Austria towards the *Reichschutzstellung*, the *III. Pz.Korps* was trying to do the same. During the night of 30/31 March, on the corps' far left wing, night attacks by Red Army units seized the towns of Klein-Nähring, Schandorf, and Schachendorf. A counterattack by *Div.Gr. Krause* that day retook Schandorf, but Soviet troops were now also on Austrian soil in the *III. Pz.Korps'* defensive sector. Although its right wing had been under considerable enemy pressure as it fell back, the corps had been able to move into its new defensive positions more or less according to plan.

During the course of the afternoon, a Hungarian unit (most likely one or several of the seven attached fortress battalions) went over to the enemy from its defensive sector between Egyházasrádóc and Ják, enabling a Soviet unit to push through the newly created gap and attack to the west.[26] As a result, they were able to take the town of Egyházasrádóc and push into the western edge of the forest east of Prostrum on the Austrian border. A counterattack by *Geb.Jg.Rgt. 99* of the *1. Volks-Geb.Div.*, that was on the march to its postion on the *III. Pz.Korps'* left wing, brought the enemy's further progress to a halt.

On account of these deep penetrations in his sector, *General der Panzertruppe* Breith was forced to order his deeply echeloned units on his right wing to begin falling back to the Austrian *Grenzschutzstellungen*. Breith himself had to displace his corps command post to the town of Kohfidisch in Austria. At 7 p.m. that night, he was informed by *6. Armee* headquarters that his corps was to make another attempt to retake Rechnitz the following day to restore contact with the right wing of the *6. Pz.Armee.*

To help Breith's corps defend its widely spaced sector on the Austrian border, it was reinforced that day by three replacement and training battalions from the city of Graz, including *SS-Gren.Ers.u.Ausb.Btl. 11.* On paper, his corps appeared numerically powerful, but with the exception of *Gen.Lt.* August Wittmann's strong *1. Volks-Geb.Div.* and *Div.Gr. Krause*, most of Breith's troops were green replacements, *Ordnungspolizei*, and *Alarm* units. Most of the attached Hungarian fortress battalions had run away, leaving him one less thing to worry about.[27] A few dozen kilometers to the south, the *IV. SS-Pz.Korps* received the news that all of the *Volkssturm* units remaining in its area had been tactically subordinated to it, based on the order issued by *H.Gr. Süd* the previous evening.[28] The only practical advantage of having such units was their knowledge of the local area; otherwise, they added scarcely any combat power to the corps.

The order specified: "The armies [will] take over the tactical command in the border positions and in the space behind them with immediate effect. All command staffs and security personnel of the *Wehrkreise* [Defense Districts, in this case *General der Gebirgstruppe* Ringel's *Wehrkreis XVIII* based in Graz] as well as the *Volkssturm* units deployed in the border positions will be subordinated to them." In regards to the *IV. SS-Pz.Korps*, which had been given the responsibility of defending the Raab and lower Lafnitz River valleys, it was to assume control of *Volkssturm-Btl. Jennersdorf*, as well as elements of *Volkssturm-Btl. 31/26*, *Volkssturm-Btl. Feldbach*, *Volkssturm-Btl. 31/51*, what remained of *Volkssturm-Btl. Graz-Land* (the few men who had not surrendered that day), and *Volkssturm-Btl. Liezen.*

In addition to these units, Gille's corps was also given authority over the 60–70 men of *Zollgrenzschutz* (Border Guard) *Kompanie Jennersdorf*, two platoons of *Sperrpioniere* (demolitions troops), 10 men and two antitank guns from *Geb.Pz.Jäg.Ausb.Kp. 137*, and a small *Volkssturm* antiaircraft defense unit, *Flak Kampfgruppe III./10957* from the town of Rax. This entire amalgamation was theoretically commanded by *Hauptmann* Lepin. While on paper this represented more than a thousand men, this did not signify any measurable increase in the corps' combat power, since no one expected that poorly equipped old men and boys of the Hitler Youth would be able to stop Soviet tank columns, as had already been clearly demonstrated earlier that day.[29]

On 31 March, the *6. Armee* reported little enemy activity in its air space, possibly because it was more difficult in a mountainous area to conduct ground-attack operations. In contrast, the *8. Armee* seems to have been the recipient of most of the Soviet 5th and 17th Air Armies' attention, as their squadrons attacked German ground troops and defensive positions in front of the advancing 7th Guards Army and 53rd Army. The *Luftwaffe* again rose to the challenge, flying numerous sorties in support of German troops fighting in the area between Güns and Wiener Neustadt, as well as in the *2. Pz.Armee* area. According to reports, *Luftwaffe* fighter-bombers destroyed five enemy tanks in the vicinity of Wiener Neustadt, while during the evening of 30/31 March, its squadrons carried out numerous attacks closely behind the front lines of the Third Ukrainian Front near Steinemanger and Csorna.

When the day dawned on 1 April, nearly all of the *IV. SS-Pz.Korps* had managed to withdraw behind the *Reichschutzstellung* along the southeastern Austrian border. In some sections of the defense line, such as the area around St Gotthard, Soviet troops had arrived before the units assigned to defend them. In some instances, German troops were able to counterattack and throw them out, but not everywhere. The initiative still lay with the Red Army, which in the case of the *IV. SS-Pz.Korps*, was embodied in the form of the XVIII Tank Corps of the 26th Army. The challenge that now lay before Gille, as with his fellow corps commanders, was the urgent necessity of reassembling his scattered forces, restoring their fighting strength as much as possible, and preparing them to mount an adequate defense before they were overwhelmed by their enemy's tank-led spearheads. Although they did not know it then, the time to do so was rapidly running out. Thus, the stage was set for the last chapter in the history of the *IV. SS-Pz.Korps*.

CHAPTER 8

Defending the Reich
1–17 April 1945

By 1 April, World War II in Europe had only 38 days remaining until it ran its course. Certainly, the nearly half a million soldiers of *H.Gr. Süd* had no way of knowing this. Still very much alive and firmly in control, Hitler and his entourage fully intended to keep fighting until they were either dead, captured, or had run out of men. As it happened, these criteria nearly coincided five weeks later. However, as long as there were armies in the field capable of obeying orders and with the ability to keep on fighting, they would. As long as they had obedient commanders to lead them, they would carry on. Consequently, the final collapse of most of the *Wehrmacht* would not begin until the last week of April, especially in the west; the Battle of Berlin would not end until 2 May, while *H.Gr. Süd* and its four armies would continue operating up to the very day of capitulation on 8 May (see Map 6).

This applied equally to the *6. Armee*, its corps, and their divisions. Although there was no longer any hope of winning, Hermann Balck continued carrying out his orders to the very end, as did Herbert Gille. Though the means to carry out these orders witnessed a rapid decline in their combat effectiveness after the army's escape from Stuhlweissenburg and its retreat into Austria, Balck and his subordinate commanders continued serving loyally, attempting—in Balck's own words—to bring order unto chaos. But even Balck's undoubted talents were insufficient for a task of this magnitude.

As mentioned earlier, the complete war diary of *H.Gr. Süd* ended on 31 March. The only official records from *H.Gr. Süd* that remain are the army group's summarized daily reports to *OKH* from 1–22 April; after that, everything leading up to 8 May has been lost—most likely destroyed or possibly not even completed. Thus, there are no detailed official accounts known to exist from that period of the activities of *H.Gr. Süd*, the *6. Armee*, or the *IV. SS-Pz.Korps*. The only complete official sources available to the author for this final phase of the war are the war diary of the *Oberkommando der Wehrmacht* and the summarized daily reports described above.

Fortunately, in his book Georg Maier provides additional information from the *Tagesmeldung Ost* (Daily Reports East) written by the *OKH* for submission to the

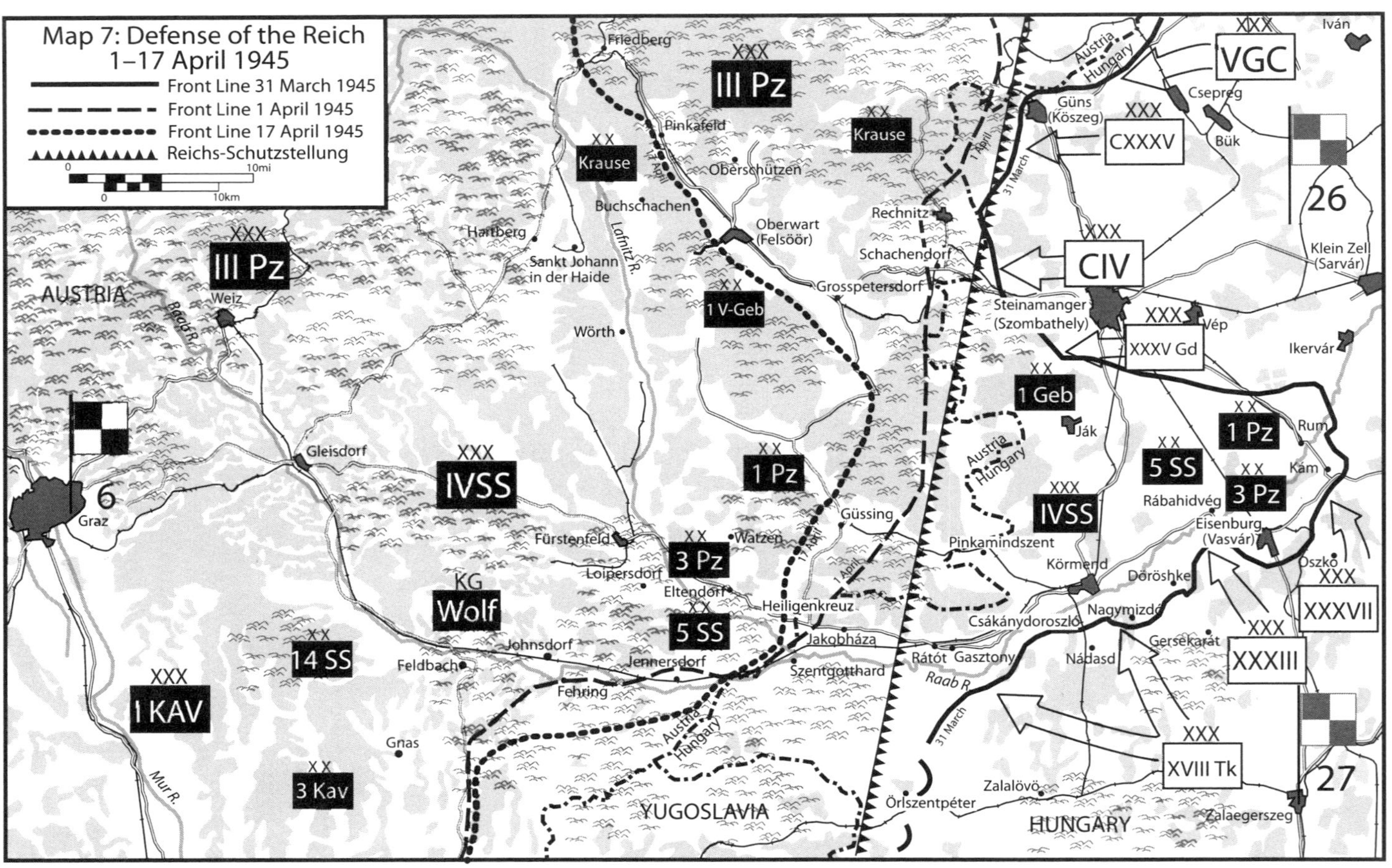

Map 7: Defense of the Reich
1–17 April 1945
Front Line 31 March 1945
Front Line 1 April 1945
Front Line 17 April 1945
Reichs-Schutzstellung
10mi
10km
VGC
CXXXV
CIV
XXXV Gd
III Pz
Krause
Krause
1 V-Geb
1 Geb
1 Pz
1 Pz
5 SS
3 Pz
IV SS
IV SS
3 Pz
5 SS
KG Wolf
14 SS
1 KAV
3 Kav
XXXVII
XXXIII
XVIII Tk
Iván
Csepreg
Bük
Güns (Köszeg)
Klein Zel (Sarvár)
Vép
Ikervár
Rum
Kám
Steinamanger (Szombathely)
Ják
Rábahidvég
Eisenburg (Vasvár)
Oszkó
Döröshke
Körmend
Nagymizda
Gersekarát
Csákánydoroszló
Rátót Gasztony
Nádasd
Raab R.
Zalalövö
Öriszentpéter
Zalaegerszeg
HUNGARY
Pinkamindszent
Austria / Hungary
Güssing
Jakobháza
Szentgotthard
Heiligenkreuz
Friedberg
Pinkafeld
Oberschützen
Buchschachen
Oberwart (Felsöör)
Rechnitz
Schachendorf
Grosspetersdorf
Hartberg
Sankt Johann in der Haide
Lafnitz R.
Wörth
Weiz
AUSTRIA
Baab R.
Gleisdorf
Graz
Fürstenfeld
Watzen
Loipersdorf
Eltendorf
Johnsdorf
Jennersdorf
Feldbach
Fehring
Gnas
Mur R.
YUGOSLAVIA
1 April
17 April
31 March
26
27
6

OKW Führungsstab at Hitler's headquarters. This provides additional information, frequently edited for brevity by the *OKW* for its own daily report. Soviet sources provide some additional information, as do contemporary eyewitness accounts, as well as division histories written 20 or 30 years after the war. Taken together, the researcher can gain an understanding of the key events that took place during the last 38 days of the war in Europe. In order to understand how the events unfolded the way they did after the *IV. SS-Pz.Korps* set foot on German soil on 31 March, a brief review of Soviet objectives is essential.

From an operational perspective, the outlines of the Red Army's Vienna Operation could clearly be seen unfolding by the last week of March. At least three Soviet armies were advancing northwest along the Danube Basin towards Vienna under the control of the Second Ukrainian Front—the 7th Guards Army and 53rd Army operating north of the Danube, and the 46th Army to the south. Northwest, west, and southwest of Lake Balaton, six Soviet armies were advancing towards the *Neusiedlersee*, Vienna, and Graz under the Third Ukrainian Front—the 6th Guards Tank Army, 4th and 9th Guards Armies, and the 26th, 27th, and 57th Armies—as well as the 1st Bulgarian Army. The 1st Guards Cavalry-Mechanized Group (aka the "Pliyev Army") was operating along the Carpathians under the Second Ukrainian Front, along with the 1st Romanian Army (see Map 6).

By following the direction of attack of these two army groups, the *STAVKA* intended Malinovsky and Tolbukhin to separate the center, left, and right wing armies of *H.Gr. Süd* and prevent them from operating in concert with one another, and that is exactly what they did. The attack along the Danube Basin forced the *6. Pz.Armee* and *8. Armee* to withdraw northwest in tandem towards Pressburg (Bratislava) and Vienna, beginning on 30 March, with Dietrich's army on the southern bank of the Danube and von Kreysing's on the northern bank.

The attack by the Third Ukrainian Front also forced the *II. SS-Pz.Korps* of the *6. Pz.Armee* to pull back around the northern end of the Neusiedlersee (Lake Neusiedl) and the *I. SS-Pz.Korps* to withdraw around the southern part of the lake. If the *6. Pz.Armee* had not successfully performed this maneuver, it would have been pinned against the lake and crushed or scattered. This movement also forced the majority of Dietrich's forces to break contact with the *6. Armee* on their right, which in turn was being forced to withdraw to the west in the direction of Graz along the Raab and Lafnitz River valleys in the south and towards the Semmering Pass in the north.

Once the Third Ukrainian Front's plan began to unfold after 31 March, the *6. Armee* was slowly pushed into the foothills of the Alps in southeast Austria (Styria) by 1 April, where it would find restoring its connection with the *6. Pz.Armee* a difficult challenge. This would make any attempt by *H.Gr. Süd* to carry out a coordinated defense of Vienna very difficult. In turn, to prevent its left wing from being exposed to envelopment, the *2. Pz.Armee* would be forced to withdraw to the northwest in order to maintain contact with the *6. Armee*, setting in motion a kind of domino effect. This move would have forced *H.Gr. E/O.B. Südost* in Croatia to begin withdrawing for the same reason, thereby causing the entire German theater of operations in southeastern Europe to shuffle to the northwest, lest it collapse. As the Vienna Operation began pressing together German forces fighting in southeastern Europe into the Alps of southeastern Austria, at the same time the Western Allies fighting in northern Italy began to push German forces north into the mountains of southern Austria, such that by mid-April they would unite and form a continuous Allied front.

Nevertheless, *H.Gr. Süd* and its four armies would fight to the end of the war until the final capitulation documents were signed on 8 May. The *IV. SS-Pz.Korps* would be there for every step of the way. Whether Balck or Gille believed the war was lost was immaterial; they would all perform their duty to the very end, carrying out their orders to the best of their ability. In this sense, like Gille, Balck was a *Nursoldat* (merely a soldier) too, even though they did not hold each other in high esteem. Because of this shared trait, there was still a great deal of fighting and dying to be done before the war finally sputtered to its long-overdue conclusion.

Before proceeding further, a review of the status of the *IV. SS-Pz.Korps* is in order to understand the conditions of its forces when it began the final phase of the campaign. On the morning of 31 March, the corps still had three *panzer* divisions subordinated to it: the *Wiking* Division and the *1.* and *3. Pz.Div.*, as well as the small *Kampfgruppe* from the *Hohenstaufen* Division's reconnaissance battalion.[1] The composition of corps troops had not changed, and it still possessed its "army troops"—*SS-ARKO 504, SS-Werf.Abt. 504, s.SS-Art.Abt. 504,* and *SS-Beob.Abt. 504*. The 15 remaining operational heavy tanks of *s.Pz.Abt. 509* were briefly attached to *IV. SS-Pz.Korps* before they were sent to assist the *III. Pz.Korps* on 6 April.[2] The identities of other *Heerestruppen* attached to the corps are unknown due to incomplete records, except for *Sturm-Pz.Abt. 219* and the remnants of *I. Abt./Pz.Rgt. 24*, which were both attached to the *1. Pz.Div.* at this time.[3]

These headquarters troops had all suffered casualties during the past three months in Hungary, though records for the most part are lacking. At least 27 SS artillerymen were still listed as missing in action, including 25 from *s.SS-Art.Abt. 504* which lost 14 men in March 1945 alone, most likely when the battalion was caught up in the chaos along the northern shore of Lake Balaton following the collapse of the *I. Kav. Korps* on 22 and 23 March. Moreover, casualty records for the *Hauptquartier* of the *IV. SS-Pz.Korps* after December 1944 are completely missing. The exact disposition of corps troops by this point in the campaign can no longer be determined; however, they had experienced the same effects from the retreat as Gille's divisions had, including straggling as well as shortages of gasoline and ammunition. How many of these corps troops, especially the artillery units, were converted into *Alarm* or *ad hoc* infantry battalions on Gille's orders can no longer be determined, though this is a distinct possibility.

Regarding the condition of the corps' three *panzer* divisions, slightly more information is available, since a weekly status report was still required to be submitted to *OKH*. Some of these survive for the period ending 31 March. On that date, *Generalmajor* Thünert's *1. Pz.Div.* reported having four operational *Pz. V* Panthers, along with three *Bergepanthers*, six captured Soviet tanks, and six antitank guns. In short-term repair, it reported two *Pz. IVs*, eight *Pz. Vs*, two *Bergepanthers*, and two captured Soviet tanks. During the past week, the division had lost 15 *Pz. Vs* listed as totally destroyed, most at the hands of their crews due to lack of fuel.[4] Not mentioned was the number of inoperable tanks taken to Graz for repair (more about them later).

On 17 March, the *1. Pz.Div.* reported having a total strength of 10,224 men, with 3,293 in its fighting units, though that number had declined considerably since then.[5] As previously mentioned, on 24 March, Thünert had reorganized his division into two components. There was a fighting element under *Oberst* Bradel that included a small *Kampf-Bataillon* from each of its two *Panzergrenadier* regiments, a self-propelled artillery battalion, a company-sized armor element, an antitank company, and a *Pionier* company.[6] Most of the fighting that the division would carry out for the remainder of the war would be carried out by Bradel's *Kampfgruppe*. The rest of the division, its *Tross* and troops without any heavy weapons, were pulled back into Austria to be reformed behind the *Reichsschützstellung*.

The condition of *Generalmajor* Söth's *3. Pz.Div.* was worse. As of 31 March, his command submitted a partial report that stated that the division had only four *Pz. V* Panthers and one *Jagd.Pz. IV* operational, seven antitank guns, and five artillery batteries.[7] This provides a stark contrast to the number on hand when the last fully complete weekly status report was submitted on 10 March, when the division reported having 67 tanks, assault guns, and tank destroyers ready for action. On 17 March, his division reported having 12,570 men assigned, with 3,728 serving in the fighting units. Like the *1. Pz.Div.*, the *3. Pz.Div.* had suffered heavy losses between 17 and 30 March, particularly during the withdrawal from its positions southeast of Stuhlweissenburg on 22 and 23 March. Its combat potential was probably very low by this point in the campaign, and logic would have forced Söth to take similar measures as Thünert had in order to preserve some form of combat capability.

In the case of the *Wiking* Division, its last complete monthly report to the Inspectorate of *Panzer* Troops for the period ending 31 March survives. Dated 1 April, it paints a sad picture in comparison to the relatively robust division it had been exactly one month earlier. After a month of campaigning, including 15 days of heavy fighting from 16 March, the number of troops assigned to the division had actually *increased*, though this paints a false picture. The report shows that the division had 19,964 men assigned, but 5,917 of these were not present for duty, being either sick or wounded, lowering the number considered "fit for duty" to 14,047. Of these, at least 1,642 were fresh transfers from the *Luftwaffe* and *Kriegsmarine*, assigned to the division's replacement depot but not yet considered trained and ready (or even armed) to be sent into combat. Thus, the actual number of men in the field at this time was approximately 12,405.[8]

In regards to losses, the real human toll begins to reveal itself. During the past month, the division suffered the loss of 482 men killed in action, 2,110 wounded, and 945 listed as missing in action, for a total of 3,537 casualties. In addition, 197 men were reported as sick and 737 absent for various reasons, such as emergency home leave, temporary duty elsewhere, or desertion, meaning that a total of 4,471 men were "not present for duty." This number was balanced by the addition of the aforementioned 1,642 replacements, as well as 83 men returning from convalescence.

To gauge the proportion of new personnel recently assigned to the number of veterans, on 31 March, the *Wiking* Division was over its authorized strength in enlisted personnel by 2,539 men. Therefore, out of the 12,405 men theoretically present for duty, 10,067 were veterans who had been assigned to the division for more than a month. But since 1,771 more replacements were assigned to the division in February, that means that as many as 3,413 men had been with it for less than two months. No matter how the numbers are calculated, the results are still the same—the number of old *Fronthasen* (*Landser* slang for front-line veterans) had continued to decline, while that of replacements from other services had increased precipitously.

As for heavy weapons, the situation for the *Wiking* on 31 March was quite bleak. On that date, it reported having only two *StuG III/IV* assault guns (both undergoing repair), two *Pz. IVs* (both in repair), two operational *Pz. V* Panther (with five in repair), and no *Jg.Pz. IVs* at all. It still fielded 51 operational *SPWs* of all types, with 55 more in short-term repair. In regards to cargo vehicles, including *Maultiere* fully tracked vehicles, the division reported 955 operational trucks and an additional 211 in repair, barely half of the 1,977 cargo vehicles it was authorized. The division still possessed 41 half-tracked prime movers, three operational antitank guns (plus nine more in repair), 21 artillery pieces (plus six in repair), and 14 *Flak* guns of all types, including six 8.8cm *Flak 37s*. Therefore, while the division was lacking in armored fighting vehicles, it still retained some degree of mobility and had slightly less than half the artillery it was required to have. In terms of combat power, it possessed the equivalent strength of an independent *Panzergrenadier* brigade.

The remarks by the division commander that accompanied the report are also available. On 1 April, *Oberführer* Karl Ullrich provided a frank assessment of this division's capabilities and what he believed was necessary for it to be restored to its authorized strength. In the realm of training, he wrote:

> Due to the hard defensive battles in the Stuhlweissenburg area and the withdrawal battles from Stuhlweissenburg to Heiligenkreuz [in Austria], a training program was not possible. Since the end of March the division's *Feldausbildungs* battalion has either been directly involved in the fighting or consolidated into the grenadier regiments. The re-establishment of the *Division-Kampfschule*, which requires 120 men [to staff it], has been delayed because [of] the width of the division's front line (38 kilometers), meaning that every man that can be spared has been committed (our *Kampfstärke* is only 48 percent); therefore, the re-establishment of a training regiment at this moment is impossible.

In regards to troop morale, Ullrich painted a vivid picture, stating that "on account of the rapid withdrawal and the ensuing fighting, the morale of the troops has declined. We have had a lot of straggling. Since the troops have stepped on German soil, they are now fighting again and after a streamlined reorganization there has been a visible improvement."

Finally, to present his corps commander and the *OKH* Inspectorate of *Panzer* Troops with a factual assessment of the special difficulties he faced as a commander, he pulls no punches:

> The division at this time possesses hardly any heavy infantry weapons and has not received an allocation of artillery ammunition (at this time, we have only 150 rounds total for both light and heavy field howitzers). Since our opponents can openly drive up with their heavy infantry weapons and fire at us beyond the range of our [light] weapons, we have suffered heavy losses. On account of shortages of fuel [for our ambulances], the evacuation of our wounded has been endangered. The rapid shifting of our infantry by truck to reinforce threatened areas is no longer possible. As a result of the last withdrawal when we ran out of fuel, we were forced to destroy the following vehicles: 35 *Maultiere*, 32 cargo trucks, seven half-tracked prime movers, seven *SPW*s, and 14 tanks and assault guns. As a result, I assess our mobility at 36 percent and our corresponding *Kampfwert* as IV.

These were the raw statistics of just one SS *panzer* division among many, but the condition of the others fighting with the *6. Pz.Armee* at this late stage of the war was probably similar to that of the *Wiking*. They all had two things in common—a lack of armored fighting vehicles caused by fuel shortages that led to their abandonment or destruction (due to their inability to recover them in a timely fashion) and lack of ammunition. Ironically, very few armored fighting vehicles were knocked out or destroyed by enemy weapons. But without armored fighting vehicles, an SS *panzer* division was nothing more than an overly large infantry division.

Another situation the *Wiking* had in common with the other SS *panzer* divisions was the low quality of the replacements it was receiving at this stage of the war. As described in Volume 1, until July 1944, the replacement system for the *Waffen-SS* had worked as it was intended. New recruits had either volunteered or were inducted, and were then subjected to three to six months of training, depending on their specialty. Upon completing their training phase, they were assigned to a field division's *Feld-Ersatz* battalion, which conducted further training designed to acclimatize the new replacements to front-line conditions. Then, depending on the need, they were parceled out to individual regiments, battalions, companies, and platoons. When these young troops arrived, they had already undergone a period of relatively good training and had been inculcated in what has been referred to as the "SS spirit."

The system collapsed in July 1944, when the field formations of the *Waffen-SS* suffered heavy casualties on all fronts. Combined with the continuing expansion of the *Waffen-SS* that was taking place at the same time, it had become impossible to provide sufficient replacements to keep the divisions in fighting trim. At the beginning of August 1944, to solve the problem, Himmler struck an arrangement with Hermann Göring to begin transferring large numbers of "excess" *Luftwaffe* personnel into the field divisions, following a one- or two-month retraining period, where they were reclassified, for the most part, as *Panzergrenadiers*. These were generally soldiers of high quality, though their introduction to combat without any sort of acclimatization period initially led to high losses until they learned the skills needed to survive on the front lines. By January 1945, most of these men had been fully assimilated within their units and had for the most part adopted a facsimile of the SS spirit from the few remaining old-timers.

By the start of 1945, most of the junior enlisted leadership positions—section or squad leaders—were being filled by these men from the so-called *Hermann Göring Spende*, and now they were the *Alte Hasen* veterans. After most SS divisions had suffered catastrophic losses in late 1944 or early 1945 (in the Ardennes, Alsace-Lorraine, Warsaw, Budapest, Kurland, etc.), tens of thousands of raw recruits from the *Reichsarbeitsdienst*, Hitler Youth, *Luftwaffe*, and *Kriegsmarine* were funneled to the field units. These men were lucky to have received two weeks of retraining at most, along with an issue of SS uniforms. Many of these men (boys, really) were immature and not physically well-developed, having suffered from inadequate diets due to wartime rationing, especially of foodstuffs containing protein. Instead of being issued an alcohol ration, many received milk to make up for this deficiency. Sprinkled among these recruits would be the occasional fanatical Hitler Youth member, who would try to inspire his peers with his warlike pronouncements. When these youngsters arrived at the front, they were probably aware that the war was rapidly coming to an end, but what that end would look like, no one knew. Seeing them as they arrived in their new uniforms, veterans could only shake their heads and wonder what had become of the *Waffen-SS*, to send such children to fight a war.

These new replacements were different from those who had come before. Most of them were very young, coming from the 1927 or 1928 year groups. The majority were barely trained and had not had time to be imbued with the SS spirit; therefore, it should have come as no surprise to anyone that they gave a poor performance when they faced combat against the Red Army, especially during their baptism of fire. Sadly, they might have made good soldiers, had there been time to train them and inculcate them with the warrior virtues. However, such an amount of time was a luxury of which there was precious little to be had. As a result, many of these recruits fled when the first shots were fired and had to be rounded up later after the fighting was over. Some deserted or became stragglers. In any case, though SS divisions at the end of March 1945 might appear strong on paper, in reality they were a weak reed, liable to break when too great a strain was placed on them. Needless to say, when Hitler heard the name of an SS division mentioned during a daily briefing, he considered all of them as being full-strength and still in possession of their previous capabilities; as we have seen, this was no longer the case.

The status of the SS replacements in the *H. Gr. Süd* theater of operations became quite a topic for discussion near the end of March 1945. After suffering crippling losses during the *Frühlingserwachen* offensive and the following Soviet counteroffensive, including the beginning of the Vienna Operation, nearly every SS division in the army group's area was understrength, especially within their *Panzergrenadier* regiments. This led to many complaints from Generals Balck, Gaedke, and Wöhler to the *OKH* and *SS-FHA*, and at least one investigation into the situation that brought Heinrich Himmler into the picture, as mentioned in a previous chapter.

In each case, when SS commanders such as Dietrich or Bittrich complained that they lacked sufficient troops to carry out their missions, *H.Gr. Süd* was ready with an answer that the SS Main Office had told Guderian that up to 6,000 replacements were sitting in the depots in the army group's rear area for each division.[9] Dietrich and Bittrich, among others, also complained about the poor quality of the replacements that they were getting, explaining that these men were being held back in the rear area because they were undergoing training to prepare them for the front. Experience had already taught them that unless some kind of acclimatization was carried out, these young recruits were useless when committed to battle. Balck, Gaedke, and Wöhler also grumbled about the large numbers of SS "stragglers" they encountered on the roads, but again failed to back up their allegations with any hard evidence. How many of these stragglers were raw recruits who had recently been assigned is not mentioned.

Dietrich ensured that stringent control measures and punishments were put in place to control the straggler problem within his army, which partially alleviated it, but as the war drew closer to its end, even threats of summary courts-martial and executions were not enough to convince many men to remain in the line.[10] Dietrich was serious about countering the desertion problem; according to official records, by 3 April he had ordered the summary execution of more than 500 deserters in his army alone.[11] Despite the risk of being caught, many potential deserters probably reasoned that if they stayed in the line, they would most certainly be killed or captured; if they deserted, at least they stood a chance of making it home alive after the war was over. It was a problem that was never fully solved, and the *Waffen-SS*, as well as *Wehrmacht* formations, were increasingly plagued with desertion and straggling during the last month of the war.

It was with this slowly disintegrating force that *H.Gr. Süd*, including the *IV. SS-Pz. Korps*, was expected to defend what remained of the ever-shrinking perimeter of the Third Reich's southeastern front. Although the corps had barely made it back to the supposed safety of the *Reichsschutzstellung*, Gille was certain that his men could hold it. Whereas a great deal of heavy fighting lay ahead of them, his men were now on native soil and would do their best to keep their relentless opponent at bay. After all, it was citizens of the Third Reich that the men of the *Wiking*, *1.* and *3. Pz.Div.* were now protecting—defenseless old men, women, and children—who were depending upon them, as exhausted as they were, to defend their homeland. Although they did not know it then, the time to do so was rapidly running out. Thus, the stage was set for the last chapter in the history of the *IV. SS-Pz.Korps*.

On 1 April, the *6. Armee* consisted of the *IV. SS-Pz.Korps* in the south, with its right flank anchored along the Raab River valley, and *Gen.d.Pz.Tr.* Hermann Breith's *III. Pz.Korps* on the left or northern flank defending the approaches to the Semmering Pass and the upper Lafnitz valley. The approaches to the Raab River valley along the army's southern boundary were still comparatively open, except for *K.Gr. Wolf* and a few *Volkssturm* units holding blocking positions. This was the source of Balck's greatest concern, leading him to cast about for enough forces to hold them at bay until a continuous front was re-established. His army's mission was to prevent a Soviet penetration towards Graz, which would have cut off not only his army, but *2. Pz.Armee* as well. Graz was also located astride the escape route through the Styrian Alps from the Balkans, and its loss would have hastened Germany's defeat in the southeastern theater (see Map 7).

Since the *6. Armee's* area of operations was located along the southeastern foothills of the Styrian Alps, virtually all of the major avenues of approach that Soviet tank forces needed to reach their operational objective of Graz lay along river valleys. Consequently, most of the fighting for the next several weeks would be for the control of the Raab, lower Lafnitz, Grazbach, and Magland River valleys in the south, as well as the area surrounding the equally important Semmering mountain pass and upper Lafnitz River valley in the north. As long as *6. Armee* could deny its opponent possession of these traffic choke points, the Soviet 26th and 27th Armies would be prevented from reaching their goals. As a result, most of the fighting that took place during the first week of April centered around the question of who would control these key terrain features and the excellent highway network running along the valley floors. It would mark some of the last successful battles fought by the *IV. SS-Pz.Korps*, including a number of small-scale engagements for control of the mountains and hilltops astride the valleys and passes, whenever the Red Army attempted to bypass German defenses using their infantry.

On 1 April, the *IV. SS-Pz.Korps* consisted of the *Wiking* and the *1.* and *3. Pz.Div.*, all of which, as we have seen, had just concluded a harrowing withdrawal from the former front north of Lake Balaton, during which they had been forced to abandon or blow up many of their remaining armored vehicles for lack of fuel. These divisions had experienced some difficulty and not a few surprises when they began settling in to their new defensive positions. In some cases, these defensive works were found to be already occupied by their opponent, who had arrived in the *Reichsschutzstellung* before they did after chasing off local *Volkssturm* units that were supposed to be guarding them. After a harrowing two weeks of constant withdrawals, during which at times its very survival was at stake, Gille's corps now found itself in the Alpine foothills, some 154 kilometers southwest of Vienna, quite a distance from its former Budapest battlefields and the relatively flat *Puszta*.

In the *Wiking* Division, some of its veterans had barely managed to make their way back in time after being separated during the hasty withdrawal from Veszprém. One of these men, *Oscha.* Siegfried Melinkat from *SS-Pz.Rgt. 5*, later wrote:

> It has stayed in my memory for a long time how our platoon was without any contact for three days at one point—fighting close combat engagements at night, hardly any ammunition left, and already considered to be missing in action by the battalion. Through the courageous effort of a messenger, contact was re-established, and the platoon was able to fight its way back to a passage point maintained by the *1. Pz.Div.*[12]

On that same day, Günther Jahnke, the *O1* of the *Wiking* Division, wrote:

> The enemy had broken through the sector of the *Reichschutzstellung* on our right [author's note: in the Jennersdorf sector]. As our units arrived, they were forced to carry out numerous small counterattacks from the march that managed to recapture the *Reichschutzstellung*. Considering the condition of our troops, this was not so easy. First of all, the units were not very cohesive, they had just been ordered to get into the trucks by officers who happened to be available and thrown into battle without any heavy weapons. Only by the personal involvement in the fighting of every commander were we able to reach the left sector of the defensive position and then throw out the enemy who had infiltrated it before us. However, it is no longer possible to occupy the position south of the road and railway line east of Jennersdorf.[13]

When the *Wiking* Division's *SS-Pz.Art.Rgt. 5* made it back to the *Reichschutzstellung* by 31 March, after a brief reorganization its commander, *Ostubaf.* Hans Bünning, reported two days later that his regiment had lost more than half of its guns. This had forced him to combine all of them into one firing battalion, which was promptly designated *Artilleriegruppe Bernau*, after its acting commander, *Stubaf.* Günter Bernau. This battalion was able to field 12 10.5cm light field howitzers and four 15cm heavy field howitzers. None of the self-propelled guns could be brought back into Austria due to lack of fuel. Still, 16 guns was a respectable number, provided they were given sufficient ammunition, but even this began to run out by mid-April. Like the *panzer* regiment, the artillery regiment had more men than heavy weapons, so it too was ordered to form an artillery–infantry company on Easter Sunday, 1 April, in Fürstenfeld.[14]

On Gille's left, Breith's *III. Pz.Korps* controlled the *1. Volks-Geb.Div.* and a miscellany of other formations such as training and replacement battalions, *Landeschützen* battalions, and bits and pieces of other combat units that had been separated from their parent organizations, which were either fighting in the *6. Pz.Armee* or *2. Pz.Armee*. Breith also had *Div.Gr. Krause*, led by the commander of the *6. Armee Rückwärtiges Gebiet, Gen.Lt.* Walther Krause. His organization was even more heterogeneous than Balck's, including *Feld-Ers.Btl. 73* of the *3. Pz.Div.*, a *Luftwaffe Flak* battalion, an SS *Panzergrenadier* training and replacement battalion, two battalions from *Volks-Werf.Rgt. 24* without launchers, several artillery batteries from different units, formations composed of rounded-up stragglers, the aforementioned *IV. Btl./SS-Rgt. Ney*, and even a *Volkssturm* battalion.[15] How Breith could mount any kind of effective defense against an opponent equipped with large numbers of tanks and mobile artillery was a mystery. The only thing working in his favor was that the narrow mountain roads and river valleys offered many opportunities to set up road blocks and antiarmor ambushes that would nullify Soviet superiority in tanks.

North of the *6. Armee*, Dietrich's *6. Pz.Armee* had been forced to withdraw beyond the *Susannestellung* along the Raab River. Its two corps had been pushed back around the southern and northern shores of the Neusiedlersee and were continuing to withdraw towards the Vienna Forest and city of Wiener Neustadt. In addition to defending the southern approaches to Vienna, Dietrich's army also had to block the east–west passes in the Leitha Mountains as well as the Bruck Gap between the Neusiedlersee and Pressburg (Bratislava).

Due to these developments, by 1 April, there were no longer any troops from the *6. Pz.Armee* remaining on Hungarian soil. Although it looked strong on paper, Dietrich's army was a shadow of its former self. All of his SS divisions had been downgraded to *Divisions-Kampfgruppen*. Consisting at that time of the *I.* and *II. SS-Pz.Korps*, Dietrich's army included the *Division-Kampfgruppen* of the *1., 2., 3.,* and *12. SS-Pz.Div., SS-K. Gr. Keitel*, the *6. Pz.Div.*, and portions of the *356. Inf.Div.* His army suffered from the same deficiencies in fuel and ammunition that plagued Balck's army. It would soon be forced back past Vienna unless his army and the neighboring *8. Armee* on the northern bank of the Danube could somehow bring the Soviet offensive to a halt.

South of the *6. Armee*, the *2. Pz.Armee* was being forced back too by the pressure exerted by the 57th Army's attack, and was fighting its way back to the *Reichsschützstellung*. A 25-kilometer-wide gap still separated it from Balck's right or southern flank near Zalagerszeg. On 1 April, *General der Artillerie* de Angelis's army finally gave up its last contact with Lake Balaton. On the same day, Hungary officially switched sides and joined the Soviet forces, though a number of loyal *Honvéd* units remained faithful to the end of the war, including the *Szent László* Division, which had been the target of Balck's misplaced ire two days before.

The second day of April, Easter Monday, promised to be a beautiful day, sunny and warm with temperatures in the low 60s Fahrenheit (above 16 degrees Centigrade). Now that most of *H.Gr. Süd* was on German soil, it had access to the area's well-paved road network, but it was questionable whether its units had enough fuel to make the best use of them. On that day, Balck's greatest concern was his army's right flank bordering the *2. Pz.Armee*, which still lay wide open south of the Raab River valley, ripe for exploitation by the Soviet XVIII Tank Corps.

Since the *IV. SS-Pz.Korps* was positioned between Fürstenfeld and Jennersdorf astride the lower Lafnitz valley and was busily preparing to carry out a counterattack to retake Jennersdorf, it had no forces available to cover the vulnerable southern boundary of *6. Armee*.[16] The neighboring *I. Kav.Korps'* left flank lay over 25 kilometers away to the south, and de Angelis, the commander of the *2. Pz.Armee*, had enough problems of his own to deal with. Therefore, he could not spare any forces to assist Balck either. To prevent the envelopment along his army's vulnerable flank, Balck did what he always did in such situations—he improvised.

The previous evening, Balck had detailed his staff *Panzerabwehr* officer, *Oberstlt.* Alfred Wolf, to create a *Kampfgruppe* from any units he could find in the Graz area within *Wehrkreis XVIII*.[17] Balck instructed the young officer: "Take a *Kübel[wagen]* with two or three men, fill it with *Panzerfausts*, and drive towards the Russian tank corps and stop them. How, I cannot tell you. Maybe it would be enough to set up a sign, 'No thoroughfare for Russian Tanks!'"[18] The enterprising Wolf rapidly formed a battle group, *K.Gr. Wolf*, consisting of convalescents from the military hospital in Graz, recruits from *Fahr-Ers.und Ausb.Abt. 18*, one company from *Pz.Jäg.Ers.und Ausb.Abt. 48*, *II. Abt/Fallschirm-Art.Rgt. 10*, and several *ad-hoc Alarm* units from the *Tross* of the *1.* and *3. Pz.Div.*

Oberstleutnant Wolf then led this mix of mostly inexperienced and poorly equipped troops to an area west of the town of Feldbach astride the Raab River valley. Here, he and his new command established a hasty defense and waited for the sound of approaching tanks. They would not have to wait long, because Soviet spearheads had already taken Feldbach and were busily engaged in the construction of a field-expedient bridge over the Raab to replace the one blown up by withdrawing German troops the previous day. As soon as this work was completed, Wolf and his men would have their hands full the next day, knowing full well that if they failed, the road to Graz would be wide open.

In the *IV. SS-Pz.Korps* sector on 2 April, the *Wiking*, *1.* and *3. Pz.Div.* began their counterattacks to retake Jennersdorf, Weichselbaum, and Rábafüzes at 4:30 a.m. The attack on the left by the *1. Pz.Div.* was led by its division commander, Thünert, riding along with the leading tanks in his *SPW*. Not expecting a German attack of such magnitude, the defending Soviet troops fled after heavy initial fighting. After liberating all these villages, both Thünert's battlegroup and *K.Gr. Medicus* from the *3. Pz.Div.* continued moving south while the *Wiking* Division consolidated its control of Jennersdorf. The counterattack by the *1. Pz.Div.* also engaged and scattered a large body of Soviet troops from an estimated three rifle divisions occupying an assembly area near Jakabháza.[19] With this, *IV. SS-Pz.Korps* was able to block the eastern access to the Raab and lower Lafnitz valleys; this still left the Soviet force occupying Feldbach 20 kilometers to the west that *K.Gr. Wolf* would have to contend with.

In addition to the heavy fighting that day, the *Wiking* Division experienced the loss of another one of its legendary commanders. That night, Günter Jahnke wrote:

> The Russians are feeling their way forward along our entire front. During an inspection trip to determine the best place to put the *Aufklärungs-Abteilung* for an upcoming action, Knight's Cross holder *Stubaf.* Vogt, while riding in his *SPW*, was mortally wounded in an air attack [by a U.S. P-38 Lightning]. That such a very brave commander fell on German soil through such a tragic circumstance.[20]

While Vogt was still being treated for his wounds in the division's *Feldlazarett*, *Wiking* Division commander Karl Ullrich visited him and presented him with his own Oak Leaves to the Knight's Cross that had been approved but not yet awarded. Vogt died the next day; his last words were "poor Germany."[21]

On Gille's left flank, Breith's *III. Pz.Korps* was able to fight off several Soviet attacks, but did not have enough troops to plug all of the isolated penetrations made by Soviet troops at several points along the *Reichschutzstellung*. The *1. Volks-Geb. Div.* reported that it had been attacked throughout the day along its *HKL* south and southwest of Pinkamindszent and Edlitz by Soviet units ranging in size from company- to battalion-strength, but its troops had managed to stand their ground. Most of the heavy fighting that day took place in the *Div.Gr. Krause* sector, where a Soviet attack north of the key position east of the town of Eisenberg an der Pinka punched an 800-meter-wide hole in the *Reichsschutzstellung*, prompting a counterattack to seal off the breach and restore the previous position. At the same time, another Soviet attack retook Schachendorf, which had been reoccupied the previous evening in the course of a German counterattack. That afternoon, *III. Pz.Korps* radioed that several enemy battalion-size units along with several antitank guns were observed pulling back from its front, but the *6. Armee* headquarters told Breith that this probably signified they were regrouping elsewhere, most likely in response to the attack that day by the *IV. SS-Pz.Korps*.[22]

That day, Soviet forces sharply pressed the *2. Pz.Armee* as its troops continued withdrawing between the Drava and Raab Rivers. Pressure was being exerted against the *6. Pz.Armee* by the 6th Guards Tank Army along both sides of Wiener Neustadt and along the Leitha River south of Vienna. North of the Danube in the *8. Armee's* defensive sector, the Second Ukrainian Front was pushing German forces back towards the *Reichschutzstellung* west of the Minor Carpathian Mountains bordering Slovakia. In the air, the *Luftwaffe* flew only 70 ground-attack sorties in support of *H.Gr. Süd*, mostly in the skies above Wiener Neustadt and Gross-Kanischa, claiming the destruction of five enemy tanks and 50 other motorized vehicles.

On Tuesday, 3 April, another warm sunny day, *H.Gr. Süd* reported that forward units of the Soviet 57th Army had reached the edge of the Nagykanizsa oilfields in the *2. Pz.Armee* area of operations and achieved a breakthrough along a wide front, forcing de Angelis to pull back his entire left flank while carrying out counterattacks in order to seal off the penetrations and rebuild a solid front. This only caused the gap between it and the neighboring *6. Armee* to grow even wider. The same applied to the gap between Balck's army and the *6. Pz.Armee* to his north, which was being slowly pushed to the northwest away from Vienna. To defend Vienna, a *Korps Bünau*, under the command of *Gen.d.Inf.* Rudolf Bünau, was established that day, but all he had to defend this large metropolitan area were some *Landeschutzen* units, *Volkssturm*, and a mixture of *Luftwaffe Flak* batteries. Northwest of Vienna, the *6. Pz.Armee* reported only a small number of *Kampfgruppen* conducting a fighting withdrawal. Another gap had been driven in the *6. Pz.Armee* front lines between Wiener Neustadt and the Neusiedlersee, which Dietrich's forces were attempting to seal off.

By 3 April, the signs of disintegration and demoralization had become so visible within the *6. Pz.Armee* that its commander was compelled to issue a dire *Armeebefehl* that applied equally to *Waffen-SS* and *Wehrmacht* personnel. Although a similar order from the commander of the *6. Armee* is no longer extant, in content and tone Dietrich's order is reflective of Balck's thinking on the matter:

Oberkommando der 6. SS-Panzerarmee

1) No soldier of the army is allowed to cross the line from this point onwards: Mariazell–Annaberg–Traisen–Traisen River where it joins the Danube to the west or crosses the Danube to the north.
2) No soldier of the army may enter the city of Vienna.
3) From now on, no soldier of the army may leave his current location and move to the rear. He must remain there until he is ordered to withdraw by a combat unit.
4) Each local commander in the army rear area shall immediately set up a reception point and assign the most senior officer to record the names of all officers, non-commissioned officers and enlisted men present. They are to be immediately assigned to the next available combat unit or used for local defense.
5) Reception points for the *Tross* are located on the road to Tulln to the south in the villages of Judenau, Gollarn, Grabensee, Rapoltenkirchen, Sankt Christofen, Stollbeg, Hainfeld, and Rohr. Each reception point will provide them information about the proper location of their division's logistics and administrative area.
6) Whoever does not obey the above orders regardless of whether he is a unit leader or an individual straggler, will be sentenced according to the law by a summary court.

signed,
Dietrich
The Commander-in-Chief
SS-Oberstgruppenführer und Generaloberst der Waffen-SS
Vienna, April 3, 1945[23]

He meant every word of it. As previously stated, Dietrich had already ordered the summary execution of over 500 men by this date, which would necessarily have included members of his own beloved *Waffen-SS*. Whether or not *der Führer* ever was aware of Dietrich's new harsh line of enforcing discipline, he certainly would have approved of it.

For its part, the *6. Armee* was forced to ward off more attacks on 3 April, but was able to carry out counterattacks of its own in the St Gotthard area and again in the Raab River valley, as well as a strong attack against Rechnitz and Schachendorf by elements of the *III. Pz.Korps*. The *IV. SS-Pz.Korps* conducted another counterattack using the *1.* and *3. Pz.Div.* against Soviet forces in the eastern Raab valley, though on its right it was unable to close the gap with the *2. Pz.Armee*—there were simply not enough troops and tanks to carry this out as well as continue holding the *Reichschutzstellung*. In the south, the *Wiking* Division was able to gain possession of the villages of Weinberg and Rax on the northern bank of the Raab and its troops were able to advance as far as the town of Mogersdorf, 8 kilometers east of

Jennersdorf, before halting for the day.[24] Although *SS-Füsilier-Btl. 14* of the Ukrainian SS division had established contact with the *Wiking* Division with foot patrols four days earlier, these successful actions had by no means sealed the gap between the *6. Armee* and the *2. Pz.Armee*—this would require far more than a single dismounted reconnaissance battalion to accomplish.

On the same day, *I. Btl./Pz.Gren.Rgt. 113* was released by the *1. Volks-Geb.Div.* and permitted to rejoin the rest of the *1. Pz.Div.* near Fürstenfeld. By this point, the *1. Pz.Div.*'s maintenance services had been able to get two dozen of its tanks up and running again, augmented by an additional seven *Jg.Pz. IV*s and three *Pz. VI* Tiger IIs attached from *s.Pz.Abt. 509*, temporarily rendering Thünert's the most powerful division in the *6. Armee*.[25] *Kampfgruppe Wolf*, defending the *6. Armee* right flank, reported that 18 Soviet tanks had attempted to cross the Raab River at Riegersburg, but when they encountered the remnants of the bridge that *Oberstleutnant* Wolf had ordered blown up, the tanks inexplicably turned around and withdrew to the east and were last reported approaching the neighboring town of Unterstang.

Little did Wolf or Balck know that Govorunenko's tank corps was being pulled out in order to reinforce the right wing of the Third Ukrainian Front in preparation for the assault against Vienna. In its place, a Soviet rifle corps would continue the attack towards Graz. It took several days for *H.Gr. Süd* to realize this; in the meantime, Balck had received a *Kampfgruppe* from the newly activated *10. Fallschirm-Div.* as a temporary reinforcement to bolster his vulnerable right flank.[26] Once this mission was accomplished, this *Kampfgruppe* was withdrawn to the Graz area, where the rest of the division was continuing its activation.

As for the *Wiking* Division, because it lacked any operational *panzers* of its own at that moment—and had no fuel for them even if it did—after the day's successful action it was relegated to defensive duties along the *Reichschutzstellung* that ran perpendicular to the lower Lafnitz River valley and along the mountain straddling the Lafnitz and Raab Rivers. Describing the events of the day, Jahnke wrote about the relief he and the rest of the staff felt when they learned that *K.Gr. Bradel* of the *1. Pz.Div.* had been positioned as the corps' reserve in their division's area, as well as mentioning the impact that the death of Fritz Vogt had upon him and his fellow officers:

> The Russians are now sending powerful groups along the road from St Gotthard to Feldbach and are incessantly attacking our thinly manned lines mainly north of Fehring with overwhelmingly strong forces. The division is able to seal off this deep penetration only through the employment of all of our available remaining forces … the *Reichschutzstellung* can now only be defended by a thin line of strong points. The *Ia* [*Stubaf.* Klose] drove [to Graz] to visit *Frau* Vogt. The new assembly area of the *1. Pz.Div.* is in our division sector.[27]

Vogt, who died at the *Hauptverbandsplatz* in Fürstenfeld near Graz, was buried nearby several days later with full military honors. His position as commander of *SS-Pz.Aufkl. Abt. 5* was temporarily assumed by *Ostuf.* Erich Stichnoth, Vogt's former *Adjutant*.

In the air that day, the Red Air Force carried out a series of powerful raids with ground-attack and fighter-bomber aircraft, particularly in the Vienna area as well as in support of Soviet troops advancing north of the Danube. The *Luftwaffe* did its best to counter the advance of the Second and Third Ukrainian Fronts, carrying out 100 ground-attack and fighter sorties of its own against enemy tank concentrations, supply convoys, and troop assembly areas south and southeast of Vienna.[28]

Wednesday, 4 April found the situation in the *2. Pz.Armee*'s area of operations relatively unchanged from the previous day, with Soviet forces continuing to roll back the army's left wing, forcing the *6. Armee* to redouble its efforts to come to its aid. Meanwhile, the forces of the Third Ukrainian Front approached to within 10–15 kilometers of Vienna as they continued their advance against the woefully overmatched *6. Pz.Armee*. The city of Baden was lost. Between the Neusiedlersee and the Danube, Soviet forces continued pressing forward and fought their way into the eastern outskirts of Pressburg, as well as through several of the passes along the Minor Carpathian Mountains north of the Danube. Fighting continued in the *8. Armee* area of operations around the Neutra Valley and near Kremnitz.

In the *6. Armee*'s area of operations, its summarized evening report stated that the *IV. SS-Pz.Korps* was ordered to press eastwards and continue to clear the Raab Valley of Soviet forces. *Kampfgruppe Wolf*, under Balck's direct control, reinforced by the *Kampfgruppe* from the *10. Fallschirm-Div.*, was able to retake the towns of Feldbach and Fehring on the corps' right flank after heavy fighting. It had managed to cut off a portion of the Soviet forces fighting in Feldbach when it blocked the road leading east out of the town, though Wolf's troops had not been able to clear the town by the evening reporting period.

Günther Jahnke reported on that day that the *1. Pz.Div.*, using its newly formed *Alarmbataillon* and seven attached *Jg.Pz. IV* tank destroyers, carried out a flanking attack towards the south at 5 p.m. against enemy forces that had broken through on the *Wiking* Division's left flank. Along the northern bank of the Raab, the *Wiking*, consolidating its new southern front along the northern bank of the Raab, launched an attack eastwards from the vicinity of Weinberg an der Raab towards the town of Hohenbrugg, with the objective of cutting off and destroying enemy forces located west of Jennersdorf. At first, Jahnke wrote, the *Kampfgruppe* had enjoyed only minor success due to the mountainous terrain that nullified its superiority in armor, but it would try again the next day.[29]

North of Gille's corps, Breith's *III. Pz.Korps* was pressed hard throughout 4 April by numerically superior Soviet infantry, as his meagre forces defended its line against several attempts to break through in the area of Rechnitz and Deutsch-Grossdorf, defended by troops from *Div.Gr. Krause*. The town of Dürnbach, held by *Geb. Ers.u.Ausb.Btl. 18*, was attacked by a tank-supported infantry force and quickly fell to the Soviet assault. Many of the *Alarm* units fighting under Krause's command simply fled when attacked, despite the efforts by their officers to rally them. *Luftwaffe* troops from *Flak-Rgt. 40*, acting as a rear guard at one point, fended off the pursuing Soviet tanks, though suffering heavy losses while doing so. The towns of Schachendorf, Burg, and Woppendorf also fell into enemy hands.[30] By this point, the gap between the *6. Armee*'s left wing and the right wing of Dietrich's *6. Pz.Armee* at Gloggnitz had widened to 50 kilometers. That evening, the *6. Armee* was also directed to redouble its efforts to establish a solid front with the *2. Pz.Armee*, though this was easier said than done.

In the *6. Pz.Armee* sector, heavy defensive fighting was reported to have taken place throughout its entire area of operations. While Dietrich's troops that day were able to deny the 4th and 9th Guards Armies and 6th Tank Army the breakthrough towards Vienna that they were seeking, his troops were not able to prevent them from advancing several kilometers into the mountains near the city of Baden bei Wien. Due to the unauthorized withdrawal of troops defending the town of Bruck an der Leitha sector ordered by their commander, Soviet troops were able to cross the Leitha River and occupy the town almost without a fight. Dietrich ordered the commander arrested, tried, and shot by a summary court martial.[31] Consequently, the *6. Pz.Armee* was ordered to retake the Leitha River sector, including Bruck, and close the gap that had arisen there by attacking towards Ödenburg.

In the *8. Armee*'s area of operations, the German garrison of Fortress Pressburg was encircled that day and was predictably ordered to stand fast instead of being allowed to evacuate the city.[32] Soviet forces were able to fight their way through the mountain pass in the Minor Carpathians and the town of Bad Pistyan was lost despite the efforts of the skillfully fighting defenders. Pressure against the army's left wing continued unabated. The only good news that day was the arrival of eight trains carrying the lead elements of the full-strength *Führer-Grenadier Division* (*Führer-Gren.Div.*) that would be initially attached to the *II. SS-Pz.Korps*.[33]

The litany of bad news continued into 5 April. On the *H.Gr. Süd* southern front, its daily summary to the *OKH* reported that the left wing of the *2. Pz.Armee* was thrown back to the Mur River, while its right was still firmly anchored to the Drava River in the south. Its front line now ran from the northwest to the southeast. Soviet forces had penetrated the defense works at Radkersburg in southeastern Austria, and the *Hohenstaufen* Division, the partially rebuilt *44. Reichs-Gren.Div. H.u.D.*, and some *Volkssturm* units were sent to throw them out, although some advanced Soviet formations were able to slip past and continue advancing west. The *6. Armee* conducted an attack across the Raab towards the left flank of the *2. Pz.Armee* and achieved some local success, while south and southeast of the *6. Pz.Armee*, advancing Soviet units were temporarily brought to a halt by another counterattack carried out by the *III. Pz.Korps*.

On 5 April, the *IV. SS-Pz.Korps* reported that its units were engaged in "mopping up actions" in the Raab River valley, where the counterattacks by the *Wiking* and *1. Pz.Div.* continued. Afterward, the *Wiking* Division moved into a new *HKL* slightly behind its old one that allowed better use of the terrain and began preparing more permanent defenses.[34] *Kampfgruppe von Hartmannsdorf* from the *1. Pz.Div.*, supported by five *Pz. VI* Tiger IIs from *s.Pz.Abt. 509*, had calmed things down in the center and right wing of the *6. Armee* for a few days, assisted by the last-minute deployment of a battalion of paratroopers from the *10. Fallschirm-Div.*[35] At the same time, *K.Gr. Bradel* succeeded in finally dislodging Soviet troops from the valley near Feldbach and in the town itself with a counterattack of its own.

On the army's left, Breith's *III. Pz.Korps*, though it had successfully prevented a breakthrough in the Semmering Gap the previous day, was forced to withdraw its left flank in the Pinka defensive sector 8 kilometers to the west after being pressed by elements of the much-stronger V Guards Cavalry Corps.[36] The defending troops from *Div.Gr. Krause* suffered heavy losses during the fighting that day, especially the *Luftwaffe's Flak* units that provided most of the antitank defense.

On 5 April, Vienna was declared a *Verteidigungsbereich* (fortified defense district), although not a *Festung*.[37] *General der Infanterie* Bünau was placed in command and was promised the *Führer-Gren.Div.* as reinforcement, since he had no real troops of his own except heavy *Flak* units, some training and replacement battalions, local Nazi Party functionaries, and local *Volkssturm* of dubious reliability. In the *6. Pz.Armee's* area of operations, between the Neusiedlersee and the Danube, Tolbukhin's forces continued their advance. The town of Bruck on the Leitha River, after being retaken the previous night, finally fell to an enemy attack, as did the town of Engerau south of Pressburg and parts of Pressburg itself. Northeast of Pressburg, troops from Malinovsky's Second Ukrainian Front managed to fight their way through several of the mountain passes in the Minor Carpathians and debouched upon the open plains below.[38]

On Friday, 6 April, the *2. Pz.Armee* withdrew its last bridgehead over the Mur River triangle, where it merged with the Drava River. That day, the *OKW* reported that significant progress had been made in drawing together the inner wings of the *6. Pz.Armee*, the *6. Armee*, and the *2. Pz.Armee*. Despite the success of the attacks launched on the right by the *IV. SS-Pz.Korps*, the *6. Armee* reported that the gap between it and the neighboring *I. Kav.Korps* of the *2. Pz.Armee* had not yet been completely closed; there was only a "loose connection" between the two armies. The *1. Pz.Div.*, which had been leading this attack, had been able to fight its way as far south as Fehring, but finally was forced to a halt due to increasing Soviet resistance.[39] What little success that the *IV. SS-Pz.Korps* was able to achieve that day was attributed to the shifting of the Soviet XVIII Tank Corps towards the Vienna axis, thereby relieving a considerable amount of pressure being exerted on German forces in the Raab valley.[40]

On the *6. Armee's* left flank, the *III. Pz.Korps* was forced to defend against a strong enemy attack that was able to penetrate its defense line along the Pinka River sector until it was finally brought to a halt that evening between the towns of Mischendorf and Buchschachen. The SS training battalion holding Rechnitz (*SS-Gren.Ers.u. Ausb.Btl. 11*) was cut off that day in the course of the attack, though it was able to reach the new German defense line early the next day after suffering a number of casualties. Krause's greatest fear was that the attack on the corps' left flank was a sign that the Soviet 26th Army was renewing its efforts to outflank the *6. Armee*. By the evening, *III. Pz.Korps* had shored up its defenses, though this position was described in that evening's report to *6. Armee* as a "weak security line."[41]

In the *6. Pz.Armee* area of operations on 6 April, Dietrich's headquarters reported that Soviet forces were pushing its troops out of the Vienna Forest in a northwesterly direction towards Klosterneuburg. Whether their spearheads had reached the Danube northwest of the city near Tulln was still unclear. Southwest of Vienna, Soviet troops continued their approach towards the city. Pressburg fell on this day, a *Festung* that was supposed to be able to withstand a siege until the autumn; its conquerors continued advancing towards Heimberg, while its rear-echelon troops enjoyed the spoils of victory in the now-liberated city. *General der Gebirgstruppe* von Kreysing's *8. Armee* was forced to establish a new *HKL* along the western edge of the Minor Carpathians; along the rest of his army's front lines, numerous breakthroughs were reported.[42]

Alarmed by the tone of the reports coming from *H.Gr. Süd* concerning the army group's rapidly dwindling armor strength, on 6 April, *Gen.Maj.* Wolfgang Thomale, Chief of the Inspectorate of *Panzer* Troops at *OKH* Headquarters, sent one of its liaison officers, *Major* Schöne, to carry out a two-day fact-finding mission. In addition to meeting with *Maj.* Graf Strachwitz, the head of the Inspectorate's *Aussenstelle* (field office) at the army group's headquarters in St Leonhard, Schöne was tasked to personally assess the situation concerning all of its *panzer* and *panzergrenadier* divisions, which by this point included nine from the *Heer* and seven from the *Waffen-SS*, as well as any remaining armored troops schools, training installations, repair facilities, and equipment depots in the *H.Gr. Süd* area of operations.[43] What he found was disconcerting.

Most of his visit was concerned with measures needed to increase the overall armor strength of the army group, such as incorporating the remnants of the *232. Pz.Div.* into the *6. Pz.Div.* He also recommended efficiency measures that could be taken, as well as where *panzer* and *panzergrenadier* replacement personnel were most badly needed. In addition, he assessed which installations needed to be evacuated further into the zone of the interior, where they would be safe from attack, such as the enormous armored troops depot at St Pölten, which contained over 4,000 metric tons of spare parts and repair-related equipment.

In addition to enumerating these duty-related tasks, Schöne could not help but record his personal thoughts concerning the overall situation within *H.Gr. Süd*. His remarkable eyewitness observations provide a measure by which to judge just how much the army group had declined in efficiency compared to other army groups. At the conclusion of his report, he recorded his personal impressions as follows:

1. The general discipline within the *H.Gr. Süd* area in comparison to that within *H.Gr. Mitte* can only be characterized as poor. Almost unbelievable examples of unsoldierly conduct seem to be the order of the day. Necessary corrective actions by officers are noticeably absent. In some places one cannot help but notice the impression that signs of dissolution are spreading.
2. Traffic discipline, including the control of columns of fleeing Hungarian civilians and soldiers, is quite lacking. Total traffic stoppages along the narrow roads are now the rule.
3. Enemy air attacks appear to be directed primarily against key transportation nodes and at the moment railroad traffic has been brought to a complete standstill.
4. The [radio and telephone] communications network within the army group area of operations is extremely bad.[44]

The incoming commander of *H.Gr. Süd*, *Gen.O.* Lothar Rendulic, was not included in the report's distribution list; he would have to learn about the problems within his new command from his own staff.

What *Generalmajor* Thomale did with Schöne's frank and shocking report remains unknown; by this point in the war, the most that the Chief of the Inspectorate of *Panzer* Troops could do was to attempt to mitigate the worst effects of the decline in the combat power of the *panzer* arm; there was little that Thomale could do to reverse this catastrophic situation. The economic effects of six years of war and the loss of most of Germany's fuel production facilities, combined with the effects of the Allied strategic bombing campaign, compounded by Hitler's bad decisions, could not be overcome by intelligent men such as Thomale or Albert Speer, Germany's Minister of Armaments and War Production.

In the *H.Gr. Süd* theater of operations on 7 April, the Soviet advance continued. Fortunately, actions taken by *6. Armee* and *2. Pz.Armee* to close the gap were beginning to bear fruit. In the *IV. SS-Pz.Korps'* sector, the situation on its right flank had calmed down considerably, especially after *K.Gr. Wolf* was able to push the front line forward as far as a kilometer south of Feldbach. Continuing its attack, after heavy fighting, *Oberstleutnant* Wolf's troops were able to retake Mühlbach and Hill 470, thereby sealing off any further Soviet attempt to penetrate into the Raab River valley. A counterattack launched that same day by *K.Gr. 3. Pz.Div.*, with four of its remaining tanks and 20 *SPWs*, stymied attempts by two Soviet battalions to resume their push towards Heiligenkreuz in the lower Lafnitz River valley.[45]

Without the tanks of the XVIII Tank Corps to lend their firepower to the attack, Trofimenko's 27th Army now had to fight against a renewed and determined German defense, whereas only a week before his troops could have gone all the way to Graz if they had concentrated their efforts. The *6. Armee's* biggest threat now lay on its northern flank, where Breith's *III. Pz.Korps* had to face a renewed attempt by Gagen's 26th Army against its left wing to force its way into the Semmering Gap and Pinka River valley. To breach the German defenses in this area, Gagen decided to commit the V Guards Cavalry Corps on 7 April in an attack aimed at the gap between the towns of Rohrbach and Oberdorf; once the Cossacks had broken through, they were instructed to continue advancing to the west. Though hard-pressed, Breith's forces, led the *1. Volks-Geb.Div.*, were able to hold their own and prevented a deep penetration, but did not have enough firepower to stop the Soviet advance completely. To counter this dangerous threat, Thünert's *K.Gr. 1. Pz.Div.* was shifted north from Gille's to Breith's sector in order to retake both towns. By that evening, Thünert's troops had succeeding in liberating Rohrbach and would continue their attack the following day.

On the same day, the *I. Btl./Norge* returned to the *Wiking* Division for the last time, though it was a shadow of its former self, especially with Vogt now gone. *Obersturmführer* Werner Radtke, Vogt's former *Adjutant*, was now serving as its acting battalion commander. He was now in command of nearly 800 new replacements, though he had few experienced NCOs and even fewer officers to lead or train them.[46] To the north, the *6. Pz.Armee* reported further Soviet advances against St Pölten in the west and towards the southern front of the Vienna Defense Zone. The *8. Armee* reported that the enemy had reached the March River west of the Minor Carpathians and was enaged in establishing several bridgeheads.

In a related development, *Gen.d.Inf.* Otto Wöhler was replaced that day by *Generaloberst* Rendulic, who had a reputation as a good tactician and stern disciplinarian, as well as being a staunch advocate of National Socialism.[47] As will be recalled, Wöhler was notified of his impending relief of command on 25 March after his defeatism had become all too evident in his communications with Berlin, but by this point Guderian was no longer at *OKH* to protect him. Wöhler had been kept on as commander of *H.Gr. Süd* until Rendulic could make his way down to Austria from his previous post in the Kurland bridgehead. Perhaps Hitler had thought that Rendulic, known as the *Führer's* "Austrian Fireman," was a miracle worker and could reinstill the desire for victory in the soldiers of *H.Gr. Süd* and succeed where Wöhler had failed.

On 8 April, Soviet forces from the 57th Army began pushing the left wing of the *2. Pz.Armee* back into the *Reichschutzstellung*. Paradoxically, de Angelis's army was finally able to establish a solid connection with the *6. Armee* because this newly shortened main defense line resulted in increased troop density along his entire front. With its right wing anchored firmly on the Drava, de Angelis's army remained in contact with *H.Gr. E*, an action that ensured German forces in Croatia and Bosnia-Hercegovina could begin withdrawing in a timely manner and escape the trap being prepared for them by Tito's partisan army and the 1st Bulgarian Army. With the situation on its right wing seemingly stabilized, the *6. Armee* began shifting some of its assets from its right to the left in order to assist the *III. Pz.Korps* in shoring up its weakening front line and its attempts to re-establish contact with the right wing of the *6. Pz.Armee*.

At midnight on 7/8 April, the *1. Pz.Div.*, now designated as the *6. Armee* reserve, began moving into an assembly area north of Fürstenfeld, where it would assist the *III. Pz.Korps* with its counterattack scheduled for the following day from the vicinity of Stegersbach.[48] This counterattack, made in conjunction with the *1. Volks-Geb. Div.*, was a success that temporarily stabilized the entire front line of the *6. Armee*. As a result of the *1. Pz.Div.*'s departure, the *Wiking* Division would have to widen its front line to take over the portion previously held by Thünert's division. That same day, Eberhard Heder's *SS-Pio.Btl. 5* was able to fight off an enemy attack at Jennersdorf. Thereafter, Soviet troops conducted frequent small-scale attacks, but the *Wiking* Division managed to ward them off with its own forces.[49]

West of Vienna, Soviet forces continued to make progress, reaching the Kahlenberg Mountain 12 kilometers north of the city that same day, where they pivoted and began to attack the city from the northwest where its defenses were the weakest. Soviet assault spearheads supported by tanks fought their way into Vienna, reaching the Franz-Josef railroad station and attempting to seize the bridges over the Danube, but the timely arrival of the *Führer-Gren.Div.* prevented any further advance. In conjunction with the *Das Reich* and *Totenkopf* Divisions, the *Fuhrer-Gren.Div.* brought the Soviet advance to a standstill and bought additional time for the city's garrison to solidify its defenses. As many as 10 T-34s were knocked out in Vienna and its outskirts on that day alone. During that day, it was reported that some of the citizens of Vienna had "lost their composure." This included accusations that some had been spotted wearing German uniforms but actively assisting the attackers, while other had been apprehended wearing red arm bands.[50]

Outside of Vienna, the bulk of the *6. Pz.Armee* was tied up in heavy fighting south, southwest, and west of the city. Soviet spearheads easily made their way through the Vienna Forest, creating suspicion among German troops that they were being led by native Austrian guides in sympathy with Stalin. Heavy fighting was reported south of the Tulln bridgehead, and at Siedling, Grünburg, and Hohe Wand. *Waffen-SS* troops from the *LSSAH* and *Hitlerjungend* Divisions fought off numerous tank attacks, destroying as many as 35 Red Army armored fighting vehicles in one day, mostly by infantry weapons. North of the Danube, the *8. Armee* was having difficulty holding its ground, as the 7th Guards Army seized four bridgeheads over the March River in one day and were only stopped when they encountered strong opposition at Lundenburg. On the *8. Armee*'s left wing, local fighting was reported in the Waag River valley.[51]

Monday, 9 April marked the 25th day since Tolbukhin had initiated the Vienna Operation, and victory was now within his grasp. In less than a month, his armies had advanced over 200 kilometers and were already at Vienna's gates. On the southernmost flank of *H.Gr. Süd*, its *2. Pz.Armee* was already defending against local attacks directed at Radkersburg. On the left flank of the *6. Armee*, Soviet troops were attempting to further their advance by seizing the approaches leading to the town of Semmering in the Mürz River valley, a sign that Tolbukhin had not given up on his plan to separate the *6. Pz.Armee* from Balck's *6. Armee*.

That day, Balck's forces were involved in an attempt to close the gap between the Bruck and the Fröschnitz valleys and eliminate the enemy elements that had penetrated into this breach. Meanwhile, the *Wiking* Division was involved in heavy fighting for Hill 365 east of Johnsdorf. Apparently, the departure of the *1. Pz.Div.* had been noticed by General Trofimenko, who ordered attacks to be carried out to seize this key terrain feature that enabled observation along the Raab valley between Fürstenfeld and St Gotthard. Finally, after three days of heavy back-and-forth combat, Soviet troops were thrown back and Ullrich's division retained possession of the key hill.[52] One of the units attached to the division at this time that probably took part in the fighting for Hill 365 that day was *IV. Btl./SS-Rgt. Ney*, which had been undergoing reorganization at St Michael.

Heavy fighting raged throughout the day in the *III. Pz.Korps'* sector, as relentless attacks by elements of the V Guards Cavalry Corps applied tremendous pressure against the *1. Volks-Geb.Div.* and *Div.Gr. Krause*, as well as *K.Gr. Semmering*, a new battle group established to block Soviet access to the Semmering Gap. Although attacks against the towns of Oberdorf and Rotenturm were driven back, Soviet troops were able to seize the village of Kreuzwirt after pushing *K.Gr. Motschmann* to the west beyond the key town of Vorau. This latter action brought a portion of the *6. Armee* reserve, *I. Btl./Pz.Gren.Rgt. 113* of the *1. Pz.Div.*, out of its assembly area and led to its commitment against enemy troops reportedly approaching the upper Lafnitz valley from the direction of Vorau.[53]

On the right flank of Dietrich's *6. Pz.Armee*, Soviet troops tried to force their way past the *I. SS-Pz.Korps* as they attempted to carry out a supporting attack against the one being undertaken against the neighboring *III. Pz.Korps*, but were unsuccessful. Enemy attempts to penetrate Vienna's defense zone from the west were also thwarted, though Soviet troops managed to make further progress in the south and the northwest, where they had entered the city the previous day. German defenders, including battle groups from the *Das Reich* and *Totenkopf* Divisions, knocked out 39 Soviet tanks in and around Vienna alone. North of the Danube, the *8. Armee* was unable to prevent Soviet forces from launching large-scale attacks from the four bridgeheads it had established over the March River. Vienna was now almost completely surrounded.

On 10 April, the *2. Pz.Armee* reported only small-scale, local attacks. Elsewhere, the dissolution of German forces accelerated. The *6. Armee* successfully repelled a series of concerted Soviet attacks along its entire front that day, with the exception of the fighting around Fürstenfeld by the *Wiking* Division, which launched an attack that retook another key terrain feature lost earlier that day, Hill 365. The *IV. SS-Pz.Korps* reported that due to the heavy fighting, many of the casualties the division suffered that day could be traced to the increasingly noticeable shortage of ammunition for its heavy weapons.[54] Even small-arms ammunition was becoming harder to get.

Combat in Hungary, Spring of 1945

Troops from the *Totenkopf* Division in the trenches north of Stuhlweissenburg in late February 1945. While the *SS-Rottenführer* in the center eats a midday meal, his comrades keep watch. (Photo by *SS-Kriegsberichter* Peter Adendorf, courtesy of Andrew Found)

An officer from the *Totenkopf* Division, visiting a front-line position near Stuhlweissenburg in late February 1945, is briefed by *SS-Hscha.* Kurt Franke (left), a Knight's Cross awardee and deputy commander of *11. Kp./SS-Pz.Gren.Rgt. 6 Theodor Eicke*. (Adendorf)

An *SS-Unterscharführer* from the *Totenkopf* Division shares a light moment with men of his squad as he cuts a slice from a loaf of *Kriegsbrot* (war bread) on the outskirts of Stuhlweissenburg in late February or early March 1945. The men shown here wear a mix of field gray and camouflage SS clothing. (Adendorf)

Waffen-SS troops from the *6. Pz.Armee* man a front-line position in the Lake Balaton area in March 1945 prior to the commencement of the Third Ukrainian Front's Vienna Operation. (Photo by *SS-Kriegsberichter* Fritz Jäckisch, courtesy of Andrew Found)

Several *Pz. IV* medium tanks from the *23. Pz.Div.* occupy an assembly area prior to commencing their attack during Operation *Frühlingserwachen* in early March 1945. (Author)

A squad of very young *Waffen-SS* troops from the *6. Pz.Armee* form up along the street of a Hungarian village in mid-March 1945, somewhere southeast of Lake Balaton. No longer strictly a force of volunteers, by the spring of 1945, most combat troops in the *Waffen-SS* were young draftees from the 1927 or 1928 year groups, involuntary transfers from the *Luftwaffe* or *Kriegsmarine*, or *Volksdeutsche* from Eastern Europe. (Photo by *SS-Kriegsberichter* Max Büschel, courtesy of Andrew Found)

A young SS trooper from the *6. Pz.Armee* leans out of a window in a village southeast of Lake Balaton in mid-March 1945. He is armed with a *Maschine-Pistole* MP 44, considered to be the world's first modern assault rifle, capable of firing semi-automatic or automatic fire. Developed in 1942, by the time it began to be issued in large numbers in late 1944, the war was nearly over. (Büschel)

SS panzer officers and an infantry officer from the 16. *SS-Pz.Gren.Div. Reichsführer SS*, assigned to the 2. *Pz.Armee*, consult a map before initiating a counterattack south of Lake Balaton during March or April 1945. (Photo by *SS-Kriegsberichter* Hans Cantzler, courtesy of Andrew Found)

An SS *Sturmgeschütz III*, most likely from the *16. SS-Pz.Gren.Div. Reichsfuhrer SS*, escorted by *Panzergrenadiers*, carries out a counterattack, somewhere south of Lake Balaton in March 1945. (Cantzler)

A column of SS vehicles from the *6. Pz.Armee* pass through a Hungarian village in mid-March 1945 as the withdrawal from the Lake Balaton front begins. A number of lightly wounded *Waffen-SS* men and troops from the *Heer* wait along the roadside for evacuation to a field hospital. (Photo by *SS-Kriegsberichter* Wilfried Woscidlo, courtesy of Günther Lange)

Two members of the *Germania* Regiment of the *Wiking* Division engage in friendly conversation with a local farmer near Várpalota in late February/early March 1945. The soldier on the right wears the ribbon for the Iron Cross, Second Class, the Infantry Assault Badge in Silver, and the Close Combat Clasp in Bronze or Silver. On his left sleeve, the *Germania* cuff title can easily be seen. (Courtesy of Andrew Found)

Three members of the *Germania* Regiment and a Hungarian comrade (far right) during a lull in the action near Stuhlweissenburg in late February/early March 1945. Their vehicle, a *Sd.Kfz. 251 Ausf. D* armored half-track, still shows signs of the white camouflage paint applied when the regiment arrived in Hungary in December 1944. (Courtesy of Andrew Found)

Two other members of the *Germania* Regiment, including the *Sturmmann* in the above photograph (right), fraternize with a Hungarian family near Várpalota in late February/early March 1945. The *SS-Rottenfuhrer* in the center wears his camouflaged cap, rather dirty white drill trousers, and a standard service tunic. On his left chest pocket, his Iron Cross, First Class, Infantry Assault Badge in Silver, and Wound Badge can be clearly seen. (Courtesy of Andrew Found)

German troops from the reconnaissance battalion of a *panzer* division atop a *Sd.Kfz. 260/261 Kleiner Panzerfunkwagen* (radio car) on the lookout along the Austrian border for approaching Soviet troops in early April 1945. The older-appearing officer on the far left is most likely a member of a *Landeschützen* home defense battalion or a leader of a local *Volkssturm* unit cooperating with the *panzer* division. (Courtesy of searchwarchiwach.gov.pl)

A platoon of destroyed *Pz. V* Panthers from the *23. Pz.Div.* lie smoldering on the highway along the northern shore of Lake Balaton on 28 or 29 March 1945. Due to a shortage of gasoline to power the *panzers*, the division was forced to order their crews to blow them up to prevent them from falling into the hands of Soviet troops, who later took this photograph. Due to shortages of essential supplies, *Gen.d.Pz.Tr.* Hermann Balck's *6. Armee* had to abandon most of its armored fighting vehicles during the last week of March 1945. (Author)

As the German retreat from Hungary begins, anxious Hungarian civilians gather around the photographer to ask questions about what is going to happen with them. The fear and disquiet on their faces is clearly visible. In the background, Gille's command car is parked next to a farmhouse. (Lange)

During the retreat from the area north of Lake Balaton towards the *Reichsschutzstellung*, troops of the *6. Armee* and other units were forced to abandon many of their soft-skinned vehicles when they broke down or ran out of fuel. Here, several trucks of various makes and models, including one assigned to the *Luftwaffe* in the foreground, lay desolate along the roadside, having been stripped by passing German or Soviet troops of anything of value. (Yuri Gubanov collection, courtesy of Kamen Nevenkin)

This photograph depicts surrendering German soldiers turning in their weapons at an American collection point in May 1945 after surrendering in Austria. The terrain shown here is similar to the area east of Graz where the *IV. SS-Pz.Korps* fought during the last month of the war. (U.S. Army Signal Corps photograph, courtesy of U.S. National Archives)

At the war's end, armored fighting vehicles were destroyed to prevent them from falling into the hands of Soviet troops. Here, two wrecked *StuG III* assault guns from either the *Wiking* Division or *3. Pz.Div.* sit in an Austrian lake after being set on fire or blown up by their crews. (Gubanov collection)

Near the demarcation line along the Enns, a number of German vehicles like these shown here were parked and abandoned to be cannibalized for spare parts, including some from units assigned to the *IV. SS-Pz.Korps*, possibly the *Wiking* Division or *3. Pz.Div.* (Gubanov collection)

After handing in their weapons, the German and Hungarian troops shown in this photograph undergo a perfunctory search by U.S. Army guards. Clearly, there were insufficient troops to watch so many prisoners; fortunately, the overwhelming majority of the troops from *H.Gr. Ostmark* surrendering between 7 and 9 May 1945 were simply glad to have survived the war and wanted nothing more than to return home as soon as possible. (U.S. Army Signal Corps photograph, courtesy of the U.S. National Archives)

After crossing the line of demarcation along the Enns, this German unit marches along a winding mountain road towards the area in Austria designated as their future internment site. They are carrying everything they need (except rations) to survive a lengthy period under U.S. guard. (U.S. Army Signal Corps photograph, courtesy of the U.S. National Archives)

This photograph depicts the huge fleet of German military vehicles under U.S. Army guard in Lieszen, Austria, after crossing over to the north side of the Enns River. This official photo was taken on 12 May 1945 at the point where most of the *IV. SS-Pz.Korps* surrendered on 8 and 9 May, and most likely includes vehicles belonging to the *1.* and *3. Pz.Div.* and the *Wiking* Division. (Photograph by Walter D. MacDonald, U.S. Army 167th Signal Photographic Company, courtesy of U.S. National Archives)

The *Totenkopf* Division, fighting with the *6. Pz. Armee* when the unconditional surrender was announced, crossed the line of demarcation near Linz, Austria. This photograph, taken by a local resident, shows a number of German vehicles, including horse-drawn wagons, attempting to reach the safety of the American lines before midnight on 8 May 1945. (Courtesy of Ian Michael Wood)

This photograph depicts the *Totenkopf* Division's initial internment area on the U.S. side of the line of demarcation near Pregarten, Austria. Little did *Brigadeführer* Becker and his men know that within a few days they would be handed over to the Red Army, and many of them would spend up to 10 years in the Soviet Union. (Courtesy of Ian Michael Wood)

The Corps Command and Staff After the War

During a postwar reunion of the *Wiking* Division in the early 1960s, Gille (foreground) talks to the former commander of the division's headquarters company, Hans Kasten. In the background between the two stands is Willi Hein, and on the far right is Fritz Wolf, former *Adjutant* of the *panzer* regiment. (Lange)

During the same reunion, Gille meets with (from L to R) Willi Hein, Fritz Wolf, and Horst Kampe. (Lange)

Gille (right) speaks with his former intelligence chief, Dr Herbert Jankuhn, who by this time had been restored to his former position as a lecturer at the University of Göttingen and who later rose to be the widely respected dean of its archaeology department. (Lange)

During a visit to his home in the mid-1950s to celebrate his birthday, three of his former staff officers pose with Gille (sitting) for a photograph. They are (from L to R) Hans Velde, Werner Westphal, and Günther Lange. Both Velde and Lange went on to have successful second careers in the *Bundeswehr* and retired respectively as *Oberst* and *Oberstleutnant*. (Lange)

In November 1958, the *Ordensgemeinschaft der Ritterkreuztrager des Eisernes Kreuz e.V.* (*OdR*, or Order of Knight's Cross Holders) presented Herbert Gille with a "new" 1957 de-Nazified version of the Knight's Cross with Oak Leaves, Swords & Diamonds during a special ceremony at its annual assembly. This ceremony was held to replace the same award stolen from him by an American officer upon his arrest in Salzburg on 28 May 1945. (Lange)

During the first large post-World War II gathering of *Waffen-SS* veterans in the small north German town of Verden on 26 October 1952, nearly 5,000 former members participated in a parade through the center of the town towards the cemetery, where they laid commemorative wreaths on the graves of many fallen comrades. In the second rank, wearing glasses and carrying his hat in his left hand, marches Herbert Otto Gille. (Lange)

During a *HIAG* meeting in the early 1960s, the three former commanders of the *Wiking* Division are photographed together in an informal moment (from L to R): Karl Ullrich, Felix Steiner, and Herbert Gille. (Photo by Ernst Baumann)

The *1. Pz.Div.* was ordered to send a battlegroup into the Lafnitz valley to carry out an armed reconnaissance to find a Soviet cavalry force that was reported in the area, the same one that had roughly handled *K.Gr. Motschmann* the previous day in Kreuzwirt. When *Oberst* Bradel, leader of the *Kampfgruppe*, and his troops entered the Austrian mountain town of Vorau, no German troops were in evidence. White flags were already flying from many buildings, and the few Austrian citizens who were seen outside their homes refused to offer the German troops from Thuringia and Hessen water, food, or any information about the Soviet force's whereabouts. This was the first time that the men of the *1. Pz.Div.* had encountered this sentiment on "German" soil.[55] Once Bradel's troops found a Cossack reconnaissance patrol a few kilometers east of the town, the Germans quickly threw them back, even without the help of the local population.

In the *6. Pz.Armee's* area, two separate battles were being fought—one west and one southwest of Vienna. In the southwest, the *I. SS-Pz.Korps* was continuing its attempts to block elements of the 6th Guards Tank Army from breaking out of the area west of Wiener Neustadt and reaching St Pölten. West of the city, the other battle was that being fought by the *II. SS-Pz.Korps* and *Korpsgruppe Bünau* in and around Vienna itself. Were it not for the mountainous area on the western edges of the Vienna Forest, the Soviet advance would have gone much more quickly; as it was, Priess's *I. SS-Pz.Korps* was barely able to maintain a continuous front as it was being slowly forced back to the west. Its troops knocked out nine tanks that day.

Bittrich's *II. SS-Pz.Korps* and the forces under von Bünau's command had been forced to abandon most of Vienna by this point, and began withdrawing north across the Danube that evening before they became trapped in the city. In the *8. Armee's* area of operations, von Kreysing began pulling his forces back along his right wing to an intermediate position, while heavy fighting was reported between Vienna and the March River, particularly against Soviet attacks out of the Lundenburg bridgehead.

On that same day, the weekly *Panzerlage* (tank strength) report was submitted by *H.Gr. Süd* to the Inspectorate of *Panzer* Troops in Berlin. It paints a sad picture of the decline of a once-legendary force that only a month before had been the most powerful assembly of combat power in the Third Reich since the Ardennes offensive. On 10 April, the *6. Pz.Armee* reported the following numbers of operational armored fighting vehicles of all types: *6. Pz.Div.*, 15; *Führer-Gren.Div.*, 29 (including eight *Pz. VI* Tigers); *LSSAH*, 20; *Das Reich*, 13; *Totenkopf*, two; and *Hitlerjugend*, eight (including one *Jagdpanther*). With these 87 operational vehicles, Dietrich's supply-constrained army was faced by several hundred tanks of the 6th Guards Tank Army plus several tank and mechanized corps with over 100 more, with access to unlimited amounts of fuel, ammunition, and replacement parts. An ominous sign that the end was near had already occurred on 5 April, when the last ammunition train arrived for *H.Gr. Süd*; after that, there would be no more.[56]

The *IV. SS-Pz.Korps* had even fewer operational vehicles than when it had crossed into Austria on 30/31 March. It reported that as of 5 April, the *1. Pz.Div.*, back once again under Gille's control, had only two operational tanks, though it did have six more in short-term repair and a further 24 undergoing depot-level repair in Graz. *Generalmajor* Thünert's tank maintenance company had gone to great lengths to recover as many of its damaged vehicles as it could during the withdrawal from Stuhlweissenburg. Using its extensive contacts in Germany (an advantage to being the oldest *panzer* division in the *Wehrmacht*), the division had been able to gather a large amount of spare parts and its maintenance personnel were working feverishly to place as many of the tanks in its Graz workshops back into operation as soon as possible. Whether there would be enough fuel to power them, as well as ammunition, was another matter.[57]

The *3. Pz.Div.* reported on 10 April that six of its armored fighting vehicles were operational, with nine more in short-term repair. Amazingly, the *Wiking* Division could still report four operational vehicles that the *SS-Pz.Rgt. 5* had been able to repair since it had arrived in Austria—two *Pz. IVs* and two *Pz. V* Panthers, with one of each in short-term repair. Therefore, on 10 May, Gille could report his corps as having 12 operational tanks and assault guns, with 17 more in short-term repair, a miniscule percentage of the nearly 400 vehicles that the corps should have at its disposal had its divisions been at full strength.[58]

On 11 April, the *OKW* consolidated daily report stated that heavy fighting had resumed along the left wing of the *2. Pz.Armee*, including numerous attacks between the Mur and Raab Rivers that its forces barely managed to seal off. The *6. Armee* experienced renewed fighting as well. On that date, the *IV. SS-Pz.Korps* reported that a tank-supported enemy regiment, originating from the Heiligenkreuz area, attacked in a north and northwesterly direction up the Lafnitz valley and was able to achieve a penetration in the vicinity of Gersdorf in the *Wiking* Division's sector. This force penetrated as far as Güssing and Grossmürbisch before it was finally brought to a halt by the *1. Pz.Div.* 12 kilometers to the southeast at Eltendorf. Using all of its combat arms—artillery, infantry, and armor—Thünert's division *Kampfgruppe* quickly and efficiently threw back the enemy force, but how much longer it could continue to do so with looming ammunition and fuel shortages was an open question.[59]

On the left flank of the *6. Armee*, the *III. Pz.Korps* was attacked by a strong armor-led Soviet force that achieved a deep penetration in the Neunkirchen area in an attempt to further separate Balck's army from Dietrich's. To hold the Semmering Pass, *K.Gr. Semmering*, commanded by *Oberst* Heribert Raithel of the Mountain Training School, carried out an attack that day to secure Hill 600 west of the town of Schottwein. In doing so, his battlegroup established a solid front line in that portion of the Austrian Alps for the first time since the corps had moved into its new positions 12 days before.[60] Much of the combat in Breith's defensive sector was now being conducted in steep mountains and narrow river valleys, where his miscellany of combat units fought Soviet units hilltop to hilltop, both seeking to gain the local advantage from possessing key terrain.

In the *I. SS-Pz.Korps'* sector, Hermann Priess's forces were able to thwart Soviet attempts to penetrate the *Hohen Wand* ("High Wall") mountain range west of Wiener Neustadt. Despite this, the 6th Guards Tank Army continued widening its breakthrough northwest of Vienna in the vicinity of Tulln. Nearly all of Vienna was now in the hands of the 4th Guards Army, except the central core of the city along the banks of the Danube. On that day, the *II. SS-Pz.Korps* with its three divisions (the *Das Reich* and *Totenkopf Panzer* Divisions and the *Führer-Grenadier* Division) reported that its troops had destroyed 25 Soviet tanks in the city and sunk four of their gunboats along the Danube.

Between Vienna and the March River, more deep breakthroughs were being reported—clearly, the main defense line of the right wing of the *8. Armee* was no longer tenable and was rapidly falling back.[61] Gehlen's Foreign Armies East reported that the Second Ukrainian Front had assembled as many as 20 rifle divisions and two mechanized corps against the *8. Armee* north of the Danube. Evidently Malinovsky was planning a thrust towards the north and northwest to get behind von Kreysing's forces before they could fall back to their intermediate defense line west of the March River. This also raised the possibility that unless it began withdrawing to the west, the *II. SS-Pz.Korps*—the bulk of which had already been withdrawn to the northern side of the Danube—would be cut off and destroyed.

On 11 April, *H.Gr. Süd's Oberquartiermeister* conducted an inventory of its remaining ammunition and fuel stockpiles, and the results were not encouraging. In terms of percentages of unit basic loads of ammunition, *Oberstleutnant* Mitlacher reported that the *6. Armee*, including the *IV. SS-Pz.Korps*, had on hand only 12 percent of its authorized level of machine-gun ammunition, 12 percent for its mortars, 3 percent of small-arms ammunition, 10 percent for its 10.5cm light field howitzers, and 6 percent for its 15cm heavy field howitzers. After the last ammunition train arrived, there was no prospect of obtaining any more. The fuel situation was simply catastrophic: the *6. Armee* had only 20 percent of its authorized daily *Verbrauchsatz* (consumption rate). The situation in the *6. Pz.Armee* was equally as bad, if not worse, since it had more armored vehicles than the *6. Armee*.[62] Clearly, *H.Gr. Süd* would soon run out of the lifeblood of war—with no fuel or ammunition, it would have no recourse but to withdraw as quickly as it could or surrender. Yet it remained fighting.

On Thursday, 12 April, the Soviet 57th Army succeeded in breaking through the center of the *2. Pz.Armee* and began advancing towards Graz from the south along the Mur River valley, only being brought to a halt after a counterattack by the *16. SS-Pz.Gren.Div. RFSS* and the *41. Inf.Div.* In the *6. Armee's* area of operations, indications of an imminent large-scale Soviet attack directed towards Güssing between the *3. Pz.Div.* and the left flank of the *Wiking* Division, as well as the *1. Volks-Geb.Div.*, led Balck to order Gille to pull back his corps to avoid the casualties that would have ensued. According to *Obersturmführer* Jahnke: "After our neighbor on our left holding the Lafnitz sector pulled back, we were forced to give up the salient north of Jennersdorf and withdraw to a position where the terrain was more favorable to the defense and where we could establish a straighter front line about 2 to 5 kilometers further back."[63]

Along the right wing of the *6. Pz.Armee*, only localized fighting in the Baden area was reported that day. West of Vienna, additional pressure was being placed on German forces by the advancing 6th Guards Tank Army, ensuring that no relief attack could be undertaken to regain control of the Austrian capital. In Vienna itself, a tiny portion of the city still in German hands continued to be held by the *II. SS-Pz.Korps* and *K.Gr. von Bünau*, though it was now only a matter of time before the entire city fell into the hands of the 4th Guards Army.

Although 15 Soviet tanks were knocked near the *Reichsbrücke*, the *Kampfgruppe* consisting of the remnants of the *Totenkopf* Division were briefly encircled near the fairgrounds before they were relieved by a counterattack from the *6. Pz.Div.* Six Soviet gunboats were sunk in the Danube by the German defenders on 12 April. The XVIII Tank Corps, recently committed against the Raab River valley, was reported at Tulln, nearly 20 kilometers northwest of Vienna. On the right wing of the *8. Armee*, the 7th Guards Army had completely broken through at Lundenburg, forcing the defenders to fall back even further.[64]

Compared to the past several days' events, the pace of operations in the *H.Gr. Süd Kampfraum* appears to have begun slackening from 13 April, although in some areas, especially in the south, heavy fighting still took place. The *2. Pz.Armee* continued its withdrawal up the Mur River valley and managed to once again put together a solid front line after the *4. Kav.Div.* of the *I. Kav.Korps* carried out a successful counterattack at Trautmannsdorf, though it suffered heavy losses in the process. Heavy and inconclusive fighting continued in the vicinity of Radkersburg, which was defended by the *XXII. Geb.Korps*.

In the sector held by the *IV. SS-Pz.Korps*, its troops were subjected to multiple attacks of up to battalion strength in the vicinity of Rittschein and Königsdorf, though in each case these Soviet attempts were repulsed. The *1. Pz.Div.* was called on to carry out several counterattacks in the Loipersdorf and Fürstenfeld areas against advancing Soviet forces that had moved in to occupy the ground that the corps had been ordered to give up the previous day.[65] Despite tough enemy resistance, *K.Gr. 1. Pz.Div.* was able to reach its objectives northeast of the town of Magland and the area a kilometer east of Oberlamm, though fighting was still ongoing when the evening report was submitted. Although it appeared that the Third Ukrainian Front had abandoned its attempt to take Graz and the Semmering Gap, Tolbukhin had no intention of granting the *6. Armee* any rest, choosing to steadily apply pressure at any point where the Germans and their remaining Hungarian allies lowered their guard. Should the opportunity for a breakthrough present itself, his troops would carry out their standing orders and advance as far as they could until they encountered a German force they could not overcome.

In the defensive sector of the *Wiking* Division located on the far right flank of the *IV. SS-Pz.Korps*, its headquarters reported that, in contrast to the day of heavy fighting experienced by the *1. Pz.Div.*, 13 April was "comparatively peaceful":

> [T]he Russians seem to have given up carrying out further massive attacks in this sector. The land is also more favorable, having a pre-Alpine character. Their little attacks can be easily driven back. The division has finally bounced back. We are receiving a constant influx of replacements. We are still experiencing serious supply problems and [are getting] no ammunition. The artillery can only fire with the corps' permission.[66]

Heavy fighting was reported that day in the *III. Pz.Korps*' area, where the departure of the *1. Pz.Div.* was sorely felt. A Soviet attack consisting of three or four rifle regiments led by 20 tanks achieved a breakthrough in the vicinity of Stegersbach that was 10 kilometers wide and 5 kilometers deep. Due to munitions shortages, there was little that Breith could do to stop them. In many instances, once troops had fired the last of their ammunition, they were forced to abandon their positions to the advancing enemy. The most dangerous attack that day managed to penetrate into the upper Lafnitz valley with as many as 25 tanks and reached as far south as the towns of Waldbach and Mönichwald. This attack, in turn would precipitate a powerful German reaction in the next several days.[67]

By 13 April, most of Vienna was in Soviet hands, though there were still some stubborn holdouts. Despite this, the Red Army declared Vienna "liberated" at 2 p.m. that day. The last German forces in Vienna, led by the *Das Reich* Division, did not actually withdraw over the Floridsdorf Bridge until late in the evening, having ensured all their wounded were evacuated. Shortly after midnight, the last troops withdrew and the bridge was blown up. Soviet historians later claimed that 47,000 German troops were taken prisoner in Vienna and 633 tanks were destroyed. This claim may be accurate if they were counting all the German losses since the fall of Stuhlweissenburg, but there were never that many troops or tanks engaged in and around Vienna during the battle for the city. West of Vienna, another Soviet breakthrough was reported. The situation in the *8. Armee* was essentially unchanged, as Soviet forces waited for their supplies to catch up.[68]

On 14 April, the right wing of the *2. Pz.Armee* had been forced back as far as Radkersburg, where its defenders—primarily troops from the *Hohenstaufen* Division—dug in. On the rest of the *H.Gr. Süd* front, from north to south, only fighting of a local nature was reported, although the Soviets did not ease up on their pressure against German forces. On that date, Gille's headquarters reported that despite efforts begun the previous day to continue its attack to clear Soviet forces out of the valley formed by the confluence of the Raab and Lafnitz Rivers, the *1. Pz.Div.* was not able to achieve any appreciable gains due to stubborn enemy resistance.

Throughout the day, Thünert's division was subjected to numerous attacks against its flanks by tank-supported enemy forces in regimental strength that forced it to shut down its assaults in order to avoid being cut off. Along the Heiligenkreuz–Fürstenfeld highway, an additional Soviet force of regimental size, supported by 10 assault guns, attempted to take advantage of the withdrawal of the *1. Pz.Div.* near the eastern outskirts of Oberdorf, but was brought to a halt by a counterattack.[69] The *Wiking* Division, southwest of Thünert's, was positioned astride the mountain overlooking the valley and could only watch the battle unfold from a safe distance.

Near Friedberg, on the *III. Pz.Korps'* left flank, Soviet tanks broke through and were able to continue their advance despite the mountainous terrain. To counter this threat, *SS-Pol.Rgt. 13* from *K.Gr. Motschmann* was sent in their direction armed with *Panzerfausts*. In the Mürzzuschlag area, the first trains carrying the *117. Jäg. Div.* began to arrive as badly needed reinforcements for *K.Gr. Semmering* of the *III. Pz.Korps* on the *6. Armee's* left wing. This division had just been sent from *H.Gr. E/O.B. Südost*, where it had been fighting on the Istrian Front, and had become available for further employment once *O.B. Südost* began to shorten its lines as it withdrew from the Balkans. Its first two battalions were quickly marched to their new defensive positions in the vicinity of Rettenegg. Although not at full strength, it was an experienced division and still fully equipped. It had arrived in the proverbial nick of time.[70]

In the Danube area on 14 April, Soviet troops approached to within 6 kilometers of St Pölten, where the *panzer* repair facility with its huge spare parts depot was being hurriedly evacuated. Along the Danube, the only German garrison still holding out had been encircled in the town of St Andrä. Unless they broke out on their own, they were lost, as there were no forces available to launch a relief attack. Most of the *6. Pz.Armee* had continued withdrawing westwards towards Krems, where it would attempt to form another defense line. On that day, Dietrich's army was augmented by the arrival of the *710. Inf.Div.* and *Sturm-Art.Brig. 261* with 18 assault guns.

Along the *8. Armee's* front, numerous attacks were reported at the upper reaches of the March River, a sign that the Soviet 53rd Army was continuing its advance towards Brno. Surprisingly, the *Luftwaffe* mounted 270 daytime sorties on 14 April, primarily in the Vienna area in an effort to disrupt and delay the advance by the 6th Guards Tank Army and 7th Guards Army.[71]

On 15 April, the *2. Pz.Armee* reported that its forces had managed to ward off a series of strong enemy attacks. However, it was forced to abandon its bridgehead at Radkersburg, which was quickly seized by Soviet forces as soon as the defenders withdrew. As a result, the army's front running along the line from north to south had to be withdrawn yet again. In the *6. Armee's* area, the *IV. SS-Pz.Korps* reported that its opponent had initiated a series of company-sized reconnaissance probes in the vicinity of Raabau, Hatzendorf, and east of Fürstenfeld, though Gille's headquarters claimed that all of them had been driven back by nightfall. The *3. Pz.Div.*, which had been enjoying a relatively quiet period, was tasked by the corps that day to strike against a battalion-sized Soviet force that had achieved a local breakthrough near the southeastern outskirts of Fürstenfeld along the railroad line; its *SPW*-battalion was able to seal off the Soviet unit in a counterattack.[72]

In the *III. Pz.Korps'* area, the armor-supported Soviet force that had penetrated as far as the Mürzzuschlag area was stopped and thrown back by a counterattack launched by *K.Gr. 1. Pz.Div.*, the SS police regiment having failed to stop them in the mountains after suffering heavy losses. Armed with hand-held antitank weapons, the *Ordnungspolizei* troops were no match for T-34s and supporting Soviet infantry, thus forcing Balck to order the commitment of Thünert's *Kampfgruppe*, the only remaining credible mobile force in the *6. Armee* order of battle. Thünert's tireless efforts directed towards rebuilding his division's capability (including increasing the number of operational tanks) had resulted in his division becoming Balck's de facto *Feuerwehr* (fire brigade), with which the *1. Pz.Div.* was being called upon on a daily basis to put out a fire somewhere on the army's widely spaced front line.[73]

Attacks against the adjoining sector held by the *I. SS-Pz.Korps* of the *6. Pz.Armee* continued throughout the day. Southwest of St Pölten, the spearheads of the XVIII Tank Corps and IX Mechanized Corps crossed the Traisen River. Here, both corps maneuvered their forces north and south of the city, despite the determined defense by *Korps Schultz*, which managed to destroy 20 Soviet tanks before withdrawing. Northwest of Vienna, on the northern bank of the Danube, the forces from the *II. SS-Pz.Korps* that had managed to withdraw from the city had fallen back to the village of Bisamberg near Neuburg, though the longer they stayed there, the greater their chances of being trapped against the river by the advancing forces of the 7th Guards Army. In the *8. Armee* area, between the Danube and March Rivers, further attacks were launched by the 7th Guards Army and 53rd Army. Near Lundenburg, Soviet forces made deep incursions in German defenses near Brno, and Lundenburg was lost that same day.[74]

Sunday, 15 April also marks the last recorded periodic armored fighting vehicle status report submitted by *H.Gr. Süd*, depicting the status of the *2. Pz.Armee, 6. Armee, 6. Pz.Armee,* and *8. Armee.* On that date, the *Wiking* Division reported having just one *Pz. IV* operational, with two in repair, three operational *Pz. V* Panthers, and three operational and one non-operational *Jg.Pz. 38t Hetzers*, for a total of only seven combat-ready vehicles and three in short-term repair. Whether the division had enough fuel for them was another question. The division also reported having eight operational and two non-operational 7.5cm antitank guns with prime movers.

The *1. Pz.Div.*, which briefly returned to the *IV. SS-Pz.Korps'* control the day after this report was submitted, stated that as of 15 April, it had one operational *Pz. III Befehlswagen* command vehicle, four operational and one non-operational *Pz. IVs*, seven operational and two non-operational *Pz. V* Panthers, two *StuG IVs*, and two *Sturmpanzer IV Brummbär* self-propelled assault howitzers from the attached

Sturm-Pz.Abt. 219, for a total of 16 operational armored fighting vehicle of all types plus three more in repair. The report also stated that it had eight 7.5cm antitank guns operational and four in repair, but made no mention of nearly two dozen of its tanks being secretly repaired in Graz.

The *3. Pz.Div.* was in roughly the same condition as the *Wiking* Division, reporting one non-operational *Pz. IV Befehlspanzer* (command tank), three operational and one non-operational *Pz. V* Panthers, two *StuG IIIs*, and two operational *Jg.Pz. 38t Hetzers*, as well as six operational and two non-operational 7.5cm antitank guns with prime movers. All told, the *IV. SS-Pz.Korps* still had 30 combat-ready tanks, assault guns, and tank destroyers, plus 22 antitank guns, amounting to a credible antitank force at this stage of the war, especially now that the mountainous terrain was working to its advantage.[75]

The readiness status of armored vehicles within the *III. Pz.Korps* defensive sector was much less robust than what Gille's corps enjoyed. On that same date, the *1. Volks-Geb.Div.* reported seven *Jg.Pz. 38 Hetzers* operational with one in repair, *Heeres-Sturm.Art.Brig. 303* reported six operational assault guns—including two 10.5cm *Sturmhaubitze* howitzers (with two in repair)—and the independent *I. Abt./Pz.Rgt. 24* also reported six operational Panthers, with one more in repair, although on this date it had apparently been subordinated to *ARKO 3* operating under the control of *III. Pz.Korps*.[76] In all, Breith's *panzer* corps had only 19 serviceable armored fighting vehicles, with four in repair. However, since Breith's corps was fighting primarily in the mountains, this was not as much of a disadvantage as it seemed.

All told, after the battle of Vienna, which began on 16 March and had concluded by 15 April, *H.Gr. Süd* and its four field armies could still report having a total of 507 armored fighting vehicles assigned, of which 284 were deemed operational. The bulk of these were within the *6. Pz.Armee*, which had a total of 269 AFV of all types (including recovery vehicles), though only 124 of these were considered combat-ready.[77] In contrast to this dwindling number, the combined strength of the Second and Third Ukrainian Fronts was nearly 1,000 tanks, assault guns, and self-propelled guns.

The losses suffered by both opponents during the Vienna Operation were simply astounding; Red Army losses alone totaled over 167,940 men, including 38,661 killed in action. As many as 603 Soviet tanks, assault guns, and self-propelled guns were reported as being irrecoverably lost, as well as 764 artillery pieces, mortars, and multiple rocket launchers. In turn, Soviet estimates indicate that *H.Gr. Süd* lost 1,345 armored fighting vehicles (which includes *SPWs* and other light armored vehicles), 2,250 artillery pieces, mortars, and rocket launchers, and approximately 30,000 men killed. Many of the German vehicles reported as lost had been undoubtedly destroyed by their own crews when they ran out of fuel. The estimate of the number of wounded suffered by *H.Gr. Süd* is not known, though the Red Army reported having captured 130,000 German and Hungarian troops during the 30-day battle, many of whom were undoubtedly wounded.[78] Civilian deaths during the fighting in Vienna were estimated to be at least 2,168 people, though the number was probably higher.[79]

While the Second and Third Ukrainian Fronts were consolidating their gains, the Red Army launched its last major offensive of the war, the Berlin Operation, on 16 April. This signaled the last act of Hitler's Third Reich. Meanwhile, Model's *H.Gr. B* was surrounded in the Ruhr Pocket, and American troops were rapidly advancing towards the Elbe River, aiming to link up with approaching Soviet forces. American and Free French forces were advancing through southern and southeastern Bavaria. The fronts in Italy and the Balkans were on the point of complete collapse. On that same day, the *OKW* issued a *Führerbefehl* intended to motivate troops fighting on the Eastern Front to continue doing their duty:

> If every soldier on the Eastern Front does his duty in these coming days and weeks, the last assault from Asia will be broken, exactly as the invasion by our enemy in the west will fail in the end in spite of everything. Berlin remains German, Vienna will be German again and Europe will never be Russian! Swear to form a community to defend not the empty concept of a fatherland, but to defend your homeland, your wives, your children and thus our future! In these hours the entire German people look to you, my Eastern Front fighters, and hope only that through your steadfastness, your fanaticism, through your weapons and under your leadership the Bolshevik onslaught will suffocate in a bloodbath. In the moment when fate has removed the greatest war criminal of all time from this earth [author's note: referring to the recent death of U.S. President Franklin Delano Roosevelt] the turn of this war will be decided. Signed, Adolf Hitler[80]

By this point, one might have asked what was the use of such meaningless exhortations to resist? Despite the order's pointless demands for each soldier to make a final sacrifice, there were apparently still enough true believers in the ranks to act upon it, at least according to one veteran of the *Wiking* Division, who wrote at the time:

> The end was long anticipated. But honestly, who at that time could already imagine it? Numerous replacements were still arriving. Intensive training was carried out, [including] instruction in hand-to-hand combat … Discipline was outstanding. Replacements likewise reached the artillery regiment from its replacement garrison as well as new guns and tractors! An additional [artillery] battery was to be established, which took place just northeast of Graz. The German war machinery appeared simply inexhaustible.[81]

On 16 April, the situation in the *2. Pz.Armee*'s sector remained relatively unchanged from what it had been the previous day. Since Radkersburg had been given up on the 15th, the town's previous defender, the *Hohenstaufen* Division, had been pinched out of the front line and was therefore available for commitment elsewhere. *Oberführer* Stadler, who had been begging to rejoin the *6. Pz.Armee* for nearly a month, finally got his wish. After receiving the necessary approvals from *H.Gr. Süd*,

Stadler learned that the *Hohenstaufen* Division—which by this point possessed not a single operational *panzer* but was nearly at full strength in personnel after absorbing thousands of replacements—would began moving north by rail by 26 April at the latest to rejoin the *II. SS-Pz.Korps* of the *6. Pz.Armee* and assist with its efforts to re-establish a solid front west of Vienna.[82]

Also that same day, in the *6. Armee*'s area of operations, the *IV. SS-Pz.Korps* reported that near Rittschein, a Soviet rifle battalion supported by four tanks attempted to take the town in a daylight attack but was brought to a halt and forced to withdraw after the *Wiking* Division carried out a counterattack. West of the adjacent town of Überbach, a company-sized enemy force was able to achieve a small breakthrough, but was sealed off shortly thereafter by a joint counterattack by the *Wiking* Division and *3. Pz.Div.* East of the town of Altenmarkt, another Soviet company- to battalion-sized force, supported by four tanks, attempted to penetrate German positions but was forced back after losing one tank.[83] Gille's own *Hauptquartier* at the time was located east of Gleisdorf, 10 kilometers west of that of the *Wiking* Division.

On 16 April, Gille's corps consisted of only the *Wiking* Division and *3. Pz.Div.* plus several smaller splinter units. Although the division *Kampfgruppe* of the *1. Pz.Div.* had been ordered that day to move north to reinforce the *III. Pz.Korps*, the rest of Thünert's division was still located in the corps' rear area near Ilz, only 8 kilometers away from the *Wiking* Division's *Gefechtstand* at Breitenfeld. During the past several days, the *Instandsetzungs-Staffel* (maintenance section) of *1. Pz.Div.* had been scavenging the entire area around Graz for fuel, ammunition, and repair parts in an effort geared towards restoring as many of its damaged tanks as possible. On that day, eight fully repaired *Pz. IVs* were delivered to the division, enough to reconstitute its *II. Abteilung*, as well as several trucks carrying fuel and 7.5cm tank ammunition.[84]

In the meantime, in the *III. Pz.Korps*' sector, the width of the gap between it and the *I. SS-Pz.Korps* of the *6. Pz.Armee* near the Semmering Pass had been further narrowed due to preliminary operations carried out the previous day by *K.Gr. Semmering* (soon to be designated as the *9. Geb.Div.*), though Soviet forces persisted in their efforts to advance to the Semmering Gap with as many as three rifle divisions supported by tanks. To counter this immediate menace, Breith ordered *Sturm-Art. Brig. 303* to counterattack in support of *SS-Pol.Rgt. 13* in the vicinity of Grafendorf until help could arrive. The SS policemen had been roughly handled the previous day near Vorau, where they had lost most of their heavy weapons and were on the point of collapse until reinforced by the assault guns.[85] The *1. Pz.Div.* was called out of reserve once more and began marching north to retrieve the situation, and in the course of doing so would achieve one of the last significant victories claimed by *H.Gr. Süd* before the war ended.

In the *6. Pz.Armee*'s area, the city of St Pölten fell to the XVIII Tank Corps, despite *Gruppe Schultz*'s efforts to retake it in a counterattack. *SS-Kampfgruppe Keitel* along with *K.Gr. 356. Inf.Div.*, fighting along the northern edge of the Hohen Wand massif southwest of Vienna, successfully warded off several Soviet attacks that day and even managed to retake two strongpoints they had lost the previous day. Heavy fighting was reported throughout the *panzer* army's area of operations, as Dietrich's forces began withdrawing to a more defensible line west of Vienna under heavy enemy pressure. He would attempt to reorganize his battered command over the next several days, including incorporating the newly activated *10. Fallschirm-Div.* into his order of battle. His headquarters reported that the *I.* and *II. SS-Pz.Korps*, along with myriad other splinter units that had attached themselves to *6. Pz.Armee*, had destroyed 70 Soviet tanks on 14 and 15 April, 47 of them in the St Pölten area alone.[86]

North of the Danube, the *8. Armee* reported numerous attacks along its entire front, especially in the Zisterdorf area, but the size and scope of these local operations had markedly decreased.[87] Heavy fighting was reported by the *XLIII. Armee-Korps* and *IV. Pz.Korps FHH*, but most of the attempts by Soviet troops to break through the thinly manned German lines were successfully thwarted. Large-scale employment of Soviet armor was conspicuously absent. Despite these ongoing local actions of battalion-size or smaller, it would have seemed to the average staff officer of *H.Gr. Süd* or any of its four field armies that the rate of advance of the Soviet juggernaut had markedly slowed to a crawl after the fall of Vienna, and that the troops of *H.Gr. Süd* might even be granted a breathing spell. Although the Red Army's intentions were unclear, what was clear was that its Second and Third Ukrainian Fronts had suffered enormous losses since 16 March (see above) and that neither could maintain such a high operational tempo indefinitely.

Upon reviewing the situation as it stood on the evening of 16 April, with so many positive developments being reported—including the stabilization of the corps' front line—it would be difficult to fault the officers and men of the *IV. SS-Pz.Korps* for believing that the military situation was looking up for a change. Deprived as they were of knowledge about the true extent of the Third Reich's looming destruction, Gille's troops could be forgiven for thinking that the tide of war was beginning to turn in their favor. Unbeknownst to them, however, the commander of the Third Ukrainian Front had been thinning out his units along the front lines in the Styrian Alps and was transferring them to the north in anticipation of an armistice being signed in the very near future. When that happened, Stalin's generals and their armies would be positioned to exploit their numerical advantage when it came to the postwar political settlement between the Soviet Union and the Western Allies. Gille, Schönfelder, Jahnke, and all the rest can be forgiven for their optimistic frame of mind; little did they know that their last and most difficult challenge still lay ahead.

CHAPTER 9

War's End
17 April–28 May 1945

The state of affairs in the *Wiking* Division's defensive sector between 17 April and 5 May 1945 was summed up by the *Wiking* Division's *O1* as follows: "The situation at the front is becoming more and more quiet. Small enemy attacks and breakthroughs are countered by our own attacks. We retain control of our own front lines."[1] While this may paint the picture of a leisurely, almost peaceful sort of war, it was certainly not peaceful elsewhere, though for once the *2. Pz.Armee*'s commander was able to report that its situation had finally stabilized and was now established firmly along a continuous front line with secure flanks. On the *IV. SS-Pz.Korps*' right flank, it had finally re-established physical contact with Harteneck's *I. Kav.Korps* of *2. Pz.Armee* after nearly two weeks of attempting to do so. As for the rest of the *IV. SS-Pz.Korps*, the *3. Pz.Div.* carried out a counterattack against Soviet forces that made another attempt to break through at Fürstenfeld. After halting the Soviet force, *Generalmajor* Söth's division was even able to retake some ground lost during a previous assault.

Söth himself would have very little time to savor the victory, because on 19 April he was replaced by *Oberst* Volkmar Schöne, a *3. Pz.Div.* veteran who had recently completed the *Panzertruppen* division commander's course. Söth's new assignment after relinquishing command was to take charge of a *Sicherungskraft*—a security force—that Balck had ordered be established to secure the *6. Armee* rear area against a possible American advance through the Austrian Alps. His mission was to safeguard the crossing points in the Pyhrn and Pötschen mountain passes and be prepared to block the valley of the Enns River near Radstadt, along which ran the major highway leading through the mountains west of Graz. To carry this out, Söth was given control of *Pz.Aufkl.Abt. 3* from his old division, some combat engineer and antitank troops, and an infantry unit. These units amounted to roughly only a reinforced regiment in strength, though American forces were to mistakenly later refer to it as "Corps Söth" when it swelled in size to 20,000 men due to the number of stragglers that had collected around it.[2] As for *Oberst* Schöne's new command, the mission of the *3. Pz.Div.* remained unchanged and it would continue being subordinated to the *IV. SS-Pz.Korps* until the end of the war.

On 17 April, the *IV. SS-Pz.Korps* reported that a Soviet force consisting of as many as six battalions launched a series of assaults along both sides of Fürstenfeld, where they managed to punch a hole in the *Wiking* Division's main defense line southwest of the town. A counterattack was made to iron out the penetration the next day. On 18 April, Gille's troops holding defensive positions northwest of Ebersbach as well as the areas southwest and west of Fürstenfeld were probed once again by Soviet reconnaissance troops before they were driven off. Fighting around the Fürstenfeld area was still underway to eliminate a local breakthrough when the evening reporting deadline arrived, though the destruction of a Soviet assault gun was mentioned.[3]

On 19 April, the corps reported that except for isolated enemy patrols and random artillery fire, no combat activity of any significance had taken place. For the following day, it reported essentially the same level of activity.[4] On 21 April, the *IV. SS-Pz.Korps* reported that the day passed quietly. It submitted an identical report for the following day. Incidentally, 22 April marked the last entry in the surviving daily reports submitted by *H.Gr. Süd* to the *OKH* and the last report submitted by Gille's corps during World War II.[5]

On 20 April, *Div.Gr. Krause* was disbanded and its units divided up within the *III. Pz.Korps*, with some going to the newly activated *9. Geb.Div.* (the former *K.Gr. Semmering*), others to *K.Gr. ARKO 3* commanded by *Oberstleutnant* Semmer, and the rest either to *K.Gr. Motschmann* or *K.Gr. Gottwald*. As for *Generalleutnant* Krause, he returned to his previous command of *Korück 593*, then located at Kapfenberg, where his activity was "limited to the control of military discipline, traffic regulation, defense against enemy incursions, training of rear detachments for defense against tanks, and local defense in areas occupied by German units."[6]

Between 17 and 24 April, the *1. Pz.Div.* played the leading role in the *6. Armee's* last large-scale counterattack of the war. Balck had designed this action to eliminate the continuing threat posed by the V Guards Cavalry Corps and XXX Rifle Corps to the upper Lafnitz valley and Semmering Pass once and for all. Thünert's *Division-Kampfgruppe* included 16 of its operational tanks, one *Panzergrenadier* battle group, and supporting artillery that began rolling up the Feistritz valley on 17 April. It would carry out this attack in cooperation with the *117. Jäg.Div.*, which had just arrived from the *H.Gr. E/O.B. Südost* area of operations after a two-day trip by rail. This division's assignment was to attack southeast between Fischbach and St Kathrein towards Vorau, where it would link up with the *Kampfgruppe* from *1. Pz.Div.* approaching from the southwest; if successful, this maneuver would trap up to three Soviet divisions in a pincer movement.

Generalmajor Thünert directed his troops to advance through the mountains via Birkfeld towards Vorau, 20 kilometers away, while another *Kampfgruppe* from the division's *Pz.Gren.Rgt. 113* under *Major* Weber attacked through the mountain pass north of Pöllau. On 22 April, the division's left assault force under *Oberstlt.*

Helmut Huppert, consisting of *Pz.Gren.Rgt. 1* and *Pz.Rgt. 1*, encountered a sizeable Soviet armored force in the shadow of the *Graue Steinwand* mountain. *Kampfgruppe Huppert* quickly outflanked it and compelled it to withdraw, though not before the enemy force had lost 20 of its own tanks when they ran into their own minefield during their attempt to pull back. Afterwards, many tanks were found that had been abandoned undamaged by their crews. After a night's rest, the main attack would continue the following day. In the meantime, the *117. Jag.Div.* had begun its own operation, seizing the villages of Ochsenkopf and Eckberg on 18 April, then Falkenstein and St Jakob by the following day. On the next day, 20 April, it had taken the town of Waldbach after overcoming stiff enemy resistance.[7]

In the fields west and southwest of Vorau, the Soviet defenders had established an elaborate defense, with minefields, *Pakfronts*, and dug-in tanks. Quickly sizing up the situation, the division commander, travelling with Huppert's group, ordered a preliminary artillery barrage that blanketed the enemy's positions while combat engineers cleared routes through the minefields. In a classic armored attack, the *1. Pz.Div.* carried out perhaps the last successful German armored assault of the war on 24 April, when Huppert's *Pz.Gren.Rgt. 1* and Weber's *Pz.Gren.Rgt. 113*—supported by nearly 20 of the division's tanks—enveloped and quickly overran the enemy's defenses.

Perhaps the Soviet commander on the scene had been lulled into a sense of complacency; most of the German forces his troops had recently encountered had not displayed much fighting spirit or military skill, such as *SS-Pol.Rgt. 13*, which had been easily swept aside when it attempted to block the advancing T-34s. However, the Soviets had not had to repel an attack by the full force of the *1. Pz.Div.* before. Most of the Soviet force was destroyed, including 35 tanks and numerous antitank guns, and a large number of troops were killed. At least 100 prisoners were taken by Huppert's force. The Soviet survivors fled to the northeast, setting fire to the village as they departed.

The town's residents, who had rejected *Oberst* Bradel's entreaties for help the week before, were now very grateful that the division had returned. A week under Soviet rule, with its attendant looting and pillaging, had convinced its citizens where their true loyalties lay. Thünert's troops even helped the townsfolk to put out the fires that the retreating Soviets had set. This was the last major action fought in the war by the *1. Pz.Div.* Shortly after the battle, it was relieved by elements of the *III. Pz.Korps* and sent to occupy a new defensive position near Ebersdorf–Hartberg, 33 kilometers to the southeast, the following day.[8] The *117. Jäg.Div.*, after playing its part, resumed its movement to the area west of St Pölten, where it was scheduled to join forces with the *6. Pz.Armee.*

In his memoirs, Balck claims that this operation destroyed three Soviet divisions and that the rest of their forces were pushed out of the Semmering Pass. This last victory enabled a relatively straight line running from north to south to be established along the entire front of the *6. Armee*, bringing a stability to the area that would last to the end of the war. From this point onwards, the situation settled down along most of the southern portion of the *H.Gr. Süd* front, while the northern part, including the *6. Pz.Armee* and *8. Armee*, were forced to continue withdrawing to the west and northwest (on 30 April, *H.Gr. Süd* was renamed *H.Gr. Ostmark*, a more accurate reflection of the area then under its control). Luckily, Dietrich's army was still able to retain contact on its right wing with the *III. Pz.Korps* on Balck's left.[9]

After the *1. Pz.Div.* had succeeded in closing off the Semmering Pass to further enemy incursions, a kind of calm seemed to settle in along the entire front of the *6. Armee*. Now firmly tied in on its right with the *2. Pz.Armee* and on its left with the *6. Pz.Armee*, the war seemed to have moved elsewhere. This was not strictly true; the opposing forces of the Red Army, though they had stopped large-scale attacks, continued to carry out low-level operations designed to gain local tactical advantages, compelling the defenders, including the *IV. SS-Pz.Korps*, to remain on their guard.

Incredibly, throughout the waning days of the war, replacements in new uniforms and weapons continued to flow into the divisions, both *Waffen-SS* and *Heer*. In order to more thoroughly cover the corps' widely dispersed front-line positions and prevent further Soviet incursions, its divisions (including the *1. Pz.Div.*, which reverted to corps control at some point after 27/28 April) were instructed to form additional provisional units from division elements that no longer had the weapons, equipment, fuel, or ammunition to fulfill their normal function. The corps troops from the *IV. SS-Pz.Korps*, primarily *s.SS-Art.Abt. 504* and *SS-Werfer-Abt. 504*, were undoubtedly included in this reorganization, since without these necessities, the artillery and rocket launcher units could serve a far more useful purpose as infantry. *Flak* troops continued carrying out their usual missions, since the Red Air Force still bombed and harassed anything they could find that was not camouflaged.

These measures also applied to the *Wiking* Division. During the middle of April, *SS-Pz.Rgt. 5* was ordered to form its own *Panzer-Infanterie* battalion using surplus crews, which were sufficient to form a full-strength battalion. The *Wiking* Division's O1 noted: "The division decided that since they no longer have tanks to ride, they had to attend an eight-day-long infantry retraining course. The battalion—all of them front-line, highly decorated veterans—present an outstanding appearance."[10] At that point, the *Wiking* Division no longer had any operational tanks. The last one, commanded by *Unterscharführer* Lasch, ran out of fuel and was blown up by its crew somewhere on the Austrian border. The remnants of *SS-Pz.Rgt. 5*, after being trucked across the Austrian border near Heiligenkreuz on 30 March, were assembled at the Hartbergen Palace near Ilz, located north of the Fürstenfeld–Graz road. The *2. Kompanie, sans* tanks, was billeted in Eichberg.[11]

According to Ewald Klapdor, the *Panzer-Infanterie Bataillon Wiking* was composed of four companies, three being "line" infantry companies and the fourth a heavy weapons company, equipped with a heavy machine-gun platoon, 8cm mortar platoon, flamethrower section, and antitank section armed with the 8.8cm *Panzerschreck*. The battalion commander was *Hstuf.* Otto Schneider, one of the *panzer* regiment's few remaining original officers.[12] Schneider picked veteran *Untersturmführer* Jakubetz of the old *6. Kompanie* as his adjutant. Veteran tank commanders such as *Oscha.* Melinkat were made a squad leader in the *2. Kompanie*. Melinkat had not been in combat since his own tank was knocked out east of Veszprém during the breakout from Stuhlweissenburg. Nearly all of the men were veterans with several years of combat behind them. Although the majority of the NCOs and officers had transferred to the *Panzerwaffe* in 1942 or 1943, most of them had begun their careers in the *Waffen-SS* as infantrymen, antitank gunners, or armored reconnaissance troops, so they were already familiar with most of the skills needed to be successful infantrymen.

While the rest of the division concentrated on getting its new replacements into shape and improving its defensive positions, Schneider's battalion was used for special assignments, such as raiding, conducting counterattacks, and night assaults. Since they were nearly all old "campaigners" from the early days of the war, they still possessed a certain amount of the old "SS spirit," unlike the new replacements they had just received, who seemed apathetic and only wanted to go home. Between its formation and the end of the war, Schneider's panzer-infantry battalion was able to carry out all of its assignments, such as "clearing up a few minor penetrations with great panache and without any casualties, just like child's play … The battalion has been committed ever since 13 April and cannot be differentiated from well-trained and well-proven front-line infantrymen," according to one observer.[13]

While the fighting north of the *6. Armee*'s area of operations shifted to the northwest as the *6. Pz.Armee* fell back towards Linz, Balck and his armies continued defending the front lines in the mountainous border of eastern Styria between 23 April and 6 May. The weather had warmed up considerably, and though Soviet or American aircraft appeared frequently in the skies, they were not nearly as aggressive as they had been. The occasional Soviet mortar or artillery harassment fire was enough to remind everyone that they were still at war with the Soviet Union and that death was never very far away. During this period, and especially after 1 May, small numbers of troops began to disappear, abandoning their positions and weapons at night and simply heading for home. Although this was not a serious problem with SS troops, the *1. Pz.Div.* began to feel its effects. On 3 May alone, 20 men from one of Thünert's regiments deserted upon hearing that Berlin had fallen, Hitler was dead, and *Grossadmiral* Karl Dönitz was now the Third Reich's head of state.[14]

On 24 April, *G.F.M.* Alfred Kesselring was named as the new *Oberbefehlshaber Süd*, the supreme commander responsible for all Axis forces remaining in southern Europe, which by this point consisted of all troops in southern Germany, what was left of Mussolini's puppet government, and Szalási's Hungarian Arrow Cross movement. Kesselring's command jurisdiction also extended to units of the *Waffen-SS*. Previously, he had been in command of all Axis forces fighting in Italy. It was he who had proposed the renaming of *H.Gr. Süd* as *H.Gr. Ostmark*, a decision that would not come into affect until on or about 1 May.[15]

In order to discern what the future course of the *6. Armee* should be, and with the war's end so clearly approaching, Balck, acting independently, met with Kesselring on the night of 6 May in Judenburg, but Kesselring was tight-lipped. Earlier that day, *Generaloberst* Rendulic, Balck's army group commander, had ordered a cease-fire to come into effect that very evening. He did not have much choice; when the Salzkammergut and Enns area was occupied by U.S. forces earlier that day, most of *H.Gr. Ostmark*'s logistics area was overrun, leaving Rendulic's army group with ammunition for only two days and rations for eight. Time was rapidly running out.[16]

General der Panzertruppe Balck had already sent his chief of staff out on a reconnaissance mission towards the American lines on 6 May "in his best uniform and [with] enough in his pack to last several days" to gauge the willingness of their leadership to reach a compromise on several points.[17] Balck had been told by Rendulic that he wanted Gaedke to carry a letter to the commander of the U.S. Third Army, Lt.Gen. George S. Patton, asking whether the Americans were serious about enforcing the terms of unconditional surrender on all German forces and whether the Third Army would allow German medical supplies to transit through its lines to reach the *6. Armee*. These items were badly needed, especially since the army group's administrative and logistics area had been overrun by American troops.

After a harrowing journey through the American lines near Steyr, where he narrowly avoided being shot by a machine-gun team posted on the bridge over the Enns, Gaedke was directed to the nearest American command post. Finally, after several hours, though he did not get to meet Patton himself, Gaedke did see the commander of the U.S. XX Corps, Lt.Gen. Walton H. Walker, who instructed him in no uncertain terms that unconditional surrender was just that—unconditional—and that the Third Army would not permit any form of supplies to be shipped to the German front lines. If there was to be any negotiation, it would have to be carried out by Rendulic in person, not by the chief of staff of one of his field armies. With that, any dream that Rendulic or Balck may have had of cooperating with the western Allies in a renewed effort against the Soviet Union collapsed.[18]

On 7 May, *Generalmajor* Söth, who had been made responsible for keeping the passes to the west clear of approaching American forces, contacted troops from the U.S. 80th Infantry Division's (I.D.) Task Force Smythe to offer the unconditional surrender of all of his forces located north and west of the Enns River. After a brief negotiation with the American division commander, Maj.Gen. Horace L. McBride, Söth accepted all of his terms and immediately ordered his troops—some 20,000 in all—to begin moving into assembly areas north of the Enns River in the rear of the 80th I.D., where they would be disarmed.[19] The following day, *SS-Kampfgruppe Keitel*—with 3,000 men—surrendered to McBride's troops too. Like Söth's command, Keitel's had been sent to protect the rear area of Dietrich's *6. Pz.Armee*.[20]

On 7 May, Balck's *Ic*, *Oberstleutnant* von Czernicki, notified his commander that he had received the cease-fire conditions from *H.Gr. Ostmark* by radio. According to Balck, the most important information was the news that "all German units were to be taken by the side that they had last fought against. That meant that we were going to have to turn around and launch a *pro forma* attack against the Americans to justify surrendering to them rather than the Russians. The big question was, would the Americans play along?"[21] Shortly afterwards, Rendulic and the entire staff of *H.Gr. Ostmark* surrendered and were taken prisoner by the Americans. At 6 p.m., Rendulic signed the articles of unconditional surrender at the headquarters of the U.S. Army's XX Corps in St Martin, Austria, and then went into captivity. Under the terms dictated to him, all of the troops under his command were required to surrender at one minute after midnight on 8 May.[22] With that, *H.Gr. Ostmark* ceased to exist, leaving Rendulic's three field army commanders to work out by themselves the movement of their troops to the line of demarcation.[23]

On that date, *H.Gr. Ostmark* consisted of three German field armies (*6. Pz.Armee*, *6. Armee*, and *8. Armee*) and one Hungarian army (*3. Armee*), with a total of six corps and 23 divisions or *Division Kampfgruppen*. *General der Artillerie* de Angelis's *2. Pz.Armee* had been subordinated to *OB Südost* several days before. According to American sources, approximately 325,630 German and Hungarian troops surrendered to the XX Corps of the Third U.S. Army between 1 and 8 May alone. In addition to having to provide for and guard this massive haul of prisoners, the XX Corps also had to sort out upwards of 200,000 displaced persons, including Hungarian refugees, Allied POWs, concentration camp inmates, and slave laborers.[24] Although the fighting soon ended, the XX Corps—as well as Patton's entire Third Army—would take several months to process so many individual cases, keeping it busy until the end of August.

By 7 May, the *6. Armee* consisted of two corps—Gille's *IV. SS-Pz.Korps* and Breith's *III. Pz.Korps*. Under Gille's direct control were the *Wiking* Division, *1. Pz.Div.*, *3. Pz.Div.*, and *1. Volks-Geb.Div.* Breith's corps consisted of the *9. Geb.Div.* and a number of smaller units, such as *K.Gr. Motschmann*, *K.Gr. Gottwald*, and *K.Gr. ARKO 3*. These units were a collection of odds and ends, including *IV. Btl./SS-Rgt. Ney*, *Bau-Pio.Btl. 504*, *SS-Gren.Ers.u.Ausb.Btl. 11*, *I. Abt./Pz.Rgt. 24*, and *Sturm-Art. Brig. 303*.[25] In all, including administrative and logistics services, Balck exercised direct control of 102,000 men, according to American sources.[26]

Having learned of Rendulic's intention of signing the document of unconditional surrender that night, Balck knew that he had to inform his subordinate commanders of his corps and divisions as quickly as possible. At 4 p.m. on 7 May, Balck convened a meeting of his corps and division commanders at his *6. Armee* headquarters in Gleisdorf, including Breith, Gille, Ullrich, Schöne, Thünert, and Krause, as well as the commander of the *1. Volks-Geb.Div.*, Wittmann, whose division had been subordinated to the *IV. SS-Pz.Korps* only several days before. He quickly briefed them on the plan, told them what he expected of them, and wished them all good luck. This was his last meeting with his subordinate commanders.

After briefing Dr Überreither, the *Gauleiter* of Graz, later that evening, Balck departed for the Enns River crossing site at Liezen with his *IIa* staff officer to seek contact with the American commander on the scene, Major General McBride, commander of the 80th I.D. Balck had already sent the rest of his staff ahead of him to find his headquarters, which was located in Kirschdorf an der Krems. When Balck arrived at the town at 7:45 p.m. on 8 May, he was ushered in by American military police to meet with McBride. The American commander informed him that no German troops or vehicles would be allowed past the demarcation line after 8 a.m. on 9 May.[27] Balck relayed word to the units still holding the line east of Graz by dispatching his staff officers, but it is questionable whether all of his commanders were notified in time. They would learn the deadline once they arrived themselves. Besides, they could not travel any faster over the mountain roads than they already were (see Map 8).

A detailed transcript of Balck's conversation with McBride was taken by Colonel S. P. Walker, McBride's chief of staff. It generally dovetails with Balck's memoirs, except that *Order in Chaos* does not mention that Balck had said that he would designate someone else to assume command of all of *6. Armee's* units south of the Enns River when he surrendered. There is no evidence that he ever did. During his conversation, Balck learned that Söth had surrendered his command the previous day, but that he was still at his headquarters and could be contacted by telephone.

Balck took pains to gain clarity of the ultimate disposition of his troops once they surrendered, for he was worried that they would be turned over to the Red Army, although McBride assured him that this would not happen. Balck then stressed that he was not affiliated with the *6. Pz.Armee*, which was known to be composed predominately of SS troops. McBride asked Balck to point out on a map the most recent location of Soviet troops; surprisingly, Balck did not know, stating that he had only an approximate idea of where they were. Finally, after stressing to Balck that he needed to tell his troops to bring all the rations they could carry since U.S. forces had little of their own to provide, McBride dismissed Balck, who returned to the crossing point at Liezen, where he remained for the next two days to supervise the movement of his troops across the Enns along with a few of his staff officers.[28] On 21 May, Balck was finally taken prisoner and taken to an Allied POW camp. His stormy tenure as commander of the *6. Armee* had come to an end.

As for Herbert Gille, after meeting with Balck and the others at Gleisdorf, he returned to his headquarters to instruct his staff to begin notifying corps troops and attached *Heerestruppen* of the situation. Balck had given Gille instructions that the *IV. SS-Pz.Korps* was to use the southern route leading through Graz to Carinthia, where he was to surrender his corps to British forces. Breith's *III. Pz.Korps* was

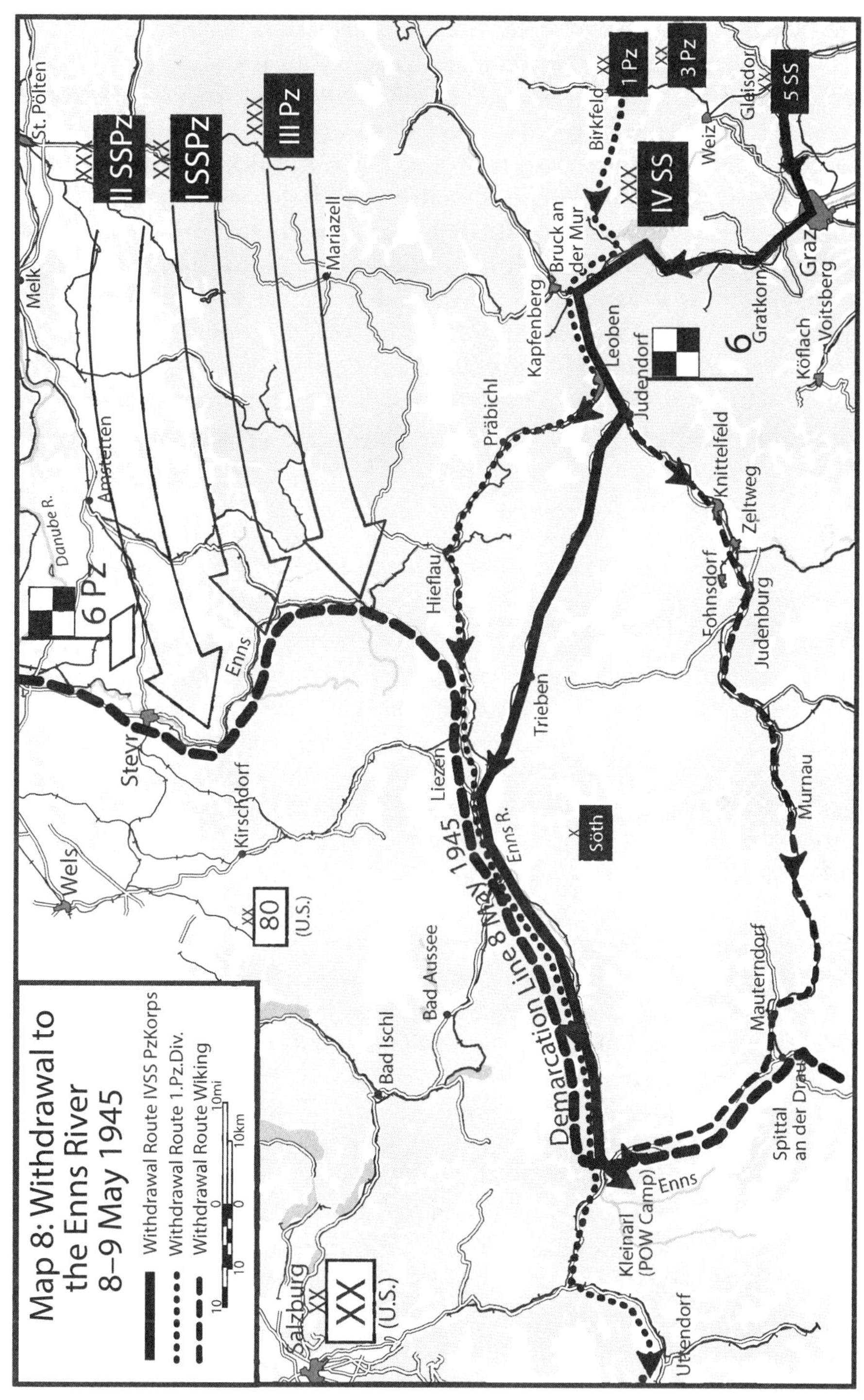

Map 8: Withdrawal to the Enns River 8–9 May 1945
Withdrawal Route IVSS PzKorps
Withdrawal Route 1.Pz.Div.
Withdrawal Route Wiking
10mi
10km
10
0
10
St. Pölten
Melk
Danube R.
Amstetten
II SSPz
I SSPz
III Pz
Mariazell
1 Pz
3 Pz
5 SS
Birkfeld
Gleisdorf
Weiz
IV SS
Bruck an der Mur
Kapfenberg
Leoben
Graz
Voitsberg
Gratkorn
Köflach
6
Judendorf
Präbichl
Knittelfeld
Zeltweg
Fohnsdorf
Judenburg
6 Pz
Enns
Hieflau
Trieben
Murau
Steyr
Kirschdorf
Liezen
Enns R.
Söth
Mauterndorf
Spittal an der Drau
Wels
80
(U.S.)
Bad Ischl
Bad Aussee
Demarcation Line 8 May 1945
Enns
Kleinarl (POW Camp)
Uttendorf
Salzburg
XX (U.S.)

directed to head directly towards Liezen to surrender to American forces at the Enns River. For once, Gille decided to disregard Balck's instructions, not only because Carinthia was further away, but because the Enns River was much closer to Germany. He informed his division commanders accordingly, who all agreed that the Enns demarcation line was a much more ideal goal. This was perhaps the first recorded instance where Gille willingly disobeyed a direct order from Hermann Balck, but as events were to prove, this was a wise decision. Had he moved to Carinthia as he had been ordered, his troops might have been forced to surrender to Tito's forces, hardly an acceptable fate, and one that would have been just as bad had they surrendered to the Red Army, which was also a possibility (indeed, de Angelis had been made to surrender his *2. Pz.Armee* to Soviet forces).

Ullrich returned to his own *Gefechtstand* at 8 p.m., called his regiment and battalion commanders together and issued the following instructions:

> Expect the capitulation shortly. We will withdraw to the west upon the issue of a pre-arranged code word in phases. After the last code word is issued, *Funkstille* [radio silence], the *6. Armee* will no longer be in command and units will be free to withdraw to the demarcation line as they see fit. The *III. Btl./Westland* under *Stubaf.* Helmut Schlupp and *Artilleriegruppe Bernau* will remain behind as the rear guard to ensure that the Soviet troops following closely behind do not try to overtake the division before it can reach the American-controlled demarcation line.[29]

The commander of the artillery regiment further instructed his regiment, telling his commanders that only two batteries were to remain behind to cover the withdrawal; the rest would be blown up and their trucks used to carry artillerymen to safety. The division commander was insistent that "none of my troops will be taken captive by the enemy so close to the end."

Ullrich's *O1* was there at the meeting at the division headquarters too, and recalled the event in his diary: "The next morning [8 May] at 7 a.m., we have our last commander's meeting. We are to hold our current positions until noon. Then we are to displace as a unit to the west … [the rearguard] will block the road at Gleisdorf until everyone has made it through. At 8 a.m., I realized that our neighbor to our left [*3. Pz.Div.*] is still there; our neighbor on the right [most likely a *Kampfgruppe* from the *14. Waffen-Gren.Div. der SS* of the *I. Kav.Korps*] has already cleared out."[30] By this point, no one wanted to be left behind to be captured by the Red Army or to be the last German soldier to die in Austria.

Beginning at noon on 8 May, the *IV. SS-Pz.Korps* began withdrawing westwards and then northwestwards with all of its subordinate units through Gleisdorf, Graz, Bruck an der Mur, Tamsweg, Judenburg, Mauterndorf and the Tauern Pass, and finally to Liezen, a nearly 184-kilometer road march from the front lines at Fürstenfeld. In the *Wiking* Division, all heavy weapons and *panzers* except those of the rear guards were left behind or blown up, once gasoline had been drained from their tanks. Everything else that moved would be used to carry troops, including the wounded, and rations. On several occasions, the rear guards had to deploy and fire on Soviet troops when they drew too close to the rear of the column or attempted to cut them off. None succeeded. In Graz, the rear guard was fired on by a handful of Austrian insurgents, but a few 7.5cm high-explosive shells fired by an *SPW* equipped with a *Stummel* (nickname for "stump." the short 7.5cm infantry howitzer) convinced them that it was better to wait until the Soviets "liberated" them.[31]

The *1. Pz.Div.* also had a long road journey ahead of it. By 8 May, it had managed to get 35 of its armored fighting vehicles running again, and possessed sufficient ammunition to fight two full-sized engagements and enough fuel for every vehicle to travel 80 kilometers. By draining the tanks of most of these *panzers* of their precious fuel, there would be enough to get everyone in the division across the Enns River, with just enough left over for the 15 Panthers constituting the division's rear guard. Just as importantly, the *1. Pz.Div.* also had enough food to provide eight days' worth of rations for its soldiers, since the commander did not know when they would be issued food again by their captors.[32]

Like that of the *Wiking* Division, the *1. Pz.Div.* rear guard would ensure that its column would not be overtaken during the withdrawal at any point. Its troops would begin pulling out of their front-line positions before the *Wiking* Division, beginning at 10 a.m. on 8 May upon receipt of the codeword *Stabsauflösung* ("staff demobilization"). When the next day drew to a close, Thünert's division—or most of it—had managed to cross the Enns to safety and began moving into camp near the town of Uttendorf, a few kilometers from Braunau, where most of it had arrived by 10 May before moving on to another camp at Mauerkirchen. On 13 May, *Generalmajor* Thünert held the last division assembly for the 6,000 survivors of his formation who had remained with him during the journey to the Enns. He thanked them for their loyalty, their service, their sacrifice, and for fulfilling their duty to the very end.[33]

Throughout 8 May, the mountains of southeastern Austria were filled with long columns of vehicles packed full of retreating troops from the *6. Armee*. To the north, the same drama was playing out southeast of Linz, where the *6. Pz.Armee* was withdrawing at the same time, though their route was over more level ground. To the south, the headquarters and divisions of the *2. Pz.Armee* and *H.Gr. E* retreated into Carinthia, while some detoured north towards the Enns like the *IV. SS-Pz.Korps* had. If one truck or Volkswagen broke down, their passengers would be distributed amongst other trucks and the broken-down vehicle would be pushed off the road. The journey took most of the day, since stops and starts along the mountain roads were frequent. Finally, the lead vehicles reached the Enns River demarcation line during the late afternoon, while the remainder continued driving throughout the night. The pursuing Soviet forces lagged behind, having learned to keep a respectful distance from the ever-alert rear guards.

Based on the available evidence, most of the headquarters and staff of the *IV. SS-Pz.Korps* and the *Wiking* Division appear not to have encountered any particular difficulty in crossing the Enns at Liezen. The American troops guarding the bridge merely waved them across throughout 8 and 9 May, only stopping them at midnight and reopening the crossing the next morning. The only instances when they would stop the column would be whenever an armored fighting vehicle or a truck towing an artillery piece attempted to cross. The U.S. guards simply told the drivers to turn around and go elsewhere or blow them up at a safe distance. Anyone who had a pistol was allowed to keep it, but only 10 percent of their rifles and no machine guns could be carried across the demarcation line. Everything else was thrown into the river—machine pistols, machine guns, mortars, *Panzerfaust*, etc. A number of the few remaining *SPWs* were also driven into the Enns at several points to prevent them from being captured.[34]

One eyewitness, who travelled that day from the front lines to the demarcation line, remembered his experiences from this period when he later wrote:

> Nearly everyone experienced the day of surrender differently … On the day of surrender, there were long march delays through the mountains. Rumors, orders, and requests buzzed through the confusion. Many men wanted to reach the mountains, where supplies, weapons, and equipment had been brought into the "Alpine Fortress." Many prepared for a long stay. Everyone was left to their own discretion. But the old discipline and [our] unequivocal orders held the mass [of troops] to maintain their cohesion. At roughly 6 p.m. [there] followed a further march to Mauterndorf, where in the night hours of 8 May the first American advance guards were encountered. However, they paid little notice to the German column. They said that they were attempting to move as quickly as possible to halt the Russians as far to the east as possible.[35]

Ullrich used the opportunity, when the column was halted near the town of Wagrain, to assemble his officers one more time to speak to them. Here, he released them from their oath of allegiance (Hitler was dead, after all) and left them free to choose whatever course they thought best for themselves—either accept imprisonment or make their way home independently as best they could. For his part, Ullrich told them he was going to remain with his troops so as to set an example and help to protect them during the rough times that he knew lay ahead. Most of his officers chose to remain with the division, come what may.[36]

One unlucky soldier, whose group was barred from crossing because they arrived after the gates were finally closed at midnight on 9 May, was *Uscha.* Henk Kistemaker, who had been a crewmember in *Ostuf.* Helmut Bauer's command tank. The American guard refused to allow them to cross the bridge, telling them they had to wait there for the Russians to come and take them prisoner. Refusing to accept that as their fate, Kistemaker and his comrades retreated to a point where they were out of the guard's sight, then struck off into woods in search of a crossing point. Satisfied that they could not be observed in the darkness, he and the others threw their pistols, awards, and decorations into the river and swam safely across.

Now resting on the opposite bank, Kistemaker and his comrades waited until it grew light. After walking a short distance, all the while keeping a lookout for any

American patrols, the exhausted men found an abandoned outbuilding and crept inside to catch a few hours of sleep. Once they awoke, they walked beyond the American-controlled bridge, which was now barred to further traffic, and began looking for a lift. After waiting a few minutes, they caught a ride on a German truck heading north. When the truck reached the German border, it was thoroughly searched by American sentries. Discovering Kistemaker and his friends hiding inside, they were ordered out of the truck and detained. Shortly thereafter, they were delivered to a temporary POW camp, where they were provided no shelter and little food, heralding a time of hunger and near-starvation. Finally, in July, their American captors began to feed Kistemaker and his fellow prisoners regular meals, but by that point the Dutch *Waffen-SS* man weighed only 121lb (55kg), far below his normal weight.[37]

Once safely beyond the demarcation line, the corps headquarters and the *Wiking* Division were directed by the Americans to proceed to the town of Mayrdörfl, another 85 kilometers away, where they camped in the valley nearby. After several days at this location, this large group of SS men (numbering over 10,000 by this point) were ordered to move to the town of Kleinarl, where they were instructed to make camp in the Kleinarl valley's meadows and pastures. By 15 May, the *Wiking* Division's rear guard finally arrived safe and sound at Kleinarl, joining the rest of the division which had arrived two days earlier. By this point, their U.S. captors had not yet issued them any food, forcing the demobilized SS men to eat whatever they had managed to carry along with them, including the five days of iron rations and hard bread they had been issued several days before. The few horses that they had managed to bring out with them were eventually slaughtered and used to make a thin goulash soup after their canned rations ran out.[38]

Unfortunately, there is no evidence that Gille gave a farewell speech to his assembled troops as Ullrich and Thünert had, although at least one regimental commander from the *Wiking* Division held a special ceremony for his troops to mark the occasion. On 16 May, *Stubaf.* Günter Bernau, acting commander of *SS-Pz.Art. Rgt. 5*, held a brief ceremony in the meadow at the temporary camp in the Kleinarl valley. Bernau thanked them for their loyalty and proven bravery, handed out the last decorations, and carried out the last promotions to men who had earned them. With tears in his eyes, he read out the text of the final *Wehrmachtsbericht* of the war to his assembled regiment. Once he finished, both Bernau and *Sturmbannführer* Wittich, one of his battalion commanders, walked up and shook the hands of every man in the formation. After that, in Bernau's own words, "the *SS-Panzerartillerie Regiment 5* ceased to exist."[39]

On 28 May, two U.S. Army officers in a jeep drove up to Gille's corps headquarters and asked for the commander of the *IV. SS-Pz.Korps*. When asked why, they told Gille's *Begleitoffizier, Ustuf.* Günther Lange, that his presence had been requested by the senior U.S. Military Commissioner to attend a meeting in Salzburg. Manfred

Schönfelder, his chief of staff, was also asked to attend. Gille was allowed to travel in his own staff car. When they arrived at the commissioner's headquarters in Salzburg, instead of meeting with the High Commissioner, a lieutenant met them instead. The unnamed lieutenant had them arrested and led them both inside the building for interrogation, where they were treated shabbily. Here, Gille's Knight's Cross with Oak Leaves, Swords, and Diamonds was taken from him, as were his other awards. He never got them back. He and Schönfelder were never permitted to return to their headquarters, but were shuttled back and forth between 13 different internment camps and not released to return home until 1948.[40]

While in one of the internment camps, Gille was approached by the military studies team of the U.S. Army Europe Historical Division, who wished to interview him for a study they were writing about the end of the war in Europe. One of the questions he was asked concerned whether he or his corps, or the *Wiking* Division, had ever fought against American forces. In his own inimitable style, he tersely replied:

> I cannot write on the questions submitted because, from the beginning of the Russian Campaign, I was engaged only in the East. Until the end of the war, my troops occupied positions east of Graz. On 7 May 1945, I received an order from [*6. Armee*] headquarters to move my corps westward behind the demarcation line. This line was to be crossed by 8 May 1945. By reason of this order I marched my corps on the indicated roads and reached the area Radstadt–Wagrain before the arrival of American troops. No combat action whatever took place between my units and U.S. troops. Signed, Herbert Gille, 27 April 1946.[41]

And that was all he said. He refused all subsequent invitations to participate in the U.S. Army's historical program. Considering the way he had been tricked into surrendering and how poorly he was treated afterwards, it is a wonder that he even answered this request.

It was a strange way to end a war. American and British troops along the demarcation line stretching from the Alps to the North Sea generally waved the withdrawing German troops across the line towards collection areas, just as freely as they allowed civilians to pass through. Pre-established POW camps seemed to be an afterthought, simply because there were suddenly millions of soldiers to take care of and no one had thought the war would end as quickly as it did. This set the stage for a several-months-long adjustment period until the Western Allies finally sorted things out, though their lack of foresight caused tremendous suffering that in some cases led to the deaths of many of their prisoners due to starvation or disease.

As for the Red Army, its forces took firm control of its German prisoners from the outset and marched them under armed guard to sites away from the demarcation line that had already been picked out in advance, where they were kept before being shipped to the Soviet Union to perform years of hard labor after undergoing thorough interrogation. By 12 May 1945, most German soldiers in uniform were prisoners. Hitler's 12-year realm had finally died a slow death and the sun would rise over it no more. Its ending was long overdue.

In the immediate aftermath of the war, many men from the *IV. SS-Pz.Korps* headquarters or the *Wiking* Division attempted to avoid captivity or escape from their POW camp, but few succeeded. Due to "automatic arrest" orders issued by the victorious Allies, anyone who had been a member of the *Waffen-SS* or any branch of the SS would be interned until they had undergone de-Nazification, war crimes investigation, and re-education so that they could be deemed "reformed" and allowed to re-enter civil society in the new West German nation. While most SS enlisted men captured by the Western Allies were released within two to three years (even less if they were an involuntary transfer from the *Luftwaffe* or *Kriegsmarine* at the end of the war), the officers were kept for longer periods, even more if they were suspected of involvement in war crimes. In contrast, many SS men held in Soviet prison camps did not secure their release until 1955, if they were lucky enough to survive 10 years in a Gulag.

One member of the *IV. SS-Pz.Korps Hauptquartier* who managed to avoid an internment camp was *Ustuf.* Günther Lange, former *O5/Begleitoffizer* for Gille. Surrendering along with the rest of the corps headquarters on 8 May, he spent most of the summer in Riegsee, upper Bavaria, at a loosely guarded POW camp with his fellow officers. The camp had no barbed wire and was guarded by a unit of African-American soldiers. Finally, on 16 August 1945, Lange and his comrades were herded into railcars at the station in Murnau. With their guards standing on the boxcar roofs, the train loaded with SS POWs chugged along through bombed-out Munich to the station in Bad Aibling, where they were unloaded and marched to a camp. Here, they were searched, their valuables taken away, and put under a heavy guard.

After three nights in the camp, Lange was fed up with his situation and decided to escape at the first chance he got. With another inmate, who had been in the SS since 1934 and had more to lose if he stayed, the 20-year-old Lange planned their escape—they would crawl through the wire, travel only by night, and hide by day. The next evening, the pair put their plan into effect. When the guard in the nearest watchtower turned to look in another direction, they made their break, crawling under the wire and dashing across an open field without being noticed. Heading north-northwest, the two former SS officers made their way through the Ebersbacher Forest that night and hid during the daytime. Growing progressively bolder, they began to travel more during daylight hours. Somewhere along the way, they procured civilian clothing and hid their uniforms.

In the town of Freising, 100 kilometers north of the camp in Riegsee, they were stopped by two U.S. soldiers who asked Lange for the time. When he showed them his bare arms (his watch had been confiscated in the camp), they let him and his comrade go. Near Pfaffenhofen, they waited on the side of the *Autobahn* in the hope of getting a ride. They did not have to wait long. Soon, a long convoy of trucks began rolling by, carrying cargoes of wrecked *Wehrmacht* vehicles towards Nuremberg. Waiting for an opportune moment, they hopped on the back of one of the trucks and climbed inside the damaged vehicle it was carrying. From here, they rode all the way into Nuremberg. As the convoy slowly passed over the Danube bridge at Ingolstadt, they stared in surprise as Heinz Huber, an old comrade from the *Wiking's panzer* regiment, rode up next to them on a bicycle. He urged them to jump off the slow-moving truck and follow him into town, where he would fix them up with proper documents.

The forged papers he gave them stated that Lange and his comrade had been civilians working at an airfield and were going home after the war. They could not believe their luck, since they could hardly be expected to make it very far with only their *SS Soldbücher* (pay books) as a means of identification. This would put them straight back into the camp. With their new identification, they walked through Ingolstadt but were stopped at the town's northwest outskirts by a G.I. who asked them for their papers. Unsure whether they would be caught, Lange and his comrade showed him their fake identity papers. Examining them, the soldier merely said "OK" and waved them on. It was a stroke of luck, especially since they had been carrying their newly minted forged papers for only an hour.

After walking the rest of the day, they moved off the road and sought shelter in a nearby field after dark. Exhausted, they found a haystack, burrowed inside, and slept warmly that night. Waking up before dawn, the two men realized that they were on the edge of an American airfield and were only yards away from a fighter aircraft. Escaping notice, they hurried back to the road and continued their journey. Soon, a truck passed by headed to the northwest, carrying household goods. After spending the night with a farmer, they reached Hammelburg the next day. Here, they grew bold and went into the town to eat a meal at a *Gasthaus* (inn) in the marketplace. Still undetected and unsuspected, the hitched another ride.

While waiting, Lange and his friend sat on a highway overpass and watched as an American jeep full of soldiers approached while an unsuspecting U.S. Army truck drove towards it. The vehicles collided with one another, causing damage and injuries to the occupants. Not wishing to be detained as eyewitnesses, Lange and the other man took off over the countryside before they were spotted. Running over the top of a low hill, when they crested the rise, they saw a huge U.S. Army camp looming ahead of them. Quickly turning around and running away again, they headed in another direction and escaped detection.

Hitching a ride on another truck, they arrived two days later in Kassel, where they had to help the driver unload furniture. In the city, they found a Red Cross tent, where they got a meal and were able to sleep for the night. Catching another ride in a truck to Hannoversch-Münden, Lange was able to purchase a seat on a train heading towards Hamburg, his hometown. His comrade wanted to go further towards the northwest, so they reluctantly parted ways after being on the road together for 10 days. When the train crossed the Elbe and rolled into Hamburg, Lange visited his beloved *Gänsemarkt* (goose market), which was still standing despite the bombing. He then walked 13 kilometers to Blankenese and the house of his uncle, who took him in when he recognized his nephew. After a hot bath and dinner at a table covered with a real tablecloth, he began to feel free again. Shortly afterwards, having got word to them that he was home, his parents came to visit. Feeling indescribable joy that their son had made it home safely after the war, they told him to come home in three days' time.

When Lange arrived at his parent's house in Altona, he went to the *Arbeitsamt* (employment bureau) to apply for a job, then to the police station to apply for a ration card, where no one questioned him about his service in the war. At the nearby British occupation authority's office, a large sign on the wall outside stated that any former members of the SS must report to the art museum, where they would be questioned. Failure to do so would be punishable by death. Lange, trusting in his lucky streak, did not report himself; no one ever suspected that he had been in the *Waffen-SS*. On 17 October 1945, he was issued a genuine identity card, and again no questions were asked. That same fall, he enrolled in an art school and, after graduating, took over his father's art studio. For Günther Lange, the war was finally over. To this day, he still has his *SS Soldbüch*, the same one that he had nearly been discovered holding in Ingolstadt, as a memento of his journey to freedom.

The 8,000 survivors of the *Totenkopf* Division were not so lucky. The division had fought side-by-side with the *Wiking* Division while serving under the *IV. SS-Pz.Korps* from the end of July 1944 until March 1945, throughout all of its battles, with the exception of the retreat to the *Reichschutzstellung*. It had also fought in Vienna, where it had inflicted heavy casualties on the attacking 4th Guards Army. After serving under Dietrich's *6. Pz.Armee* from the end of March until 8 May 1945, the *Totenkopf* Division crossed the line of demarcation on 8 May. *Brigadeführer* Helmuth Becker surrendered himself and his entire division to the U.S. 11th Armored Division of Patton's Third Army near Linz, Austria.

On 14 May, he and his entire division were handed over to the Red Army, which many of its members regarded as an act of betrayal by their American captors. Many of Becker's men were tried and sentenced to 25 years' hard labor as war criminals; many disappeared in the Soviet prison camp system forever, never to be seen again.[42] Helmuth Becker and four other officers were tried on trumped-up charges of sabotage and executed by a Soviet firing squad on 28 February 1953. His widow did not learn of his death until 1961. After 10 years in a Gulag, most of it spent performing hard labor, many of the division's survivors were eventually released from Soviet captivity in 1955, thanks to the personal intervention of West German Chancellor Konrad Adenauer, who took advantage of the political thaw that set in after Nikita Khrushchev became the Premier of the Soviet Union.[43]

Some of the survivors of the *IV. SS-Pz.Korps*, especially the officers, were kept in American, British, or French detention camps longer than members of the *Wehrmacht* because they were deemed unrepentant Nazis, upon whom the Allied "re-education" program had no effect. Those among them who were Dutch, Belgian, Danish, or Norwegian citizens were deported in chains to their home countries, where many were put on trial, found guilty of collaboration, and sentenced to additional prison terms or even put to death. But even most of the surviving prisoners were finally released by 1950, except for those who had been accused of war crimes or were still serving lengthy prison sentences in Soviet Gulags.

Herbert Gille was initially held at Dachau with other high-ranking SS officers. During his internment, in 1946, he also spent time at what had originally been designated as the U.S. Army's "War Criminals Camp," POW Camp 78, at Stuttgart-Zuffenhausen, where he served as *Lagerführer* (camp leader). In this position, he worked for the welfare of his fellow prisoners, including obtaining materials needed to help them repair their worn-out clothing and shoes, since their captors rarely provided any such necessities. He was also moved around to several other camps during his internment, including those at Sandbostel and Fallingbostel. Deemed to have been sufficiently "de-Nazified," Gille was finally released on 21 May 1948 and allowed to return to his wife and daughter in the town of Stemmen.

While interned, in June 1946, Gille was briefly transferred to Nuremberg to play what he thought would be a small part in the notorious war crimes trials that were then taking place. He later related that he assumed he was to be a witness for the prosecution during the trial of some of the major war criminals. However, both the trials' prosecution and defense teams decided not to have Gille testify after all. He felt this was due to the Western Allies' belief that his testimony would have revealed the voluntary membership of so many foreigners in the *Waffen-SS*, which might have proven embarrassing in the immediate postwar political atmosphere.[44] Gille himself was never charged with having committed any war crimes. Yet as a senior leader within the *Wiking* Division's artillery regiment since its inception, he must have been aware of the atrocities committed by other elements of the division during its initial commitment in support of Operation *Barbarossa* in June and July 1941.[45] How much he knew about this sordid chapter in the division's history will probably never be known.

By no means was his ordeal over. In April 1949, Gille was charged by the *Entnazifizierungs-Spruchkammer* (de-Nazification court) in Hannover with having been a member of a criminal organization (i.e., the *Waffen-SS*) and found guilty, making him essentially the victim of a case of double jeopardy, since he had already been kept in Allied detention for the same offense. He spent six months in prison waiting for his sentence to be pronounced. When brought before the trial judge, he learned that he was condemned to serve 18 more months' imprisonment. However, the judge decided to release him that same day due to his good behavior and the three years he had already served in detention. Additionally, the judge placed him in de-Nazification Category V, which marked him as a "minor offender," thus allowing him to reclaim the full rights of West German citizenship.[46]

Some former SS officers were confused with others of the same last name and bound over for war crimes trials. One such unlucky individual was former *Stubaf.* Richard Pauly, who had been the corps' first *Ia* from May–July 1944. Surrendering along with the rest of the division staff of the *38. SS-Grenadier-Division Nibelungen* in southern Bavaria on 8 May 1945, Pauly was plucked out of a U.S. Army internment camp on 25 February 1947 and sent to Poland to face trial for atrocities allegedly committed againt Polish prisoners in Danzig in 1939. At first mistakenly identified as his older brother Max Pauly, who had been involved in the incident, his Polish captors nevertheless sentenced Richard to eight years in prison in Warsaw on unspecified charges.[47] While waiting for his case to be appealed as a case of mistaken identity, he died in prison on 6 December 1951 from tuberculosis. It was a sad ending for an officer who had served throughout the war in an exemplary fashion and had never actually been implicated in any war crimes.

After the war, *Waffen-SS* veterans encountered significant difficulties in returning to normal life in West Germany, especially in regards to employment. Postwar prejudice against them was very strong during the early 1950s, and former officers of the *Wehrmacht* laid the blame for the majority of the Third Reich's crimes on their heads as part of their highly successful "pure *Wehrmacht*" narrative. Because the entire SS had been declared a criminal organization during the Nuremberg war crimes trials, many West German companies did not want to hire former members of the *Waffen-SS*, even though membership of it was not considered criminal on an individual level. Unlike former members of the *Wehrmacht*, they were ruled ineligible for veterans' pensions or veterans' rights in accordance with Article 131 of the Federal Government's *Grundgesetz* (Basic Law) passed in 1951.[48]

Life was hard for nearly all German citizens between 1945 and 1950, but that of former *Waffen-SS* members was even more difficult. Many men had to take menial jobs to make a living, and many others found it difficult to gain admission to institutes of higher learning due to the "Mark of Cain" that adhered to former members of Himmler's command. In order to assist one another in transition during this period before the German *Wirtschaftswunder* (economic miracle) of the 1950s took hold, many former SS veterans joined veterans' associations such as the *Stahlhelm* or *Verband deutscher Soldaten* (League of German Soldiers) or formed local mutual aid associations.

Some former leaders of the *Waffen-SS*, such as Felix Steiner and Herbert Gille, collaborated in the publication of a veterans' newsletter mailed out initially to former members of the *Wiking* Division, with the first edition appearing in November 1951. Due to increasing interest, it began to be distributed in greater numbers, as the number of *Waffen-SS* veterans began to make their impact in public life during the early 1950s. Steiner and Gille's first publication, *der Wiking Ruf* (The *Wiking* Call), was composed and written by Gille in his tiny bookstore in Stemmen, where he eked out a living for himself and his family by selling military history books to a growing audience throughout Western Europe. The print run of each edition soon grew to as many as 10,000 copies.

Slowly, postwar *Waffen-SS* veterans' organizations began to form during the late 1940s and early 1950s. Sensing their growing clout, these organizations began to seek political influence as a means of having their full rights of citizenship restored, including the rights to employment, to serve in the civil service and police, a military pension, and full acceptance by the German national community. Gille's small *Wiking* veterans' organization had already merged in late 1950 with other *Waffen-SS* veterans' groups to found the *Hilfsgemeinschaft auf Gegenseitigkeit der Angehörigen der ehemaligen Waffen-SS* (*HIAG*, or Mutual Aid Association of the *Waffen-SS*).

The stated goals of the *HIAG* were to "legally put former members of the *Waffen-SS* on an equal footing with soldiers of the *Wehrmacht* and to rehabilitate the *Waffen-SS*." The denunciation and rejection of the accusations of war crimes and the rehabilitation of the *Waffen-SS* continued to be part of the *HIAG's* program for the next 40 years.[49] At its peak in the early 1960s, it reached a membership of over 20,000 within 376 local branches, though at one time it claimed to have over 150,000 members. Gille's *Wiking Ruf* newsletter was renamed *Der Freiwillige* (The Volunteer) in 1955 and became a polished monthly periodical sold by subscription from the *Waffen-SS*-owned publishing house, Munin Verlag.[50] After anti-SS sentiment among the civilian populace in Germany began increasing in the 1980s and 1990s, the national organization was officially disbanded in 1992, though many local chapters still remain to this day.

The *HIAG's* political lobbying effort gradually began to bear fruit. In 1953, Chancellor Adenauer announced in a public speech in Hannover that members of the combat formations of the *Waffen-SS* had been "soldiers just like the rest" who had been "simply drafted," which even then was considered a controversial statement, not least by former SS men, who believed that they had belonged to an "elite" arm of the *Wehrmacht*, and not an army of conscripts.[51] In 1955, when the new *Bundeswehr* (West German Federal Armed Forces) was established, former members of the *Waffen-SS* were initially not permitted to volunteer, but after an intensive lobbying effort by Gille and Felix Steiner, with the assistance of former *G.F.M.* Erich von Manstein, the Federal Government relented.

After very stringent vetting by the Blank Commission's screening board, SS men were finally allowed to serve from 1955, including many officers who had reached the rank of *Hauptsturmführer* (with few exceptions, those who had reached the more senior ranks were automatically excluded).[52] Initially, the acceptance rate of former SS officers was only 3 percent, while that of enlisted men was a somewhat greater 20 percent.[53]

Eventually, the *Bundeswehr's* need for experienced officers and non-commissioned officers led to a gradual relaxation of the vetting requirements, leading to more *Waffen-SS* veterans being accepted. By 1961, at least 3,838 former members of the

Waffen-SS, including 236 officers, were able to transition into the *Bundeswehr*, with the majority going into the new *Bundesheer* (Federal Army). Another 648 former SS men joined the *Bundesgrenschutz* (Federal Border Police).[54] By the mid-1960s though, the few former SS applicants seeking *Bundeswehr* careers were considered too old; by that point, the war had been over for 20 years and most of them had already found other, more lucrative or satisfying ways of making a living.

Some of the former members of the *IV. SS-Pz.Korps* and the *Wiking* Division who had second full careers in the *Bundeswehr* included *Stubaf.* Günther Bernau (*Oberst*), *Hstuf.* Georg Glanert (*Oberst*), *Hstuf.* Eberhard Heder (*Oberst*), *Ustuf.* Helmuth Krause (*Major*), *Hstuf.* Werner Meyer (*Oberstleutnant*), *Ustuf.* Günther Lange (*Oberstleutnant der Reserve*), *Hascha.* Josef Loibel (*Hauptfeldwebel*), *Hstuf.* Hans-Helmut Luers (*Major der Reserve*), and *Hstuf.* Werner Strecker (*Oberst*), the latter having served in both the *Wiking* and *Totenkopf* Divisions. Hans Velde, a former resident of Denmark and the last *O1* of the *IV. SS-Pz.Korps*, retired as an *Oberst*, after serving in the office of the *Bundeswehr*'s Inspectorate of *Panzer* Troops.[55]

The highest rank attained by any former member of the *Waffen-SS* was *Generalmajor*, a distinction held by Gerhard Deckert, who rose to the lofty position of Chief of Staff of *Führungsstab des Heeres* (Land Forces Command). At the end of World War II, Deckert had been a 21-year-old *Untersturmführer* in the artillery regiment of the *Das Reich* Division. Other officers who had been in the *IV. SS-Pz.Korps* who later served in the West German equivalent of the C.I.A., the *Bundesnachrichtendienst* (Federal Intelligence Service), included former *Stubaf.* Herbert Schmeisser, the last commander of *SS-Nachr.Abt. 5*, and *Hstuf.* Otto Bronke, a former battery commander in the *Totenkopf* Division's *SS-Pz.Art.Rgt. 3*.[56]

In November 1958, the *Ordensgemeinschaft der Ritterkreuztrager des Eisernes Kreuz e.V.* (*OdR*, or Order of Knight's Cross Holders) presented member Herbert Gille with a "new" 1957 de-Nazified version of the *Ritterkreuz mit Eichenlaub, Schwertern und Brillanten* (Knight's Cross with Oak Leaves, Swords, and Diamonds) during a special ceremony at its annual assembly. This was held to replace the same award stolen from him by an American officer upon his arrest in Salzburg on 28 May 1945, and was seen as long overdue.

Gille remained a tireless promoter of the interests of *Waffen-SS* veterans throughout the remainder of his life. During the early stages of the *HIAG* during the mid-1950s, however, he and Steiner were embroiled in a controversy with a significant portion of its membership, who insisted that it focus more on the mutual aid and missing-in-action *Suchdienst* (search service) aspect of the organization instead of striving to be a power broker in contemporary West German politics. Many members, such as former *Standartenoberjunker* and *HIAG* functionary Werner Drewes, felt that these two leaders were focused too much on concentrating their control over the organization to make it a more effective political tool, and prosecuting their agenda of rehabilitating the image of the *Waffen-SS* as well as the restoration of pension rights for senior SS officers, rather than improving the lot of the average former SS man.[57]

Several years later, Gille and Steiner's faction had won out, though the disagreement about the objectives of the organization was to continue festering for a number of years. The results of the *HIAG's* lobbying of West German political parties and members of the *Bundestag* were mixed; though they had won their goals of allowing former *Waffen-SS* members to enlist in the *Bundeswehr* (albeit at a much lower rate than they deemed desirable) and gaining partial pension rights for those who had served in uniform for 10 years or more, most of the organization's goals remained unmet. The *Deutsche Rote Kreuz* made it known that the *HIAG's Suchdienst* was little more than a duplication of its own efforts and felt that it tended to overly politicize the issue to the detriment of the families concerned, though the *HIAG* disputed this.[58]

Gille also exercised a great deal of editorial discretion with *der Wiking Ruf*, using it as a sounding board to express his own unapologetically militaristic, anti-communist, and Germany-centric opinions on a variety of matters, especially those touching upon his beloved *Wiking* Division. For example, in the first issue appearing in 1951, Gille complained about the manner in which the victorious Allies had declared the *Waffen-SS* part of a criminal organization, when the Allies were just as guilty of having committed the same offenses as his former comrades were accused of, writing: "We have known since the [Korean War] that the soldiers fighting there do not behave any differently from our own. We know that the declaration of criminality against our association was made only in order to take revenge on a defeated but [militarily] superior opponent [i.e., the *Waffen-SS*]."[59] In this and other similar editorials, Gille also expressed his mistrust of the U.S., adhering to an editorial line that encouraged Germany to follow a more independent line *vis-à-vis* one that featured Germany being enmeshed as an unwilling participant in the Cold War between the West and the Communist bloc.

At some point during 1959, editorial duties for the now-renamed *Der Freiwillige* magazine were passed on from Herbert Gille to Erich Kern, a right-wing activist and "unrepentant and unreconstructed Nazi," according to one noted authority. During the war, Kern had been an SS *Untersturmführer*, war correspondent, and sometime psychological warfare expert who served under his real last name of Kernmayr. He had worked for several months in the *IV. SS-Pz.Korps'* headquarters under Herbert Jankuhn during the Hungarian campaign, where he became acquainted with Gille. A prolific author and untiring advocate for rehabilitating the image of the *Waffen-SS* and advocating an unabashedly German nationalist worldview, he served as the editor at large of *Der Freiwillige* until his death in 1991.[60]

As for Herbert Gille, after an active life serving in the *Kaiserheer* and the *Waffen-SS*, and being a post-war advocate for SS veterans' rights, he passed away from a heart attack in his home town of Stemmen on 26 December 1966 at the age of 69. He had been a heavy smoker throughout his life, which probably hastened his death. Over 700 former members of his division and corps headquarters, other divisions of the *Waffen-SS*, and several *Bundeswehr* officers in uniform attended his funeral (despite the ban prohibiting such attendance). Fittingly, Karl Ullrich, the last commander of the *Wiking* Division, gave the memorial speech.[61]

Instead of seeking to join the West German military or security services, other former members of *IV. SS-Pz.Korps* returned to their pre-war civilian pursuits. For instance, Manfred Schönfelder took up the reins to his father's company, while Dr Herbert Jankuhn returned to the faculty of the University of Göttingen, where he continued to teach archaeology until 1973, when he retired.[62] His Nazi past did not catch up with him until 1968, when he was denied a planned guest appearance at the University of Bergen in Norway because students and faculty members resented his uncritical approach to his own Nazi activities in Norway during the war.[63]

By 1960, nearly all former members of the *Waffen-SS* had successfully reintegrated into West German society. But by the 1980s, time began to take its inevitable toll: Schönfelder passed away in March 1983, Jankuhn in April 1990, Hans Velde in March 1995, and former acting corps *Ia* Werner Westphal in 1992. Former *Bundeswehr Oberst* and *Waffen-SS Hauptsturmführer* Eberhard Heder died on 18 November 2017 at the aged of 99. As of writing this account in 2020, the only former member of the *IV. SS-Pz.Korps* headquarters known to be living is Gille's former *Begleitoffizier* Günther Lange.

For those living in East Germany, life under Communism was more problematic. They could not speak openly of their former membership of the *Waffen-SS* and were not able to enjoy the full benefits of a free society, such as freedom of association or freedom of speech, until the Wall came down in 1989. After the end of the Cold War and the dissolution of the U.S.S.R., many Estonian, Latvian, Finnish, Ukrainian, Romanian, and Hungarian veterans who volunteered for or were drafted by the *Waffen-SS* became members of the *HIAG* and were able to reconnect with their former comrades living in the West. Many attended annual commemoration ceremonies under the flags of their former units, such as the Estonian survivors of the *SS-Panzergrenadier Battalion Narwa* at the annual Cherkassy survivors' gathering in Bad Windsheim, Germany.

In Austria, the situation was somewhat different. Jointly occupied by the Western Allies and the Soviet Union until October 1955, Austria was considered a victim of the Third Reich, having participated in World War II involuntarily. The de-Nazification of Austria was therefore somewhat less systematic and extreme than it had been in Germany. Having been a member of the *Waffen-SS* did not carry nearly the same degree of stigma, and SS veterans were not subjected to the restrictions and limitations on their citizenship that they were in West Germany. They were also able to form their own veterans' organizations with relatively little interference from their government after 1955. Some former Austrian *Waffen-SS* members who had served in the ranks of the *IV. SS-Pz.Korps* were also very active in postwar espionage and intelligence-gathering for the Western Allies in Austria and Hungary during the late 1940s and early 1950s, such as Erich Kernmayr, former corps staff officer Franz Wehofsich, and dual Austrian-Hungarian citizen Károly Ney, former commander of the Hungarian SS brigade that carried his name.[64]

The members of the *Totenkopf* Division who had survived their imprisonment in the Soviet Union and returned home by 1955 also reconnected with thousands of their former *Totenkopf* comrades who had avoided being taken prisoner by the Red Army, whether because of hospitalization due to wounds at war's end, service in training and replacement units within the Reich, or having been transferred to other *Waffen-SS* divisions after initially serving in the *Totenkopf*. They soon established a division veterans' association, known unofficially under the cover name of the *Urlaubergemeinschaft Ilmensee* (Lake Ilmen Holiday Association), and held reunions of their own.

In March 1984, despite the threat of protest demonstrations in the town, over 300 survivors of the *Totenkopf* Division and their families conducted their annual meeting in the Hessian town of Oberaula. Defiant even in their old age, the veterans stood firm in the face of 4,000 demonstrators, who equated their service in the division with service in concentration camps, from whence the division sprang in 1940. Stating that their reunions were motivated by "friendships formed in battle and not furtive yearnings to keep alive the spirit of Nazism," its treasurer, former SS officer Kurt Meyer (no relation to the famous *Panzermeyer* of the *Leibstandarte*), told the press: "We are children of Germany … a country has only one history and you cannot throw away the bad and just keep the good."[65] As of writing this account, there are few survivors of either division, and for the most part their annual reunions, such as they are, are limited to the gathering of a few grizzled veterans around their local *Stammtisch* (regulars table) in some out-of-the-way local *Gasthaus*. Soon they will be no more, but their legacy will live on, for good or ill.

The histories of the *Wiking* and *Totenkopf* Divisions have been well documented, not only by their own former members, but by many Western historians since the 1950s, and continue to be a popular topic even to this day. Members of the staff and corps troops of the *IV. SS-Pz.Korps* did not establish their own separate veterans' organization (with the exception of *SS-Werf.Abt. 504*), choosing instead to join those from whence they had begun their initial service in the *SS-Verfügungstruppe* or *Waffen-SS*, such as the *Wiking* or *Totenkopf,* the *LSSAH, Das Reich,* or *Nord* Divisions. As such, there are few veterans' accounts of their experience in Gille's corps headquarters, only scattered vignettes. Gille himself only occasionally answered requests from authors seeking his personal insights and did not compose his own memoirs. All we have are his few wartime notes, but he might have already decided that his corps' deeds alone were enough of a testament. That is all a true *Nursoldat* could ask for.

Like the other more famous SS *panzer* corps, the *IV. SS-Pz.Korps* has earned its place in history. Though only in existence for slightly over a year, it fought in eight major battles that were equally as significant as any of those fought in the West, such as Normandy, Arnhem, or the Ardennes, or even Berlin for that matter. These battles—the tank battle of Praga, the three battles of Warsaw, the three relief attempts of Budapest, and the battle of Stuhlweissenburg—have all gone down in the annals of the Eastern Front as some of its most savage, bitter, and costly battles. The toll in human lives was enormous. During the six months between October 1944 and the end of March 1945, the *Wiking* Division alone lost 12,136 men, more than 67.6 percent of its authorized strength of 17,797 men. During this same period, the division received 9,813 replacements.[66] The losses suffered by the *Totenkopf* Division were even higher, reported as 13,000 men killed in action and another 6,000 missing during the entire war, not counting tens of thousands who were wounded in action.[67]

With "Papa" Gille's passing, the *Waffen-SS* lost one of its most legendary and celebrated commanders. However, the question remains: just how good a commander was he? He had certainly excelled as an artillery officer, having successfully commanded at the battery, battalion, and regimental levels. After benefitting from Felix Steiner's tutelage for nearly three years, Gille succeeded him as commander of the *Wiking* Division, leading it competently from the spring of 1943 until July 1944 through some of its toughest battles, including the harrowing breakout from the Cherkassy Pocket. When elevated to command of the *IV. SS-Pz.Korps* at the end of July 1944, he had amassed more than four years of active campaigning experience, as much or more than most of his contemporaries had. By that point, he was as ready as he ever would be to exercise corps command. Besides his abovementioned leadership qualities, he also cared deeply for the lives of his men, who returned his affection, and was always to be found "up front" where the fighting was.

What was Gille's legacy? George H. Stein, one of the earliest and most impartial historians of the *Waffen-SS*, wrote:

> Of far greater significance was the influence of the former regular Army officers who had commanded the *SS-Verfügungstruppen*—men like Paul Hausser, Felix Steiner, Herbert Gille, Wilhelm Bittrich, and Georg Keppler. If the divisions of the *Waffen-SS* seemed at times indistinguishable from those of the *Heer*, it was in no small measure due to the efforts of these men.[68]

As mentioned in Volume I of this work, Gille had received praise from several *Wehrmacht* field army commanders he had previously served under, such as *9. Armee* commanders *Gen.d.Pz.Tr.* Nikolaus von Vormann and Freiherr von Lüttwitz, who recognized his ability to demand nearly impossible feats of arms from the troops of his corps while fighting at the gates of Warsaw during the late summer and fall of 1944.

These distinguished *Heer* generals were not the only ones who recognized Gille's ability as a leader. On 9 April 1944, in his recommendation for his award of the

Diamonds to his Knight's Cross with Oak Leaves and Swords for his successful defense of Kovel during March and April 1944 as division commander, *Gen.d.Inf.* Friedrich Hossbach of the *LVI. Pz.Korps* and Gille's corps commander at the time, wrote: "In spite of the greatest supply difficulties and considerable losses against a far superior enemy, the weeks-long heroic defense of *Festen Platz* [Fortress] *Kowel* was possible only due to [Gille's] determined leadership and great personal bravery."[69] Seconding Hossbach's recommendation for the award, *Gen.O.* Walter Weiss, commander of the *2. Armee*, wrote:

> [Gille] has once again distinguished himself through outstanding leadership and heroic commitment of his person at the highest level. During the several weeks of defense of the completely surrounded *Festen Platz Kowel*, he was the soul of resistance of the small garrison in relation to the far superior and ruthlessly and continuously attacking enemy. His living example made the admirable defense of the city possible. What he demonstrated here was his highest determination and hardness as well as his superior calmness and prudence, even in the moment of an almost hopeless-seeming fight that deserves the highest recognition.

Eight months later, Weiss signed Gille's fitness report on 31 December 1944 that covered the second time that his *IV. SS-Pz.Korps* had been subordinated to the *2. Armee* from November–December 1944. This leadership evaluation, countersigned by *H.Gr. Süd* commander *Gen.O.* Dr Lothar Rendulic several months later, described Gille as "an aggressive leader, hard and efficient with a very active intellect. He always maintains a cheerful mood even in the most difficult and dangerous situations, thereby providing an inspiration to those under him." This of course contradicts Balck's negative assessment of Gille, leading one to wonder whether the source of disagreement and constant strife between the two officers can be traced to a conflict of equally strong personalities, rather than a question of basic competency. After all, Gille received the highest recognition for valor and leadership that a soldier in the German Armed Forces could possibly earn during the war—the Knight's Cross with Oak Leaves, Swords, and Diamonds, an award not bestowed lightly. The only other soldier in the *Waffen-SS* to earn that distinction was Sepp Dietrich himself, who gained his while serving as a corps commander of the *I. SS-Pz.Korps*.

Awards and honors aside, how well did Gille perform as a corps commander? Given the increasingly rigid constraints being placed upon *Wehrmacht* and *Waffen-SS* leaders at all levels of command after the 20 July 1944 Bomb Plot, commanders became mere executors of orders emanating from *OKH* Headquarters in Berlin, with less and less leeway allowed to practice the art of operational or tactical command. Opportunities for independent thinking and the exercise of one's own initiative became rarer as the war ground to its bloody climax.

However, some things can be discerned from the original records. Certainly, Gille was technically and tactically proficient. He was sufficiently senior in the rankings of the *SS-Dienstalterliste* to merit elevation to corps command.[70] Most of all, he could be relied upon to carry out his orders without question. Of course, those were the primary reasons why he was chosen to command the *IV. SS-Pz. Korps* in the first place. The available evidence seems to indicate that he was an above-average regimental commander, a good (though not brilliant) division commander, and an average corps commander. This latter comment should not be seen as a slight against him; in fact, most general officers commanding at division, corps, or army have an average amount of abilities needed to adequately perform their duties at their individual level. That is the most that any army can hope for. Only a very select few commanders have the ability, the talent, and (most of all) the luck needed to rise above the pack and display the kind of battlefield brilliance—the *Fingerspitzengefühl*—that sets a Rommel apart from a Busch, a Model apart from a Wöhler.

Gille's greatest strengths were his willpower, his ability to inspire his troops, and that most underestimated strength that all successful generals bring to a battle—the sheer physical stamina that allows one to keep going with little rest for two or three days at a time yet still maintain poise and judgement. Given a relatively proficient general staff to work with, enough food, fuel, and ammunition, and most of all, two of the greatest armored divisions the world has ever seen—the *Wiking* and *Totenkopf* Divisions—it should have come as no surprise that the *IV. SS-Pz. Korps* stopped Rokossovsky's First Belorussian Front at the gates of Warsaw and nearly liberated Budapest after three separate attempts in the face of the determined defense offered by Tolbukhin's Third Ukrainian Front. Although he served a tyrannical regime dedicated to the enslavement of an entire continent and the genocide of entire peoples whom Hitler and Himmler deemed "racially inferior," Gille fought as honorably and as decently as only a *Nursoldat* could. He probably would have been satisfied with that epitaph.

And what of his nemesis, *Gen.d.Pz. Tr.* Hermann Balck? After formally surrendering to Major General McBride on 8 May 1945, he was arrested on 21 May and shipped off to a POW camp for senior German officers, where he remained until 1947. In 1948, he was brought to trial by a West German de-Nazification court in northern Württemberg, on charges that he had an officer illegally executed on 28 November 1944 for dereliction of duty when he was found drunk during the middle of an important attack, rendering him unfit to carry out his responsibilities. Balck was acquitted by that court, but shortly thereafter that same year was brought before a civilian court on charges of murder for the same act.

Despite his defense argument that his actions were in keeping with the *Wehrmacht's* code of military justice and were appropriate under the circumstances, the court disagreed and found him guilty. Sentenced to three years in prison, he served only 18 months before he was released to his home near Stuttgart. He was tried for war crimes by a French court in 1950 for having ordered the destruction of the French village of Gérardmer in mid-November 1944 during the Lorraine campaign. Found guilty *in absentia* (for the Americans and West German government both refused to release him), he was sentenced to 20 years in prison but never served time for what he believed as a necessary act of war.

Unlike most of his fellow senior officers, Balck did not participate in the postwar U.S. Army Foreign Military Studies project spearheaded by S. L. A. Marshall. Rather, he earned a living following non-military pursuits, though he consulted occasionally with other former leaders tasked with organizing the West German *Bundeswehr* in the 1950s. He did not begin composing his memoirs until the early 1970s, using the copious notes he had managed to preserve during and after the war. After they were completed in the late 1970s, they were published in 1981 in Germany as *Ordnung in Chaos: Erinnerungen 1893–1948* (Order in Chaos: Memories). He died at his home in Asberg, Germany, one year later.

Balck became somewhat of a minor sensation in the United States during the early 1980s, especially within U.S. Army doctrinal and historical circles. Heralded as "The Greatest German General No One Ever Heard Of," Balck had risen to public fame on the shoulders of a book written by his former chief of staff, *Gen.Maj.* Friedrich-Wilhelm von Mellenthin. His book, *Panzer Battles*, was reprinted in the U.S. in 1971, appearing at the time when the U.S. Army was trying to find its way after the debacle of the Vietnam War. The tales of the team of Balck and von Mellenthin and their tactical brilliance, as they fought effectively as a team leading a *panzer* corps against overwhelming odds on the Eastern Front, inspired many U.S. Army officers to think about using their brand of maneuver warfare as an antidote to Soviet numerical superiority along NATO's border with the Warsaw Pact.

In the late 1970s, Balck and von Mellenthin were invited to the United States, where, as guests of the U.S. Army, they were featured as guest speakers and lecturers on operations and tactics in seminars and panel discussions with American and other senior NATO leaders at the U.S. Army War College in Carlisle, Pennsylvania. The two veterans collaborated on two projects commissioned by the U.S. Army and carried out by Battelle–Columbus Laboratories between July and November 1979, and another by the BDM Corporation a year later. Both projects focused on Balck's and von Mellenthin's understanding of tactical doctrine as practiced by the Wehrmacht in World War II, lessons learned, and their applicability to the situation in which NATO found itself the late 1970s and early 1980s.

Especially noteworthy was their espousal of *Auftragstaktik* (mission-type orders), a feature of *Wehrmacht* officer training during the 1930s which was seen as a groundbreaking idea by those within U.S. Army doctrinal circles who were looking for a better way to train division and corps commanders and their staffs.[71] With the publication of his memoirs in 1981 (finally translated into English by the University Press of Kentucky in 2015), Balck's reputation as a tactical and technical genius was finally secured more than 35 years after the war ended and after many of his peers (and opponents) had already passed away

In evaluating his performance, it can easily be said that Balck, especially when teamed with von Mellenthin, *was* brilliant. Imaginative, driven, and ruthless, he brought the right qualities to the table that enabled him to function extremely effectively as a brigade, division, and corps commander. Like Hitler had said, Balck got results. But when he was forced to part with von Mellenthin at the end of November 1944, he found himself operating without his "modulator" for the first time since assuming senior command. His long-time chief of staff's calm demeanor, knack for detail, and planning capability had previously kept his mercurial commander well-grounded in the realm of the possible. Without von Mellenthin, especially in Hungary when commanding the *6. Armee*, Balck lacked that which had made him a whole person. Prone to flights of fancy and over-optimistic assessments of what was possible, he repeatedly took on more tasks than his troops were capable of carrying out as quickly as he wanted. His *6. Armee* chief of staff, Heinz Gaedke, was small-minded in comparison to von Mellenthin and lacked the talent, maturity, and even-handedness of his predecessor. Together, Balck and Gaedke brought out the worst in each other's personalities.

This found its full expression in the dislike and even loathing both men felt for the *Waffen-SS*, a simmering hate in Balck that Gaedke stoked only too gladly. This animosity expressed towards Gille, the *IV. SS-Pz.Korps*, and all things *Waffen-SS-*related soon resulted in battlefield repercussions that ironically affected the lives of the poor soldiers tasked with fighting in the mud attempting to achieve unrealistic goals rather than the officers who were the targets of Balck's ire. As the war turned increasingly against the fortunes of the Third Reich, Balck, who was not used to failure, sought an outlet for his anger and disappointment, and found it in Gille and his staff.

Whether Gille or Schönfelder, *et al.*, were as incompetent as Balck and Gaedke alleged they were has already been amply demonstrated in this manuscript; clearly, they were not. Yet despite the war crashing about their ears, the commander of the *6. Armee* and his chief of staff persisted in nursing their grievances and continuing their petty campaign against Gille and his corps, even when their primary mission of keeping the Soviet Union at bay suffered as a consequence. Sadly, Balck was a better man than that; the dark side of his nature had unfortunately gotten the better of him, a not unusual occurrence in leaders during wartime, especially when facing a situation as hopeless as the one that *H.Gr. Süd* faced after March 1945. Had he been able to retain von Mellenthin by his side, who knows what he would have been able to achieve in Hungary in January 1945? Budapest may very well have been relieved and the Nagykanizsa oilfields might have been safeguarded from the Third Ukrainian Front long after they actually fell in April 1945.

The *IV. SS-Pz.Korps* has left no monuments, save the headstones and grave markers of thousands of its troops buried in a number of cemeteries stretching from Modlin to Warsaw, and Budapest to Veszprem, before finally ending at the German War Graves cemetery outside of Graz. Most of its members have passed on, leaving only their corps motto: *Der Kämpfer des Fuhrers*—The Führer's Warriors. Indeed, they were. Together, the *Totenkopf* and *Wiking* Divisions, fighting together under the leadership of their corps commander, nearly achieved the impossible, and for a while seemed to have been in reach of turning the tide of the war in the East. But it was not to be, fortunately for the Allied cause and the fates of millions whose lives depended upon who won the titanic struggle between Nazi Germany and the Soviet Union.

The author hopes that this concluding volume of the history of the *IV. SS-Pz. Korps* has shed some light on this turbulent era and the corps' history as a prominent member of a very exclusive type of organization—the four *panzer* corps of the *Waffen-SS*. Thus ends this account of its short and momentous history, during which it led more divisions of the *Heer* than those from Heinrich Himmler's "Black Corps." Perhaps at some point, future historians will locate additional records in the Russian State Military Archives or the German Federal Archives or its Military Archives that will shed more light on its campaigns and battles, its personnel, equipment, and organizational details, but until such time, the author hopes that this modest work will suffice.

IV. SS-Pz.Korps Battle and Campaign Participation Credits awarded for the period 23 February to 8 May 1945

Heeresgruppe Süd, on 1 May 1945 *Heeresgruppe Ostmark* (*General der Infanterie* Otto Wöhler, after 7 April 1945 *Gen.O.* Lothar Rendulic)

Withdrawal battles in northwest Hungary and Lower Austria, Pressburg, and Vienna, 21 March–8 May 1945

6. *Armee* (*General der Panzertruppe* Hermann Balck) 6 March–8 May 1945

Tank battle on the Hungarian Plain at Stuhlweissenburg (Székesfehérvár), 6–23 March 1945

Defensive and withdrawal battles south of the Danube to the eastern Alps, 24 March–8 May 1945

IV. SS-Pz.Korps (*SS-Obergruppenführer* Herbert Gille)

Defensive battles in Stuhlweissenburg area, 23 February–15 March 1945
Battle of Stuhlweissenburg, 16–21 March 1945
Withdrawal battles towards the *Reichsschutzstellung* (Heiligenkreuz), 22–30 March 1945
Defensive battles in the *Reichsschutzstellung* and south of Fürstenfeld, 31 March–8 May 1945
Capitulation of the *Wehrmacht,* 8 May 1945

IV. SS-Pz.Korps Orders of Battle, 5 February to 8 May 1945

5 February–18 March 1945—Defense of Stuhlweissenburg

Corps Staff and Corps Headquarters Command

Divisions

3. SS-Pz.Div. Totenkopf
5. SS-Pz.Div. Wiking
356. Inf.Div.
4. Kav.Brig.
2. Ung.Pz.Div.

Army Troops

SS-Rgt. Ney
I. Btl./SS-Pz.Gren.Rgt. 23 Norge
I. Btl./SS-Pz.Gren.Rgt. 24 Danmark
SS-ARKO 504
SS-Werfer-Abt. 504
s.SS-Art.Abt. 504
SS-Beob.Abt. 504

Corps Troops

SS-Korps-Nachr.Abt. 104
SS-San.Abt. 104
SS-Kraft-Fahr Kp. 104
SS-Bekl.Inst. Zug 504
SS-Feldpostamt 104

22–31 March 1945—Withdrawal from Stuhlweissenburg to *Reichschutzstellung*

Corps Staff and Corps Headquarters Command

Divisions

1.Pz.Div.
    s.Pz.Abt. 509
    I. Abt./Pz.Rgt. 24
    Sturm-Pz.Abt. 219
3. Pz.Div.
5. SS-Pz.Div. Wiking
9. SS-Pz.Div. Hohenstaufen
Div.K.Gr. LSSAH

Army Troops

SS-ARKO 504
SS-Werfer-Abt. 504
s.SS-Art.Abt. 504
SS-Beob.Abt. 504
IV. Btl./SS-Rgt. Ney
Volkssturm-Btl. Jennersdorf
Volkssturm-Btl. Feldbach
Volkssturm-Btl. Liezen
Flak-K.Gr. III./10957
Zollgrenzschutz-Kp. Jennersdorf

Corps Troops

SS-Korps-Nachr.Abt. 104
SS-San.Abt. 104
SS-Kraft-Fahr Kp. 104
SS-Bekl.Inst. Zug 504
SS-Feldpostamt 104

15 April 1945

Corps Staff and Corps Headquarters Command

Divisions

K.Gr. 3. Pz.Div.
K.Gr. 5. SS-Pz.Div. Wiking
    I.Btl./SS-Pz.Gren.Rgt. 23 Norge

Army Troops

SS-ARKO 504
SS-Werfer-Abt. 504
s.SS-Art.Abt. 504
SS-Beob.Abt. 504
Festungs-Pak Verband IX (2 companies)
Volkssturm-Btl. Jennersdorf

Corps Troops

SS-Korps-Nachr.Abt. 104
SS-San.Abt. 104
SS-Kraft-Fahr Kp. 104
SS-Bekl.Inst. Zug 504
SS-Feldpostamt 104

8 May 1945—End of the War

Corps Staff and Corps Headquarters Command
Divisions

K.Gr. 1. Pz.Div.
 I. Abt./Pz.Rgt. 24
1. Volks-Geb.Div.
K.Gr. 3. Pz.Div.
K.Gr. 5. SS-Pz.Div. Wiking
 I. Btl./SS-Pz.Gren.Rgt. 23 Norge

Army Troops

SS-ARKO 504
SS-Werfer-Abt. 504
s.SS-Art.Abt. 504
SS-Beob.Abt. 504

Corps Troops

SS-Korps-Nachr.Abt. 104
SS-San.Abt. 104
SS-Kraft-Fahr Kp. 104
SS-Bekl.Inst. Zug 504
SS-Feldpostamt 104

6. *Armee* Orders of Battle, 1 and 17 April 1945

1 April 1945

K.Gr. Wolf (*Wehrkreis XVIII*)
  Fahr-Ausb.u.Ers.Abt. 18 Graz
  1 Kp./Pz.Jäg.Ausb.u.Ers.Abt. 48
  II. Abt./Fallschirm-Art.Rgt. 10
  Convalescents from the military hospitals in Graz

IV. SS-Pz.Korps (Gille)
  K.Gr. 1. Pz.Div. (Thünert)
    s.Pz.Abt. 509
    I. Abt./Pz.Rgt. 24 (Panther)
    Sturm-Pz.Abt. 219
    Pz.-Flamm Kp. 351
  K.Gr. 3. Pz.Div. (Söth)
  K.Gr. 5. SS-Pz.Div. Wiking (Ullrich)
    I.Btl./SS-Pz.Gren.Rgt. 23 Norge
  Volkssturm-Btl. Jennersdorf
  Festungs-Pak Verband IX (without *2. Kp.*)

III. Pz.Korps (Breith)
  1.Volks-Geb.Div. (Wittmann)
    Hungarian Fortress Units (7 battalions)
    Feld-Ers.Btl. 75 (*3. Pz.Div.*)
    Elements *SS-Rgt. Ney*
  Kampfgruppe Krause (Krause)
    K.Gr. Gottwald
      Btl. Büttner
      Volks-Werfer Rgt. 24

> *Beob.Abt. 34*
> *Feld-Ers.Btl. 73 (1. Pz.Div.)*
> *K.Gr. Siegers*
> > *Geb.Ers.u.Ausb.Btl. 18 Graz*
> > *Geb.Jag. Alarm-Einheiten*
> > *Alarm-Einheiten Volks-Werfer Rgt. 24*
> *K.Gr. Schweitzer*
> > *SS-Gren.Ers.u.Ausb.Btl. 11 Graz*
> > *IV. Btl./SS-Rgt. Ney*
> > *Volks-Werfer Brig. 17* and *19* (as infantry)

Sturm-Art.Brig. 303
Heeres-Art.Abt. 171

17 April 1945

Army Reserve
> *K.Gr. 1. Pz.Div.* (Thünert)
> > *Sturm-Pz.Abt. 219*
> > *Pz.Flamm-Kp. 351*

> *IV. SS-Pz.Korps* (Gille)
> > *K.Gr. 3. Pz.Div.* (Schöne)
> > *K.Gr. 5. SS-Pz.Div. Wiking* (Ullrich)
> > > *I.Btl./SS-Pz.Gren.Rgt. 23 Norge*
> > *Volkssturm-Btl. Jennersdorf*
> > *Festungs-Pak Verband IX* (without *2. Kp.*)

> *III. Pz.Korps* (Breith)
> > *1.Volks-Geb.Div.* (Wittmann)
> > > Hungarian *Fest.Btl.* (remnants)
> > *117. Jäg.Div.* (Kreppel)
> > *K.Gr. ARKO 3* (Semmer)
> > > *IV. Btl./SS-Rgt. Ney*
> > > *Bau-Pio.Btl. 504*
> > > *SS-Gren.Ers.u.Ausb.Btl. 11 Graz*
> > > *I.Abt./Pz.Rgt. 24* (Panther)
> > > *Sturm-Art.Brig. 303*
> > *K.Gr. Motschmann* (Motschmann)
> > > *SS-Pol.Rgt. 13*
> > > *Stab/Geb.Ers.u.Ausb.Btl. 36*
> > > *Geb.Pio.Ers.u.Ausb.Btl. 83*
> > > *Nachrichten-Zug*

    Panzer-Zerstörer-Zug
    Radfahrer-Schwadron
K.Gr. Gottwald (Gottwald)
    Marsch-Kp. 118. Jäg.Div.
    Gruppe Borsán
    Sturmboot-Kp. 117
    Volkssturm-Btl. Hanisch
    Alarm-Einheit Volks-Werfer Rgt. 24
    Art.Beob.Abt. 32
K.Gr. Siebert (Siebert)
    Geb.Ers.u.Ausb.Btl. 18
    Geb.Jäg.Kp. Wendt
    Alarm-Btl. Volks-Werfer Rgt. 24
    Versprengten-Kp.
K.Gr. Schweitzer
Heeres-Art.Abt. 171

K.Gr. Semmering aka *K.Gr. Raithel* (renamed *9. Geb.Div.* on 25 April 1945)
    Div.Stab (from Mountain Artillery Gunnery School)
    Geb.Jäg.Rgt 154
    Geb.Jäg.Rgt 155 (From from *RAD Brigade Steiermark)*
    Landesschützen-Btl. 851
    Wehrkreis-Unterführer-Lehrgang XVIII
    Ordnungspolizei units
    Kriegsmarine units (U-Boat crews, Danube flotilla)
    Luftwaffe units (elements of *Kampfgeschwader 27 Bölcke* and *Zeltweg*
        airfield personnel)
    Geb.Aufkl.Abt. 56 (from *SS-Geb.Jäg.Ers.Abt. 13)*
    Pz.Jäg.Kp. 48 (from *Pz.Jäg.Ers.Abt. 48)*
    Geb.Art.Rgt. 56 (from *Geb.Art.* Gunnery School Dachstein)
    Geb.Pio.Kp.

German Order of Battle, Operation *Frühlingserwachen*, 5 March 1945

Heeresgruppe Süd (Wöhler)
   6. Pz.Armee (Dietrich)
      I. SS-Pz.Korps (Priess)
         1. SS-Pz.Div. Leibstandarte SS Adolf Hitler (Kumm)
         12. SS-Pz.Div. Hitlerjugend (Kraas)
      II. SS-Pz.Korps (Bittrich)
         2. SS-Pz.Div. Das Reich (Ostendorff/Lehmann)
         9. SS-Pz.Div. Hohenstaufen (Stadler)
         23. Pz.Div. (von Radowitz)
         44. Reichs-Gren.Div. Hoch und Deutschmeister (von Rost)
      I. Kav.Korps (Harteneck)
         3. Kav.Div. (von der Groeben)
         4. Kav.Div. (von Grolman)
         25. Ung.Inf.Div. (Kalkó)
   6. Armee (Balck)
      III. Pz.Korps (Breith)
         1. Pz.Div. (Thünert)
         3. Pz.Div. (Söth)
         356. Inf.Div. (Kühl)
      IV. SS-Pz.Korps (Gille)
         3. SS-Pz.Div. Totenkopf (Becker)
         5. SS-Pz.Div. Wiking (Ullrich)
         2. Ung.Pz.Div. (vitéz-Zador)

   3. Ung. Armee (vitéz-Heszlényi)
      III. Ung. Armee-Korps (Hankovsky)
         1. Ung.Hussar-Div. (Schell)
         23. Ung.Inf.Div. (Feher)
         6. Pz.Div. (von Waldenfels)
         96. Inf.Div. (Harrendorf)

    711. Inf.Div. (Reichert)
    SS-K.Gr. Ameiser
    SS-Regiment Ney
2. Pz.Armee (de Angelis)
  LXVIII. Armee-Korps (Konrad)
    71. Inf.Div. (von Schuckmann)
    13. SS-Waffen-Geb.Div. Handschar (Hampel)
    16. SS-Pz.Gren.Div. Reichsführer-SS (Baum)
  XXII. Geb.Armee-Korps (Lanz)
    1. Volks-Geb.Div. (Kuebler)
    118. Jäg.Div. (Lamey)
    Gren.Brig. (mot.) 92 (Grosser)

Oberbefehlshaber Südost/Heeresgruppe F (von Weichs)
  Heeresgruppe E (Löhr)
    LXXXI. Armee-Korps (von Erdmannsdorff)
      104. Jäg.Div. (von Ludwiger)
      11. Luftwaffe Feld-Div. (Henke)

Third Ukrainian Front Order of Battle, Vienna Operation, 16 March 1945

Third Ukrainian Front (Marshal Fyodor Tolbukhin)
    1st Bulgarian Army (Stojčev)
        III Bulgarian Rifle Corps (Toshev)
        IV Bulgarian Rifle Corps (Trendafilov)
    57th Army (Sarokhin)
        VI Guards Rifle Corps (Dreyer)
        LXIV Rifle Corps (Kravcov)
        CXXXIII Rifle Corps (Artyushenko)
    9th Guards Army (Glagolev)—parts used at Rechnitz
        XXXVII Guards Rifle Corps (Mironov)
            98th Guards Rifle Division
            99th Guards Rifle Division
            103rd Guards Rifle Division
    26th Army (Gagen)
        CXXXV Rifle Corps (Gnedin)
            74th Rifle Division
            151st Rifle Division
            155th Rifle Division
        XXX Rifle Corps (Lazko)
            36th Guards Rifle Division
            68th Guards Rifle Division
            74th Rifle Division
        CIV Rifle Corps
            66th Guards Rifle Division
            93rd Rifle Division
            233rd Rifle Division
        In reserve: LXXV Rifle Corps (no structure known)

V Guard Cavalry Corps (Gorshkov)—taken over by the 27th Army on 12 April 1945
    11th Guards Cavalry Division
    12th Guards Cavalry Division
    63rd Cavalry Division
    57th Tank Regiment
    60th Tank Regiment
    71st Tank Regiment
    150th Guard Tank Regiment
    1896th Assault Gun Regiment

27th Army (Trofimenko)
  XVIII Tank Corps (Govorunenko)
    110th Tank Brigade
    170th Tank Brigade
    181st Tank Brigade
    32nd Mechanized Brigade
    1438th, 1453rd, 1479th, and 1894th Assault Gun Regiments
  XXXV Rifle Corps (Gorbachev)
    78th Rifle Division
    163rd Rifle Division
    202nd Rifle Division
    1691st Assault Gun Regiment
  XXXIII Rifle Corps (Semenov)
    206th Rifle Division
    337th Rifle Division
    3rd Guard Airborne Division
  XXXVII Rifle Corps (Kolcuk)
    108th Guards Rifle Division
    316th Rifle Division
    320th Rifle Division
    1011st Assault Gun Regiment

6th Guards Tank Army (Kravchenko)
  V Guards Tank Corps (Savelyev)
    20th Guards Tank Brigade
    21st Guards Tank Brigade
    22nd Guards Tank Brigade
    6th Guards Mechanized Brigade
    48th Guards Antitank Brigade
    1458th, 1462nd, and 1484th Assault Gun Regiments
  II Guards Mechanized Corps* (Sviridov)
    4th Guards Mechanized Brigade
    5th Guards Mechanized Brigade

  6th Guards Mechanized Brigade
  37th Guards Tank Brigade
  22nd, 23rd, 24th, and 25th Guards Tank Regiments
 IX Guards Mechanized Corps (Volkov)
  18th Guards Mechanized Brigade
  30th Guards Mechanized Brigade
  31st Guards Mechanized Brigade
  46th Guards Tank Brigade
  83rd, 84th, 85th Guards Tank Regiments and 252nd Tank Regiment
4th Guards Army (Zakharov, Zakhvatayev)
 XX Guards Rifle Corps (Biryukov)
  5th Guards Airborne Division
  7th Guards Airborne Division
  80th Guards Rifle Division
 XXI Guards Rifle Corps (Kozak)
  62nd Guards Rifle Division
  69th Guards Rifle Division
  41st Guards Rifle Division
 XXXI Guards Rifle Corps (Bobruk)
  4th Guards Rifle Division
  34th Guards Rifle Division
  40th Guards Rifle Division
 I Guards Mechanized Corps (Russianov)
  1st Guards Mechanized Brigade
  2nd Guards Mechanized Brigade
  3rd Guards Mechanized Brigade
  9th Guards Tank Brigade
  207th Combat Engineer Brigade
  17th, 18th, 19th, and 20th Guards Tank Regiments
  1544th Assault Gun Regiment
46th Army* (Petrushevskiy)
 LXXV Rifle Corps (Akimenko)
  223rd Rifle Division
 LXVIII Rifle Corps (Skodunovich)
  53rd Rifle Division
  59th Guards Rifle Division
  297th Rifle Division
 XXIII Rifle Corps (Grigorovich)
  19th Rifle Division
  99th Rifle Division
  252nd Rifle Division

X Guards Rifle Corps (Rubanyuk)
    49th Guards Rifle Division
    86th Guards Rifle Division
    180th Rifle Division

*April 1945 transferred to Second Ukrainian Front

German Army, *Waffen-SS* and U.S. Army Rank Equivalents

Wehrmacht-Heer	*Waffen-SS*	Abbreviation	U.S. Equivalent
Generalfeldmarschall	N/A	*G.F.M.*	General of the Army
Generaloberst	*SS-Oberstgruppenführer und Generaloberst der Waffen-SS*	*Gen.O./Obstgruf.*	General
General der Infantrie, Kavallerie, etc.	*SS-Obergruppenführer und General der Waffen-SS*	*Gen.d.Inf./Ogruf.*	Lieutenant General
Generalleutnant	*SS-Gruppenführer und Generalleutnant der Waffen-SS*	*Gen.Lt./Gruf.*	Major General
Generalmajor	*SS-Brigadeführer und Generalmajor der Waffen-SS*	*Gen.Maj./Brig.Fhr.*	Brigadier General
Oberst	*SS-Oberführer*	*Oberf.*	Senior Colonel
Oberst	*SS-Standartenführer*	*O./Staf.*	Colonel
Oberstleutnant	*SS-Obersturmbannführer*	*Oberstlt./Ostubaf.*	Lieutenant Colonel
Major	*SS-Sturmbannführer*	*Maj./Stubaf.*	Major
Hauptmann or *Rittmeister*	*SS-Hauptsturmführer*	*Hptm./Hstuf.*	Captain
Oberleutnant	*SS-Obersturmführer*	*Oberlt./Ostuf.*	First Lieutenant
Leutnant	*SS-Untersturmführer*	*Lt./Ustuf.*	Second Lieutenant
Stabsfeldwebel	*SS-Sturmscharführer*	*Stabs Fw./none*	Sergeant Major
Oberfeldwebel	*SS-Hauptscharführer*	*Ofw./Hscha.*	Master Sergeant
Feldwebel	*SS-Oberscharführer*	*Fw./Oscha.*	Sergeant First Class
Unteroffizier	*SS-Unterscharführer*	*Uffz./Uscha.*	Staff Sergeant
Obergefreiter	*SS-Rottenführer*	*Ogefr./Rttf.*	Corporal/Specialist
Gefreiter	*SS-Sturmann*	*Gef./Strm.*	Private First Class
Obergrenadier, Oberkannonier, etc.	*SS-Obergrenadier, etc.*	none	Private Second Class
Grenadier, Kanonier, Funker, etc.	*SS-Grenadier, etc.*	none	Private

Glossary

Abteilung (Abt.): Literally, detachment. A German unit of company size or greater, though normally of battalion size. Traditionally used to designate artillery, armor, or reconnaissance battalions.

Abteilungsartzt: Unit physician or medical doctor.

Alte Hase: Old hare, German Army slang for front-line veterans who have served for a significant time in a unit.

Armee: Field army. Its headquarters was designated as an *Armeeoberkommando (AOK)*.

Armeegruppe: Field army-level task force, normally consisting of one or more armies, including those from allied nations.

Armee-Korps: German infantry corps headquarters, capable of controlling two to four tank, armored infantry, or infantry divisions as well as various corps troops, such as artillery, engineer, antiaircraft, and antitank battalions or regiments.

Armee-Oberkommando (AOK): Field army headquarters, under which several *Armee-Korps* or divisions might operate.

Auffrischung: Reconstitution, a weeks-long process wherein a unit that has been destroyed or in combat for a prolonged period of time is pulled out of the line and rebuilt in a rest area behind the front lines, including the absorption of replacement personnel, weapons, and equipment.

Aufgefrischt: Description of a unit that has recently undergone reconstitution.

Aufklärungsabteilung (Aufkl.Abt.): Reconnaissance Battalion.

Ausbildung: Training, including individual and unit level. Normally carried out when not involved in direct combat.

Befehlshaber: Field army commander.

Befehlspanzer: Command tank, equipped with necessary radio equipment to command and control armored formations and to communicate with adjacent and higher units.

Bergepanther: Tank recovery vehicle built on the chassis of a *Pz. V* Panther

Berichtszeit: Reporting time stated for morning, midday, and daily reports.

Divisionsgruppe (Div.Gr.): A temporary division-sized task force, normally created to accomplish short-term objectives or missions, that may consist of companies, battalions, or regiments from different divisions or *Heerestruppen*, as in *Div.Gr. Pape*. Also may be defined as a late-1943 measure instituted by the *OKH* in which a composite regiment is formed from the remnants of other destroyed or deactivated regiments from the same division and controlled by a *Korpsgruppe* headquarters formed from the headquarters of another destroyed or deactivated division.

Drückeberger: German Army slang for deserter (*Deserteur*), shirker, or malingerer; i.e., one who seeks to avoid duty or flee from fighting. Often conflated with *Versprengte*.

Einsatzbereit: Operational, especially in regards to armor vehicles, meaning that the vehicle is fully capable of shooting, driving, and communicating.

Ersatzheer: The Replacement or Home Army, responsible for training replacements and sustaining the forces of the Field Army (*Feldheer*) fighting on the various fronts.

Fahnenflucht: Desertion.

Fahrer: Vehicle driver; implies that the soldier also maintains the vehicle.

Fallschirmjäger: Paratrooper.

Feldausbildungs: Designation of a training unit located in close proximity to the front lines established to provide advanced individual training or reclassification training for soldiers from other branches of the *Wehrmacht* being transferred to ground combat branches, such as the infantry.

Feldgendarmerie: Field police. Normally tasked with traffic regulation, but also serve a disciplinary role or assisting a division's intelligence staff with counterespionage work.

Feldlazarett: Field hospital.

Fernschreiben: Telex message sent via *Hellschreiber* or teletype.

Flakvierling: Four-barreled 20 mm *Flak*, often on a self-propelled mount.

Fliegerabwehrkanonone (Flak): Any kind of German antiaircraft gun.

Fliegerverbindungsoffizier (Flivo): *Luftwaffe* officer, usually a qualified pilot, assigned or attached to a ground unit to coordinate the employment of air assets in support of combat operations.

Freiwilligen: Volunteer; pertains especially to the *Waffen-SS* or foreign units serving under the German banner.

Frontschwein: Front-line pig. Slang for veterans who have survived serving in the front lines for several months or even years.

Führungsabteilung: The operations and intelligence staff of a German brigade-level unit or higher, usually consisting of the *Ia* (Operations) and *Ic* (Intelligence) officers and their assistants. Has same connotation as *Führungstaffel*.

Gebirgs-Korps (*Geb.Korps*): German mountain corps headquarters, capable of controlling two to four infantry, mountain, or light infantry divisions as well as various corps troops, such as artillery, engineer, antiaircraft, and antitank battalions or regiments.

Gefechtstand: Command post of the *Führungsabteilung*, usually located closer to the front than a *Hauptquartier*.

Gefechtsvorposten: Screen line, or forward line of troops who serve as an early warning to spot or delay an approaching enemy. Usually designates a thin line of troops who are required to fall back into the main defense line upon contact with the enemy.

Gruppe: Group; in an infantry company, usually denotes a rifle squad.

Hauptquartier: Headquarters; may denote the main headquarters installation of a division, corps, or field army. Often located separately from the forward-positioned *Gefechtstand*.

Heer: German Army.

Heeresgruppe (*H.Gr.*): Army Group, consisting of two or more field armies.

Heeresrüstungsamt: The ordnance department of the German Army responsible for managing the provision of weapons and equipment, including armored vehicles, for the field forces.

Heerestruppen: Independent general headquarters (GHQ) troops organized, trained, and equipped to carry out specific functions, including supply and transportation, medical care, construction, communications, and rear-area security. Also may include artillery, combat engineer, antitank, tank, antiaircraft, and specialized assault units, as well as penal or rehabilitation units, that operate in the army, corps, or division areas within a designated *Kampfraum* (area of operations).

Honvéd: Title of the Royal Hungarian Army.

Hussar: Hungarian mounted infantryman.

Infanterie-Division (*Inf.Div.*, or *I.D.*): German Army infantry division.

Jagdpanzer: Tank destroyer mounting a 7.5 cm gun built on the chassis of a *Pz. IV* or Czech 38t chassis.

Jäger: Luftwaffe designation for fighter aircraft or infantry troops in *Luftwaffe* field divisions, the Hermann Göring Division, or paratroopers. Also designation of *Heer* light infantry units.

Kampfgruppe (*K.Gr.*): A temporary task-organized body of troops, which may range in size from a company to brigade plus attached troops, normally identified by its commander's name, and used to achieve a given, short-term military objective.

Kampfraum: Operational area, combat area, or combat zone.

Kampfstärke: Combat strength, used as a means to measure the combat power of an infantry, mechanized, or armored division, focusing on the number of ground troops serving in the front line, specifically infantry, combat engineer, and reconnaissance troops. Used by higher headquarters as a tool to measure a unit's combat power or to calculate the number of troops holding a given length of front line.

Kommandeur: Unit commander, designated by official orders confirming an officer in that position, as opposed to being a *Führer*, an officer acting in a temporary command capacity.

Kommandierender General (*K.G.*): Commanding general of a corps or service command.

Korpstruppen: Corps troops, consisting of those created specifically to provide the corps' *Hauptquartier* with logistical, communications, medical, traffic control, and security support. Generally remained with the corps throughout their existence, unlike *Heerestruppen*, which were moved around constantly.

Korück: Abbreviation for *Kommando Rückwärtiges Gebiet*, the rear area or communications zone of a field army, normally commanded by a *Generalleutnant*.

Kraftfahrzeug (*Kfz.*): Any German motor vehicle, except armor.

Kraftrad (*Krad*): Motorcycle.

Kriegsberichter (*KB*): War correspondent.

Kriegsmarine: German Navy.

Kriegsstärkenachweisung (*K.St.N*): War Strength Inventory Directive, a document similar to the modern U.S. Army's table of organization that describes an organization's structure and lists the total number of personnel and major end items authorized.

Kübelwagen: Bucket car, slang term for Volkswagen equivalent of U.S. Jeep.

Landeschützen-Bataillon (*Ldsch.Btl.*): German local defense battalion, formed from older reservists. Often used for local security duties in the occupied regions or during emergencies as front-line infantry.

Landser: German slang for infantryman.

Luftflotte: Air Fleet, *Luftwaffe* administrative headquarters similar in function to an army headquarters, or *Armee-Oberkommando* (*AOK*).

Luftwaffe: German Air Force.

Mannschaften: Enlisted men.

Marder: Self-propelled antitank gun, usually mounted on an obsolete tank chassis such as a *Pz. II* or Czech 38t.

Nationalsozialistische-Führungs Offizier (*NSFO*): National Socialist Leadership Officer, who acted somewhat in the capability of cheerleader and commissar responsible not only for ensuring that everyone in the command continued to display the proper Nazi attitude, but for monitoring troops' morale and welfare. In the *Waffen-SS*, the *NSFO* was usually assigned as the VI Staff Officer. Assigned to division, corps, and field army staffs.

Nebelwerfer: "Smoke Launcher" or mobile rocket launcher firing high-explosive projectiles ranging in in size from 15 cm to 32 cm; had a distinctive moaning sound when fired, giving rise to the nickname "moaning minnies."

Oberbefehlshaber (*O.B.*): Army group commander.

Ordnungspolizei (*OrPo*): Order Police; paramilitary police force, frequently organized into battalions and regiments operating under the auspices of the SS, often used for rear-area security duties as well as for combatting partisans. During the waning months of the war, increasingly incorporated into the front lines as ordinary infantry, a task for which they were neither trained nor equipped to carry out.

Pakfront: German term for an integrated Red Army antitank gun defense, usually consisting of multiple antitank gun units, employing everything up to and including the 12.2 cm gun.

Panzerfaust: A recoilless antitank grenade launcher designed to be used against armor at ranges from 25–100 meters. It consisted of a steel launching tube, which contained a percussion-fired propellant charge, and a hollow-charge antitank grenade mounted at the end. Could penetrate up to 6 inches of rolled steel plate.

Panzerabwehrkanone (*PaK*): Antitank gun.

Panzergrenadier (*Pz.Gren.*): Armored or mechanized infantryman.

Panzerjäger: Antitank troops.

Panzergruppe (*Pz.Gr.*): Armored Group, could range in size from battalion to field army.

Panzerkampfwagen (*Pz.Kfw.*): Armored battle vehicle, or tank, called *panzer* for short.

Panzer-Korps (*Pz.Korps*): Armored corps, controlling two or more divisions of various types, though primarily trained and equipped to control armored or *Panzergrenadier* divisions.

Rollbahn: "Trunk road" or main supply route for divisions and higher.

Ritterkreuz: Knight's Cross of the Iron Cross. The *Ritterkreuz* was the highest class of the Iron Cross and the most prized of the German World War II military decorations, awarded for bravery in combat or decisive leadership in critical situations.

Sanitäter: Medic or corpsman.

Schützenpanzerwagen (*SPW*): Armored Personnel Carrier of the *Sd.Kfz. 250* or *251* type.

Schwere Panzerabteilung (*s.Pz.Abt.*): Heavy tank battalion, usually equipped with *Pz. VI* Tiger I/E or King Tiger IIb tanks.

Schwerpunkt: German term of the military art that designates where the point of main effort is for any given operation, whether offensive or defensive.

Schwimmwagen: Amphibious version of the Volkswagen.

Sicherheitsdienst (*SD*): Security Service of the SS; charged with combating or carrying out espionage.

Sicherungs-Regiment (*Sich.Rgt.*): Line of communications security regiment, often consisted of older *Landes-Schüzten* personnel. Often committed to front-line combat when situations dictated.

Sperrverbände: Blocking formations, established for the purpose of barring or blocking important roads or highways to prevent breakthroughs by enemy mobile formations. Normally formed using *Bau-Pionier* (construction engineers) or *Pioniere* equipped with his explosives, barrier materials, and antitank weapons.

SS-Führungshauptamt (*SS-FHA*): The main leadership office of the SS, responsible for coordinating the manning, equipping, and training of SS units, including the *Waffen-SS*.

Strafbataillon: Punishment battalion, usually consisting of men who have been charged with non-capital offenses and have been sent to one of these units to serve out their term of punishment, usually near the front lines and in conditions that are considered extremely hazardous. Survivors are usually restored to their previous ranks or may be posted to a *Bewährungsbataillon* (see above) for further rehabilitation.

Stuka: Short for *Sturzkampfflugzeug*, or dive bomber. Generally refers to the Junkers *Ju–87*.

Sturmabteilungen (SA): Paramilitary arm of the Nazi Party which propelled Hitler to power. Its influence was severely reduced when it attempted to compete with the SS.

Sturmgeschütz (StuG): Armored assault gun specifically built to provide close-in infantry support using its 7.5 cm or 10.5 cm howitzer. Normally built on a *Pz.Kfw. III* or *IV* chassis, they were at a disadvantage when fighting tanks in open terrain due to their lack of a rotating turret, but were formidable when employed in built-up areas or as a tank destroyer firing from hide positions.

Totenköpfler: Informal term of endearment relating to the men of the *Totenkopf* Division.

Tross: The "Trains" where a unit's logistical and administrative units were located, from company to regimental level.

Versprengte: Stragglers, i.e., soldiers separated from their unit during or after combat.

Volksgrenadier: Honorific title of an infantryman, or the divisions formed during September 1944 under a new infantry division structure designed to economize on manpower by adding additional weaponry, such as more heavy weapons and the MP-44 assault rifle.

Volkssturm: German People's Militia, founded in October 1944 by the Nazi Party. It included all German men between the ages of 16 and 60 who were not in the *Wehrmacht* or *Waffen-SS* and able to bear arms. Raising and leadership of *Volkssturm* units was entrusted to the local *Gauleiter* (District Leader) unless subordinated to field armies responsible for defending a given area. Often poorly trained and equipped, and generally unreliable in combat.

Vorgeschobener Gefechtstand: Forward command post, usually staffed by a minimum number of personnel needed for a commanding officer to control an ongoing engagement near the front lines.

Vorübergehend unterstellt: A German military term, designating a unit (company, battalion, regiment, etc.) that has been placed under the temporary tactical control of a higher level organization other than its own. The unit concerned will normally remain the administrative and logistical responsibility of its parent organization, and usually reverts to its control once a particular mission or tactical objective has been accomplished. Similar to U.S. Army/NATO terminology of TACON (tactical control).

Waffen-SS: Militarized SS; the combat arm of Heinrich Himmler's SS. When deployed in a combat zone, normally fell under the operational or tactical control of an appropriate field army or corps headquarters of the *Heer*.

Waffenwillig (*Wawis*): Term used to describe foreign "volunteers" who were willing to take up arms and fight alongside German forces. Frequently were integrated within individual German infantry squads.

Wehrkreis: Defense District, geographically designated areas in Germany and occupied areas of Europe that were designed to serve as the *Ersatzheer's* (Home Army) base for the generation and constitution of forces for the *Feldheer* (Field Army), as well as to serve as the headquarters for controlling the various local security forces and POW camps in the zone of the interior.

Wehrmacht: The German Armed Forces, which included the *Heer*, *Luftwaffe*, and *Kriegsmarine*. Technically, the *Waffen-SS* was not a part of the *Wehrmacht*.

Wehrmachtbefehlshaber: Commander of the German armed forces in a geographic area; technically, had control over all three branches of the *Wehrmacht* but not the *Waffen-SS*.

Wikinger: Informal term of endearment relating to the men of the *Wiking* Division.

Zugführer: Platoon leader, usually a senior NCO but occasionally a junior grade officer, such as a *Leutnant* or *Untersturmführer*.

Zugkraftwagen (*ZgKw*): Artillery half-tracked prime mover.

Endnotes

Chapter 1: A South Wind Brings Hope

1 Soviet General Staff, *The Budapest Operation 1945: An Operational-Strategic Study.* (Solihull, U.K.: Helion & Company Ltd, 2017), p. 324.

2 Günther Jahnke, Diary December 1944–4 August 1945 in *Truppenkameradschaft Wiking* Archives (Munich, Germany: Undated private manuscript), entry dated 12 February 1945, p. 11.

3 *H.G. Süd, Ia Tagesmeldung* dated 14 February 1945, p. 4.

4 Wolfgang Vopersal. *Soldaten, Kämpfer, Kameraden, Marsch und Kämpfe der SS-Totenkopf Division*, Vol. Vb (Bielefeld, Germany: Selbstverlag der Truppenkameradschaft der 3. SS-Pz.Div. e.V., 1991), p. 676.

5 *H.Gr. Süd, Ia KTB Anlage, Abschlussmeldung Budapest*, p. 521.

6 Vopersal, p. 676, quoting the *Wehrmachtsbericht* for 17 February 1945.

7 On 18 February, most of these "surplus" tank crewmen were shipped to Sennelager to supposedly accept the delivery of new armored vehicles. However, they were incorporated instead into other scratch SS armored units at the end of the war and did not rejoin their parent divisions (Vopersal, p. 677, and p. Klapdor, 439).

8 Erich Klapdor. *Viking Panzers: The German 5th SS Tank Regiment in the East in World War II* (Mechanicsburg, PA: Stackpole Books, 2011; translation of 1981 edition), p. 405.

9 Ian M. Wood. *Tigers of the Death's Head: SS Totenkopf Division's Tiger Company* (Mechanicsburg, VA: Stackpole Books, 2013), p. 238.

10 Vopersal, p. 677.

11 Manfred Schönfelder. "Einsatz der Verbänder der Waffen-SS auf dem Kriegsschauplatz in Ungarn in der Zeit vom 1 January–31 März 1945" (Hamburg, Germany: Unpublished manuscript in author's possession, 1 December 1981), p. 10.

12 Vopersal, 677, and Wilhelm Tieke, *Ein ruheloser Marsch war unser Leben* (Osnabrück: Munin Verlag, 1977), p. 231.

13 Vopersal, p. 678.

14 Vopersal, p. 679.

15 Jahnke Diary, entry dated 23 February 1945, p. 12.

16 Georg Maier. *Drama Between Budapest and Vienna: The Final Battles of the 6. Pz.Armee in the East—1945* (Winnipeg, Canada: J. J. Fedorowicz Publishing, 2004), pp. 429–30 quoting *H.Gr. Süd an OKH: Medlung der Absichten, Kräftegliederung und Ansatz beim Unternehmen Südwind (Gran-Brückenkopf), H.Gr. Süd Ia Nr. 42/45 gKdos. Chefs*, dated 6 p.m., 14 February 1945.

17 Maier, pp. 424–25, quoting *Befehl H.Gr. Süd: Unterbringung des I. SS-Panzerkorps, Ia Nr. 20/45 G.Kdos.*, dated 1 February 1945.

18 Despite numerous postwar comments, assertions, and claims to the contrary, Dietrich's army was never officially designated as the "6. SS-Pz.Armee." Although there is evidence in contemporary accounts that describe it as such, this title was never officially recognized by the *OKH Führungsstab*. Therefore, the writer will continue to refer to it by its official designation.

19 Maier, pp. 426–27, quoting *Befehl H.Gr. Süd: Tarn und Geheimhaltungsmassnahmen beim I. und II. SS-Panzerkorps, Ia Nr. 29/45 G.Kdos*, dated 7 February 1945.

20 Számvéber, Norbert, *Days of Battle: Armoured operations north of the river Danube, Hungary 1944–45* (Solihull, U.K.: Helion & Company, 2013), p. 226.

21 *H.Gr. Süd Ia KTB, Fernschreiben Betr: Personelle und Materielle Verluste Abschnittsstab Süd während Bereinigung Gran Brückenkopf*, dated 6:35 p.m., 9 March 1945.

22 Maier, pp. 142–43.

23 Maier, p. 142.

24 *H.Gr. Süd, Ia KTB Anlage Betr: Wochenmeldung, Stand vom 24.2.45, Ia/Id Nr. 319/45 geheim*, dated 27 January 1945, p. 5, and *Stärkemeldung alle unterstehende SS-Verbände mit Stand vom 1.3.45, Höherer Pionier-Fuhrer Ungarn, Ia/Id, Nr. 1027/45 g.kdos*, dated 18 March 1945 (Maier, p. 440).

25 *H.Gr. Süd, Ia KTB Anlage Betr: Wochenmeldung, Stand vom 24.2.45, Ia/Id Nr. 319/45 geheim*, dated 27 January 1945, p. 5, and *Stärkemeldung alle unterstehende SS-Verbände mit Stand vom 1.3.45, Höherer Pionier-Fuhrer Ungarn, Ia/Id, Nr. 1027/45 G.Kdos*, dated 18 March 1945 (Maier, p. 440).

26 Aleksei Isaev and Kolomiets Maksim. *Tomb of the Panzerwaffe: The Defeat of the Sixth SS Panzer Army in Hungary 1945* (Solihull, UK: Helion & Company Ltd, 2014). Isaev, Aleksei and Kolomiets, Maksim, *Tomb of the Panzerwaffe: The Defeat of the Sixth SS Panzer Army in Hungary 1945* (Solihull, UK: Helion & Company Ltd, 2014), pp. 101–102.

27 Maier, pp. 141–42.

28 Jahnke Diary, entry dated 24 February 1945, p. 12.

Chapter 2: Operation *Spring Awakening*

1 The interesting debate between the advocates of the different courses of actions, including the pros and cons of each, are laid out in an admirable manner in Maier's *Drama Between Budapest and Vienna*. Although it is easy to see which course of action that Maier, as the *Ia* of the 6. *Pz.Armee*, preferred, he gives all of the courses of action a fair hearing. Due to the length and scope of the debate, it will not be covered here, suffice to say that those interested in learning more about the planning leading up to the battle should read pages 148–52 in the J. J. Fedorowicz English language edition or pages 165–70 in the Munin Verlag German language edition.

2 *H.Gr. Süd Ia KTB*, entry dated 20 February 1945, p. 9.

3 Maier, the *Ia* of the 6. *Pz.Armee*, lays out a convincing argument that *Unternehmen Südwind* was a grave error, and that the gains made in reducing the Soviet bridgehead could not compensate for the loss of the element of surprise for *Frühlingserwachen* in his *Drama Between Budapest and Vienna*, pp. 141–43.

4 Jahnke Diary, entry dated 24 February 1945, p. 12.

5 *SS-Führungshauptamt, Amt. II Org.Abt. Ia/II, Betr: SS-Panzer und SS-Panzergrenadier Divisionen, Tagebuch Nr. 948/45 g.kdos*, dated 14 February 1945, and Navenkin, p. 47.

6 *H.Gr. Süd Ia KTB, Tagesmeldung*, 25 February 1945, p. 2.

7 Vopersal, p. 683.

8 *H.Gr. Süd Ia KTB, Tagesmeldung*, 25 February 1945, p. 5.

9 *H.Gr. Süd Ia KTB, Tagesmeldung*, 26 February 1945, pp. 3, 5, and Vopersal, p. 684.

10 Vopersal, p. 685.

11 *H.Gr. Süd Ia KTB, Tagesmeldung*, 27 February 1945, p. 3.

12 Maier, p. 153.

13 Maier, p. 167.

14 Maier, p. 166.

15 *3. SS-Pz.Div. Totenkopf, Zustandbericht*, 1 March 1945.

16 *5. SS-Pz.Div. Wiking, Zustandbericht*, 1 March 1945.

17 Maier, p. 166, and *H.Gr. Süd, Chef des Generalstabes, Fernschreiben Ia Nr. 2846/45 geheim, Betr: Massnahmen gegen ungarische Überläufer*, dated 3 March 1945.

18 Maier, p. 167.

19 *H.Gr. Süd Ia KTB, Tagesmeldung*, 2 March 1945, pp. 2–3.

20 Vopersal, p. 690.

21 *H.Gr. Süd Ia KTB, Tagesmeldung*, 3 March 1945, p. 4.

22 Vopersal, p. 691.

23 Vopersal, p. 691.

24 *Stärkemeldungen der 3. SS-Pz.Div. Totenkopf* and *5. SS-Pz.Div. Wiking vom 4.3.45*, dated 4 March 1945.

25 *H.Gr. Süd Ia KTB, Tagesmeldung*, 5 March 1945, p. 3.

26 Center for Land Warfare, U.S. Army War College, David Glantz, ed. *1986 Art of War Symposium*, "From the Vistula to the Oder: Soviet Offensive Operations—October 1944 to March 1945" (Carlisle, PA: U.S. Army War College, May 1986), p. 722 (Hereafter referred to as Glantz, *From the Vistual to the Oder*).

27 Karl-Heinz Frieser (editor and contributing author), Klaus Schmider, Klaus Schönherr, Gerhard Schreiber, Krisztian Ungvary and Bernd Wegner. *Germany and the Second World War, Vol. VIII: The Eastern Front 1943–1944—The War in the East and on Neighboring Fronts* (Oxford: Clarendon Press, 2017), p. 945.

28 *H.Gr. Süd Ia KTB, Tagesmeldung*, 7 March 1945, p. 3, and Vopersal, p. 699.

29 Vopersal, p. 699.

30 Vopersal, p. 700.

31 Maier, p. 192, and Vopersal, pp. 699–700.

32 *H.Gr. Süd Ia KTB, Tagesmeldung*, 9 March 1945, p. 5.

33 Maier, pp. 194–95, and Vopersal, pp. 700–01.

34 *H.Gr. Süd Hauptquartier, Ia KTB, Fährten des O.B. in der ersten Märzhalfte*, dated 12 March 1945.

35 *Gen.Kdo. IV. SS-Pz.Korps, Adjutantur IIa, Korps-Gefechtstand*, 9 March 1915.

36 Maier, p. 197.

37 Maier, pp. 197–98.

38 Maier, pp. 197–98, Vopersal, pp. 703–04, and *Planung H.Gr. Süd für Teilangriff des IV. SS-Pz. Korps nördlich Stuhlweissenburg, H.Gr. Süd Ia Nr. 100/45 g.Kdos. Chef*, dated 10 February 1945, reproduced in Maier (Munin Verlag German Language version), p. 571.

39 Vopersal, p. 704, and Young, Desmond, *Rommel the Desert Fox* (New York: Harper and Row, 1964), pp. 12, 195. Ranks in the *Waffen-SS* and *Allgemeine-SS* were not considered interchangeable, especially since many of the ranks in the *Allgemeine-SS* were politically based or honorary. Usually, whenever an officer who had served in the *Allgemeine-SS* in a non-military capacity was transferred to the *Waffen-SS*, his rank would be downgraded by one or two grades.

40 Maier, p. 203.

41 Vopersal, p. 207.

42 *H.Gr. Süd Ia KTB, Tagesmeldung*, 13 March 1945, p. 3.

43 Maier, p. 207.

44 Vopersal, p. 708.

45 Vopersal, p. 709.

46 Maier, p. 211.

47   Schönfelder Manuscript, entry dated 14 March 1945, p. 12.

48   Maier, p. 211.

49   Maier, p. 212.

50   Schönfelder Manuscript, entry dated 14 March 1945, p. 12. On 14 March, Balck directed one of his staff officers, *Hauptmann* Rabe, to personally conduct an inventory of the available reserves within the *IV. SS-Pz.Korps. Aktennotiz H.Gr. Süd, Betr: Reserven des IV. SS-Panzerkorps*, dated 14 March 1945.

51   *H.Gr. Süd Ia KTB, Tagesmeldung*, 14 March 1945, p. 5.

52   Maier, p. 212.

53   Schönfelder Manuscript, entry dated 14 March 1945, p. 12.

54   *H.Gr. Süd Ia KTB, Tagesmeldung*, 14 March 1945, p. 3; Maier, p. 210; Vopersal, p. 711; and *Kriegstagebuch des OKW 1944–1945, Teilband 2*, entry dated 15 March 1945, p. 1173.

55   Maier, p. 213.

56   *H.Gr. Süd Ia KTB, Morgenmeldung*, 15 March 1945, p. 2.

57   Vopersal, p. 715.

58   Erich Kern. *Die Letzte Schlacht, Ungarn 1944–45* (Göttingen: Verlag K. W. Schütz, 1960), pp. 218–22. Incidentally, Graf von Rittberg was arrested by a flying court-martial and shot in Haidholz, Austria, for treason on 12 April 1945. What act of treason he actually or allegedly committed is unknown, although some sources believe that it was the belated discovery of his complicity in the 20 July 1944 assassination plot against Hitler (source: http://www.sagen.at/fotos/showphoto. php/photo/21271, accessed 4 March 2018, which depicts the large monument erected in Austria to honor his memory).

59   Frieser, *et al.*, *Germany and the Second World War*, Vol. VIII, p. 940.

60   Maier, pp. 221–22.

61   Peter Goszton. *Endkampf an der Donau, 1944/45* (Vienna: Verlag Fritz Molden, 1969), p. 231.

62   Kuznetzov, P. G., *Marschall Tolbukhin 1894–1949* (Moscow: Progress Publishers, 1966), p. 235.

63   Maier, p. 233, quotes *H.Gr. Süd Ia KTB, Tagesmeldung* for 17 March 1945, p. 9. This number does not account for Soviet troops wounded or missing.

64   G.F. Krivosheyev, *Soviet Casualties and Combat Losses in the Twentieth Century* (London: Greenhill Books, 1997), p. 110.

Chapter 3: The Defense of Stuhlweissenburg

1   Frieser, *et al.*, *Germany and the Second World War*, Vol. VIII, pp. 942–43.

2   On 1 March 1945, Col.Gen. N. D. Zakhvatayev replaced General Zakharov, who was transferred to become the deputy commander of the Fourth Ukrainian Front (Source: http://www.warheroes. ru/hero/hero.asp?Hero_id=5460, accessed on 15 May 2020).

3   Frieser, p. 944.

4   Gosztony, p. 233.

5   Frieser, p. 943.

6   Glantz, *From the Vistula to the Oder*, pp. 721, 755.

7   Frieser, p. 943.

8   Earl F. Ziemke. *Stalingrad to Berlin: The German Defeat in the East* (Washington, D.C.: U.S. Army Center of Military History, 2002), p. 455.

9   Vopersal, p. 716.

10   A Major Feuchtleben of the Hungarian Army, who survived the attack, later wrote that the Germans "sent me an *SS-Untersturmführer* with 20 men as a reserve, which could only be employed on the direction of their own commanders. Therefore, they were positioned behind us, possibly to keep us in check." (Vopersal, p. 709).

11 Maier, p. 228.

12 *H.Gr Süd Ia KTB, Morgenmeldung*, dated 16 March 1945.

13 Maier, pp. 213–14.

14 Jahnke Diary, entry dated 16 March 1945, p. 12; Herbert O. Gille, "Angriff zum Entsatz der Stadt Budapest, Dezember 1944–8 Mai 1945" In *Truppenkameradschaft Wiking* Archives (Stemmen, Germany: Undated private manuscript), p. 4; Klapdor, p. 417, quoting Kerckhoff; and Vopersal, quoting Brunst, p. 717.

15 Schönfelder Manuscript, entry dated 16 March 1945, p. 12.

16 Gosztony, p. 233.

17 *H.Gr Süd Ia KTB, Tagesmeldung*, dated 16 March 1945, pp. 4–5.

18 Maier, p. 223.

19 Maier, p. 224.

20 Maier, pp. 228–29, quoting letter from Herbert Brunst to Peter Gosztony, dated 5 January 1974.

21 Maier, p. 224. In the *H.Gr. Süd KTB*, von Grolman's note stated "on 15 March 1945 the commander in chief [i.e., *Generaloberst* Wöhler] went to *A.Gr. Balck* and to the *6. Pz.Armee* to discuss the situation and other details as well … *Gen.d.Pz.Tr.* Balck displayed his well-known optimism in his estimate of the situation, [but] even there it was out of place," which Maier interpreted as Balck's erroneous evaluation of the situation. By this point, Maier claims, Wöhler was becoming increasingly annoyed by Balck's "carefree high-handedness towards *H.Gr. Süd*," but also characterized it as a typical case of Balck's "situation estimates" being used as "self-serving estimates" as well (Maier, p. 223).

22 Klapdor, p. 417.

23 Vopersal, quoting Hack, p. 717.

24 Vopersal, p. 717.

25 Vopersal, p. 717, quoting Messerle.

26 Vopersal, p. 718.

27 Vopersal, p. 718.

28 Vopersal, p. 718.

29 *H.Gr Süd Ia KTB, Tagesmeldung*, dated 16 March 1945, p. 5.

30 *H.Gr Süd Ia KTB, Morgenmeldung*, dated 17 March 1945, p. 2.

31 *H.Gr Süd Ia KTB, Tagesmeldung*, dated 17 March 1945, p. 1.

32 *H.Gr. Süd Ia KTB, Fernschreiben Ia Nr. 960/45 g.Kdos., Betr: Unterstellung des. III. Pz.Korps unter 6. Pz.Armee*, dated 16 March 1945.

33 *H.Gr Süd Ia KTB, Tagesmeldung*, dated 17 March 1945, p. 5.

34 Maier, p. 227.

35 Maier, pp. 227–28.

36 Maier, p. 228.

37 Maier, p. 229.

38 Maier, p. 233.

39 *H.Gr Süd Ia KTB, Morgenmeldung*, dated 18 March 1945, p. 1.

40 Maier, p. 234.

41 Jahnke Diary, entry dated 18 March 1945, p. 13.

42 *Deutsches Rotes Kreuz, Suchdients München: Heimkehrer-Erklärungen von Hans Penckwitt*, dated 4 May 1960, and Wilhelm Kisling, 6 July 1968, and Oskar Stanzel, 10 April 1959 (Courtesy of Tommy Natedal), as well as John Moore's *SS-Führerliste*.

43 Kursietis and Munoz, p. 57, and "RFSS-Brigade Ney" at *Hungarian formations of the Waffen SS and Sondertruppen der Reichsführung-SS*, found at http://www.hunyadi.co.uk/page5.php, accessed 18 May 2020.

44 *H.Gr Süd Ia KTB, Tagesmeldung*, dated 18 March 1945, pp. 4–5.

45 Klapdor, pp. 417–18.

46 Vopersal, p. 727.

47 Wood, pp. 241–42.

48 Wood, p. 241.

49 *Rochade*, a German chess term for a castling move.

50 Maier, pp. 240–41.

51 Schönfelder Manuscript, entry dated 18 March 1945, p. 14.

52 Maier, p. 240, and Balck, p. 422.

53 *H.Gr Süd Ia KTB, Morgenmeldung*, dated 19 March 1945, pp. 1–2.

54 Jahnke Diary, entry dated 19 March 1945, p. 13.

55 *H.Gr Süd Ia KTB, Tagesmeldung*, dated 19 March 1945, pp. 1–4.

56 Schönfelder Manuscript, entry dated 19 March 1945, p. 14.

57 Rolf Stoves. 1. *Panzer-Division 1935–1945: Chronik einer der drei Stamm-Divisionen der deutschen Panzerwaffe* (Bad Nauheim, Germany: Verlag Hans-Henning Podzun, 1961), p. 755.

58 *H.Gr Süd Ia KTB, Tagesmeldung*, dated 19 March 1945, p. 8.

59 Maier, pp. 244–45.

Chapter 4: The Storm Breaks

1 *H.Gr. Süd Ia KTB, Morgenmeldung*, dated 20 March 1945, p. 1.

2 *H.Gr. Süd Ia KTB, Tagesmeldung*, dated 20 March 1945, pp. 5–6.

3 *H.Gr. Süd Ia KTB, Tagesmeldung*, dated 20 March 1945, p. 4.

4 *H.Gr. Süd Ia KTB Anlage, Fernschreiben an OKH/Gen.St.d.H./Opr.Abt, Betr: Nachmeldung zur Wochenmeldung, H.Gr. Süd Ia/Id Nr. 1021.45 g.Kdos*, dated 12:35 p.m., 20 March 1945, p. 2.

5 Maier, pp. 241, 244–45. Friction between the two field army headquarters persisted concerning this issue; *Gen.d.Pz.Tr.* Balck continued holding on to the main body of the *Hohenstaufen* Division despite numerous orders given by *H.Gr. Süd* to release it to the *6. Pz.Armee*.

6 Maier, p. 249.

7 Gosztony, p. 239.

8 *H.Gr Süd Ia KTB, Tagesmeldung*, dated 20 March 1945, pp. 1–6.

9 *H.Gr Süd Ia KTB, Tagesmeldung*, dated 20 March 1945, p. 6.

10 *Brigadeführer* Fritz Kraemer, the talented chief of staff of the *6. Pz.Armee*, was a graduate of the *Kriegsakademie* class of 1935 and had been serving as a general staff army in the *Heer* until he was *Abkommandiert* (detailed to serve in a temporary duty capacity) to the *Waffen-SS* on 1 August 1944 due to its lack of qualified general staff officers (refer to Volume 1).

11 Schönfelder Manuscript, entry dated 20 March 1945, p. 15. Csór was still under German control, held by a small *Kampfgruppe* centered around one of the *Wiking* Division's artillery battalions and a *Sturmgeschütz* battery.

12 Maier, pp. 251–53. Admittedly, Maier is a partisan concerning this particular issue, but a simple review of the daily reports of *H.Gr. Süd* between 18 and 23 March reflect that Wöhler repeatedly directed Balck to release this division to the *6. Pz.Armee*. It does not seem that Balck suffered any repercussions for his curious actions that very nearly resulted in the complete destruction of the *Wiking* Division as well as his own army.

13 *H.Gr Süd Ia KTB, Tagesmeldung*, dated 20 March 1945, pp. 9–10.

14 *H.Gr Süd Ia KTB, Anlage Meldungen und Befehle, Ia/O.Qu. Nr. 1011/45 g.Kdos.*, dated 1:41 p.m., 20 March 1945.

15 Vopersal, pp. 756–57.

16 *H.Gr Süd Ia KTB, Tagesmeldung*, dated 21 March 1945, p. 9.

17 Jahnke Diary, entry dated 21 March 1945, pp. 13–14.

18 *H.Gr Süd Ia KTB, Tagesmeldung*, dated 21 March 1945, 3, pp. 7–8.

19 *H.Gr Süd Ia KTB, Tagesmeldung*, dated 21 March 1945, p. 1.

20 Ibid.

21 Klapdor, p. 421.

22 *H.Gr Süd Ia KTB, Tagesmeldung*, dated 21 March 1945, p. 18, and Klapdor, p. 426.

23 Franz Hack and Fritz Hahl. *Panzergrenadiere der Panzerdivision Wiking im Bild.* (Osnabruck: Munin Verlag GmbH, 1984), pp. 234–235. Hereafter referred to as Hack and Hahl, *Panzergrenadiere der Panzerdivision Wiking im Bild.*

24 Jahnke Diary, entry dated 21 March 1945, p. 14.

25 Klapdor, p. 427.

26 Darges account in Klapdor, pp. 422–23.

27 *H.Gr Süd Ia KTB, Tagesmeldung*, dated 22 March 1945, p. 7. Between 19 and 23 March 1945, the *Hohenstaufen* Division had been subordinated to the *II. SS-Pz.Korps*, the *III. Pz.Korps*, the *I. Kav.Korps*, the *IV. SS-Pz.Korps*, and finally back to the *I. Kav.Korps*, in that order. Therefore, it is not surprising that *Oberf.* Stadler and his staff were having such a difficult time in carrying out the division's mission, faced as they were with so many conflicting orders and guidance from so many different higher headquarters during such a chaotic and action-filled point in time when radio and land-line telephone communications were lacking or infrequent.

28 Gunter Bernau. *SS-Panzer Artillerie-Regiment 5 in der Panzer-Division Wiking* (Wuppertal, Germany: Eigenverlag Kameradschaft ehem. Pz.Art.Rgt. 5, 1990), p. 150.

29 Jahnke Diary, entry dated 22 March 1945, p. 15.

30 Klapdor, p. 425.

31 Peter Strassner. *European Volunteers: 5 SS Panzer Division Wiking* (Winnipeg, Canada: J. J. Fedorowicz Publishing, 1988), p. 207.

32 Jahnke Diary, entries dated 21–22 March 1945, pp. 14–15.

33 Bernau, pp. 148–49.

34 Gille Notebook, entry dated 23 March 1945, p. 4.

35 Maier, pp. 256–58. Maier provides a good accounting of the blizzard of messages that passed back and forth from 21–23 March, which gives the reader a good idea of just how dysfunctional the Third Reich's military leadership in general had become, particularly under the guidance of Adolf Hitler, whose poor judgement and inflexible commands often made a bad situation worse. It was further complicated when some of the actors, notably Hermann Balck, bypassed the normal chain of command and violated military protocol by contacting Guderian directly, skipping over his immediate commander, Otto Wöhler. Ironically, this was the same violation of military protocol that Balck had repeatedly accused Gille and other SS officers of committing.

36 Balck, p. 421.

37 *H.Gr Süd Ia KTB, Tagesmeldung*, dated 21 March 1945, p. 8.

38 *H.Gr Süd Ia KTB, Morgenmeldung*, dated 22 March 1945, p. 1.

39 *H.Gr Süd Ia KTB, Tagesmeldung*, dated 22 March 1945, pp. 2–3.

40 *H.Gr Süd Ia KTB, Tagesmeldung*, dated 22 March 1945, p. 2.

41 Balck, p. 421.

42 Schimak, Anton, Lamprechts, Karl and Dettmer, Friedrich, *Die 44. Infanterie-Division: Tagebuch Hoch und Deutschmeister* (Vienna: Verlag Austria Press, 1969), pp. 343–44.

43 Stoves, pp. 761–68.

44 *H.Gr Süd Ia KTB, Tagesmeldung*, dated 22 March 1945, p. 2.

45 *H.Gr Süd Ia KTB, Tagesmeldung*, dated 22 March 1945, p. 1.

46 Andreas Kunz, *Wehrmacht und Niederlage: Die bewaffnete Macht n der Endphase der nationalso-zialistischen Herrschaft 1944 bis 1945* (Munich: R. Oldenbourg Verlag, 2007), p. 278.

47 Kunz, p. 278.

48 *H.Gr Süd Ia KTB, Tagesmeldung*, dated 22 March 1945, p. 11.

49 *H.Gr. Süd Ia KTB, Oberbefehlshaber H.Gr. Süd für KTB*, dated 24 March 1945.

50 *H.Gr Süd Ia KTB, Tagesmeldung*, dated 22 March 1945, p. 7.

51 *H.Gr. Süd Ia KTB, Meldungen und Befehle, Ia Nr. 1068/45*, dated 11:15 p.m., 22 March 1945.

52 *H.Gr Süd Ia KTB, Tagesmeldung*, dated 23 March 1945, p. 1.

53 *H.Gr Süd Ia KTB, Stärkemeldung der Heeresgruppe, Ia/Id Nr. 1038/45 g.kdos.*, dated 21 March 1945, Muster I.

54 *H.Gr Süd Ia KTB, Anlage, Zustandbericht der Divisionen der H.Gr. Süd*, 17 March 1945.

55 *H.Gr. Süd Ia KTB*, dated 23 March 1945, p. 2.

56 While the war diary of *H.Gr. Süd* does not mention the *Hohenstaufen* as actually having been attached to the *IV. SS-Pz.Korps* on that date, the manner in which it was employed on 23 March makes it clear that it was fighting in the sector held by Gille's corps and was operating under his control. On account of the extremely fluid tactical situation, of which the headquarters of the 6. *Armee* seemed to be having difficulty keeping itself fully cognizant, it is understandable that there was confusion about the status of the *Hohenstaufen's* higher command.

57 Ralf Tiemann, *The Leibstandarte IV/2* (Winnipeg, Canada: J. J. Fedorowicz Publishing, 1998), pp. 255–56. This is the authorized English language edition of Tiemann's German language version published by Munin-Verlag in 1986.

58 Tiemann, pp. 256–57.

59 Teimann, p. 256.

60 *H.Gr. Süd Ia KTB*, dated 23 March 1945, p. 11. It would have made more sense to subordinate *Div.K.Gr. LSSAH* to Gille's corps, which was responsible for defending Veszprem. Although Balck could not directly contact Kumm by radio, Gille's headquarters was less than 10 kilometers away and could very well have executed direct command and control of *Div.K.Gr. LSSAH* by the use of liaison officers to transmit instructions.

61 *H.Gr. Süd Ia KTB*, dated 23 March 1945, p. 15.

62 Ibid. Wöhler should have called Balck's bluff; by this point, his insubordinate field army commander had become an obstacle to the effective conduct of operations by the two armies and should have been immediately replaced. As it turned out, Wöhler and his chief of staff were the ones to be fired by Hitler, not Balck or Gaedke.

63 Maier, pp. 287–88, 290. When reading about it, this entire episode conveys a certain amount of unreality; for a field army commander to repeatedly ignore the direct orders of his army group commander, not once, but numerous times, is certainly a rarity in the history of the German Armed Forces. Unaccountably, Balck fails to mention this rather inexplicable incident in his memoirs.

64 *H.Gr Süd Ia KTB, Tagesmeldung*, dated 23 March 1945, p. 2.

65 Frieser, *et al.*, *Germany in the Second World War*, Vol. VIII, p. 946.

66 Herbert Fürbringer, *9. SS-Panzer-Division 1944: Normanie–Tarnopol–Arnhem* (Paris: Editions Heimdahl, 1984), p. 519.

67 Frieser, *et al.*, *Germany in the Second World War*, Vol. VIII, p. 946.

68 Fürbringer, p. 518.

69 Hermann Black. *Order in Chaos: The Memoirs of General of Panzer Troops Hermann Balck* (Lexington, KY: The University Press of Kentucky, 2015), p. 421.

70 Ibid.

71 Fürbringer, 521.

72 Wilhelm Tieke, *In the Firestorm of the Last Years of the War: The II. SS-Panzerkorps with the 9. and 10. SS-Divisions "Hohenstaufen" and "Frundsberg"* (Winnipeg, Canada: J. J. Fedorowicz Publishing, 1999,

English translation of the original 1975 Munin-Verlag edition), pp. 389–90. Interestingly, Balck had a previous encounter with the *Hohenstaufen* Division a year before during the battle of Ternopol, when he was commanding the *XLVIII. Pz.Korps*. During this battle in April 1944, he claimed that the division had not attacked when it was supposed to and failed to hold its position when it was later attacked. These accusations were proven to be unfounded at the time, as shown in the official records. Evidently, Balck, who never forgot a perceived slight, carried this animus towards yet another formation of the *Waffen-SS* with him to Hungary, manifesting itself when Balck needed yet another convenient scapegoat upon which he could place the blame for his own shortcomings (Tieke, p. 390).

73 Maier, p. 262.

74 Maier, pp. 465–66. In the Munin Verlag edition, the actual telex messages are reproduced.

75 Maier, p. 272.

76 Gille Notebook, entry dated 23 March 1945, p. 4.

77 Maier, p. 271.

78 *H.Gr Süd Ia KTB, Tagesmeldung*, dated 23 March 1945, p. 3. The term "special judicial powers" (*mit besondern Vollmachten*) generally connotes flying courts martial empowered to use summary execution if necessary.

79 Balck, p. 422.

80 Edgar F. Puryear Jr, *Nineteen Stars: a Study in Military Character and Leadership* (Fairfax, Virginia: Coiner Publications, Ltd, 1971), p. 289.

81 *H.Gr Süd Ia KTB, Tagesmeldung*, dated 23 March 1945, pp. 18–19, and Balck, pp. 421–22.

82 *H.Gr. Süd KTB, Fernschreiben Ia Nr. 1100/45 g.Kdos. Betr: Waffen-SS*, dated 11:50 p.m., 23 March 1945. English translation courtesy of Fedorowicz edition of *Drama Between Budapest and Vienna*, Appendix 105, p. 466.

83 For more, refer to Maier, pp. 271–72, 275, 278–79 (Fedorowicz English edition). Upon reading it, one must come away with the impression that the German high command in Hungary was out of its mind, indulging as it did in such controversies when its leaders should have been focused instead on winning the ongoing battle.

84 Jahnke Diary, entry dated 23 March 1945, p. 16.

85 Gille Notebook, entry dated 23 March 1945, p. 4.

86 *H.Gr Süd Ia KTB, Tagesmeldung*, dated 23 March 1945, p. 3.

87 Ibid.

88 Tieke, p. 388.

89 Vopersal, p. 793.

Chapter 5: The Retreat from Hungary

1 Balck, p. 421.

2 Maier, p. 283, Endnote 669.

3 Gaedke, p. 240.

4 *H.Gr. Süd Ia KTB Anlage, Meldungen und Befehle, Ia Nr. 1091/45*, dated 8:05 p.m., 24 March 1945.

5 *H.Gr. Süd Ia KTB, Tagesmeldung*, dated 24 March 1945, p. 1.

6 The *Hohenstaufen* Division was attached once again to the *I. Kav.Korps* during the evening of 23/24 March 1945 (Tieke, p. 389). In addition, the battered 44. Reichs-Gren.Div. HuD was temporarily subordinated to the 23. Pz.Div. until it could be withdrawn for reconstitution in the 2. Pz.Armee area of operations.

7 *H.Gr. Süd Ia KTB, Tagesmeldung*, dated 24 March 1945, p. 2. *Div.K.Gr. LSSAH* was one of two battle groups formed by the division at this time, one to fight in the north in the defense of Papa as part of the *I. SS-Pz.Korps* and the other with the *6. Armee*. It consisted of *SS-Pz.Gren.Rgt. 1*,

most of *SS-Pz.Rgt. 1*, elements of *SS-Flak.Abt. 1*, and the division's antitank battalion, led by the division commander, *Brig.Fhr.* Otto Kumm.

8   Vopersal, p. 805, and Strassner, pp. 207–08.

9   Ralf Tiemann, *The Leibstandarte*, IV/2 (Winnipeg, Canada: J. J. Fedorowicz Publishing, 1998), pp. 259–60.

10 *H.Gr. Süd Ia KTB, Tagesmeldung*, dated 24 March 1945, p. 6. On 23 March 1945, the *232. Pz.Div.* had only one *Pz. IV*, 13 *SPW*s, four self-propelled *Pak*s, and seven towed *Pak*s (Navenkin, p. 604).

11 Tiemann, p. 259–60.

12 *H.Gr. Süd Ia KTB, Tagesmeldung*, dated 24 March 1945, pp. 2, 7.

13 *H.Gr. Süd Ia KTB Tagesmeldung*, dated 24 March 1945, p. 7.

14 Maier, pp. 269–70.

15 Tieke, p. 259.

16 On this same day, Balck complained to Wöhler when the latter visited his command post that the *IV. SS-Pz.Korps* had failed to position a battalion behind the Hungarian *1. Hus.Div.*, which led to its collapse when attacked on 16 March. This is patently untrue, as previously detailed in Chapter 1. Gille had ordered Becker to place a battalion at that location, which he did, though one *Waffen-SS* battalion was not nearly strong enough to hold back the onrushing tide of the vastly superior Soviet attacking force (*H.Gr. Süd Ia KTB, Tagesmeldung*, dated 24 March 1945, p. 16).

17 The *6. Armee*'s material readiness reports (*Panzerlage*) for the period 18–27 March are lacking, except for that of the *1. Pz.Div.* On 24 March, after the breakout from the "Jenö Pocket" east of Lake Balaton, it reported having five operational *Pz. V* Panthers, four 7.5cm *Pak*s, five 2cm *Flak*s, and 16 artillery and field pieces. It had many more damaged or broken down tanks that its repair services had been able to recover. As weak as these figures reveal it to be, it was still the most powerful division in Balck's army. (*H.Gr. Süd KTB, Anlage, Fernschreiben, Betr: Zustand der 1. Pz.Div. nach dem Stand vom 24.3.45*, dated 10:50 a.m., 25 March 1945).

18 *H.Gr. Süd KTB, Anlage, Fernschreiben Ia Nr. 119/45*, dated 2:20 p.m., 24 March 1945. This order specifically singled out *Waffen-SS* units, informing them that they were also required to obey a *Führerbefehl* in regards to the treatment of deserters.

19 *H.Gr. Süd KTB, Anlage, Fernschreiben Ia Nr. 1200/45*, dated 2:10 a.m., 28 March 1945.

20 Frieser, *et al.*, 948, quoting a *Meldung von Chef des Stabes der H.Gr. Süd am 3.4.1945*.

21 *H.Gr. Süd KTB, Anlage, Fernschreiben Ia Nr. 4039/45*, dated 1:50 p.m., 24 March 1945, referenced in Maier, pp. 467–68.

22 Glantz, Situation Briefing 23 March 1945 in *From the Vistula to the Oder*, pp. 700–01.

23 *H.Gr. Süd KTB, Anlage, Fernschreiben Ia Nr. 1110/45*, dated 12:45 p.m., 24 March 1945, referenced in Maier, p. 468.

24 *H.Gr. Süd KTB, Anlage, Fernschreiben Ia Nr. 1115/45*, dated 8:30 p.m., 24 March 1945, referenced in Maier, p. 468.

25 *H.Gr. Süd KTB, Anlage, Fernschreiben Ia Nr. 116/45, Betr: KR-Blitz Nr. 45124/45 g.Kdos.Chefsache von 23.3.45*, dated 12:10 p.m., 24 March 1945, referenced in Maier, pp. 468–69.

26 Heinz Guderian. *Panzer Leader* (New York: Ballantyne Books, 1957), pp. 356–57.

27 Wolf Keilig. *Das Deutsche Heer*, Vol. III, Section 211, "Die Generalität des Heeres im 2. Weltkrieg." (Bad Neuheim: Podzun-Verlag, 1956), p. 112.

28 Balck, pp. 421–22.

29 Traditionsverband der 3. Pz.Div., *Geschichte der 3. Panzer-Division Berlin-Brandenburg 1935–1945* (Berlin: Gunter Richter Verlag, 1967), p. 471.

30 *H.Gr. Süd Ia KTB, Morgenmeldung*, dated 25 March 1945, p. 1.

31 *H.Gr. Süd Ia KTB, Tagesmeldung*, dated 25 March 1945, p. 1.

32 *H.Gr. Süd Ia KTB, Tagesmeldung*, dated 25 March 1945, p. 2.

33 Frieser, *et al.*, p. 948. According to Soviet sources, on 25 March 1945, as many as 57 captured German armored fighting vehicles were placed back into operation by troops of the Third Ukrainian Front against their former owners.

34 *KTB, s.Pz.Abt. 509*, entry dated 25 March 1945, p. 26.

35 *Geschichte der 3. Panzer-Division*, p. 471.

36 *H.Gr. Süd Ia KTB, Tagesmeldung*, dated 25 March 1945, p. 12.

37 Jahnke Diary, entry dated 25 March 1945, p. 16.

38 Strassner, p. 208.

39 *H.Gr. Süd Ia KTB, Tagesmeldung*, dated 25 March 1945, pp. 2, 7.

40 *H.Gr. Süd Ia KTB, Tagesmeldung*, dated 25 March 1945, p. 9.

41 Tiemann, pp. 259–60.

42 Tiemann, pp. 260–61.

43 *H.Gr. Süd, Ia KTB Anlage, Fernschreiben, Ia Nr. 1135/45 g.Kdos.*, dated 2:30 a.m., 25 March 1945.

44 Schimak, *et al.*, pp. 344–45. Apparently, *Geb.Art.Rgt. 96* was temporarily attached to *III. Pz.Korps* because its movement route led it around to the northern flank of *6. Armee*, causing it to be employed in support of Breith's corps.

45 *H.Gr. Süd, Ia KTB Anlage, Fernschreiben, Ia Nr. 1123/45 g.Kdos.*, dated 1:50 a.m., 25 March 1945. It also had managed to evacuate 30–35 of the *panzer* regiment's damaged tanks along with its tank repair shop to a safe location within Austria (Stoves, pp. 775–76).

46 *H.Gr. Süd, Ia KTB Anlage, Fernschreiben, Ia Nr. 1131/45 g.Kdos.*, dated 12:40 a.m., 25 March 1945.

47 *H.Gr. Süd Ia KTB, Tagesmeldung*, dated 25 March 1945, p. 5.

48 Manfried Rauchsteiner, *Der Krieg in Österreich* 1945 (Vienna: Österreichischer Bundesverlag 1984), pp. 99–101.

49 *H.Gr. Süd Ia KTB, Tagesmeldung*, dated 26 March 1945, p. 1.

50 Jahnke Diary, entry dated 26 March 1945, p. 16.

51 Schönfelder Manuscript, entry dated 26 March 1945, p. 17.

52 Balck, p. 423.

53 Maier, p. 267, and Schönfelder, pp. 19–21.

54 Heinz Gaedke and Gerhard Brugmann. *Wege eines Soldaten* (Norderstedt: Books on Demand, 2005), p. 240.

55 *H.Gr. Süd Ia KTB, Tagesmeldung*, dated 26 March 1945, pp. 1–2.

56 *Geschichte der 3. Panzer-Division*, p. 470.

57 Karl Reuther and Ulrich Ulms, MS # B-735, *Reflections and Experiences, Command Mission of Corps Headquarters (XII. SS-Armee Korps)* (Neustadt: U.S. Army Europe Historical Division, 11 January 1948), p. 5.

58 *H.Gr. Süd Ia KTB, Anlage, Fernschreiben Ia Nr. 1162/45 g.Kdos.*, dated 8:50 p.m., 26 March 1945.

59 The official records do not specify the exact size and composition of this *Kampfgruppe*; it was most likely of battalion size or less, since the rest of *Div.K.Gr. LSSAH* had already departed the area.

60 *Kampfgruppe Bradel* consisted of the two *Kampf* battalions of the *1. Pz.Div.*, its few remaining armored fighting vehicles, and its SP artillery. The rest of the division, consisting essentially of its non-fighting elements, remained in the army's rear area.

61 *H.Gr. Süd Ia KTB, Tagesmeldung*, dated 27 March 1945, p. 1.

62 *Geschichte der 3. Panzer-Division*, p. 472.

63 *Ibid.*

64 Schönfelder Manuscript, entry dated 27 March 1945, p. 17.

65 Jahnke Diary, entry dated 27 March 1945, p. 17.

66 *H.Gr. Süd Ia KTB*, dated 27 March 1945, p. 10.

67 *H.Gr. Süd Ia KTB, Tagesmeldung*, dated 27 March 1945, p. 7.

68 Tieke, p. 261.

69 *H.Gr. Süd Ia KTB Anlage, Fernschreiben Ia Nr. 1154/45 g.Kdos.*, dated 10:30 p.m., 26 March 1945.

70 *H.Gr. Süd Ia KTB Anlage, Fernschreiben Ia Nr. 1186/45 g.Kdos.*, dated 12:00 p.m., 27 March 1945.

71 *H.Gr. Süd Ia KTB, Tagesmeldung*, dated 27 March 1945, pp. 3–4.

72 *H.Gr. Süd Ia KTB, Tagesmeldung*, dated 28 March 1945, p. 1.

73 Stoves, pp. 775–76, and *Geschichte der 3. Panzer-Division*, p. 472.

74 Jahnke Diary, entry dated 28 March 1945, p. 17.

75 *Geschichte der 3. Panzer-Division*, p. 472.

76 *H.Gr. Süd Ia KTB, Tagesmeldung*, dated 28 March 1945, p. 6. The strongest combat element of *III. Pz.Korps* was the aforementioned *1. Volks-Geb.Div.*, which was assessed as having one medium-strong infantry battalion, four average battalions, two weak battalions, and one average combat engineer battalion. It had 10 heavy antitank guns (including two attached from the *1. Pz.Div.*), 10 light and one heavy artillery batteries, and a mobility rating of 70 percent. Its commander awarded it a *Kampfwert* of "II." The rest of *III. Pz.Korps'* infantry forces were grouped under *K.Gr. Krause*, consisting of four subordinate battle groups composed of men from a variety of units with varying composition.

77 *H.Gr. Süd Ia KTB Anlage, Panzerlage Stand 1.4.45*, dated 1 April 1945.

78 Schönfelder Manuscript, entry dated 28 March 1945, p. 17.

79 *Ibid.*

80 Maier, pp. 311–13. In his book, Maier goes into additional details concerning the behind-the-scenes tug of war between Generals Balck and de Angelis about the ultimate control of the *I. Kav.Korps*. De Angelis ultimately presents a more convincing argument than Balck.

81 *H.Gr. Süd Ia KTB Anlage, Nachmeldung zur Wochenmeldung, Ia/Id Nr. 1187/45 g.Kdos.*, dated 7 p.m., 28 March 1945, p. 1.

82 *H.Gr. Süd Ia KTB Anlage, Nachmeldung zur Wochenmeldung*, dated 31 March 1945, found in Traditionsverband der 3. Pz.Div., p. 474.

83 Eleonore Lapin. Yad Vashem, "The Death Marches of Hungarian Jews Through Austria in the Spring of 1945" at https://www.yadvashem.org/articles/academic/the-death-marches-of-hungarian-jews-through-austria.html#footnote89_u161xg0, accessed 11 August 2020.

84 *Ibid.* Incidentally, Storms survived the war and never stood trial for his crimes. Discovered living openly in Austria in 2008, he died in 2010 before criminal proceedings could be brought against him. For more information, refer to https://de.wikipedia.org/wiki/Adolf_Storms, accessed 11 August 2020, or the book about his case by Walter Manoschek, *Dann bin ich ja ein Mörder! Adolf Storms und das Massaker an Juden in Deutsch-Schützen* (Göttingen, Germany: Wallstein, 2015).

85 *H.Gr. Süd Ia KTB, Tagesmeldung*, dated 29 March 1945, p. 1.

86 Maier, p. 312.

87 *H.Gr. Süd Ia KTB, Tagesmeldung*, 29 March 1945, p. 6.

88 Jahnke Diary, entry dated 29 March 1945, p. 17.

89 Stoves, p. 777.

90   Schönfelder Manuscript, entry dated 29 March 1945, p. 18.

91   *H.Gr. Süd Ia KTB, Tagesmeldung*, dated 29 March 1945, p. 16.

92   *H.Gr. Süd Ia KTB, Tagesmeldung*, dated 29 March 1945, p. 7.

93   *H.Gr. Süd Ia KTB Anlage, Funkspruch*, dated 6:20 p.m., 29 March 1945.

Chapter 6: The Cuff Title Order

1   Frieser, *et al.*, pp. 948–49, and George H. Stein. *The Waffen SS: Hitler's Elite Guard at War, 1939–45* (New York: Cornell University Press, 1984), p. 237.

2   Maier, p. 304.

3   Guderian, pp. 347–48.

4   Maier, pp. 303–04. In an endnote on page 337 of the English language edition, Maier mentions that he corresponded directly with Günsche concerning this matter, and received a copy of his unpublished account of what happened in the *Führerbunker* on 1 February 1982.

5   *H.Gr. Süd Ia KTB, Tagesmeldung*, dated 26 March 1945, p. 14.

6   Maier, p. 303.

7   Maier, p. 305. Incidentally, in his book *Drama Between Budapest and Vienna*, Maier devotes a considerable amount of attention to this event, as could be expected. He is considered the most reliable eyewitness to what happened, except perhaps Dietrich himself, who never wrote an account of what had occurred.

8   Maier, p. 305.

9   Maier, p. 304.

10   Balck, pp. 422–23.

11   Perry Pierek. *Hungary 1944–1945: The Forgotten Tragedy* (Nieuwegein, The Netherlands: Aspekt Publishing, 1996), pp. 243–44.

12   Maier, p. 304.

13   Maier, p. 305.

14   Gerald Reitlinger, *The SS: Alibi of a Nation* (New York: Viking Books, 1957), p. 370.

15   Götz von Berlichingen was a well-known German free knight and robber baron from the late 15th/early 16th century made famous in the eponymous play written by Johann Wolfgang von Goethe. When ordered to surrender his castle to the Bishop of Bamberg in 1512 or 1513 to answer charges of plundering merchant convoys, he reportedly replied, *"Er kann mich im Arsche lecken!"* (He can kiss my ass). Since then, the mere mention of Götz's name, also known as the Swabian salute, has served as a feisty response to a challenge made by anyone in a position of authority. Incidentally, the SS division by that name was fighting on the Western Front at the time.

16   *H.Gr. Süd Ia KTB Anlage, Besprechungspunkte für Reichsführer-SS*, dated 27 March 1945.

17   Maier, p. 313.

18   Maier, p. 313, quoting *H.Gr. Süd Ia KTB*, entry dated 28 March 1945, pp. 14–15.

19   *H.Gr. Süd Ia KTB*, entry dated 28 March 1945, p. 15.

20   *H.Gr. Süd Ia KTB Anlage, Fernschreiben Ia Nr. 1215/45 g.Kdos.*, dated 8:20 p.m., 28 March 1945.

21   Maier, p. 305.

Chapter 7: Withdrawal to the *Reichsschutzstellung*

1   *H.Gr. Süd Ia KTB, Tagesmeldung*, dated 30 March 1945, p. 1.

2 Strassner, p. 208. Ullrich had issued this order to Jahnke the same day. Additionally, there were actually two bridgeheads occupied by the corps on this date: the one he mentions at Körmend and the other at Steinamanger.

3 Jahnke Diary, entry dated 30 March 1945, p. 17.

4 Schönfelder Manuscript, entry dated 30 March 1945, p. 18.

5 *H.Gr. Süd Ia KTB*, dated 30 March 1945, pp. 11–12.

6 *Geschichte der 3. Panzer-Division*, p. 473.

7 *H.Gr. Süd Ia KTB*, dated 30 March 1945, p. 7.

8 Gille Notebook, entry dated 30 March 1945, p. 4.

9 Rauchensteiner, p. 426f, citing Harteneck, in M. A. Freiburg, RH 24-202/23, "*Das deutsche Kavallerie-Korps.*" *Nachträgliche Ausarbeitung des Kommandierender Generals: General d. Kav. a.D. Gustav Harteneck, 18.2.1963.*

10 Evidently, when the *Hohenstaufen* Division passed into the *2. Pz.Armee* sector along with the rest of the *I. Kav.Korps*, Balck, as was his habit, kept a portion of its armored element for use in his own army sector, despite orders to give them up. His high-handedness had become almost routine, but nothing of substance was ever done against him. The evidence of the mixed *Kampfgruppe* from the *1. Pz.Div.* and the *Hohenstaufen* Division being assigned to defend Eisenburg are found in a directive from *H.Gr. Süd* to *6. Armee* dated 28 March 1945.

11 *H.Gr. Süd Ia KTB*, dated 30 March 1945, p. 3, and Walther Krause, MS # B-139, "Fighting in West Hungary and East Steiermark in the Area of the Sixth Army from March 25 to May 8, 1945" (Frankfurt: Headquarters U.S. Army Europe Historical Division, 13 June 1952), pp. 9–10.

12 *H.Gr. Süd Ia KTB*, dated 30 March 1945, pp. 6–7.

13 Wöhler would be officially replaced on 7 April 1945 by *Gen.O.* Lothar Rendulic.

14 Michael O. Logusz, *Galicia Division: The Waffen-SS 14th Grenadier Division 1943–1945* (Atglen, PA: Schiffer Publishing Ltd, 1997), pp. 342–43.

15 Balck, p. 425.

16 Krause, p. 5.

17 *H.Gr. Süd Ia KTB, Tagesmeldung*, dated 30 March 1945, p. 8.

18 Rauchensteiner, p. 250.

19 *H.Gr. Süd Ia KTB, Tagesmeldung*, dated 31 March 1945, pp. 1–3.

20 Rauchensteiner, pp. 249–50.

21 *Ibid.*, p. 250.

22 Jahnke Diary, entry dated 31 March 1945, p. 18. Incidentally, the *Volkssturm* units responsible for defending this area had only been mobilized on 25 March 1945, less than a week before (Rauchensteiner, p. 99).

23 Schönfelder Manuscript, entry dated 31 March 1945, pp. 18–19. Incidentally, this was the last date entered in Schönfelder's papers, but he left a closing remark concerning the relationship between Balck and Gille that we will refer to later.

24 Balck, p. 420.

25 Maier, p. 335, and *H.Gr. Süd Ia KTB*, dated 31 March 1945, p. 13.

26 *H.Gr. Süd Ia KTB*, dated 31 March 1945, p. 2. At first, *III. Pz.Korps* believed that this had been the *Szent Lazlo* Division, but this later proved to be incorrect since that division was fighting several dozen kilometers to the south as part of the *2. Pz.Armee*. This incident resulted in a flurry of messages concerning whether or not the *Honvéd* units still fighting alongside *H.Gr. Süd* should be allowed to bear arms. Even after the war, Balck refused to acknowledge his error, continuing to blame the *Szent Lazlo* Division for this fiasco, when in fact it was probably Hungarian fortress battalions assigned to the *III. Pz.Korps* who fled from their positions or went over to the Soviet side.

27 *H.Gr. Süd Ia KTB, Tagesmeldung*, dated 31 March 1945, p. 2.

28 *H.Gr. Süd Ia KTB Fernschreiben, Ia Nr. 1228/45 g.kdos., Betr: OKH/Gen.St.d.H/Op.Abt./Abt.Lds. Bef, OB Südost*, dated 10:15 p.m., 29 March 1945.

29 Rauchensteiner, p. 499.

Chapter 8: Defending the Reich

1 Apparently, the portion of the *Hohenstaufen's SS-Pz.Aufkl.Abt. 9* fighting with the *1. Pz.Div.* shortly after this engagement was allowed to rejoin the rest of its battalion fighting in the neighboring sector under the *6. Pz.Armee.*

2 *Kriegstagebuch s.Pz.Abt. 509*, entry dated 1 April 1945, p. 20.

3 Rauchensteiner, p. 430f.

4 *H.Gr. Süd, Ia KTB Anlage, Panzerlage Teilmeldung, Stand 1.4.45*, dated 1 April 1945, p. 1. This number does not include the 30–35 vehicles that had been recovered behind the *Reichsschutzstellung* awaiting repair.

5 Maier, p. 314. This page reproduces the contents of the original report of 17 March 1945 for all divisions and division-sized units in the *H.Gr. Süd* order of battle, including the *3. Panzer* and *Wiking* Divisions.

6 *H.Gr. Süd Ia KTB, Anlage, Betr: Zustand der 1. Pz.Div. nach dem Stande vom 24.3.45*, dated 1:50 a.m., 25 March 1945.

7 *H.Gr. Süd, Ia KTB Anlage, Panzerlage Teilmeldung, Stand 1.4.45*, dated 1 April 1945, p. 1.

8 *5. SS-Pz.Div. Wiking, Ia KTB, Zustandmeldung*, 1 April 1945.

9 Maier, p. 288, referring to message from *H.Gr. Süd, Generaloberst* Wöhler, to *OKH Operationsabteilung, Betr: Ersatzzuführung 6. Pz.Armee, Ia/Id Nr. 1039/45 geh*, dated 1:50 p.m., 24 March 1945.

10 *Ibid.* For example, on 23 March, *6. Pz.Armee* reported 700 stragglers behind the lines; after his stringent anti-straggling measures were put into place the next day, only 60 were reported.

11 *H.Gr. Süd KTB, Chefsachen, Meldung von Chef des Stabes der Heeresgruppe Süd am 3.4.1945*, dated 3 April 1945 (referenced in Frieser *et al.*, p. 948).

12 Klapdor, p. 436.

13 Jahnke Diary, entry dated 1 April 1945, p. 18.

14 Bernau, pp. 151–52.

15 Krause, pp. 5–10.

16 In his memoirs, Balck accused Gille's corps of being a "tangled mess," but in reality on 2 April it was carrying out a counterattack towards Jennersdorf with its three divisions, just as Balck had ordered (Balck, p. 427).

17 Wolf had previously served as the commander of *II. Abt./Pz.Rgt. 23* of the *23. Pz.Div.*

18 Balck, p. 427.

19 *H.Gr. Süd, Tagesmeldung*, dated 2 April 1945 (Rauchensteiner, Annex 1: *Die Tagesmeldungen der Heeresgruppe Süd vom 29. März bis 22. April 1945*), p. 456. After reoccupying Jennersdorf, troops from the *Wiking* Division allegedly murdered as many as 40 ill Hungarian Jews who were being treated for typhus by Soviet medical personnel in a tent set up next to the brickworks. It was also alleged that troops from the *Wiking* Division were implicated in the summary execution of several dozen escaped Jewish forced laborers who had sought hiding places within the area immediately behind the front lines, considered a capital offense. For more information, refer to Eleonore Lappin-Eppel's *Hungarian-Jewish forced laborers in Austria 1944/45: Labor deployment—Death Marches—Consequences* (Vienna: LIT Publishing House, 2010), p. 344.

20   Jahnke Diary, entry dated 2 April 1945, p. 18.

21   Meyer, Hans. "Der Letzte Einsatz des Kommandeurs der SS-Aufklärungs-Abteilung 5 Wiking, SS-Sturmbannführer Fritz Vogt" in *Unser Wiking Ruf* (Hamburg: Truppenkameradschaft 5. SS-Panzer-Division Wiking e.V., 1997), pp. 74–75.

22   *H.Gr. Süd, Tagesmeldung*, dated 2 April 1945 (in Rauchensteiner, p. 456).

23   *Oberkommando der 6. Pz.Armee, Armeebefehl*, dated 3 April 1945 (Note: this document actually states that it originated in the headquarters of the "*6. SS-Panzerarmee*," one of the several instances of this informal title being used by Dietrich himself).

24   *H.Gr. Süd, Tagesmeldung*, dated 3 April 1945 (in Rauchensteiner, p. 457).

25   Stoves, pp. 781–82.

26   Rauchensteiner, p. 252.

27   Jahnke Diary, entry dated 3 April 1945, pp. 18–19. Vogt's wife had been visiting her husband and was staying in a hotel in Graz shortly before he was wounded.

28   *H.Gr. Süd, Tagesmeldung*, dated 3 April 1945 (Rauchensteiner, p. 457).

29   Stoves, pp. 781–82, and Jahnke Diary, entry dated 4 April 1945, p. 19.

30   *H.Gr. Süd, Tagesmeldung*, dated 4 April 1945 (in Rauchensteiner, p. 459), and Krause, p. 16.

31   *H.Gr. Süd, Tagesmeldung*, dated 4 April 1945 (Rauchensteiner, p. 458).

32   *KTB des OKW*, Vol. 8/2, entry dated 4 April 1945, pp. 1221–22.

33   The *Führer-Grenadier* Division was established on 26 January 1945 in the Cottbus area by expanding the existing *Führer-Grenadier* Brigade. It consisted of two *Panzergrenadier* regiments, a *panzer* regiment, an artillery regiment, and division troops. Considered a top-notch unit, it was intended to become part of the *Grossdeutschland* family of elite units but was shifted to the Austrian front in early April 1945 instead of joining the new *Führer-Panzerkorps* in the planning stages (which never came to pass). Its arrival on the battlefield around Vienna was a major boost to the dwindling combat power of Dietrich's *6. Pz.Armee*. Its commander was *Gen.Maj.* Erich von Hassenstein (Georg Tessin. *Verbände und Truppen der deutschen Wehrmacht und Waffen-SS im Zweiten Weltkrieg 1939–1945*, Vol. I-XVI (Osnabrück, Germany: Biblio-Verlag, 1979), pp. 76–77).

34   Stoves, p. 782, and Jahnke Diary, entry dated 5 April 1945, p. 19.

35   According to the diarist of *s.Pz.Abt. 509*, the battalion's Tiger tanks were used for the first time as mobile artillery, the first time that the battalion had ever been used in such a fashion (*s.Pz. Abt. 509 KTB*, entry dated 5 April 1945, p. 26).

36   Maier, p. 348.

37   The difference was that Vienna was not to be organized for an all-round defense like a *Festung*, but rather as an element in an integrated defense line. In practice, depending how Hitler felt on that particular day, this was a distinction without a difference.

38   *KTB des OKW*, Vol. 8/2, entry dated 5 April 1945, pp. 1223–24.

39   *H.Gr. Süd KTB, Tagesmeldung*, dated 6 April 1945 (Rauchensteiner, p. 461).

40   Maier, p. 349.

41   *H.Gr. Süd, Tagesmeldung*, dated 6 April 1945 (Rauchensteiner, p. 461), and Krause, pp. 15–16.

42   *KTB des OKW*, Vol. 8/2, entry dated 6 April 1945, p. 1225.

43   *Heeres-Panzer* Divisions included the *1., 3., 6., 23., 25., 232.,* and *FHH 1*; *Panzergrenadier* divisions included the *Fuhrer-Gren.* and the *FHH 2. Waffen-SS Panzer* Divisions included the *1., 2., 3., 5., 9.,* and *12.,* and the *16. SS-Pz.Gren.Div.*

44   *Stab Gen.Insp.d.Pz.Tr., Verbindungs-Offz. Nr. F 492/45 g.Kdos. Betr: Reisebericht über dem Besuch der Heeres-Gruppe Süd und der Aussenstelle des Gen.Insp.d.Pz.Tr. bei H.Gr. Süd am 6.4.1945*, dated 7 April 1945.

45   *H.Gr. Süd, Tagesmeldung*, dated 7 April 1945 (Rauchensteiner, p. 463).

46   Karl Martini, "Die Apokalypse: Der Untergang des Bataillons 'Norge' SS-Pz.Gren.Reg. 23" (Helmstedt, Gemany: Unpublished manuscript), p. 2 (courtesy of Tommy Natedal).

47   Strassner, p. 210. He was also a wearer of the Golden *NSDAP* Badge.

48   Stoves, pp. 782–83.

49   Jahnke Diary, entry dated 8 April 1945, p. 19.

50   *H.Gr. Süd, Tagesmeldung*, dated 7 and 8 April 1945 (Rauchensteiner, pp. 463–64, 466).

51   *KTB des OKW*, Vol. 8/2, entry dated 7 April 1945, pp. 1228–29, and Maier, pp. 352–53.

52   Jahnke Diary, entry dated 9 April 1945, p. 19, and Maier, p. 353.

53   *H.Gr. Süd, Tagesmeldung*, dated 9 April 1945 (Rauchensteiner, p. 467).

54   *H.Gr. Süd, Tagesmeldung*, dated 10 April 1945 (Rauchensteiner, p. 469).

55   Stoves, p. 783.

56   Maier, p. 358.

57   Stoves, p. 783.

58   *H.Gr. Süd, Ia KTB Anlage, Panzerlage Teilmeldung, Stand 10.4.45*, dated 10 April 1945, pp. 1–2.

59   Stoves, p. 784.

60   *H.Gr. Süd, Tagesmeldung*, dated 11 April 1945 (Rauchensteiner, pp. 471–72).

61   *KTB des OKW*, Vol. 8/2, entry dated 11 April 1945, pp. 1233–34, and Maier, p. 358.

62   Maier, p. 377.

63   Jahnke Diary, entry dated 12 April 1945, p. 19.

64   *KTB des OKW*, Vol. 8/2, entry dated 12 April 1945, p. 1236, and Maier, p. 359.

65   Stoves, pp. 785–86.

66   Jahnke Diary, entry dated 13 April 1945, p. 19.

67   *H.Gr. Süd, Tagesmeldung*, dated 13 April 1945 (Rauchensteiner, p. 475).

68   *KTB des OKW*, Vol. 8/2, entry dated 13 April 1945, p. 1238, and Maier, p. 360.

69   *H.Gr. Süd, Tagesmeldung*, entry dated 14 April 1945 (Rauchensteiner, p. 477).

70   *Ibid.*

71   *KTB des OKW*, Vol. 8/2, entry dated 14 April 1945, p. 1240, and Maier, p. 362.

72   *H.Gr. Süd, Tagesmeldung*, dated 15 April 1945 (Rauchensteiner, p. 479).

73   *Ibid.*

74   *KTB des OKW*, Vol. 8/2, entry dated 15 April 1945, p. 1242, and Maier, p. 363.

75   *H.Gr. Süd, Panzerlage 15.4.45*, dated 15 April 1945.

76   *H.Gr. Süd Ia KTB, Anlage, Unterstellung und Kampfgruppen Heeresgruppe Süd, Stand 15.04.45*, dated 19 April 1945.

77   *Ibid.*

78   Frieser *et al.*, p. 953.

79   Rauchensteiner, p. 393.

80   *Führerbefehl* dated 16 April 1945, reproduced in full in Vopersal, p. 940, and Strassner, p. 210

81   Strassner, p. 210.

82   Tieke, p. 438.

83   *H.Gr. Süd, Tagesmeldung*, dated 16 April 1945 (Rauchensteiner, p. 481).

84   Stoves, p. 787.

85   *H.Gr. Süd, Tagesmeldung*, dated 16 April 1945 (Rauchensteiner, p. 481).

86   *Ibid.*, p. 482, and Maier, pp. 364–65.

87   *KTB des OKW*, Vol. 8/2, entry dated 16 April 1945, p. 1244, and Maier, pp. 364–65.

Chapter 9: War's End

1   Jahnke Diary, entry dated 17 April 1945, p. 19.

2   Rauchensteiner, p. 376, and G-2 After-Action Report, U.S. 80th Infantry Division, 1–9 May 1945, p. 3.

3   *H.Gr. Süd, Tagesmeldung*, entries dated 17–20 April 1945 (Rauchensteiner, pp. 483–84).

4   *Ibid.*, pp. 486–87.

5   *Ibid.*, p. 488.

6   Krause, pp. 22–23.

7   *H.Gr. Süd, Tagesmeldung*, entries dated 17–20 April 1945 (Rauchensteiner, pp. 483–87).

8   Stoves, pp. 790–92.

9   Balck, pp. 428–29.

10   Jahnke Diary, entry dated 16 April 1945, p. 19.

11   Klapdor, pp. 434–35.

12   Klapdor, p. 435.

13   Jahnke Diary, entry dated 16 April 1945, p. 19.

14   Stoves, p. 794. Hitler had committed suicide in his bunker in Berlin the previous day, 30 April.

15   Maier, p. 369.

16   Dr Lothar Rendulic, *Report of the Commander: Stabilization of the Eastern Front*, MS #B-328 (Frankfurt: U.S. Army Europe Historical Division, 1 April 1947), pp. 7–8.

17   Gaedke, p. 241.

18   Balck, p. 437, Rauchensteiner, pp. 373–74, and Gaedke, pp. 242–43.

19   Headquarters, 80th Infantry Division, G-3 After-Action Report, 1–9 May 1945 (Headquarters, Third United States Army, 1945), p. 1.

20   *SS-Obersturmbannführer* Karl-Heinz Keitel was the son of *G.F.M.* Wilhelm Keitel, the chief of staff of the *OKW*. He had transferred into the *Waffen-SS* from the *Heer* on 5 August 1944. At the time of his appointment to lead the *Kampfgruppe* bearing his name, he had been commanding *SS-Freiwilligen Kavallerie Regiment 92* of the *37. SS-Freiwilligen-Kavallerie Division Lützow*.

21   Balck, p. 439.

22   Headquarters, XX Corps, Report of Combat Operations, 1 May to 8 May 1945 (Headquarters, Third United States Army, 12 June 1945), p. 5.

23   The *2. Pz.Armee* had been detached from *H.Gr. Ostmark* and subordinated to *H.Gr. E* on 7 May 1945 (Rauchensteiner, p. 385).

24   *Ibid.*, pp. 3, 14.

25   *H.Gr. Ostmark, Ia KTB Schematische Kriegsgliederung H.Gr. Ostmark*, dated 7 May 1945.

26   Headquarters, 80th Infantry Division, G-2 After-Action Report, 1–9 May 1945 (Headquarters, Third United States Army, 1945), p. 3.

27   Balck, p. 439. This turned out to be a rather flexible timeline, at least in the *6. Armee*'s case.

28   Headquarters, 80th Infantry Division, "Surrender of Sixth German Army, a Conversation between MajGen Horace L. McBride and *General der Panzer Troops* Balck, CG Sixth German Army at 1945 hours in Kirschdorf, Austria 8 May 1945" (Headquarters, Third United States Army, 1945), pp. 1–3.

29   Bernau, p. 156.

30   *Ibid.*

31   *Ibid.*, pp. 156–57.

32   Stoves, pp. 797–801.

33   *Ibid.*, pp. 803–04.

34   Strassner, pp. 211–13.

35   *Ibid.*, p. 212.

36   *Ibid.*, pp. 212–13.

37   Ron Erlings, Hans Fischer and Paul Oosterling. *Standartenführer Johannes Mühlenkamp und seine Männer* (Erpe, The Netherlands: Uitgeverij De Krijger, 2003), pp. 398–99.

38   Bernau, p. 157.

39 *Ibid.*

40 Günther Lange, "Der 29. Mai 1945," in *Unser Wiking Ruf,* 11/2006 (Handeloh, Germany: Truppenkameradschaft 5. SS-Panzer-Division Wiking, 2006), pp. 20–21.

41 Herbert Gille, MS # B-166, "The IV SS Panzer Corps" (Frankfurt: Headquarters U.S. Army Europe Historical Division, 1946), p. 1.

42 Charles W. Sydnor Jr. *Soldiers of Destruction: The SS Death's Head Division, 1933–45* (Princeton: Princeton University Press, 1977), p. 311; Hugh Page Taylor and Roger J. Bender. *Uniforms, Organization, and History of the Waffen-SS*, Vol. 2 (San Jose, CA: R. James Bender Publishing, 1971), p. 105, and Vopersal, p. 969.

43 Vopersal, pp. 997, 999.

44 Ronald Smelser and Enrico Syring. *Die SS: Elite unter dem Totenkopf—30 Lebensläufe* (Paderborn, Germany: Ferdinand Schöningh, 2000), pp. 184–85.

45 For more information about the *Wiking* Division's implications in war crimes during the early stages of the war against the U.S.S.R., refer to Lars Westerlund's fine study, *The Finnish SS-Volunteers and Atrocities 1941–1943* (Helsinki: The Finnish Literary Society and the National Archives of Finland, 2019).

46 Smelser and Syring, p. 185.

47 His brother, *Ostubaf.* Max Pauly, had been the commandant of the Neuengamme and Stutthof concentration camps from 1941–45. Placed on trial by the Western Allies, he was sentenced to death by hanging and executed at the Hameln prison on 8 October 1946. He had led the execution squads in Danzig and had been responsible for the 5 October 1939 murder of the Polish militiamen captured after the fall of the Danzig Post Office on 1 September (Source: French MacLean, *The Camp Men: The SS Officers who ran the Nazi Concentration Camp System*, pp. 174–75).

48 David C. Large, "Reckoning without the Past: The HIAG of the Waffen-SS and the Politics of Rehabilitation in the Bonn Republic, 1950–1961" in *The Journal of Modern History*, 59 (Chicago: University of Chicago Press, 1987), p. 83. This law concerned West German citizens who had been dismissed from public service after 8 May 1945 and had thereby lost pension rights. It was specifically directed against former officials of the Nazi Party, the SA, Hitler Youth, and the SS.

49 Reinhard Opitz, *Faschismus und Neofaschismus*, Volume 2: "Neofaschismus in der Bundesrepublik," p. 34.

50 Large, pp. 84, 98. The first books printed on behalf of HIAG were produced by Plesse Verlag in Gottingen before it established Munin-Verlag as its own in-house publisher.

51 Large, p. 89.

52 Hagen Frieser, "Wiederbewaffnet: Ehemalige Waffen-SS Soldaten in der Bundeswehr" in *Deutsche Militärzeitschrift*, Sonderausgabe Waffen-SS, 1/2007 (Martinsrade, Germany: Verlag Deutsche Militärzeitschrift, 2007), pp. 35–36.

53 Large, p. 108.

54 Frieser, p. 36. The number of former *Waffen-SS* members allowed to join the *Bundeswehr* is based on official numbers released by the *Bundesministers für Verteidigung* (Federal Ministry of Defense) for the years 1955–56 and 1961; the actual number is probably higher, since the totals for 1958–60 are not available. For more information, refer to Frederick Zilian's *From Confrontation to Cooperation: The Takeover of the National People's (East German) Army by the Bundeswehr* (New York: Praeger Studies in Diplomacy and Strategic Thought, 1997), pp. 16–17, or Reimund Schnabel, *Macht ohne Moral: Eine Dokumentation über die SS* (Frankfurt: Rodenberg, 1957), p. 548f.

55 Eberhard Heder, "Wikinger in der Bundeswehr" in *Unser Wiking Ruf,* No. 10, 2005 (Handeloh, Germany: Truppenkameradschaft 5. SS-Panzer-Division Wiking, 2005), pp. 102–03.

56 Correspondence with John P. Moore, 7 January 2017.

57 Large, p. 93.

58 *Ibid.*, pp. 92–93.

59 Smelser and Syring, p. 185.

60 Jonathan Petropoulos, *The Faustian Bargain: The Art World in Nazi Germany* (New York: Oxford University Press, 2000), p. 151.

61 Smelser and Syring, pp. 185–86.

62 Monika E. Steinel, "Science and Service in the National Socialist State: A Case-Study of the German Archaeologist Herbert Jankuhn (1905–1990)," Doctoral Dissertation (London: University College of London, Institute of Archaeology, 2009), p. 22.

63 Heather Pringle, *The Master Plan: Himmler's Scholars and the Holocaust* (New York: Hyperion, 2009), p. 312.

64 U.S. Army Counter-Intelligence Corps (C.I.C.) Networks in Eastern Europe, Net Project "Montgomery" and "Mount Vernon" (Washington, D.C.: Central Intelligence Agency, 1948). Declassified and approved for release by the C.I.A. under the provisions of the Nazi War Crimes Disclosure Act, 2001.

65 William Drozdiak, "Like School Chums, Nazi Veterans Gather: Despite Protests, Former SS Men Meet in Village" in *New York Times*, 2 April 1984 (New York: New York Times, Inc., 1984).

66 Oosterling, *et al.*, p. 399.

67 Vopersal, p. 1002.

68 Stein, p. 291.

69 Moore, Gille SS Officer File, *Führerliste der Waffen-SS Personalakten*, Part 4.

70 The *SS-Dienstalterliste* was the list of names of all mid-grade and senior officers of the SS, including the *Allgemeine SS*, *Sicherheitsdienst*, *Waffen-SS*, and Gestapo. It was published by the *SS Personalamt*, arranged in order of rank and time in grade. First published in 1934, it was periodically updated throughout the war. In July 1944, a *Dienstalterliste der Waffen-SS* first appeared, which included only officers who were serving in the *Waffen-SS*. The last one appeared on 30 January 1945.

71 *Auftragstaktik*: the theory and practice and training in the use of mission-type orders, in order to amplify the advantages which flow from the full exploitation of the battlefield initiative of the German officer and soldier (Source: BDM Study, 19 December 1980, "Generals Balck and von Mellenthin on Tactics: Implications for NATO Military Doctrine," p. 17).

Bibliography

Books and Journal Articles

Anonymous, "SS-Werfer-Abteilung 504—Solche Kerle!" in *Der Freiwillige*, Vol. 9, 1965 (Osnabrück, Germany: Verlag der Freiwillige GmbH, 1965).

Bacyk, Norbert, *Warsaw II The Tank Battle at Praga July—September 1944: The 4th SS Panzer Corps vs. the 1st Belorussian Front* (Stockholm: Leandoer & Eckholm Publishing, 2006).

Balck, Hermann, *Order in Chaos: The Memoirs of General of Panzer Troops Hermann Balck* (Lexington, KY: The University Press of Kentucky, 2015).

Barstein, Jan, "Norwegische Freiwillige im Kampf in Ungarn 1945" and "Pettend fest in unserer Hand" in *Der Freiwillige*, 2/2000 and 3/2000, respectively (Osnabrück, Germany: Munin Verlag GmbH, 2000), 24, 10.

Batov, Pavel I., *Campaigns and Battles* (Moscow: Progress Publishing, 1965).

Bayerl, Mirko, "Husarenstreich: The Attack on Stuhlweissenburg January 22nd 1945" in *Nordic Edge Model Gallery*, Volume 2 (Stockholm: Canfora Grafisk Form & Förlag, 2007), pp. 94–98.

Bender, Roger J. and Taylor, Hugh-Page, *Uniforms, Organization and History of the Waffen-SS* Vol. 2 (San Jose: R. James Bender Publishing, 1971).

Bernau, Gunter, *SS-Panzer Artillerie-Regiment 5 in der Panzer-Division Wiking* (Wuppertal, Germany: Eigenverlag Kameradschaft ehem. Pz.Art.Rgt. 5, 1990).

Brenden, Geir, Kjellander, Petter and Westberg, Lennart, *III. Germanic SS Panzer-Korps: The History of Himmler's Favourite SS-Panzer-Korps, 1943–1945, Vol. 1: Creation—September 1944* (Warwick, U.K.: Helion & Company Ltd, 2019).

Center for Land Warfare, U.S. Army War College, *1986 Art of War Symposium*, "From the Vistula to the Oder: Soviet Offensive Operations—October 1944 to March 1945" (Carlisle, PA: U.S. Army War College, May 1986).

Condell, Bruce and Zabecki, David T. (eds), *On the German Art of War: Truppenführung: German Army Manual for Unit Command in World War II* (Mechanicsburg, PA: Stackpole Books, 2008).

Davies, Norman, *Rising '44: The Battle for Warsaw* (New York: Viking Press, 2003).

Drozdiak, William, "Like School Chums, Nazi Veterans Gather: Despite Protests, Former SS Men Meet in Village" in *New York Times*, 2 April 1984 (New York: New York Times, Inc., 1984).

Erlings, Ron, Fischer, Hans and Oosterling, Paul, *Standartenführer Johannes Mühlenkamp und seine Männer* (Erpe, The Netherlands: Uitgeverij De Krijger, 2003).

Fey, Willi, *Armor Battles of the Waffen-SS, 1943–45* (Winnipeg, Canada: J. J. Fedorowicz, 1990).

Fraschka, Günter, *Mit Schwertern und Brillanten: Die Träger der höchsten deutschen Tapferkeitsauszeichnung* (Munich: Limes Verlag Niedermayer & Schlüter GmbH, 1977).

Frieser, Hagen, "Wiederbewaffnet: Ehemalige Waffen-SS Soldaten in der Bundeswehr" in *Deutsche Militärzeitschrift*, Sonderausgabe Waffen-SS, 1/2007 (Martinsrade, Germany: Verlag Deutsche Militärzeitschrift, 2007).

Frieser, Karl-Heinz (editor and contributing author), Schmider, Klaus, Schönherr, Klaus, Schreiber, Gerhard, Ungvary, Krisztian and Wegner, Bernd, *Germany and the Second World War, Vol. VIII: The Eastern Front 1943–1944—The War in the East and on Neighboring Fronts* (Oxford: Clarendon Press, 2017).

Fürbringer, Herbert, *9. SS-Panzer-Division 1944: Normanie–Tarnopol–Arnhem* (Paris: Editions Heimdahl, 1984).

Gaedke, Heinz and Brugmann,Gerhard, *Wege eines Soldaten* (Norderstedt: Books on Demand, 2005).

Glantz, David M., *Atlas of the Lublin–Brest Operation and the Advance on Warsaw* (Carlisle, PA: Privately published, 2005).

Glantz, David M., "The Red Army's Lublin–Brest Offensive and Advance on Warsaw (18 July–30 September 1944): An Overview and Documentary Survey" in *Journal of Slavic Military Studies*, 19 (London: Taylor & Francis Group, LLC. 2006), pp. 401–41.

Gosztony, Peter, *Endkampf an der Donau, 1944/45* (Vienna: Verlag Fritz Molden, 1969).

Guderian, Heinz, *Panzer Leader* (New York: Ballantyne Books, 1957).

Hack, Franz and Hahl, Fritz. *Panzergrenadiere der Panzerdivision Wiking im Bild.* (Osnabruck: Munin Verlag GmbH, 1984).

Hack, Franz, "Kämpfe in Ungarn" in *Unsere Wiking Ruf*, 7/2002 (Ziegenhain, Germany: Truppenkameradschaft 5. SS-Panzer Division Wiking, Geschichtlicher Verein Treysa, 2002).

Hahl, Fritz, *Mit "Westland" im Osten* (Osnabrück, Germany: Munin Verlag, 2000).

Haupt, Werner, *Army Group Center: The Wehrmacht in Russia 1941–1945* (Atglen, PA: Schiffer Military History, 1997).

Haupt, Werner, *Die Schlachten der Heeresgruppe Mitte aus der Sicht der Divisionen* (Friedberg, Germany: Podzun-Pallas Verlag, 1983).

Heder, Eberhard, "Der Kampf des IV. SS-Panzerkorps um Budapest" in *Unsere Wiking Ruf*, 7/2002 (Ziegenhain, Germany: Truppenkameradschaft 5. SS-Panzer Division Wiking, Geschichtlicher Verein Treysa, 2002).

Heder, Eberhard, "Wikinger in der Bundeswehr" in *Unser Wiking Ruf*, No. 10, 2005 (Handeloh, Germany: Truppenkameradschaft 5. SS-Panzer-Division Wiking, 2005).

Heiber, Helmut and Glantz, David M. (eds), *Hitler and His Generals: Military Conferences 1942–1945* (New York: Enigma Books, 2003).

Hinze, Rolf, *East Front Drama—1944* (Winnipeg, Canada: J. J. Fedorowicz Publishing, Inc., 1996).

Husemann, Franz, *Die guten Glaubens waren*, Band II (Osnabrück, Germany: Munin Verlag GmbH, 1977).

Isaev, Aleksei and Kolomiets, Maksim, *Tomb of the Panzerwaffe: The Defeat of the Sixth SS Panzer Army in Hungary 1945* (Solihull, UK: Helion & Company Ltd, 2014).

Jauss, Karl, *Glück Allein Kann Es Nicht Gewesen Sein* (Göppingen, Germany: Privately published, 1984).

Kathagen, Friedhelm and Lechtenböhmer, Heinz, *Chronik der 2./SS Pz.Nachr.Abt. 5, 1940/45* (Witten, Germany: Selbstverlag, 1991).

Keilig, Wolf. *Das Deutsche Heer*, Vol. III, Section 211, "Die Generalität des Heeres im 2. Weltkrieg." (Bad Neuheim: Podzun-Verlag, 1956).

Kern, Erich, *Dance of Death* (London: Collins, 1951).

Kern, Erich, *Die Letzte Schlacht, Ungarn 1944–45* (Göttingen: Verlag K. W. Schütz, 1960).

Klapdor, Erich, *Viking Panzers: The German 5th SS Tank Regiment in the East in World War II* (Mechanicsburg, PA: Stackpole Books, 2011; translation of 1981 edition).

Knobelsdorff, Otto von, *Geschichte der niedersächichen 19. Panzer-Division 1939–1945* (Friedberg, Germany: Podzun-Pallas Verlag GmbH, 1985).

Kunz, Andreas, *Wehrmacht und Niederlage: Die bewaffnete Macht n der Endphase der nationalsozialistischen Herrschaft 1944 bis 1945* (Munich: R. Oldenbourg Verlag, 2007).

Kurowski, Franz, *Panzer Aces II: Battle Stories of German Tank Commanders of WWII* (Mechanicsburg, PA: Stackpole Books, 2004).

Kursietis, Andris J., *The Hungarian Army and its Military Leadership in World War II* (New York: Axis Europa Books & Magazines, 1999).

Lange, Günther (ed.), "Der Mai 1945" and "Ein Flucht durch Deutschland—Glück Gehabt!" in *Unser Wiking Ruf*, Nr. 11/2006 (Handeloh, Germany: Truppenkameradschaft 5. SS-Panzer Division Wiking, 2006).

Lappin-Eppel, Eleonore, *Hungarian-Jewish forced laborers in Austria 1944/45: Labor deployment—Death Marches—Consequences* (Vienna: LIT Publishing House, 2010), p. 344.

Large, David C., "Reckoning without the Past: The *HIAG* of the *Waffen-SS* and the Politics of Rehabilitation in the Bonn Republic, 1950–1961" in *The Journal of Modern History*, 59 (Chicago: University of Chicago Press, 1987).

MacLean, French, *The Camp Men: The SS Officers who ran the Nazi Concentration Camp System* (Atglen, PA: Schiffer Publishing, Ltd, 1999).

Maier, Georg, *Drama Between Budapest and Vienna: The Final Battles of the 6. Pz.Armee in the East—1945* (Winnipeg, Canada: J. J. Fedorowicz Publishing, 2004), p. 509.

Maier, Georg, *Drama Zwischen Budapest und Wien: Der 6. Panzerarmee, 1945* (Osnabrück, Germany: Munin Verlag, 1985), p. 672.

Mehner, Kurt, *Die Deutsche Wehrmacht 1939–1945: Führung und Truppe* (Norderstedt, Germany: Militair-Verlag Klaus D. Patzwall, 1993).

Model, Hans-Georg, *Der deutsche Generalstabsoffizier* (Frankfurt am Main, Germany: Bernard Graefe Verlag für Wehrwesen, 1968).

Moore, John P., *Führerliste der Waffen-SS: Personalakten*, Vols 1–6 (Portland, Oregon: Self-published, 2003).

Munoz, Antonio J., *Forgotten Legions: Obscure Combat Formations of the Waffen-SS* (New York: Axis Europa Book, 1991).

Munoz, Antonio J., "Teutonic Magyars: Hungarian Volunteers in the Waffen-SS 1944–1945" in Kursietis, Andris J., *The Hungarian Army and its Military Leadership in World War II* (New York: Axis Europa Books, 1999).

Nebolsin, Igor, *Stalin's Favorite: The Combat History of the 2nd Guards Tank Army from Kursk to Berlin* (Solihull, U.K: Helion & Company, 2016).

Nevenkin, Kamen, *Fire Brigades: The Panzer Divisions 1943–1945* (Winnipeg, Canada: J. J. Fedorowicz, 2008).

Niehorster, Leo W., *The Royal Hungarian Army 1920–1945* (New York: Axis Europa Books, 1998).

Opitz, Reinhard, "Neofaschismus in der Bundesrepublik" in *Faschismus und Neofaschismus*, Vol. 2. (Cologne, Germany: Pahl-Rugenstein Verlag, 1996).

Petropoulos, Jonathan, *The Faustian Bargain: The Art World in Nazi Germany* (New York: Oxford University Press, 2000).

Pierek, Perry, *Hungary 1944–1945: The Forgotten Tragedy* (Nieuwegein, The Netherlands: Aspekt Publishing, 1996).

Pohlmann, Hartwig, *Geschichte der 96. Infanterie Division* (Bad Nauheim, Germany: Podzun-Verlag, 1959).

Pringle, Heather, *The Master Plan: Himmler's Scholars and the Holocaust* (New York: Hyperion, 2009).

Rauchensteiner, Manfred, *Der Krieg in Österreich 1945* (Vienna, Austria: Österreicher Bundesverlag, 1984).

Regiments-Kameradschaft des ehemaligen SS-Panzergrenadier Regiment 10 "Westland," *Panzergrenadiere der Panzerdivision "Wiking" im Bild* (Osnabrück, Germany: Munin Verlag GmBH, 1984).

Regiments-Kameradschaft Panzerregiment 5 "Wiking," *Verweht sind die Spuren: Bilddokumentation 5. SS-Panzerregiment "Wiking"* (Osnabrück, Germany: Munin Verlag GmBH, 1979).

Reitlinger, Gerald, *The SS: Alibi of a Nation 1922–1945* (New York: The Viking Press, 1957).

Rikmenspoel, Marc, *Soldiers of the Waffen-SS: Many Nations, One Motto* (Winnipeg, Canada: J. J. Fedorowicz Publishing, Inc., 1999).

Rokossovsky, Konstantin, *A Soldier's Duty* (Moscow: Progress Publishers, 1985).

Sanchez, Alfonso E., *Feldherrnhalle: Forgotten Elite: The Panzerkorps Feldherrnhalle and Antecedent Formations, Eastern and Other Fronts, 1942–1945* (Bradford, U.K.: Shelf Books, 1996).

Schimak, Anton, Lamprecht, Karl and Dettmer, Friedrich, *Die 44. Infanterie-Division: Tagebuch der Hoch- und Deutschmeister* (Vienna, Austria: Verlag Austria Press; herausgeben von der Kameradschaft der 44. Inf.Div., 1969).

Schmeisser, Herbert, *Panzer-Nachrichten-Abteilung Wiking: Männer mit Mikrofon + Morsetaste* (Welzheim, Germany: Eigenverlag, 1985).

Schneider, Jost W., *Their Honor Was Loyalty! An Illustrated and Documentary History of the Knight's Cross Holders of the Waffen-SS and Police 1940–1945* (San Jose, CA: R. James Bender Publishing, 1977).

Schulze-Kossens, Richard, *Militärischer Führernachwuchs der Waffen-SS* (Osnabrück, Germany: Munin Verlag, 1982).

Smelser, Ronald and Syring, Enrico, *Die SS: Elite unter dem Totenkopf—30 Lebensläufe* (Paderborn, Germany: Ferdinand Schöningh, 2000).

Stein, George H., *The Waffen SS: Hitler's Elite Guard at War, 1939–45* (New York: Cornell University Press, 1984).

Steinel, Monika E., "Science and Service in the National Socialist State: A Case-Study of the German Archaeologist Herbert Jankuhn (1905–1990)," Doctoral dissertation (London: University College of London, Institute of Archaeology, 2009).

Stöber, Hans, *Die lettischen Divisionen im VI. SS-Armeekorps* (Osnabrück, Germany: Munin Verlag GmbH, 1981).

Stocker, Peter, "Mit Kopfverband und Armschlinge: SS-Obersturmbannführer Hans Dorr" in *Schwertträger*, 2, October–December 2017 (Selent, Germany: Verlag Deutsche Militärzeitschrift, 2017), pp. 3–21.

Stoves, Rolf, *1. Panzer-Division 1935–1945: Chronik einer der drei Stamm-Divisionen der deutschen Panzerwaffe* (Bad Nauheim, Germany: Verlag Hans-Henning Podzun, 1961).

Strassner, Peter, *European Volunteers: 5 SS Panzer Division Wiking* (Winnipeg, Canada: J. J. Fedorowicz Publishing, 1988).

Sydnor, Charles W. Jr. *Soldiers of Destruction: The SS Death's Head Division, 1933–45* (Princeton: Princeton University Press, 1977).

Számvéber, Norbert, *Days of Battle: Armoured operations north of the River Danube, Hungary 1944–45* (Solihull, U.K.: Helion & Company Ltd, 2013).

Számvéber, Norbert, *The Sword Behind the Shield: a Combat History of the German Efforts to Relieve Budapest 1945—Operation "Konrad" I, II, III* (Solihull, U.K.: Helion & Company Ltd, 2015).

Tessin, Georg. *Verbände und Truppen der deutschen Wehrmacht und Waffen-SS im Zweiten Weltkrieg 1939–1945*, Vol. I–XVI (Osnabrück, Germany: Biblio-Verlag, 1979).

Tieke, Wilhelm, *Tragedy of the Faithful: A History of the III. (germanisches) SS-Panzer-Korps* (Winnipeg, Canada: J. J. Fedorowicz Publishing, Inc., 2001).

Tiemann, Ralf, *The Leibstandarte*, Vol. IV/2 (Winnipeg, Canada: J. J. Fedorowicz Publishing, Inc., 1998).

Traditionsverband der 3. Panzer-Division, *Geschichte der 3. Panzer-Division Berlin-Brandenburg 1935–1945* (Berlin, Germany: Gunther Richter Verlag, 1967).

Trevor-Roper, H. R., *Hitler's Secret Conversations, 1941–1944* (New York: Farrar, Straus and Young, Inc., 1953).

Ulrich, Karl, *Wie ein Fels im Meer: 3. SS-Panzerdivision "Totenkopf,"* Vol. 2 (Osnabrück, Germany: Munin-Verlag, 1984).

Ungváry, Krisztián, *The Siege of Budapest: 100 Days in World War II* (New Haven, CT: Yale University Press, 2002).

Vopersal, Wolfgang, *Soldaten, Kämpfer, Kameraden, Marsch und Kämpfe der SS-Totenkopf Division*, Vols Va and Vb (Bielefeld, Germany: Selbstverlag der Truppenkameradschaft der 3. SS-Pz.Div. e.V., 1991).

Vuksic, Velimir, *SS Armor on the Eastern Front 1943–1945* (Winnipeg, Canada: J. J. Fedorowicz Publishing, Inc., 2005).

Wegner, Bernd, *The Waffen-SS: Organization, Ideology and Function* (Oxford, U.K.: Basil Blackwell Ltd, 1990).

Westerlund, Lars, *The Finnish SS-Volunteers and Atrocities, 1941–1943* (Helsinki, Finland: The National Archives of Finland, 2019).

Wood, Ian M., *Tigers of the Death's Head: SS Totenkopf Division's Tiger Company* (Mechanicsburg, VA: Stackpole Books, 2013).

Yerger, Mark, *German Cross in Gold Holders of the SS and Police*, Vols 8 & 9 (San Jose, CA: R. James Bender Publishing, 2015.)

Yerger, Mark, *Waffen-SS Commanders: The Army, Corps and Divisional Leaders of a Legend*, Vols 1 and 2 (Atglen, PA: Schiffer Military History, 1997).

Ziemke, Earl F., *Stalingrad to Berlin: The German Defeat in the East* (Washington, D.C.: U.S. Army Center of Military History, 2002).

Diaries, Notes and Manuscripts

Barstein, Jan, "Bericht Jan Barstein" (Unpublished private manuscript, courtesy of Tommy Natedal), four pages.

Gille, Herbert O., "Angriff zum Entsatz der Stadt Budapest, Dezember 1944–8 Mai 1945" In *Truppenkameradschaft Wiking* Archives (Stemmen, Germany: Undated private manuscript), four pages.

Jahnke, Günther, Diary December 1944–4 August 1945 in *Truppenkameradschaft Wiking* Archives (Munich, Germany: Undated private manuscript), 18 pages.

Kovács, Zoltán András and Számvéber, Norbert, "RF-SS Brigade 'Ney' (Kampfgruppe Ney)" (Budapest, 2001), http://www.hunyadi.co.uk/; accessed 20 November 2015.

Kovács, Zoltán András and Számvéber, Norbert, "The 1st Hungarian Sturmjäger Regiment" (Budapest, 2001), *http://www.hunyadi.co.uk/*; accessed 20 November 2015.

Mallis, Herbert, "Chronik 1. SS-Pz.Gren.Btl.—Norge 1944–1945" (Lalling, Germany: Unpublished manuscript, 1981), 51 pages.

Martini, Karl, "Die Apokalypse: Der Untergang des Bataillons 'Norge' SS-Pz.Gren.Reg. 23" (Helmstedt, Germany: Unpublished undated manuscript), 20 pages.

Nash, Douglas, "73. Infanterie-Division at Warsaw, September 1944" (Dumfries, VA: September 2017).

Pfeiffer, Roland, "Das Generalkommando IV. SS-Panzer-Korps" (Unpublished timeline, May 2015).

Pfeiffer, Roland, "Zur Geschichte der schweren Artillerie-Einheiten der Waffen-SS" (Unpublished outline, 5 December 2012) from *Forum der Wehrmacht* at https://www.forum-der-wehrmacht.de/index.php?thread/32759-zur-geschichte-der-schweren-artillerie-einheiten-der-waffen-ss/; accessed 27 January 2017.

Renz, Manfred, "Battles in Hungary 1945" (Heilbronn, Germany: Unpublished private manuscript), four pages.

Schönfelder, Manfred, "Einsatz der Verbänder der Waffen-SS auf dem Kriegsschauplatz in Ungarn in der Zeit vom 1 January–31 März 1945" (Hamburg, Germany: Unpublished manuscript in author's possession, 1 December 1981).

Skarlo, I. Ivar, "Tarjan—5 Januar 1945" (Unpublished private manuscript, courtesy of Tommy Natedal), eight pages.

Wood, Ian M., "Short History of I./SS-Pz.Rgt. 3 (Panther), 1942 to 1945."

Published Official Government Records, Manuals and Internal Publications

Foreign Military Studies

Berlin, Wilhelm, *Comments on the Study "Russian Artillery in the Battle for Modlin and German Countermeasures,"* MS C-030, undated manuscript (Heidelberg, Germany: Historical Division, U.S. European Command).

Brasack, Kurt, *Russian Artillery in the Battle for Modlin and German Countermeasures*, MS D-228 (Heidelberg, Germany: Historical Division, U.S. European Command, 29 July 1952).

Dörffler-Schuband, Werner, *Officer Procurement in the Waffen-SS: Reception, Processing and Training*, MS D-178 (Heidelberg, Germany: Office of the Chief Historian, Headquarters, U.S. European Command, Ref. Draft published 13 July 1945).

Förtsch, Hermann, *Training and Development of German General Staff Officers*, MS P-031b, Project # 6, Vol. VIII (Heidelberg, Germany: Historical Division, U.S. European Command, 22 June 1951).

Gille, Herbert Otto, *The 4th SS Panzer Corps May 1945*, MS #B-166 (Heidelberg, Germany: Historical Division, U.S. European Command, 27 April 1946).

Krause, Walther, *Fighting in West Hungary and East Steiermark in the Area of the Sixth Army from March 25 to May 8, 1945*, MS B-139 (Heidelberg, Germany: Historical Division, U.S. Army Europe, 13 June 1952).

Reinhardt, Helmuth, *Size and Composition of Divisional and Higher Staffs in the German Army*, MS P-139 (Karlsruhe, Germany: Historical Division, Headquarters, U.S. European Command, 1954).

Rendulic, Lothar Dr, *Report of the Commander: Stabilization of Eastern Front*, MS #B-328 (Frankfurt, Germany: Historical Division, U.S. European Command, 1 April 1947).

Reuther, Karl and Ulms, Ulrich, *XII SS Corps: Reflections and Experiences* (Heidelberg, Germany: Historical Division, U.S. European Command, 8 December 1947).

Westphal, Siegfried, *German General Staff Training and Development of German General Staff Officers*, MS P-031b, Project # 6, Vol. XXI (Heidelberg, Germany: Historical Division, U.S. European Command, August 1948).

Contemporary German Operational and Doctrinal Sources

Deutscher Rotes Kreuz—Suchdienst Munchen. Vermisstenbildliste, Hauptquartier IV. SS-Pz.Korps, Band WA Seite 60, 1944–1945. This finding aid, located at http://193.159.223.62:8081/vbl/Truppenanschrift-Polizei/TA_P.aspx identifies 54 members of the headquarters and headquarters troops of the *IV. SS-Pz.Korps* who were still declared as missing in action as late as 1958.

Gen.Kdo. IV. SS-Pz.Korps Adjutantur IIa, Verleihungsliste Nr. 5, Korpsgefechtstand, 16 February 1945. Bundesarhiv: Zentralnachweisstelle Heerespersonalampt, Verleihungsliste für Verleihung des Eisernes Kreuzes, RH 7A/1338 Folio 1.

Gen.Kdo. IV. SS-Pz.Korps Führungsabteilung, various reports, orders, and records of conversations, 12 January to 2 February 1945, from captured documents held in the Central Archive of the Russian Ministry of Defense, TsAMO Podolsk, Fund: 243, Inventory No. 2900, Case: 2011, pp. 281–85, folio. Originals translated into Russian by Lieutenant Glushkin on 2 February 1945, translated into English 2020 by Viktor Ukhov, Rostov-on-Don, Russia.

Gen.Kdo. IV. SS-Pz.Korps Adjutantur IIa, Korps Gefechtstand, Führerbefehl, 5 March 1945. "Im Auftrage Hitlers vom Chef des Oberkommandos der Wehrmacht, Generalfeldmarschall Wilhelm Keitel, unterzeichneter Befehl über Sippenhaft," issued 9 March 1945.

H.Gr. Ostmark, Ia KTB Schematische Kriegsgliederung H.Gr. Ostmark, dated 7 May 1945.

Kriegsarchiv der Waffen-SS, IIb. an Gen.Kdo. IV. SS-Pz.Korps, Betr: Kriegstagebücher, Gefechts- und Tätigkeitsberichte sowie im V.Bl.d.W.-SS verlautbare Schlacht- und Gefechtsbezeichnungen, dated 5 January 1945.

Kriegstagebuch (Ia), SS-Pz.Rgt. 5, 26 March–30 November 1944.

Kriegstagebuch (Ia), I. Abteilung, SS-Pz.Rgt. 5, 9 February–30 November 1944.

Kriegstagebuch (Ia), schwere-Pz.Abt. 509, 12 January–9 May 1945, pp. 18–27.

Kriegstagebuch (Ib) und Anlagen, Armeeoberkommando (AOK) 2, 1 October–31 December 1944. (This includes daily reports, including ammunition, fuel, and food expenditures, tank and other armored vehicles losses, and daily supply status for the *IV. SS-Pz.Korps* compiled by the *Quartiermeister*).

Kreigstagebuch (Ia) Anlage: Meldungen und Befehle, Armeegruppe Balck/6. Armee, 16 December 1944–3 February 1945. (This includes daily orders, armor and infantry strengths, transcripts of radio and/or telephone message traffic, reports from subordinate units, rail and highway movement status, and orders/instructions from higher headquarters, including *Heeresgruppe Süd*, located in Documents Inventory Number 12472, Case Folders 408–410. Accessed on the "German Documents in Russia" website at http://wwii.germandocsinrussia.org.

Kreigstagebuch (Ia), Armeeoberkommando (AOK) 9, 1 August–31 December 1944.

Kreigstagebuch (Ia) Anlagen, Armeeoberkommando (AOK) 9, 1 August–31 December 1944. This includes morning, midday, evening, and daily reports, as well as armor and infantry strengths, radio and/or telephone message transcripts, reports from subordinate units, commanders' daily summaries, rail and highway movement status, and orders/instructions from higher headquarters, including *Heeresgruppe Mitte*.

Kriegstagebuch (Ia), Heeresgruppe Süd, 1 February–31 March 1945.

Kriegstagebuch (Ia), Meldungen und Befehle, Heeresgruppe Süd, 1 February–31 March 1945. This includes morning, midday, evening, and daily reports, as well as armor and infantry strengths, radio and/or telephone message transcripts, reports from subordinate units, commanders' daily summaries, and orders/instructions from higher headquarters, including message traffic with the *Oberkommando des Heeres (OKH) Führungsabteilung*.

Kriegstagebuch (Ic), Armeegruppe Balck/6. Armee, Documents of the Ic department of *AOK 6*: KTB, File H, Volume 21, January 1945—Activity reports of the *Ic/AO* of the *AOK 6* and the departments and units subordinated to it for January 1945, *Ic* reports, enemy order of battle updates for *AOK 6*, located in Documents Inventory Number 12472, Case Folder 411. Accessed on the "German Documents in Russia" website at http://wwii.germandocsinrussia.org.

Kriegstagebuch (Ia), Armeegruppe Balck/6. Armee, Documents of the *Ia* department of *AOK 6*: KTB, 1 December 1944–3 February 1945, including daily orders and reports, combat strengths, *Heeresgruppe Süd* messages and other related items located in Documents Inventory Number 12472, Case Folders 382, 387–388, 408–410, and 447. Accessed on the "German Documents in Russia" website at http://wwii.germandocsinrussia.org.

Kriegstagebuch (Ia), Armeegruppe Balck/6. Armee, Documents of the *Ia* department of *AOK 6*: KTB, 1 December 1944–3 February 1945 daily situation maps, located in Documents Inventory Number 12472, Case Folders 396–404, 412, and 415–445. Accessed on the "German Documents in Russia" website at http://wwii.germandocsinrussia.org.

Oberbefehlshaber der 8. Armee, Armee Gefechtstand, Massnahmen in der nationalsozialistischen Führung der Truppe für die jetzige Lage, 8 April 1945.

Personnel and Matériel Strength Reports, including monthly *Kriegsgliederung*, for *3. SS-Pz.Div. Totenkopf* July 1944–March 1945.

Personnel and Matériel Strength Reports, including monthly *Kriegsgliederung*, for *5. SS-Pz.Div. Wiking* July 1944–April 1945.

SS-Führungshauptamt, Amt II, Org. Abt. Ia/II SS-Führungshauptampt. Kriegsgliederungen der Panzer Divisionen der Waffen-SS. (Berlin: *SS-Führungshauptampt*, 24 October 1944).

SS-Personalamt, Org.Abt. IIb, Verlustmeldungen der Waffen-SS, Band Ws 664–666, Gen.Kdo. IV. SS-Pz. Korps, schw.SS-Beob.Bttr. 104, and SS-Nachr.Abt. 104, March–August 1944, Band Ws 703, *SS-Werfer Abt. 504*, September–November 1944. Documents now stored at the *Deutsche Dienststelle* (*Wehrmachtauskunftstelle, WASt*), Berlin, and administered by the *Bundesarchiv*.

Wehrmachtführungsstab (Percy Schramm *et al.*), *Kriegstagebuch des Oberkommando der Wehrmacht 1944–1945: Eine Dokumentation, Band 8, Teilband 2* (Augsburg, Germany: Verlagsgruppe Weltbild GmbH, 2005).

Contemporary Allied Sources

Headquarters, XX Corps, Report of Combat Operations, 1–8 May 1945 (Headquarters, United States Army Europe, 12 June 1945).

Headquarters, XX Corps, Report of Combat Operations, 9–31 May 1945 (Headquarters, United States Army Europe, 27 June 1945).

Headquarters, 80th Infantry Division, Operational History of the 80th Infantry Division, May 1945 (Headquarters, United States Army Europe, 1945).

Headquarters, 80th Infantry Division, G-2 After-Action Report 1–9 May 1945 (Headquarters, United States Army Europe, 1945).

Headquarters, 80th Infantry Division, G-3 After-Action Report 1–9 May 1945 (Headquarters, United States Army Europe, 1945).

Headquarters, 80th Infantry Division, "Conversation between Maj.Gen. Horace L. McBride, Commanding General, 80th Infantry Division and General der Panzer Truppe (U.S. Lt.Gen.) Balck, Commanding General Sixth German Army at 1945 hours 8 May 1945 in Kirchdorf, Austria" (Headquarters, United States Army Europe, 1945).

Headquarters, 318th Infantry Regiment, 80th Infantry Division. After-Action Report 1–9 May 1945 (Headquarters, United States Army Europe, 1945).

Joint Intelligence Staff, JIC, Chiefs of Staff Committee, Joint Intelligence Sub-Committee, *Germany's War Effort and its Failure, The Eastern Front 1944–1945*, 1945 (aka "the ULTRA History of the Russian Front"), 273 pages.

Task Force Smyth, "Surrender of 6th German Army at Garstan, Austria and account of last shot fired by American forces in World War II 6–8 May 1945" (Headquarters, 80th Infantry Division, Kaufbeuren, Austria, 19 June 1945).

U.S. Army Counter-Intelligence Corps (C.I.C.), "C.I.C. Networks in Eastern Europe (Net Project 'Montgomery' and 'Mount Vernon')" (Washington, D.C.: Central Intelligence Agency, 1948). Declassified and approved for release by the C.I.A. under the provisions of the Nazi War Crimes Disclosure Act, 2001.

War Department, Military Intelligence Division, Special Series No. 12, *German Military Abbreviations*, 12 April 1943 (Washington, D.C.: U.S. War Department, 1943).

War Department, Military Intelligence Division, *German Military Symbols*, Vols I and II, 1 April 1944 (Washington, D.C.: U.S. War Department, 1944).

War Department, Military Intelligence Division, *Order of Battle and Handbook of the Hungarian Armed Forces* (Washington, D.C.: U.S. War Department, February 1944).

War Department, War Department Technical Manual TM 30-506, *German Military Dictionary, German–English, English–German*, 20 May 1944 (Washington, D.C.: U.S. War Department, 1944).

Contemporary Red Army Operational and Doctrinal Sources

Central Archive of the Russian Ministry of Defense [TsAMO], Podolsk, "Armored Replenishment of the Third Ukrainian Front in January 1945," f. 243, op. 2928, gy. 340, l. 129, available at https://pamyat-naroda.ru/.

Central Archive of the Russian Ministry of Defense [TsAMO], Podolsk, "Tank and self-propelled gun strength of the Third Ukrainian Front on 1 February 1945," f. 243, op. 2928, gy. 340, l. 23–128, available at https://pamyat-naroda.ru/.

Soviet General Staff, *The Budapest Operation 1945: An Operational–Strategic Study*. (Solihull, U.K.: Helion & Company Ltd, 2017). This publication, translated by Richard W. Harrision, consists of two separate documents. The first one is Volume 21 of the *Sbornik Materialov po Izucheniyu Opyta Voiny* series (Collection of Materials on the Study of War Experience) titled "The Budapest Operation (28 October 1944–13 February 1945)," and was originally published by the *STAVKA* in 1945. The second document, "The Third Ukrainian Front's Activities in the Budapest Operation (An Operational-Tactical Sketch)," was written by Major General S. P. Tarasov and issued to students at the Red Army's General Staff Academy in 1957.

Trophy (captured) documents of the *IV. SS-Pz. Korps* held in the Central Archive of the Russian Ministry of Defense, TsAMO Podolsk, Fund: 243, Inventory No. 2900, Case: 2011, pp. 281–323, folio. Original translation by Lieutenant Glushkin on 2 February 1945, translated into English 2019 by Olivia J. Allison, Kiev, and in 2020 by Viktor Ukhov, Rostov.

Interviews

Interview with *Oberstleutnant der Bundeswehr a.D.* Günther Lange, Handeloh, Germany, 7 October 2017, and continuing correspondence 2005–2020.

Index

References to notes are indicated by n; references to images are in *italics*.

Acs 85, 94
Adenauer, Konrad 253, 256
aircraft:
    Douglas A-20 Boston 73, 93
    Focke-Wulf Fw 190 78
    Ilyushin IL-2 *Sturmovik* 73, 160, 169
    Junkers Ju-52 129
    Junkers Ju-87 Stuka 78
    Lavochkin-Gorbunov-Gudkov *LaGG-3* 78
Aka Súr 77
Aldrian, *Gen.Lt.* Eduard 27
Alsőgalla 76, 78, 93, 99–100, 101
Altenmarkt 234
Ameiser, *SS-Stubaf.* Anton 35
Angelis, *Gen.d.Art.* Maximilian de 38, 192,
    222, 243, 246
    and 24–29 March 163, 167, 170–2, 174
    and 1–17 April 212, 214

Bachmann, *SS-Hstuf.* Christian 61, 67–8, 72
Baden 217, 218, 228
Bajka 148
Bakony Forest 23, 24, 47–8, 177
    and 20–23 March 96, 108, 112, 115, 120,
        128, 130
    and 24–29 March 138–40, 142, 148–9,
        152–4, 160, 163
    and Stuhlweissenburg 69, 76, 77, 86
Bakonycsernye 86, 88, 90
Bakonykúti 85, 86, 89
Balaton *see* Lake Balaton
Balatonalmádi 122
Balatonfökajar 108, 111
Balatonfüred 141, 148, 149
Balatonfüzfő 45, 105, 110–11
Balatonkenese 108, 115, 122

Balck, *Gen.d.Pz.Tr.* Hermann x, xi, 1, 3–4, 10,
    179–81, 183, 262–5
    and 20–23 March 91, 94–6, 98, 100–2,
        104, 107–8, 109–11, 113–14, 119–28,
        298n12, 299n35, 300n60–3, 300n72
    and 24–29 March 91, 94–6, 98, 100–2,
        104, 107–8, 109–11, 113–14, 119–28
    and 30–31 March 188–90, 192–5, 197–8
    and 1–17 April 201, 204, 209–10, 211–17,
        223–4, 226–7, 231
    and *Spring Awakening* 20, 40–2, 46–9,
        50–1
    and Stuhlweissenburg 62, 65–6, 68–70,
        72–3, 78, 81–8, 297n21
    and war's end 237–8, 239–44, 246
Balinka 80, 84, 90, 92
Barthel, *SS-Ustuf.* Joachim 26
Bauer, *SS-Ostuf.* Helmut 80, 248
Becker, *SS-Brig.Fhr.* Helmuth *vii*, 5, 10, 90,
    99, 131, 253
    and *Spring Awakening* 29, 30, 32–3, 39,
        43–6
    and Stuhlweissenburg 61–2, 65, 68, 77, 80
Berhida 99, 109–11, 115, 122
Bernau, *SS-Stubaf.* Günther 211, 249, 257
Bittrich, *SS-Ogruf.* Wilhelm 23, 36–7, 86, 140,
    144
    and 20–23 March 91, 124, 126
    and war's end 209, 225, 261
Börgönd 91, 96
Böttger, *Ltn.* Werner 8
Bradel, *Oberst* Ernst-Joachim 111, 164, 205,
    225, 239
Bratislava *see* Pressburg
Breith, *Gen.d.Pz.Tr.* Hermann 58, 71–2, 86–7,
    189, 198–9, 234

and 24–29 March 138, 165–6, 170, 172,
   173
and 1–17 April 210, 211, 214, 217, 219,
   220–2, 226, 229, 232, 234
and *Spring Awakening* 21, 24, 36, 42–3
and war's end 243–4, 246
Brno 230, 231
Bruck an der Leitha 218, 219, 224
Bruck an der Mur 246
Bruck Gap 212
Brumbär see weaponry
Brunst, *SS-Hstuf.* Herbert 62, 66
Bühler, *SS-Stubaf.* Karl-Heinz 150
Bünau, *Gen.d.Inf.* Rudolf 214, 225, 228
Bundeswehr (West German Armed Forces) xi,
   256–9, 264, 311n54
Bünning, *SS-Ostubaf.* Hans 211
Busse, *Gen.d.Inf.* Theodor 146

Csabdi 35, 65, 72
Csákberény 38, 49, 51, 61, 63, 65, 67
Csakvár 45, 46, 78
Császár 76, 85
Csillaki Puszta 67, 80
Csólkakő 77, 86
Csór 76–7, 83–6, 90–2, 95–6, 98, 103, 107
Csorna 164, 199
Czelldömölk *see* Kleinmariazell
Czernicki, *Oberstlt.* von 243

Dachau 254
Danube Flotilla 112
Darges, *SS-Ostubaf.* Fritz 5–6, 66, 103–4, 130
Deutsch-Schützen 169–70
Devecser 138, 149, 151, 157
Dietrich, *SS-Obstgruf.* Sepp xi, 16, 177–82,
   183, 189
   and 20–23 March 90–1, 93–6, 99, 101,
      108, 111, 113, 114–16, 120, 123–4,
      126–30
   and 24–29 March 133, 135, 137, 139–40,
      143–4, 146, 148, 159, 162, 165, 171,
      174
   and 1–17 April 203, 209, 212, 214–15,
      218, 220, 224, 225, 226, 230, 235
   and *Spring Awakening* 20–1, 25, 36, 41,
      53, 55
   and Stuhlweissenburg 57, 58, 62, 69, 81–3,
      86, 88

and war's end 240, 242, 253, 262
Dönitz, *Grossadmiral* Karl 241
Drava River 19, 21, 36, 37, 116, 214, 218–19,
   222
Dürnbach 217–18

Ebersbach 238, 251
Eckert, *SS-Stubaf.* Fritz 9
Egyházasrádóc 198
Eisbrecher (Operation *Icebreaker*) 20, 37
Eisenburg (Vasvár) 172, 189, 190, 191, 193,
   196, 197
Eisenstadt 164, 183
Enns River (Demarcation Line) x, 137, 237,
   242, 244, 246–8
Entnazifizierungs-Spruchkammer (de-
   Nazification court) 254
Ersatzheer (Replacement Army) 181
Esterháza Palace 12, 51, 147, 164

Falubattyán 91, 96, 99, 104, 108, 110
Fegelein, *SS-Gruf.* Hermann 5, 144, 178
Fehring 196, 198, 216, 217, 219
Feldbach 197, 199, 213, 216–17, 219, 221
Felsőgalla 10, 58, 65, 69, 75–6, 78, 93, 99,
   101
field hospitals *(Feldlazarett)* 6, 69, 79, 103, 213
Fingerspitzengefühl (sense of unfolding action)
   263
Floridsdorf Bridge 229
Freiwillige, Der (HIAG periodical) 256, 258
Friessner, *Gen.d.Inf.* Johannes 28
Frühlingserwachen (Operation *Spring
   Awakening*) ix–x, 19–57, 58, 60, 72, 75
   and losses 108, 209
   and order of battle 277–8
   and SS units 82, 180
   and Wöhler 69
Führerbefehl (*Führer* directive) 41, 135, 145,
   177, 191, 193, 233
   and 20–23 March 99–100, 102–4, 105,
      107, 123
Führerbunker 5, 177, 181
Führungsabteilung (key operations and
   intelligence staff) 7, 12, 80, 194
   and *Spring Awakening* 25, 27, 40–1, 42
Fürstenfeld 137, 173, 188, 196–8, 237–8, 246
   and 1–17 April 211–12, 216, 222, 224,
      228, 230–1

Füzitö oil refinery 60, 85, 97

Gaedke, *Gen.Maj.* Heinz 3, 20, 82, 179–80,
    209, 242, 265
    and 20–23 March 94, 101–2, 113
    and 24–29 March 135, 156, 165
Gagen, *Lt.Gen.* N. A. 1, 36, 37, 221
Gaja Canal 77, 80, 82
Gehlen, *Gen.Maj.* Reinhard 49, 141, 227
Gerecse Mountains 28, 47, 57–8, 85, 90
German Units:
    Oberbefehlshaber (Theater Commands):
    OB Südost 243
    Heeresgruppen:
    H.Gr. E 19–21, 36–8, 53, 204, 222, 230,
        238, 247
    H.Gr. F 147
    H.Gr. Mitte 11, 195, 221
    H.Gr. Nord 11
    H.Gr. Ostmark 240, 242–3
    H.Gr. Süd xi–xii, 4–5, 8, 10, 14, 15, 19–
        20, 23, 28–31, 33, 36, 39, 40–2, 46–54,
        60, 62–3, 66, 68–71, 73–5, 77, 80–1,
        83–4, 87–8, 91, 93, 95–8, 100–1, 107–
        17, 120–1, 123–7, 129–30, 133–5, 137–
        9, 141, 143–4, 146–7, 151–4, 157–64,
        166–71, 173–5, 177–81, 183–4, 187,
        189–95, 198–9, 201, 203–4, 208–9,
        212, 214, 216, 218, 220–3, 225, 227–9,
        231–5, 238, 240, 242, 262, 265
    H.Gr. Weichsel 11, 147
    Armeegruppen:
    Armeegruppe Balck 83
    Armies:
    2. Armee ix, 262
    2. Pz.Armee 19–20, 36–8, 48, 55, 60,
        65, 74–5, 80, 108, 135, 139, 153,
        163, 167–71, 174, 187–90, 192–3,
        195, 199, 203, 210–12, 214–19,
        221–4, 226–31, 233, 237, 240, 243,
        246–7
    6. Armee x–xi, 1, 3–4, 8–11, 19, 21,
        28, 35–6, 39–40, 42–3, 46–7, 50,
        52–3, 57–8, 62, 65, 68–71, 74–5,
        80–3, 85–8, 89–91, 94–6, 99–100,
        102, 104, 107–19, 121–4, 126–8,
        130–1, 133–5, 137–42, 145, 147–9,
        151–6, 158–67, 170–1, 173–5, 177,
        179–81, 184–5, 187–8, 190, 192–5,

197–9, 201, 203, 210–12, 214–24,
    226–8, 230–1, 234, 237–8, 240–4,
    246–7, 250, 265, 267, 273–6
    6. Pz.Armee xi, 6, 9–10, 12–14, 16, 19–
        21, 23–4, 27–9, 35–6, 38, 39–42,
        45–6, 49, 52–4, 57–8, 60–3, 69–70,
        72–5, 81–3, 85–8, 89–91, 93–5,
        97, 99–102, 104, 107–8, 111–16,
        119–20, 123–4, 126–8, 130–1,
        133–5, 137, 139–45, 148, 152–4,
        157, 159–60, 162–3, 165–6, 174–5,
        177–85, 187, 189, 192, 195, 198,
        203, 207, 211–12, 214–15, 217–20,
        222–5, 227–8, 230–5, 239–44, 247,
        253, 277
    8. Armee 11–12, 14, 27, 48, 58, 60,
        80, 87, 95, 108, 112, 128–9, 139,
        147–8, 154, 162–4, 169, 174–5,
        187, 195, 199, 203, 212, 214,
        217–18, 220, 222–5, 227–31, 235,
        240, 243
    9. Armee 146, 263
    Korpsgruppen:
    Korpsgruppe Harteneck 4, 11, 12, 28
    Korps:
    I.Kav.Korps 4, 12, 28, 35, 36, 53, 75,
        82, 87, 96, 100, 102, 104–5, 109–
        11, 114–15, 118, 121–5, 129–30,
        138, 141, 147–9, 152–5, 159–61,
        163–4, 167–8, 171–2, 174, 189,
        191–2, 204, 212, 219, 228, 237, 246
    I. SS-Pz.Korps 13–16, 23, 25, 35–7,
        42, 52–3, 62, 69–71, 74–5, 81–4,
        86–7, 89–93, 95–6, 99, 101, 108–9,
        111–12, 118, 120–1, 126, 128,
        130–1, 139–40, 143, 148, 152,
        157, 162, 165, 195, 203, 212, 218,
        224–5, 227–8, 231, 234–5, 262
    II. SS-Pz.Korps 23, 25, 36, 37, 42,
        52–3, 70–1, 75, 81–3, 86–7, 90–1,
        93, 95, 99, 101, 112, 126, 128, 130,
        140, 143, 148, 203, 212, 218, 225,
        227–8, 231, 234–5
    III. Pz.Korps 21, 24, 28–9, 36–7, 42–3,
        47, 52–3, 57–8, 62, 65, 69, 71–3,
        75–6, 81–2, 86–7, 90–1, 98, 100,
        102–5, 107–12, 114, 118, 123,
        138, 147, 165–7, 170, 172–3, 189,
        191–4, 198, 204, 210–11, 214–15,

217–24, 226, 229–32, 234, 238–40, 243, 244

IV. SS-Pz.Korps ix–xi, 1, 3, 5–10, 17, 19, 21, 23–30, 33–5, 39–52, 55, 57–8, 60–3, 65, 67, 69–77, 81–2, 84–8, 89–98, 104–5, 108–9, 115, 117–19, 121, 125, 127–8, 130–1, 134–5, 137–8, 141–3, 145, 147–50, 152, 154–6, 159–61, 163–8, 170, 172–4, 179–81, 188–90, 192–4, 196–200, 201, 203–4, 209–10, 212–15, 217–19, 221, 224, 226–32, 234–5, 237–8, 240, 243–4, 246–7, 249, 251, 253, 257–63, 265–6, 269–72

Korück 593 238

LXXII.Armee-Korps 169

Volks-Art.Korps 403 3, 29, 74, 99

XLIII. Armee-Korps 81, 85–7, 90, 93, 95, 99, 112, 128, 140, 148, 162, 195, 235

XXII. Geb.Korps 190, 228

Infantry/*Volksgrenadier*/*Gebirgs*/*Jäger*/ *Fallschirm* Divisions:

1. Volks-Geb.Div. 36, 139, 140, 151–2, 156, 159, 161–2, 165–6, 170, 172–3, 189, 193, 198–9, 211, 214, 216, 222–4, 227, 232, 243

9. Geb.Div. 234, 238, 243

10. Fallschirm-Div. 216, 217, 219, 235

44. Reichs-Gren.Div. Hoch und Deutschmeister 34

96. Inf.Div. 12, 14, 35, 46, 58, 63, 65, 69, 72, 75, 78, 93, 112

117. Jag.Div. 230, 238–9

118. Jäg.Div. 36

211. V.G.D. 195

356. Inf.Div. 3, 10, 29, 36, 37, 39, 73–5, 81, 85, 86–7, 93, 95, 128, 140, 162, 212, 235

357. Inf.Div. 148

710. Inf.Div. 230

711. Inf.Div. 12, 14, 46, 65, 78, 85, 90, 100, 128–9, 154, 162

Panzer/*Kavallerie*/*Panzergrenadier* Divisions:

1. Pz.Div. 36–7, 72, 85, 87, 89–91, 96, 98–9, 101, 104, 110–11, 115, 121, 138, 141–2, 153, 159, 164–5, 167–8, 172, 189–91, 196, 197,

204–5, 211, 213, 216–19, 222–6, 228–31, 234, 238–41, 243, 247

1. SS-Pz.Div. Leibstandarte SS Adolf Hitler 13

2. SS-Pz.Div. Das Reich 36, 86, 181

3. Kav.Div. 100, 110, 111, 164, 167

3. Pz.Div. 3, 36–7, 42, 87, 96, 99, 103, 108–11, 115, 118–19, 121, 127, 130, 141–2, 148, 150, 152, 156–7, 159, 164–8, 172, 189–90, 197, 204–5, 209–11, 213, 215, 221, 226–7, 230, 232, 234, 237, 243, 246

4. Kav.Div. 34, 35, 108, 109, 111, 115, 121, 138, 141, 147, 155–6, 167–8, 228

5. SS-Pz.Div. Wiking 110, 115, 156

6. Pz.Div. 3, 35, 40–3, 47, 65, 70–1, 81, 86–7, 93, 95, 112, 128, 162, 212, 220, 225, 228

9. SS-Pz.Div. Hohenstaufen 36, 86, 96, 109, 123, 126

12. SS-Pz.Div. Hitlerjugend 13, 182

16. SS-Pz.Gren.Div. Reichsführer-SS 37, 139

23. Pz.Div. 36–7, 87, 100, 111, 115, 121, 138, 141, 155–6, 167

Fuhrer-Gren.Div. 218, 219, 223, 225

Brigades/Artillery Commands:

4. Kav.Brig. 3, 8, 9, 10, 28

ARKO 3 232, 238, 243

Gren.Brig. (mot.) 92 48, 65, 68, 71–5, 78, 93, 99–100, 129, 154

HARKO 306 27

Heeres-Art.Brig. 959 48

SS-ARKO 504 27, 60, 204

SS-Werf.Abt. 504 32, 68, 204, 260

Sturm-Art.Brig. 239 14

Sturm-Art.Brig. 261 230

Sturm-Art.Brig. 303 39, 166, 234, 243

Sturm-Art.Brig. 325 48, 72

Volks-Werf.Brig. 17 3, 29, 166

Infantry/*Panzergrenadier* Regiments:

Gren.Rgt. 283 78

Pz.Gren.Rgt. 1 119–20, 239

Pz.Gren.Rgt. 113 216, 224, 238, 239

SS-Pol.Rgt. 13 230, 234, 239

SS-Pz.Gren.Rgt. 5 Totenkopf 9

SS-Pz.Gren.Rgt. 19 122

SS-Rgt. Ney 28, 44, 51, 68, 77, 155,
    166, 189, 211, 224, 243
Artillery Regiments:
  SS-Pz.Art.Rgt. 3 27, 38, 67, 131, 257
  SS-Pz.Art.Rgt. 5 98, 105, 150, 169, 211,
    249
Panzer Regiments:
  Pz.Rgt. 1 14, 118, 239
  Pz.Rgt. 24 7, 204, 232, 243
  SS-Pz.Rgt. 1 14, 118
  SS-Pz.Rgt. 3 6, 8–9, 67, 80
  SS-Pz.Rgt. 5 6, 26, 43, 98, 102, 103,
    105, 130, 211, 226, 240
Kampfgruppen:
  Div.K.Gr. LSSAH 118–21, 130,
    138–40, 142, 149, 151–2, 155–6,
    159, 162
  Flak Kampfgruppe III./10957 199
  K.Gr. Ameiser 35, 72, 85, 91, 128–9,
    154
  K.Gr. Bradel 138, 153, 159, 164, 172,
    196, 216, 219
  K.Gr. Gottwald 238, 243
  K.Gr. Keitel 162, 212
  K.Gr. Medicus 213
  K.Gr. Motschmann 224–5, 230, 238,
    243
  K.Gr. Semmering 224, 226, 230, 234,
    238
  K.Gr. Wolf 85, 93, 210, 213, 221
Battalions:
  Pz.Abt. 208 12
  Pz.Aufkl.Abt. 1 72, 73, 93
  Pz.Aufkl.Abt. 3 50, 61, 237
  s.Pz.Abt. 509 8, 149, 166, 204, 216,
    219
  SS-Beob.Abt. 504 3, 204
  SS-Füsilier-Btl. 14 216
  SS-Gren.Ers.u.Ausb.Btl. 11 199, 220,
    243
  SS-Nachr.Abt. 104 8, 26
  SS-Pio.Btl. 5 223
  SS-Pz.Aufkl.Abt. 3 50, 61
  SS-Pz.Aufkl.Abt. 5 98, 138, 155, 216
  SS-Werf.Abt. 504 32, 68, 204, 260
  s.SS-Art.Abt. 504 3, 7, 32, 68, 204, 240
Volkssturm Units 196, 199
Gerse 172, 189, 191

Gille, SS-Ogruf. Herbert Otto vi, x–xii, 3–4,
    7–8, 11, 13, 17
  and 20–23 March 89–92, 94, 96, 98–9,
    102, 104, 107, 109, 114, 115–16, 118–
    19, 121, 124, 127–8, 130–1
  and 24–29 March 134–5, 137–9, 141–2,
    148–9, 151, 153, 156–9, 161, 164–5,
    167, 170–5
  and 26–28 March 179–80, 183
  and 30–31 March 188–92, 194, 196–200
  and 1–17 April 201, 204, 209–11, 214,
    217, 222, 226–8, 229–32, 234, 235
  and Spring Awakening 21, 25–6, 28–9,
    31–2, 35, 38, 39–46, 48–52
  and Stuhlweissenburg 60–1, 63, 65–6,
    68–70, 72, 77, 78, 81–2, 85, 87
  and war's end 238, 243–4, 246, 249–51,
    254, 255–63, 265
Glagolev, Col.Gen. Vasily 58
Glanert, SS-Hstuf. Georg 103, 257
Gleisdorf 234, 243, 244, 246
Göring, Reichsmarschall Hermann 178, 183,
    207–8
Govorunenko, Maj.Gen. P. D. 188, 196, 216
Gran (Hron) River 11–16, 23, 28, 34, 82
  and 20–23 March 95, 100, 128
  and 24–29 March 141, 147, 162, 174–5
Graz x, 165, 169, 192, 199
  and 1–17 April 203, 210, 213, 216, 221,
    226–8, 232–4
  and war's end 237, 244, 246–7, 250, 265
Grenzschutzstellungen 172, 196, 197, 198
Groeben, Oberst Peter von der 167
Grolman, Gen.Lt. Helmuth von 20, 55, 94,
    113, 120
  and 24–29 March 139, 147, 168
  and Stuhlweissenburg 62, 66, 76, 81
Grosser, Oberst Herbert 68, 78
Grossrock, SS-Ostuf. Alfred 79
Guderian, Gen.Oberst Heinz 177–8, 180–1,
    209, 222, 299n35
  and 20–23 March 94, 102, 107, 125–6
  and 24–29 March 135, 139, 143–4, 146,
    158
  and Spring Awakening 20, 40–2, 53, 55
  and Stuhlweissenburg 60, 73, 75, 80–1,
    83–4
Güns (Köszeg) 171, 187, 191, 195, 199

Güssing 226, 227
Guttámási 77, 80, 83
Gyldenfeldt, *Gen.Lt.* Heinz von 147, 174, 194
Györ *see* Raab

Hack, *SS-Ostubaf.* Franz 66–7, 92, 97, 102–5,
    107, 109, 131
Hajmáskér 112, 115, 117, 118, 119
Harrendorf, *Gen.Maj.* Hermann 65
Harteneck, *Gen.d.Kav.* Gustav 28, 111, 114,
    122–3, 130, 237
    and 24–29 March 138, 149–50, 152–3,
        155–6, 159, 160, 164, 167, 171, 174
Heder, *SS-Hstuf.* Eberhard 223, 257, 259
Heiligenkreuz 196–7, 206, 221, 226, 230, 240
Heszlényi, *Gen.Lt.* vitéz József 28, 44, 78, 85,
    90, 93, 95, 99, 129
Hidegkút 138, 141, 148–9
Hilfsgemeinschaft auf Gegenseitigkeit der
    Angehörigen der ehemaligen Waffen-SS
    (HIAG, or Mutual Aid Association of the
    Waffen-SS) 256
Himmler, *Reichsführer-SS* Heinrich 11, 13, 43,
    125–6, 135, 146
    and 26–28 March 178–84
    and Jews 169, 263
    and SS 207–9, 255, 266
Hitler, *Reichskanzler* Adolf 7, 12–14, 16, 177–
    84, 192–4, 299n35, 310n14
    and 20–23 March 94, 100–1, 107–8,
        125–7, 129, 134–5
    and 24–29 March 134–5, 137, 139, 143–6,
        157–8, 162, 170–1, 175
    and 1–17 April 201, 203, 208, 221, 222,
        233
    and *Spring Awakening* 19–21, 34, 38, 53–4
    and Stuhlweissenburg 58, 60, 62, 69, 74–5,
        80
    and war's end 241, 248, 250, 263, 265
    see also *Führerbefehl* (*Führer* directive)
Hofmann, *SS-Ostubaf.* Bernhard 122
Holste, *Gen.Maj.* Rudolf 3, 9, 10
Honvéd see Hungarian Units
Hron *see* Gran (Hron) River
Hungarian *(Honvéd)* Units:
    Armies:
        3. Armee 28, 35, 44–8, 50–1, 57–8,
            69–70, 72–3, 75, 77–8, 81, 83–6,

            90, 93–5, 99, 101, 108, 112, 115,
            128–9, 153, 243
    Corps:
        II. Armee-Korps 152
        VIII. Armee-Korps 9–10, 39, 42, 57,
            62–3, 65–6, 68, 70, 72, 77, 84–6, 93
    Divisions:
        1. Hus.Div. 10, 39, 43, 51–2, 58,
            61–2, 65–6, 69, 72, 76, 77–8, 85–6,
            302n16
        2. Pz.Div. 3, 10, 27, 29, 33, 39, 44, 45,
            50, 58, 61–3, 65–7, 71–2, 77, 86,
            89, 130
        20. Inf.Div. 3, 39, 67, 152
        23. Inf.Div. 3, 72, 78, 86, 91, 95, 129
        25. Inf.Div. 35, 87, 111, 115, 152
    Regiments:
        Inf.Rgt. 14 39, 40
    Battalions:
        Btl. Holczer 3, 10, 39, 40
Hüppe, *SS-Ostubaf.* Herbert 26

Inota 38, 45, 51–2, 90, 92, 95, 107
    and Stuhlweissenberg 68, 77, 81, 85
Iszkaszentgyörgy 10, 29, 76–7, 80
Isztimér 84, 86, 90

Jankuhn, *SS-Stubaf.* Herbert 27, 51, 258–9
Jennersdorf 196, 211, 212–13, 216, 217, 223,
    228
Jenö Pocket 109–11, 121, 122, 153
Judenburg 242, 246

Kalbskopf, *SS-Ostuf.* Dr Edwin 105
Kampfraum (area of operations) 9, 124, 228
Kampfstärke (combat strength) 6, 15, 29, 91,
    140, 153, 206
Kampfwert (combat value) 5, 16, 29, 30, 32,
    44, 167–8, 207
Kaposvár 20, 36, 37
Kecskéd 75, 78
Keitel, *Generalfeldmarschall* Wilhelm 41, 146,
    242
Kerckhoff, *SS-Ostuf.* Heinrich 66
Kernmayr, *SS-Ustuf.* Erich 51–2, 260
Kesselring, *Generalfeldmarschall* Albert 241–2
Keszthely 171–2
Kirschdorf an der Krems 244

Kirschner, *Gen.d.Pz.Tr.* Friedrich 11
Kirva 65, 72
Kisber 48, 76, 80–1, 85, 87, 140, 155, 162
    and 20–23 March 89, 90, 95, 99, 112,
    128, 129
Kiskecskemét 75, 92
Kislőd 142, 151, 152
Kistemaker, *SS-Uscha.* Henk 248–9
Klarastellung (Clara Position) 117, 121, 131,
    138, 141
Kleemann, *Gen.d.Pz.Tr.* Ulrich 3, 12
Kleffner, *SS-Ostubaf.* Franz 67
Kleinarl Valley 249
Kleinmariazell (Czelldömölk) 155, 159–60
Kleinzell (Sárvár) 161–2, 164, 166, 170, 173,
    174
Kocs 85, 108
Komorn (Komarom) 11, 13, 16, 47, 49
    and 16–19 March 58, 60, 69–70, 85–7
    and 20–23 March 91, 93–5, 97, 102, 108,
    112, 128
    and 24–29 March 140, 155, 157, 162, 163,
    166, 174
Königsdorf 190, 197, 228
Körmend 165, 172, 188–90, 193
Környe 65, 72, 75, 78
Kőszeg *see* Güns
Kraas, *SS-Brig.Fhr.* Hugo 92
Krause, *Gen.Lt.* Walther 193, 198, 211, 217,
    220, 238, 243
Kravchenko, Col.Gen. Andrei 58, 88, 96, 130,
    139, 170
Krebs, *Gen.Lt.* Hans 146–7
Kreuzwirt 224, 225
Kreysing, *Gen.d.Geb.Tr.* Hans 11–12, 58, 195,
    203, 220, 225, 227
Kriegsmarine (German Navy) 9, 15, 31, 48,
    182, 251
    and 24–29 March 140, 143
    and 1–17 April 205, 208
Küngös 108, 111, 121
Küstrin 133, 146

Lafnitz River 192, 196–7, 199
    and 1–17 April 203, 210, 212–13, 216,
    221, 224–6, 228–9
Lake Balaton 3–4, 187, 191, 203–4, 210, 212
    and 20–23 March 93–4, 96, 100–2, 104–5,
    108–10, 112, 114–17, 122–3, 125,
    129–30
    and 24–29 March 133–5, 137, 146–7, 149,
    152, 157, 158–60, 163, 167, 170–1
    and *Spring Awakening* 19, 21, 23, 25, 28,
    36, 38, 40, 45–6, 49, 54
    and Stuhlweissenburg 57, 60, 69, 74, 80–3,
    87–8
Lake Sóstó 89, 103–4
Lake Velencze 8, 10, 91, 94, 100, 101
    and *Spring Awakening* 19, 21, 23, 25, 29,
    37–8, 40, 42–3, 45–7, 49, 51, 53–4
    and Stuhlweissenburg 62–3, 69, 71, 72,
    81–2, 87
Landeschützen 211, 214
Lange, *SS-Ustuf.* Günther xii, 26, 249, 251–3,
    257, 259
Leitha Mountains 212
Leitha River 214, 218, 219
Liezen 244, 246, 248
Linz 241, 247, 253
Litér 115, 118
Lókút 128
Lovasberény 40, 42, 45, 46
Luftwaffe (German Air Force) 4, 9, 15, 178,
    182, 199, 251
    and 1–17 April 205, 207–8, 211, 214,
    217–19, 230
    and 20–23 March 113, 117, 126, 129
    and 24–29 March 143, 148, 157, 159–60,
    169
    Luftflotte 4 68, 78, 86, 93–4, 141, 154,
    162, 163, 174
    and *Spring Awakening* 31, 46, 48
    and Stuhlweissenberg 61, 69, 73
Lundenburg 223, 225, 228, 231

McBride, Maj.Gen. Horace L. 242, 244, 263
Magland 210, 218
Magyaralmás 6, 63, 71, 77, 80
Maier, *SS-Ostubaf.* Georg xi, 82, 135, 156,
    167, 201
    and 20–23 March 123–4, 127
    and 26–28 March 179, 180–2, 184
Malinovsky, Marshal Rodion 57–8, 148, 157,
    164, 203, 219, 227

maps:
defence of the Reich *202*
Frühlingserwachen Offensive *22*
situation 12 February 1945 *2*
situation 16 March 1945 *59*
Stuhlweissenburg escape *106*
Vienna Operation *64, 136*
withdrawal to Enns River *245*
Marcaltö 160, 166
Marczal Canal 154–5, 157, 160, 161, 163, 177
Margarethestellung (Margaret Position) 1, 10, 21, 23, 87, 100, 121, 170, 187
Máriahalom *see* Kirva
Martinsberg 90, 93, 114–15
Melinkat, *SS-Oscha.* Siegfried 211, 241
Mellenthin, *Gen.Maj.* Friedrich W. von 264–5
Messerle, *SS-Stubaf.* Friedrich 45–6, 65
Minor Carpathian Mountains 214, 217, 218, 219, 220, 222
Mitlacher, *Oberstlt.* Otto 227
Mocsa 85, 90, 95, 112
Modlin ix, 265
Mór 6, 10, 90, 92, 96
and *Spring Awakening* 34, 42, 47–9, 51
and Stuhlweissenburg 58, 62, 66, 68, 71–2, 75–7, 79–82
Müller, *SS-Stubaf.* Helmut 150
Mürz River 223
Mürzzuschlag 230, 231

Nádasdladány 73, 84, 91, 98–9, 104, 110
Nagybajom 36, 170, 187
Nagyigmánd 69, 76, 85, 90, 95, 99, 112, 129, 140
Nagykanizsa oilfields 19, 38, 74, 135, 139, 171, 214, 265
Nagyvázsony 150, 152, 155
Naszály 85, 90
Nemesvámos 109, 128, 138, 141, 148
Neuhäusel (Nové Zámky) 49, 162, 164, 171, 174
Neumarkt an der Raab 193, 196–8
Neusiedlersee 164, 187, 189, 195, 203, 212, 214, 217, 219
and 1–17 April 203, 212, 214, 217, 219
Neutra (Nitra) River 164, 171, 174, 187, 191, 217
Ney, *SS-Ostubaf.* Károly 44, 77, 260
Nuremberg Trials 254, 255

Nyerges Ujfalu 90–1, 94, 112

Oberdorf 221, 224, 230
Oberkommando der Wehrmacht (OKW) 4, 41, 49, 144
and 1–17 April 203, 219, 226, 233
Oberkommando des Heeres (OKH) xi, 4–6, 8, 13–14, 60, 74
and 20–23 March 92, 95, 100–1, 107, 117, 126
and 24–19 March 134–5, 139, 143–4, 146, 157, 162, 163, 166
and 26–28 March 177, 181
and 30–31 March 187, 191, 193
and 1–17 April 201, 205, 209, 218, 220, 222
and *Spring Awakening* 20, 28–9, 32, 34, 42, 52
and war's end 238, 262
Ödenburg (Sopron) 164, 195, 218
Ordnungspolizei (Order Police) 15, 144, 169–70, 184, 199, 231
Oroszlány 71–2, 78
Ösi 98–9, 108, 110, 126
Öskü 85, 90, 98

Pakfronts (antitank defences) 24, 239
Pákozd 42, 50
Papa 100, 120, 138, 148–9, 153, 154, 301n7
Pape, *Gen.Maj.* Günther 87, 95, 112, 140, 162
Papkeszi 105, 108, 109, 119–20, 122
Parkány 11, 12–13, 14
Patton, Lt.Gen. George S. 242–3, 253
Pauly, *SS-Stubaf.* Richard 255
Pétfurdő oil refinery 122, 150
Petrushevskiy, Lt.Gen. Alexander 58
Pfeffer-Wildenbruch, *SS-Ogruf.* Karl von 107
Pfefferkorn, *SS-Oberscharführer* 80
Pilis Mountains 28, 57, 90
Pinka River 192, 219–22
Plattensee *see* Lake Balaton
Polgárdi 108, 110, 111
Pressburg (Bratislava) 162, 191, 195, 203, 212, 217, 219–20
Priess, *SS-Gruf.* Hermann 13, 15–16, 23, 35–7, 62, 139–40, 144
and 20–23 March 90, 96, 99, 111, 119, 120, 128
and war's end 225, 227

Pusztavám 39, 72, 77, 85

Raab (Györ) 13, 47, 69, 85, 94, 177
    and 24–29 March 140, 155, 160–7, 171–3
    and 30–31 March 187–8, 190–3, 196–9
    and 1–17 April 203, 210, 212–19, 221,
        224, 226, 228–30
Rábadorosló 188, 190, 197
Radkersburg 153, 154, 218, 223, 228–30, 233
Radowitz, *Gen.Maj.* Josef von 167
Radstadt 237, 250
Radtke, *Ostuf.* Werner 222
Raithel, *Oberst* Heribert 226
Rausch, *SS-Stubaf.* Friedrich 25
Rax 199, 215
Rechnitz 154, 191–3, 198, 215, 217, 220
Red Army Units *see* Soviet Units
Reichert, *Gen.Lt.* Josef 65
Reichsarbeitsdienst (Reich Labor Service) 15,
    196, 208
Reichsführer-SS see Himmler, Heinrich
Reichsschutzstellung x, xii, 97, 137, 185
    and 24–29 March 154, 169, 175
    and 1–17 April 205, 209, 210, 212, 214
    and withdrawal 187, 190–1, 196
Rendulic, *Gen.O.* Lothar 221–2, 242–3, 262
Renold, *SS-Ustuf.* Peter 61, 67–8, 79
Rentrop, *SS-Stubaf.* Fritz 7, 25
Riegsee 251
Ringel, *Gen.d.Geb.Tr.* Julius 193, 199
Rost, *Gen.Maj.* Hans-Günther von 110

St Gotthard (Szent Gotthard) 196–7, 200,
    215, 216, 224
St Pölten 220, 222, 225, 230, 231, 235, 239
Salzburg 249–50, 257
Sárkeresztes 43, 63, 67, 71, 76, 90
Sárkeresztur 37, 69, 70, 96
Sárvár *see* Kleinzell
Sárviz Canal 3, 36–8, 57, 73, 75, 100
Schachendorf 191, 198, 214, 215, 218
Schandorf 198
Schmeisser, *SS-Stubaf.* Herbert 26, 257
Schneider, *SS-Ostuf.* Otto 40, 241
Schöne, *Oberst* Volkmar 220–1, 237, 243
Schönfelder, *SS-Ostubaf.* Manfred 27, 42, 48,
    63, 82, 179, 183
    and 24–29 March 135, 155–6, 158, 161,
        167, 171–2, 174

and 30–31 March 188–90, 194, 197
    and war's end 235, 250, 259, 265
Schumacher, *SS-Ostuf.* Kurt 103
Semmer, *Oberst* Gerhard 238
Semmering Gap 203, 210, 219, 221, 223–4,
    228, 234, 238–40
Sennelager 9
Seregélyes 10, 91, 96, 99, 114
    and *Spring Awakening* 37, 39, 42
    and Stuhlweissenburg 65, 75, 83, 85, 87
Sharokhin, Lt.Gen. Mikhail N. 170
Simontornya 35, 37, 54, 70
Sió River 35, 37, 53, 70, 75
Sóly 109, 117, 118
Sonnenwende, Operation 11
Sopron *see* Ödenburg
Söréd 45, 49, 61, 68, 71, 77, 79–80
Söth, *Oberst* (later *Gen.Maj.*) Wilhelm 118,
    120, 205, 237, 242, 244
    and 24–29 March 141, 148, 168
Soviet Units:
    Fronts:
        First Belorussian 263
        Second Ukrainian 14, 23, 26, 57–8,
            60, 100, 141, 147, 148, 154, 157,
            162–4, 171, 203, 214, 219, 227
        Third Ukrainian x, 13, 16–17, 19, 21,
            23–4, 36, 38, 40, 47, 52, 54, 57–60,
            62, 69–70, 75, 82–3, 88, 96, 108,
            134, 137, 147, 154, 163, 169, 180,
            184, 193, 199, 203, 216–17, 228,
            232–3, 235, 263, 265, 279–83
    Armies/Groups:
        1st Bulgarian 36, 203, 222
        1st Romanian 203
        4th Guards 1, 10, 23, 27, 52, 58, 90,
            98, 108, 120, 195, 227–8, 253
        6th Guards Tank 11, 13, 38, 47, 58,
            73, 88, 92, 94, 96, 99, 101, 103,
            108, 110, 114, 117, 120, 130, 139,
            141, 148–9, 157, 160, 163, 165–6,
            170, 173, 190, 195, 203, 214, 225,
            227–8, 230
        7th Guards 11, 13, 14, 23, 141, 163,
            171, 195, 199, 203, 223, 228, 230–1
        9th Guards 23, 38, 47, 55, 58, 60, 63,
            69, 74, 75–6, 83, 87, 94, 96, 108,
            112, 141, 160, 163, 173, 195, 203,
            218

26th Army 1, 23, 36–7, 138–9, 191, 200, 220, 221
27th Army 23, 37, 138–9, 160, 164, 188–9, 221
46th Army 58, 65, 70, 73, 75–6, 78, 85–7, 90, 94, 99, 101, 108, 112, 128, 140, 148, 162, 195, 203
53rd Army 141, 163, 199, 203, 230, 231
57th Army 36, 37, 163, 170, 174, 195, 212, 214, 222, 227
Air Armies:
5th Air Army 93
17th Air Army 68, 73
Corps:
CXXXIII Rifle 37
I Guards Mechanized 1, 23, 100, 118, 195
II Guards Mechanized 58
IX Guards Mechanized 195
V Guards Cavalry 52, 191, 219, 221, 224, 238
V Guards Tank 118, 135, 161, 195
XVIII Tank 37, 161, 188, 194, 196, 198, 200, 212, 219, 221, 228, 231, 235
XX Guards Rifle 27
XXI Guards Rifle 1, 98
XXIII Tank 23
XXV Guards Rifle 13–14
XXX Rifle 238
Divisions:
62nd Guards Rifle 90
80th Guards Rifle 92, 98
93rd Guards Rifle 14
Brigades:
27th Tank 13
Spätlese, Operation 4, 21
Spring Awakening see *Frühlingserwachen* (Operation *Spring Awakening*)
Stalin, Josef 16, 52, 57, 223, 235
STAVKA (Soviet High Command) 16, 23, 36, 40, 52, 57–8, 92, 203
Stegersbach 197, 223, 229
Steinamanger (Szombathely) 165, 171, 173, 187, 191–2, 196–7
Steiner, *SS-Ogruf.* Felix xi, 11, 255–8, 261
Stichnoth, *SS-Ostuf.* Erich 98, 216

Stienen, *SS-Hstuf.* Peter 29
Storch see aircraft
Stuhlweissenburg (Székesfehérvár) x, 1, 3, 10, 17, 57–88, 141, 177
and 20–23 March 89–94, 96–105, 107–10, 130–1
and 1–17 April 201, 205–6, 226, 229
and *Spring Awakening* 21, 28–9, 33–4, 38–43, 45–7, 49–51
and war's end 241, 261
Sturmovik see aircraft
Südwind, Operation 4, 11, 12–13, 15–17, 19, 23
Sümeg 150, 159, 160–1, 164, 168
Súr 28, 44, 68, 77
Susannestellung (Susan Position) 160, 163, 165, 169, 177, 212
Szalási, Arrow Cross Leader Ferenc 44, 241
Székesfehérvár *see* Stuhlweissenburg
Szentkirályszabadja 118, 122, 138
Szombathely *see* Steinamanger

T-34 tank 67–8, 103, 160, 223, 231, 239
Tapolca 149, 161
Tata 28, 81
Tata Tóváros 85, 90
Tatra Mountains 195
Thomale, *Gen.Maj.* Wolfgang 220–1
Tolbukhin, Marshal Fyodor x, 1, 99, 108, 117, 263
and 24–29 March 134, 137, 148–9, 164, 193
and 1–17 April 203, 219, 223, 228
and *Spring Awakening* 23, 36, 42, 52–4
and Stuhlweissenburg 57–8, 70, 72, 74, 83, 87–8
Tótvázsony 128, 149, 152
Traisen River 215, 231
Trofimenko, Lt.Gen. Sergei 37, 221, 224
Tulln 215, 220, 223, 227, 228

Überreither, *Gauleiter* Dr Sigfried 244
Ullrich, *SS-Oberf.* Karl 3, 5, 7, 8, 61, 68, 76
and 20–23 March 98, 100, 102, 107, 109
and 24–29 March 141, 149, 158, 168–9
and 1–17 April 206–7, 213, 224
and *Spring Awakening* 27, 29, 32, 44
and war's end 243, 246, 248–9, 259

United States Army 242, 243
Urhida 103–4

Váli River 42, 101
Várpalota 10, 23
   and 20–23 March 89, 92, 98–9, 108, 109,
     111
   and Stuhlweissenburg 58, 69–70, 74, 76–7,
     81, 84, 86–8
Vasvár *see* Eisenberg
Velde, *SS-Hstuf.* Johann-Friedrich (Hans) 25,
   27, 257, 259
Velencze *see* Lake Velencze
Versock, *Gen.d.Geb.Tr.* Kurt 85, 162
Vértes Mountains 10, 90, 94, 101, 130
   and *Spring Awakening* 21, 23, 28, 38, 39,
     46–9
   and Stuhlweissenburg 57–8, 65, 70–1,
     73–6, 78, 82, 85
Vértessomlo 72
Veszprém 9–10, 23, 28, 58, 68–9, 182, 265
   and 20–23 March 102, 107, 109, 111–12,
     115–20, 122, 124, 125, 127–9
   and 24–29 March 138, 140–1, 147, 150–1,
     163, 169
   and 1–17 April 211, 241
Vienna Forest (Wiener Wald) 212, 220, 223,
   225
Vilonya 99, 102, 109, 115, 117
Vogt, *SS-Stubaf.* Fritz 7, 28, 68, 138, 155
   and death 213, 216, 222
Volksdeutsche (ethnic Germans) 61
Volkssturm (People's Militia) xii, 154, 169, 191,
   196, 199
   and 1–17 April 210–11, 214, 218, 219
Vorau 224–5, 234, 238–9
Vörösto 150, 152

Waag River 195, 223
Wagner, *SS-Stubaf.* Heinz 138
Wagrain 248, 250
Waldbach 229, 239
Walker, Col. S. P. 244

Walker, Lt. Gen. Walton H. 242
weaponry:
   Panzerfausts (antitank grenade launchers)
     68, 79, 145, 150, 213, 230, 248
   Stümmel 7.5cm SP Infantry Howitzer 247
   Sturmgeschütz (StuG) III/IV Assault Gun
     107
   Sturmpanzer IV Brumbär 231
Wehofsich, *SS-Hstuf.* Dr Franz 260
Wehrkreis (Defence District) *XVIII* 154, 193,
   196, 199, 213
Wehrmachtsbericht 4, 249
Weichselbaum 196, 213
Wenck, *Gen.d.Pz.Tr.* Walter 146–7
Wiener Neustadt 195, 199, 212, 214, 225,
   227
Wiking Ruf, Der (*The Wiking Call*) (periodical)
   255–6, 258
Wittmann, *Gen.Lt.* August 140, 152, 161,
   199, 243
Wöhler, *Gen.O.* Otto 4, 8, 11–12, 14, 263
   and 20–23 March 92–7, 102, 107, 111,
     113–16, 120–1, 123–7
   and 24–29 March 135, 139, 142–7, 150,
     152, 162–3, 165, 172, 175
   and 26–28 March 177–8, 180–4
   and 30–31 March 189, 192, 194
   and 1–17 April 209, 222
   and *Spring Awakening* 20–1, 40–1, 44, 51,
     53, 55
   and Stuhlweissenburg 62, 69–70, 74–5,
     80–2, 84, 86–7
Wolf, *Oberstlt.* Alfred 213, 216, 217, 221

Zakharov, Gen. G. F. 1, 296n2
Zakhvatayev, Col.Gen. Nikanor 58
Zala River 164, 166, 172
Zalagerszeg 161, 171, 172, 212
Zámoly 1, 6, 8, 9–10, 65, 71, 75
   and *Spring Awakening* 27, 45–7, 49–50
Zingel, *SS-Oscha.* August 68
Zirc 48, 99, 128, 141
Zsedényi, *Gen.Maj.* vitéz Zoltán 33, 44, 65, 68